Date Due

Nov 23	NOV 11		
NOV 7	NOV 24		
NOV 22	DEC 9		
DEC 5	JAN 4		
DEC 20	MAR 29		
MAY 26	MAR 7		
MAR 7			
APR 1			
APR 18			
MAY 2			
SEP 30			
OCT 24			
NOV 28 '56			
DEC 12			
OCT 4			
DEC 6			
DEC 18			
FEB 5			
FEB 19			
OCT 24			
OCT 7			

No. 293   DEMCO-MADISON-WIS

CHRIST AND
THE CRITICS

CHRIST AND THE CRITICS

A DEFENCE OF THE DIVINITY OF
JESUS AGAINST THE ATTACKS OF
MODERN SCEPTICAL CRITICISM

BY HILARIN FELDER, O.M.Cap.

TRANSLATED FROM the ORIGINAL GERMAN

BY JOHN L. STODDARD

Author of "Rebuilding a Lost Faith"

VOLUME I

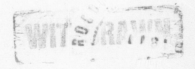

LONDON

**BURNS OATES AND
WASHBOURNE LTD.**

PUBLISHERS TO THE HOLY SEE

APPROBATIO ORDINIS

PRAESENTIUM vigore annuimus, ut opus cui titulus *Christ and the Critics* [*Jesus Christus*] (t. I et II, editio anglica) a P. Hilarino Felder, in Provincia Helvetica S. Theologiae Doctore et Lectore exaratum et a duobus Ordinis nostri theologis examinatum, servatis aliunde servandis, typis mandari et publici juris fieri possit et valeat.

Romae, e Curia nostra generali, die 15 Julii, 1922.

FR. JOSEPHUS ANT. A PERSICETO.

O.F.M.CAP., MINISTER GENERALIS.

Nibil Obstat

F THOMAS BERGH, O.S.B.,

CENSOR DEPUTATUS

Imprimatur

EDM. CAN. SURM NT,

VICARIUS GENERALIS

WESTMONASTERII
die 3a Januarii, 1924.

First Edition . 1924
Second Edition . 1933

CONTENTS

v

PART III.—THE DIVINE CONSCIOUSNESS OF CHRIST

Τίνα λέγουσιν οἱ ἄνθρωποι εἶναι τὸν υἱὸν τοῦ ἀνθρώπου;
Σὺ εἶ ὁ Χριστὸς ὁ Υἱὸς τοῦ Θεοῦ τοῦ ζῶντος.

Whom do men say that the Son of man is?
Thou art the Christ, the Son of the living God.

MATT. xvi, 13, 16.

INTRODUCTION

I.—CHRIST AND SCEPTICAL CRITICISM

JESUS CHRIST! No other problem arouses to-day keener, more universal and more serious attention. Even if we leave out of consideration the world of professing Christians and Christian believers, seekers after Christ are at present found in all classes of society, of all degrees of education and in all categories of doubters, including that of the wholly sceptical.

The proof of this is seen in the enormous increase in the literature treating of the life of Jesus. Professor Albrecht Schweitzer of Strasbourg recently asserted that the mere enumeration of all the "Lives of Jesus" which have appeared would alone wellnigh fill a volume.[1]

"It is touching to see how everyone, from his own standpoint and sphere of interest, finds himself occupied with Jesus Christ, or wishes to have some part in him. Ever anew is the spectacle, which the second century offered in Gnosticism, repeated, revealing itself as a conflict between all conceivable schools of thought for the possession of Jesus Christ. We may commend our century at least for this, that it is earnestly engaged with the question of the essential character and value of Christianity, and that there is now more research and inquiry into this subject than there was thirty years ago. And in its method of groping its way and experimenting, in the extraordinary and abstruse answers which it evolves, in its caricatures and chaotic confusion— yes, even in its hate, we see real life and a serious struggle."[2] Thus does Adolf Harnack, the head of liberal Protestant theology, characterize the present longing for Christ; and, God be thanked, he is perfectly right. Despite all appearances to the contrary, the non-believing, intellectual world of Christendom to-day is thrilled by *a mighty feeling of homesickness and a feverish longing for Christ.*

The profoundest *causes for this phenomenon* lie, doubtless, first of all, not in the modern intellectual world itself, but in that fulness of truth and holiness which has manifested itself in the person and religion of Christ, and always continues to attract man, even when he would like by every effort to escape it. Mankind, as such, undergoes the same experience as Goethe, one of the greatest and most intelligent of men,

---

[1] *Von Reimarus zu Wrede,* viii (Tübingen, 1906).
[2] *Wesen des Christentums,* 2 f. (Leipzig, 1905).

and one whom many have sought to put upon the same level
with Christ, personally underwent.[1] The old philosopher of
Weimar, who was anything but a believing Christian, and
expressed himself for the most part only æsthetically about
the mighty revelation of Christ and Christianity, sometimes,
in the intimacy of the family circle, " praised the sublimity
of Christ . . . always more seriously, more ardently and
with ever increasing emotion until he burst into tears." On
one occasion he said : " I regard all the four Gospels as
absolutely genuine, for there is in them the reflection of a
greatness which emanated from the person of Christ, and
is of as godlike a kind as has ever appeared on this earth.
I bow before him, as the divine manifestation of the highest
principle of morality. . . . Let intellectual culture continue
to advance, let the natural sciences continue to grow in
breadth and depth, and the human mind expand as much
as it may, it will never go beyond the elevation and the moral
culture of Christianity as it shines resplendent in the
Gospels."[2]

The profoundest minds have always experienced in themselves the truth of these words of Goethe,[3] and discovered it
also in reading the history of the centuries. The higher
human civilization rises, and the more exalted the pinnacle of
the truth is from which it surveys the conduct of mortals, the
more it observes and admires the unique and mighty manifestation of Christ and Christianity, before which all others
fade and disappear like mist before the sun.

If the interest in Christ, and in all problems connected with
his person and activity, is even greater and more general in
our modern unchristian, or only half-christian, society than
it perhaps has ever been, this is not to be ascribed merely to
the circumstance that our age, in contrast to the rationalistic
period, exhibits a high degree of sense and comprehension
for historical considerations (though only such considerations
will ever do justice to Christ and Christianity) ; the credit for
it is rather due—though very undeservedly—to the very unbelief of rationalism. And strange as this may sound, it is
nevertheless true.

On the one hand, the fruit which has gradually ripened
from the anti-christian rationalism of the last century is so
clearly poisonous and universally dangerous that mankind
now sees itself compelled to creep on its knees to the Cross,
if it is not to fall a victim to nihilism, atheism and satanism.
On the other hand, those rationalistic critics of Christ, whose
aim was to destroy all living faith in the incarnate God,

---

[1] Friedrich Daab, *Jesus von Nazareth,* 49 (Düsseldorf, 1907) ; Weidel,
Jesu Persönlichkeit (Halle, 1908).

[2] Goethe, *Conversations with Eckermann,* viii, 148 f., 203 (Leipzig,
1890).

[3] *cf.* Pfannmüller, *Jesus im Urtheil der Jahrhunderte* (Leipzig, 1908).

themselves helped to force science to consider again more seriously and thoroughly the life of the Saviour. No less a person than the rationalistic writer on civilization, Houston Stewart Chamberlain, has said : " Such men as Strauss and Renan, two concave mirrors (one distorting all the perpendicular lines, the other all the lateral), have nevertheless effected an important work by directing the attention of thousands to the great miracle of the manifestation of Christ, and by thus preparing an audience ready to listen subsequently to profounder thinkers and more sagacious men."[1]

As a matter of fact, *the majority of modern investigators of the life of Jesus have already become more sagacious, juster and—on that very account—also more conservative.* Moreover, this state of things will increase with every year. We shall soon see that the rationalistic sons of those men regard both the documents which treat of the life of Jesus, and also the main outlines of that life, as having been made, in a great measure, absolutely certain by critical research. Yet these sons had inherited from their rationalistic fathers the dogma that the Gospel in general, and all the separate Gospels, had either been already historically condemned, or were still in a state of arrest pending examination. Yes, even though the majority of those atavistic prejudices have still remained, the fundamental, *a priori* one against whatever of Christianity has been handed down to us by tradition is disappearing. Indeed, a most " modern " rationalistic investigator of this subject thinks that he can safely predict of his school that " Modern theology will one day become perfectly honourable " (Albrecht Schweitzer). " Yet," he at once prudently adds, " this is a prediction awaiting the future." And to this draft on the future, a still more rationalistic colleague from the ranks of the laity adds the malicious comment : *Quousque, tandem, Catilina ?*[2]

However this may be, rationalistic criticism, in spite of its clearer insight into the original sources of the life of Jesus, has not yet deigned to correct its inherited antagonistic christology in a single point.

As for liberal Protestant research into the life of Jesus, it is historically more conservative than in previous decades ; but, theologically, it can still rival the worst periods of rationalism. Schweitzer, in speaking of this, rightly says : " Historical research into the life of Jesus did not proceed from a purely *historic* interest, but sought the Jesus of history, so that he might be an ally in its fight for freedom from dogma. . . . Thus each succeeding theological epoch has found in Jesus its own thoughts, and could not conceive of his life otherwise."[3]

---

[1] *Die Grundlagen des XIX Jahrhunderts,* 8th ed., I, 227 f. note (München, 1907).
[2] Arthur Drews, *Die Christusmythe,* ix (Jena, 1909).   [3] *ibid.,* 4.

This is even truer of the latest period of liberal theology than of any which preceded it, for it recklessly cuts out from the original Christian frame (which it then endeavours to restore) the figure of Christ in order to copy it again according to the foreshortened and distorted scale of its own subjective, and therefore wholly arbitrary, conception. Externally, it holds fast to Christ and Christianity, but inwardly, and practically, everything which is precious in them has a new valuation put upon it, according to the critics' private estimate, and all the Christian ideas are falsified or replaced by modern, incommensurable properties.

On the whole, rationalistic theology becomes enthusiastic about Christ and Christianity only so far as it thinks that these represent freedom from dogma, contempt for the Church, modern civilization and the modern ideal of humanity. There remains in it hardly more than a faint semblance of what has, at all times and from the very beginning, been understood by the terms " Christ " and " Christianity."

We are fully aware of the severity of this reproach, and shall bring forward detailed proof for its justification in the course of our work. Suffice it for the moment to refer to the judgement of the philosopher and investigator of the life of Jesus, Edward von Hartmann. He maintains that the " Christianity " of Christ in liberal Protestantism is actually more sceptical than Islam, and is not essentially different from reformed Judaism; and that ideas of modern civilization are sailing about in it under a Christian flag, and adorned with merely the name of Christianity. Yet this is heralded as normal Christianity !¹ It is therefore undeniable that liberal Protestantism " can no longer claim the right, in any sense, to be included in Christianity, and that it is as irreligious as it is unchristian."²

" Modern theology has become completely absorbed in the idea of attributing its own religious ideals to Jesus."³

This inward falling away from Christ and Christianity, perceptible in present-day Protestantism, is not limited to scholarly books and learned men. It makes itself felt in one college and school after another. It is already the fashion in most of the universities, and forces its way into all the guilds of the students, and into all departments of study. D. Odland, Professor of Lutheran theology in Christiania, justly complains that, for the last twenty-five years, in the high schools of Germany there has prevailed a regular system of " counterfeiting " in regard to religious ideas.⁴ Dr. Emil

¹ *Die Selbstersetzung des Christentums und die Religion der Zukunft,* 11, 57, 60, 64 (Berlin, 1874).
² *Krisis des Christentums in der modernen Theologie,* 2nd ed., xi (Berlin, 1882).
³ *Das Christentum des Neuen Testaments,* xiii (Sachsa i. Harz, 1905).
⁴ Hartl, *Moderne Leben Jesu für das Volk,* in *Theol.-prakt. Quartalschrift,* 722 (Linz, 1906).

Rasmussen even gloats over the fact that "in Protestant countries half of the theological professorial chairs are occupied by men who no longer believe in the divinity of Jesus."[1] Professor W. Krüger has uttered the appalling statement that the vocation of theological instructors is to destroy the faith of youthful students and to cause scandal.[2]

More and more does this unchristian Christianity of liberal criticism transplant itself to the pulpit, acquire control of the daily press, and make its way into all branches of polite literature. The novels of Peter Rosegger[3] and Gustav Frenssen,[4] founded on the life of Jesus, exert an especially baneful influence on both the higher and lower classes of society. With these also are associated the rationalistic *popular books on the History of Religion,* and a thoroughly sceptical kind of literature for the masses, on the *Life of Jesus,* of which an extreme " Modernist " sarcastically says : " While the criticism of the Gospel manuscripts advances with ever increasing boldness, and leaves to us less and less of an historical Jesus, in popular religious literature the number of works is increasing enormously which aim at the glorification of the *man* Jesus, and seek to make up for the lack of assured historical material with unctuous phrases and a loud assertion of conviction. As for the fine rhetoric, which is at present so conspicuous in the treatment of this subject, the less historical material it has to work with, the more approval it seems to receive."[5]

Thus the masses of the people are gradually becoming ripe for spiritual apostasy from Christ and Christianity. Even our youth are taught that the history of Jesus, as related in the Gospels, is very legendary and that his sublime deeds are largely inventions.

Naturally there remains only one more step to take, from the surviving external semblance and shadow of liberal Christianity to the complete denial of the historical existence of Christ. We have, therefore, recently observed without astonishment that the left radical wing of rationalistic criticism has dared to take this final step also, and has even *denied the very existence of Jesus.* Yet in this there is really only one thing to excite astonishment, and that is the fact that liberal theology showed itself so amazed and indignant about it.

Certainly every attempt to undermine the complete historicity of Jesus, and to make the rise of Christianity comprehensible without a personal founder, must " go to pieces

[1] *Jesus, eine vergleichende psychopathologische Studie,* 158 (Leipzig, 1905).
[2] Philipp Huppert, *Der deutsche Protestantismus zu Beginn des XX Jahrhunderts,* 22 (Köln, 1902).
[3] *Frohe Botschaft des armen Sündners* (Leipzig, 1906).
[4] *Hilligenlei* (Berlin, 1905).
[5] A. Drews, *Christusmythe,* viii f.

on the reef of facts."[1] Houston Stewart Chamberlain writes : " The fact that the nineteenth century has fed itself on books in which it was shown that Christianity originated quite casually, by chance, as a phase of mythology or a dialectical antithesis, or I know not what, or again as a necessary product of Judaism, etc., will give in later ages eloquent testimony to the childishness of our judgement."[2] And yet it was precisely the critical world of the nineteenth century, the age of the sceptical criticism of the Gospels by Bruno Bauer, and that of the mythical theory of Strauss, that could allow such a thing to be put forward. From the standpoint of the latest investigation of the Gospels and the other sources of information about the life of Jesus, such an attempt is, how-ever, at once condemned by every serious critic and historian, whether he belongs to the rationalistic or the orthodox Chris-tian school of thought. We need waste no more words on this point here, especially as we must revert to the unpleasant subject at another place (chap. II). So far, however, the indignation in the camp of liberal theologians is compre-hensible.

On the other hand, it must again be emphasized that *the liberal school of investigators of the life of Jesus has no right to be excited over the latest deniers of Christ's existence.* In any case, it reminds us forcibly of Assuerus, who flees from his own shadow. For, however much it may refuse to acknowledge it, the latest form of radical criticism, which has become a veritable scandal, is really the offspring of the liberal school. It is true, as we have already acknowledged, this school has become, historically, more conservative, so long as it is not necessary to apply these clearer historical decisions to the domain of theology and christology. Tried by this test, however, it is certain to fail at once. The Gospel documents and the Gospels' representation of Jesus are genuine, it says, but in case these go beyond the Pro-crustean bed of the liberal theory, they must be transformed and abbreviated in the name of "criticism," until almost nothing more remains.

Liberal investigation of the life of Jesus is thoroughly imbued with the spirit of negation. Its historian, Albrecht Schweitzer, who holds such views, confesses frankly : " There is nothing more negative than the result of research into the life of Jesus." This means nothing else than " con-fusion and uncertainty about the historic Jesus."[3] Harnack, who is acclaimed enthusiastically by almost the entire rising generation of modern Protestant theologians, has already proclaimed a Christianity without Christ and christology. " Not the Son, but the Father only, has a place in the

---

[1] H. von Soden, *Die wichtigsten Fragen im Leben Jesu,* i (Berlin, 1907).
[2] *Die Grundlagen,* i, 294.   [3] *Von Reimarus zu Wrede,* viii, 396.

Gospel, as Jesus preached it."[1]   The Zürich theologian, P. Schmiedel, has written the discriminating preface to Smith's *Der vorchristliche Jesus,* and elsewhere even affirms lightheartedly : " No harm would be done to my innermost religious assets if I were convinced to-day that Jesus never lived."

From that standpoint to Albrecht Kalthoff's assertion that we do not possess, for certain, a single word of Jesus, and must reject entirely the historical character of the Saviour,[2] and then to the *Christ-myth* of Arthur Drews is evidently not far to go.

Moreover, both these spokesmen, in their attack upon the existence of Jesus, expressly confess that the origin of the views which they champion is to be ascribed to liberal research into the life of Jesus. Kalthoff characterizes his own mistakes with the remark that the " prodigal son "—the modern sceptic—who does not yet wish to go back into the sheepfold of the Church and to the old " Christianity *en bloc*," cannot satisfy himself with the husks of liberal Protestant theology, which " empties Christianity of all that once constituted its great strength and fulness," and " clutches at the straw of the historic Jesus," of whom, however, nothing certain remains, except that he once existed.   The whole liberal system of research into Jesus rests upon the assumption that " all the characteristics of ancient Christianity, which are no longer suited to the man of to-day, are to be treated as spurious accessories to the Bible, or as additions and elaborations of a later age, or as the work of incipient ' Catholic corruption,' and consequently are to be eliminated from the constituents of original Christianity."   It is only necessary to carry out this simple method to its logical conclusion to see that there will then remain nothing more of the historical Jesus of liberal theology.[3]

Still more plainly does Arthur Drews assert that *from the standpoint of liberal investigation into the life of Jesus, " the most advanced theologians proceed to controvert the fact that Jesus ever existed at all."*[4]   They are " encouraged to do this by the essentially negative results of so-called critical theology. . . .   The critical and historical theology of Protestantism has itself poured such a flood of light into the origins of the Christian religion that the question of the historical existence of Jesus loses all the paradoxical char- acter which may have up to this time still adhered to it in

---

[1] *Wesen des Christentums,* 91.
[2] *Die Entstehung des Christentums,* 1 ff.
[3] Kalthoff, *Das Christusproblem,* 19; *Religiöse Weltanschauung,* 184; *Die Religion der Modernen,* 290.
[4] *Die Religion als Selbstbewusstsein Gottes,* 108 n.

the eyes of many. It has, then, really no longer any occasion to get excited if anyone answers this question in a contrary sense."[1]

The resultant despair *in regard to Jesus Christ lies, therefore, wholly in the line of descent from such liberal Protestant research, and is a certain symptom of the malady from which it suffers.* It is a confused, fevered dream of rationalistic theology, not its wide-awake consciousness; for the latter is not only permeated with the historical reality of Jesus, but, in general, draws nearer and nearer to the traditional conception of historical Christianity. No, it is its rationalistic sub-consciousness, which excludes every supernatural characteristic from the personality and religion of Jesus, and finally has nothing left but a shadowy image, for which we seek in vain to feel enthusiasm.

It is pathetic that the majority of those who are to-day taking part most zealously in the study of Christ are once more chasing a mere phantom—a *fata morgana;* so that the paths of modern seekers after Christ lead them away from him just in proportion as they fancy they are approaching him. Even though a goodly number of believing critics and theologians are still to be found in the Protestant camp—in England far more than in Germany—it is, nevertheless, true that the Catholic Church, as a Church, is the only one that enters into the intellectual conflict in behalf of the divine Saviour, with whom it alone throughout the centuries has never broken faith.

II.—CHRIST AND HIS BELIEVING APOLOGISTS

For positive Christianity Christ is everything. No believing Christian permits this sacred conviction to be contested. Even those who hold aloof from the faith also declare " that the earthly life of Jesus Christ constitutes the origin, source, strength, and in the deepest sense the content of all that has ever been known under the name of the Christian religion " (Chamberlain). This even those who dream of a Christianity without Christ do not deny.

Adolf Harnack has written : " The confession of the Christian Church is that there is salvation in none other, and that there is also no other name given unto men, by which we can be saved, than the name of Jesus Christ. With this confession it has begun; in this confession its martyrs have died; and from this confession it still derives its strength, as it did 1,800 years ago. It identifies with this Person the whole substance of religion—life in God, the forgiveness of sins, and consolation in suffering."[2]

[1] Drews, *Christusmythe,* vi, ix.
[2] *Das Christentum und die Geschichte,* 3 (Leipzig, 1904).

In a word, Jesus Christ is the beginning, centre, final aim, and heart of Christianity. No more is necessary in order to perceive *the whole purport of the defence of Christ against the modern, negative standpoint in regard to Jesus.* Whoever co-operates in showing scientifically to the world the portrait of the divine Saviour, and in establishing it firmly in his own soul by the vital power of faith, accomplishes for himself and for humanity a high and ever-enduring intellectual and civilizing work, because Christ is " full of grace and truth."

In view, then, of the conclusions which we have thus far reached, it will not be surprising if we prefer to use the words " a defence of *Christ* " instead of " a defence of *Christianity.*" Yet, in accordance with an old established habit, we must make Christianity, as such, the principal object of our investigation, and bring in the person of the Saviour simply as a constituent, though certainly the most important part, of this principal question.

Christianity in its foundation, expansion and development, in its persecutions, its triumphs, its victorious course through the centuries, and in its creative activity in the spheres of religion and morals, science, art, culture, public life, the family and the individual soul, is really not only the greatest, mightiest and sublimest phenomenon of history, but a phenomenon which can never be explained without divine intervention. The mere fact that Christianity exists is and remains an obvious proof that its origin was divine, and that its founder was an ambassador of God.

But to such considerations modern criticism is blind; and if we could at one stroke eliminate from the world the phenomenon of Christianity and its history, the inferences drawn from them to Christ would nevertheless be rejected as unscientific. In fact, in the circles of our opponents there is not the least agreement as to what Christianity really is, and it is always asserted—and it must be owned with some justice—that " the historical importance of Christianity cannot be measured and correctly estimated without an accurate acquaintance with this phenomenon [of the person of Jesus Christ]. On the other hand, the contrary is not true, and the figure of Jesus Christ is to-day obscured and removed from us, rather than unveiled to our scrutinizing gaze by the historical evolution of the Churches."[1] Nevertheless, in consequence of the latest criticism of the Gospels, " the manifestation of the one divine Man has been made so prominent that unbelievers as well as believers cannot but recognize it as the source and central point of Christianity."[2]

Thus the defence of Christianity cannot easily become a

[1] *Die Grundlagen*, i, 221.
[2] *ibid.*, p. 228.

defence of Christ, which shall suit the modern world. But, on the contrary, *the defence of Christ is always the best defence of Christianity,* and is, above all, the one best suited to our time.

Even apart from this, however, it is a welcome circumstance that, both among believers and unbelievers, interest centres more and more upon the innermost core, the head and heart of the Christian religion—the one and only Lord and Saviour Jesus Christ. Nothing is more adapted to deepen and strengthen the orthodox point of view than to rivet one's gaze upon the God-Man. And if there exists any hope whatever of reconciling the modern civilized world with Christianity, the reconciliation will surely be effected in the name and person of him of whom it was written : " He is our peace, who hath made both one, and hath broken down the middle wall of partition between us, having abolished in his flesh the enmity " (Eph. ii, 14).

Yet in order to meet the needs and demands of the present age, the defence of Jesus Christ must, *in reference to its subject-matter,* be otherwise constructed than a few years ago. It is not radically different, for its essential substance is and remains the old, unchangeable confession of the primitive Church, that " *Jesus is the Christ, the Son of God* " (John xx, 31). Truth and error remain the same, and with them also the *apologia perennis* remains the same. But the enemy, according to the temporary condition of the world and science, continually changes his method of attack, and thereby forces the apologist to adapt himself to it in his vindication of the truth. This is especially true in reference to the Messiahship and divinity of Jesus Christ.

Thus our opponents' attitude towards the *foundations* on which the proofs of the Messiahship and divinity of Jesus rest—namely, towards the sources and documents relating to the life of Jesus—has become, almost over night, an entirely different one. While sceptical criticism, until recently, almost universally altogether denied the genuineness and apostolic origin of the Gospels and of the New Testament writings, to-day it is more and more disposed, as we have already remarked, once more to assign these books to their original authors and their proper age. It even condescends to recognize, on the whole, the honesty and literary integrity of the New Testament writers. Yet it evades the necessary conclusion as to the scientific credibility of the sources of the life of Jesus by assuming that the sacred writers have, consciously or unconsciously, not written the true and actual history of Jesus, but have designed the portrait of Christ according to the standards of the belief of that time and with the embellishments characteristic of the period.

If, therefore, the genuineness of the original New Testament sources has to be proved, another question also arises to-day—perhaps the most important of all—whether the Apostles and their pupils wished to write, and have actually recorded, the *history of Jesus,* or merely the *belief about Jesus.* That sufficient attention has not been paid to this question in our apologetic handbooks and our larger works, anyone can easily convince himself.

Also those who are concerned with the vindication of the Messiahship and divinity of Christ ought, in the *formation* of their lines of defence, to keep the attitude of modern criticism, especially in its latest phase, more clearly in view than is usually the case. We leave out of consideration here how far this wish is justified in respect of the selection and exposition of the *proofs* of the Messiahship and divinity of Jesus. We shall have occasion to express our opinion on that point in another volume of this work. But the *consciousness* which Jesus had of his Messiahship and divinity is almost invariably treated, in the presentation of the evidence, too briefly and superficially.

Whoever has come into close touch with modern liberal criticism—and it is against this that every defence of Christ must be to-day directed—will confess that the problems of the consciousness and personal testimony of our Lord have forced, and are still forcing, all other problems into the background. Did Jesus really know, and did he really confess, that he was the Christ? Whence comes his Messianic consciousness? What is the nature of it? What did he think of his Messianic activity and character? Did he mean to imply that he was absolutely a supernatural, divine being or not? Did he conceive himself to be the Son of God in the strict metaphysical sense, or has the divine christology of the Church's faith been formed only gradually under the influence of Pauline, synoptical and Johannine ideas?

These and other questions are now of paramount interest, and justify us in dividing our defence of Christ into two parts—the first of which deals with the consciousness of Jesus, and the second with the evidence given by Jesus himself for his Messiahship and divinity. Whether this conception corresponds to the nature of the subject, in itself considered, we do not inquire. It certainly does correspond to the nature of antagonistic criticism at the present time, and to the standpoint of its representatives. It is, however, the duty and task of the peace-loving apologist to be as conciliatory as possible to his opponent, and to take the latter's standpoint into consideration, although he may not be able to share it.

Apart from its subject-matter, this is especially true of the *method* of the defence of Christ. Who is Christ? Are the

Gospel, the person, the doctrine, the life and deeds of Christ
—that is to say, is *Christianity*—actual history? Did Christ
declare himself to be really the Messiah and God, and did he
furnish the evidence for his Messiahship and deity? That is
the one great *historical question* to which all others lead at
last.

Only *by means of historical science* is this question to be
answered, and only thus is the appearance of Jesus Christ
and Christianity on this earth to be comprehended and explained. It is true history cannot immediately and plainly
demonstrate the truth of the Christian revelation and of the
divinity of Jesus Christ, but it can prove the truth of the *fact*
that Christ represented himself as God, and his religion as
divine, and that he undoubtedly furnished proofs for this
assertion. And precisely in this do we see the scientific
guarantee for the credibility of Christianity. Faith cannot
be *attested* by means of history, but credibility can and
must be *demonstrated*. Faith is not a matter of science;
but it is the affair of science, and in this case also the affair
of history, to prove that our faith is scientifically based upon
the facts of revelation and Christianity, and is therefore
reasonable.

Now, it is true, modern criticism is always boasting of its
purely historical method, and asserting that it has passed
judgement upon primitive Christianity and its belief in Christ
scientifically by means of history. Nothing is, however,
more unhistorical than the procedure of negative criticism.
This has been already pointed out, and we shall, step by step,
be able to observe this everywhere. From Reimarus and
Bauer to Harnack and Wrede, all the adherents of the so-
called critical school approach the manifestation of Christ
with the *philosophical* presumptions of *rationalism*, which
claim that any supramundane intervention of God in Nature
and any supernatural revelation are impossible, and therefore
that everything supernatural in the life, words and works of
Jesus must at the very outset be stricken out of his history.
Richard Rothe and, after him, Otto Ritschl, utter the following " fundamental thoughts of an easy-going, cheerful Christianity "—characteristic of the liberal school of Schleiermacher, Albrecht Ritschl and Harnack : " *We know* that
nature does not allow herself to be disturbed in her sacred
law of necessity by any miracles ; we know that the fulness of
the idea of humanity is not poured into one individual, and
that even Jesus can have been only one genius among many ;
we know that the accounts of his life are only fables, which
the childish imagination of his first, immature churches
lovingly wove about the portrait which had imprinted itself
indistinctly upon their recollection. . . . The historian must
not expect our age to accept the old ecclesiastical ideas,

however true they may be. For this age necessarily repudiates everything *superhuman* and extraordinary."[1]

To the majority of the rationalistic critics even these views are not extreme enough. Consciously or unconsciously, they judge of the facts of Christianity from the philosophical standpoint of *agnosticism*. According to this, "human reason is entirely limited, first, to phenomena—that is, to the objects which come to external manifestation; and, secondly, to the manner of their manifestation. Beyond this reason may not and cannot go. Hence it cannot also lift itself to God, and cannot know his existence outside of visible things. It follows, therefore, that God can in no way be the direct subject of scientific research; and as for history, God has in no sense any part in it as an historical person. . . . In the person of Christ science and history can discern nothing but a man. Accordingly, everything is to be eliminated from his history which bears any semblance to the divine, and all his discourses and deeds—in short, everything which is not in keeping with his human character, position, education and local and temporal environment is to be denied him."[2]

This is not the place to disprove *philosophically* the error of rationalism and agnosticism. But it ought to be evident at once that it is contradictory to the *historical* method to adopt the rationalistic and agnostic point of view as a standard by which to estimate the person of Jesus Christ. Only that method is historical which, without any previous assumption, examines the facts of Christianity, and supplements, or possibly corrects, one's own religious and philosophic opinions and views according to the result which has been historically established. If the modern investigation of the life of Jesus had been conducted thus, it would never have come, as it has, to the brink of ruin—a fact which is acknowledged even by its adherents.[3]

All the problems of this modern christology, and the whole opposition of Modernists to the Christ of the Gospels, find their explanation in the preconceived assumptions of rationalistic and agnostic philosophy.

If we, however, summon the opponents of the Christian revelation before the bar of fair, unclouded history, we, on our side, must of course be equally scrupulous. In this case we must not, as apologists, presuppose either the faith or the scientific credibility of Christianity. Thus, all those matters of christology which become knowable *only in faith and through faith* are excluded in advance from the defence of Christ. To these belong the mystery of the hypostatic

[1] Martin Kahler, *Dogmatische Zeitfragen*, i, 48 ff. (Leipzig, 1898).
[2] Pius X, *Pascendi*.
[3] A. Schweitzer, *Von Reimarus zu Wrede*, 4-11; Fr. Lipsius, *Protestantenblatt*, 702 (Berlin, 1906).

union and the trinitarian relation of the Son of God to the Father and the Holy Ghost.

But also the sources from which the truth about Christ and Christianity comes to us must be here estimated merely from the point of view of *historical science, not from that of faith.* According to Christian belief, the stream of ancient Church tradition bears along with it the gold of revelation, and Catholic consciousness recognizes tradition as a true witness, and, hence, as a source of supernatural faith. By the apologist, however, the wealth of Christian tradition must be weighed with the usual scales of historical criticism, and regarded as purely historical material. According to faith and theology, the Holy Scriptures of the Old and New Testaments have also a twofold significance. They are, first, "divine books"—that is, books written under the special inspiration and guidance of the Holy Ghost, so that God himself is their chief author, although the human writer has done his work in them as a free instrument of God. In the second place, they are reliable, historical works concerning the origin and development of revealed religion.

The apologist, however, must, from his standpoint, pay no attention to the alleged inspired character of the Bible. He must see in the sacred books of the New Testament merely historical documents treating of the life of Jesus and primitive Christianity, and he has first to prove that these documents are original and credible before he builds up from them the defence of Christ.

PART I
THE SOURCES

REVIEW OF CHRISTIAN AND NON-CHRISTIAN SOURCES

SINCE Jesus Christ, even if considered merely as an historical person, is the greatest man in the world's history, it is fortunate that more and better authenticated accounts of him have been handed down to us than of any other personality of the ancient world. These accounts are partly *Christian* and partly *non-christian*.

The latter are few in number, but this is not to be wondered at, if we reflect that " Christ crucified was to the Jews a stumbling-block and to the Gentiles foolishness " (1 Cor. i, 23). Christianity appeared to the *pagan Romans* at first only as a Jewish sect. As such, they naturally felt little interest in it. There were also, in the first century after Christ, innumerable cults and religious confessions in the broad empire. Moreover, the Founder of the Christian religious movement had lived only in a corner of the Roman world, had been active for a very brief time, and had called forth no political revolution whatsoever. We cannot, therefore, expect that Roman writers would pay attention to him. Suetonius mentions him cursorily in his biography of the Emperor Claudius.[1] Tacitus, the sole consul in the year 97, speaks of the execution of Christ under Pontius Pilate, and of the rapid spread of Christianity and its persecution.[2] Pliny, Governor of Bithynia, testifies in his letter to the Emperor Trajan that the believers worship Christ as God, and have been admonished by him to observe a strict morality.[3] Phlegon, the freedman of Hadrian, knows of the eclipse of the sun at the death of Jesus, and mentions that the latter predicted many events which had since then actually taken place. Phlegon's utterances must, however, be taken with precaution, since he even confounds Christ with Peter.[4] The philosopher, Celsus, who, in the reign of Marcus Aurelius, first undertook to study Christianity minutely and to refute it, boasts indeed of being acquainted with sources of information concerning the life of Jesus until then completely unknown.[5] But in reality he had not at his disposal one single new fact. Apart from the Gospels, he was acquainted only with current Jewish gossip.[6]

---

[1] *Vita Claudii*, c. 25. [2] *Anal.*, xv, 44.
[3] *Epist.*, x, 96. [4] Origen, *Contra Celsum*, ii, 13, 33, 59.
[5] *id.*, *l.c.*, ii, 13.
[6] See Seitz, *Christuszeugnisse aus dem klassischen Altertum von un gläubiger Seite* (Cöln, 1906).

It is evident, especially in the Gospels of Matthew and John, that *the Jews* gave themselves, from the first, all imaginable trouble to pourtray the life of Jesus after their own fashion. Even before the first Gospel had been written, a nucleus of malicious legends had formed itself about the name of the hated Nazarene.[1] In the course of the first and at the beginning of the second century, the oral calumnies of the Jews against Christ increased in number. We learn this from Justin,[2] Tertullian,[3] and Hegesippus,[4] as well as from the scoffer Celsus.[5] Soon after, some of these false stories about Jesus were established in written form in the *Talmud,* the great organ of the Rabbis after Christ, and were thereby introduced into official Jewish theology.[6] After the fourth century, the oral and written web of lies consolidated itself more and more in a caricature of the life of Jesus (*Toldoth Jeshu*), which is even now in the hands of many children of Israel.[7] According to the confession of Jewish investigators themselves, however, this whole tradition of the life of Jesus does not represent the truth concerning the Saviour, but merely the subjective views, wishes and feelings of post-christian Judaism.[8] This is certainly the mildest judgement that one could pronounce upon it. The Christians, beginning with the Apostle Matthew,[9] have always stigmatized the Jewish calumnies against Christ as patent lies and intentional slanders. The most important Jewish source of information concerning the life of Jesus is an unfortunately much con-tested passage from the "Jewish Antiquities" of Flavius Josephus, a Jewish patriot and subsequently Roman renegade, towards the end of the first century.[10] We shall refer to this later.[11]

But so much the more zealously did *Christian writers* endeavour to preserve the portrait and the words of the Master after he himself no more walked on earth. Already the Evangelist Luke can point to the fact that "Many have taken in hand to set forth in order a narration of the things

---

[1] Matt. xxviii, 15.
[2] *Dialogus cum Tryphone Judæo,* 17, 108, 117.
[3] *Ad nationes,* i, 14; *de spectaculis,* c. 30.
[4] Eusebius, *H. E.* ii, 23.
[5] Origen, *Contra Celsum,* ii, 13 *sqq.*
[6] See Franz Delitzsch, *Ernste Fragen an die Gebildeten der jüdischen Nation* (Leipzig, 1880); Laible, *Jesus Christus im Talmud* (Leipzig, 1900); A. Marmorstein, *Talmud und Neues Testament* (1908), together with the comprehensive article *Jesus im Talmud,* by Arnold Meyer, in Edgar Hennecke's *Handbuch zu den N. T. Apokryphen,* 49 ff. (Tübingen, 1904).
[7] Samuel Krauss, *Das Leben Jesu nach jüdischen Quellen,* 22 (Berlin, 1902).
[8] See Krauss's admissions, *op. cit.,* 237.   [9] Matt. xxviii, 15.
[10] *Antiquitates Jos. Flavii,* xviii, 3, 3.
[11] In the second volume of this work, "The Miracles of Jesus."

that have been accomplished among us, according as they have delivered them unto us, who from the beginning were eye-witnesses and ministers of the word " (Luke i, 1). Hereby well meant, but not wholly satisfactory, records of small extent seem to have been in the mind of Luke. The authors of our Gospels added indeed the sifted material of these written documents to the substance of their own Gospels, which they already knew from the testimony of their own eyes and ears and those of others, and thus created finally their portraitures of the life of Christ. Critics of the Gospel sources have busied themselves for decades with the attempt to find out and reproduce the different sources used by the Evangelists. But even if they should ever succeed in finding a satisfactory solution of this literally and historically im-portant problem, they would not thereby bring to light any previously unknown documents of the life of Jesus. Those original sources are already hidden in our Gospels, and their historical worth is, in the last analysis, guaranteed only by the Evangelists.

The so-called *Logia,* or " Sayings," or " Discourses " of the Lord still always form the principal theme for discus-sion. Probably, or even only possibly, there was in the very earliest times a collection of the sayings and discourses of the Lord. Schleiermacher in 1832 " discovered" this when he misunderstood a note of Papias of Hierapolis. Papias reports :[1] " Now Matthew wrote down the Logia in the Hebrew tongue. But everyone translated them as best he could." These words have been always and only referred to our Matthew—that is, to his original Aramaic text, while Schleiermacher wrongly applied[2] it to only one collection of sayings and discourses.[3] The mischief that has since then been made with these Logia borders on the incredible. As a matter of fact, up to this time no one has succeeded in establishing with certainty any trace of them outside the Bible. The " Sayings of Jesus " which have been found in recent times—as, for example, on the papyrus of Fayum in Central Egypt, on that of Behnesa in Lower Egypt,[4] and elsewhere—are interpolated Logia-texts. On the other hand, many critics think that the collection of Sayings lies at the basis of that special property which is common to the Gospels of Matthew and Luke, in contrast to the Gospel of Mark. Harnack has lately even attempted to reconstruct

[1] Eusebius, *H. E.,* iii, 39.
[2] Proof given by Belser, *Einleitung in das N. T.,* 251-253 (Freiburg, 1901).
[3] Schleiermacher, *Ueber die Zeugnisse des Papias von unseren beiden ersten Evangelien* in *Theolog. Studien,* 735 (1832).
[4] See the complete literature on this subject in Ehrhard, *Die altchrist-liche Literatur und ihre Erforschung von* 1884-1900, i, 124 (1900) ; and Otto Bardenhewer, *Geschichte der altkirchlichen Literatur,* i, 389-391 (1902). (All published by Herder, Freiburg.)

the text of the Logia out of Matthew and Luke.[1]   Yet it
remains questionable whether the Logia, or only a part of
them, are thus recovered.   But even if Harnack's supposition
should prove true, we should (let us once more emphasize the
fact) even in the Logia find no new source of information
about the life of Jesus, but only a new source of the Gospels.

Quite without reason some modern critics assert that the
Logia are identical with an original Gospel written by
Matthew.   Not only does this identity rest on mere imagination, but " probably the whole so-called *original Matthew* is
not the Aramaic primitive form of our Matthew, but a
fantasy, which first began to exist in the nineteenth century
through the mistake of an old passage in the writings of a
Church Father[2] . . . and has been already buried again at
the commencement of the twentieth century."[3]   In any case,
it is a biting irony on the impartiality of the criticism of
negation that anyone, with a total disregard of the real
Gospels, should have built up repeatedly the most airy
hypotheses on Matthew's alleged original book of Sayings,
and have drawn from this " authentic " views about Christ
and Christianity.[4]

Exactly the same thing is true of the so-called *original
Mark*.   Ever since the middle of the nineteenth century all
" critical " heads have been haunted by the dogma that a
short primitive Gospel forms the basis of our Gospel of Mark,
and, at a greater distance, of the other two synoptic Gospels
also.   And how many times have we seen the text of
this original Mark reconstructed to the smallest details before
our astonished eyes.   On closer scrutiny and more serious
investigation, however, the much-vaunted discovery of the
original Mark dissolved into thin air.   Harnack already some
years ago was able to assert : " The hypothesis that our
canonical Mark has replaced an ' original Mark ' rightly
loses more and more adherents."[5]   At present this " mutila-
tion [of the Gospel of Mark] through the hypothesis of a
primitive Mark, as well as its historical depreciation,"[6] is
almost universally given up as uncritical.   We have said
that the original ante-evangelical documents concerning the

[1] A. Harnack, *Sprüche und Reden Jesu, die zweite Quelle des Matthäus
und Lukas,* 88 ff, 175 ff. (Leipzig, 1907).

[2] Of Papias. (See above.)

[3] Richard Grützmacher, *Die Jungfraugeburt,* 22 (Berlin, 1906); *cf.*
Th. Zahn, *Einleitung in das N. T.,* ii, 294 ff (Leipzig, 1899).

[4] So recently still Adolf Hausrath, *Jesus und die N. T. Schriftsteller,*
i, 178 (Berlin, 1908); *cf.* Otto Pfleiderer, *Das Urchristentum, seine
Schriften und Lehren,* ii, 161 (Berlin, 1902).

[5] *Chronologie der altchristlichen Literatur,* i, 700 (Leipzig, 1897).

[6] B. Weiss, *Die Quellen der synoptischen Überlieferung,* 222 (Leipzig,
1908).

life of Jesus are incorporated in our canonical Gospels and have thereby been saved for history. This statement must, nevertheless, be a little modified. It appears that at least a small part of those old materials was not used by the New Testament writers. In old Christian literature there are found here and there various utterances of the Lord, and further items of information about Jesus Christ, or from him, which we seek for in vain in the canonical writings of the New Testament. These uncanonical fragments—the so-called *Agrapha,* or " unclaimed " words of the Lord—may perhaps in part contain the remainder of the so-called ante-evangelical accounts. Yet the yield in historical material which the Agrapha offer is very small, and in all cases very problematical. Moreover, in the best authenticated specimen of the Agrapha, there remains the possibility that it can just as well be a later addition to the Gospels, as a fragment antedating the Gospels, or a fragment of the Gospel itself.[1]

Only those Agrapha can be seriously considered which go back to the oldest uncanonical literary monuments of Christianity, to the writings of the *apostolic* Fathers. Apart from the New Testament books, we possess a number of old Christian writings from the years A.D. 70 to 140, which contain individual items of information about Jesus Christ —*the Doctrine of the Apostles, the Epistle of Barnabas, the Epistle of Clement, the Epistles of SS Ignatius and Polycarp, and the Apologies of Quadratus and Aristides.* Their utterances are, indeed, very important, since they confirm in all essential features the Gospel portrait of the Saviour. Yet they do not offer any new, important narrations exceeding those of the Gospels. Evidently there was nothing really new to be learned about Jesus. Moreover, the Gospels enjoyed such high esteem, and Christianity held so firmly to the purely apostolical tradition, that representations of Christ, which did not originate with the Apostles, would have had no prospect of success.

For that very reason writers eager for novelties sought to put forged books into circulation bearing the names of the Apostles. Such, for example, were the *Proclamation of Peter,* the *Acts of Peter,* the *Gospel of Peter,* the *Gospel of the Twelve,* the *Gospels of Matthias, Philip* and *Thomas,* and

---

[1] See Nestle, *Novi Testamenti Græci Supplementum,* 89 ff. (Lipsiæ, 1896); Erwin Preusschen, *Antilegomena. Die Reste der ausserkanonischen Evangelien und urchrist. Überlieferungen,* 2nd ed., 26 (Giessen, 1905); Alfred Resch, *Agrapha,* in *Texte und Untersuchungen zur Gesch. der altchrist. Literatur,* vol. XXX (1906); in regard to the value of the Agrapha for Gospel research Resch expresses himself perhaps too optimistically, pp. 387-398.

even a *Gospel of Judas.*[1] The most of these *apocryphal* ("*secret*") *writings* were invented by heretics for the palliation of error.

Sometimes, however, even foolish believers allowed themselves to commit such a "pious fraud." The apocryphal literature originating thus is, indeed, not without value for the history of the genuine apostolic writings, yet it cannot be considered as a source of information concerning the life of Jesus. Otto Pfleiderer is certainly right when he thus expresses his opinion regarding the apocryphal writings : "We see that in this débris of apocryphal remnants of the Gospels a great variety of materials has been jumbled together; together with primitive rock from the primary stratum of tradition are found also wonderful petrifications from late formations. But as literary and historical monuments, they have their incontestable importance."[2]

Moreover, the Apocrypha have come down to us only in a fragmentary form. In the gradually increasing flood of genuine and forged literary productions about Christ and Christianity the Church accepted finally only such books as she regarded as inspired, and therefore as *Holy Scriptures of the New Testament.* But the science of history, which does not allow the inspired character of the Bible, is also bound to recognize the thousand-year-old tradition that the truth about Jesus is to be found only in the New Testament.[3]

The majority of the New Testament books belong to the literary category of *didactic writings.* They bring out the teachings of Jesus, but only here and there make an allusion to his life. Of all the didactic writings the *Epistles of the Apostle Paul* contain most historical information. The genuineness of the Pauline writings, if we make no reference to the pastoral writings and the Epistle to the Hebrews, is regarded, even in liberal circles, as an established fact. Wilhelm Wrede, an extremely liberal critic, has written on this subject the following incisive words : "The view which is so widespread in Holland and uttered also sporadically in Germany—namely, that all of Paul's Epistles belonged to a later age, we can now regard only as a great mistake of criticism. Epistles like the First to the Thessalonians, the Epistle to the Galatians, and the Second to the Corinthians, refer in a hundred particulars and allusions with the greatest definiteness to conditions such as are conceivable only but a few decades after the death of Jesus. And the forger is yet

---

1 Tischendorf edited the editions of all the remnants of the apocryphal Gospels, *Evangelia apocrypha* (Lipsiæ, 1853); Nestle, *N. T. Græci Supplementum* (Lipsiæ, 1896); Preusschen, *Antilegomena* (Giessen, 1905); E. Hennecke, *Neutestamentliche Apokryphen,* and *Handbuch zu den N. T. Apokryphen* (Tübingen, 1904).
2 *Das Urchristentum,* 2nd ed., ii, 171.
3 Oskar Holtzmann, *Christus,* 27 (Leipzig, 1907).

to be born who would know how to invent such unintentional, individual, purely personal and instantly conceived expressions as are here so numerous, and who could, moreover, in the whole range of the Epistles put forward fraudulently a finished and original personality as their author."[1] Otto Schmiedel[2] remarks, in agreement with the foregoing : " It is settled, therefore, that the genuineness of the chief Pauline Epistles, and therewith the fundamental facts of the life of Jesus, are assured."

" It is true," adds Adolf Harnack, " as the criticism of the early history of Christianity has even to-day not yet overcome the furthest extreme of radical censorship, there are not wanting a few scholars who declare that all the Epistles of Paul are ungenuine and forgeries of the second century."[3] By serious critics, however, as has been said, only the Epistle to the Hebrews and the pastoral Epistles—that is, the two Epistles to Timothy and the Epistle to Titus—are often objected to.

The Pauline origin of the *pastoral Epistles* is, nevertheless, recognized more universally from year to year even in Protestant circles.   B. Weiss, for example, makes them really equally genuine with the other Pauline writings.[4]   Th. Zahn alleges that " the confidence with which for several generations the genuiness of these Epistles has been denied, before that of all other Epistles bearing the name of Paul, finds no support in tradition."[5]   Rather do the pastoral Epistles have to suffer simply because their contents will not everywhere coincide with the preconceived doctrinal opinions of the liberal critics.[6]   It is, moreover, undoubted even by our opponents—and that is the principal thing—that the pastoral Epistles elaborate " Pauline material."[7]   " That they are built up from the Pauline Epistles is a result of criticism which need not again be proved."[8]

Also in regard to the *Epistle to the Hebrews,* its Pauline

---

[1] *Paulus,* 2 f. (Tübingen, 1907).

[2] *Die Hauptprobleme der Leben-Jesu Forschung,* 2nd ed., 16 (Tübingen, 1906).

[3] A. Harnack, *Ueber die Glaubwürdigkeit der evangel. Geschichte,* in *Christliche Welt,* 19th year, 318 (1905).   Harnack publishes here extracts from the lectures which he delivered at the Berlin University in the winter term of 1904-1905.

[4] B. Weiss, *Lehrbuch der Einleitung in das N. T.,* 3rd ed. (Berlin, 1897), and *Das Neue Testament,* ii (1902).

[5] *Einleitung in das N. T.* i, 457 (Leipzig, 1897).

[6] See proof in Zahn, *op. cit.,* pp. 459-489 : *Die Echtheit der Briefe an Timotheus und Titus;* Johannes Belser, *Einleitung in das N. T.,* 630-652 (Freiburg, 1901), *Die Eigenart und Echtheit der Briefe an Timotheus und Titus;* Cornely, *Introductio in utriusque Testamenti libros sacros,* iii, 551 ff., ed. altera (Paris, 1892).

[7] Harnack, *Die Chronologie der altchrist. Literatur bis Eusebius,* i, 480 (Leipzig, 1897).

[8] Harnack, *id.*

character is more and more conceded. Barth. Heigl[1] recently came, after thorough investigation, to the conclusion that there is no decisive argument against the direct authorship of Paul. And even those investigators who deny the Pauline origin of the Epistle do not call in question the fact that in its import it goes back to Paul, or at least is intimately related to him. On the other hand, they concede that the Epistle was written in the lifetime of the Apostle to the Gentiles, or, in any case, shortly after his death.[2] Thus it unquestionably is to be regarded as a witness for Christian opinions in the time of Paul. In case it was not a work of the great Apostle its importance would rather gain than lose thereby. It would then take its place near St Paul as an independent witness to inform us about the original Christian Church of those days, and to confirm the statements of the Apostle to the Gentiles.

For research into the life of Christ the Pauline writings, in particular, are invaluable. The powerful personality of Jesus stood so vividly and constantly before the mental vision of Paul that it lives again in his Epistles and takes plastic form. Harnack estimates the historical value of his utterances as follows :[3] " We may be certain that what Paul informs us about Jesus, as fact, is almost as reliable and valuable as if the disciples had related it personally. I say almost as reliable because a subjective element is never to be quite excluded. But, on the whole, what Paul imparts to us of the historical Jesus, as fact, must have corresponded to the very earliest Christian preaching. There was never a controversy on this point between the Apostles. . . . If one sums up what the post-pauline Christian writers down to the beginning of the second century report, and what Paul himself tells us of Jesus, one can truly speak of a *fifth unwritten Gospel;* and in a certain way this Gospel is even more important than the four which we possess. However many or however few details that fifth ecumenical may contain, the great features of that portrait—the Teacher, the Prophet, the Saviour,[4] sublimity in humiliation, holiness, love of enemies, intercourse with sinners, the Cross and the manifestations after death—are testified to. Before all, however, it is certain that this life of Jesus, however it may have terminated, and this personality, whatever characteristics it

---

[1] *Verfasser und Addresse des Briefes an die Hebräer* (Freiburg, 1905).

[2] B. Weiss, *Lehrbuch der Einleitung in das N. T.,* puts its date at A.D. 65-66; Th. Zahn about A.D. 80; A. Jülicher, *Einleitung in das N. T.,* 136, at about 75-85; Harnack, *Chronologie,* 479, declares, " as the only sure thing," that the Epistle was written between 65 and 95.

[3] *Ueber die Glaubwürdigkeit der evan. Geschichte,* 319, 436.

[4] Harnack adds : " But not one miracle is reported by him." But how about Paul in 1 Cor. xv? And Quadratus (Eusebius, *H. E.,* iv, 3, 2)?

may have had, have laid the foundation for the declaration of faith : ' This is the Lord and the Son of God.' "

Formal pourtrayals of the life of Jesus are contained, however, only in the *four canonical Gospels*. Precisely for the reason that they proclaimed the Gospel—" the glad tidings "—of Jesus Christ and his salvation, they received already in the earliest times the name : " Gospels of our Lord Jesus Christ, according to Matthew, Mark, Luke and John." The Gospels are, in fact, nothing else than the classic sources of information and the documents of the divine-human life and history of Jesus Christ.

It becomes at once comprehensible, therefore, why, ever since the days of incipient rationalism—that is, for about one hundred and forty years—the question of the historical value of these fundamental books of our religion has been always over and over again asked and answered. From this side and from that, out of the conflict of opinions and out of serious research there has grown up an exceedingly rich and almost unlimited literature connected with the criticism of the Gospels. Attack and defence have been renewed innumerable times, in all conceivable positions, and with the sharpest intellectual weapons. To-day we can estimate with perfect confidence the results gained, which mean a brilliant vindication of the Gospels. Even if the conflict may enter into many a new phase, another answer to these questions is simply impossible.

The historical value of our Gospels depends, of course, like that of every other source of history, upon two points. One question is, whether they are *authentic*—that is, whether they really originate from an epoch near, and from men who themselves stood in proximity to the events described; the second is, whether they are *credible*—that is, whether we may rely upon these men and their narrative. Accordingly, we have now to examine and put to the test the *authenticity* and the *credibility* of the Gospels.

CHAPTER I

THE GENUINENESS OF THE GOSPELS

I.—Genuineness of the Gospels and Recent Criticism.

ACCORDING to Christian *tradition*, the four Gospels had their origin in the second half of the first century; the three so-called " synoptic " Gospels —that is, Gospels written from a common point of view—originating between the years A.D. 50 and 70; the fourth, however, between 80 and 100. Tradition also points out as the authors of the four Gospels, the publican Levi, subsequently the Apostle Matthew; the disciple of St Peter, Mark; the physician and pupil of St Paul, Luke; and John, the son of Zebedee, one of the original twelve Apostles.

It was *rationalism* that first attacked the correctness of these assertions. In so doing it admittedly[1] did not allow itself to be guided by historical arguments (though these are the only ones which are decisive), but by preconceived religio-philosophical opinions. It wanted especially at any price to eliminate the supernatural entirely, and for this purpose sought for a long time to undermine the credibility of the Gospels, which are themselves in complete harmony with the supernatural. Yet all the attempts to attain this end broke down before the indubitable fact that we here have to do with writings issuing from the immediate circle of the disciples of Jesus and the Apostles.

Then Ferdinand Christian Baur and his pupil, David Friedrich Strauss, were bold enough totally to ignore the genuineness of the Gospels in order to create thus a clear path for the rationalistic explanation of Christianity.

Strauss placed the origin of the Gospels at 150 years after Christ, and certainly needed all that time as a support for his airy hypothesis that the Christianity of the Gospels grew gradually out of legends.

It was *Baur* himself who gave the death-blow to the mythical theory of his pupil, but he invented the hypothesis of " deception," which, by the way, is equally valueless. Appealing to the " higher criticism," he maintained that the early history of Christianity ran its course in continual

---

[1] Strauss, *Das Leben Jesu,* 3rd ed., pp. 86, 94 ff. (Tübingen, 1838); Renan, *Vie de Jésus,* vi (Berlin, 1863); Schweitzer, *Von Reimarus zu Wrede,* pp. 4, 9, 15 (Tübingen, 1907).

antagonism between the so-called Gentile-Christian policy of
Paul and that of the party of Peter and the other Apostles,
which was more friendly to the Jews; but that finally the
hostile brothers became reconciled, and that then, in order
to close the previous line of cleavage, the four Gospels were
composed, being in reality documents resulting from a compromise.

According to Baur, " Matthew's Gospel " appeared about
A.D. 130, and this was made use of about the year 150 to
produce the Gospel of the heretic Marcion, and to the work
thus formed was given the name of " Luke." Soon after, out
of Matthew and Luke was compiled the work known as
" Mark "; and, finally, about A.D. 170, the Gospel of " John "
first saw the light.[1]

It was considered a great piece of good fortune to have
suddenly found all this out at one stroke, and thereby to have
turned all the old literature of Christianity topsy-turvy.
Baur became, on this account, the founder of the " younger
Tübingen school," which was very properly designated as
" critical, with a distinct purpose," although it called itself
" historical." Whoever did not agree with it was simply
declared to be lacking in a comprehension of " higher
historical criticism." Köstlin, Zeller, Schwegler and Holsten
went over entirely, Keim, Hilgenfeld, Volkmar and others
partially, into the camp of Baur.

Bruno Bauer went even further than the " Master of
Tübingen " in his unlimited criticism of primitive Christian
literature.[2] In the name of " higher criticism " the whole of
early Christianity and with it also the Gospels were transformed into a seething cauldron, full of controversies, lies
and subtleties.[3]

That was too much. These " fantastic ideas "[4] could not
maintain themselves permanently. Even De Wette[5] predicted that such extravagant criticism would destroy itself;
and, like him, other thorough-going rationalists such as
Karl Hase, Ewald, Schenkel and even Renan, refused to
follow the school of Baur. Soon every honourable investigator was ashamed to be numbered with the " Tübingens,"
and once more men called to mind seriously the declarations
of primitive Christian literature, and sought to determine
thereby the age of the Gospels.

Th·1s, *in the second half of the nineteenth century,* criticism

[1] Baur, *Paulus der Apostel Jesu Christi* (Tübingen, 1845); *Kritische
Untersuchungen über die kanonischen Evangelien* (1847).
[2] Harnack, *Lehrbuch der Dogmengeschichte,* 3rd ed., 51 note.
[3] Bauer, *Kritik d. evang. Geschichte des Johannes; Kritik d. evang.
Geschichte der Synoptiker; Kritik der Evangelien; Kritik der paulinischen Briefe*   [4] Schweitzer, *Von Reimarus zu Wrede,* 9.
[5] *Kurzgefasstes exeget. Handbuch zum N. T. Apostelgeschichte,*
vol. V (Leipzig, 1848).

approached always nearer to the traditional views. The first three, or *synoptic Gospels,* in the opinion of Theodor Keim,[1] originated between A.D. 70 and 117; according to Hilgenfeld[2] from A.D. 70 to 100; according to H. J. Holtzmann[3] between A.D. 68 and 100; according to B. Weiss[4] between A.D. 69 and 95; according to Adolf Harnack[5] between A.D. 65 and 93, or very likely still earlier;[6] and according to T. Zahn[7] between A.D. 60 and 75. Thus criticism comes in touch again with what tradition has to say in regard to the time of the composition of the first three Gospels.

In the question of their *authorship* also tradition has proved itself more and more correct. Even if the school of Baur had made use of such late dates in order forcibly to take away the authorship of the New Testament from the Apostles and their contemporaries, and thereby to diminish its credibility, the Gospels, nevertheless, together with the earlier statements about their age, came back again to Matthew, Mark and Luke.

That Matthew was the author of one Gospel will, indeed, be contested by no one; but, according to modern criticism, it is questionable whether Matthew wrote only a very old Gospel in the Aramaic tongue, or also in Greek the book named after him.

The second Gospel is unanimously ascribed to the pupil of Peter, *Mark.* Only Schmiedel and Loisy raise objections to this idea, and thus give the impression of people who are continually grumbling about something.[8]

Liberal theology, however, refuses obstinately to allow the third synoptic Gospel and the Acts of the Apostles connected with it to be accepted as the work of *Luke.* Harnack had recently to complain : " The untenableness of the tradition in regard to this is so generally taken now for granted that scarcely anyone takes any more trouble to prove it, or even to consider in the least the arguments of its opponents. One seems no longer willing to acknowledge that such arguments even exist. Jülicher[9] sees in the ascription of the book to Luke merely a ' quixotic ' wish. So quickly does criticism forget, and in such a partisan spirit does it entrench itself in its theories !"[10] To-day, after Harnack's exhaustive pre-

[1] *Geschichte Jesu von Nazara,* I, 47 (1867); III, 129 ff. (1872).
[2] *Historisch-Kritische Einleitung in das N. T.,* 461 ff., 515, 609 (1875).
[3] *Einleitung in das N. T.,* 2nd ed (1886).
[4] *Lehrbuch der Einleitung in das N. T.,* 3rd ed. (1897).
[5] *Die Chronologie der altchristl. Literatur,* I, 651 ff. (1897).
[6] *Die Apostelgeschichte,* 217-277 (1908).
[7] *Einleitung in das N. T.,* II, 432 ff., 440 (1899).
[8] E. Wendling, *Die Entstehung des Markus-Evangeliums* (1908).
[9] *Einleitung,* 5th and 6th ed., 406 (1908).
[10] *Lukas der Arzt, der Verfasser des dritten Evangeliums und der Apostelgeschichte,* 5 (Leipzig, 1906).

sentation[1] of the case, these theories also are finally condemned.

The *Gospel of John* has had from the earliest times a difficult position. On the one hand, it was already by tradition assigned to a later date; on the other, its contents constitute a great offence in the eyes of liberal critics. It has even been believed that the Fourth Gospel may be discarded as of no value. The most incredible views about its age and origin have been advanced. In recent years, however, critics have been forced, in this respect also, to come nearer and nearer to tradition. Thus, from A.D. 160-170 (according to Baur and Bruno Bauer), they have gone back to 150-160 (Schwegler), 155 (Volkmar), 150 (Zeller), about 150 (Bretschneider, Scholten and Matthes), 135-163 (Taylor), about 140 (Hilgenfeld, Hausrath, Thoma), 130-135 (Lützelberger), 130 (Keim), 110-115 (Nicholas, Renan, Schenkel), and 100 (Aubé).[2]

To-day the *origin* of the Fourth Gospel is again generally assigned to the years of transition from the first to the second century, although the *authorship* of John is for the most part still doubted or positively denied by liberal criticism. A synopsis of the controversy over the authenticity of this Gospel is given by Watkins,[3] who at the same time cites also the wellnigh endless list of modern critics who defend the genuineness of the Johannine Gospel.

This list could now be still further increased by many names, such as Karl Müller, B. Brückner, Gess, Kahnis, Schnedermann, Leuschner, Paul Ewald, F. Barth, Lobstein, Kaftan, Resch, Koehler, Reynolds, Godet and others who are noncatholics, to say nothing of the Catholics. On the Protestant side there are arrayed against the latest attacks on the Gospel of John especially the following : Stanton, Drummond, Sanday, J. Robinson, J. H. A. Hart, E. H. Asquith, and C. R. Gregory. F. W. Worsley remains undecided whether he should ascribe the Fourth Gospel to the Apostle John or to the Presbyter John.

A large number of the later liberal investigators concede that it is not possible to fail to recognize the Apostolic-Johannine character of the Fourth Gospel. They seek, nevertheless, to eliminate its, to them, disagreeable doctrines by making these out to be later insertions made in an earlier Johannine manuscript—that is to say, they deny the unity of the Gospel. This is the standpoint of Ammon, Christ. Weisse, Renan, Alex. Schweitzer, Bertling, Delff, Wendt, Becker, Linder, Bacon, Frey, Fries, Lepsius, Völter, v. Dobschütz,

---

[1] *In Lukas der Arzt* and *Die Apostelgeschichte; cf.* Weiss, *Die Quellen des Lukasevangeliums* (Stuttgart, 1907).
[2] H. J. Holtzmann, *Einleitung in das N. T.*, 2nd ed., p. 476.
[3] *Modern Criticism in its Relation to the Fourth Gospel*, pp. 313-350 (London, 1890).

Schütz, Soltau, Johannes Weiss. The extremely liberal Prof. Jülicher of Marburg writes in opposition to all these theories of dismemberment : " The hypotheses of dismemberment are already almost innumerable. Their aim is to prove that entire passages of John's Gospel have disappeared, while others have been transplanted into erroneous contexts, and others still are subsequent interpolations. Or else a considerably shorter original Gospel of John is constructed, since it is claimed by some that the ' Galilean portions,' by others that most of the accounts of miracles, and by others still that the lengthy discourses of Jesus, were inserted later. These hypotheses, however, are to be rejected absolutely, for they break down completely before the homogeneity, both in form and content, of all the constituent parts of John's Gospel."[1]

The latest of such hypotheses also, elaborated by Wellhausen[2] and G. Schwartz[3] on the ground of Oriental and Greek philology, and by Frederick Spitta[4] rather from a critical-theological standpoint, merely confirm the judgement of Jülicher., The whole Johannine question can be clearly stated thus : Is the canonical Fourth Gospel Johannine at all, or is it not? The fact that a large number of liberal critics seek to answer this question by Yes and No demonstrates clearly that in the controversy over the Fourth Gospel, as well as in the few remaining questions which are still disputed, *Tradition* proves itself right after all.

Harnack wrote some years ago the well-known words : " In the criticism of the sources of primitive Christianity we are, without doubt, returning to tradition."[5] To-day he can say positively that this frank utterance, which then met with violent contradiction, has been proven[6] by the facts. In reality, the rationalistic criticism of the Gospels has made a complete fiasco, and even the liberal school of Ritschl and Harnack surrenders one position after another to the historic tradition of the Church. Especially in the matter of the authenticity of the Gospels, the points of difference have already been reduced to an insignificant minimum. This authenticity must have been, therefore, powerfully and manifestly established; that, at least, is the teaching which the latest sceptical criticism gives us—namely, the *negative* proof of the correctness of the Christian view of the origin of the historical books of the New Testament.

Let us now scrutinize the *positive* proofs, which we divide into ecclesiastical and non-ecclesiastical testimony.

1 *Einleitung in das N. T.*, 6th ed., p. 353 (Tübingen, 1906).
2 *Das Evangelium Johannis* (Berlin, 1908).
3 *Aporien im 4 Evangelium* (Göttingen, 1907).
4 *Das Johannes-Evangelium als Quelle der Geschichte Jesu* (Göttingen, 1910).
5 *Geschichte der altchrist. Lit.*, 3rd ed., II, 1, p. x.
6 *Lukas der Artzt*, III, f.

II.—NON-CATHOLIC PROOFS OF THE GENUINENESS OF THE GOSPELS.

1. *The Uncanonical or Apocryphal Gospels.*

THE uncanonical or apocryphal Gospels have been often used, since the time of Volkmar, as a pretext for attacking the genuineness of the canonical, historical books of the New Testament. " There are also," it is said, " numerous false Gospels; and if it was possible to ascribe *these* to the Apostles, the possibility exists that the four Gospels recognized by the Church may also have been attributed to the wrong authors, and are therefore spurious !"

This objection can, however, in any case rest only on an ignorance of the Apocrypha. These uncanonical fragments, on the contrary, confirm clearly and in a threefold way the apostolicity of the canonical Gospels.

First, in respect of their *contents*, the apocryphal are imitations of the canonical Gospels. Whether they introduce, under the false name of an Apostle, narratives which are not found in the Gospels, or whether they adorn and amplify the stories actually contained in them, they have always at their disposal matter already existing in the genuine Gospels. The oldest Church Fathers already called attention to this fact; and now that the still existing fragments of the Apocrypha have been collected and examined carefully, we can convince ourselves of this step by step.[1]

In the first place, the so-called " Gospel to the Hebrews," the oldest piece of apocryphal writing and the one most closely related to the canonical, had the text of Matthew as a subject to work on, and introduced into it clumsy additions which reveal themselves at once as forgeries. Thus, for example, in the narrative of our Lord's temptation it makes him say : " So my mother seized me, and the Holy Ghost took me by one of the hairs of my head and carried me off to the lofty mountain of Thabor."[2]

The " Egyptian Gospel " of the Encratites (a sect of the Gnostics) transforms the text of the genuine Gospels as much as possible into a polemic against matrimony, and accordingly changes the redemptive plan of Jesus expressed in his words, " I am come that they might have life," into " I am come to destroy the works of the Feminine."[3]

All that we possess of the " Gospel of the Ebionites " (the Gospel of the twelve Apostles) endeavours in the same clumsy way to distort the words of our Lord in the canonical Gospels,

---

[1] See Walter Bauer, *Das Leben Jesu im Zeitalter der neutestamentl. Apokryphen* (Tübingen, 1909).
[2] Edgar Hennecke, *Neutestamentliche Apokryphen,* p. 19.
[3] *ibid.,* p. 23.

and to give them an exactly opposite meaning. According to this, the main purpose of the life of Jesus was the suppression of sacrifices and the eating of meat.[1] The contents of the fragmentary " Gospel of Peter " correspond in their main features to the parallel contents of the canonical Gospels, only they are disfigured by " coarseness and amplifications."[2] The Gnostic Gospels correct the received apostolic Gospel text by an appeal to private revelations, which are said to date back to the Apostles.[3]

Finally, the numerous " Childhood Gospels " indulge in insipid legends about the birth and childhood of the Saviour, in order to supply the deficiencies found in the Gospels of Matthew and Luke. How well or how badly they succeed in doing so may be seen from a few examples.

The " Gospel of Thomas " represents the five-year-old child Jesus as playing by the ford of a stream, collecting some of the flowing water into little pools and making it there wonderfully pure. Then the child amuses himself by making a paste of moist clay and forming out of it twelve sparrows, and as he is disturbed in this by an intruder, he cries to him in anger : " Thou unjust, godless blockhead, what have the pools and the water done to thee? Lo, thou also shalt now wither like a tree." And so it happened. On another occasion Jesus was jostled by a boy, and forthwith causes him to die. Being reproved by Joseph for such a " naughty deed," and " having had his ear suitably pulled for it . . . the child becomes indignant, and says : ' May it be thy lot to seek and not to find. Thou hast acted very unwisely.' "[4] In similar ways Jesus makes himself conspicuous in school and synagogue as a genuine *enfant terrible*.[5]

Even the " First Gospel of James," the least repulsive of the " Childhood Gospels," is distinguished by " the desire to tell fabulous tales, and by curiosity to know all the details about the birth of Christ and how his mother arrived at her wonderful decision.[6] There is not wanting even a legend about it, including a somewhat indecent story of a midwife and some old wives' gossip."[7]

If we compare, therefore, the fabulous, fantastic, involved and often comical passages, which for the most part fill the Apocrypha, with the text of the canonical Gospels, we find at once that the former are imitations, distortions, amplifications and falsifications of the latter.

But shadow presupposes light, imitation implies an original, and counterfeit coin proves the existence of the genuine, from which these are copied. Consequently there must also have

---

[1] *Cf.* Edgar Hennecke, *Neutestamentliche Apokryphen,* p. 26.
[2] *ibid.,* pp. 28-32.   [3] *ibid.,* pp. 34-44.   [4] *ibid.,* pp. 67 ff.
[5] *ibid.,* pp. 68 ff.   [6] *ibid.,* p. 49.   [7] *ibid.,* pp. 54-63.

been true Gospels for the very reason that there were false ones; and the true must have stood in the highest esteem, for otherwise so much trouble would not have been taken to invent and circulate the spurious.

In respect to their *origin,* the apocryphal writings, together and separately, claim to be derived from the Apostles or the disciples of the Apostles.

Whether their writers thus attributed to some Apostle their own ideas about Christianity and popular traditions about Christ from an innocent attempt to do good or from misplaced zeal, in any case it was thought necessary to declare the Gospel in question to be the work of either Peter, Andrew, Philip, Thomas, Matthew, James or Judas; and the reason why every such apocryphal Gospel was ascribed to the Apostles or the Lord's disciples can be found only in the firm conviction prevailing at the time that only Apostles and disciples had composed the Gospels which were universally acknowledged, and, hence, that every Gospel which did not claim to be apostolic, must itself be worthless.

Yet, even if the Apocrypha were not apostolic, the majority of them are certainly very old. Hegesippus, who died about A.D. 180, already writes of the apocryphal books, and says that some of them had been written in his day.[1] The contemporary of Hegesippus, Irenæus, also complains that " The heretics appeal to an incredible number of apocryphal and supposititious writings, which they themselves have invented. . . . In these they distort certain narratives which are found in the Gospel."[2]

In fact, we possess even now fragments of apocryphal Gospels which were written about the year A.D. 150.[3] The Gospel to the Hebrews, which may be assigned to a date between A.D. 65 and 125, appears to have been merely a free translation and elaboration of the canonical Matthew.[4] But if there was already, soon after the apostolic era, such an extensive apocryphal Gospel-literature, then the models of these—the canonical Gospels—must undoubtedly have originated in the apostolic age itself.

The *fate* of the Apocrypha was irretrievably sealed by the fact that these false Gospels first appeared after the time of the Apostles. For the reason that they were *not* apostolic, they were, from the moment of their appearance, almost universally rejected by the Christian communities, were excluded from public reading at divine service, and were condemned by the pastors and Fathers of the Churches as

---

[1] Eusebius, *H. E.*, iv, c. 22.   [2] *Advers. Hæres.*, i, c. 20.
[3] S. Nestle, *N. T. Græci Supplementum;* Harnack, *Chronologie der altchristl. Literatur,* i, 589; Bardenhewer, *Geschichte der altkirch. Literatur,* I, 377 ff.; Hennecke, *Neutestamentl. Apokryphen,* 22, 29, 46.
[4] Bardenhewer, *id.,* 379 f.; Hennecke, *id.,* 11-21.

I.

spurious productions. While in the Church there was never expressed the least doubt of the genuineness of the canonical Gospels, the spuriousness and insignificance of the apocryphal, on the other hand, were positively established.

Thus the argument with which Volkmar tries to impugn the authenticity of the canonical Gospels by means of the apocryphal is finally answered. He says, indeed, that the canonical Gospels in the " Catholic Episcopate " of the early times did find " universal recognition," but that other (heretical) Churches had already at that time recognized other Gospels also.[1] That is true; but such Gospels were immediately exposed as being non-ecclesiastical, and their heretical defenders were characterized as renegade Christians, because they introduced surreptitiously false, non-apostolic Gospels.

The Apocrypha, therefore, in regard to their contents, origin and fate give the clearest testimony in favour of the genuineness of our four sacred Gospels.

We come now to speak of the position which the earliest heretics took towards the Gospels.

2. The Non-Catholic Teachers.

The heretics of primitive Christianity were as firmly convinced of the authenticity of the Gospels as was the Catholic Church.

It is true, as has been said, that some heretics made use of other, apocryphal Gospels also, in connection with the canonical, in order to put their non-evangelical doctrines in a better light. Moreover, they often chose out of the four canonical Gospels one special favourite which best corresponded to their views, and this they altered, on their own responsibility, to suit their own requirements. The Ebionites, for example, accepted only the Gospel of Matthew; the Marcionites a mutilated version of Luke; the Cerinthians the Gospel of Mark; and the Valentinians that of John.[2]

Yet they contested only the *credibility* of the other Gospels —that is, they asserted that the remaining Evangelists had misunderstood or misinterpreted the teaching of the Lord; but that all four Gospels originated from the Apostles and their disciples, Matthew, Mark, Luke and John—that is to say, that they were genuine—the heretics never doubted.

Marcion indeed (about A.D. 117-138) swears by his version of Luke's Gospel, which he cut to his own pattern, according to the bitter reproaches of Tertullian,[3] much as he liked. But he never disputes the genuineness of the four canonical Gospels. On the contrary, he alleges only that Matthew, Mark and

---

[1] *Der Ursprung unserer Evangelien,* 24 f. (1866).
[2] Iren., *Adv. Hær.,* i, 3.
[3] *Adv. Marcionem,* iv, c. 2, 3; *De carne Christi,* c. 2.

John have put a false interpretation on the apostolic doctrine, while Paul and his pupil Luke have alone written it down correctly.

" Marcion first and Marcion only," says Tertullian, " he, the improver of the Gospels ; he, who so long had yearned for Christ, has discovered this, lamenting that Jesus had sent the Apostles too soon into the world, without waiting for the protection of Marcion ! . . . Thus Marcion corroborates two things : first, that our Gospels were earlier, for otherwise he would not have been able to improve them ; and second, that his Gospel appeared later, because it came out, as a novelty, from an attempt to improve ours."[1]

Basilides, who died in A.D. 130, also acknowledges the Gospels, and " relates the history of Jesus exactly as they do."[2]

He quotes also the text of the Gospels with the preliminary remarks : " Thus saith the Scripture," or " Thus it is written," or " So it is said in the Gospel," or " Thus speaks the Lord in the Gospel."[3]

Basilides quotes especially Matthew,[4] Luke,[5] and (immediately after the year A.D. 100) John.[6]

He even wrote twenty-four books *Concerning the Gospel.*[7] But in order to establish his Gnostic fabulous stories, he saw himself obliged to invent his own fifth Gospel. This he ascribed to Matthias, the subsequently chosen Apostle, and maintained that the Redeemer had entrusted to him his (Gnostic) secret doctrine, which had remained unknown to the other Apostles and Evangelists.[8]

The Gnostic Valentinus (about A.D. 160) prefers to quote John,[9] but cites also the other Gospels.[10] In order, however, to provide for his doctrine of æons and " conjugations,"[11] he does not interpret the Gospels literally, but purely in an allegorical sense.

Much more important, however, is the attitude which the Syrian *Tatian* assumes towards the Gospels.

He had been converted to Christianity by his teacher, the philosopher and martyr, Justin, and had been received into the Church at Rome. In consequence of the exaggerated severity of his views, he nevertheless soon left the Catholic Church, returned to his home, and became head of the sect of the Encratites, who were ascetics in regard to food.

In this capacity, between A.D. 172 and 180, he introduced into the Syrian Church a Gospel which he had already com-

---

[1] Tertullian, *Adv. Marcionem,* c. 4.
[2] Hippolytus, *Philosophum.,* vii, n. 27.   [3] *ibid.,* n. 22, 27.
[4] Clem. Alex., *Stromata,* iii, c. 1 ; *Epiph., Hær.,* xxiv, 5.
[5] Hippolytus, *Philos.,* vii, n. 26.   [6] *ibid.,* n. 22, 27.
[7] Eusebius, *H. E.,* iv, c. 7.   [8] Hippolytus, *Philos.,* vii, n. 20.
[9] Irenæus, *Adv. Hær.,* I, viii, 5 ; III, xi, 7.
[10] *ibid.,* I, vii, 4 ; viii, 2.
[11] *ibid.,* III, xi, 7.

posed during the period of his Catholic life at Rome.[1] He called this the *Diatessaron,* or *The Gospel written by the Four,* or *The Gospel of the Four.* It contains a history of the life and activity of Jesus, compiled out of the four canonical Gospels—a harmony of the Gospels.

Even in the fourth century this *Diatessaron* was still the only Gospel which was used in the Syrian churches, both Catholic and non-catholic.[2] Ephraem, the light of the Syrian Church, himself wrote a commentary on the Gospels, having for its basis the *Diatessaron.* After the latter had disappeared for 1,500 years, its text was reconstructed as far as possible from Ephraem's commentary,[3] and soon after an Arabic translation of the *Diatessaron*[4] was also found, as well as fragments of the original Syriac text.[5] According to these publications, there is no doubt that Tatian regarded our Gospels, and ours only, as genuine, and used them as such ; and these lay before him in the form and extent in which we still possess them.[6]

With Tatian is connected the Syriac manuscript of the Gospels, which was discovered in the year 1892 in the monastery of St Catherine on Mount Sina. This so-called *Syrus Sinaiticus,*[7] which contains the four Gospels, " was translated about the year A.D. 400 from a Greek original, which can hardly be later than the second century. Since the text is almost perfectly preserved, this *Syrus Sinaiticus* remains one of the most important—in fact, very probably the most important—of all the witnesses for our Gospels. . . . Whoever reads the Gospels in this form has them before him as the Christians of 1,700 years ago read them. It is noteworthy that the text of Tatian is most closely related to this text, and that both texts prove the essential integrity of our Gospels since the time of Marcus Aurelius."[8]

Irenæus, the keenest and best informed student of the history of heresies in the earliest times, is able, about A.D. 180, to proclaim the fact before the whole world, Catholic and non-catholic, that " so great is the certainty in regard to our Gospels that the heretics themselves give testimony for them, and everyone proceeds to found his own doctrine out of them. If, therefore, our enemies testify for us, and make

[1] *Cf.* Harnack, *Chronologie,* i, 284 ff. ; Bardenhewer, *Geschichte der altt. Literatur,* i, 258.

[2] Theodoret of Cyrus, *Hæret. fab. comp.,* i, 20.

[3] By Zahn, *Forsch. zu Geschicht. d. neutest. Kanons,* i, 112 ff.

[4] A. Ciasca, *Tatiani Evangeliorum harmoniæ arabice* (Romæ, 1888).

[5] H. Goussen, *Studia theologica,* i, 62-67 ; Harris, *Fragments of the Commentary of Ephraem Syrus upon the Diatessaron* (London, 1895).

[6] *Cf.* M. Maher, S.J., *Recent Evidence for the Authenticity of the Gospels : Tatian's Diatessaron* (London, 1893).

[7] German translation by Merx, *Die vier Kanonischen Evangelien nach ihrem ältesten Texte* (Berlin, 1897).

[8] Harnack, *Reden und Aufsätze,* 2nd ed., i, 320 (Giessen, 1906).

use of our Gospels, the proof which they produce in their behalf stands sure and true."[1]

The *Alogians* alone, of all the heretics (A.D. 165-175), form an exception. They rejected especially the Gospel of John as unauthentic. In this, however, it is a question only of a handful of foolish people, who appeared and disappeared, without having left behind them any perceptible trace in the early Christian Church.

Not even the keen-eyed Church historian *Eusebius* considers it worth while to make mention of them. Only *Irenæus*,[2] their contemporary, and somewhat later *Epiphanius*,[3] give them a thought. From the description given by both these writers we perceive that the Alogians contested the authenticity of the Gospel of John in defiance of all history and all historical foundation, and purely out of doctrinal considerations. They believed that this Gospel formed the chief support of the views of the Montanists, which were diametrically opposed to theirs; and in self-defence against the latter, and as a downright falsehood, they made the assertion that not John, but the heretic Cerinthus, had been the author of the Fourth Gospel.

This was, however, the most foolish assertion imaginable. John's Gospel is devoted almost entirely to the defence of the real divinity of Jesus, while the doctrine of Cerinthus is aimed essentially at the denial of this divinity and of the supernaturalism of the Saviour.[4] Cerinthus was the intellectual leader of a judaizing sect which wanted to whitewash over the old rabbinical Mosaic law with a light coating of Christianity. In contrast to this, John proclaims the full, spiritual kingdom of Heaven, founded by Christ, the Son of God. How, then, could Cerinthus have written the Fourth, or Johannine, Gospel?

But even apart from this, the statement of the Alogians—which was made much later—is proved to be a mere fiction by the fact that Ignatius, Polycarp, Papias and the whole school of John's disciples in Asia Minor (the place where the Fourth Gospel originated) ascribe this Gospel unanimously to the Apostle John. Far from furnishing, therefore, an argument against the authenticity of the Johannine writings, the desperate attempt of the Alogians proves only that it was impossible, even in one single point, to break down the conviction of all Christendom concerning the apostolicity of the Gospels.[5]

---

[1] *Adv. Hær.*, III, xi, 8.
[2] *Adv. Hær.*, III, xi, 9.   [3] *Hæret.*, li, 3.
[4] Irenæus, *id.*, I, xxvi, 1; Epiphanius, *id.*, xxviii, 1; and xxx, 14.
[5] The Alogi. *cf.* Harnack, *Chronologie der altchristl. Literatur,* i, 376 ff.; Zahn, *Einleitung in d. N. T.*, ii, p. 460; L. Duchesne, *Histoire ancienne de l'Eglise,* i, p. 304; M. Lepin, *L'origine du quatrième Evangile,* pp. 211 ff. (Paris, 1907).

3. *The Non-Christian Writers.*

The non-christian writers, Jews as well as Pagans, testify to the authenticity of the Gospels whenever they have occasion to speak of them.

Judaism was pleased to assume the part of Mephistopheles towards the Gospels—that is, it everywhere sought to distort the facts related in them, and to make the Gospel's conception of the persons of Christ and of his followers laughable.

While the Christians were bringing the Gospel to the pagans, the Jews—according to St Justin—also sent ambassadors into the whole civilized world who calumniated[1] the Christian name to everyone who did not know of it, and accused Christ of the blackest crimes.[2] The vilest means were good enough for them in their fight against Christianity.[3] Wherever a pagan set himself to work to ridicule the Gospels, the Jew also offered him his services in furnishing him with the most childish absurdities about the Gospel history.[4] This mass of lies was naturally transmitted from generation to generation, till it found in the *Talmud* a permanent abode, and developed finally, in the *Toldoth Jeshu,* into a popular pseudo-gospel.

Of the *real* Gospel the Jews themselves, even the Rabbis, knew in general extremely little. In the whole *Talmud* the Gospel is mentioned only once,[5] and even in this passage, which it is believed dates from A.D. 90 to 110, the text of the Gospel is incorrect and quoted merely from hearsay.[6] The dense ignorance of the Jews in regard to the Gospels, as well as their ardent hatred for them, is shown in the words of Rabban Tarphon : " By the life of my children, should the writings of the Christians fall into my hands, I would burn them, together with the names of God which they contain."[7]

However little confidence, therefore, the Jewish tradition about the New Testament writings can inspire, reaching back though it does into primitive Christianity, it is, nevertheless, very important for us, because it never and nowhere dared to cast a doubt upon the genuineness of the Gospels. And yet the proof of their spuriousness would have been equivalent to saving the national honour of Judaism and to an annihilating criticism of Christianity.

The *pagan writers* at first referred to the Gospels slightingly and contemptuously. Lactantius[8] gives the reason for this. Made fastidious by the brilliant and attractive language

---

1 Justin, *Dialog. cum Tryphone,* c. 17, 117.   2 *id.,* c. 108.
3 Tertullian, *Ad Nationes,* i, 14.
4 Origen, *Contra Celsum,* ii, 13 *et passim.*
5 Treatise on *Sabbath.*
6 *Cf.* Laible, *Christus im Talmud,* 62 ff. (Leipzig, 1900); A. Meyer, *Jesus im Talmud* in Hennecke's *Handbuch,* p. 70.
7 Treatise on *Sabbath.*   8 *Institution.,* v, 1 ; vi, 1.

and descriptions of the classical writers, the educated pagans felt no interest whatever in the books of the Bible, which were written in a popular style and with a most unusual manner of thought and speech. Moreover, the Christians were anxious to conceal their sacred books from the pagans in order not to expose them to dishonour.

Nevertheless, the Roman controversialists and sophists knew how to get possession of them little by little, and then began the fearful attacks of pagan science on the contents of the Gospels. The eclectic *Celsus,* the Epicurean and satirist *Lucian of Samosata,* the Neopythagorean *Flavius Philostratus,* the Neoplatonist *Porphyrius, Julian the Apostate* and others employed the whole power of their eloquence, the most trenchant acuteness of their logic and the biting sarcasm of their wit, to prove that the Evangelists had written nothing but incredible absurdities. Yet never did the Pagans let a doubt arise as to whether the Evangelists were really the authors of the books ascribed to them. Rather do they everywhere take it for granted that the Christian view of the apostolic origin of the Gospels is based upon the truth.[1]

Passing over all the others, let us refer to Celsus only, who is not merely the oldest but also the ablest of these writers who are hostile to Christianity, and of whom we, at the same time, possess the most definite information. Celsus's book, entitled *The True Word,* was written in A.D. 178, and was refuted by Origen practically sentence by sentence. In fact, the latter has quoted in his reply nearly the whole text of Celsus, so that Theodore Keim[2] could reconstruct the greater part of it out of Origen's answer.

There results from this, first, that Celsus knew our Gospels well and had studied them. He even asserts[3] that he is thoroughly familiar with the entire doctrinal system of this Christianity of recent date and understands it perfectly. He even boasts : " I could still say much about the history of Jesus—that is, much that is true, and not like the written stories of his disciples ; but I prefer to leave it unsaid."[4] He wishes to argue from the Gospels alone, as the books which form the basis of Christianity, and thus to impale the Christians on their own swords.[5] Then he actually quotes, in the course of his expositions, four passages from the Gospels. He uses preferably the work of Matthew, yet brings in a great number of texts also from the other Gospels,[6] and these prove unquestionably that our Gospels lay before the pagan philosopher in their present textual form.

[1] *Cf.* Seitz, *Christuszeugnisse aus dem Klassischen Altertum von ungläubiger Seite,* pp. 40-81.
[2] *Celsus, Wahres Wort.* (Zürich, 1873).
[3] Origen, *Contra Celsum,* i, 12, 26.
[4] *id.,* ii, 13.   [5] *id.,* ii, 74.
[6] Fr. Seraph. Muth, *Der Kampf. des heidnischen Philosophen Celsus gegen das Christentum,* 176-183 (Mainz, 1899).

Of these he informs his readers expressly and repeatedly that they were written by the disciples,[1] and that subsequently many believers had fallen away from the " Great Church,"[2] and had altered the text of the Gospels : " Three or four times, and even more frequently, they have changed and spoiled the original, primitive text " until it exactly suited their fancy.[3] But Celsus attacks and ridicules only the *contents and credibility* of the Gospels. That these *originated with the Apostles,* and that the apocryphal Gospels are merely imitations and counterfeits of the real ones, is for him a certainty. This testimony is crushing. Celsus criticises Christianity, and especially the Gospels, in the sharpest way, and was able to convince himself as to their genuineness or spuriousness, and must have done so. Proof of their *post*-apostolic origin would have been a veritable death-blow to the hated Christianity.

If, then, he does not produce such a proof, it was only because he felt himself unable to awaken a single doubt of the fact.

Thus do the *non*-ecclesiastical authorities of antiquity assert unanimously that the Gospels originate from the time of the primitive Church, and, indeed, from apostolic circles. But the *ecclesiastical* witnesses will give us still more exact and certain information on this point.

III.—Catholic Witnesses for the Authenticity of the Gospels.

1. *The Canonical Gospels Themselves.*

The canonical Gospels themselves indicate with the greatest distinctness their apostolic origin.

The most obvious proof of the great antiquity of the Gospels would, of course, be the existence of the original copies or autographs of the Evangelists. We must, however, give up this idea at once. Not one of the older manuscripts, whether of a secular or religious character, has come down to us as an original manuscript of its author. They were all written on papyrus leaves—the only writing material of that time—unless we accept clay tablets and stone inscriptions. The papyrus, however, lasted only a short time, especially since the Gospels suffered greatly by reason of their frequent, almost daily, use. Thus the manuscripts of the Evangelists had already disappeared, it seems, before the end of the second century. Only the second and third hand copies of them resisted the ravages of time, and after the end of the third century parchment volumes replaced the papyrus rolls.

[1] Origen, *ibid.,* 13, 15, 16. [2] *ibid.,* v, 59.
[3] *ibid.,* ii, 27.

Our oldest *manuscripts of the Bible* date from the fourth and fifth centuries. Nevertheless, even that is a very great age when we think that the earliest manuscripts of the Greek and Latin classics come to us only with the eighth and ninth centuries. Moreover, the biblical manuscripts of the times immediately succeeding this era are incomparably more numerous than the classical. The latter could be saved only with difficulty and in very few copies, while we possess of the New Testament alone over 3,800 manuscripts.[1]

A comparison of these different manuscripts with one another brings us, moreover, to a time much more remote than the dates at which the individual copies originated. It is true all agree with one another in the immense majority of the texts. The different readings refer almost entirely to small details, and even the most striking variations change neither the least article of faith, nor the most insignificant moral doctrine.[2]

It is, nevertheless, a fact that a great number of these textual discrepancies are found already in the biblical manuscripts of the fourth and fifth centuries, and, indeed, are of such a kind that we must suppose that we have to do here with copies of earlier models which, in their turn also, did not belong to one and the same family of manuscripts, but represent different revisions of a still earlier epoch.

This brings us already into the third or, indeed, into the second century. In this period, however, there existed not merely one or two manuscripts of the Bible; it is true rather, as we can conclude from the works of the Fathers, that the New Testament was spread over the whole Roman Empire. In all the churches it was read aloud at divine service, either in the original Greek, or in the Latin and Syriac translations, which were composed already in the second century.

But in those days the circulation and the multiplication of books proceeded much more slowly than now, because everything had to be written by hand. Plainly, therefore, the original models were already existent at the beginning of the second century. The Gospels must, then, certainly go back to the period of the Apostles.

Not only have the latest comparisons of the Gospel manuscripts with the quotations made from them by the Fathers—compiled by Hermann von Soden with astonishing technical knowledge and patience—led to the evident result that the ecclesiastical writers about A.D. 140 already used the predecessors of those Gospel texts and Gospel manuscripts, as we possess them still to-day, but the interval between the

---

[1] *Cf.* C. R. Gregory, *Die Griechischen Handschriften des N. T.* (Leipzig, 1908) ; H. von Soden, *Die Schriften des N. T. in ihrer ältesten erreichbareu Textgestalt.*, i, vol. 1-3 (Berlin, 1902, 1906, 1907).

[2] See article *Bibeltext* in Wetzer and Weltes, *Kirchenlexikon.*

composition of the Gospels and the year A.D. 140 is "so small that scarcely enough time remains for any essential changes in the text."[1] Consequently the *external historical and critical stability* of the New Testament proves that our four Gospels go back to the apostolic age, and have come down to us from that apostolic era essentially unchanged.

But the *internal features* of the Gospels give us a still clearer and more definite light upon this point. The knowledge of languages and linguistic forms displayed in them is at once characteristic. From these we perceive that the Evangelists, with the exception of Luke, were Semites, *speaking Aramaic.*

The language of the New Testament has been studied thoroughly in recent years, and examined in its minutest idioms. Philologists have analysed sentence after sentence, and have even numbered and weighed, so to speak, all its phrases; and there has gradually arisen an entire library of dictionaries and grammatical works concerning the New Testament, in which the elements of the Gospel language are established and compared with other contemporaneous writings and documents.

The result of all these labours is that the Greek idiom of the Gospels is proved to rest upon an essentially Aramaic basis. We not only find there single Aramaic expressions, such as *Corban, Ephpheta, Talitha Cumi, Eloi, lamma sabacthani,* but the Gospels are thoroughly permeated with Aramaic phrases and opinions.

Moreover, the most exact acquaintance with the popular Greek dialects of that time never fully discloses the meaning of the Gospels. Only a knowledge of the Hebrew-Aramaic colloquial, popular speech furnishes the key to a complete understanding of the New Testament writings. These are composed in that Hebraic-Greek idiom, which the Jews of the first century acquired from their varied intercourse with Hellenic Romans, and introduced into their literature through their most important scholars, Philo (born 20 B.C.) and Flavius Josephus (born A.D. 37).

The Gospels originate, therefore, from the pens of Christian writers who had learned the Greek language more or less accurately, but whose mother-tongue was the Aramaic dialect which Christ and his Apostles used.

If the Evangelists are to be recognized from their speech as Jews, they appear from their *acquaintance with their country* to be *inhabitants of Palestine.*

They describe very minutely, with information about innumerable details, the places in which Jesus Christ lived and worked. Geographical, topographical, political, historic and religious conditions are mirrored on almost every page. The Galilæan landscape; the lake of Genesareth and the life upon

---

[1] H. von Soden. *op. cit.,* 1646 ff.

its shores; the region bordering on the Jordan; the local peculiarities of the smallest hamlets; the distances from one village to another; the springs, gates, routes and paths; the environs of Jerusalem; the monuments and objects of interest of the Holy City—all these and a thousand other details are clearly delineated. Accordingly, wherever the Palestine of Christ's time is now properly excavated and thoroughly investigated, it is seen that all the statements of the Gospels agree precisely with what has been discovered. Only men who had originated in Palestine, or who, at least, had dwelt or passed some time there could write thus.

If the preceding considerations make it extremely probable that these Jewish-Christian Palestinians lived and wrote in *the first century of our Christian era,* the supposition becomes certainty from the knowledge of history which the Evangelists possessed.

An historical event of the first importance coincided with the early life of the primitive Church in Palestine—the destruction of Jerusalem, which took place in the year A.D. 70, razed ancient Israel to the ground and created new and absolutely different conditions in Palestine. Before that event there had been Roman dominion, tempered by an extensive autonomy under the Jewish Sanhedrim; after that time there prevailed a complete and exclusive supremacy of the foreign, Roman, rulers. Formerly there had been a predominant influence of the Jewish national population and parties; afterwards, a powerful subjugation of all nationalistic efforts. Previously, a multiform religious life had existed, passing from synagogue to synagogue under the leadership of the Scribes and Pharisees, and, above all, an imposing temple ceremonial at Jerusalem; subsequently, the Temple, the heart of the Jewish nation, was swept away, the ceremonial was made impossible, and the children of Israel were left without a sacrifice, without an altar, without a sanctuary, their whole religious life having been drained away. Before then there had been an unrivalled national unity of the people; afterwards, an Israel scattered throughout all the world, without its own city, an alien among all nations—the "Wandering Jew." In short, the scene of the history of the Jewish nation, that history itself, and the conditions of the people were all completely transformed by the capture and destruction of Jerusalem.[1]

Now, whenever we open the Gospels, we are confronted plainly by the Palestinian Judaism before the destruction of Jerusalem. In clear, brilliant colours the Evangelists paint for us the political, religious and social life of the time of

---

[1] Josephus, *Wars of the Jews,* vi and vii; Schürer, *Geschichte des Judischen Volkes im Zeitalter Jesu Christi,* 3rd ed., i, 455-656; Bousset, *Die Religion des Judentums im neutestamentlichen Zeitalter,* pp. 91-168 (Berlin, 1903).

Christ. The relations between the pagan Chief of State and his Jewish vassals; the delicate conditions prevailing between the foreign officials and the local Great Council; the fine lines of demarcation in which the rights of the Roman judges collided with those of the Sanhedrim—all take for granted the continued existence of the Holy City.

Even to the smallest details the Evangelists are fully conversant with those times. The Roman-Jewish census, under the Emperor Augustus and the Governor of Syria, Quirinus;[1] the Greek and Roman coins, which were in circulation together with the former Hebrew ones;[2] the famine under Claudius;[3] the expulsion of the Jews from Rome under that Emperor;[4] the tragic ending of Herod Agrippa I;[5] the members of the whole Herodian dynasty;[6] as well as other personal conditions, are all well known to the Evangelists. They understand also the complicated dealings of the religious and political parties of those days—the Pharisees, the Sadducees and Herodians, as well as those of the philosophical schools of the Stoics and Epicureans. Before their eyes still stands the magnificent capital of the country, with its monumental belt of walls and buildings of the temple, together with its priests and scribes, its gorgeous ceremonial and intricate observances of the Mosaic Law.

Thus could write only those who had lived in Palestine before the decisive war with Rome, and who, partly before, partly after, the catastrophe of the year A.D. 70 had put their experiences on paper and transmitted them to posterity. John wrote only after the destruction of Jerusalem. The conflict against the Gnostic heresy, which forced him to take pen in hand, began to be powerful only towards the end of the first century. The three synoptic Gospels must, however, have appeared before the Jewish war. The prophecy of the destruction of the city and of the rejection of the Jewish people is set forth in these Gospels as still unfulfilled.[7] If the frightful ruin had already stood before the eyes of the synoptists as an accomplished fact, they certainly would not have kept silent about the event. Indeed, the prophecy and the fulfilment of that fearful tragedy would have thrilled their hearts and affected their entire representation profoundly.

We may, however, go still further, and determine even more exactly the personality of the Evangelists. From their

[1] Luke ii, 1 ff.; Acts v, 37; Tacitus, *Annal.,* i, 11; Cassiodorus, *Varia,* iii, 52.
[2] Matt., xvii, 26; xxii, 19.
[3] Acts xi, 23; Josephus, *Antiquitates Judaicæ,* III, xv, 3; Suetonius, *Vita Claudii,* xviii.
[4] Acts xviii, 2; *id.,* xxv.   [5] Acts xii, 23.
[6] Matt. ii, 1, 19; Luke iii, 1; xxiii, 7; Acts xii, 1; xxv, 13.
[7] Matt. xxiii, 36; xxiv, 15, 24; Mark xiii, 1 ff.; Luke xix, 41 ff.; xxi, 32.

knowledge of the life and activity of Jesus it is evident that they belonged either to the immediate or collateral circle of the Saviour's *disciples*.

The personality of Jesus, his appearance in public, his discourses and his deeds are drawn from life, and adhered to with striking vividness. The Evangelists conduct us to all the roads and paths trodden by his feet; they accompany us into all the cities and villages where he preached; to the solitary regions and the mountains where he prayed; and into the houses and market-places where he healed the sick and raised the dead.

The whole Gospel history is related not only with astonishing exactitude and certainty, but also with touching candour and simplicity. Nowhere does the narrator obtrude himself; nowhere does he bring out his own personal views and feelings; and scarcely even does he mention now and then the successes of the Saviour and the impression which his words and miracles produced. Only that is recorded which transpired before the eyes of the Evangelists, or had been seen and heard by immediate eye and ear witnesses.

No later or foreign historian could have represented that, and in such a way. The Evangelists must themselves have been present, or at least have received the verbal accounts or written documents concerning the " glad tidings " from associates and disciples of the Saviour.

Nor is this all. By means of the *individual characteristics of the separate Gospels,* even the traditional account can be tested and confirmed, in accordance with which *Matthew, Mark, Luke* and *John* composed the historical works in question.

First, *Matthew.* The earlier Church Fathers already recognized the fact that the Evangelists pass over in silence whatever honours them, and report whatever humiliates them. In the first Gospel the repast which Matthew gave to the Lord after having been called to him is mentioned only casually, while into the list of the Apostles the (to Matthew) unpleasant surname of " the Publican " is inserted. This of itself should indicate that Matthew himself is the narrator.

Moreover, the first Gospel emphasizes in particular the prophecies of the Old Testament and their fulfilment. On this account it rightly became the Gospel of the Jewish Christians—a fact which agrees remarkably well with the primitive tradition that " Matthew published a Gospel among the Hebrews, and in their language."[1]

Mark. In contrast to this, the second Gospel is evidently intended for the pagans, and primarily for the Romans. Jewish manners and usages are explained in this Gospel because they were unknown to its readers. The Jewish money-value is given in small Roman coinage, and we also meet

[1] Irenæus, *Adv. Hær.*, iii, 1.

with Latin—instead of Greek—nomenclature in several places. Everywhere Peter and the Petrine mode of preaching to the pagans are here given the foremost place. Even the extremest of the liberal critics[1] see in this a confirmation of the tradition that Mark has written this Gospel, as the Prince of the Apostles preached it in the capital of the Roman Empire, and especially for these Romans.[2]

Luke. The third Gospel and the Acts of the Apostles develop most fully the universalist programme of St Paul— that of the Gospel, as " the power of God unto salvation to everyone that believeth, to the Jew first, and also to the Greek " (Rom. i, 16). In respect to contents, form and expression, these writings are thoroughly Pauline.[3] Their author must have been a pupil of the Apostle to the Gentiles, and by his use of technical medical expressions, observations and opinions he shows himself clearly to have been a physician.[4] No other can have written the third Gospel and the Acts of the Apostles than " Luke, the beloved physician,"[5] and companion of Paul.

John. Finally, the character of the Apostle John is imprinted on the Fourth Gospel throughout. The plastic certainty, the sublime serenity, the tender, glowing enthusiasm, with which the portrait of the Saviour is brought before us; the simplicity, the depth of feeling, and the ideal flights of the thoughts, contents and representation of the entire book are all undoubtedly Johannine.[6] Moreover, as opposed to Harnack's undemonstrable assertion,[7] John expressly claims for himself the authorship of the Fourth Gospel with the clearly defined words : " This is that disciple who giveth testimony of these things and hath written these things " (John xxi, 24); the disciple whom Jesus loved (John xxi, 20); who also leaned on his breast at the Last Supper, and said : " Lord, who is he that shall betray thee?" who stood also beneath the Cross, and to whom the Saviour commended his mother (John xix, 26)—the beloved disciple—John.

Thus we derive from the Gospels themselves the conviction that these writings of Jewish Christians from Palestine were composed in part before, in part shortly after, the destruction of Jerusalem ; and that the Gospels themselves bring us into

---

[1] Jülicher, *Realenzyklopädie für protestant. Theologie,* 3rd ed., xii, 293; Wernle, *Die synoptische Frage,* 208-223 (Freiburg, 1899).
[2] Eusebius, *H. E.,* iii, 39; Clement of Alexandria, *Hypotyp.* in 1 Pet. v, 13; Eusebius, *id.,* vi, 14.
[3] Harnack, *Lukas der Arzt; Die Apostelgeschichte* (Leipzig, 1907).
[4] Harnack, *Lukas,* 122-137; Hobart, *The Medical Language of St Luke* (1882).
[5] Col. iv, 14.
[6] *Cf.* Zahn, *Einleitung in das N. T.,* ii, pp. 466 ff. ; Belser, *Einleitung in das N. T.,* pp. 343 ff. ; *Das Evangelium des hl. Johannes* (Freiburg, 1905).
[7] *Die Chronologie der altchristlichen Literatur,* i, 677; *Wesen des Christentums,* 13; see Zahn, *id.,* and in *Realenzyklopädie,* ix, 2807.

the immediate circle of the Apostles and their pupils, and name for us as their authors the Saints Matthew, Mark, Luke and John. Moreover, before the last Gospel has yet concluded its testimony to itself, and before the Apostle of love has published his book, the oldest writers of the Church already raise their voices to testify clearly and unmistakably, first, to the existence of the Gospels in general; then to the three Synoptics; and, soon after, to all the Evangelists together.

2. Early Church Literature.

The ancient literature of the Church appears from the very first as an eye and ear witness for the Gospels.

Of course, only a few wholly casual utterances and reports are to be expected from it *in the first century*. Only a few, because we possess from that remote period hardly more than a few small writings of Christian origin. These were, moreover, simply pamphlets, and for the most part of such a special character, that there was no reason for their touching on the question of the Gospels.

But even aside from this, primitive Christian literature can at most only by chance define its position towards the subject we are considering, for that was precisely an age which had still seen and heard the Apostles and their pupils. The Apostolic words and living tradition meant to it almost everything. No need was felt of appealing to the writings of those whose preaching was still in the memories of all. It had not yet occurred to anyone to defend the Holy Scriptures, for the reason that no one ventured to attack them. All primitive Christian records, however, show an acquaintance with the Gospels, make use of them, and take it for granted that they are highly honoured by the Church.

The Syrian and the Alexandrian-Egyptian Churches are in this respect represented by the so-called *Teaching of the Twelve Apostles* and the *Epistle of Barnabas*—the former composed in the last third of the first century, the latter at its termination.[1]

In the *Epistle of Barnabas* texts from the writings of St Matthew[2] are twice quoted literally, while the sense of other passages is lightly referred to.[3] The *Teaching of the Twelve Apostles* quietly makes use of some thirty passages from Matthew, one from Mark, and four from Luke.[4] In four

---

[1] Funk, *Opera Patrum apostolicorum*, ed. 2a, I, xii, xxii, ff. ; Batiffol, *Anciennes littératures chrétiennes; La littérature grecque*, p. 72; Harnack, *Chronologie der altchristlichen Literatur*, i, pp. 410 ff. ; Ehrhard, *Die altchristliche Literatur und ihre Erforschung*, i, pp. 37 ff. ; Bardenhewer, *Geschichte der altkirchlichen Literatur*, i, 76-98.

[2] *Ep. Barnabas*, iv, 14. All patristic quotations are taken from Funk's edition.

[3] See Funk, *id.*, i, pp. 642 ff.   [4] *ibid.*, pp. 640 ff.

other places it refers expressly to the Gospel in such words
as : " Thus it stands in the Gospel,"[1] " Thus you find it
stated in the Gospel of our Lord,"[2] " Act according to the
precept of the Gospel,"[3] and " As the Lord commands in his
Gospel."[4]

Therefore, exactly as we to-day quote the Gospels after
nineteen centuries, so they were quoted already at the end of
the first century, and taken for granted as well known. Yet
they are said to have originated in the second century.

Clement, whom Paul calls his fellow-worker, and whom
Peter appointed Bishop of the Church at Rome, wrote in the
years A.D. 95-97 a letter to the Corinthians, in which he
certainly does not quote and transcribe the Gospels word for
word, but makes use of at least ten passages out of the
synoptic Gospels of Matthew, Mark and Luke.[5] Hence,
the successor of St Peter, " in whose ears still echoed the
preaching of the Apostles,"[6] and with him " many others
also who had been instructed by the Apostles,"[7] received the
synoptic Gospels directly from the hands of their authors,
watched over them and transmitted them to posterity as a
precious treasure. Whether the Gospel of St John also was
in their possession cannot be positively determined. But if
not, it need not surprise us, for this Gospel originated almost
at the same time as the letter of Clement, and first appeared
in Asia Minor, so that it had scarcely become known yet in
Rome.

Immediately *at the beginning and during the first half of
the second century* we encounter in Asia Minor and Greece,
as well as in Rome, a number of the pupils of the Apostles
and witnesses of the apostolic era who already mention the
Gospels much more clearly and frequently. The more the
recollection of the direct, oral instruction of the disciples of
the Lord disappeared, the more the teachers of the Church
saw themselves compelled to remind the people of the written
records of the Gospel, although the main emphasis was always
laid on the unbroken doctrinal tradition of the Church.

Of the existence of the Gospels in the Syrian Church we
are informed by *Ignatius,* Bishop of Antioch. Ignatius goes
back far into the first century. He must have been born, at
the latest, between A.D. 50 and 60, and was already a man
while several of the Apostles, and above all his kindred spirit,
John, the beloved Apostle, were still living. Soon after the
latter's death, Ignatius himself died at Rome, where he was
thrown to the wild beasts during the reign of the Emperor
Trajan (A.D. 98-117). While awaiting martyrdom he wrote
seven letters, the genuineness of which is no longer doubted

[1] *Didache,* xv, 3. [2] *ibid.,* 4. [3] *id.,* xi, 3.
[4] *id.,* viii, 2. [5] Funk, *Opera PP. apost.,* i, 645.
[6] Irenæus, *Adv. Hær.,* III, iii, 3. [7] *ibid.*

by anyone. In this testament of his faith and love the words
and thoughts of the Gospels are forever on his lips. They are
not literal citations which he thus recalls to his churches—for
the earlier writers were accustomed to quote for the most
part only freely; but Ignatius on every occasion puts his
reliance on the apostolic books, and is thoroughly identified
with their ideas and even their expressions.

The synoptic Gospels certainly were in his possession. His
acquaintance with them is evident in most of the letters.[1]
But he adheres with especial fondness to the Gospel of John.[2]
His intimate knowledge of this Fourth Gospel is, in fact, so
extensive that the Protestant scholar, Theodor Zahn, is
moved to make this admirable observation : " The amplifications of the utterances of Jesus found in John's Gospel, and
the application of these to quite different conditions, presupposes that Ignatius had already for a long time, both as
reader and preacher, paid much attention to the Fourth
Gospel. And he takes for granted a similar condition of
things also among the Christians in Rome and Asia Minor."[3]
Even Alfred Loisy[4] writes in agreement with this statement,
that Ignatius is penetrated with the teaching and spirit of
the Fourth Gospel to such an extent that he evidently must
have been acquainted with this Gospel for a long time before
the composition of his letters.

Remarkable also are the utterances of St Ignatius about
the Gospels in general. When he occasionally imparted
admonitions, which he enforced by an appeal to the " Doctrine
of Christ," some Christians, as he himself informs us,
answered him : " If I do not find that written in the
archives—that is, in the Gospel—I will not believe it."[5]

The written Gospel, therefore, then existed; and men in
matters of dispute appealed to it, and held its words to be the
faithful exposition of apostolic truth. Ignatius even adds[6]
that certain heretics were only too ready to be one-sided and
to swear by the letter of the Gospel instead of taking in
comprehensively the spirit of the whole written and oral
teaching of Christ. Comprehended in this sense, the Gospels
are " the fulfilment of eternal life,"[7] and are "as worthy of
honour as was Christ, when actually present."[8]

In *Asia Minor* Ignatius is immediately connected with his
friend *Polycarp*. The latter was a pupil of the Apostle John,

---

[1] *Eph.* xiv, 2; *Trall.* xi, 1; *Philad.* iii, 1; *Smyrn.* i, 2 ff.; vi, 1; *Polyc.*
i, 3; ii, 2.

[2] *Eph.* xx, 2; *Magn.* vii, 1 ff.; viii, 2; *Rom.* vii, 2 ff.; *Philad.* ii, 2;
vii, 1; ix, 1. *Cf.* Boese, *Die Glaubwürdigkeit unserer Evangelien,*
71-83 (Freiburg, Herder, 1895).

[3] Zahn, *Geschichte des neutestamentlichen Kanons,* i, 905 (Leipzig,
1888).

[4] *Le Quatrième Evangile,* i, 6 ff. (Paris, 1903).   [5] *Philipp.* viii, 2.

[6] *id.*   [7] *Philad.* ix, 2   [8] *id.,* v, i, 2.

I.   4

and was appointed by him to be the head of the Church of
Smyrna;[1] but he enjoyed also the instruction of other
Apostles " and associated with many who had seen Christ."[2]
With visible emotion St Irenæus relates of his teacher : " I
can still indicate the place where the blessed Polycarp
preached . . . the addresses which he delivered to the
people, as he described his association with John and with
the others who had seen the Lord, and how he quoted their
words. Polycarp also reported all that he had heard from
them about the Lord, about his miracles and his teaching, as
one who had received it from those who had seen with their
own eyes the Word of Life, and it was all in perfect agreement with the Holy Scriptures."[3]

Of Polycarp's works we possess only one piece of writing
which he sent to the church at Philippi in Macedonia[4] in the
year of the death of St Ignatius, together with the latter's
letters. The whole communication is interwoven with quotations from and allusions to the writings of the whole New
Testament. Besides the first three Gospels and the Acts of
the Apostles, almost all the Epistles of St Paul, the first
Epistle of Peter, and the first Epistle of John are made use
of.[5] The Gospel of John itself is not cited, yet even Holtzmann concedes that " from the appearance of the satellite
(that is, the first Epistle of John) we can infer the existence
of the complete sun."[6]

The third authority at this time in Asia Minor is *Papias,*
Bishop of Hierapolis in Lesser Phrygia, " a pupil of John,
a friend of Polycarp, a man of the olden time."[7] He also
can claim to have seen and heard, together with his teacher,
John, many disciples of the Lord. " From them," he writes,
" I found out what Andrew or Peter had said, or what Philip
or Thomas, or James, or John, or Matthew, or any other of
the disciples of the Lord had said."[8] What he thus had
" learned and had deeply impressed upon his memory "[9] from
the most trustworthy sources, he compiled later in his work
entitled *Explanations of the Sayings of the Lord.* Unfortunately we possess from this only small extracts, which
Eusebius, the father of Church history, has preserved.

Passing over the Gospel of John, the origin of which in
Asia Minor, where it appeared, was moreover known, Papias

---

[1] Irenæus, *Adv. Hær.*, III, iii, 4; Eusebius, *H. E.*, v, 20, 24.

[2] Irenæus, *op. cit.*

[3] Irenæus, *Ad Florinum* in Eusebius, *H. E.*, v. 20.

[4] See Lightfoot, *The Apostolic Fathers, Polycarp,* i, 629 (London,
1885); Funk, *PP. apost.*, I, xc ff.; Harnack, *Chronologie der altchristl.
Literatur,* i, 384 ff.; Bardenhewer, *Gesch. d. altkirchl. Literatur,* i, 149.

[5] Funk, *id.,* 573; Bardenhewer, *id.,* 151; Boese, *id.,* 56 ff.

[6] H. T. Holtzmann, *Lehrbuch der hist.-kritischen Einleitung ins
N. T.*, 3rd ed., p. 469 (Freiburg, Mohr, 1892).

[7] Irenæus, *Adv. Hær.*, V, xxxiii, 4.

[8] Eusebius, *H. E.*, iii, 39.   [9] *ibid.*

gives in this work information about the synoptic Gospels. He makes use of the third of these, without referring to it by name.[1] But in regard to the origin of the other two, he goes into details, as follows : " Mark, who had been an interpreter for Peter, wrote exactly all that Christ had said and done, so far as he recollected it. Not in its precise order certainly ; for he himself had not heard the Lord, and also had not followed him as a disciple, but only later had accompanied Peter. The latter arranged his discourses with a view to the needs of his hearers, not as one who wished to present an orderly compilation of the utterances of the Lord. Hence Mark has made no mistake, since he noted down everything just as he recalled it, for he was intent on one thing only—to leave out nothing which he had heard, or in any point whatever to be guilty of falsehood. . . . Matthew, on the contrary, wrote down the utterances [of Jesus] in the Hebrew tongue, and on this account everyone translated them as best he could."[2]

From these words the critics have concluded that there was at first only a Hebrew, or rather an Aramaic, manuscript of Matthew, which contained merely a short collection of the discourses of Jesus. This compilation of his words was, later, made use of and enlarged by the separate Evangelists until there grew out of it the first three Gospels, to which was subsequently added the fourth—all of them being written in Greek. Now, by the adoption of this theory the apostolic origin of our Gospels would also certainly be established. At most, the testimony of Papias about Matthew would be shattered. But it will not do to play off a so-called primitive Gospel of Matthew against a final Gospel of Matthew with an appeal to Papias. The worthy Bishop of Hierapolis evidently wishes to say only that the original Hebrew Matthew, in contrast to the Greek Gospel of Mark, has not been wholly understood by some who were scarcely half acquainted with Hebrew, and " everyone translated it as best he could." That the synoptics have elaborated and enlarged a collection of sayings from a primitive Matthew Papias does not say.

It was desired to infer the existence of a " collection of sayings " from the fact that Papias designates the writings of Matthew as *Logia* (utterances), not as a Gospel. But he names the real Gospel of Mark in precisely the same way, and calls his own work also *Explanations of the Logia of the Lord,* and yet it was concerned with the discourses and deeds of Christ and with the Gospel in the broadest sense of the word. The *Logia* of Matthew, of which Papias speaks, are, therefore, not only " sayings," but words and deeds of the Lord, narratives and reports about the Lord—in short, the

---

[1] Holtzmann, *l.c.,* p. 96.   [2] Eusebius, *l.c.*

Gospel of Jesus Christ according to Matthew. Thus did
Irenæus[1] and Eusebius[2] understand Papias, whose entire
work they knew. From him, indeed, they wish to produce
the proof that our Gospels, already in that "ancient time,"
were well known in Asia Minor and recognized as apostolic
documents.

In the *Greek Church* it was just the same. *Aristides,* a
Christian philosopher of Athens, addressed to the Roman
Emperor, Antoninus Pius, about the year A.D. 140,[3] a manuscript in defence of the Christians. The apologist refers in
this to the Christian teaching with the remark : " This is
the teaching of that Gospel which has recently been proclaimed. You also, if you read it, will perceive the force
which it contains."[4] Then Aristides concisely summarizes
the principal events in the life of Jesus, and adds : All this
can be learned " from the book of the Christians."[5] Several
times more does this philosopher mention " the writings " of
the New Testament, which together constitute " the evangelical Holy Scripture."[6] Aristides, therefore, before the
pagan emperor and the great Roman public, is able to
appeal to the fact that the Christians possess several original
sources of history, which they call a Gospel, or evangelical
Holy Scriptures, and what he recounts of these agrees completely with the essential, fundamental characteristics of our
present Gospels.

About ten years later, the *Roman* philosopher, *Justin*
(A.D. 100-165), composed two works in defence of the Christian religion, as well as a controversial pamphlet, entitled
A Dialogue with the Jew Trypho. In the first Apology,[7]
which he presented to the Emperor in Rome, Justin mentions
The Memoirs of the Apostles, called Gospels,[8] and certifies
that " these memoirs of the Apostles and the writings of the
Prophets " are read aloud on Sunday at the divine service of
the Christians.[9] In the *Dialogue* also he asserts that these
memoirs *were composed by the* " *Apostles and disciples of
Christ.*"[10]

In view of the fact that he uses the plural here both times,
he evidently speaks of two " Apostles " (Matthew and John),
and of two " disciples " (Mark and Luke)—that is to say,

---

[1] *Adv. Hær.,* V, xxxiii, 4.   [2] *H. E.,* III, xxiv, 6.

[3] *Cf.* Zahn's *Forschungen zur Geschichte des N. T. Kanons,* V, 268-
280. Seeberg on Aristides' Apology ; Bardenhewer, *op. cit.,* ii, 181 ff.

[4] Rendel Harris, *The Apology of Aristides,* xvii, p. 36 (Cambridge,
1891).

[5] *id.,* xvi, p. 5.   [6] *id.,* xv, i ; xvi, 3 ; xvii, 1.

[7] Written after 148 : see Veil, *Justinus der Phil. und Märt. Rechtfertigung des Christentums,* xxxi ; Harnack, *Chronologie der altchristl.
Literatur,* i, 278 ; Bardenhewer, *Geschichte des altkirchlichen Literatur,*
i, 205.

[8] *Apologia Prima.* n. 66. (The quotations are taken from Migne.)

[9] *ibid.,* n. 67.   [10] *Dialog.* n. 103.

of all four Evangelists. Moreover, a little before this, he had quoted in one and the same sentence passages from all four Gospels.[1] From the first three especially he quotes so often that even the most outspoken rationalists concede that he was in possession of our synoptic Gospels.[2] Traces of the Gospel of John we find less frequently in Justin, yet several passages appear there which can be taken only from him.[3]

Hilgenfeld remarks in regard to this : " It is difficult to deny even the use (by Justin) of the Gospel of John."[4] Harnack expresses a similar opinion : " I will not deny that Justin held the Fourth Gospel to have been written by the Apostle John, and his judgement in regard to the origin of the Apocalypse of the Twelve Apostles seems to me also to be of great importance for the Gospel."[5] Loisy also finds that the christology of Justin is thoroughly Johannine, and that the apologist makes use of this Gospel as an authority of the same value as the Synoptics.[6]

During the *latter half of the second century* heresies increased in number as well as, to a remarkable degree, the apocryphal Gospels of the heretics. Accordingly, the ecclesiastical writers were obliged to defend the genuine apostolic writings much more decidedly and positively. From their testimony we see not only that the four canonical Gospels were then in existence, and were ascribed to the well-known Apostles and their pupils, but also that they existed exactly in the textual form and contents in which they still remain to-day. Let us again select our authorities from different provinces of the Church, so that the universality of the Christian faith in the Gospels may appear more clearly.

First of all, we come to the *Canon of the Roman Church*— that is to say, the catalogue of the sacred writings which were attributed to the Prophets and Apostles, and for that reason could be read aloud at divine service. Such a catalogue, originating about the year A.D. 170, was discovered by the distinguished scholar, Muratori, in the Ambrosiana in Milan,[7] and since then has been reprinted, dated and discussed over and over again.[8] It is called, therefore, the *Muratorian Fragment.* Among the books of the New Testament which are allowed in the "Catholic Church," the Canon of Muratori names four and only four Gospels—

[1] *Dialog.* n. 88.
[2] Volkmar, *Der Ursprung unserer Evangelien,* 91 (Zürich, 1866).
[3] *Cf.* Boese, *Glaubwürdigkeit unserer Evangelien,* 33 ff. ; Cornely, *Introductio,* iii, 2nd ed., 220 ff. ; Alfred Leonard Feder, S.J., *Justins des Märtyrers Lehre von Jesus Christus* (Freiburg, 1906).
[4] *Einleitung ins N. T.,* 66.   [5] Harnack, *Chronologie,* i, 674.
[6] *Le Quatrième Evangile* (1903), 14.
[7] *Antiquitates italicæ medii ævi,* iii, 854 (Milan, 1740).
[8] We follow the text of Tregelles's facsimile *Muratorian Canon* (Oxford, 1867).

namely, those which are still called the canonical ones. On the contrary, another book, the so-called *Shepherd,* is rejected, because it "was first written recently, in our own time, under the pontificate of Pius [the First] in Rome, by Hermas, the brother of the aforesaid Bishop," who reigned from A.D. 142-157.

Soon after the year A.D. 150, therefore, in contradistinction to the *Shepherd of Hermas,* which had been published "recently and in our own time," the Gospels were recognized as writings of earlier times. But works of the second century certainly were not called so. The Gospels, therefore, were in use in Rome at the very latest about the year A.D. 100, and, moreover, were already then all united together in one harmonious whole, consisting of four books. "For," remarks the Canon, "although different teachings are presented in the separate books of the Gospels, yet this variety does no harm to the faith of believers, because all that the separate Gospels contain concerning the birth of the Lord, his sufferings and his resurrection, his life with his disciples and his second coming, is revealed by one spirit of God."[1]

The more precise information contained in the Muratorian Canon regarding the authors of the first two Gospels we do not know, because the fragment breaks off at this place. There can, however, be no doubt that it ascribes these Gospels, in accordance with the universal tradition of the time, to Matthew and Mark. The third it attributes expressly to Luke, the physician and companion of Paul, and the fourth to " John, of the number of the disciples."

Soon after this, *Tertullian* (born A.D. 160), lived and wrote in *Africa,* first as a Catholic and later as an adherent of the Montanist heresy. His learned works are entirely interwoven with texts from the Gospels, and from all his citations we see that our Gospels were in his possession actually in their precise and complete form. In fact, they could be reconstructed for the most part out of Tertullian's writings, so that a German scholar, Rönsch, was really able to write a book with the significant title : *The New Testament of Tertullian; reconstructed as perfectly as possible from his Writings* (Leipzig, 1871).

Tertullian emphasizes frequently and decidedly the apostolic origin of the Gospels. In his work against Marcion, who had produced a false *Gospel of Luke,* he says : "We affirm, first of all, that the source of proof which the Gospels furnish indicates the Apostles as their authors. . . . I maintain that this Gospel of Luke existed, from the very beginning of its publication, in the apostolic churches and in all those which were united with them through a common bond of faith, while that of Marcion was unknown to most of the

---

[1] Zahn's reconstructed Muratorian Fragment. See *Geschichte,* ii, 139.

congregations, and, if known to any, was bitterly condemned. The same authority of the apostolic churches supports also the other Gospels, which we possess through them and after them—namely, the Gospels of John and Matthew, as well as the Gospel of Mark, which is designated as that of Peter, whose interpreter Mark was. Similarly, the Gospel composed by Luke is wont to be ascribed to Paul. What their pupils have published the prestige of the masters preserves."[1]

Contemporaneously with Tertullian there taught in *Egypt Clement of Alexandria* (born about A.D. 150). His youth, as he himself says, went back to the first successors of the Apostles. His teacher, Pantænus, was actually a pupil of those very old men who had known and heard the Apostles.[2] Appealing to the testimony of these elders, Clement first mentions the formation of the three synoptic Gospels as the work of Matthew, Mark and Luke, and then adds that John wrote the last of all; for when he (John) had remarked that in the other Gospels it is rather the physical side of the manifestation of Jesus that is presented, he, at the solicitation of his friends, and moved by the Spirit of God, wrote a spiritual Gospel.[3]

This statement of facts is entirely confirmed by *Irenæus of Lyons*, who wrote, between the years A.D. 174-189, his learned work entitled *Against Heresies,* in which he gives his opinion of the Gospels with great clearness, thoroughness and completeness. He was so familiar with them that their words flow spontaneously from his pen at every opportunity. From each of the Gospels of Matthew, Luke and John he quotes nearly a hundred passages, and from Mark about a dozen. Some of these are of considerable extent, and he also gives repeatedly exhaustive reports about the contents of the Gospels. His citations and records would, as in the case of Tertullian, make it possible to reconstruct a great part of the Gospels from his work alone. A comparison between the review of the Gospels made by Irenæus and that of the editions of to-day reveals the incontestable fact that the great Bishop of Lyons used and commented on our Gospels actually text by text.

Of their origin he relates the following: "Matthew published his Gospel among the Hebrews, and in their language, at the time when Peter and Paul were preaching the glad tidings in Rome and founding the Church there. After their decease, Mark also, the pupil and interpreter of Peter, has given us what had been preached by Peter. Luke, however, a companion of Paul, has chronicled in his work the Gospel

---

[1] Tertullian, *Adv. Marcion.,* IV, ii, 4, 5.
[2] Clem. Alex., *Stromat.,* i, 1; *Hypot.* in Eusebius, *H. E.,* v, 11, vi, 13.
[3] Eusebius, *H. E.,* vi, 14.

as it was preached by that Apostle. After that, John, the
disciple of the Lord, who reclined upon his breast, published
his Gospel also while he was residing at Ephesus in Asia."[1]

Far, however, from presenting his judgement about the
apostolic origin of the Gospels as his own view only, Irenæus
appeals to a *threefold guarantee* for its truthfulness. First,
he is able to assert that he is uttering only *the universal
faith of the Church of his time ;*[2] and he knew what this faith
was better than anyone else. Born and instructed in Asia
Minor, he had also lived in Rome for a long time, and completed his education there; and, finally, had also become
acquainted with the Church in France. Everywhere he had
investigated the doctrines of the Church with such an intense
desire for knowledge that Tertullian had already honoured
him with the title : *Omnium doctrinarum curiosissimus ex-
plorator.*[3] His statements about the universal belief at that
time in the authenticity of the Gospels are, therefore, indisputable.

Irenæus, however, goes further than the views of his contemporaries in the way of proof, and collects *the reports of
the primitive ecclesiastical authorities* almost up to the beginning of Christianity. He tests every question in the light of
this oldest tradition, as he assures us very positively : " When
a dispute arises over a question of any importance, must one
not go back to the most ancient churches in which the Apostles
have lived, and learn from them in regard to the affair under
consideration what is certain and well known? And even if
the Apostles had left us no writings, would not we have
been obliged to hold to the guiding line of the traditions
which they bequeathed to those to whom they entrusted the
churches ?"[4] Above all, he wishes to have the question of the
Gospels settled by ancient tradition, and he accompanies his
information about the origin of the Gospels with the oft
repeated reference to the importance of tradition, from which
we ought not to depart; and Irenæus finds this information
precisely in the men and writings of early Christian times.

Moreover, he can appeal to these also *from his own experience*. His teacher and predecessor in office in the
bishopric of Lyons, the saintly Pothinus, died in A.D. 177
a martyr's death[5] as an old man of ninety years. He could,
therefore, give to his eager pupils the most precise information about the proceedings in the Church as far back as the
first century. Furthermore, before Irenæus had come to
France, he had enjoyed in his youth in Asia Minor the instruction and intimacy of several pupils of John. Again and

---

[1] *Adv. Hær.*, III, i, 1. *Cf.* Gutjahr, *Die Glaubwürdigkeit des
Irenäischen Zeugnisses über die Abfassung des 4 kan. Evangeliums*
(Graz, 1904).
[2] *id.*, III, xi, 8.
[3] *Adv. Valentinum*, v.
[4] Irenæus, *Adv. Hær.*, III, iv, 1.
[5] Eusebius, *H. E.*, v, 5.

again he refers to their testimony.[1] In important points of
doctrine he appeals expressly to them : " As those bishops
remember, who have seen John, the disciple of the Lord ;[2]
. . . As they testify, who have seen John face to face ;[3]
. . . As the Gospel and all the oldest Christians testify,
who have met John, the disciple of the Lord, and who assure
us that John has imparted this to them."[4]

The deepest and most lasting impression had been made
upon the youthful Irenæus by Polycarp, the old pupil of John
in the bishopric of Smyrna. Polycarp is always present to
his memory, and he sees him as he explained to him Christian truth, and as he had spoken of his intimate friendship
with the beloved disciple and other disciples of the Lord ; and
had quoted their words.[5] Nothing had imprinted itself upon
his mind and heart so strongly and immovably as these impressions received in youth from Polycarp.[6] He reminds his
former fellow-student, Florinus, who was about to fall into
the Valentinian heresy, of this teacher whom they had both
had in Smyrna : " In the sight of God I can testify that this
blessed, apostolic bishop, if he had heard anything of this
sort [the heresy], would have cried aloud, stopped his ears,
and exclaimed, as he was wont to do : ' O good God, for
what times hast thou preserved me, that I must experience
this !' and he would have fled from the place where, sitting or
standing, he had heard such things."[7]

The reason, however, why Irenæus always finds his support in Polycarp and the other bishops in Asia Minor in the
matter of the Gospels, as well as in his entire doctrinal system,
lies in the fact that they were pupils of John, and that the
" oldest " who had transmitted the faith to him " had been
the pupils of the Apostles,[8] had gone to school to the
Apostles, and had remained faithful to their teachings."[9]

Thus the latest witnesses whom we appeal to for the genuineness of the Gospels are still, as it were, borne upon the
shoulders of the pupils of the Apostles ; and their utterances
can be traced back, in connection with the older testimony
which had preceded them, even into apostolic times. From
Clement of Alexandria through Pantænus to the Alexandrian
disciples of the Apostles ; from Irenæus through Polycarp
and the other apostolic pupils in Asia Minor to " John and

---

[1] Funk, *Opera PP. apost.,* 2nd ed., i, 378-389 ; *Presbyterorum reliquiæ
ab Irenæo servatæ.*

[2] *Adv. Hær.,* V, xxxiii, 3.

[3] *l.c.,* V, xxx, 1.

[4] *l.c.,* II, xxii, 5.

[5] Irenæus, *Ad Florin.* in Eusebius, *H. E.,* v, 20.

[6] *ibid.*   [7] *ibid.*

[8] *Des hl. Irenäus Schrift . . . herausgegeben von* Karapet Ter-
Mekerttschian u. Erwand Ter-Minassiantz, in *Texte und Untersuchungen,* xxxi, 1. Heft, p. 26 (Leipzig, 1907).

[9] Irenæus, *Adv. Hær.,* v, 20.

the others who had seen the Lord "; from Irenæus to Papias, " the man of antiquity," who had himself sat at the feet of John and other disciples of Jesus; from Ignatius and his circle of friends directly into the times of the Apostles; from the most ancient Roman canon, which we still possess, through Justin and Aristides to Clement, the successor of the Princes of the Apostles, Peter and Paul, who had preached in Rome the Gospel, which their listeners, Mark and Luke, had then written down—these and many other lines of antiquity, which cross and recross, all lead us in an unbroken course back to the origin of the Gospels themselves. It is, however, conceded by all our opponents that the Gospels were considered genuine by Irenæus, Tertullian and Clement of Alexandria down to Origen, Eusebius and the whole theology of early times. We come, therefore, to the last proof for the apostolic origin of the historical books of the New Testament—viz. :

3. *The Universal Church Tradition.*

The concordant witnesses of early Christian literature do not give merely their own personal views concerning the Gospels. The declaration of Irenæus, Tertullian and Clement of Alexandria and the Muratorian Fragment show that they regard their opinions as an expression of the universal faith of the Church. The whole Church ascribes the authorship of the four Gospels to the apostolic men—Matthew, Mark, Luke and John. In Alexandria, in Carthage, in Rome, Lyons, Asia Minor and Greece this conviction is met with everywhere and among all.

According to evidence, therefore, *after the year* A.D. 150 *belief in the authenticity of the Gospels is universal in the Church.* Now this universal faith must go back to a genuine fact. It would be truly a miracle of mystification and an unheard-of falsification of history, if, from fifty to a hundred years after the Apostles, such a unanimous tradition, recognized alike by friend and foe, could be formed if it had not corresponded to reality.

To this may be added another consideration of great weight. The above mentioned *universal belief of the Church in the origin of the Gospels appeals to apostolic tradition,* and to the teaching and express testimony of the Apostles and the apostolic era. Nothing is clearer and more evident than this from the literature of the second century.

Origen, for example (born A.D. 185), sums up the result of this in the following concise words : " I have learned from tradition that the four Gospels, recognized without contradiction by the whole Church of God throughout the world, were written by Matthew, Mark, Luke and John."[1] Clement

---

[1] *Comment. in Matt.* Prolog.

of Alexandria, the great teacher of Origen, repudiates indignantly any appeal to the apocryphal Gospels, precisely because they are not recognized as apostolic by hereditary tradition.[1] In writing to the followers of Marcion, Tertullian lays stress upon the statute of limitation of the *canonical* Gospels, since their authenticity is supported by the testimony of the apostolic Church, and this again rests on the guarantee of the Apostles themselves.[2]

That Irenæus continually appeals to the old apostolic tradition for the authenticity of the Gospels has been already shown. The author of the Muratorian Fragment also expresses the Church principle with the utmost clearness : " No writing, however old and venerable it may be, may be considered as sacred or canonical unless it is proven to be apostolic."

Apostolicity is, therefore, made the principle of testing the New Testament books. The test of apostolicity itself, however, was the apostolic tradition. Transmitted or not, that was, in every case and in regard to every single book and in all the churches, the decisive question. However Christian in spirit the contents of a book might be ; however old it was ; however worthy of esteem its author ; and though upon its title page might stand the name of an Apostle—all that was useless if the writing in question was not proven to be *apostolic* by the unbroken chain of Church tradition.

When the Syrian bishop, Serapion, learned that in a corner of his diocese the apocryphal Gospel of Peter was accepted as genuine, he forbade it with the severe reproof : " Brothers, we accept Peter and the other Apostles as we accept Christ ; but whatever falsely bears their names we, as being well-informed, repudiate, since we know that no such book has been handed down to us."[3]

Even documents really written by Apostles were rejected by some individual churches, so long as the universal tradition in regard to them was not established beyond a doubt. And thus it came to pass that some apostolic Epistles, as well as the Apocalypse of St. John, were not at once in all the churches adopted and considered as part of the Bible. The apostolic tradition in regard to them had to be ascertained before their authenticity could be recognized.

Now, the Gospels were accepted as apostolic in the years A.D. 130-170. So far as the memory of teachers in the year A.D. 170 could go back, the genuineness of the four Gospels had been always firmly established on the basis of apostolic tradition. The men, however, from whose hands the generation of that time had received this tradition had themselves received it directly from the Apostles and the pupils of the

[1] *Stromat.*, iii, 13. [2] Tertullian, *Adv. Marc.*, iv, 4, 5.
[3] Eusebius, *H. E.*, vi, 12, 3.

Apostles. The chain between the first and second century, between apostolic and post-apostolic tradition, is, therefore, complete. Link by link, it stretches back to the days when Matthew, Mark, Luke and John wrote their books. The Gospels must be apostolic.

The apostolic tradition originated and moreover maintained itself under such strict measures and precautionary rules that fraud and deception are simply inconceivable.

The apostolic authors usually addressed their writings to well-defined circles, parishes, or individuals. Matthew wrote for the Christian communities in Palestine; Mark for the Church in Rome; Paul intended his Epistles for the " saints in Ephesus, in Philippi, in Rome " . . . or " for the Church in Corinth, in Thessalonica, in Galatia " . . . or " for Titus, Timothy or Philemon."

In order to prevent those thus addressed from having any doubt about the origin of their writings, the authors added their own signatures (1 Cor. xvi, 21 ; Col. iv, 18), and sometimes even called attention especially to the character of the written letters (Gal. vi, 11 ; 2 Thess. iii, 17). If they did not give these writings personally to those addressed, they chose as the bearers of them thoroughly reliable messengers, whom they provided, when necessary, with personal letters of introduction. In this way the first Epistle of St John is a voucher for the authorship of the Fourth Gospel. Sometimes the severest threats are made against those who should alter anything in the text thus sent (Apoc. xxii, 18 ff.). In general the Apostles themselves took great pains to preserve intact their written and oral teaching (Gal. i, 7 ff. ; 2 Thess. ii, 2, 15).

Under their supervision the New Testament writings were still further circulated by the churches originally addressed. Many writers of the sacred books were still living at the time when their writings, and especially the Gospels, had become already wellnigh the common property of the entire Church. A mistake about the origin of the Gospels was, therefore, among the contemporaries of the Evangelists, impossible.

The succeeding generations of Christendom also watched over this inherited treasure with an equally great and painstaking anxiety and care. The copies of the original apostolic autographs were, then, recognized as such only if there was impressed upon them the attestation of those Christian churches or persons who had received them from the Apostles.[1] This attestation was verified, according to the procedure common in apostolic times, by means of its own credentials. Even the genuineness of the oldest writings of the Fathers had to be vouched for in this way. The church of Philippi had the collection of the letters of St Ignatius

[1] Tertullian, *Adv. Marc.*, iv, 4.

confirmed and sealed only by Polycarp, the friend of the
disciple of John from Antioch.[1] Irenæus conjures the copyist
of one of his books to compare the copy with the original
conscientiously, and also to enclose with it this confirmation.[2]
So much the more, then, did they watch over the origin and
preservation in their original form of the apostolic writings,
which enjoyed an incomparably higher esteem and importance
in the Church than the most venerable writings of the Fathers.
If, however, doubts did arise about the authenticity of any
writing, of even of any single text in it, recourse was had to the
ancient copies of the Apostles, which were preserved as long
as possible. Tertullian still admonishes the heretical teachers :
" Go through the apostolic churches, in which the professional chairs of the Apostles still stand, wherein their
authentic writings themselves are still read—those writings
in which the voice of each Apostle still leaves its echoes, and
from the pages of which his face looks out again upon us."[3]

In addition to all this, the manuscripts of every church
were subjected to a continual *twofold control—one, official,
by the superintendents ; the other, public, by the faithful.*

The guardianship of the sacred books was made the official
duty of the bishops and priests, and the copies intended for
divine service were preserved at their residences.[4] Under
their supervision, the readers—a special class of clerics—
guarded the treasure of the sacred scriptures ;[5] and it was
the duty of these men in case of necessity to defend them
with their lives. Whoever handed over the sacred books to
the pagans was regarded as an apostate and excluded from
the Church.[6] Also the falsification of the Bible was visited
with the severest penalties. A bishop of Asia Minor who,
out of imprudent zeal, had composed the *Acts of Paul and
Thekla,* and ascribed the work to the Apostle to the Gentiles,
was removed from office.[7] The apostolic Canon (60 or 59),
which, as regards its contents, belongs still to the second
century, orders the removal from office of anyone who allows
the forbidden writings to be read aloud as sacred, " to the
ruin of the clergy and people."[8]

The Christian people, for their part, were very familiar
with the Holy Scriptures. These were read to them publicly

[1] Polycarp, *Ep. ad Philipp.,* iii and xiii.
[2] Irenæus, in Eusebius, *H. E.,* V, xxxii, 2.
[3] Tertullian, *De præscr.,* xxxvi.
[4] Irenæus, *Adv. Hær.,* iv, 32.
[5] Justin, *Apolog.,* i, 67.
[6] Augustine, *De Baptismo,* vii, 2.
[7] Tertullian, *De Baptismo,* xvii.
[8] *Can. Apost.,* Ed. Hardouin, *Acta Concil.,* i, 23. *Cf.* Funk, *Das
achte Buch der apost. Konstitutionen und verwandte Schriften; Das
Testament unseres Herrn u. die verwandten Schriften* in *Forschungen
zur christ. Literatur u. Dogmengesch.,* ii, 179 ff. (Ehrhard-Kirsch,
Mainz, 1901).

at divine service.[1]   Justin mentions[2] particularly that every
Sunday there are brought out before the eyes of the congregations by the readers " the memoirs of the Apostles, called
Gospels."   Thus the people were well acquainted with their
contents and even with the text; and owing to their un-
bounded veneration for them they spied out with argus eyes
every innovation in regard to the transmitted Scriptures.   The
churches also mutually supervised each other by means of the
constant and intimate intercourse which prevailed between
them, especially between mother and daughter churches, and
all important elections, decrees and events were communicated to each other.   How great the sensation would have
been if any one church had palmed off apocryphal writings
as apostolic, or even merely changed the text of an apostolic
manuscript.

The attempt in some churches to associate the Epistles of
Barnabas and Clement or the third Epistle to the Corinthians
with the apostolic books met with a veritable storm of indignation.[3]   Indeed, in the age of SS Augustine and Jerome,
the people of one province rose as one man in protest when
a bishop in the biblical story of Jonas had the name of a
plant translated as "ivy" instead of, as formerly, "a gourd."
Nor did the disturbance cease until the gourd had once more
replaced the ivy in the text.[4]

Thus the universal Church tradition is not only a living
proof of the genuineness of the sacred books, but also an
incontrovertible guarantee of their integrity.

Let us recapitulate.   *The Gospels are genuine.*

The apocryphal as well as the canonical Gospels, the non-
ecclesiastical teachers and the ecclesiastical literature of the
earliest times, and the non-christian as well as the universal
Church tradition, all testify to the great age and the apostolic origin of our Gospel writings.   Whoever is not willing
to recognize this gigantic, critically indisputable body of proof
as compelling, must, with much more reason, reject all the
profane sources of history of ancient times, and therewith
abolish history itself.   To deny the authenticity of the
Gospels is, therefore, a highly uncritical and unhistoric
procedure.

All the Gospels are genuine.

Modern liberal criticism, compelled by the evidence of
facts, has finally consented to recognize the authenticity of
the three synoptic Gospels.   Those who still contest it out

---

[1] Tertullian, *De præscr.*, xxxvi; Justin, *Apol.*, i, 67; 1 Thess. v, 27;
Col. iv, 16.
[2] *Apol.*, i, 66, 67.
[3] Zahn, *Geschichte des neutest. Kanons,* i, 326 ff.
[4] Augustine, *Ep.* 104, al. 88; Jerome, *Ep.* 112, al. 89, n. 21 ff.

of a morbid desire to criticize have at most a claim to the sincere sympathy of their colleagues. On the other hand, the majority of liberal Bible critics still persist in disputing the Johannine origin of the Fourth Gospel. But this negative attitude of many critics should not intimidate us. There was a time—and it lies only a little way behind us—when men declared much more loudly and triumphantly that the un-authenticity of the Synoptics was manifestly and for ever proven. Yet a few years passed, and the whole proud strong-hold of the enemies of revelation was overthrown, and already the leader of the liberal school announces that the positions still remaining will, one after another, also fall, acknowledging that the ancient tradition was right.[1]

This event, as regards the authenticity of the Fourth Gospel, ought to be realized all the sooner for the reason that the argu-ments of the enemy stand in inverse ratio to his certainty of victory. It is, above all, significant that this hostile criticism appeals only to *internal evidences,* on which alone reliance can seldom or never be placed. Some, like Otto Schmiedel, reject this Gospel on account of its " difference from the Synoptics."[2] Others, on the contrary, like Oscar Holtzmann, condemn it because its narratives " are, in a literary sense, dependent on similar passages in the first three Gospels, and therefore certainly none of the twelve Apostles has written the Gospel of John."[3] But while Oscar Holtzmann is always sus-pecting John's dependence on the Synoptics, Harnack[4] says : " There is *some* indication that John has read Luke, but more than that cannot be said." But neither dependence on the Synoptics nor difference from them, so far as these really exist, contradict the Johannine authorship. These difficulties could at most be considered in a study of the credibility of this Gospel. Whether they have any foundation or not, this is not the place to investigate them. That should be done rather in connection with an inquiry into the trustworthiness of the Johannine Gospel.

In reality, all the prejudices against the genuineness of John's Gospel proceed, from first to last, from the alleged incredibility of its contents. The doubts of the Johannine origin of this document are not based upon " positive observa-tion of the text and positive far-reaching knowledge of tradi-tion . . . but the representatives of such hypotheses were united only in the negative decision that a personal disciple could not have written the book, since its contents are held to be incredible for various reasons, partly historical, partly psychological, partly philosophical and partly dogmatic."[5]

[1] Harnack, *Chronologie der altchristl. Literatur,* I, x ff.
[2] *Die Hauptprobleme der Leben-Jesu-Forschung,* 18 (Tübingen, 1906).
[3] *Christus,* 33 (Berlin, 1903).   [4] *Lukas der Arzt,* 159.
[5] Zahn, *Realenzyklopädie für protestantische Theologie,* ix, 280 (3rd ed.).

The genuineness of John's Gospel can, therefore, be doubted only in so far as its credibility is doubtful. That the latter is not the case will be shown later. *Meanwhile, the external evidence for the Johannine authorship is for us a guarantee that the internal proofs, derived from the Gospel, also cannot testify against its authenticity.* If this is vouched for by the unanimous, universally well-informed external tradition, then a conflict between external and inner criticism is impossible. Otherwise, it would be truly an unheard of and unique phenomenon in the history of literature.

But, as appears from the investigation which we have just made, the ancient tradition of the Church testifies to the genuineness of the Fourth Gospel with the same unanimity as it does to that of the other three. And this tradition shows itself to be even more directly and clearly informed about the origin of the Fourth Gospel than about that of the synoptic ones. John, the author in dispute, lived considerably longer than the synoptic writers, and, even at the close of the first century, was still imparting to his pupils information, which these in turn transmitted to us, partly directly, partly through their disciple Irenæus.

One single consideration in favour of the claim of this negative criticism is derived from the testimony of the disciples of John. According to Eusebius, Papias stated that there had lived in Asia Minor, contemporaneously with the Apostle John, a presbyter of the same name.[1] Of course, the critics did not hesitate for a moment to claim that this bishop was the teacher of Papias and the author of the Gospel.

But Eusebius himself admits that this supposition that another John, besides the Apostle, lived in Asia Minor is based merely upon the mentioning of the name of John twice in the preface of the work of Papias. It is clear how doubtful such a conclusion is. " John the Presbyter appears to be, on the whole, an immature creation of critical necessity and the imperfect knowledge of Eusebius."[2] Without doubt John the Presbyter is identical with the Apostle of the same name.[3]

But even if the existence of this " double " of John, in the writing of Papias, were proved, the question would still at once present itself whether he, or the Apostle, had instructed Papias and had written the Gospel. Now it is Eusebius himself who indicates Papias as a hearer of the theologian and Apostle John, and Irenæus cites the latter as an Evangelist, with constant reference to his teacher, Polycarp, who was also a pupil of John. This alone would be sufficient to establish the genuineness of the Fourth Gospel,

[1] Eusebius, *H. E.*, iii, 39.   [2] Zahn, *op. cit.*, 284.
[3] Bardenhewer, *Geschichte der altchristl, Literatur*, i, 538 ff. ; Lepin, *L'origine du 4me Evangile*, 87 ff. (Paris, 1907).

A thorough treatment of the Johannine question could be given only in a monograph devoted exclusively to it; but, apart from the previously mentioned Protestant authors, the reader is referred to the investigations and representations of Schanz,[1] Cornely,[2] Fillion,[3] Batiffol,[4] Knabenbauer,[5] Mangenot,[6] Fouard,[7] Calmes,[8] Belser,[9] Lepin,[10] E. Lahousse,[11] Dausch,[12] and L. Murillo.[13]

The Gospels are genuine in the essential form of their text as we still possess it. Our text of the Gospels is essentially, that of Origen, Clement of Alexandria, Tertullian, Tatian, Syrus Sinaiticus, Irenæus and Justin—in fact, that of the whole second century.

And the Gospels of the second century are in every respect identical with those of the pupils of the Apostles and of the Apostles themselves. Whoever, therefore, denies the essential integrity of the Gospels is reduced to one of two alternatives : either to assume that all those illustrious men of the second century were deceivers, since they claim to have received these Gospels from the first century; or else to assert that the Church authorities of the first century betrayed the Apostles and their pupils, since they falsified the texts of the Gospels almost as soon as they appeared, and handed them down in that form to their successors. Both these alternatives are evidently incorrect. The universal tradition of the Church and criticism of the text both give us the vital proof that the Gospels (some unimportant and unavoidable variations excepted) have been transmitted to us from generation to generation *unimpaired*.

---

[1] *Kommentar über das Evangelium des hl. Johannes* (Tübingen, 1885).
[2] *Historica et critica Introductio*, iii, ed. altera (Paris, 1897).
[3] *Evangile selon S Jean* (Paris, 1887).
[4] *Six leçons sur les Evangiles*, 4me ed. (Paris, 1892).
[5] *Commentarius in Ev. secundum Joannem* (Paris, 1898).
[6] *Dictionnaire de la Bible*, iii, 1167 ff. (Paris, 1903).
[7] *Saint Jean et la fin de l'âge apostolique.*
[8] *L'évangile selon S Jean,* 1904; also L. Fonck in *Zeitschrift für kath. Théologie,* 28th year (Innsbruck, 1904), pp. 545-570.
[9] *Das Evangelium des hl. Johannes,* also *Einleitung in d. N. T.,* i, 259-368 (Freiburg, 1901).
[10] *L'origine du* 4me *Evangile; La valeur historique du* 4me *Evangile.*
[11] *Le problème Johannique* (Bruxelles, 1908).
[12] *Das Johannes-Evang.* (Münster i. W., 1909).
[13] *San Juan, Estudio critico-exegetico,* 9-135 (Barcelona, 1908).

CHAPTER II
THE CREDIBILITY OF THE GOSPELS

I.—THEIR CREDIBILITY DISPUTED.

THE result of the investigations which we have thus far made is that the Gospels bearing the names of Matthew, Mark, Luke and John, are the work of apostolic hands. The problem of the credibility of the Gospel history is thus brought nearer to its solution. Quite apart from the question of inspiration, *the Christian Church* saw, from earliest times, in the apostolic origin of the historical books of the New Testament the scientific guarantee that everything related in them is true, reliable and credible.

" This conviction," writes Irenæus, " is so strong that even *heretics* join in defending the Gospels, and everyone proceeds to strengthen his doctrine by appealing to them."[1] As often as the heretics attack the Christian faith, they take refuge, first, in the canonical Gospels, and, later, in the apocryphal ones, which must to some extent have been based upon the apostolic Gospels. No doctrine could then be successfully defended otherwise than by its real or pretended agreement with the Gospel. Even in defending their positions against the orthodoxy of the Church the heretics assumed, as a matter of course, that the Catholic teachers would also appeal to the Gospels. The rejection of the testimony of the Gospels would, of course, have blunted the Catholics' weapons ; hence, since the heretical teachers recognized the right to appeal to the Gospels, they prove clearly how firmly convinced both sides were of the credibility of the Gospel accounts.

If ever a sect, like the Alogi, made assertions to the contrary, we may be sure in advance that it was already outside the pale of the Christian confession.

It is plain that the *non*-christians were obliged to attack the contents of the Gospel as being unhistorical. The pagan polemical writers—Celsus, Lucian, Porphyrius and Julian the Apostate, like the Talmudists and Rabbis of the whole of non-christian Judaism—attribute the Gospel narratives, for the most part, to deception.

They found willing pupils within the Christian Church first among the older *rationalists* of the eighteenth century. The whole superficial philosophy of that century tended to sever

[1] *Adv. Hær.*, III, xi, 7.

66

the connection between nature and revelation, and between history and the truths of reason.

It considered true only that which it called " natural " and " rational." Nature and reason were regarded as the only great, eternal and unchangeable facts. That age, influenced by the teachings of Rousseau, believed that man has within his reason all that he needs for time and eternity, and that he has only to develop himself " according to nature " in order to realize the ideal of humanity. A divine revelation, or, indeed, anything supernatural, is neither desirable nor possible. Moreover, this conception of the world had no more need of history. An historical event was neither a product of reason nor of nature; yet it held within itself nothing that was not already contained in reason and nature.

Thus did rationalism sunder the bond uniting religion and revelation, and that between natural religion and revealed religion. Every " historical " or " revealed " religion, including even the Christian, when placed before the forum of that " philosophical " century, was at best merely an obscuration of the only true, natural religion; but for the most part it was nothing but deceit and humbug.[1] It was from this rationalistic point of vantage that the approach was made to the critical attack upon the revelation and history of the New Testament, so permeated with the supernatural.

1. The Theory of Deception.

The first to apply the incendiary torch of rationalism to the Gospel was the Hamburg professor, Hermann Samuel *Reimarus* (1694-1768).

Besides some other works, he wrote a book of 4,000 pages, entitled *A Vindication of the Rational Worshippers of God.*[2] Yet he died without having published it.

Soon after, *Lessing* got possession of it, and published the most important parts of it under the title of *Wolfenbüttler Fragments*. It has been said of these that Lessing put muzzles on them, as if they were dogs, yet that the dogs by their barking and snapping frightened many people.

The most incisive Fragments are the third, called *The Impossibility of a Revelation which all Men could Believe as Being Proven,* and the seventh (also the last) *On the Purpose of Jesus and his Disciples.* The impossibility of any supernatural revelation is therein proclaimed as a principle, and the whole biblical history, especially that of the New Testament, is stamped as a fraud. We quote here several leading passages of these Fragments, that the reader may be able to appreciate their author's mode of thinking.

---

[1] *Cf.* Harnack, *Das Christentum und die Geschichte,* 5th ed., 4.
[2] D. F. Strauss, *Reimarus und seine Schutzschrift, etc.* (Leipzig, 1862).

Thus, in the third Fragment we read : " Christianity profited by the circumstance that it at first opposed to the pagans nothing but the religion of nature and reason ; reserving, subject to strict discipline, the mysteries of the faith, which were already in existence, until the new converts had been brought into complete obedience. For the purpose of strengthening the Christian doctrine by means of pious frauds, there were also composed all sorts of books, prophecies and miracles, which, in the state of ignorance then prevailing, found credence, thanks to an audacious system of deception " (p. 337). Again, " The Christians are mere parrots (p. 343), who do not fail to repeat what has been said to them." If, on the contrary, " a rationally educated man, with strong and well trained mental powers, and devoid of prejudice, should come upon the Bible without knowing at all what kind of a book it was, he would not only read it without emotion, but would consider it to be either a romance and collection of old fables of history, or a record of the folly and wickedness of the best among the Jewish people, or an incomprehensible ecstasy, or a perfectly comprehensible piece of trickery on the part of priests " (p. 343).

Like the Bible in general, the Gospel also is bluntly characterized by Reimarus as a fraud. Christ (he claims) had merely the intention of freeing his country from foreign domination by plotting an insurrection against the Romans. When this " system " of his had been frustrated, and the disciples saw themselves betrayed, they tried to extricate themselves from their dilemma by attributing to their crucified Master another intention and a second " system," alleging that in reality he had wanted to be not a political liberator, but a spiritual Redeemer. To return to their old handicraft was for them too unpleasant, for, through their continual wandering about, they had become unaccustomed to work ; and they had also seen that the preaching of the kingdom of Heaven had given their leader enough to eat, for the women who cared for them had always provided well for them and their Master.

Why not, then, continue this business? There would surely be found simpletons enough to believe in the second " system " about a Redeemer of all men. Hence they stole the corpse, hid it, and announced to the world that he had risen from the dead and would shortly come again to complete his redemption. " Now, since the history of Jesus in the records of his disciples, after the alteration of the system, is worded in the most important points otherwise than it would have been worded before the change ; and since they relate as having happened, things on which their new system chiefly depended, and of which, before the alteration of their system, they knew absolutely nothing ; and since they omit from the history other things about which, before that alteration, they must necessarily have thought; the result was that their new system did not adapt itself to history, but history had to be made to suit their new system. Jesus, therefore, during his life, had to be made to say and promise—in fact, the whole Council had to be made to do—things of which they had not previously the slightest knowledge " (p. 125).

" So," he continues, " we cannot but think that the disciples of Jesus devised a different system for the presentation of his views (whereby he becomes a suffering, spiritual Redeemer of men), only on account of their disappointed hopes after his death. For this reason also they composed the narrative of his discourses and deeds. This narrative and system therefore are, so far, groundless and false " (p. 127).

This was, however, going much too far. Even Semler, a contemporary of Reimarus and Lessing, and himself a rationalist and the father of " critical historical research," felt himself compelled to refute these Fragments sentence by sentence. They did not, however, really deserve so much honour. Subsequent generations turned from them with shame.

David Friedrich Strauss, the biographer of Reimarus, was himself disgusted that the writer of the Fragments " declared at times that the *facts* in the Gospels, and at other times that the Gospel narratives themselves also, were the impostures and clumsy inventions of swindlers."

Albrecht Schweitzer, who otherwise defends Reimarus, nevertheless calls this hate-inspired apology " a polemical piece of writing, but certainly not an objective, historical study. . . . It was only a desperate hypothesis on his part, adopted in order to ascribe the origin of primitive Christianity to fraud."[1]

" The Fragments," says Schmiedel, " are so thoroughly rationalistic, in the bad sense of the word, and betray in most respects so little historical and religious comprehension, that science has long since turned from them to really important considerations."[2] Otto Pfleiderer adds : " This example is significant of that want of a true historical sense and psychological understanding of religious questions, which is generally characteristic of that sort of rationalism."[3]

2. The " Natural" Explanation of the Gospels.

The problem before which rationalism saw itself placed called always more loudly for a satisfactory solution. Reimarus and Lessing had shown more clearly than ever how immense the contrast was between the rationalistic denial of a revelation and the Gospel history.

[1] *Von Reimarus zu Wrede,* 22 ff., (Tübingen, 1906).
[2] *Die Hauptprobleme der Leben-Jesu-Forschung,* p. 3, (Tübingen, 1906).
[3] *Die Entstehung des Christentums,* p. 4 (München, 1904).

Previous endeavours to reconcile rationalism and biblical Christianity with each other had broken down, and therefore the Heidelberg professor, Gottlieb *Paulus* (died 1851), attempted a new solution of the problem.[1]

Mindful of the pitiable fiasco of the Wolfenbüttler Fragments, and yet true to his rationalistic views, he let the Gospel apparently pass for history, but interpreted it " naturally and rationally." All its miraculous facts and all its supernatural truths in general, whether it was feasible or not to do so, were brought down to the level of purely natural occurrences, and in every case the Gospel text was condensed, abbreviated or enlarged, or else interpreted in new and strange ways, till nothing more of the supernatural was left in it.

To this end the " natural " explanation assumed that the Evangelists had adapted themselves to the credulous, superstitious and otherwise false ideas of their readers and hearers, and had either altered facts for certain psychological purposes and reasons, or had simply repeated incorrect traditions. They had also, in many places, left out connecting links in the story, or added accessory circumstances, which had been erroneously understood, or wrongly reported. Consequently the text and facts of the Gospel had retained their " miraculous appearance," of which they must be divested by the " natural " explanation.

Here we have for the first time real, thorough-going Bible criticism—complete, historical, philosophic rationalism. In our subsequent treatment of Christ's miracles, we shall have to occupy ourselves with this " natural " explanation. Suffice it now to say that it turned out to be so unnatural, insipid and arbitrary, that it was easy for Strauss, who in other respects held somewhat similar views, to destroy it scientifically a few years later. Subsequently, however, it became the favourite theory on which were constructed the romantic biographies of Christ.

It was this alone that made possible the fanciful Life of Christ by *Ernest Renan*.[2] This *Life of Jesus* lacks not only all scientific value, but also all " moral consciousness," as Luthardt[3] has remarked. " It is a book in which only the topography of Palestine, where the author travelled, is true, and only the language of the writer is beautiful. All the rest of it offends equally at every step both those experienced in such matters, and also the Christian by its superficiality and godlessness."[4]

The book owes its unparalleled success—in the first three

[1] *Kommentar über das N. T.* (Lübeck, 1800); *Das Leben Jesu als Grundlage einer reinen Geschichte des Urchristentums* (Heidelberg, 1828).
[2] *La Vie de Jésus.* I refer to the first French edition (Berlin, 1863).
[3] Schill, *Die modernen Darstellungen des Lebens Jesu* (Leipzig, 1864).
[4] *Theologische Prinzipienlehre*, p. 302 (Paderborn, 1905).

months eight editions were exhausted—to its fascinating
form and manner of presenting the subject, and above all to
the sentimental, frivolous and sexually suggestive style of the
French society novel. Renan, under the mask of assumed
piety, became to Jesus the modern Judas, with the sole difference that he made thereby much the better bargain. While
Judas had to be satisfied with thirty pieces of silver, Renan,
as the younger Dumas has informed us, received from the
Jew Rothschild a million francs for his *Life of Jesus*.

Renan, however, had sunk into obscurity long before his
death in 1892, and to-day no one would have the courage to
profess himself any longer an adherent of the " natural "
explanation of the Gospels which Paulus invented. Nevertheless, for the most part it is precisely the so-called critical
Lives of Jesus of recent times which have retained in many
respects the romantic mode of treatment peculiar to Renan;
and, if nothing else is possible, they too do not hesitate to
explain themselves " naturally," like Paulus, if only thus to
get rid of miracles and revelation.

3. *The Mythical Hypothesis.*

It was truly the irony of fate that David Friedrich *Strauss*
(1808-1874), who had condemned the father of the " natural "
explanation, Paulus, subsequently greeted the son, Renan,
as a kindred spirit, and stretched out to him " his hand
across the Rhine."[1] In fact, he practically returned to the
views of Reimarus.

But in Strauss's mythical theory intentional deceit is replaced by the delusive " undesigned, poetical legend."
According to Strauss, the Christian legend simply developed
the equally fictitious Messianic expectations of the Old
Testament still further, and wove out of both the Old and
New Testament myths a many-coloured mantle, which it
threw about the Jesus of history, in order to make of him the
Jesus whom we find in the Gospels. In his opinion, the
miracles especially are the " mythical garlands, which en-
wreathe the portrait of Jesus of Nazareth."

Already before Strauss various critics had applied the
mythical theory to the first and last pages of the Gospels—
that is, to the story of the childhood of Jesus and his resurrection—while they left undisturbed the real pith of the
Gospel narrative, from the baptism to the crucifixion.

The myth was, up to this time, as Strauss expressed it,
the State Portal through which one entered into the Gospel
history, and through which one also left it again; but
between the entrance and exit lay the crooked and winding
passage-ways of the " natural " explanation of Dr. Paulus.

[1] *Leben Jesu für das deutsche Volk* (Vorrede, Leipzig, 1864).

In his first *Life of Jesus,*[1] Strauss applied the mythical hypothesis to the entire Gospel.

His bold undertaking was, however, already condemned in advance by the fact that it is based *upon three unproven and thoroughly incorrect suppositions.* In the first place, *he puts historical, primitive Christianity on the same footing with prehistoric mythologies.* Like these, he claims that early Christianity originated from the pious imagination of the people and its poets. This is, however, absolutely contrary to common sense.

The legends of ancient peoples could come into existence only because they lose themselves in prehistoric times. The formation of myths takes place in the night of antiquity, which knew of no writing, no chronology and no history, which did not distinguish carefully between the world of fancy and that of reality, and for that very reason dreamed the dream of legends. Primitive Christianity, however, existed in a time which was thoroughly historical, had even reached the highest degree of excellence in historic composition, and passed by the myths of antiquity with a sceptical smile. Such an age may still devise anecdotes connected with important personages or legends associated with great events ; but it does not create a new mythical world.

The second basis of the mythical hypothesis is the alleged *spuriousness of the Gospels.* Strauss was well aware that myths can be formed only a long time after the events in question. The generations directly following the event would indeed be simpletons if they allowed themselves to be deluded by mythical inventions. Hence Strauss transfers the origin of the Gospels far down into the second century.[2] If, indeed, one single Gospel should prove to belong to the first century, the whole mythical hypothesis would dissolve into thin air, as the critic himself acknowledges. And it actually does so dissolve, since we have proved the genuineness of all the Gospels, and since liberal criticism also ascribes at least the three synoptic Gospels to the first century.

Moreover, Strauss had, first of all, rejected the genuineness of the Gospels in order to complete the third support for his hypothesis—*the impossibility of miracles.* In his second *Life of Jesus* he confesses unreservedly : " If the Gospels are really historic documents, the miraculous cannot be eliminated from the biography of Jesus ; if, on the contrary, the miraculous is incompatible with history, the Gospels cannot be sources of historical authority."[3] With Strauss everything, therefore, depends on proving the impossibility

---

[1] *Das Leben Jesu kritisch bearbeitet,* vol I (1835) ; II (Tübingen, 1836).

[2] *Leben Jesu kritisch bearbeitet,* p. 23, 13th ed. (Leipzig, 1904).

[3] *Leben Jesu für das deutsche Volk,* p. 18 (Leipzig, 1864).

of miracles. Otherwise, his whole hypothesis falls to the ground, and the Gospels are proven to be perfectly correct.

Now, in the works of Strauss no attempt is made to disprove the possibility of miracles. He merely asserts that "through Hume's discussion of miracles the matter can be looked upon as settled."[1] Whatever has been presented in favour of miracles seems to him like "apologetic jungles"; numerous certainly, "as field-mice in a dry autumn," but "it cannot be expected from a scientific man that he should mix himself up with such a rabble."[2] Then he has recourse to his "peculiar apparatus for causing miracles to evaporate into myths,"[3] expands his chest, and declares : "The miraculous is the heterogeneous element in the Gospel accounts of Jesus, which is opposed to the historic treatment of them . . . historical research nowhere and under no conditions recognizes such a thing as having really happened."[4]

In other words, if we apply his pet names to the apologists who believe in miracles, and some other remarks of his, to the facts in the case, Strauss argues thus : "Miracles are impossible, because I assert their impossibility ; but since, nevertheless, miracles are actually related in the Gospel, the Gospel history must evidently be a collection of legends."

If it were not so sad, it would be comical to skip over the most important problems of philosophy and history in such an utterly frivolous way. On the whole, only one who, like Strauss, surrenders himself blindly to the pantheistic philosophy of Hegel, will, without evidence, consider the impossibility of miracles to be philosophically proved, and recognize this as a standard for judging all historical reality and statements of facts.

It is true this repudiation of miracles has found, and still finds to-day, the hearty approval of rationalistic and liberal criticism. Nevertheless, this too now rejects the mythical theory as such. Harnack dismisses it with the words : "The assertion of Strauss that the Gospels contained very much that is mythical has not been verified, even if we allow the very indefinite and erroneous idea of the mythical of which Strauss makes use."[5]

Chamberlain remarks : "At the beginning of the nineteenth century . . . it had become the fashion to explain everything as ' mythical.' In the year 1835, David Strauss followed the example given him on all sides, and offered, as a ' key ' to the Gospels, the ' idea of the myth.' To-day everyone sees that this alleged key was nothing more than a new, obscure transcription of the still unsolved problem, and that not an ' idea,' but simply a being, who once actually lived, as well as the incomparable impression of a Person-

---

[1] *Leben Jesu für das deutsche Volk,* p. 118 (Leipzig, 1864).
[2] *id.,* pp. 161 ff.   [3] *id.,* p. 159.   [4] *id.,* p. 146.
[5] *Wesen des Christentums,* 16.

ality, such as the world had never previously known, give
the ' key ' to the origin of Christianity. . . . That Strauss
never had a conception of what a myth is and what mythology
means—as is evident from his confused jumble of popular
myths, poetry and legends—is a matter by itself. A later
age will be unable to comprehend at all the success of such
dreary productions as those of Strauss; learned, it is true,
but devoid of any profound insight or creative inspiration.
It seems as if, just as the bees and ants have need of entire
cohorts of sexless workers in their colonies, so we men could
not get along without the industry and the temporarily far-
reaching activity of such minds as, marked with the stamp
of sterility, flourished so abundantly about the middle of the
nineteenth century. The progress of historical and critical
research . . . causes Strauss's mythological theory to be
regarded to-day as so dead, even from its inception, that one
cannot look through the pages of this worthy man without
yawning audibly."[1]

Moreover, even Strauss's contemporaries and adherents,
especially his teacher, Baur, already saw that no undesigned,
poetical legend could create the Gospel, and that there was no
other way of escape than to return either to the historical
credibility of the Gospels or to intentional fraud on the part
of the Evangelists.

4. *The Tendency-Hypothesis.*

Ferdinand Christian *Baur* in reality dug up again the rusty
war sword of Reimarus. He thought that he could grind
down its ragged edges by transferring the fraud from the
evangelists of the first century to those of the second, and
by representing the Gospels as products of the post-apostolic
period, which deceived intentionally.

According to Baur, the Gospels were invented in the
course of the second century, as writings with a definite
purpose, in order to settle the conflict between Jewish and
Gentile Christianity, the Petrists and the Paulists—a conflict which had split in twain the early Christian Church—
and to enable the Catholic Church to subdue its opponents.
The pupils and adherents of Baur built still more extensively on the same foundation, even if they adopted different
styles. Strauss also, although still retaining the word
" myth," gave a partial adherence, in his *Life of Jesus for
the German People,* to Baur's tendency-hypothesis, for he
now designated conscious inventions as myths.

But all those arguments which had already crushed
Reimarus testify also against the theory of Baur. Whether

---

[1] Chamberlain, *Die Grundlagen des* 19 *Jahrhunderts* (8th ed.), i, 227 ff.

the fraud was committed in the first century or in the second, Christianity and the Gospels cannot be the result of deception. Baur's criticism of the New Testament was much more severely condemned by serious scientists than that of Reimarus, for the reason that he was just neither to the first century, by flatly denying that it possessed the Gospels, nor to the second, which he stigmatized as a perfect tangle of quarrels and biassed lying.

Historical criticism, therefore, whether Christian or non-christian, has thoroughly unmasked Baur's style of making history. " The whole critical apparatus with which Baur has disputed the old tradition rightly passes to-day for worthless."[1] And yet the abandoned root-stock of the old Tübingen school still puts forth in modern theology many a new shoot. We can almost say that the assumptions of the school of Baur have been universally abandoned; yet there has remained in the criticism of the old Christian writings an undefined mistrust, a mode of procedure suggestive of an ill-tempered prosecuting attorney, or at least a straw-splitting method, which still continually fastens on all sorts of details, and tries to argue from them against plain and decisive observations. Instead of adopting conscientiously a " fixed-intention hypothesis," attempts have been made to spy out all kinds of " tendencies," and to prove the existence of a vast number of interpolations.

5. The Sceptical Criticism of the Gospels.

Bruno *Bauer* (1809-1882), an offshoot of the Tübingen school of Baur, and at the same time a kindred spirit of Strauss, adopted only the latest conclusions arising from the fallacies of critics up to his time.

These had, little by little, undermined the whole Gospel history—with the exception of the actual existence of Christ—in order to get rid of revelation and miracles. They had not succeeded. All efforts in that direction had proved arbitrary and inadequate. Bauer went, therefore, to the extreme limit, in order to dispute boldly not only the shell and kernel of the Gospel, but also the historical existence of Jesus itself.

According to him, not merely the miracles, discourses and events recorded, but the very personality of Jesus, which is taken as the starting-point of the whole Gospel movement, are a piece of religious fiction. He claims that Jesus is not an historical figure, but an ideal portrait ; and that the Greco-Roman ideal of virtue had blended, at the commencement of the Christian era, with the Jewish ideal of the Messiah. The ideal of man, resulting from this, was what the most pious pagans, as well as the most orthodox Jews, desired. A great

---

[1] Harnack, *Chronologie der altchristl. Literatur,* i. p. 244, note.

poet—the " very first Evangelist "—personified this ideal, and created the figure of Jesus. Then from among the readers of this oldest of the Gospels primitive Christianity arose; and, later, through further poetical activity, the four Gospels themselves originated. Finally, what was really only religious poesy and deep religious art, was conceived by theology and faith as history.[1]

Nothing but hate on the part of Bauer could have dictated such a strange theory. " In view of this hatred, which is fully as pathological in character as is his senseless method of punctuation, one has the impression of having to do with a man who reasons perfectly rationally, but who talks to himself, as if possessed with a fixed idea. . . . This holds him always more firmly in its grasp, and makes him burst out laughing ironically. What, then, are convinced apologists of Christianity to make of the scraps of the Gospel which remain thus in their hands? . . . Violent hatred and a wild desire to deprive the theologians of absolutely everything, drive Bauer much further than his critical acumen would have otherwise led him."[2] " Endowed with an unlimited subjectivity, which subordinates the facts transmitted by tradition to a preconceived idea, he has for forty years, in opposition to all science and historic truth, indefatigably taught men to regard the great figures of the New Testament, Jesus and Paul, as literary inventions."[3]

Naturally not only the " theologians," but also the critics of all shades were indignant at such unheard-of vagaries, which are their own strongest refutation. In fact, when Bauer's last book appeared, his life-work had been already long condemned and forgotten. Nevertheless (and if it were not true, one would not believe it possible), the banner of Bauer's worthless theory has recently been again unfurled. The Dutch writer Loman,[4] the Englishmen Edwin Johnson[5] and John Robertson,[6] the Frenchmen Emile Burnouf[7] and Hochard,[8] as well as the anonymous German writer, Verus,[9] have tried, with a manifest leaning towards the school of

---

[1] Bauer, *Kritik der evang. Gesch. des Johannes* (Bremen, 1840); *Kritik der evang. Gesch. der Synoptiker* (Leipzig, 1841-42); *Kritik der Evangelien* (Berlin, 1850-51); *Kritik der Apostelgeschichte* (Berlin, 1850); *Kritik der paulin. Briefe* (1850-52); *Christus und die Cäsaren* (Berlin, 1877).

[2] Schweitzer, *Von Reimarus zu Wrede*, 144, 153.

[3] H. Köhler, *Sozialistische Irrlehren von der Entstehung des Christentums und ihre Widerlegung* (Leipzig, 1899).

[4] *Theologisch Tijdschrift* (1882, 1883, 1886).

[5] *Antiqua Mater* (1887).

[6] *Christianity and Mythology* (1900); *A Short History of Christianity* (1902); *Pagan Christs* (1903).

[7] *La Science des Religions,* 4me ed. (1885).

[8] *Études d'histoire religieuse* (1890).

[9] *Vergleichende Uebersicht der vier Evangelien* (Leipzig, 1897).

Bauer and Strauss, to make the Gospel portrait of Jesus comprehensible, as a result of the formation of pagan and Jewish myths. Their assertions have met, however, almost everywhere with the contempt they deserve.

More attention was paid to the equally worthless attacks of the Bremen pastor, *Albrecht Kalthoff.* He knew how to interest the socialists by the never failing trick of supporting proletarian wishes and the Marxian view of history. He derived the origin of Christianity from a socialistic popular movement, and excluded an actual historical Founder, Jesus.

According to Kalthoff, Jesus is merely a personification of the social hopes and needs of ancient socialism, which originated from the general ideal and the general wretchedness of the Jewish-Grecian proletariat.[1] But this socialistic novelty could not, of course, make thinking men doubt for a moment the historic existence of Jesus. It was not only an exaggeration of Bauer's criticism, but a lack of real criticism in the highest degree.[2]

The latest denial of the historical existence of Jesus seems to assume a more scientific character. The American William Benjamin Smith[3] and the German Orientalists A. Jeremias,[4] P. Jensen[5] and Karl Vollers[6] developed the unsubstantial theory of Bauer and his successors still further by the aid of Oriental mythology and the comparative history of religions. Finally, the lay-theologian, *Arthur Drews,* made a résumé of all previous attempts in this line, and conceived from them his impossible book—*The Christ-Myth.*[7]

He conceived it, but certainly did not write it according to historical reality. "It is the book of a critical theorist, who merely through philosophic thinking and his own critical view-point has lost all sense of the living marks of a personal reality. He rambles into the distance, yet does not see what lies nearest him; he labours over the details of mythical research and the representations of Oriental cults;

---

[1] *Das Christusproblem, Grundlinien einer Sozialtheologie,* 2nd ed. (Jena, 1903); *Die Entstehung des Christentums* (Jena, 1904); *Was wissen wir von Jesus?* (Schmargendorf-Berlin, Renaissance, 1904).

[2] See Kalthoff answered by Franz Messert, *Die geschichtliche Existenz Christi,* 4th ed. (1905); Thikötter, *Kalthoff's Schrift "Das Christusproblem" beleuchtet* (Bremen, 1903); Henke, *Die Zeugnisse aus der Profanliteratur über die Entstehung des Christentums, Protestantenblatt* (1903), Nos. 19, 20, 25, 26; Weinel, *Das Christusproblem, Ibid.,* Nos. 32-34; Steck, *Die Entstehung des Christentums, Prot. Monatshefte,* VIII, viii, 288 ff. (1904); Ad. Harnack, *Christl. Welt* (nineteenth year of issue), p. 316 (1905); O. Schmiedel, *Die Hauptprobleme der Leben-Jesu-Forschung,* p. 105 ff., 2nd ed. (Tübingen, 1906); Paul Mehlhorn, *Wahrheit und Dichtung im Leben Jesu* (Leipzig, 1906).

[3] *Der vorchristliche Jesus* (1906).

[4] *Altbabylonisches im N. T.* (1905).

[5] *Das Gilgamesch-Epos in der Weltliteratur* (1906).

[6] *Die Weltreligionen in ihrem geschichlichen Zusammenhange,* 163 (1907).   [7] Published at Jena, 1909.

puts all this together; unites it with mere academic intelligence; finds out what suits the perspective he desires; and, consciously or unconsciously, rejects what could disturb the course of his argument; and the whole is cut up with the shears of an unsympathetic logician, who would like to represent himself as wholly without preconceived ideas, but who, in reality, is the most prejudiced person imaginable. He is at heart dominated by his own critical point of view, and indeed by the whole disintegrating tendency of our radical age. He *will have it* that the whole figure of Christ is nothing but a mere myth, a fantastic invention of a religious purpose; and he insists that there has never been a Jesus; hence his *will* becomes the father to his whole scheme of reasoning. Only thus is the whole incredible artificiality of his combinations and interpretations to be comprehended."[1] Serious criticism, therefore, both liberal and orthodox Christian, have in fact condemned this clumsy compilation unanimously and with indignation.[2]

Moreover, it deserves the honour of a refutation just as little as does the sceptical theory of Bauer; or, to speak more correctly, it bears within itself, like all the doubts of the existence of Jesus since Bauer's time, the most decisive refutation. Whoever must first deny Gospels which were written by eye and ear witnesses, and then must artificially remodel the so-called "ante-christian" Christ out of all possible varieties of old Oriental and Grecian fables, in order to be able to doubt the real, historic Christ, has forfeited every claim to be taken seriously.

And even if he should be able to tear the Gospels to pieces and to weave his mythological patches into a winding-sheet for them, the person of the living Christ would even then, in spite of everything, shine forth, uncontroverted and indisputable, from the "fifth Gospel"—that is, from Paul, and from the testimonials to Jesus, both Christian and non-christian, found outside the Bible. These alone are sufficient to lift the existence of Jesus and the fundamental facts of his life far above all doubt.

In addition to this, however, the fact that the Gospels—so far as their essential characteristics and the historical truth of the person of Jesus are concerned—are scientifically sure and credible, can, in the present state of criticism, even in that

---

[1] Fr. W. Förster, *Autorität und Freiheit*, 89 (1910).

[2] See refutations by Fillion, *L'existence historique de Jésus et le Rationalisme contemporain* (Paris, 1909); R. Saitschick, *Gedanken über Christus und Christentum, Hochland* (May, 1909); K. Dunckmann, *Der historische Jesus, der mythologische Christus und Jesus der Christ* (Leipzig, 1910); K. Beth, *Hat Jesus gelebt?* (Berlin, 1910); C. Delbrück, *Hat Jesus Christus gelebt?* (Berlin, 1910); J. Weiss and G. Grützmacher, *Die Geschichtlichkeit Jesu* (Tübingen, 1910); Chwolson, *Über die Frage, ob Jesus gelebt hat* (Leipzig, 1910).

of thoroughly sceptical criticism, no longer be doubted by
anyone who has any idea of what the Gospels and criticism
really are.

6. *The Evolutionary Hypothesis.*

If radical scepticism of the Bible need not be any further
considered, then conservative Christian faith in the Gospels
has only one enemy left—the *liberal School,* whose founder
was Albrecht *Ritschl,* who died in 1889.

Its present chief is Adolf *Harnack,* and its most important
representatives are Hausrath, Weizsäcker, Schürer, Bousset,
Heinrich Julius, and Oscar Holtzmann, Jülicher and Wellhausen. Their host of followers includes also by far the
majority of Protestant theologians. These are joined by
some deserters from Catholic circles, the so-called Modernists
—Loisy, Tyrrell, Minocchi and others.

Adolf Harnack's *Essence of Christianity* may be described
as the most popular scientific catechism of the liberal line of
thought.

Inasmuch as this school, for nearly twenty years, has
occupied itself especially with historical matters, it calls itself
by preference the *historical-critical School,* and it has really
won for itself great distinction by its researches into ancient
Christian and biblical literature and history. It has freed
itself, in particular, entirely from the rationalistic and sceptical
criticism of the Gospels advocated by Reimarus, Baur,
Strauss, Renan and Bruno Bauer; has destroyed the last
doubts of the genuineness of the synoptic Gospels; and has
also, within certain limits, defended their credibility.

It cannot, however, rise to a full recognition of their
historic value.

According to this school, the Gospels are not at all historic
pourtrayals of the life and teaching of Jesus, but the intellectual precipitate of what Christians thought of Jesus and
his teaching at the time of the origin of the Gospels. There
is thus deposited in them, not the history of Jesus, or the
actual occurrences of his life, but the belief of the older
Churches. " Their devotional character was for them the
standard of credibility. . . . They have described (of course
without any idea of the possibility of such a contrast), not
Jesus as he really was, but the Christ, as he appeared to the
heart of his Church, and as the faithful needed him."[1]
" This biographical sketch [of Jesus] was, from the outset
drawn from the standpoint of faith, not from that of historical
fidelity."[2]

[1] Ad. Jülicher, *Einleitung in das N. T.,* 327, 5th and 6th ed. (Tübingen, 1906).
[2] Bousset, *Jesus,* 76, 3rd ed. (Tübingen, 1907); *cf.* J. Denner, *Jesus
and the Gospel; Christianity justified in the Mind of Christ* (New
York, 1909).

Moreover, when the Evangelists set about writing their works, the original facts had already acquired, so to speak, a history of their own, and thereby also had attained a considerable development. " The oldest records betray already the most unmistakable traces of an elaboration of the historical element, in combination with the ideal motives of dogmatic speculation. . . . Jewish prophecy, rabbinical teaching, oriental gnosis, and Greek philosophy had already mingled their colours on the palette, from which the portrait of Christ in the New Testament writings was composed."[1] " They surrounded his life with myths,[2] and, moreover, made out of the Gospels a pourtrayal of the primitive Christian faith and of their own wishes and hopes."[3]

From remote times, and indeed already during the life of Jesus, there was mirrored in the minds of the disciples, not a clear, historic picture of the Saviour, but *the impression which he had made on them.* And the more forcible this impression was, so much the more did it continually force itself upon their minds. Every further reconsideration of this picture meant, however, a restoration and further development of it.

Especially after the death of the Saviour, the disciples wreathed about the portrait of Christ ever new embellishments, and when they had presented to the believing masses, which had not seen or heard the Lord, a memorial of the Master characterized by enthusiastic eulogy, many a man, from well-intentioned motives of love, wanted to add to it some individual traits, acquired either from hearsay or from inward experience, or from an unrestrained imagination (the usual way of forming legends), until the portrait of the Christ of faith was finally completed, which the Evangelists then adhered to piously and faithfully.

The situation, frame of mind and intellectual tendency of the Evangelists made it unavoidable that this portrait should prove, through writing, still less historical than it was before. " How much had already become uncertain in their recollection is shown by the contradictions between these ' synoptists ' in regard to wholly indifferent things, such as names, or statements about a place or time, or the occasion for a discourse. To this (still further obscuring the question) must be added religious interest as the only motive of their writing, which yet is so entirely unlike that of the unprejudiced historian. The Gospels are, in fact, not books of history at all, but didactic writings intended to win believers. To pre-

---

[1] Pfleiderer, *Das Christusbild des urchristl. Glaubens,* p. 4 (Berlin 1903).

[2] Or " legends " ; but Hess can no more distinguish " myth " from " legend " than Strauss could in the century before him.

[3] Hess, *Jesus von Nazareth in seiner gesch. Lebensentwicklung* (Tübingen, 1906).

suppose in them any consideration for historical connection
would be unreasonable, and still more so to demand from
them an objective, historical understanding of the religion of
Jesus. The important thing to the Evangelists was to set
forth powerfully the supernatural, the incomparable and the
incomprehensible in their subject-matter. What has for them
the highest value is not what we should consider the best
attested facts, but what seemed best adapted to suppress
doubts about the divinity of Jesus, and to strengthen confidence in him and his cause—such as the story of his transfiguration, his opened tomb, and his raising of the dead.

" In the synoptic Gospels the writers wrestle too forcibly
with material often not understood by them, and frequently
actually repugnant to them. The real Jesus, whom they have
received, stands at an exalted height above the man, the
sketch of whose life they give us, with additions from the
Old Testament, Babylonian mythology, Jewish literature,
popular lore, primitive Christian theology, and poetic
art." [1]

According to this, the Christ of the Gospels is the Christ
of faith—the Christ of the churches and the faith-producing
legends, but not the Christ of history.

Historic criticism now desires " to put the Jesus of history
in the place of the Christ of faith." [2] The former stands far
below the latter. He is much more human ; his teaching is
much more moderate, the actual facts in the case incomparably more natural and plain. " To establish the real course
of events, one must go back further than the Gospels and
seek information from the earliest tradition." [3] Historical
research must " cut away the rank growth of legend " [4] and
remove the historic kernel from a confused mass of evangelical
tendrils, leaves and faith-entanglements, and thus bring to
light the underlying Christ, buried beneath a superimposed
Christianity—the " Gospel within the Gospel." [5]

That is, however, according to the assurance of some
critics, a desperately difficult undertaking. " Only late
accounts, and those not written by eye-witnesses, testify to
us of Jesus," sighs Wilhelm Wrede ; " over the amount of
true information which they undoubtedly contain, have been
deposited thick layers of legendary embellishments and historical formations, furnished by the faith of later churches.
Only after a wearisome work of elimination, attended with

[1] Ad. Jülicher in Paul Hinneberg's *Die Kultur der Gegenwart,* I, iv,
43, 45 (*Die Christliche Religion,* Berlin, 1906) ; *cf.* Jülicher, *Neue
Linien in der Kritik der Evangelienüberlieferung* (Giessen, 1906).
[2] Ad. Hausrath, *Jesus und die neutestl. Schriftsteller,* I, x (Berlin,
1908).
[3] O. Holtzmann, *Christus,* 41 (Leipzig, 1907).
[4] Bousset, *Jesus,* 26 (Halle, 1904).
[5] Harnack, *Wesen,* 9.

many uncertainties, can we reach the kernel."[1] " Only with effort," says Wilhelm Bousset also, " and often perhaps not at all, is it possible to separate in the tradition of our Gospels what was the faith and conviction of the Church and what was the real opinion of Jesus. . . . The belief of the Church has painted over and gilded the portrait of Jesus."[2]

Other liberal critics find, on the contrary, that this work of sifting and separation is not so difficult. According to Harnack, " The Gospel within the Gospel is something so simple, something that speaks to us so powerfully, that it is not easy to miss it. Extensive, methodical directions and long introductions are not necessary to find the way to it. Whoever possesses a clear apprehension of what is vital and a true appreciation of what is really great, must be able to see and distinguish it from the wrappings of contemporaneous history."[3] " For the most part the extraneous stands out in contrast to the original so clearly—like the cut glass from the diamond—that confidence in the genuine, which maintains its unique brilliancy when placed beside any glittering sham, is truly not misplaced."[4]

Already at the first glance the critically trained eye will find that the Gospel of John can " scarcely anywhere be claimed as an authority for the history of Jesus. Only a little is to be accepted from him, and that with caution."[5] " So far as any ' history ' at all is to be found in him, it has only the purpose of being a transparent medium for profound thoughts . . . an allegory of the idea."[6] " The Jesus of John's Gospel can be held to be the hero of a religious poem."[7]

On the other hand, " the first three Gospels are not incapable of being used as sources of history."[8] " Certainly these writings leave very much to be desired . . . and they suffer from many imperfections. It is true, gross interpolations from a later age are not found in them; but here and there we see reflected in them also the conditions of the primitive Church and the experiences which it had passed through at a subsequent period."[9] Of course " the good faith of the three Gospels cannot be doubted . . . nevertheless, they have undoubtedly contained, even in their ancient form, much that is legendary."[10] What they report is " a mixture of truth and fiction."[11] Thus, the story of Christ's childhood is not to be looked on as " sacred history," but as " sacred legend,"[12] the " product of a pious imagination."[13]

---

[1] *Paulus,* 2nd ed., 1 (Tübingen, 1907).   [2] *Jesus,* 76.
[3] *Wesen,* 9.   [4] Jülicher, *Die Religion Jesu,* 45.   [5] *Wesen,* 13.
[6] Rudolf Otto, *Leben und Wirken Jesu,* 15 (Göttingen, 1905).
[7] Jülicher, *Die Quellen,* 45.   [8] Harnack, *Wesen,* 14.
[9] *ibid.,* 15.   [10] Jülicher, *Die Religion Jesu,* 44.
[11] Jülicher, *Einleitung in das N. T.,* 325, 5th and 6th ed.
[12] Otto, *id.,* 22.   [13] Jülicher, *id.,* 327.

The narratives of miracles appear either to have been " evidently exaggerated," as Harnack[1] thinks, or they are entirely later introductions and legendary accounts, " which had for a long time been passing from mouth to mouth . . . and land to land, before they succeeded in being permanently located in the written text."[2]

Finally, whenever facts or doctrines are brought out, which are explainable only by supernatural power or revelation, we must suppose that these do not belong to history, but to legend and to the belief of the Church at the time of the Evangelists. Even Mark—according to the majority of liberal investigators the oldest Gospel—" does not present to us the first and most original deposit of evangelical tradition. It is no more a *source,* but already a reservoir."[3]

The above is substantially the view of the modern liberal school; and even though this hypothesis is presented by individual investigators in very different shades of thought, in the main they all agree, from the historical-positivist wing of Harnack to the extreme left of the liberal-radical group. The Modernists also, like Loisy, join in the chorus.[4] In substance, all the liberal critics assert that the Gospels are simply unreliable. That is to say, they do not contain the original history of Jesus, but the belief of the Christian Church between the years A.D. 70 and 100. This belief, however, does not agree with what really occurred from the beginning. Is such an asumption justified?

II.—The Proofs of Credibility.

1. *The Gospels Themselves.*

The Gospels themselves are taken as the starting-point of the evolutionary theory. In fact, no other support for it can either be stated or thought of ; in the latter case because the procedure of our opponents is one of purely internal, evolutionary criticism ; in the former because it will be shown that all external criteria militate against our opponents' view. It is, therefore, only a question whether this view can in the least appeal for support to the Gospels themselves. We must investigate first the Synoptics, and then the Gospel of John.

---

[1] *Wesen,* 16.

[2] H. von Soden, *Die wichtigsten Fragen im Leben Jesu,* 41, 3rd ed. (Berlin, 1907).

[3] J. Weiss, *Das älteste Evangelium,* 2 (Göttingen, 1903).

[4] Loisy, *Le 4me Evangile,* 72 (Paris, 1903) ; *Autour d'un petit livre,* 44, 83 (Paris, 1903) ; *L'Evangile et l'Eglise,* 1, 15, 33, 2me ed. (Bellevue, 1903).

(a) The Synoptic Gospels.

Against the credibility of the Gospel history an appeal is made to *the relation of the first three Gospels to one another* —that is, to the so-called " synoptic question."

Prof. P. *Wernle*,[1] of Bâle, whose presentation of the case may be pointed out as typical, " solves " the synoptic question as follows. According to him, there is noticeable at the first glance, " in contrast to John, the extraordinarily great affinity between the three Gospels of Matthew, Mark and Luke. . . . Not only are the histories and the words of Jesus in them for the most part identical, but even in the sequence of the narratives sometimes two, sometimes all three, continue a long time in harmony, and the text in many verses agrees in every letter. This intimate resemblance would already be a sufficient reason for inquiring into the mutual relationship of the three documents. Still more pressing, however, does this question become in consequence of their differences. Although they form a homogeneous group, as contrasted with John, they show a strong lack of harmony, as soon as they are carefully compared with one another. . . . The problem which bears the name of the ' synoptic question ' arises from the, at first sight, puzzling connection between such great similarity and such profound differences. . . . Our hope of finding at once in the synoptics the genuine, oldest tradition, after the exclusion of John, proves deceitful, as is shown by the above-mentioned differences."[2]

On this account, the three Gospels are to be characterized as works derived from others, and present the further questions : " Where do we find in the synoptic Gospels the oldest traditions?" and " Which accounts prove themselves to have been ' derived ' and historically incapable of use?"[3] In answering these questions, the critic finds that the synoptic material was derived from a number of sources —perhaps from an " original Mark," or a Greek " Collection of Discourses," or from other " Traditions."[4]

In this case, we should have no more to do with the three synoptics; and the question now would be, whether at least the sources used by them (the original Mark, Sayings and Traditions) are reliable.[5] This is, however, not necessarily the case, since these go back in their turn to still more ancient, and of course rarer, traditions, as the " ultimate source " of information.[6] " In the course of this long journey very much has fallen away, which for centuries formed a

[1] *Die Quellen des Lebens Jesu*, pp. 32-87 (Tübingen, 1906); cf. *Die synoptische Frage* (Tübingen, 1899); *Die Anfänge unserer Religion*, 2nd ed. (Tübingen, 1904).
[2] *Die Quellen*, 33.   [3] *id.*, 34.   [4] *id.*, 34-54.
[5] *id.*, 54 ff.   [6] *id.*, 55-81.

part of the established portrait of Jesus; ₂ . . . but, after all, that is no great harm.''[1]

Only now, however, do we encounter '' the last and greatest difficulty. . . . The ultimate sources of information, which we have reached in our investigation of the authorities— viz., those oldest traditions, which Mark and the ' Collection of Sayings ' had gathered together, and the gleanings of which Matthew and Luke retained . . . are always something different from Jesus himself. They contain the possibility of indistinctness and remodelling. They give us, first, the belief of the earliest Christians—a belief which had grown up in the course of four decades, and had also been changed. Between Jesus and ourselves there stands always the belief of the primitive Church, as the object first to be investigated. This belief of the primitive Church *can* go back to Jesus himself wholly, or in part; it can also only be carried back thither in the words and life of Jesus. There is, therefore, no reason to despair or to give up the search. A part of the work is already done when the task and its difficulties are clearly recognized. And finally all this is still not at all the principal thing. . . . For us to-day all this is of only secondary importance and the last thing to be considered. Saturated to excess with christology, we are longing for God.''[2]

Now, even one who is '' saturated to excess with christology '' will find the lynch-law justice meted out to the history of Jesus, to say the least, poignant. Yet neither this rectilinear '' solution '' of the synoptic problem, nor the synoptic question in general, has the least thing to do with the sum total of our knowledge of Christ and the credibility of the first three Gospels. It is a purely literary, and not simply an historical, question. It would be decisive for the historical credibility of the Gospels only in case the Evangelists had not themselves been contemporaries, and truth-loving eye and ear witnesses of the life of Jesus. In that case, what they report would have value, only so far as they drew it from the old original sources.

But the Evangelists are themselves the original witnesses and the original sources of Gospel history, and if they amplify their personal knowledge of Jesus through the use of other, written or unwritten, authorities, then they assume also the guarantee for their purity and clearness. Whoever might wish to contest this, and to cast doubts upon the reliability of the synoptists, would have first to prove that the Evangelists either used untrustworthy sources, or augmented the trustworthy sources with untrustworthy material, and thus beclouded them. To prove this, however,

---

[1] *Die Quellen,* 81-83.　　　　[2] *id.,* 83, 85, 87.

is not possible; and so the synoptic question cannot be used against the credibility of the Gospels.

On the contrary, should the critics succeed in giving any scientifically certain answer to the synoptic question (until now they have unfortunately not succeeded in doing so, and all the alleged " solutions " are mere interrogation points), the credibility of the synoptists would thereby be only strengthened. Every proof to the effect that the synoptists made use of this or that authority of an earlier date is also a fresh indication that they did not look upon their task superficially. They were not satisfied with what they themselves had seen, or learned from eye-witnesses, but took their information also from older and original documents.

The critics who still always rely so bravely on the synoptic question as a means of discrediting the synoptic writers,[1] should consider most seriously the warning of Harnack :[1] " In the criticism of the origins of primitive Christianity we are unquestionably retracing our steps towards tradition. The task of criticizing internally these sources, and (in a still higher degree) that of discovering the origin of doctrinal and historical tradition, and the way in which the real history [of early Christianity] was formed, will probably, a few years hence, appear to the majority of our colleagues essentially otherwise than it does to-day. . . . There will come a time—and it is already drawing near—when men will trouble themselves very little more about the solution of literary and historical problems in regard to primitive Christianity, because, in any case, all that is to be gained by it will have become universally recognized. This, with a few unimportant exceptions, will be the essential truth of tradition."

The comparison of the synoptic Gospels between themselves would turn out to the detriment of their credibility only in case the presentation of history in the three Gospels should contain *substantial contradictions*.

Contradictions, not mere differences. Considered from the purely natural standpoint, as well as from that of the Catholic doctrine of inspiration, the individuality of the separate Evangelists, their personal talents, the origin and aim of their creations are all so different, that their works also must reveal numerous differences. The Protestant-orthodox doctrine of verbal inspiration certainly cannot concede this, as may be easily conceived. And the Protestant-liberal higher criticism, acting at the opposite extreme, will not adopt it. " They act as if they had before them documentary records concerning the life of Jesus, and then subject these to a hearing before a criminal court, where every contradiction

[1] *Chronologie der altchristl. Literatur,* I, x, f.

which has been brought out by cross-examination must serve to prove the incredibility of one Gospel, or logically, in the last analysis, of all four."[1]

Instead of this, the conscientious historian should remember that it is a question here of fragmentary writings, which are far removed from formal historical composition. If, therefore, the planes of the Gospel representations do not exactly coincide, it is to be remembered that the Evangelists did not work at all according to one pattern, and that what they report finds its complement in what they do not report.

Should, however, a thorough agreement prove impossible, and should there remain as a result some vanishing remnants of different readings, nevertheless, historical research—and this is also true from the standpoint of inspiration—is not at all concerned with it. A. Deissmann also acknowledges : "For the history of the Gospels, and of their written and oral origins, which often present questions of the most perplexing difficulty, these different readings are, as far as the history of the Gospel and the delineation of Jesus are concerned, for the most part no greater problems than the critic of texts has also to solve elsewhere" in the treatment of biblical and non-biblical authorities.

These different readings are clearly present "by reason of the character of that mass of tradition, which is a mosaic of many separate reminiscences."[2] Together with Deissmann, Prof. Fritz Barth,[3] of Berne, rejects both the narrow-minded method of Protestant verbal inspiration and also that of liberal criticism. The far-sighted harmony of the Gospels, characteristic of the Catholic school, as represented by Joseph Grimm,[4] proves itself more and more to be the only scientific method.[5]

Accordingly, the comparison of the first three Gospels with one another offers no support whatever for the liberal, evolutionary hypothesis. If now we fix our glance solely *on the mass of facts contained in the synoptic Gospels,* we gain the positive and very definite impression that here the original reality of the history of Jesus lies before us, and not a later remodelling of facts, according to the standard of belief in the Church, and, as is asserted, of a speculative delineation of Christ, partly legendary, partly an outgrowth of history.

Of course, within the limits of our study the entire Gospel narrative cannot be examined and tested as to its earlier or

---

[1] B. Heigl, *Die Differenzen und Widersprüche in den Evangelien, Monatsblätter für kath. Religionsunterricht,* 338 (Köln, 1907).

[2] Deissmann, *Evangelium und Urchristentum,* in *Beiträge zur Weiterentwicklung der christl. Religion,* 86 (München, 1905).

[3] *Die Hauptprobleme des Lebens Jesu,* 4-34 (Gütersloh, 1907).

[4] *Die Einheit der vier Evangelien* (Regensburg, 1868).

[5] *Cf.* B. Bonkamp, *Zur Evangelienfrage* (Münster, 1909).

later origin. We single out one point only, and this assuredly the most salient, most difficult and most important—the one on which everything depends, and which concerns almost exclusively both our opponents and ourselves—*the views of the Gospels concerning the Messiahship and Divinity of Christ.*

In the synoptic Gospels we find the Messianic views, as the disciples held them just before the resurrection of the Saviour. They expect the Son of David as an earthly potentate and conqueror of the Romans. They revel in the anticipation of his royal splendour, and are frankly eager to secure for themselves the best places and posts of honour in his kingdom, and all this not without jealousy, and in spite of all the Master's instructions. This idea of the Messiah, however, corresponds exactly to the popular view. It is a living example of Jewish popular life.

But the death of Jesus, his resurrection, the sending of the Holy Ghost, and all that followed till the days when the synoptists wrote, had given a drastic denial to that Messianic faith. All was different; everything was the very opposite of what had been hoped for, expected, and greedily enjoyed in anticipation. Instead of flesh, there was spirit; instead of a kingdom on earth, a kingdom of heaven; instead of the national hero, a universally redeeming Saviour of sinners.

If the Gospels, as is alleged, had accommodated themselves to the belief of the days in which they were written, then that previous conception of the Messiah, which men had now been forced sharply to reject, both from the necessary recognition of events and from personal conviction, would have no more been presented. At this point surely, if anywhere in the Gospels, the former history would have been varnished over with the then existing theology of the Church. How natural it would have been, for practical pastoral reasons and out of tender consideration for the Apostles, to regard the old Messianic dreams of the disciples as idle fancies, and to consign them to oblivion! But no; the expectations concerning Christ, prevalent in those days, are outlined in precise agreement with history, although they were in contradiction to the Messianic belief of the Church. Yet we are told that the Gospels are a portraiture of the Church between A.D. 70 and 100.

Let us consider, first, the complete synoptic representation of Jesus. This puts the divinity of Christ so much into the background that our opponents sometimes actually maintain that the writers did not know or teach it. Even if that is incorrect, it nevertheless remains true that the first three Gospels reveal to us the glory and divinity of Jesus in a subdued light only, as it were through a veil.

His human nature, on the contrary, stands out in bold

relief, powerfully and plastically, everywhere in the first three Gospels.

"The synoptic Christ is a being of flesh and blood, who mingles with men, like one of them, in spite of—or rather in consequence of—the consciousness of his high mission. He speaks and acts like a man; he seats himself at the tables of the Pharisee and the publican; he is touched by the woman who was a sinner; he converses, as a friend, with his disciples; he is tempted by the devil; he is filled with sadness in the garden of Gethsemani; he works miracles out of sympathy, and hides them from observation rather than use them as a proof of his mission; he is quiet and dignified before his judges, and allows himself to be smitten and insulted; the cry which he utters before his death is one of anguish of heart and physical agony.

"Even if we discover everywhere in his discourses, deeds and sufferings, a breath of the divine, which raises him above ordinary humanity—and even humanity at its best—it does not remain less true that everything that he does and says is profoundly human, permeated through and through, if we may so say, with human reality."[1]

Now it is precisely our opponents who declare that at the time when the Gospels came into existence, theological speculation had already forced the *Man* Jesus quite into the background, and emphasized only his divinity; and that formerly, and at the beginning especially, it had been entirely different.

But in that case it is impossible that the synoptic Gospels should be a feeble reproduction of the beliefs of the early Church in contrast to real history, since their portrait of the Saviour exhibits throughout those characteristics which are pointed out by liberal critics as absolutely original and entirely genuine, in contrast to the portrait of Christ in later decades.

It is a most striking fact that it is precisely in Luke, who writes the Gospel of Paul, that the human element in the figure of Christ comes so decidedly into the foreground, while its divine majesty is seen as through a veil.

Paul is usually made responsible for the adoption of the doctrines of the divinity of Jesus, his supernatural existence and atoning death. In any case, it must be conceded that he brought out these doctrines with special emphasis, and deepened the speculative belief in them which he had found already in the Church, and that he in a certain sense created this theology.

But, if this were the case, we should certainly expect that Paul's pupil, writing soon after his death, would bring

---

[1] Loisy, *Le 4me Evangile*, 72 (Paris, 1903).

this speculative theology into his Gospel, if he had produced the contemporaneous, didactic theology of the Church,
and not the actual, original history.[1] Yet there is nothing
to be seen of any such infiltration. Luke is, in fact, so little
speculative and didactic that Harnack declares that the
Church, " as soon as it became didactic—and that soon happened—preferred Matthew, and let Luke retire into the background."[2]

At the time when the synoptists wrote there were, therefore, in the Church two lines of thought—one speculative, the
other historical. The first occupied itself with the theology
of the Church—that is, with didactic writings; the second
with the history of Jesus Christ, the Gospels. The fact that
both currents of thought flowed on quietly, side by side, is
also a complete proof that both the theology of the Church
and its belief were in harmony with the original history, and
that their mutual antagonism, insisted on by the liberal critics,
had no existence whatever.

(b) The Gospel of John.

As the synoptic Gospels are said to mirror the legendary
belief of their time, so in a still higher degree is the Gospel
of John believed to represent the views of the Church from
the end of the first century on, in opposition to history.

The Fourth Gospel is designated by critics as a theological
textbook, from which the state of the *development of the faith*
of that time can be exactly learned, but from which not the
slightest information about the life of Jesus ought to be
accepted.

In this Gospel not the actual, but the idealized life of the
Saviour is said to be described. John offers, therefore, not a
history, but a kind of religious philosophy—" a piece of
theological, didactic writing in the form of a Gospel history,
. . . a doctrinal poem, which skims over the ground of
reality so boldly, that no historical biography of Jesus can
be derived from it."[3]

This " solution of the Johannine problem " is declared to
be one of the principal dogmas of historic criticism by nearly
all adherents of the liberal-protestant school.[4] Many liberal
investigators discover, nevertheless, here and there in John

[1] Even Jülicher notes this. See his *Einleitung in das N. T.*, p. 292,
6th ed.

[2] Harnack, *Lukas der Arzt*, p. 121 (Leipzig, 1906).

[3] Pfleiderer, *Die Entstehung des Christentums*, 224, 229 (München,
1905).

[4] Thoma, *Die Genesis des Johannesevangeliums* (Berlin, 1882);
J. Réville, *Le 4me Evangile* (Paris, 1901); O. Pfleiderer, *Das Urchristen-
tum*, ii, 281-503, 2nd ed. (Berlin); *Die Entstehung des Christentums*,
224 ff; W. Wrede, *Charakter und Tendenz des Johannesevangeliums,*
(Tübingen, 1903); P. W. Schmiedel, *Die Johanneschriften des N. T.*
(Halle a. S., 1906); *Das vierte Evangelium* (Tübingen, 1906); Jülicher,
Einleitung, 6th ed., p. 382 (Tübingen, 1906).

a grain of historical tradition, or even a small amount of authentic information.[1]

J. Wellhausen has recently seen himself obliged to acknowledge the existence in John's Gospel of important historical constituents, which come near to the synoptic Gospels; and this in spite of his effort to represent the original text of the Fourth Gospel as free, poetic fiction about Christ.[2]

Frederick Spitta wishes, on the contrary, to prove that even the original text of the Fourth Gospel, and indeed precisely that text, is Johannine and historical. Wellhausen has, in Spitta's opinion, underrated the historical value of this Gospel, and says that serious, thorough-going research gives, as a result, " a joyful confidence in the essential character of a document which has always seemed to many to be the most conclusive thing that the New Testament—yes, that all the literature about the person and history of Jesus—possesses; . . . so that the Fourth Gospel, even though it be only within certain limits, becomes again the harmonious, tender and principal Gospel—that of the disciple whom the Lord loved."[3] Spitta even cannot, however, rise to the recognition of its full historicity. But he often arbitrarily and even despotically separates the text into historical and unhistorical[4] constituents, and gives it as his judicial opinion that " The conservatives and the radicals, in their judgement concerning this Gospel, are equally right and equally wrong."[5]

In his attempt to land these views on Catholic soil, Alfred Loisy suffered shipwreck. First he undermined, in part, the historicity of the Fourth Gospel,[6] and then rejected it entirely, declaring that the Johannine Gospel was only an allegorical, didactic document, which clothed its deep religious ideas in the form of a life of Jesus.[7]

[1] H. J. Holtzmann, *Evang., Briefe u. Offenbarung Johannes,* p. 23, 2nd ed. (Freiburg i. Breisgau, 1893); Bousset, *Die Offenbarung Johannis,* p. 45 (Göttingen, 1896); Harnack, *Wesen des Christentums,* 13; Wendt, *Das Johannesev.,* etc. (Göttingen, 1900); *Die Lehre Jesu,* 33 ff., 2nd ed. (Göttingen, 1901); Abbott, " Gospels " in Cheyne and Black's *Encyclopædia Biblica,* ii, col. 1794 ff.; Soltau, *Zum Problem des Johannesev. in Zeitschrift für neutest. Wissensch,* 147 ff. (1901); O. Holtzmann, *Leben Jesu,* 34 ff. (Tübingen, 1901); Weizsäcker, *Das apostolische Zeitalter,* 517, 3rd ed. (Tübingen, 1902); H. von Soden, *Urchristl. Literaturgeschichte,* 211, 230 (Berlin, 1905); G. Wobbermin, *Das Wesen des Christentums,* in *Beiträge zur Weiterentwicklung der christl. Religion,* 351 ff. (München, 1905); Konrad Furrer, *Das Leben Christi,* 2nd. ed., 19 (Leipzig, 1905).
[2] Wellhausen, *Das Evang. Johannis* (Berlin, 1908).
[3] Spitta, *Das Johannesev. als Quelle der Geschichte Jesu,* 401, 466 (Göttingen, 1910).   [4] *id.,* ix-xlvii.   [5] *id.,* viii.
[6] *Revue du Clergé français,* Nov. 1, 1899; *Etudes bibliques* (Paris, 1901).
[7] *Le 4me Evangile,* 75 ff. (Paris, 1903); *Autour d'un petit livre,* 85 ff. (Paris, 1903); against Loisy, see Lepin, *L'origine du 4me Evang.* (Paris, 1905); *La valeur historique du 4me Evang.* (Paris, 1907).

Otto Schmiedel argues that : " The chief stumbling-block is the *fundamental difference between the Fourth Gospel and the Synoptics,* so that investigation into the subject results in the statement : ' If John has the genuine tradition of the life of Jesus, then that of the synoptists is untenable ; if the synoptists, however, are right, then the fourth Evangelist must be rejected as an authority. There is no possibility of a compromise. Every historian decides this matter immediately, as the critical theologian does.' "[1]

If we ask in what the fundamental differences consist which necessitate this categorical " either-or," our attention is called to the fact that the Gospel of John, both in style and content, does not agree with the synoptics ; and that, in particular, the figure of Jesus here and there appears to be different ; being, in regard to its nature, genuinely human in the synoptics, but thoroughly divine in the Gospel of John. Moreover, in respect to the outward delineation of Jesus, it is claimed that, according to the synoptics, he worked principally in Galilee and for the Jews, while in John's Gospel the theatre of his activity was preferably Judea and Jerusalem, and he bestowed his salvation also upon the Gentiles. These are the points of difference.[2]

Far from setting the synoptists against John we claim that, when carefully studied, all four Gospels unite in peaceful harmony. In reality, merely a consideration of the *aim and purpose* of John's Gospel is sufficient to explain all.

The last Evangelist wishes for his part to supplement what the first three have either omitted or barely touched on. This explains his silence about the parables and many of the miracles which are recorded by the synoptists, and about the institution of the Last Supper. This accounts, too, for his giving us words and deeds of Jesus which had been left out of the other Gospels, especially those of the eucharistic and high-priestly discourses, and those concerning the washing of the disciples' feet, additional features of the scene of the Last Supper, as given in the synoptics. Also the detailed accounts of the activity of Jesus in Judea and Jerusalem, which are rendered in a more condensed form by the synoptists, as well as the concise summary of his Galilæan achievements, which had been already minutely described in the first Gospels, are all comprehensible from this point of view.

Another aim is also discoverable in John's Gospel. The synoptists wrote before the destruction of the Jewish nation. They still hoped always to win over the chosen people to the kingdom of God. They therefore laid as much stress as possible on the points of connection between the Old and

---

[1] *Die Hauptprobleme der Leben-Jesu-Forschung,* pp. 18 ff, 120.
[2] *id.,* 19 f.

New Testaments—the purely human element in Christ which united Jew and Christian.

John takes his pen in hand, after God's judgement has already fallen upon Jerusalem, and after the Church has, fortunately, wholly freed itself from the embrace of the dead synagogue. Accordingly, he accentuates the points of separation between them—the thoroughly *non*-Jewish element in Christianity, whereby the Church revealed itself in its full spiritual independence and thus became sympathetic to the pagans. Even in his wording and representation of Christian doctrine, John, who is writing in Asia Minor, comes as closely as possible to classic ways of thinking, feeling and speaking, and even adopts the Greek idea and expressions about the Logos, because these seemed to him admirably adapted to serve as a vessel for the doctrine of the incarnate Son of God.

The incarnate Son of God was, on the whole, the great thesis of this prophet among the Evangelists. While the synoptists, out of consideration for the Jews, had to emphasize the human side, and the Old Testament's Messianic conception, of the Saviour, John, in opposition to the Jewish-Christian heresy, which represented Christ as merely a man, was obliged to defend the supernatural grandeur and essential divinity of Jesus. And not only that; in mind and heart alike he feels the necessity of revealing to men, in his entire glory and sublimity, the Master, whom he loved supremely, and whom he, better than anyone else, had learned to know from a most intimate companionship.

That was indeed one more reason why John preferred for his pourtrayal the later Judaic and Jerusalem period, during which the divine-human manifestations had already made further progress than in the Galilæan period, when the Lord first imparted to his disciples the fundamental ideas of the new plan of salvation. The Apostle also, in accordance with his purpose, selects for narration those episodes which contain the most striking proofs of his thesis. Even the miracles are chosen from the "point of view of the self-revelation and manifestation of the glory of the Son of God."[1]

The Christ of John is the true Son of God, who, out of love to men, has come down to earth from the glory of the Father, and has become flesh in order, as a man, to live with men and for men. The Christ of the synoptists is the true Son of Man, flesh of our flesh and blood of our blood, but sustained by his Messianic dignity, and thoroughly imbued with divine power and essence, in order to lift us up to God.

Thus are the alleged contradictions between John and the synoptists solved by the higher unity of the entire Gospel.[2]

---

[1] Julius Grill, *Die Entstehung des vierten Evang.*, i, 45 (Tübingen, 1902).
[2] *Cf.* Worsley, *The Fourth Gospel and the Synoptics* (Edinburgh, 1909).

From this it is evident that there is no justification for the idea that Christ and christology are in John's Gospel essentially different in character from those in the synoptic Gospels. Harnack acknowledges expressly : " If we have called John a glorified Matthew because he shares with him his didactic, apologetic purpose, one can just as well call him a glorified Mark and Luke; for he agrees with the former in his dominating intention of making clear the divine sonship of Jesus ; and like the latter (Luke) he wishes to pourtray Jesus as the Saviour of the world by means of an historical narrative, especially designed for the unbelieving Jews and the disciples of the Baptist."[1]

Still more decidedly does Harnack's colleague, Pfleiderer, express himself : " It must be acknowledged that *all* our Gospels occupy in principle the same standpoint, and the difference between Mark and the other two synoptists, on the one hand, and John, on the other, is *only a relative difference of degree.*"[2] The Gospel of John can, therefore, be real history, in spite of its dissimilarity from the synoptists.

If, in addition to this, we consider in itself *the essence of John's Gospel,* we come to the conclusion that this is truly history, and not an allegorical or symbolical vestment of philosophical and theological ideas.[3]

Personal occurrences in the life of Jesus are not presented in general, undefined features, as is necessarily the case with the hero of an allegory, but are carved plastically, concretely and vividly from life, with an exact statement of place, time and other circumstances.

When the Evangelist describes how the forerunner of the Saviour bears witness to him, he introduces Jesus as follows : "These things were done in Bethania beyond the Jordan, where John was baptizing. The next day John saw Jesus coming to him, and he saith : Behold the Lamb of God (i, 28). The next day again, John stood, and two of his disciples, and beholding Jesus walking, he saith, Behold the Lamb of God ! (i, 35). It was about the tenth hour (i, 39). The following day, Jesus would go forth into Galilee (i, 43). The third day there was a marriage in Cana of Galilee, and the mother of Jesus was there (ii, 1). After this he went down to Capharnaum, he and his mother and his brethren and his disciples ; and they remained there not many days. And the pasch of the Jews was at hand, and Jesus went up to Jerusalem (ii, 12, 13). After these things Jesus and his disciples came into the land of Judea, and there he abode with them

---

[1] *Lukas der Arzt,* 119 note (Leipzig, 1906).

[2] *Das Urchristentum,* i, 666, 2nd ed. (1902).

[3] *Cf.* Knabenbauer, *Commentarius in Evang. secundum Joannem,* 27-53 (Paris, 1898); see also *Stimmen aus Maria Laach,* vol. LXVII, 361-371 (1904).

and baptized. And John also was baptizing in Ennon near Salim, because there was much water there (iii, 22, 23). He left Judea and went again into Galilee. And he was of necessity to pass through Samaria. He cometh therefore to a city of Samaria, which is called Sichar, near the land which Jacob gave to his son Joseph . . . Jesus therefore, being wearied with his journey, sat thus on the well. It was about the sixth hour. There cometh a woman of Samaria to draw water " (iv, 3-7). Then follows the whole lifelike scene at Jacob's well.

And so the narrative goes on from chapter to chapter, from event to event, through all the activity of Jesus to the very days of his Passion.[1] Everywhere we find luminous, radiant colours and definite outlines, instantaneous photographs, so to speak, eloquent, active, lifelike history, and not a trace of mere allegory. Loisy himself cannot but acknowledge that in many places the Evangelist gives accounts character- ized by astonishing exactitude, but thinks he does so " in order to give to his narrations the appearance of having been reported by an eye-witness of the events."[2]

Then, above all, the days of *Jesus' Passion*. With almost the precision of a statistician, and with the deep emotion of the disciple most closely concerned in them, John describes them faithfully to the minutest details. " Jesus went forth over the brook Cedron, and entered into a garden on the other side. Peter stood at the door without (xviii, 16). The servants and ministers stood there, who had made a fire of coals, for it was cold, and warmed themselves; and Peter stood with them (xviii, 18). It was early when they led Jesus from Caiphas to the hall of judgement. They themselves went not in, but Pilate went out to them (xviii, 28, 29). Then Pilate went into the judgement hall again (xviii, 33); Pilate went forth again (xix, 4). He entered into the judgement hall again (xix, 9); He brought Jesus forth, and sat down in the judgement seat in the place that is called Lithostrotos, and in Hebrew Gabbatha (xix, 13). And it was the parasceve of the pasch, and about the sixth hour (xix, 14). The place where they crucified him was nigh to the city (xix, 20). On account of the Sabbath—for that Sabbath day was an especi- ally solemn one—the bodies ought not to remain on the crosses (xix, 31). Near by was a garden and in the garden a sepulchre—a new and unused one; there they buried him because of the Jews' preparation day, for the sepulchre was nigh at hand (xix, 41, 42). The first day of the week, Mary Magdalen cometh early, when it was yet dark, to the sepulchre (xx, 1). Mary stood at the sepulchre without (xx, 11). Late in the evening of that day, the first of the week, when the doors were shut where the disciples were gathered together

---

[1] *ibid.*, p. 365.   [2] *Le 4me Evangile*, 87.

for fear of the Jews, Jesus came, and stood in the midst (xx, 19). And after eight days again his disciples were within; Jesus cometh, the doors being shut, and stood in the midst '' (xx, 26).[1]

Whoever has the least understanding of what history is feels here its spirit—warm, living and pulsating. The trembling, painful, sanguinary history of suffering is found in every verse and every observation. How will the advocate of the allegorical character of the Gospel fight his way out of this difficulty? To say nothing of the portraiture in general, how will he deal with the *history of the Passion?* It is for him an enigma—a development and culmination of the didactic poetry found in the Gospel—appealing powerfully to the heart, yet in reality saying nothing. But the Passion cannot in the least be interpreted symbolically, either as a whole or in detail.

The allegorists believe that *the discourses of Jesus* especially should be characterized as merely poetical, or didactic personal creations of the Evangelist, invented for the purpose of ascribing his own ideas to the Saviour. "The Evangelist does not separate what the historic Christ has said or done from what he himself makes him say and do. . . . For us such a procedure would mean a lack of honesty. . . . Yet the Evangelist is not conscious of this lack of honesty, because it corresponds to his vague manner of thinking and his absolute indifference to mere facts." Thus speaks Loisy.[2] In other words, owing to his state of mind, the Evangelist is not responsible for his sins against loyalty and honesty! After such a compliment, Loisy, with a gracious wave of the hand towards the discourses of Jesus, writes : "The Evangelist *makes Jesus say*"; and with these words it is supposed to be proved that the discourse of the Saviour which follows them is not the language of the Lord, but a lifelike invention of the Evangelist, who puts the words into the Saviour's mouth.

Yet the Evangelist gives us also clearly to understand, by the comments which he adds, that the utterances and discourses reported by him are to be considered as historical. In regard to the scene in the Temple, for example, the Evangelist remarks by way of explanation : "But he spoke of the temple of his body. When, therefore, he was risen again from the dead, his disciples remembered that he had said this; and they believed the scripture and the word that Jesus had said" (ii, 21, 22). The language used by Jesus in regard to Lazarus, John explains thus : "Jesus spoke of his death, and they thought that he spoke of the repose of sleep" (xi, 13). At his entry into Jerusalem, Jesus connects with it a Messianic prophecy of Zacharias;

---

[1] Knabenbauer, *ibid.,* 366.   [2] *Le 4me Evangile,* 891.

whereupon the Evangelist remarks : " These things his disciples did not know at the first, but when Jesus was glorified, then they remembered that these things were written of him, and that they had done these things to him " (xii, 16). By means of these and similar[1] explanations John represents positively the words and discourses of Jesus, quoted by him, as historical.

These discourses are not monologues, as we might expect in an allegorical work. On the contrary, they are interrupted by objections, refutations, questions and answers. Now it is the Apostles—the most ardent and zealous of all; now it is the representatives of the people; or, again, priests and Pharisees who interfere, turn aside, check or lead on again the current of his words. (See chapters iii, iv, vi, vii, viii, xi, xiii and xiv.) Only reality speaks and discourses in this way.

Loisy, however, naïvely replies : " The intervals which occur during the teachings of the Saviour, such as interruptions, questions, murmurs and disputes among those present are merely literary expedients to enliven and make easier the development of the Johannine thesis."[2] But one tries in vain to find in Loisy's writings any proof for this incredible assertion.

Loisy treats also the *miracles of Jesus* equally lightly. Yet the narrations of John referring to these, too, evidently bear the stamp of history. Think only of the miracles—reported with astonishing clearness and preciseness—which Jesus performs upon the paralytic, the man who was born blind, the young man of Naim, the daughter of Jairus, and Lazarus. To this Loisy can only proffer the objection that the entire biographies of the people healed thus, or brought back from death, are not reported![3] For this reason it is not a question of actual facts, but only of symbolical representation !

But whenever the critic really attempts to carry out to its conclusion the purely symbolical explanation of the miracles, the whole inadequacy of his method is revealed.

Take, as one example only, the first miracle of Christ— that of Cana. Loisy maintains that it has no historic character, and that it is all to be understood allegorically. By the " mother of Jesus " must be understood the synagogue; by the " water " the Old Testament teaching; by the " wine " the blood of Christ; by the " bridegroom " the Saviour; by the " bride " the Christian Church.[4] What, then, do the " stone jars " signify? and Cana? and Capharnaum, whither Jesus goes immediately after? and what do the " brethren " and the " disciples " mean, who accompany him? What

---

[1] Knabenbauer, *ibid.*, 367 ff.   [2] Loisy, *id.*, 86.
[3] *ibid.*, 83.   [4] *id.*, 281-284.

I.   7

must all that be, if it has no historic sense? "Scenic effects," Loisy thinks; "concrete scenic effects." But whatever he cannot drag into his system is for him "concrete scenic effect," from the day at Cana down to Malchus and his cousin, who are the "concrete scenic effect" of the purely symbolic box on the ear[1] delivered by Peter!

Truly nothing more is needed in order to perceive that the allegorical conception of the Fourth Gospel has broken down, and that the only correct interpretation of John is the historic one.

Yet let us first question the Evangelists themselves.

2. The Evangelists.

Did the *Evangelists* wish to present the real, actual *history of Jesus,* or only that history in a legendary garb? And, in the former event, *were they capable of writing the history of Jesus,* just as he lived, without any legendary additions and misrepresentations? The whole point lies there.

The answer to the first question is given in what has been already said. The works of the Evangelists themselves, from the first line to the last, from their first deep, fundamental idea to their ultimate completion, are so constructed, that no possibility of doubt remains that these men wish themselves to be regarded as historians, and their writings as historically faithful representations.

Luke especially, whose critical ability is most highly prized by our opponents, and John, to whom, least of all, historical importance is conceded, both speak most plainly on this subject. "Forasmuch as many," it is said in the introduction to Luke's Gospel, "have taken in hand to set forth in order a narration of the things that have been accomplished among us, according as they delivered them unto us, who from the beginning were eye-witnesses and ministers of the word, it seemed good to me also, having diligently attained to all things from the beginning, to write to thee in order, most excellent Theophilus, that thou mayest know the verity of those words in which thou hast been instructed" (Luke i, 1-3). The determination to write *history—pure, unadulterated history*—could not be more definitely stated.

Like Luke, at the beginning of his Gospel, so John, at the conclusion of his, writes: "Many other signs also did Jesus in the sight of his disciples, which are not written in this book; but these are written that you may believe that Jesus is the Christ, the Son of God, and that, believing, you may have life in his name (xx, 30, 31; xxi, 24). This is the disciple who giveth testimony of these things and hath written

[1] *id.,* 281-841.

these things, and we [the Evangelist and his pupil] know that his testimony is true" (xxi, 24). It is evident, therefore, that the Evangelist wishes to report what eye-witnesses have seen; and he himself, as an eye-witness, guarantees the truth and reality of the facts related.

Moreover, the facts and the testimony of John are, so to speak, audited and approved by the earliest readers of his Gospel : "We know that his testimony is true." And, therefore, on these facts and testimony is built up the beatific faith that Jesus Christ is really and truly the Son of God. All this proves clearly that John considers himself to be an historian, and that the reality and actuality of the narratives contained in his book ought not to be in the least assailed.

It is true, there was a time, and not so long ago either, when this personal testimony was abruptly rejected, with the assertion that no reliance is to be placed on the veracity of the Evangelists. And so the Christian apologist, until a few years ago, had to be able to prove the honesty of the Evangelists from their personal character, no less than from the contents, form and statements of their writings. To-day the critics have done justice to them, at least in that respect. In contrast to Reimarus, Baur, and their older as well as their latest adepts, they now take pride in recognizing the Evangelists' universal love of truth.

Even in the case of John, to whom they still obstinately refuse the rank of an historian, liberal critics reject any suspicion of deception on his part. Indeed, it is precisely because they will not, on the one hand, allow him to pass for an historian, and, on the other, cannot doubt his veracity, that they take refuge in the desperate hypothesis of "John the allegorist" and "poet-evangelist."

The Evangelists, therefore, wish most conscientiously to report the historic truth about Jesus, his life, deeds and teaching. They write no line which they do not consider absolutely correct. They relate no episode in the life of Jesus, the actuality of which they do not believe. They do not ascribe to the Saviour one single doctrine which they do not, with absolute conviction, regard as a part of his teaching. It would be a waste of time to expend more words on this point.

Quite different, however, is the question : *Were the Evangelists capable of writing the history of Jesus?* Did they know the *objective* truth of the life of Jesus, and were they qualified *subjectively* to report it correctly?

The *subjective* ability to make a suitable report was as little wanting in the Evangelists as an honest wish to do so. It is true they had not a high, scientific education[1] and

---

[1] Luke alone " had an education above the average and an unusual facility in writing." Harnack, *Lukas der Arzt*, 104.

critical precision; but these they did not need. It was not a matter of solving deep problems, or of extracting the truth from old bundles of documents, and examining it critically. The task of the Evangelists was merely to write down perfectly concrete deeds, which had been enacted for the most part in public and in broad daylight, and were of the greatest simplicity.

Among these even the supernatural deeds and teachings of Jesus make no exception. Their supernatural character in no way alters or impairs their natural, outward phenomena. The Evangelists had, moreover, neither to place a value on the supernatural element in the miracles of Jesus, nor to pass judgement on the supernatural element in his teaching. They merely relate the deeds and words of Jesus. They simply state, for example, that he caused the blind to see, instantly stilled a tempest on the lake, called back the dead to life, etc. For this there is no need either of critical training or of high intellectual culture. *Normal senses,* clear vision, an unprejudiced judgement, practical common sense— these are the principal things wanted. But these qualities the Evangelists did possess to a high degree.

Nothing is more unjust than the assertion that they were overwrought, credulous, and fond of the miraculous. There is not a trace of fanaticism in their writings. On the contrary, we find everywhere calm, sober, passionless conceptions and descriptions.

Even where we should certainly expect an admixture of personal temperament and judgement, they adhere to the bare delineation of facts. They even relate miraculous acts of healing, raisings of the dead and marvellous deeds in the sphere of nature without the least expression of astonishment. They also give accounts of the ill-treatment, abuse and condemnation of their Master without allowing one word of indignation or disapproval to pass their lips. They pourtray even the death and resurrection of their beloved Master as simply as if in those events they had only the interest of the observer and narrator. Hence, although they were not historians in the sense of Thucydides, the father of critical historical composition, nevertheless they did possess the most pronounced subjective ability to write down the facts of the Gospels in accordance with truth.

But were they sufficiently acquainted with these facts? How far did their *objective* knowledge extend?

Certainly a complete knowledge of the *chronological sequence* and concatenation of events was not theirs. Papias, the disciple of John, had already noticed this in regard to Mark's Gospel.[1] It is at once evident also in Matthew and John. Luke wishes, it is true, to " write in

[1] Eusebius, *H. E.*, iii, 39.

order " (Luke 1, 3) the facts of the Gospels; yet it is not probable that he means by this the exact chronological order. For this reason the Gospels are not historical works in the strictest sense of the term, and do not offer, therefore, a real, thorough-going " life " of the Saviour. Indeed, such an one could not have been written on the basis of the Gospels.

It is, moreover, clear that the Evangelists do not report all the *words* of Jesus with absolute fidelity. Even the inspiration of the Gospels, according to faith, does not extend to every word of the text. This limitation of the idea of inspiration rests upon a law of natural history with which alone we have to do here—namely, that words cannot easily be handed down from one age to another without alteration, even were it only from the first generation to the second. Some words have, indeed, preserved their imprint indelibly for centuries, but they form the exception. It follows from this that we, in many cases, cannot exactly determine the expressions which our Lord used, especially when his words are not understood by the individual Evangelists in entire agreement; but the decisive words of Jesus certainly did stamp themselves on the memories of his hearers with imperishable fidelity, as we see from the Gospels.

As in regard to single words, so too in respect to individual, secondary *circumstances,* the Evangelists sometimes differ from one another. This proves that we should not expect from them an infallibly certain and complete representation of the accessory circumstances of historic facts either by appealing to natural knowledge of the facts, or to supernatural inspiration.

All this, however, has nothing essentially to do with our question. We are concerned only to know whether the Evangelists were well informed about the subject-matter of the history of Jesus, and about its real facts and the actual substance of his teaching. That must be answered emphatically in the affirmative.

In the first place, the last Evangelist, John, whose testimony is most disputed, claims to be an *eye-witness*. In a great number of passages in his Gospel also the eye-witness reveals himself unmistakably.[1]

He can expressly state : " And he that saw it hath given testimony; and his testimony is true; and he knoweth that he saith true, that you also may believe " (John xix, 35). " That which was from the beginning, which we have heard, which we have seen with our eyes, which we have looked upon, and our hands have handled, of the word of life—that we declare unto you " (1 John i, 1, 3). Even though this ocular obser-

---

[1] *Cf.* Knabenbauer, *Der geschichtliche Charakter des 4 Evangeliums, l.c.,* p. 368 ff.

vation may not refer, mathematically, to *all* the details of the life of Jesus, it does concern itself with all its essential events.

Under certain limitations this is true also of Matthew. True, he was not an Apostle of the first hour, as John was; and cannot therefore, as we perceive at once from his book, be appealed to as an eye-witness for the whole Gospel. Nevertheless, he lived through the most important period and the most momentous events of the life of Jesus in company with the Master.

We reach, then, the conclusion that the first Gospel rests for the most part, and the Fourth Gospel almost entirely, upon personal experience and ocular observation. And since both these Gospels contain all the critical events in the history of Jesus, we know these events themselves substantially from the reports of veracious eye-witnesses.

As for the other narratives of things which they did not know from personal experience, they had at their disposal the oral, individual reports of the mother of Jesus and their fellow-apostles.

This is wholly true also of Mark and Luke. These did not themselves belong to the Lord's circle of disciples, yet they were for many years in daily and most intimate intercourse with the Apostles and disciples. They were, therefore, the best qualified *ear-witnesses* of the life of Jesus. We know especially that Mark wrote down in substance the teachings of Peter; while Luke based his writings, in particular, on the sermons of Paul. For his history of the Acts of the Apostles, St Luke made use of the most reliable accounts of numerous eye-witnesses and of the teacher of the Gentile nations, Paul himself—to say nothing of the fact that the author also participated personally in many of the occurrences described.

Moreover, all four Evangelists had also, together with the oral reports, *written documents* of the first generation. Luke expressly tells us this in the words already quoted : " Many have taken in hand to set forth in order a narration of the things that have been accomplished among us, according as they delivered them unto us, who from the beginning were eye-witnesses and ministers of the word " (Luke i, 1, 2).

The form of the text of the Gospels also—at least, that of the synoptists—indicates the use made of such written sources of information. On this the liberal critics especially lay great emphasis. With considerable unanimity they assume that Mark wrote the oldest Gospel. This and a further document—" The Sayings (*Logia*) of the Lord "—were, they think, made use of by Matthew and Luke. Luke has, in any case, profited by still another original manuscript—probably the earliest—which was not known to the other two synoptists. Perhaps also some special material of Matthew, which we do not find in Mark and Luke, comes from an unknown written source of a still older time.

We must, however, take great care not to ascribe too much certainty to these assertions of New Testament literary criticism, and above all must not attach too much importance to them. It is remarkable how precipitately mere hypotheses are credited as assured results, and how thoughtlessly even some Catholic critics, especially in France, at once adopt the separation of authorities advocated by the liberals, and therewith assume[1] the priority of Mark's Gospel and the dependency of Matthew and Luke on the second synoptist, although our traditional chronological order of the Gospels cannot be weakened by any decisive arguments.[2]

Our opponents reveal only too plainly that their standard for answering the synoptical question is, from first to last, nothing but the degree of the " Catholicity " of the Gospels. Thus, Jülicher, in his introduction to the New Testament, now so extensively used, says : " In my opinion the religious attitude of Matthew turns the scales (in favour of the late entry of Matthew's Gospel). . . . He wrote a Catholic Gospel, and its purely Catholic tone has won for it the first place among the Gospels. . . . To put this genuinely Catholic Gospel at the head of the writings of the ancient Church is, however, a most stupendous mistake."[3] Of this " unprejudiced " theory of the sources of authority, even the Berlin theologian, Bernhard Weiss, writes as follows : " We shall progress no further in our attempt to solve the principal problems in the life of Jesus if we do not, by a study of the original sources, learn to discriminate between the various strata of tradition, present in our three oldest Gospels, *instead of construing them according to preconceived notions.*"[4]

From the investigations of the origins of the Gospels thus far made there results with complete certainty only this—that the Evangelists had some written documents at their disposal. It remains problematical what form those documents had and how far they were consulted by the writers of the Gospels. In any case, it must be characterized as an act of great injustice that liberal critics remodel our Gospels by referring to documents which perhaps may never have existed elsewhere than in the imagination of some modern bookworm, and the contents of which cannot now be determined at all. That "notes " of great antiquity existed antecedently

---

[1] Lagrange, *Bulletin de Littérature ecclésiastique,* p. 19 (1904); Batiffol, *Six leçons sur les Evangiles,* p. 65 ff., 8th ed. (Paris, 1907).

[2] See *Introductions* by Kaulen, Danko, Cornely, Zahn, Belser, Bonkamp.

[3] *Einleitung in das N. T.,* p. 265 ff., 6th ed. (Tübingen, 1906).

[4] *Die Quellen der synopt. Evang.* in *Texte und Untersuchungen,* edited by Harnack and Schmidt, XXXII, iii, 255 ff. (Leipzig, 1908).

to the Gospels, from which the Evangelists could, when necessary, draw their material, is of great interest for the historian. But practically such notes have only a hypothetical value, because they are not accessible as literary productions. Compared with these objects of unknown and often imaginary importance, not only the genuine texts of the Gospels, but even the scanty traditions of primitive Christian times also, retain their full validity.

So much the more weighty, therefore, as a source of authority for the Gospels, is the unanimous testimony of the primitive Christian Church, which may be truly called *the unwritten, original Gospel*. No matter how many oral, or written, individual testimonies may have been accessible to the Evangelists, the universal tradition of the earliest Church was for the Gospel, as a whole, of fundamental importance. The whole "paleontological" period of Christianity is dependent upon that.

It relies less upon individual oral reports, and still less[1] upon written sketches dating from the first generation, than upon the universally known public tradition. The constant admonition in the time of the Apostles[2] was, in effect, the following : "Remember the words of the Lord Jesus. Keep his word and testimony, his commandment and teaching, which you have heard from the beginning. Think of the commandment of the Saviour, brought and delivered unto you by your Apostles." (See Acts xx, 35 ; 1 John ii, 5, 7 ; 2 Peter ii, 21 ; iii, 2.)

Throughout their writings the Evangelists always adhered closely to this unwritten Gospel of the primitive Church. In this opinion we are at one with the liberal school; but the conclusions which they draw from this fact are in opposition to those which we deduce from it. We see in it the clearest and fullest proof of the historicity of those portions of the Gospels which were not written down by eye-witnesses. In fact, in so far as the Evangelists were not themselves eye-witnesses of the events which they reported, they deserve unlimited confidence only because their testimony is the testimony of everyone else, and their representation the representation of the whole primitive Christian community—the entire apostolic Church.

Now, since the whole Church, soon after the year A.D. 50, unanimously held this opinion of Christ, as the Evangelists tell us was the case, it must have evidently thought and spoken of him thus also ten or twenty years before; for an inference from the unanimous opinion of the second generation to the corresponding opinion of the first generation, which had seen and experienced all those things with Jesus, forces itself upon us as an historically necessary consequence.

---

[1] In N. T. only Luke i, 1 ff.   [2] Zahn, *Einleitung*, ii, 158-172.

The Evangelists pourtray correctly the real history of Jesus precisely because they hold fast to the belief of the Church of their time. The history of Jesus and the belief of the earliest Christian Church must essentially agree.

Liberal criticism, however, sets them up in opposition to each other. Instead of starting from the primitive Church, in order to reason back thence to the real Christ, it starts from its own modern views, and applies these, as a standard, to the measurement of the primitive Church. And because the difference between them is insurmountable, it does not reach the conclusion that the liberal portrait of Christ is unhistorical, but that the portrait of Christ made by the primitive Church is legendary. This is the Achilles heel of the whole liberal theology and history. In the following section we shall examine still more closely the unreliability of such Gospel criticism.

3. *The Contemporaries.*

Liberal evolutionary criticism starts from the influence, growth and development of historical events caused by legend. "Legend," says Harnack, "is in many respects the worst and never resting enemy of true history. It may be compared to the climbing plant, which grows wherever history grows. Almost contemporaneously with the great event and the great man legend begins to climb upward, and the greater those become the more rankly it grows. It surrounds and encircles elementary events as well as mighty deeds, facts no less than persons. It sends forth its creepers from tree to tree, and the higher the trunk the more densely and compactly it is covered. At last, the whole forest is interwoven with a tangle of tendrils and foliage. One tree after another is sucked dry and withers away. We see no more the natural variety of different trees. Everywhere appears merely the uniform foliage of the climbing plant. Only the insignificant undergrowth on the floor of the forest remains unharmed."[1] Thus does Harnack with equal beauty and exactitude describe the rank growth of legend.

Unwritten history, passing on without restraint and growing wild, becomes in time through the evolutionary working of the legend actually transformed, and is finally crushed by it. This may pass for a law of the science of history.

But this law cannot be applied to the Gospels : first, because the Gospels are the *contemporary representations* of recent facts ; and, secondly, because their authors were *put to the test of accuracy by their own generation.*

The school of sceptical criticism cannot yet entirely forget

---

[1] *Reden und Aufsätze,* I, 4, 2nd ed., (Giessen, 1906).

its experiences with the great conclusions of Baur, however much it is convinced of their inaccuracy. To proclaim the Gospel history to be a legendary caricature of true history would indeed have some sense if one placed the origin of the Gospels between the years 140-170, as the old Tübingen school did. Then, at least, there would be, relatively, enough time for the parasitic processes of the legend to have spread themselves out; although even then only under the supposition of our opponents that Church tradition had not checked the formation of legends, but, on the contrary, promoted it.

But we stand no longer under the spell of Baur's dates for the Gospels. The last Gospel was already written about the year 100; and Matthew's Gospel, according to the calculation of liberals, was already in existence about the year A.D. 70. On the ground of "very important observations," some critics assume that the Gospel of Luke "was already composed even at the beginning of the sixties."[1] The Gospel of Mark is universally looked upon as still older. Moreover, in so far as Matthew and John are veracious eye-witnesses, the starting-point of their Gospels must coincide with the events described. Where, then, remains the time necessary for legend-building? How could such legends have so altered the history of Jesus within a period of from twenty to thirty years?

At the most, within such a limited amount of time, the growth of some small, unimportant accretions, suitable for the formation of legends, might be thought possible. But it is not a supposition of such things that our opponents present. It is true, liberal criticism at one moment expresses the opinion that the original events are only partially transformed by the synoptists, but at another time it conceives the contents of the Gospel and the entire portraiture of Christ as being opposed not only to John and Paul, but in an equal degree also to the synoptists themselves.

The "liberal" Gospel is a Gospel without a revelation, without miracles, without a Messiah, and without an incarnate God—a mere product of modern civilization and modern humanity—a Gospel without Christ or Christianity.

And now are we to believe that legend, within the space of one generation, made this journey from the Gospel of the primitive Church and the Evangelists to the modern "original" Gospel? Such a supposition belongs to the domain of fables.

The difficulty cannot be waved aside by paraphrasing the notion and extent of the Gospel legend-formation, as being what "the first generation had experienced with Jesus Christ"; or as the "impression which the powerful person-

---

[1] Harnack, *Apostelgeschichte,* 219 (Leipzig, 1908).

ality of Jesus made on his disciples"; or as the "subsequent effect of the words and experiences of Christ"; or as the disciples' estimate of the portrait of their Master; or as "the history of thoughts about the facts" of the life of Jesus Christ.[1]

However appropriate such a characterization of a real legend may be, it has no application to the Gospels. The Evangelists have left to us not their personal experiences with Christ, nor the impression which he made upon them, nor the subsequent effects of his words and actions, nor their estimate of his worth, nor their thoughts about the facts, but rather the facts, the words, the teaching, and the life of Christ himself. They do not pourtray the Christ of experience, but the living Christ. And for that very reason their representations contain the history of Jesus Christ, and have nothing to do with legends.

Another consideration which will confirm us in this view is the *checking of the Gospel history and its records by contemporaries.*

Liberal criticism takes no notice whatever of this circumstance. It builds up its evolutionary hypothesis with as much boldness as credulous naïveté, but it all rests on—air. The foundation from which it starts is, in any case, the supposition that the wild shoots of legend have in perfect freedom more and more overrun the field of early Christian history until the Evangelists welded history and legends together to form the Gospel, and this without the opposition of anyone; in fact, amid the unanimous applause of the entire Church of that time. This fundamental supposition of our opponents does not, however, hold good at all in this case.

It could at best have done so only if the whole generation of Christ's contemporaries, the generation which had known him, seen him and heard him, had died out with him, and had given place to another which knew very little positively about him. But this was not the case. A great number of those who had known the Saviour, his life and public career through daily experience, lived through the subsequent period also, down to the writing and publication of the Gospels.

Hegesippus, in his *Memorabilia* (written about A.D. 180), relates that "Simeon, the son of Cleophas, who was of the tribe of David," suffered martyrdom at the beginning of the second century, at the age of 120 years. Up to this time, adds Hegesippus, the Church of Jerusalem had been guided by men "who had been privileged to hear with their own

---

[1] Harnack, *Reden und Aufsätze,* ii, 10 f., 22 f.; *Wesen des Christentums,* 6 f.

ears the divine truth."[1] The apologist, Quadratus,[2] and
Papias of Hierapolis,[3] affirm that some of those who were
healed by Christ and were raised by him from the dead lived
until the time of Hadrian (117-138). When, therefore, the
Gospel of John appeared the generation of the contemporaries
of Jesus had not yet died out, and when the synoptists wrote,
a few decades before, those who had been of the same age
as Christ, and were still living, were in the sixties. Of the
somewhat younger contemporaries and hearers of the Saviour,
considering the tenacity of the Jewish race, probably about
half had survived (cf. 1 Cor. xv, 6). Whether they were
believers or unbelievers, they could not possibly have allowed
the real history of Jesus to be so caricatured by grotesque
legends, and these to be circulated everywhere as a true
Gospel.

I say expressly " caricatured by grotesque legends," for
in reality it might have been still worse. According to our
enemies' supposition, the mere man, Jesus, sprang at a bound
before the eyes of his believing contemporaries into the
position of a worker of miracles, the Lord of life and death,
and a pre-existing supernatural being—yes, even to an actual
God, such as we find him, in the fifties, in the writings of
Paul, in the belief of the Church and almost simultaneously
in the Gospels. And everyone—Evangelists as well as their
readers and hearers—believed in this transformation ; the
Gospel was to them neither poetry nor deception ; they wanted
to deceive neither others nor themselves ; they accepted the
masquerade as sacred truth, and regarded the legend of the
Son of God as the true history of him whom they had known
as a mere man. But, then, surely this whole Christian society
would have been crazy, to use the mildest expression admis-
sible. Yet that is still the least difficulty.

If it were merely a case of some elaborated system, some
phantastic transformation, or a deification of the portrait of
Jesus, on the ground of " inward sentiments," " impressions," " feelings," and " soul-experiences," as Harnack's
school imagines, all would still be relatively comprehensible.
But, as has been already remarked, the evolution of the
Church's faith was accomplished in company with, and by
reason of, external, tangible facts and obvious, manifold and
well-known history. The time, the scene, the circumstances
of the superhuman life and activity of Jesus, and the persons
participating in them, are characterized in minutest detail.[4]

It was, for example, in Corozain, Bethsaida and Capharnaum

---

[1] Eusebius, H. E., iii, 32.   [2] id., iv, 3.
[3] cf. Gebhardt and Harnack, Texte und Untersuchungen, V, ii, 170
(Leipzig, 1889).
[4] cf. Boese, Die Glaubwürdigkeit unserer Evangelien, 114 (Freiburg,
1895).

that his divine power of performing miracles was proved in broad daylight and in the presence of all the people. In the synagogue at Capharnaum, still used by the Jews, he drove out the devil (Mark i, 21 ff.). In the house of Simon, whose inmates were still there, he cured Peter's mother-in-law of her fever. To this house, on the day before the Sabbath, the people brought their sick, and he healed them (Matt. viii, 14 ff.). Under circumstances which are minutely described he also healed the man sick of the palsy and the servant of the centurion, and raised from the dead the daughter of Jairus, the ruler of the synagogue (Matt. viii, 5 ff.).

Would it have occurred to the community of Christians to invent these and similar details, and would the Evangelists have had the audacity to record them, if they had been wholly or even partially invented? Must not the persons appealed to, as witnesses, have disclosed the falsity of these legends? And there were among them not merely believers in Christ, but also enemies of Christ—individuals, groups and entire villages.

Capharnaum and its neighbouring cities are reminded of the miracles worked in them, and the severest accusations, reproaches and condemnations are on that account pronounced upon them : " Woe to thee, Corozain ! woe to thee, Bethsaida ! for if in Tyre and Sidon had been wrought the miracles that have been wrought in you, they had long ago done penance in sackcloth and ashes. But I say unto you, it shall be more tolerable for Tyre and Sidon in the day of judgement, than for you. And thou, Capharnaum, shalt thou be exalted up to heaven? Thou shalt go down even unto hell. For if in Sodom had been wrought the miracles that have been wrought in thee, perhaps it had remained unto this day. But I say unto you that it shall be more tolerable for the land of Sodom in the day of judgement than for thee " (Matt. xi, 21 ff.).

And as the Gospels reproach the country towns and country people in Galilee, so do they upbraid also the leaders of the nation at Jerusalem and the Scribes and Pharisees for their unbelief, and the judicial murder which they had committed in the case of Jesus, although the latter had by his miracles proved himself to be the legitimate Messiah. It would, however, have been madness to write thus, if those reports of his miracles and many other statements had rested on nothing but fraud. The accused party-leaders, who were well acquainted with the life and deeds of the hated Nazarene, and who closely and scrutinizingly examined every report concerning him, would have needed only to point out the deception to be able, at one blow, to strike down these annoying accusers and their followers.

Instead of this, they had to hear, day after day, how this

Gospel was preached, both before and after its committal to writing, in the public streets and squares, and how the reproach of the judicial murder of the Messiah and the Son of God was continually repeated anew. Yet not one of the pharisaical leaders in the controversy dared to give the lie to these preachers and thus save his own honour and that of his party and the nation. It is true, the Apostles were summoned from time to time to appear before the tribunal, and were commanded to keep silent (Acts iv, 5, 27 ff. ; 2 Tim. iv, 9 ff.). But the charge was never brought against them that their preaching and their Gospel did not coincide with the actual history of Jesus.

This silence on the part of contemporaneous enemies is the most eloquent defence of Gospel history ; and we may add that the liberal critics of to-day give their consent to this compulsory vindication.

4. The Enemies.

The Gospels themselves, their authors and the contemporaries of the Evangelists emphatically contradict the supposition that the historical books of the New Testament are merely legends, in which historic facts are mixed up with romantic additions and pious embellishments. Consequently, it is not the Gospels, but the liberal theories about them, that are unhistorical. The more furious the enemy's attack, the more impressively does the superior historical power of the Gospels prove its failure. We need not add anything more to what has been already said, since all the objections raised against the reliability of the Gospel history are refuted.

Yet there still remains unsolved the psychological problem, especially persistent at the present time, How comes the historical-critical school to put upon its programme for the complete investigation of the Gospels and for the entire conception of primitive Christianity the " legendary hypothesis," which is, scientifically, simply untenable? Only the solution of this problem will bring about full understanding both of our foregoing defence of the Gospels and of our opponents' criticism of them. Only through the solution of this problem shall we succeed in perceiving that all that has been thus far said was only a skirmish on the outer battle lines, while fundamentally a much deeper intellectual conflict, based on principle, is going on.

It would be, in fact, incomprehensible if the historical-critical school persisted in misunderstanding the Gospel in consequence of such frivolous pretexts as those which it puts forward, and it would be most unjust for us to doubt the scientific rectitude of so many able men. Some of them, and above all Harnack, have rendered great services to the history of primitive Christianity, as we have repeatedly acknowledged, and in this connection most gladly recognize again.

The criticism of former times attached great importance to the fact that the primitive Christian tradition in regard to history and faith reached its full development only after one, or even two, centuries; that the most diverse peoples and lands contributed to its contents; and that, in consequence, old Christian literature, which asserts the contrary, is absolutely unreliable. To-day, the "historical-critical school" concedes that both the outer frame and the historical and doctrinal tradition originating within it have been correctly outlined by primitive Christianity. "During the years from A.D. 30 to 70, in Palestine, and more particularly in Jerusalem, practically everything came into being and took place, which subsequently underwent development."[1] "The chronological framework, in which tradition has put the documents together, is correct in all the principal points, from the Epistles of Paul to Irenæus, and compels the historian to take no account of all the hypotheses about the historical course of things which deny this framework."[2]

In particular the "retrograde movement to tradition" is more and more favourable to the age, authenticity and reliability of the Gospels, owing to the historical researches of men of all camps. Harnack announces that even in the sphere of primitive Christianity the "essential truth of tradition (a few insignificant exceptions left out of consideration) will, in a few years, acquire universal importance."[3] In a word, *because modern criticism has bethought itself again of strictly historical research, and in proportion as it remains true to the historic method of investigation, it is coming more and more to the perception that the Gospels and the tradition concerning them are right.*

But why, then, does it not, after all this, accept these historical books as they are? Why does it raise again in the last court of appeal such objections to their reliability that all previous decisions in the case are once more made illusory? Why does it declare, in spite of the Gospels and their authors and contemporaries, that the New Testament reports are for the most part legendary creations?

For the simple reason that the Gospel history *opposes the modern liberal view.* Whenever this view comes in collision with Gospel history, the latter is measured by the standard of the former, and so historical research is subordinated to philosophic presuppositions.

The Gospel claims to rest essentially upon divine revelation. Liberal rationalism, "warmed up with fresh flavour, and

---

[1] Harnack, *Lukas der Arzt,* iv.
[2] Harnack, *Chronologie der altchr. Lit.,* I, x.   [3] *ibid.*

tempered by indistinctness'' (Schnehen), wishes to explain every religion, the Christian included, by the purely natural evolution and development of humanity. There is no question of a revelation of God to men, or of any higher intervention of divine power in human history. Only faith—blind, legend-loving credulity—can dream of a revelation and the supernatural.

It is this thoroughly prejudiced philosophy of history and this historical method alone which have produced the evolutionary criticism of the Gospels. So long as the text of the Gospels presupposes nothing supernatural, it is considered historical; but in so far as it speaks '' supernaturally,'' it is legendary. Either supernatural or natural—that is the starting-point of sceptical criticism. According to this biassed scheme the credibility of the Gospels is finally settled.

Renan confesses openly : '' The question of the supernatural forms the basis of every discussion about matters of this kind. . . . That the Gospels are partly legendary is evident, since they are full of miracles and the supernatural. . . . Not because it has been proved to me that the Gospels are undeserving of an absolute faith in them, but because they relate miracles, do I say : the Gospels are legends; it is possible that they contain history, but not everything in them is historic. A rapid work of transformation was effected in the first twenty or thirty years after the death of Christ, and this imprinted everywhere on his biography the characteristics of a legend.''[1]

In this respect the liberal school has never got beyond Renan. It is true it does not acknowledge it with such smiling cynicism as he uses. It is busily occupied, rather, in covering its philosophical subconsciousness with rich historical-critical drapery. Yet it would protest energetically should one attribute to it any other than the purely naturalistic conception and practical criticism of the Gospel.[2] Every '' absolutely marvellous, wholly incomprehensible event . . . and everything inscrutable, shows itself, in advance, according to its subject-matter, to be dogmatic legend,'' and must be cut out, as a legendary excrescence.[3]

Thus and similarly the watchword goes through all the ranks of '' theologians engaged in historical research.'' *The starting-point of the legendary theory is, therefore, the evolutionary view of life—a philosophical principle.* This principle is now, along the whole line, applied to the Gospels, and the Gospel's texts and facts are judged in accordance with it. The critics curtly declare, with Harnack, that they '' frequently cannot accept the representations and explana-

---

[1] *Vie de Jésus,* vi, ix, xlviii, xci, 13th ed.
[2] *cf.* Harnack, *Lukas der Arzt,* iii f.
[3] Bousset, *Jesus,* 2, 5, 3rd ed. (Tübingen, 1907).

tions of the first reporters."[1]   That is enough to characterize a text or a fact as legendary.

Harnack's Berlin colleague, Bernhard Weiss, himself severely criticizes this method of procedure against the Gospels with the words : " At the root of many new representations of the life of Jesus lies the idea that one must, in order to comprehend correctly the essence of Christianity, go back from the apostolic doctrine of Christ to the teaching of Jesus himself . . . in order then to cut out what may have been formed first in the apostolic teaching under the influences of contemporaneous history from descriptions of the person and the words of Christ.   To a real historical-critical student especially, the complete hopelessness of this undertaking must be at once evident. . . .   The eliminating process, attempted by criticism, is begun in accordance with thoroughly subjective points of view and philosophical presuppositions which are entirely foreign to historical investigation."[2]

Prof. Wilhelm Wrede, certainly a good liberal investigator, thus characterizes the historical method of his school : " Features which are considered incredible are cut out of the text, and the sense is altered so that it may become historically usable "—from the rationalistic standpoint, of course— " that is, something is substituted in the report which the author never thought of, and this is given out as its historical purport . . . although no one ever asks whether the real essence of the report is not thereby destroyed. . . .   This is why so many judgements based upon ' taste ' abound.   The number of arbitrary psychological interpretations of the words, facts and contexts of the Gospels in literature is legion. . . .   Two things are common to all these manifold attempts—the taking away of parts and the making of new interpretations. . . .   Every investigator proceeds finally in such a way that he retains of the words handed down to us just what can be adapted to his own construction of the facts and his conception of historical possibility.   Everything else he rejects.   The fact that the words lose thus more or less the sense in which they were transmitted to us gives him little concern."[3]

H. J. Holtzmann confesses : " That there is justification for such a charge cannot be doubted.   Psychological suppositions,

---

[1] Harnack, *Lukas der Arzt*, iv.   In *Gegenwart*, No. 1 of 1901, it is interesting to watch E. von Hartmann balancing accounts with Harnack's *Wesen des Christentums*—" to show that even to-day an historico-critical theologian of the highest impartiality is unfaithful to critical methods and evolutionary viewpoints as soon as he comes to the teaching of Jesus."   E. von Hartmann, *Das Christentum des N. T.*, x (Sachsa, 1905).

[2] *Das Leben Jesu*, i, 11, 4th ed. (Stuttgart u. Berlin, 1902).

[3] *Das Messiasgeheimnis in den Evangelien*, 2 ff., 85 ff. (Göttingen, 1901).

I.

amateurish fancies, and adventurous guessing play almost as
fatal a part in all this literature, as do efforts to ' harmonize
the Gospels ' from dogmatic motives and the violent treatment of the authorities."[1]

The ultra-radical pastor, Albrecht Kalthoff, adds : " The
numerous passages in the Gospels, which must be struck
out by this liberal theology, stand on precisely the same
literary level as those passages out of which theology
constructs its historic Jesus."[2]

*The separation of the historic from the legendary features
of the Gospels rests, therefore, on nothing but personal
choice.* " The transpositions and new connections made
are as numerous as the internal and external perversions of
the text."[3] Most of the representatives of the so-called
modern theology, in making their excerpts, use the shears
according to the critical method loved by David Strauss :
that is, " The mythical element in the Gospel is to be cut
out, and what remains is to form the historical core."[4]

In fact, even the most zealous adherents of the liberal
school confess that *the Gospel criticism of the last few years
is nothing else than a return to David Strauss*[5] *and F.
Christian Baur.*[6]

In regard to W. Wrede, the latest renowned representative
of the " historical-critical " line of thought, the following
complaint is made by a modern theologian : " We must, to
our regret, state it as a fact that the latest attempt to test
the material of Gospel history in regard to its historical value
leads us again at once into the track even of Bruno Bauer."[7]
Schweitzer declares the same thing in reference to the
criticisms of Otto Schmiedel and Hermann von Soden :
" They run straight into the hands of Bruno Bauer."[8]

That is not quite correct, since the liberal school wishes to
save for the most part the external compass of the Gospels ;
but it is true in so far as this school empties the Gospels of
much of their inner contents, denies all that is supernatural
and miraculous in them, and explains this as a legendary,
" mythical " ingredient. But now, according to Pfleiderer's
own confession, " the mythical and the possibly historical
features of the text are so inseparably interwoven that the

---

[1] *Das messianische Bewusstsein Jesu,* 44 (Tübingen, 1907).

[2] *Das Christusproblem,* 20.

[3] Schweitzer, *Von Reimarus zu Wrede,* 294.

[4] Kalthoff, *Das Christusproblem,* 27

[5] W. Brandt, *Die evang. Geschichte und der Ursprung des Christentums,* x (Leipzig, 1893).

[6] Schmiedel, *Hauptprobleme der Leben-Jesu-Forschung,* vi, 2nd ed.
(Tübingen, 1906).

[7] H. Zimmermann, *Der historische Werth der ältesten Überlieferung
von der Geschichte Jesu im Markusevangelium,* 1 ff. (Leipzig, 1905).

[8] *Von Reimarus zu Wrede,* 303.

two cannot be divided from each other without depriving the latter also of their definite significance and retaining only an indistinct shadow."[1]

Here, then, we really reach the final result of the liberal criticism of the Gospels : " Almost everywhere we are left standing helplessly in the midst of uncertainties and suppositions."[2] In his search for the " Gospel in the Gospel," Harnack writes : " We ought not to be like the child who, in his attempt to find the heart of a plant, kept stripping it of its leaves until he had nothing more left in his hand, and was forced to perceive that precisely the leaves were the heart itself."[3] Such, however, has been his own experience and that of his school. They thought they could tear out of the Gospel one leaf after another, and transfer them to the account of legend-formation, without detriment to the Gospel's heart. What one critic, however, for personal reasons allowed to remain, another, just as autocratically, cut away, until finally the whole was stripped bare.

Let us recapitulate. The *starting point,* the real stronghold from which liberal criticism proceeds and finally pronounces our Gospels to be legends, is the rationalistic and agnostic view. So long as the historical-critical school proceeds historically, and so long as modern historians occupy themselves with history, they recognize more and more the sterling value of the Gospels. Only in so far as they depart from the strictly historical method of research does the legendary theory gain importance. It is, however, an act of violence to science to destroy a purely historic question by means of a philosophical principle. Even if this philosophical principle were not false, the procedure of liberal criticism would be, nevertheless, unscientific.

The procedure of the legendary theory is no less unhistorical and arbitrary than its starting point. Liberal criticism proceeds always in the very error which it wishes to shift off upon the Gospels. According to its theory, the authors of the Gospels allowed themselves unconsciously to be influenced by the views of the contemporaneous Church in such a way that they painted over the golden ground of objective history, with the variegated colours of subjective impressions. Yet in reality this reproach falls precisely upon liberal criticism.

It starts out from its subjective view, constructs according to that the modern " Gospel in the Gospel," and finally produces a Gospel history which changes its hues to suit all shades of the modern world of scepticism and of the personal scholarly ideas of individual critics. As the radical W. von

[1] *Protest. Monatschrift,* 172 (1906).
[2] Bousset, *Jesus,* 9, 3rd ed. (Tübingen, 1907).
[3] *Wesen des Christentums,* 9.

Schnehen remarks : " As a permanent and essential nucleus
of the Gospel, practically nothing is of value which was held
to be most important by Jesus himself or his disciples—no,
only that is designated a 'nucleus,' which appears acceptable
to the theological freethought of to-day, or to which a new
interpretation can be easily given."[1]

According to this, not the Gospel of the Evangelists, but
the Gospel of liberal criticism, is, in the full sense of the
word, a romantic and fantastic pourtrayal of the history of
Christ and of primitive Christianity. " All the latest literature
(of the school of Ritschl) about the life of Jesus can be
looked upon as the climax of theological romanticism, which
considers its ideals realized, and strives to prove that the
historic Jesus was the realization of this ideal."[2]

The *final result* of liberal Gospel-criticism is such that it
invalidates the criticism itself. In the name of historical
research it declares at first that the Gospels are in substance
trustworthy, and that " there are no gross interpolations of
a later date. Only here and there we see reflected in them
the conditions prevailing in the primitive Church." Finally,
however, the Gospels and their contents are, in the name of
its philosophical point of view, so transformed, that " the
newly found presentation of the life of Jesus produces an
impression almost the opposite of that which the description
of our Evangelists makes."[3] This contradiction between
the beginning and the end of liberal criticism is the sharpest
conceivable condemnation of that criticism. Like all other
attempts to explain the Gospel, without the essential historical
truth of the events related in it, so this one also shows itself
to be a hopeless task.

We have now reached the conclusion of our investigation
of the Gospels. We have had the experience of everyone
who is laying foundations. The work and effort are always
greater than they at first seemed. Yet, after all, not only
the foundation, but also a good part of the edifice itself is thus
built.

So is it with the composition of a defence of Christianity.
The Gospels form its *foundation*. When the authenticity
and credibility of these historical books are once established,
the apologist moves on firm ground. He has then the right
unhesitatingly to draw his proofs from every part of the
Gospels for the solution of all the problems which present
themselves. He is, therefore, freed from the trouble of
always examining anew the foundations, as he passes from
question to question and from text to text. The Gospels are
for him, in their full extent and in the strictest sense of the
word, historical authorities and scientific evidence.

---

[1] *Der moderne Jesuskultus,* 34, 2nd ed. (Frankfurt a. M., 1906).
[2] Ed. von Hartmann, *Das Christentum des N. T.,* 16.
[3] M. Kähler, *Dogmatische Zeitfragen,* ii, 116.

If we, however, in subsequent pages now and then demonstrate again in particular the reliability of certain individual parts or passages of the Gospels; if we lay greater stress upon the synoptic Gospels than on the Gospel of John; if we finally give more prominence in the Gospels to the words and personal testimony of Jesus than to the testimony of the Evangelists, we do so for two reasons. First, in order to meet the objections and prejudices of the critics in a peaceful way, and to dispel them; and secondly, to show that the enemies of Christianity exert themselves to no purpose in appealing from the unity of the Gospel text to isolated textual difficulties, from the synoptic Gospels to the Gospel of John, and from the Evangelists to Jesus Christ himself.

With this acceptance of the results of the affirmative criticism of the Gospels, the groundwork of the defence of Christ and Christianity is, in a certain sense, completed. Whoever comes to the Gospels with the firm conviction that he has before him genuine and entirely trustworthy sources of history will at once find in them also convincing motives for the Christian faith.

Thus and in no other way did the Christians of the first century and of all subsequent time, the learned and the unlearned, come to a belief in the truth of the Gospels.

To-day also the Gospel still retains its divine power. But it is necessary to read and hear it with an *unprejudiced mind, an honest will, and a prayerful heart*. With an unprejudiced mind; for whoever is pledged to a preconceived view, and takes that as a standard by which to judge of the Gospel, will naturally become confused in regard to it. With an honest will, to seek Christ and the truth of Christianity, and to accept them when found; for faith is not alone a matter of the understanding, but fully as much, and indeed in a higher degree, an affair of the will. With a prayerful heart; for faith must, above all, be considered as a precious grace from God, " coming down from the Father of lights, from whom cometh every best and perfect gift " (James i, 17).

PART II
THE MESSIANIC CONSCIOUSNESS OF CHRIST

INTRODUCTORY

AFTER *liberal criticism* has fashioned the Gospels to suit its purposes, it sketches approximately the *following portrait of the person of the Saviour.* The man of Nazareth appears, first of all, as a real man among his fellow-men. He is nothing more, and claims to be no more. There is no trace of his having looked upon himself as the Messiah, expected by the Jewish people, or of his having had even a faint idea of the Messianic vocation. He only knew himself already very early in life as a " Son of God," that is, as a human being specially favoured and endowed by God. By means of this consciousness he came, either naturally or in consequence of self-suggestion, gradually to the conviction of his Messianic mission and dignity. He did not, however, yet dare to come out openly as the Messiah and to declare himself as such. Only at the end of his life, and especially before his judges, did he energetically declare himself to be the Messiah-King, and went to death for the conviction that he would come again, in order to establish his Messianic kingdom.

Overpowered by the force of his words and personality, the first disciples and the believers of the first century idealized the portrait of the Saviour. They promulgated the assertion that Jesus would not only unfold the spiritual activity of the Messiah, at his second coming, but that he had already unfolded it in his earthly life, which was a matter of history. Yes, not only his life, but his death also was a Messianic deed. He had died in order to redeem the world from sin and spiritual bondage. Moreover, the Redeemer had already existed previously, before his earthly life, in heaven with God, and after his death had risen from the dead, to return to his heavenly Father.

From this assertion to the complete deification of Jesus had then been only a step. This step also has been taken unquestioningly. The claims of the Saviour to be a child of God have been interpreted physically and metaphysically, and he has accordingly been declared to be the incarnate, consubstantial Son of God.

In the synoptic Gospels, it is said, are still found trifling additions showing the traces of such a retouching of the historical portrait of Christ. But this process had already made great progress in the faith of the Church of that time.

Paul has seen to it that the theology and christology thus formed were practically and theoretically established and developed. The imaginative formation of the faith, freely exercised in the second and third generations of Christians, did the rest, until the development of christological dogma reached its conclusion in the writings of John.

This, in a few sentences, is the portrait of Christ as drawn by Protestant liberalism as well as by Catholic Modernism. Both consider this conception of him the only scientific one. But while the Protestant school consistently condemns the Christ of faith as a caricature, the Modernists, who call themselves Catholic, utter the incomprehensible absurdity that faith has, positively, or at least possibly, idealized the historical portrait of Jesus, and has been right in doing so.

The honest searcher after truth, however, can have nothing to do with such ambiguity. Either the Christ of faith is identical with the Christ of historical science, or he is wholly an illusion. Either the Messiah and the Son of God—and about these two essential elements of christology the entire question turns—proves himself to be a real manifestation of history, or he cannot be for us an object of faith and conviction. For faith holds firmly that its portrait of Christ is based upon history, and agrees essentially with history.

Briefly, therefore, it is a question whether the Gospels and other early Christian documents, which we have come to know as reliable sources of information about the historical life of Jesus, *represent the Saviour as the Messiah and the Son of God in the sense adopted by faith, or not.* We should have a perfect right to answer this life-or-death question for Christianity by appealing to all the declarations of the above-mentioned sources, whether they are made directly by Christ himself or by the disciples. For our line of argument to prove the reliability of the Gospel sources reaches its climax precisely in the evidence that the views and reports of the Evangelists are not to be regarded as the expressions of a faith at variance with history, but as thoroughly authentic reports, which are in accord with history.

Nevertheless, because our opponents are always hunting out in the views of the disciples infiltrations of the later faith of the Church, and appeal from them to the testimony of Jesus to himself, it is expedient to deal with his artifice of liberal criticism. What Christ has thought of himself and said of himself must in any case be decisive in solving the problem of his Messiahship and divinity. We take our stand, therefore, first of all, on the *direct consciousness of Jesus and his testimony to himself,* on the utterances critically conceded as certain, which Jesus personally made *regarding his Messiahship and divinity.* Moreover, provided, especially in the inquiry into Christ's consciousness of divinity, the Apostles and disciples also are admitted as witnesses, that can happen only in so far as their views may be traced back again directly to Christ.

The *problem of the Messiahship,* which we first encounter
here, is a *life-or-death question for Christianity.* It is true,
among freethinking theologians, there are not wanting
those who would willingly give up the point of the Messiahship with no fear that thereby Christianity would lose anything.[1] Such a view, however, is comprehensible only from
the standpoint of a Christianity without Christ. For one
who does not adopt this singular standpoint the Messiahship of Jesus is of central importance. Not only the believing representatives of supernatural Christianity, but also
good liberal partisans of a purely natural, evolutionary
Christianity are agreed in this, that " if Jesus did not regard
himself as the Messiah that means the death-blow to
the Christian faith."[2] " The name ' Messiah ' includes the
assertion of the pre-eminence of Christianity . . . and contains the certainty of a salvation to be found at most in Jesus;
hence Christianity will never give up this thought. . . ."[3]
" For what can ' Christ ' mean other than the religion *of
Christ,* whether it be of Christ or by Christ? ' Christ ' is,
however, really the translation of ' Messiah.' "[4]

We understand thus why *the Messiahship of Jesus stands
in the very front of modern research into the life and character of Christ.* A veritable flood of books and treatises about
the Saviour's Messianic consciousness and testimony to himself has been poured out over the literary world in recent
times. It already needs real courage to toil through all these,
and yet the number still increases from year to year.

And just as the fulfilment of the Messianic hopes is a life-
or-death question for Christianity, *so was the Messianic hope
the very heart of Judaism.* The whole Old Testament drew
its vitality from the Messianic prophecy. The expectation
of the Messiah and the prospect of the Redeemer of Israel
formed in particular, shortly before the commencement of the
Christian era, the only great hereditary property of Judaism.

Everything else Israel had at this time wholly or nearly
lost. Its political freedom and independence were ended.
Since the year 63 B.C. the city of Jerusalem had been in
Roman hands. Twenty-three years later Herod of Idumea

---

[1] Thus Harnack, *Das Wesen des Christentums,* 81-89 (1900); R. Steck,
in *Protestantische Monatshefte,* 91 (1903); J. Wellhausen, *Israelitische
und jüdische Geschichte,* p. 380 (1907); *Das Evangelium Marci,* p. 71
(1903); Ed. von Hartmann, *Das Christentum des Neuen Testaments,* 110
(1905); O. Frommel, *Die Poesie des Evangeliums Jesu,* 150 (1906);
O. Kluge, *Die Idee des Priestertums in Israel-Juda und im Urchristentum,* 40 (1906); A. Deissmann, *Evangelium und Urchristentum* in
Beiträge zur Weiterentwicklung der christlich. Religion, 107.

[2] Albrecht Schweitzer, *Das Messiantäts- und Leidensgeheimnis, eine
Skizze des Lebens Jesu,* vi (1901).

[3] Oskar Holtzmann, *Das Messiasbewusstsein Jesu und seine neueste
Bestreitung,* 25 (1902).

[4] H. J. Holtzmann, *Das messianische Bewusstsein Jesu,* 1 (1907).

ascended the throne of David. The national temple stood
under the dominion of the Romans; the Jewish people paid
to Roman emperors the interest and taxes due to Jehovah;
the sons of God were conscripted into the legions of the
pagans and forced to daily defilements and to participation
in unlawful abominations. Nor was it better in the sphere
of spiritual religion. The narrow, statutory system of rabbinical theology had replaced the elevating religious teaching
of the Old Testament. The learned Rabbis had, by their
eternal fault-finding, not only taken the spirit completely out
of the service of the Law, but had also in part deformed its
letter, and in part enveloped it with so thick a hull that the
original kernel could no longer be discerned. Everything
was ruined.[1]

But Israel did not forget her Messianic vocation. All the
Jews looked with unfaltering confidence for the Messiah, in
whom their fathers had already believed, and whose portrait
and appearance the Prophets had delineated in ever clearer
outlines. The rabbinical interpretation of the Law had even
increased this longing still more powerfully. The writings
of the New Testament, as well as the oldest literature of the
Synagogue, point out to us *the impatient expectation of the
Messiah prevalent among the Israelites contemporary with
Christ*. The history of the Jewish war and of the destruction
of Jerusalem show that people ran after every phantom of
the so-called Messiahs, so thoroughly convinced were they of
the nearness of their Redeemer. For the fulness of time
had come. All the prophecies ran out about the reign of
Augustus.

Then suddenly came the news that in Bethlehem in the
land of Juda the "Messiah," the son of David, the
anointed of the Lord, had been born—the light to enlighten
the Gentiles and the honour of the people of Israel. The
annunciation, the birth, the first years of the child Jesus are
surrounded by a garland of wonderful events and heavenly
testimonials, which alone exclude every doubt that the child
of Bethlehem, so long anticipated, was the divinely sent
Messiah.[2]

This *Gospel of the childhood of Jesus* is rejected by liberal
critics simply because, in consequence of its supernatural
contents, it does not agree with the philosophical views of
that school of criticism. Reasons of an exegetical-historical
nature are said to oppose the credibility of the Gospel of
Christ's youth. His enemies content themselves with pointing out the supernatural and miraculous elements in it in
order simply to pronounce the verdict: "We have no

[1] See H. Felder, *Die Krisis des religiösen Judentums zur Zeit Christi*
(Stans, 1903).
[2] See the first chapters of Matthew and Luke.

historical information about the childhood and youth of
Jesus, for what the Gospels of Matthew and Luke relate of
them is nothing but religious legends with no historical worth
whatever—all that belongs to the domain of pious myth, the
origin of which must be explained by the faith of the
Church.''[1] In the light of unprejudiced historical research
the statements of the first and third Gospels concerning the
youth of Jesus must be recognized as, historically, wholly
unobjectionable representations.

Jesus, however, wraps himself in silence even after these
revelations—with the exception of his unique appearance,
when twelve years old, in the temple—until the day when he
publicly enters upon his Messianic vocation and begins to
bear witness to it.

[1] Otto Pfleiderer, *Die Entstehung des Christentums,* 61, 93 (München, 1905).

CHAPTER I
THE FACT OF CHRIST'S MESSIANIC CONSCIOUSNESS

I.—The Messianic Testimony of Jesus to himself in General.

FORMER *thorough-going rationalists* dealt summarily with the testimony of the Saviour to himself as the Messiah. In the good old days when David Friedrich Strauss saw in the Gospels only a collection of legends and fables, which originated long after Christ's death, and when Ferd. Christian Baur ascribed the historical writings of the New Testament, all and singly, to a date far in the second century, it was the custom to reject every proof of Messianic consciousness, and in general every objectionable text of Scripture, with a wave of the hand and the simple statement : " That is not an utterance of the Lord; that is a later addition.'' We are, it is true, accustomed also even now to hear such forcible language from many a " historical-critical '' investigator. But it finds no longer such a ready acceptance as formerly, since they themselves now concede that the synoptic Gospels were composed soon after the middle of the first century and even by Matthew, Mark and Luke. Since the commencement of this " retrograde movement '' of Gospel criticism the denial of the Messianic consciousness of Jesus has been for the most part characteristic only of those radical controversialists who, notwithstanding all the signs of the times, have still learned nothing from, and forgotten nothing of, the precipitous collapse of rationalistic and historical criticism. Only thus is it explicable that, after the example of Bruno Bauer, Strauss, Volkmar, and A. Jakobsen, *many radical critics of recent times,* such as A. Loman[1] and A. Bruins[2] in Holland, E. Havet[3] in France, James Martineau[4] in England, G. L. Cary[5] and Nathaniel Schmidt[6] in America, P. de Lagarde[7] and Meinhold[8] in Germany, dispute the Messianic consciousness of Jesus. But these attempts, as has been said, start

[1] *De Gids,* ii, 118 (1888).
[2] *Heeft Jesus sich zelven als den Messias beschouwd?* (1893).
[3] *Le Christianisme et ses Origines,* iv, pp. 15, 75 (1884).
[4] *The Seat of Authority in Religion,* 326, 349 (1890).
[5] *The Synoptic Gospels,* 360 (1900).
[6] *The Prophet of Nazareth,* 131 (1905).
[7] *Deutsche Schriften,* i, p. 69 (1887).
[8] *Jesus und das Alte Testament,* 89, 101 (1896).

out with such a destructive criticism of the Gospels, and have in themselves so little solid foundation that even the liberal school of research would hardly pay serious attention to them any longer.

The question entered an entirely new phase, however, with the sensational book of W. Wrede, *The Messianic Mystery in the Gospels*.[1] With a rare exhibition of criticism, as intelligent as it is one-sided, this book seeks to establish the thesis that the idea of the Messiahship was inserted only subsequently into the record of the life of Jesus.

Partly in connection with Wrede, partly on their own independent lines, these views have been advocated lately by Adalbert Merx,[2] W. Stark,[3] Nathaniel Schmidt,[4] W. B. Smith,[5] Bolliger,[6] and P. Kölbing.[7]

Julius Wellhausen takes his place at least among the doubters. According to him, "Jesus appears to have acknowledged himself to be the Messiah in Jerusalem itself."[8] The Saviour has not, however, declared himself as the Messiah "freely and in plain words," and "doubts whether it ever was done at all cannot be suppressed."[9]

Yet with all this multiformity of views the above-named critics with tolerable unanimity justify their antagonistic attitude as follows : According to the representation of the Gospels, they say, Jesus sometimes wishes to pass for the Messiah, and at other times forbids any mention of his Messiahship. This contradiction is explained by the supposition that Messianic ideas were only subsequently ascribed to the Saviour. During his lifetime Jesus did not regard himself as the Messiah. But after his death the disciples imagined that he had risen from the dead, and precisely through the fact of that resurrection had become the Messiah. If, however, he was actually the Messiah after his resurrection, then he had been already during his lifetime on the way to the Messiahship. So at all events concluded the disciples, and the oldest faith of the Church added that Jesus had been the Messiah already during his earthly life, and had also professed to be such. The synoptists made this belief an enduring one by their writings. Yet in their representations the historical substratum, to which the Lord's

[1] Göttingen, Vandenhoeck und Ruprecht (1901).

[2] *Das Evangelium Matthäus* (1902); *Die Evangelien des Markus und Lukas* (1905).

[3] *Jesu Stellung zum jüdischen Messiasbegriff, Protest. Monatshefte*, vi, 291-309 (1902).

[4] *The Prophet of Nazareth*, 131 (1905).

[5] *Der vorchristliche Christus*, 71, 81, 88 (1906).

[6] *Das Messiasgeheimnis bei Markus*, in *Schweiz. Theol. Zeitschrift*, 98-132 (1906).

[7] *Die geistige Einwirkung der Person Jesu auf Paulus* (1906).

[8] *Israelitische und jüdische Geschichte*, 6th ed., 379.

[9] *Einleitung in die drei ersten Evangelien*, 92; cf. 79-98 (1905).

Messiahship was unknown, is still always apparent under the Messianic retouching furnished by faith.

So runs this fine hypothesis, so ingeniously worked out. It is, however, only "worked out"; it is neither an historical composition nor an historical pourtrayal. *It coincides at once with the theory of the Gospels already rejected by us,* according to which the Gospels are said to contain, not the real history of Jesus, but the history of him in the legendary form given it by faith. Yet also, apart from this, that view is, even *from the standpoint of liberal criticism, wholly untenable.*

According to this criticism, as has been said, the Gospels (in the present instance the Messianic passages written by the Evangelists) merely represent the belief of the disciples and the Church in the Messiahship of Jesus. But how is this belief to be explained psychologically if Jesus had not professed to be the Messiah?

"The disciples believed in his Messiahship on the ground of their belief in his resurrection," it is said. But evidently the exact contrary is true. They believed in his resurrection because of their belief in his Messiahship. Liberal criticism repudiates indeed the reality of the resurrection. According to it, the belief in the resurrection is founded on purely subjective imagination, not upon actual objective appearances of Jesus after his death.

Those fantasies and the belief in the resurrection and Messiahship which grew out of them presuppose, however, that Jesus, during his life, had spoken to the disciples of his Messiahship, and of his resurrection as a proof of his Messiahship, and had thereby inflamed their powers of imagination. Otherwise, how should this have produced the belief in the resurrection and in the Messiah precisely at the time when the life of the Master had come to such a tragical ending, and when his adherents despaired of him, of his cause, and even of themselves? "Where has anything similar occurred in the history of mankind," Harnack himself asks, "that those who had eaten and drunk with their Master and had seen him in the characteristics of his human nature, not only proclaimed him as the great prophet and revealer of God, but also as the divine director of history, as the 'beginning' of the creation of God and as the spiritual force of a new life? . . . That they were able to grasp and firmly to hold *this* sure hope; that in spite of his suffering and death they beheld in him the promised Messiah; and that they, while under the influence of the usual Messianic conception, had felt that he was the Lord and Saviour actually present with them, and had taken him into their hearts—that is what is astounding!"[1] And not only that. We must call it also

---

[1] Harnack, *Wesen des Christentums,* 97.

something problematical and psychologically and historically impossible if the disciples' belief in the Messiah had sprung merely from an imaginary resurrection, and if it had subsequently been transferred thence into the life of Jesus.

Just as little as Wellhausen and Wrede are able to explain the origin of the *disciples' belief in the Messiahship,* just so little can they explain the *testimonies of the Gospels to the Messiahship.* We place ourselves again on the ground of our opponents' criticism of the New Testament. This recognizes that the synoptic Gospels, even if they are enlarged by legends, nevertheless contain a thoroughly reliable historical foundation. Wellhausen and Wrede acknowledge this no less positively than Harnack, Schürer, Jülicher and the whole liberal school.

If, however, *one* thing in the Gospel is historical, it is certainly the fact that Christ considered himself as the Messiah, and professed to be so. Johannes Weiss says forcibly : " Our best and oldest (Gospel) tradition testifies with a hundred voices to the fact that he (Jesus) understood the movement which he started as Messianic in the full sense of the word, and that he considered himself to be the specifically chosen one, who was more than a prophet. Simply to push aside this whole tradition, or to interpret it to suit oneself, and to explain everything Messianic out of the text is an unheard of abuse of power."[1]

Like Johannes Weiss, Harnack also declares plainly : " Important scholars, and among them Wellhausen, have doubted whether Jesus ever designated himself as the Messiah. I cannot, however, agree with him ; in fact, I find that we must do violence to our Gospel reports to reach that desired result. Already the expression ' Son of Man,' it seems to me, can be understood only in a Messianic sense (that Jesus himself used it is not to be doubted), and we should have to strike out entirely a story like that of the entry of Christ into Jerusalem in order to carry out the theory that he did not consider himself as the promised Messiah, and did not wish to be so regarded. Moreover, the forms of speech in which Jesus expressed his self-consciousness and his vocation are quite incomprehensible if they are not determined by the Messianic idea. Finally, since the positive reasons, which are brought forward for that view, are very weak and in the highest degree questionable, we can with confidence adhere to the supposition that Jesus has called himself the Messiah."[2] " This part of the Gospel narrative appears to me to stand the severest examination," adds Harnack in his *History of*

---

[1] *Die Predigt Jesu vom Reiche Gottes,* 2nd ed., p. 64 (Göttingen, 1900). Johannes Weiss also gives a thorough contradiction to Wrede in his book *Das älteste Evangelium* (1903).

[2] *Wesen des Christentums,* 82 ff.

I.

Dogma.[1] " The backbone of Christianity would be broken, if belief in the Messiah were taken from it."[2]

The recent utterances of Emil Schürer,[3] Adolf Jülicher,[4] Oskar Holtzmann,[5] Paul Wernle,[6] O. Schmiedel,[7] Ad. Deissmann,[8] A. Schlatter,[9] Fritz Schubart,[10] H. J. Holtzmann,[11] Loisy[12] and other trustworthy representatives of modern liberalism[13] are just as positive.

In following out this idea, Wrede also is finally forced to go over to the most radical sort of scepticism. In order to further his purpose, not only does he refashion the synoptic Gospels by designating all their Messianic features as unhistorical,[14] but he says precisely of Mark, the oldest and " most reliable " of the Evangelists : " Mark has no longer any real conception of the life of Jesus."[15] Only by such presuppositions can Wrede derive the " Messianic mystery of the Gospels " from " the effort to make the life of Jesus on earth Messianic in character."[16] This critic, therefore, willingly or unwillingly, comes back again to the " tendency " hypothesis of Ferd. Christian Baur, and, in fact, " enters once more into even Bruno Bauer's line of argument."[17]

The Messianic consciousness and the Messianic testimony of Jesus would, however, still be undeniable even if we should accede to this destructive criticism of the Gospels, or should actually destroy them altogether. The mere fact, contested by no one, that *the oldest Christian Church held Jesus to be the Messiah,* would alone prove incontestably that Jesus professed to be the Messiah. Wilhelm Bousset well says : " One of the positions which appears to be sure and impregnable, in spite of multiform controversy and ever-repeated examinations, is the fact that Jesus considered himself the Messiah of his people. For our Gospels this pre-

---

[1] Third edition, i, 62 (1894).

[2] O. Holtzmann, *War Jesus Ekstatiker?* 133 (1903).

[3] *Das messianische Selbstbewusstsein Jesu Christi,* 12 (1903).

[4] *Die Religion Jesu und die Anfänge des Christentums* in *Die Kultur der Gegenwart,* i, abteil 4, 55.

[5] *Das Leben Jesu,* p. 107 (1901) ; *Das Messiasbewusstsein Jesu und seine neueste Bestreitung* (1903) ; *War Jesus Ekstatiker?* 23, 28, 133 (1903).

[6] *Die Anfänge unserer Religion,* 31 (1904).

[7] *Die Hauptprobleme der Leben-Jesu-Forschung,* 2nd ed., 55-65 (1906).

[8] *Evangelium und Urchristentum,* 107.

[9] *Der Zweifel an der Messianität Jesu* (1907).

[10] *Der Messiasglaube der ersten Jünger in seiner Entwicklung auf Grund des synoptischen Selbstzeugnisses Jesu untersucht* (1907).

[11] *Das messianische Bewusstsein Jesu,* 1-39 (1907).

[12] *L'Evangile et l'Eglise,* 2nd ed., 19 ff., 104.

[13] The Jew B. Kellermann, *Kritische Beiträge zur Entstehungs-geschichte des Christentums,* 9 (1906), severely and justly criticizes the prejudiced, equivocal work of theological liberalism.

[14] *Das Messiasgeheimnis,* 30 ff., 47 ff., 61 f., 87 f.

[15] *id.,* 129.   [16] Wrede, *id.,* 228.

[17] Heinrich Zimmermann, *Der historische Wert der ältesten Ueber-lieferung von der Geschichte Jesu im Markusevangelium,* 1 ff. (1905).

supposition is a matter of course . . . but we can gain from our assertion a still surer point of departure than a line of argument drawn from single passages of the tradition. We know positively that from the beginning the belief prevailed in the Christian Church that Jesus was the Messiah, and, reasoning backwards, we can maintain that the origin of this belief is simply inexplicable if Jesus had not acknowledged to his disciples during his lifetime that he was the Messiah. For it is indeed comprehensible that the earliest disciples of Jesus, all of whose hopes had been shattered by his death and burial, and all of whose notions of the Messiahship of Jesus had been destroyed, should have *returned* to the belief that Jesus was the Messiah under the impression of their experiences with their risen Lord, if they had acquired this belief earlier on the ground of the utterances and conduct of Jesus. But it remains wholly inexplicable how this belief could have *originated among the disciples as something new* after the catastrophe. One must, then, suppose that those wonderful experiences during the days of Easter created something absolutely new in their souls in a purely super-natural way and without any psychological means. But precisely from a strictly historical point of view, this cannot be accepted. From this retrospective consideration we arrive at the result that Jesus, in some form or other, must have considered himself as the Messiah, and must have imparted this conviction to the disciples also. . . . It will become more and more evident that it is wholly useless to try to invalidate by criticism this point of Christian tradition."[1]

In spite, therefore, of Wellhausen, Wrede and those who agree with them, the fact may be accepted by both friend and foe that Jesus did bear witness to himself as the Messiah.

On the other hand, most of the modern critics contest the statement that he knew himself to be the Messiah and testified to that fact from the *beginning* of his public activity. Jülicher, for example, affirms that "It is hardly true that Jesus from the very beginning felt himself to be the Messiah, or destined later to become so."[2] Pfleiderer[3] writes categorically : "It is certain, in any case, that Jesus did not make his appearance at the outset with the Messianic claims." Paul Wernle thinks that "It would indeed be too much to deny to him a belief in his Messianic vocation, but how and from what point of time he considered himself as the Messiah . . . these are questions which we can answer only partially and approximately."[4]

For the most part, it is asserted that Jesus confessed him-self positively to be the Messiah only towards the end of his life, or for the first time before his judges. In this sense

---

[1] *Jesus,* 3rd ed., 77 ff. (Tübingen, 1907).   [2] *id.,* p. 55.
[3] *id.,* p. 100.   [4] *Die Quellen des Lebens Jesu,* 83 (Tübingen, 1906).

Loisy says : " It seems indubitable that the Saviour was condemned to death because he made claims to the kingdom of Israel—that is, to the character of the Messiah. Yet, as far as one can conclude from the memorials of tradition, this occurred first before the High Priest and then before Pilate."[1] " In the course of his activity Jesus did not preach in order to inform people of his Messianic character, nor did he perform his miracles as proofs of his Messiahship."[2] According to Bousset also : " The activity of Jesus was not in any way decidedly Messianic. Perhaps it was first at the entry into Jerusalem that Jesus proclaimed himself to the people as the Messiah."[3] Still more positively does E. von Hartmann inform us that " in the first period (of his public activity) he is only the prophet of the approaching end of the world and kingdom of God, and there is wanting in him . . . at first, all consciousness of his Messiahship. Only at the conclusion of the first period does this idea begin gradually to take root in him, but even in the second period he alludes to it only indirectly at first, and seeks in the judgement of others a confirmation of the fact. In the third period he proclaims himself the Messiah, first before his disciples and then openly before the tribunal."[4]

It will be shown later, in connection with the inquiry into the origin of Christ's Messianic consciousness, why modern rationalism lays such great stress upon this belated testimony of the Saviour to his Messiahship. Meanwhile, it is possible for us, by use of the Gospels, to bring proof of the contrary, and to disclose the different degrees of Christ's revelation of himself as the Messiah.

II.—ANNOUNCEMENT OF CHRIST'S TESTIMONY TO HIMSELF AS THE MESSIAH.

In this connection we must go back to the *appearance of the forerunner.* The preaching and baptism of John indicate with such definiteness the nearness of the Messiah and his kingdom (Matt. iii, 1-12; Mark i, 1-8; Luke iii, 2-18) that the multitudes surmised that the Baptist himself was the Saviour, and a formal delegation of the Sanhedrim went to him to learn the real facts of the case (John i, 19). " I am not the Messiah," John declares positively, " but there hath stood one in the midst of you, whom you know not. The same is he that shall come after me, who is preferred before me, the latchet of whose shoe I am not worthy to loose "— the intensely longed-for Messiah.

[1] *L'Evangile et l'Eglise,* p. 52 (Paris, 1902). Also see Loisy in his *Les Evangiles synoptiques,* i, 192 (Mâcon, 1907).
[2] *Autour d'un petit livre,* 83 (Paris, 1903). [3] *Jesus,* 10.
[4] *Das Christentum des neuen Testaments,* 55 (Sachsa, 1905).

Soon after, *Jesus presents himself for baptism.* John recognizes in him the one sent by God (Matt. iii, 13-15). Heaven opens. The Spirit of God descends upon Jesus in the form of a dove, and from above the voice of the Father is heard clearly and distinctly : " This is my beloved Son, in whom I am well pleased " (Matt. iii, 16 and parallels). It cannot be doubted that Jesus saw in this procedure the Messianic spiritual consecration and the recognition of himself as the Messiah by the heavenly Father (Luke iv, 18; Isa. lxi, 1; Matt. xii, 18; Isa. xl, 1-4; Acts x, 38). It will be shown later that the expression " Son of God," in its application to Jesus, and in the mouth of Jesus himself, denotes, if not always his divinity, yet always at least his Messiahship.

It has this meaning also in the *history of the temptation,* which immediately follows the baptism. The tempter supposes and fears in Jesus the existence of the Messiah, the Son of God. Yet he wishes first to assure himself of this. " If thou art the Son of God—that is, at least, the Messiah— prove thyself to be so by thy works. The Saviour is predicted as being a miracle-worker; work, then, his miracles ! The Messiah is expected to be the destroyer of the satanic power over the world, and the founder of a universal kingdom of God; hence, receive from my hands the kingdoms of the world !" That is, in substance, the language of the tempter. Jesus indignantly repudiates the impostures of Satan, but he silently accepts for himself the Messianic title " Son of God " (Matt. iv, 1-11 and parallels).

The Messiahship of Jesus forms, therefore, the very essence of the first episodes of the public life of Jesus. John the Baptist announces and acknowledges Jesus as the Messiah; heaven consecrates him and equips him audibly and visibly with the means to be the Messiah; the spirits also fear him and testify to him as the Messiah; and Jesus himself in all this possesses the calm consciousness of his Messianic dignity and mission.

Liberal investigators, of course, explain this prelude of the Messianic revelation of Jesus in such a way that the miraculous and supernatural disappear from it altogether. They assume, for this purpose, that it is a question here merely of a vision, in which the supernatural occurrences at the baptism and temptation took place only in the mind of Jesus. But the question whether it was a vision or an affair of the senses, does not affect our problem at all. That the accounts of the baptism and temptation are genuine, and that Jesus appears in them as the Messiah, is universally conceded. We shall later establish the fact that our opponents, with the exception of the extremest radicals, are forced to the confession that Jesus really reveals at the very outset of his career a positive Messianic consciousness.

In this sense Harnack writes : " The oldest tradition saw in a spiritual experience of Jesus on the occasion of his baptism the foundation of his Messianic consciousness. We cannot verify it, but we are still less able to contradict it; it is rather entirely probable that, when he made his public appearance, he was fully convinced on that point. The Gospels place the remarkable history of the temptation of Jesus before the beginning of his public activity. This presupposes that he already knew himself to be the Son of God and the one entrusted with a definite work for the people of God, and that he withstood the temptations which were intimately connected with this consciousness."[1]

Now begins also the first indication of his Messianic proclamation—at first only a gleam, as of the dawn. At the beginning " Jesus naturally observed a modest reticence about this mystery of his person and this sublime faith in himself."[2] But he had especially to take into consideration the capacity of apprehension in those about him and their Messianic ideas and preconceived notions, in spite of the fact, and indeed precisely because of it, that he did not share these notions. *The necessity of reckoning with the ingrained, misguided conception of the Messiah, characteristic of the Judaism of the Synagogue and the Rabbis*—that is the point of view from which the whole testimony of Jesus to himself as the Messiah must be judged. The defenders of the Messiahship of Jesus have not sufficiently considered this. On the other hand, all the difficulties of our opponents, who deny wholly or in part the Messianic testimony of Jesus to himself, would find their solution from this point of view. Only thus, indeed, can it be understood why Jesus appears to wish sometimes to proclaim and sometimes to conceal his Messiahship; why he speaks of it so clearly at one time and with so much reserve at another; and why, after such vast efforts, he still finds so little faith.

Consideration of the popular views about the Messiah determined him, already on his first appearance, to adopt the title of the *Son of Man*. G. Volkmar,[3] W. Brandt,[4] Lietzmann[5] and J. Wellhausen[6] try to prove that Jesus has not himself assumed the designation of the Son of Man, but has only received this title owing to the subsequent transformation of the Gospel history by believers. Yet this view not only rests on a wholly distorted criticism of the Gospels, but has

[1] *Wesen des Christentums,* 88.

[2] Heinrich Weinel, *Jesus im XIX Jahrhundert,* 109 (Tübingen, 1907).

[3] *Die Evangelien, oder Markus und die Synopsis,* 197 (Leipzig, 1869); *Jesus Nazarenus,* p. 153 (Zürich, 1882).

[4] *Die evangelische Geschichte und der Ursprung des Christentums,* 562 (1893).   [5] *Der Menschensohn* (Tübingen, 1896).

[6] *Skizzen u. Vorarbeiten,* vi (Berlin, 1899); *Das Evangelium Marci,* 66 (Berlin, 1903); *Einleitung in die drei ersten Evangelien,* 2nd ed., 123-130 (Berlin, 1911).

also been rejected by chosen experts in this field for the very philological reasons on which that criticism thought it could support itself.[1] As a matter of fact, Jesus calls himself, from the very outset and down to his condemnation by the Sanhedrim, continually and by preference the Son of Man (Matt. xxvi, 64; Mark xiv, 62; Luke xxii, 69). The name " Son of Man " occurs thirty-two times in Matthew, fourteen in Mark, twenty-five in Luke, and eleven times in John. Outside of the Gospels it is found only three times in the New Testament writings,[2] and also in the Gospels no one but the Saviour gives himself this title. He never receives it from his disciples.[3]

This name did not have the national and political significance which the other Messianic titles had by degrees acquired, such as " Christ " (Messiah, the Anointed), " Son of David," " Prince of Peace " and " King of Israel." For that very reason, also, it did not excite, as the others did, national hopes and passions.[4] It was thus best adapted to become representative of the Messianic views of Jesus, and a token of his silent, gradual revelation of himself.

In the Aramaic mother-tongue of Jesus, " Son of Man " (*barnaša*) meant certainly merely a man. But ever since the prophecy of Daniel (vii, 13) it had signified also the Messiah, as he had been heralded in advance in the holy Scripture of the Old Testament as the founder and Prince of the Messianic kingdom, who was at some time to come again in the clouds of heaven. Both interpretations were well known to the people.[5]

Now, because Jesus called himself the Son of Man in contrast to all other men, he evidently did not understand the word in its first meaning. He did not call himself " man " in the general and usual sense of that word, but in the particular sense connected with the Messianic passage in Daniel.[6] Moreover, from the first day on, he himself declared unequivocally that he applied to himself the title of Son of Man in a Messianic sense (*cf.* John i, 41, 45 and 49 with John i, 51). As

---

[1] S. Dalman, *Die Worte Jesu*, 191-219 (Leipzig, 1898); P. Fiebig, *Der Menschensohn* (Tübingen, 1901); Fritz Tillmann, *Der Menschensohn,* 60-147 (Freiburg, 1907).

[2] Acts vii, 56; Apoc. i, 13 and xiv, 14.

[3] For the reasons of this, see Tillmann, *Der Menschensohn,* 169-176.

[4] H. Wendt, *Die Lehre Jesu*, 436 (Göttingen, 1901); Weizsäcker, *Das apostolische Zeitalter*, 106 (Tübingen, 1902); B. Weiss, *Lehrbuch der biblischen Theologie des N. T.*, 55 (Berlin, 1895).

[5] For the proof of this double signification of the expression *barnaša* and its use, see G. Dalman, *Die Worte Jesu*, i, 191-217; P. Fiebig *Der Menschensohn*, 56; Tillmann, *Der Menschensohn*, 60-106.

[6] See Dalman, *id.*, 210, 217; H. J. Holtzmann, *Lehrbuch der N. T. Theologie*, 250 (1897); W. Baldensperger, *Das Selbstbewusstsein Jesu,* 169 (1892); J. Weiss, *Die Predigt Jesu vom Reiche Gottes,* 160 (1900); H. H. Wendt, *Die Lehre Jesu,* 426; Derambure, *Le Fils de l'homme dans les Evangiles* in *Revue Augustin.*, 708-720 (1908) and 319-340 (1909).

his activity progressed he concentrated into this title, as we shall see, an ever-greater amount of dignity, character, deeds of benevolence, rights and the vocation of the teaching, working, suffering and glorified Messiah.

Also extreme liberal critics like Renan,[1] Harnack,[2] Loisy,[3] H. J. Holtzmann[4] and others acknowledge that the name Son of Man in the mouth of Jesus is undoubtedly Messianic in meaning. Tillmann, after deep research, comes to the result that "no passage referring to the Son of Man is free from a Messianic meaning, and that by far the greater number of them allow this interpretation only."[5]

Jesus' testimony to himself as the Son of Man was, therefore, equivalent to testimony to himself as the Messiah. The Son of Man ascribes to himself absolutely the vocation and the dignity of the Messiah, although he does not at first bear the name Messiah. Indeed, precisely because he claimed to be the Messiah was he at the outset obliged to renounce the use of the name in public.

In any case, the name *Messiah-Christ* was not necessarily connected with the plan of salvation promised in the Old Testament. In consequence of their being anointed, kings and priests had always borne this name. And because the future Saviour was to be Priest and King in the full sense of the word, this designation also suited him pre-eminently. It is, however, given to him only three times in the whole Old Testament.[6] Only shortly before the dawn of the Christian era,[7] and only together with other titles (" Son of David," " King of Israel ") was the expression " Messiah " made one of the official titles of the expected Saviour.[8] Precisely at this time, however, there came at length to be connected with the name Messiah an idea *which compromised the Messianic cause itself.*

In the popular imagination *the Messiah was, first of all, a political liberator.* As the Son of David, he was, by his mere appearance, to shatter with one blow the Roman yoke, reestablish the Jewish throne, and, as King of Israel, lead the people of the Law, and the life according to the Law, to triumph.[9] Where such a frame of mind was prevalent it needed only a breath to cause the flame of national aspiration to flare up at once. A popular rumour of the presence of the Messiah—that is, of the national hero—would be sufficient to

---

[1] *Vie de Jésus,* 93 (Berlin, 1863).   [2] *Wesen des Christentums,* 82.
[3] *Les Evangiles synoptiques,* i, 193.
[4] *Das messianische Bewusstsein Jesu,* 50-75 (Tübingen, 1907).
[5] *id.,* 147.   [6] 1 Kings ii, 10; Ps. ii, 2; Dan. ix, 25.
[7] *Psalms of Solomon* xvii, 36; xviii, 6, 8; *Apoc. of Baruch,* xxxix, 7; xl, 1; lxxii, 2.
[8] S. Philipp Friedrich, *Der Christusname im Lichte der alt- und neutest. Theologie,* 29 ff. (Cöln, 1905); Lagrange, *Le Messianisme chez les Juifs,* 213 (Paris, 1909).
[9] The proof of this is given in the next chapter.

kindle boundless political enthusiasm and call forth a general "Messianic" revolution.

Willingly or unwillingly, Jesus would have been forced into the leadership of this if he had simply called himself the Messiah. A fatal conflict with the authorities would have put a precipitous ending to his scarcely begun career and frustrated his whole work. Jesus would have been at once condemned, as, indeed, finally was the case, by the Jewish Sanhedrim and Roman tribunal; by the former under the charge of having been unable to prove himself the Messiah-King; by the latter under the pretext of having wished to prove himself the Messiah-King. In order to escape this premature catastrophe, he prevented the too precipitate proclamation of his Messiahship, and himself avoided assuming the name Messiah.

It is true *the first disciples,* overpowered by the impression produced by his language and his personality, *suspect in him at once the Messiah, and give him the Messianic title.* "We have found the Messiah!" cries out Andrew to his brother Simon, after his first meeting with Jesus (John i, 41). "We have found him of whom Moses in the Law and the Prophets did write," announces Philip to Nathanael (John i, 45). And shortly after his meeting with Jesus, Nathanael also confesses : "Rabbi, thou art the Son of God; thou art the King of Israel" (John i, 49).

The *demons* also seek to proclaim his Messiahship through the mouths of those they possessed. For "they knew him" (Mark i, 34),[1] "they knew that he was the Messiah" (Luke iv, 41), "the Holy One of God," "the Anointed One of God," the "Son of God," the "Son of the most high God," who had come to destroy them.[2]

Jesus accepts with joy the acknowledgement of the first disciples, although, as it proved later, it was only a joyful expression of faith and hope that the Master would prove himself to be the Messiah (John i, 50). Yet he substitutes for the titles "Messiah," the "Prophet" and "King of Israel" (to the Jews all these had the same significance) the title "Son of Man." Also, he does not contradict the utterances of the devils, although he admonishes them severely not to proclaim him publicly as the Messiah.

Modern critics are greatly shocked at *these prohibitions of Jesus,* and Wellhausen and Wrede conclude from them that Jesus never felt himself to be the Messiah, while other adherents of the liberal school maintain that at least at the beginning of his career he had not yet believed in his Messiahship.

[1] "That the devils recognize in Jesus the Messiah is now in any case seldom contested." Wrede, *Das Messiasgeheimniss,* 24.

[2] Mark i, 24; iii, 12; v, 7; Luke iv, 34, 41; viii, 28; Matt. viii, 29.

Yet the very contrary is evident from the conduct of the Saviour in this regard. He did not forbid the publication of the testimony of the devils to his Messiahship because he did not consider it to be true, but precisely because he did consider it true. The Evangelists mention expressly that " he suffered not the devils to speak, because they knew him " (Mark i, 34). " And rebuking them, he suffered them not to speak, for they knew that he was Christ " (Luke iv, 41). " He strictly charged them that they should not make him known " (Mark iii, 12).

Jesus, therefore, does not repudiate faith in his Messiah-ship, but forbids the publication of it, the spreading of the report that he was the Messiah in the sense in which the people had been waiting for their Christ so long and so impatiently. By a quiet, intensive mode of education, Jesus wanted to convince, first his disciples, and then the wider circle of his associates, of his Messiahship, his supernatural Messianic nature and his spiritual Messianic vocation. Belief in him as the Messiah was to originate and become purified from within, and by reason of actual proofs; and his disciples and the people were, from his own words and, above all, from his works, to come gradually to the conviction that he was the Messiah, even though he did not usher in the hoped-for Messianic revolution.[1]

III.—DEVELOPMENT OF CHRIST'S TESTIMONY TO HIMSELF AS THE MESSIAH.

In order to render the minds of the people more receptive, Jesus starts out immediately from the standpoint of the preaching of the Baptist : " Repent, for the kingdom of Heaven is at hand " (Mark iv, 17). *The announcement of the kingdom of Heaven—that is, of the kingdom of the Messiah—forms the substance of his Galilean activity.*

But how entirely different this message of the Son of Man sounds from that of the forerunner! Above the Son of Man heaven stands open, and the angels of God ascend and descend above his head (John i, 51). The Son of Man has himself descended from heaven, and will return thither again (John iii, 1 and vi, 32, 33).

The Son of Man claims for himself, therefore, the whole spiritual dignity and spiritual task of his vocation of the Messiah, prophesied by Isaias (lxi, 1 ; Luke iv, 18). The Son of Man is come to proclaim the Gospel of the kingdom of God (Mark i, 38), to call sinners to his kingdom (Matt. ix, 13),

---

[1] Weizsäcker says pertinently, *Das apostolische Zeitalter der christlichen Kirche,* p. 106 (1902) : " It is on the whole to be concluded from the whole course of the history of Jesus that he did not at first present himself to his countrymen as the Messiah, but rather led them on to accept him as such themselves."

and to save the lost sheep of the House of Israel (Matt. xv, 24). On this account the Son of Man speaks—as a teacher, with absolute authority (Matt. v, 22, 28, 32-44) and as one who has superior force, unexampled wisdom and divine power (Matt. vii, 29; Mark i, 22).

The Son of Man is not bound by the Law of Moses (Matt. xii, 8). In contrast to this Law and to the Old Testament, the Son of Man, in his parables, discourses, and, above all, in his Sermon on the Mount, announces the Law of the Messianic kingdom (Matt. v, 1-7, 29). If the kingdom of the Son of Man is superior to the Synagogue of the Old Testament, it forms, on the other hand, a complete antithesis to the kingdom of Satan. An insult to the Son of Man is equivalent to blasphemy (Matt. xii, 31). The Son of Man will return at the end of the world to act as Judge over the kingdom of God (Matt. xiii, 37, 41).[1]

To strengthen and to seal his supernatural Messianic mission and preaching, the Son of Man also performs the *miraculous works*, which were prophesied of the Messiah, and served as evidence of his Messiahship. He subdues the elements, heals the sick, frees those possessed of devils, raises the dead, remits sins and performs new miracles in order to prove his full authority to forgive sins (Matt. ix, 1-8; Mark ii, 1-12; Luke v, 17-26). *A continual, positive and overpowering revelation of his Messiahship!*

It is true he also often seeks to prevent the publication of these Messianic deeds,[2] in order to free himself of any appearance of vanity, and always in order not to stir up political Messianic enthusiasm. How well grounded this foresight was is shown on the occasion of the first multiplication of the loaves of bread (John vi, 14). Moreover, in the working of his miracles the chief point was not to endanger the Messianic cause by a storm of enthusiasm, but to change the minds of the people by a continual definite work, and to capture, as it were, one position after another (see John vii, 3-6). In this way, however, all the people gradually learned to know him as a worker of miracles, and were able to conclude from his works that he was the divinely sent Christ,[3] although this Messiah did not correspond to the national expectations of the masses.

Jesus also recalls this to the mind of the impatiently expectant Baptist, who had sent to him from his prison the inquiry: "Art thou he that art to come, or look we for another?" Jesus answers: "Go and relate to John what you have heard and seen: the blind see, the lame walk, the lepers are cleansed, the deaf hear, the dead rise again, the

---

[1] The later utterances on the Parousia we pass over here because at present we have to do merely with the Galilean period.

[2] Matt. viii, 2; ix, 30; Mark i, 43; v, 43; vii, 36; viii, 26; Luke v, 12; viii, 56.

[3] John v, 36; vi, 28; ix, 3; x, 25-38; xiv, 10; xv, 24.

poor have the Gospel preached to them " (Matt. xi, 2-16;
Luke vii, 18-23).

These *words of Jesus to the disciples of John* are only the
repetition of the words of Isaias, in which he depicts the
blessings of the Messianic period (Isa. xxix, 18; xxxv, 2;
lxi, 1). The main thought in the answer of Jesus is, therefore,
this : " Compare what the Prophets, especially Isaias, have
predicted of the Messiah with what you see me do, and then
decide for yourself whether I am the Messiah or not." The
proof is convincing and compelling for one who is acquainted
with the Prophets, recognizes their truth and has an open
eye and ear. The Lord concludes this solemn testimony to
his own person with the serious, significant words : " And
blessed is he whosoever shall not be offended in me." Blessed
is he who shall not be offended in the Messiah, notwithstanding the fact that the expected, popular Messianic deeds and
the national and political rebellion and liberation are not
accomplished. For this one thing was the stumbling-block.
All else agreed with the predictions; all the proofs of his
Messiahship had been furnished by him a hundred times. One
thing only was lacking—the great political act, which the
narrow-mindedness and blindness of the Jews regarded as the
special work of the Messiah. But he could not effect this bold
stroke without becoming a traitor to his spiritual Messianic
dignity and task. *He could not declare himself to be the
Messiah in the sense in which the people wanted to have the
Messiah.*

On the other hand, however, the people could not be
induced to recognize his Messiahship. They praised God, it
is true, for his wonderful deeds, and said : " A great prophet
is risen up among us, and God hath visited his people "
(Luke vii, 16). " *A great prophet* "—*that was about the idea
of him that was generally held.* Some said that John the
Baptist, who had just been beheaded, had risen from the
dead ; others that Elias had appeared, who, according to
Jewish tradition, was to be the forerunner of the Messiah;
while others still declared that one of the old Prophets,
perhaps Jeremias, " had arisen " (Luke ix, 8, 19; Matt.
xvi, 14). Only occasionally did anyone ask in astonishment :
" Is not this the Son of David?" (Matt. xii, 23). " Son of
David, have mercy on us," was the cry of the two blind men
of Capharnaum and of the Canaanite woman (Matt. ix, 27;
xv, 22).

These utterances of the people certainly show also that *some
classes of the population were already near believing in the
Messiahship of Jesus.* In Samaria, which did not share the
political ideas of the Jews regarding the Messiah, Jesus could,
without danger, expressly declare himself to be the Messiah,
and found many who believed in him (John iv, 39-42). Indi-

viduals also, and entire families from among his Jewish hearers, joined immediately the number of his disciples (John iv, 53). Under the impression produced by his miracles, great multitudes of people thought, for a time at least, that they had discovered in him the coming Christ[1] (John ii, 23), although his own relatives refused to believe in him (John vii, 5). After the multiplication of the loaves at Bethsaida the people felt such enthusiasm that they cried out : " This is truly that Prophet that should come into the world "—the Messiah. And they " wanted to take him by force and make him king " (John vi, 14 and 15); that is, to proclaim him the Messianic national hero.

Only under the condition that he would carry out the definite " Messianic " revolution of the State were the people ready to recognize his Messiahship. How little reliance, anyhow, could be placed upon the belief of the crowd, and even on that of the larger circle of his disciples, was shown at the conclusion of the Galilean period of his life. As soon as Jesus put the coarse-minded notions of that larger circle to the test, most of them fell away. Only the Twelve held out through the crisis and remained steadfast (John vi, 66, 67, 70).

Among the twelve disciples faith had indeed taken root more and more deeply. As we have seen already, from the beginning the original disciples had shown a disposition to believe.[2] It would, in fact, be absolutely unthinkable that without such a disposition they would have followed the Saviour. The first miracle at Cana also confirmed them in their conviction (John ii, 11).

Yet the way to a positive, immutable and supernatural faith in his Messiahship was still a long one. For a long time yet they had to learn in the Messianic school of Jesus. Only little by little did their minds open to the mysteries of the kingdom of God, which the Master revealed frankly and confidentially to them, in contrast to the mass of the people, so far, indeed, as their powers of comprehension sufficed (Matt. xiii, 10-12; Mark iv, 11). All the infinite patience of the Lord was necessary in order not to despair of their progress (Mark iv, 13, 40; vi, 50; vii, 18). Nevertheless, their faith grew stronger from

---

[1] A comparison of this passage with Matt. xvi, 13-15 and John vii, 12 proves certainly that there cannot have been a complete conviction and belief on the part of the masses.

[2] John i, 37; F. Spitta in *Das Johannes-Evangelium als Quelle der Geschichte Jesu,* p. 424 (Göttingen, 1910), remarks with reason : " The assertion that the disciples of Jesus had recognized him as the Messiah first at Cesarea Philippi, and that the Baptist had proved by his question (Matt. xi, 3 and Luke vii, 19) that he could not have recognized him as the Messiah, rests upon incompetent investigation. By the synoptists nothing is reported differing from what we find in the Fourth Gospel—viz., that the Messiahship of Jesus became manifest from the time of his baptism."

day to day, incited, above all, by the unbroken series of his
miracles. In their astonishment at the stilling of the waves,
they fell at the feet of Jesus and cried out : " Of a truth thou
art the Son of God !" Moreover, they proved, immediately
afterwards, that this had not been merely an act of passing
enthusiasm, but the expression of a profound conviction.

It was at *Cesarea Philippi,* quite at the conclusion of the
Galilean teaching and activity, that Jesus put to them the
searching question : " Who do men say that the Son of Man
is?" But they said, " Some John the Baptist, and other some
Elias, and others Jeremias, or one of the Prophets," who,
according to Jewish opinion, was to precede the Messiah.
He saith unto them : " But whom do you say that I am?"
And he receives for the first time from the mouth of Peter
the positive answer : " Thou art Christ, the Son of the living
God." In his joy over this confession Jesus pronounced him
blessed. " Blessed art thou, Simon Bar-Jona, because flesh
and blood hath not revealed it to thee, but my Father who is
in heaven " (Matt. xvi, 13-19).

Peter was not offended in regard to the Messiah, notwithstanding the fact that he did not see him establishing the
material Messianic kingdom. Hence the blessing. The other
disciples also were now already equally advanced in the faith
(John vi, 69). Jesus was to them the Messiah, the Son of the
living God, although he still was not a Jewish Messianic king.
But that he would eventually become such a king and would
thus fulfil his essential task, as the Messiah in the Jewish
sense, they all still held for certain.

IV.—COMPLETION OF CHRIST'S OWN TESTIMONY TO HIS MESSIAHSHIP.

And now there began a new phase in Christ's testimony
to himself as the Messiah. The disciples recognized his
Messianic dignity and his Messianic character. They also
believed in his absolutely supernatural origin and nature,
although as yet they had not, as we shall see later on, entirely
clear ideas about his divinity. *On the other hand, they conceived of the vocation of the Messiah in itself and in its realization in Jesus quite erroneously.* It was most difficult to free
them from the idea *that the Messiah was to appear radiantly
in worldly power and splendour on the throne of David.*

Hence Jesus, from now on (*i.e.,* after the confession of
Peter), began to show to his disciples that he must go up to
Jerusalem and suffer much from the Elders, the Scribes, and
the High Priests, and must be put to death, and on the third
day rise again (Matt. xvi, 21), and thus " enter into his glory "
(Luke xxiv, 26).

Formerly he had referred to the sufferings of the Messiah

only transiently and figuratively (Mark ii. 19 and parallels). But now that the disciples believed on him, even though they still mistakenly identified his Messianic vocation with a brilliant political achievement, he taught them that *the Messiah's work reaches its climax in suffering and death and in the glorification ensuing therefrom.* This thought fills almost the whole last part of the Gospels. And as he holds up the spiritual and suffering Messiah in contrast to the political Messiah, so does he set up, by word and deed (John xviii, 36), in contrast to the worldly and secularized Messianic kingdom, the religious and supernatural kingdom of God, which will be developed from the smallest beginnings to world-wide and heaven-high dimensions, and is not, as the Jews supposed, to be conjured up at one stroke. From the day of Cesarea Philippi on, the teaching of Jesus to his disciples is concerned with this transformation and rectification of the Messianic faith and the Messianic idea.

The success was not very pronounced. Even Peter, who on that day had distinguished himself so brilliantly, was the first who earnestly reproached the Saviour for his idea of suffering (Matt. xvi, 22; Mark viii, 32), and who, even in the hours of his Passion, thought the time had arrived to strike a blow for the political kingdom of the Messiah (Luke xxii, 49; Matt. xxvi, 51, etc.). The two sons of Zebedee, James and John, disputed, even at a late hour in Christ's life, about the most influential and honourable positions in the Messianic kingdom (Mark x, 37, 45; Matt. xx, 20-28). Yes, even after the resurrection the disciples will not understand the teaching about the suffering Saviour (Luke xxiv, 20-27), and the old catchword still prevails among them, that now at last, and now at once, must come the Messianic liberation from the Roman yoke (Luke xxiv, 21), and the Messianic re-establishment of the kingdom of Israel (Acts i, 6). Jesus had explained to them plainly and forcibly the whole doctrine of his spiritual Messianic vocation and work, but, though they knew this doctrine, they did not yet apprehend it.

From this intellectual standpoint of the disciples we now understand also the simultaneous *attitude of Jesus towards the people after the conclusion of his Galilean activity.* However little understanding the disciples may have shown of the revelation of his Messianic vocation, they yet believed, with a few vacillations (John xvi, 30), absolutely in his Messiahship. But in the great majority of the people both faith and understanding were still wanting. Even the more progressive among them doubted whether they had before them the Messiah or only a prophet. Consequently Jesus could not yet openly say to the crowd either that he was the Messiah, or, still less, that he was the suffering Messiah and that his kingdom was wholly spiritual.

Upon the confession of Peter, therefore, he again enjoins upon the disciples to wait awhile for the public announcement of his Messiahship (Matt. xvi, 20). Soon after occurred the Transfiguration on Mount Thabor, glorified by the voice of his Father in the presence of the pillars of the Law and the prophets. Nothing was more calculated to confirm the disciples in their faith in his Messianic vocation. Yet Jesus at once repeats his positive prohibition to speak to anyone of this Messianic manifestation until the Son of Man should have risen from the dead (Mark ix, 6 and parallels)—that is, until he should have passed through suffering and humiliation into glory, and thus should have proved unmistakably that he was the Messiah and that only the spiritual idea of the Messiah is the correct one.

Yet even if the keeping secret of the name of Messiah from the people was still always enjoined, Jesus nevertheless preached his Messianic mission always more and more clearly during the last period of his activity.

Scarcely had Peter at Cesarea Philippi confessed the faith of the disciples in his Messiahship, when Jesus collected " the people also with the disciples " and addressed to " all " the burning words : " Whosoever shall lose his life for my sake and the Gospel shall save it. . . . He that shall be ashamed of me and of my words in this adulterous and sinful generation, the Son of Man also will be ashamed of him, when he shall come in the glory of his Father with the holy angels " (Mark viii, 34-38). And another time, " when great multitudes stood about him, so that they trod one upon another, he began to say . . . Whosoever shall confess me before men, him shall the Son of Man also confess before the angels of God, but he that shall deny me before men, shall be denied before the angels of God " (Luke xii, 1 and 8, 9). In this and similar ways does he proclaim himself before all to be the One sent by God, upon the faithful recognition or denial of whom depends eternal salvation or eternal condemnation.

The more plain, emphatic and public his testimony to himself as the Messiah becomes, the more evident also becomes the *miraculous Messianic proof* of the absolute reliability of his testimony. If previously he had somewhat limited the publication of his miracles " because his hour was not yet come " (John vii, 6)—the hour of his suffering and of his glorification (John vii, 30)—towards the end of his activity he more and more dispenses with those former precautions. He no longer forbids people to spread abroad the fame of his works, and performs his mighty deeds, for the most part, before great multitudes and before the priests, the Scribes and the Pharisees; in fact, even in the temple itself at Jerusalem (Matt. xii, 9 ; Mark xi, 15 ; Luke xix, 45). And he continually characterizes his miracles as a test of his having been sent by

God, and demands in this absolute faith (John ix, 3; x, 25, 32, 37; xiv, 10; xv, 24).

The eye-witness John continually mentions the success with which this increasing Messianic revelation was attended.[1] "There was much murmuring among the multitude concerning him : for some said, He is a good man : and others said, No ; but he seduceth the people. Yet no man spoke openly of him for fear of the Jews "—that is, of the Scribes and Pharisees (John vii, 12 and 13).

Nevertheless, many from among the people believed on him and said : " When the Christ cometh, shall he do more miracles than these which this man doth? The Pharisees heard the people murmuring these things concerning him, and the rulers and Pharisees sent ministers to apprehend him " (John vii, 31, 32). But as Jesus, in spite of this, continued to make his impressive revelation, the faith of the people increased also. Some said : " This is the prophet indeed. Others said, This is the Christ. But some said, Doth the Christ come out of Galilee? So there arose a dissension among the people because of him " (John vii, 40-43). Yet the number of those who believed steadily increased (John viii, 30). In vain did the Pharisees determine to put out of the synagogue every one who should confess him to be the Christ (John ix, 22). They could no longer control this great wave of popular enthusiasm. " If we let him alone so, all will believe in him " (John xi, 48), said the supreme council. And, in fact, Jesus was already quite commonly spoken of among the people as " Christ the Messiah " (Matt. xxvii, 17, 22), and with each day the army of his adherents grew greater (John x, 42 ; xi, 27 and 45).

Already the week of his Passion was approaching ; and now that the multitude, for the most part, believed in his Messiahship, Jesus set to work, as he had long tried to do with his disciples, *to correct publicly the popular notion of the Messiah,* prevalent even among the masses who believed on him. The Son of Man, he says, is not the longed-for Messianic king, and his kingdom and his glory are not of this world. He is not come to be ministered unto, but to minister, and to give his life a redemption for many (Mark x, 38, 45). The way to his infinite Messianic dominion and glory leads through suffering, death and the grave (Matt. xxvi, 10-12 ; Luke xix, 11, etc.). "For as the lightning that lighteneth from under heaven, shineth unto the parts that are under heaven, so

---

[1] It is simply impossible to controvert the genuineness of this Johannine delineation. Only an eye-witness could observe so sharply and feel so keenly. P. M. Strayer in *The Self-Revelation of Christ, with special reference to the Fourth Gospel,* in the *Biblical World,* xxxii, 327-334, rightly points out that the development of the Messianic consciousness and its acceptance by the people is pourtrayed most clearly and precisely in the Fourth Gospel and is corroborated by the synoptists.

shall the Son of Man be in his day.   But first he must suffer many things and be rejected by this generation'' (Luke xvii, 24, 25).

Such words, however, were, to the people, absolutely incomprehensible (John xii, 37).   They still unanimously adhered to the idea that he was indeed the Messiah, but that, being so, he was the *Deus ex machina,* who would soon ascend the throne of David.

Such was the popular sentiment, under the influence of which *the great Messianic demonstration*[1] was prepared and realized *at the beginning of the holy week*.   On the eve of that week an exhibition of miraculous power, following closely that of the calling of Lazarus to life, contributed the last impulse to this movement.   Two blind men of Jericho hastened towards the Saviour, who was passing by with the multitude, with the cry : '' Jesus, thou Son of David, have mercy on us !'' And they received their sight (Matt. xx, 30 and parallels).

When Jesus thereupon was about to enter Jerusalem, the people met him with shouts of '' Hosanna to the Son of David !'' (Matt. xxi, 9) '' Blessed be the King that cometh !'' (Luke xix, 38) '' Blessed is the King of Israel !'' (John xii, 13) '' Blessed is the kingdom of our father David, that cometh !'' (Mark xi, 10) '' Blessed is he that cometh in the name of the Lord !'' to establish it (Matt. xxi, 9).   These were merely acclamations to the *national and political Messiah* which they discerned in Jesus, and this made the Pharisees furious : '' Behold, the world is gone after him !'' (John xii, 19).   And they resolved to destroy him at once.

Some days later Jesus stands before the highest tribunal of the land.   *He is accused of being a popular agitator who lays claim to the throne*.   That meant to the Romans a revolutionary, to the Jews a false Messiah.   But both the Roman charge of his claiming to be a king of the Jews, and the Jewish charge of his claiming to be a Messianic king, are refuted by Jesus with the single utterance : '' My kingdom is not of this world '' (John xviii, 36).   Then he develops the true, spiritually supernatural idea of the Messiah, and sets the official seal upon his whole revelation of himself as the Messiah, when he, under a sacred oath, affirms that he is '' the Christ, the Son of God,'' '' the Son of the Blessed,'' he who, in his own character as the '' Son of Man,'' shall sit at the right hand of almighty God, and shall one day come again in the clouds of heaven (Matt. xxvi, 63 ; Mark xiv, 61 ; Luke xxii, 69).

But the more decidedly he rejected for himself the notion of the Messiah, held by the Pharisees and the people, and the more positively he applied to himself the true conception of

[1] That the entry of Jesus into Jerusalem was a Messianic scene is conceded also by Loisy, *Les Evangiles synoptiques*, i, 110,

the Christ, the more clearly he appeared to all classes of Jewish society as a false Messiah.

A few hours later there were to be read upon his cross the words, "Jesus of Nazareth, the King of the Jews" (John xix, 19). The Romans read this as meaning "This Jesus of Nazareth claimed to be a Jewish pretender to the throne." The Jews understood it as signifying "This Jesus of Nazareth claimed to be the Messianic King promised to the Jews." Jesus, however, had contended his whole life long against this conception of his person and the Messianic office. The steadily progressive revelation of himself as the Messiah had had precisely for its object the avoidance of this terrible misunderstanding. At the commencement, in the centre and at the conclusion of his career he uniformly professed to be the Messiah. Yet in an entirely different sense from that held by his expectant Jewish contemporaries.

CHAPTER II

CONTENT OF THE MESSIANIC CONSCIOUSNESS OF CHRIST

THAT the views concerning the Messiah, held by Jesus, did not agree with the official Messianic ideas of Jewish society is clear from the foregoing explanations. Christ's positive notion of the Messiah also is thereby partially revealed. Not completely, however. The question remains: Did Jesus entirely reject the common idea of the Messiah, characteristic of rabbinical Judaism, or did he merely seek to correct it? And, in the latter case, did he correct the popular notion of the Messiah in regard to a special Messianic movement of that time, or did he appeal from the Judaism of his contemporaries back to the canonical writings of the Old Testament, fulfilling and transfiguring the Messianic prophecies of the Prophets? Or did he give to the respective names and titles of Messiah and Son of Man, which he assumed, a wholly new and individual sense and substance?

The answer to this question is extremely important. According to this, Jesus will appear to the world as a universal Saviour in the sense of Christianity, or, on the contrary, as an eccentric among the Jewish Rabbis, an apocalyptical enthusiast, or even as a modern superman. Hence the feverish interest which the latest criticism of this question excites. These critics must concede to orthodox Christianity the fact of Christ's testimony to himself as the Messiah; and so they try at least to diminish the substance of this testimony, so that nothing positively Christian is left in it, and Jesus appears only as an enthusiast or a Messiah of civilization.

I.—THE CONCEPTION OF THE MESSIAH BEFORE JESUS CHRIST.

In order to appreciate the point at issue, and at the same time better to understand the attitude of Judaism to Jesus, we must first sketch briefly the Israelitish and Jewish notion of the Messiah in its fundamental lines up to the time of Christ's appearance. I say " sketch briefly," for it is only a matter of gaining a general survey of the subject, from which the Messianic views of the Saviour will then detach themselves more clearly. We must refer whoever wishes to inform himself more thoroughly about ante-christian Messiahship, whether of the Old Testament or of later Judaism, to the special literature on that subject.

1. *The Conception of the Messiah in Old Testament Prophecies*

We present the prophetical conception of the Messiah found in the Old Testament much more briefly than the rabbinical and apocalyptical ideas of him, and for an obvious reason. The modern evolutionary-historical criticism, with which we are concerned, measures Christ's Messianic conception, first of all, not by the Old Testament ideas of the Messiah, but by the rabbinical and apocalyptic notions of him, which were nearer in time to the Saviour, and from which Christ's Messianic claim is said to be taken. Also the following quotations of Old Testament passages are here valued only as historical expressions of the older prophetic ideas and expectations of the Messiah. The question whether they are, in the strict sense of the word, *prophecies*, and were fulfilled in Christ, does not belong to our present task. But that these passages refer to the Messianic hope and person cannot be seriously controverted.[1]

The essence of the old idea of the Messiah is expressed in the words *Son of David, Son of Man, Servant of God, God with us and the kingdom of God.*

Son of David. According to revelation, God promised, immediately after the Fall, to the misguided mother of the race a descendant who should vanquish the seducer and establish in opposition to his kingdom a kingdom of goodness. " I will put enmities between thee [the serpent] and the woman, and thy seed and her seed; she shall crush thy head, and thou shalt lie in wait for her heel " (Gen. iii, 15).[2] After the flood the promise goes over *to the Semites through Noe* (Gen. ix, 25-27), and later particularly to *Abraham, the first*

---

[1] The following works give more detailed information : Bade, *Christologie des A. T.* (1850-1852) ; Hengstenberg, *Christologie des A. T.* (1854-1857) ; Reinke, *Die messianischen Weissagungen bei den grossen und kleinen Propheten des A. T.,* five vols. (1859-1862) ; Böhl, *Christologie des A. T.* (1882) ; Becker, *Die Weissagungen als Kriterien der Offenbarung* (1890) ; Orelli, *Die alttestamentl. Weissagungen von der Vollendung des Gottesreiches* (1882) ; Meignan, *Les Prophètes d' Israel et le Messie* (1894) ; Hühn, *Die messianischen Weissagungen* (1899) ; Riehm, *Die messianischen Weissagungen des israelitisch-jüdischen Volkes bis zu den Targumim* (1899) ; Caillard, *Jésus-Christ et les prophéties messianiques* (1905) ; Möller, *Die messianischen Erwartung der vorexilischen Propheten* (1906) ; A. Schulte, *Die messianischen Weissagungen des A. T.* (1908) ; Leimbach, *Messianische Weissagungen des A. T.* (1909) ; Ernst Sellin, *Die israelitisch-jüdische Heilandserwartung* (1909) ; A. Lémann, *Histoire complète de l'idée messianique chez le peuple d'Israel* (1909) ; Richter, *Die messianische Weissagung in ihre Erfüllung* (1905).

[2] See also Zapletal, *Alttestamentliches,* 16-25 (1903).

ancestor of the Israelitish people. " I will bless thee," God says to Abraham, "and thou shalt be blessed. I will bless them that bless thee, and curse them that curse thee, and in thee shall all the kindred of the earth be blessed" (Gen. xii, 2, 3). "In thy seed shall all the nations of the earth be blessed" (Gen. xxii, 18). *Jacob,* Abraham's grandson, bequeathed the promise of the blessing and the Saviour of the nations to the tribe of Juda : " The sceptre shall not be taken away from Juda, nor a ruler from his thigh, till he come that is to be sent, and he shall be the expectation of nations " (Gen. xlix, 10).[1]

This supremacy of Juda is handed down to *David,* to whom again the promise is made : " I will raise up thy seed after thee . . . and will establish his kingdom. . . . He shall build a house to my name, and I will establish the throne of his kingdom for ever " (2 Kings vii, 11-16). Long after David and his immediate successors had departed this life, and their power had fallen, it is still always announced that *David, the Son of David, the offspring of the house of David, at some future time shall reign for ever over Israel:* " And I will set up one shepherd over them, and he shall feed them, even my servant David ; he shall feed them and he shall be their shepherd, and I the Lord will be their God, and my servant David the prince in the midst of them. I the Lord have spoken it " (Ezek. xxxiv, 23, 24).[2]

But not only Israel, but also the Gentile nations are to be the heirs of this Son of David, whom God will place as an everlasting king upon Sion, the holy hill (Ps. ii, xliv, cix). For he will replace the old covenant, concluded only with Israel, by a new covenant, and the Jewish theocracy by a new Messianic kingdom (Jer. xxxi, 31-34) : " And in that day the root of Jesse [David], who standeth for an ensign of people, him the Gentiles shall beseech, and his sepulchre shall be glorious " (Isa. xi, 10). " And many people shall go and say : Come, and let us go up to the mountain of the Lord, to the house of the God of Jacob ; and he will teach us of his ways, and we will walk in his paths. For the Law shall come forth from Sion and the word of the Lord from Jerusalem " (Isa. ii, 3 ; Mic. iv, 1-3). " The earth is filled with the knowledge of the Lord, as the covering waters of the sea " (Isa. xi, 9). In justice, peace, compassion and blessings shall David's Son reign " from sea to sea and from the river unto the ends of the earth . . . and all kings of the earth shall

[1] See Lagrange, *La prophétie de Jacob, Revue biblique,* pp. 525 ff. (1898); Seydl, *Donec veniat qui mittendus est, Katholik,* xxi, pp. 159 ff. (1900); Zapletal, *Alttestamentliches,* 26-54 (1903); Posmanski, *Shiloh ein Beitrag zur Geschichte der Messiaslehre,* part I (1904).

[2] See also Ezech. xxxvii, 21-28 ; Jer. xxiii, 5, 6 ; xxx, 8, 9 ; xxxiii, 15-26 ; Osee iii, 5 ; Amos ix, 11.

adore him, all nations shall serve him . . . and in him shall all the tribes of the earth be blessed " (Ps. lxxi).[1]

If in the " Son of David " there is conspicuous almost nothing but the brilliant and beneficent glory of the Messiah who is to govern as the head of the universal kingdom, yet, on the other hand, he is depicted as the *Servant of God,* who is to suffer and die vicariously for the sins of men, and thus is to acquire the Messianic supremacy and glory. This side of the Messianic expectation is especially emphasized in the Psalms descriptive of the Man of Sorrows (Ps. xxi and lxviii) and in the songs of Isaias concerning the Servant of God.[2]

. The Servant of God, chosen and anointed by Jehovah, and equipped with all the gifts of the Spirit of God (Isa. xi, 2, 3), is to be a teacher, a prophet, a worker of miracles, and a saviour in the full sense of the words. As such he is called, not only for the salvation of Israel, but " for a light and redeemer of the Gentiles unto the ends of the earth " (Isa. xlii, 1-7; xlix, 6). Nevertheless, he will be despised by men, abhorred by the people, and proscribed by kings (Isa. xlix, 1-9). " Despised and rejected of men, a man of sorrows " (liii, 3), he gives his body to the strikers and his cheeks to them that plucked them, and turns not away his face from them that rebuked him and spit upon him (Isa. l, 6). " He was offered . . . and opened not his mouth; he shall be led as a sheep to the slaughter " (Isa. liii, 7). Under nameless sufferings, deserted by heaven and rejected by earth (Ps. xxi, lxviii), with pierced hands and feet (Ps. xxi, 17; Zach. xii, 10), he dies in the company of malefactors, he who had done no iniquity, neither was there deceit in his mouth (Isa. liii, 8, 9).

. Suffering, distress and death come upon him only on our account. " He hath borne our infirmities and carried our sorrows. . . . He was wounded for our iniquities, he was bruised for our sins, the chastisement of our peace was upon him, and by his bruises we are healed. All we like sheep have gone astray; everyone hath turned aside into his own way, and the Lord hath laid on him the iniquity of us all " (Isa. liii, 4-6). He atones to God for the sins of the world (Isa. liii, 8, 11). Thus does he fulfil the redemptive plan of

---

[1] M. Güdemann, *Jüdische Apologetik,* pp. 51, 211 (1906), rightly says that in the historic plan of the Jewish religion there was nothing which could have promoted the subsequent national chauvinism; the Old Testament notion of God, the notion of a united humanity, and the duty of universal charity exclude in advance a national, chauvinistic character of the Messianic vision of the future. See Meinertz, *Jesus und die Heidenmission,* pp. 17-35 (1908).

[2] Isa. xlii, 1-16; xlix, 1-9; l, 4-10; lii, 13; liii, 12; lv, 4. The proof that these songs refer to the person of the Messiah and not to the Jewish nation does not belong here. See the copious literature on this subject and on the Messianic prophecies, and in particular see Feldmann, *Der Knecht Gottes in Isaias* (Freiburg, 1907); Conrad v. Orelli, *Der Knecht Jahves im Jesajabuche* (Lichterfelde, Berlin, 1908).

the Lord, " and shall justify many " (Isa. liii, 11). Through
him " all the ends of the earth shall remember and shall be
converted to the Lord, and all the kindreds of the Gentiles
shall adore in his sight " (Ps. xxi, 28). The murdered Servant
of God shall, however, rise to a new life, and at the right
hand of God shall be satisfied with fulness of joy and pleasures
for evermore (Ps. xv, 10 and 11).

From this proximity to God he will one day return for the
Last Judgement, as the *Son of Man,* in the clouds of heaven, in
order to enter into his everlasting dominion over the Messianic
kingdom of God, which he had established and inherited
through his sufferings, death and resurrection. That is the
meaning of Daniel's prophecy of the Son of Man : " I beheld
in the vision of the night, and lo, one like the Son of Man
came with the clouds of heaven, and he came even to the
Ancient of Days, and they presented him before him. And he
gave him power and glory and a kingdom ; and all people,
tribes and tongues shall serve him ; his power is an everlasting
power that shall not be taken away, and his kingdom that
shall not be destroyed " (Dan. vii, 9, 13, 14).[1]

In view of this unheard-of dignity and these supernatural
official functions of the Messiah, it is scarcely to be wondered
at that he is announced as God in human form, as *Emmanuel*
—God with us.

In numberless passages, which it is neither necessary nor
possible to quote here separately, the Old Testament proclaims the fact that God himself will come in his own person
to redeem his people. In the second psalm the Redeemer is
designated more exactly as the *Son of God.* The Psalmist
here attributes to the Messiah, constituted and anointed by
God, the words : " The Lord hath said to me : Thou art my
Son, this day have I begotten thee " (Ps. ii, 7). But most
clearly and emphatically does Isaias utter his prophecy concerning the divine redeemer : " The Lord himself shall give
you a sign. Behold, a virgin shall conceive and bear a son,
and his name shall be called Emmanuel " (Isa. vii, 14). That
God is really meant in the metaphysical sense of the word by
this Emmanuel, born miraculously of a virgin, is shown by the
fact that he is designated immediately after as the highest
Lord and possessor of the land of Israel, and is therefore
identified with Jehovah (Isa. viii, 10).

Then the prophet describes Emmanuel still more plainly as
the divine Messiah : " The people that walked in darkness
have seen a great light ; to them that dwelt in the region of
the shadow of death, light is risen. . . . For a child is born
to us, and a son is given to us, and the government is upon

---

[1] In regard to the Messianic character of this passage, see the pre
viously mentioned literature about the Son of Man, and Lagrange, *Les
prophéties messianiques de Daniel, Revue biblique,* 494 ff. (1904).

his shoulder; and his name shall be called Wonderful, Counsellor, God the Mighty, the Father of the world to come, the Prince of Peace. His empire shall be multiplied, and there shall be no end of peace; he shall sit upon the throne of David, and upon his kingdom, to establish it and strengthen it with judgement and with justice from henceforth and for ever. The zeal of the Lord of Hosts will perform this" (Isa. ix, 2, 6, 7).[1]

The dominion of God over the world, or the *kingdom of God* in the world, was in general the sum total of all hopes for the future. The whole Old Testament is filled with the idea, which Jesus summarized in the words: "Thy kingdom come." By the *Malkuth Jahwe,* the kingdom of God, or the kingdom of Heaven—Heaven is only a metonymic designation of God[2]—the Holy Scripture means, according to the use of the Semitic language, exactly the concrete royal rights which God possesses over the world, and the exercise of these by God on his part, and the recognition of them by men on their part—that is, a kingdom which is governed from heaven and consents to be entirely subject to heaven.[3]

Precisely the latter—the recognition by men of the inalienable rights of God—is to be made a reality by the Messiah. *The kingdom of God and the Messiah are, therefore, correlative ideas.* All the traits of the Messiah unite here in one central point. As the suffering Servant of God he makes the founding of the kingdom possible; as the Son of David he comes to its head; and as the Son of Man he will some day return to establish it in glory. Since, finally, the Messiah himself is "God with us," his dominion will be one with that of God, and the kingdom of the Messiah becomes in the highest sense God's kingdom.

It is likewise clearly said in the prophetic announcements that in this kingdom the *earthly and political aspirations* of the people of the revelation also have their part. It does not at all appear that the prophecies on this subject are to be interpreted wholly and exclusively in a spiritual and religious sense. Rather is it to be supposed that Israel, provided it had not rejected the Messiah, would have inherited that temporal and national blessing which from time immemorial had been the reward for its fidelity to Jehovah, and which was promised no less for the Messianic period than as an accom-

---

[1] A more exact examination of the passages quoted from the Psalmist and Isaias cannot be given in this space. The proof that the Messiah was expected as God, in accordance with Old Testament prophecies, is abundantly furnished by Simon Weber, *Die Gottheit Jesu in der alttestl. Offenbarungsgeschichte,* in *Jesus Christus,* Vorträge zu Freiburg im Br., 43-68 (1908).

[2] E. Schürer, *Geschichte des jüdischen Volkes,* 539 (Leipzig, 1898).

[3] Lagrange, *Le règne de Dieu dans l'Ancien Testament, Revue biblique,* 36-61 (1908).

paniment of the *spiritual and religious blessings of the Messianic kingdom.* These formed, however, unquestionably the principal thing, as is sufficiently evident from the statements thus far made. The Messianic kingdom will bring the perfect knowledge of God (Isa. ii, 2-4; xi, 9; Mic. iv, 1-3). The whole people will be blessed through God's presence, and will find in him a refuge and help in every kind of distress and time of need (Isa. iv, 4; xxv, 4). Above all, however, the kingdom of God will be blessed by the full abundance of the forgiveness of sins, promised by the Messiah and purchased by his death. "In that day there shall be a fountain open to the house of David and the inhabitants of Jerusalem, for the washing of the sinner and of the unclean woman" (Zach. xiii, 1). "In those days and at that time, saith the Lord, the iniquity of Israel shall be sought for, and there shall be none; and the sin of Juda, and there shall none be found; for I will be merciful to them" (Jer. l, 20). "I will forgive their iniquity and I will remember their sin no more" (Jer. xxxi, 34). "If your sins be as scarlet, they shall be made as white as snow; and if they be red as crimson, they shall be white as wool" (Isa. i, 18). "I have blotted out thy iniquities as a cloud, and thy sins as a mist; return to me, for I have redeemed thee" (Isa. xliv, 22).

2. *The Pharisaical and Rabbinical Concept of the Messiah.*

The pharisaical and rabbinical theology developed after the return from exile, reached its climax about the time of Jesus, and was thereupon edited in the writings of the Synagogue, and especially in the literature of the Talmud. Although for this reason the publication of almost all the rabbinical literature is subsequent to the time of Christ, it forms, nevertheless, "a source of priceless information for the age of Jesus Christ; for the foundations of the current of tradition here established go back, not only to the lifetime of Christ, but far beyond it."[1]

For this reason we present in the following pages the rabbinical views of the Messiah according to the oldest writings of the Synagogue, if still older sources are not at hand.[2]

---

[1] E. Schürer, *Geschichte des jüdischen Volkes,* p. 112 (1901); also W. Bousset, *Die Religion des Judentums im neutestamentlichen Zeitalter,* 41 (Berlin, 1903).

[2] Thus the *Talmud* will be quoted, according to custom, simply by treatise and folio page, and the *Mishna* by treatise, chapter and paragraph. From the *Midrashim* we have made use of *Mechilta,* ed. Weiss (Vienna, 1846); *Sifra,* ed. Malbim (Bukarest, 1860); *Sifre,* ed. Friedmann (Vienna, 1864); *Pesikta des R. Kohana,* ed. Buber (Lyck, 1868). Together with this oldest *Midrash* from the third century, some other *Midrashim* have been used, the publication of which is later, but whose essential contents rest, as is acknowledged, on ancient synagogal traditions—namely, *Tanchuma,* ed. Buber (Wilna, 1885), and several *Rabboth,* ed. Wünsche (*Bibliotheca rabbinica,* Leipzig, 1880).

The picture thus gained will correspond essentially to the rabbinical ideas about the Messiah prevailing at the time of Christ. But no one at the present stage of investigation into Jewish theology can guarantee that every particular feature of them goes back to a period preceding the Christian era.[1]

At the first glance it seems strange that the rabbinical theology, and with it later Judaism, was not able to maintain itself at the height of that notion of the Messiah, entertained by the prophets, which we have just observed. It laid, on the whole, little stress any longer on the prophetic writings. In order to strengthen practical Jewish life as opposed to the influences of their pagan environment, *the Law*—that is, the 613 Torah commandments (for such was the number that the Scribes found in the Pentateuch)—*became more and more exaggerated at the expense of the real meaning of the prophetical Messianic revelation.* The Rabbis not only caused the religious private life of the people to be entirely absorbed in devotion to the Law, in comparison with which prayers and sacrifices were much less important,[2] and not only made the reading of the Torah also the central point of public worship and of the whole religious consciousness of the community,[3] but, according to them, the books of the Law contain the whole of religion, and the Torah is the revelation, in which God has included everything that he in any way can reveal[4] through all eternity. The Law[5] existed even *before* the world, and, accordingly, God already circumcised Adam before he breathed into him the breath of life,[6] while the prophetical and doctrinal books of Holy Scripture came only later and, as it were, by chance.[7] The books of the Law will also exist

---

[1] See Klausner, *Die Messianischen Vorstellungen des jüdischen Volkes im Zeitalter der Tannaiten* (Berlin, 1904); Robinson, *Le Messianisme dans le Talmud et les Midraschim* (Paris, 1907); B. Stakemeier, *Il Messianismo degli Ebrei al tempo di Gesù, Rivista di scienze teologiche,* 35-45 (1910). On a broader scale write Schürer, Bousset, and especially A. Hausrath, *Neutestamentliche Zeitgeschichte* (1868-1873); Alfred Edersheim, *The Life and Times of Jesus, the Messiah,* 1-110 (London, 1890); H. Kellner, *Jesus von Nazareth und seine Apostel im Rahmen der Zeitgeschichte* (1908); J. Felten, *Neutest. Zeitgeschichte, oder Judentum und Heidentum zur Zeit Christi u. der Apostel,* 133-189 (1910).

[2] *Shabbath* 10 a and 30 a; *Jebamoth* 105 a; *Wajjikra rabba* 29. After the destruction of the Temple, study of the Torah replaces sacrifices for the atonement of all sins (*Jebamoth* 105 a; *Tanchuma Achare moth* 10), even for past murders (*Sifre* 1316).

[3] *Sifre* 13 b and 40 a, *jer Shabbath* 12 c; *Shemoth rabba* c. 34. Other books were only introduced as appended to the reading of the Law (*Tanchuma, Debarim Reëh* 1; *Rosh Hashshana* iv, 6).

[4] *Debarim rabba* c. 8 on 5. *Mos.* xxx, 12; *Taanith* 9 a.

[5] *Sebachim* 116 a; *Shabbath* 88 b; *Pirke Aboth* vi, 10; *Mechilta* 64 b; *Bereshith rabba* c. 1.

[6] *Tanchuma Parasha Noach* 5. It is often stated that Sem had his own school of instruction in the Law—*e.g., Maccoth* 23 b. According to *Bereshith rabba* 63 Esau and Jacob had a dispute on the interpretation of Law in their mother's womb.

[7] *Nedarim* 226; *Koheleth rabba* on i, 13.

eternally, while all the rest of the revelation will at some future time pass out of validity and use.[1]

This frightful exaggeration [of the Law] destroyed the whole prophetical expectation of salvation. If the Mosaic Law—that is, the Law as interpreted by rabbinical and kabbalistic[2] exegesis, as the highest good and the only thing which remains eternally—is all, then *Mosaism* can no longer be a means to the end of Messianic redemption, and no more a transient institution; it is then *itself redemption and perfection.*

And it was really looked upon as such by the rabbinical theology. According to this, Jehovah, by the revelation of the Law on Sina, in order to make up for Adam's fall, offered to the chosen people his loving union,[3] and Israel acceded to the proposal of its divine Bridegroom through its acceptance of the Law.[4] Thus *Judaism was redeemed on Sina.*[5] This act of redemption was to be the end of God's dealings, and the nuptial relation which had been created thus between God and his people was to last for ever. Even though Israel had frustrated this plan of God by its worship of the golden calf,[6] yet so much at least is certain, that all the revelation of salvation cannot surpass what was given on Sinai. The aim of the historical development of the plan of salvation is, therefore, to get back again, through the fulfilment of the Law, what, through the episode of the golden calf, had been lost.[7] It is no more a matter of inward justification and of an atoning redemption from sin; sin, atonement, healing and justification, in the sense of Holy Scripture, are unknown to rabbinical theology. *The great means of redemption and the great act of redemption is excellence in matters of the Law, and that only.*

To complete this act of redemption is, however, not, of course, *the work of the Messiah.* If justice and justification are conceived of only as legal notions and as the outward, legal justice of the nation and individual, then the nation or

[1] *Shemoth rabba* c. 33; *jer. Megilla* i, 7.

[2] See F. Weber, *Jüdische Theologie auf Grund des Talmud und verwandter Schriften,* edited by F. Delitzsch and G. Schnedermann, pp. 109-124 (Leipzig, 1897); Schürer, *op. cit.,* pp. 419 ff.; Bousset, *op. cit.,* 128-138.   [3] *Bammidbar rabba* c. 5 and 13.

[4] *Shir rabba* on 1, 2; *Shabbath* 88 a; *Pesikta* 124 b. God offered the Law even to the heathen, but they refused it (*Pesikta* 199 b, 200 a; *Shemoth rabba* c. 13). Therefore God cast them away for ever (*Wajjikra rabba* c. 13; *Bammidbar rabba* c. 2), while confiding for ever in Israel (*Debarim rabba* c. 3; *Shemoth rabba* c. 51), so that Jehovah and Israel can never deny one another (*Wajjikra rabba* c. 6) without committing unfaithfulness (*Shemoth rabba* c. 33).

[5] *Shir rabba* on 1, 2; 4, 7; *Bammidbar rabba* c. 16; *Shemoth rabba* c. 32.

[6] *Pesikta* 124 b; *Shabbath* 88 a; *Shir rabba* on 1, 3.

[7] *Bammidbar rabba* c. 17: "The Holy One, to whom be praise, hath established the Law and the commandments that Israel may obtain the life of the world to come."

individual must alone and on its own account make itself just through a mathematically strict balancing between debit and credit, between the demands of the Law and their fulfilment. These demands and fulfilments are noted down day by day, reckoned up, credited and balanced.[1] He is wholly just whose legal performances numerically equal the sum of the commandments;[2] relatively just is he whose life-balance shows at least an absolute surplus of legal achievements.[3]

Only when the balance of all the individuals and of the whole nation corresponds to the budget of the Law—in other words, only when all Israel is justified and made holy—does the Messiah begin his work. Only then will the Redeemer come.[4]

It is true his coming is immediately preceded by a period of absolute lawlessness. The appearance of that period is "like that of a dog."[5] Elias will, however, appear in order to create again respect for the Law, and thereby fully and absolutely to justify Israel and to make it holy for the Messiah.[6] Then, and only then, will the Messiah appear, as the well-earned reward for fidelity to the Law; not as a grace, much less as an act of redemption.[7]

His redeeming work—if one can still speak of it as such—consists in the fact that *he, by word and example, encourages and perpetuates faithfulness to the Law.* As a perfectly competent scribe, he will instruct[8] all the people in the Torah, and even take upon himself its unbearable yoke;[9] and he will be "loaded down, like a mill, with fulfilments of rabbinical commandments."[10]

That is all. A great Rabbi—nothing more; that is the Messiah of the theology of the Synagogue. But a Messiah who makes his appearance as a preacher of morals, and who accuses this people, so faithful to the Law, and, above all, the flower and intelligence of the nation—the Scribes and Pharisees—of guilt and sin, is at once condemned as a false Messiah. Should he once disclose the necessity of a religious regeneration for Israel, or should he wish to proclaim a religion surpassing the Mosaism of the Rabbis, he is a traitor to the Holy of Holies, a blasphemer. But also even the censure, and still more the violation of one single rabbinical iota, the healing of a sick man, or the plucking an ear of corn

---

[1] *Wajjikra rabba* c. 26; *Tanchuma, Wajjelech* 2; *Aboda Sara* 2 a.

[2] *Shabbath* 32 a.   [3] *Kiddushin* 40 b; *Pesikta* 176 a.

[4] *Sanhedrin* 97 b; *Shabbath* 118 a; *Shemoth rabba* c. 25; *Wajjikra rabba* c. 3.

[5] *Sota* ix, 15; *Sanhedrin* 97 a; *Shir rabba* on 2, 13.

[6] *Pirke de-Rabbi Eliezer* c. 43; *cf.* Matt. xvii, 10 ff.; Mark ix, 10 ff.; Luke i, 16 ff.

[7] It needed all the intellectual power of St Paul to make even the Jews who had become Christians understand that they had not been justified by the Law, but must become justified by Christ (see Rom. iii, 4, 7; Phil. iii).

[8] *Jonathan Targum* on Is. liii, 5, 10-12; *Shir rabba* on 2, 13.

[9] *Jonathan Targum* on Is. ix, 3.   [10] *Sanhedrin* 93 b.

upon the Sabbath, association with a publican, or the omission of an ablution, marked him as a disciple of Beelzebub. He only can be recognized as the true Messiah who, like the Scribes, and even more than they, observes the Law with all its additional stipulations, in all its subtleties, and with the whole rabbinical barrier drawn around it.[1]

The religious efficacy and redemptive activity of the Messiah are, accordingly, not specifically Messianic; they do not surpass those of Hillel or of an extraordinarily gifted scribe. The Messianic activity and work of the Redeemer lie essentially elsewhere. He has simply to toss the reward into the lap of self-redeemed Judaism by *founding the Messianic kingdom; or*, rather, *by the re-establishment of the kingdom of God* in the form in which it had already existed on Sinai, according to the fancy of the Rabbis; as a worldly—yes, exceedingly worldly—theocracy.

In the opinion of the Rabbis, the kingdom of Heaven itself came down to earth with the Lord on Sinai.[2] From that time on, politics and religion were one and the same thing. To be subject to any other sovereign than Jehovah meant to deny the religious supremacy of God and even religion itself. Since God had taken up his abode in the midst of his people, he alone was that people's King and supreme Lord, and his dominion assured not only Israel's predominance over the Gentiles, who served him as his footstool, but it created paradisaical conditions of every kind. God's nearness banished all the consequences of original sin and re-established the blessed primitive state of the Garden of Eden in this terrestrial kingdom of Heaven, until the earth should be merged into heaven itself, and time into eternity. Thus did Nomism imagine the first redemptive kingdom on Sinai[3] to have been, and thus it logically imagined would be also its rehabilitation by the Messiah.

On the first day that the entire nation shall keep the Law[4] the Messiah will appear, drive back the enemies of Israel, compel the Gentiles to respect the Torah,[5] and establish the Messianic dominion.[6]

---

[1] See Döllinger, *Heidentum und Judentum*, 773 (Regensburg, 1857).

[2] *Mechilta* 73 b; *Pesikta* 16 b; *Shemoth rabba* c. 23.

[3] Weber, *op. cit.*, p. 271 ff.

[4] If all Israel would repent even for only one day, and would keep only one Sabbath perfectly holy, the Messiah would at once appear. *Pesikta* 163 b; *Shemoth rabba* c. 25.

[5] Weber, p. 385 ff. In this procedure, however, the formal conversion to the Law and thereby the hope of Messianic salvation for the godless Gentiles are excluded, according to *Aboda Sara* 3 b; *Jebamoth* 24 b, etc. Jewish proselytising propaganda had its justification only before the coming of the Messianic era. Whoever is not already a Jew when the Messiah comes cannot any more become one, and is at once excluded from participation in the Messianic blessings (see Lagrange, *Le Messianisme chez les Juifs*, 284-287).

[6] *Mechilta* 59 b; *Pesikta* 51 a; *Debarim rabba* c. 1.

This is regarded as the *continuation of the kingdom of David and Solomon*,[1] which, however, will be far surpassed by the Messianic kingdom in brilliancy, splendour, might and happiness. Jerusalem, the capital of the kingdom, will, at the same time, be the metropolis of all the cities of the world.[2] Its ascendancy, grandeur and magnificence will be something until then unknown.[3] In the midst of the city God will pile up Carmel, Thabor and Sina, one on top of the other, and will erect upon the summit the Temple,[4] visible to the whole world. From there the Messiah, in the name of Jehovah, will extend his sceptre. The vast Roman Empire,[5] which arose only on account of Israel's sins, will lie in ruins at his feet.[6] The non-Roman pagan nations will be obliged to pay tribute to him and to the pious Israelites, as vassal states.[7]

To serve the Messiah and the Jews in Palestine will be the sole *raison d'être* of the nations living outside Palestine. As a beneficent Messianic king, the Messiah offers himself only to the children of Abraham and only in the Promised Land.[8] Hence all the scattered remnants of Israel will return from the dispersion under Divine leadership and assemble in Palestine.[9]

There he will lavishly bestow the *blessings of the Messianic kingdom and era*. All the sensuous delights of the Israelitish kingdom of the Torah ever dreamed of will be realized—the removal by the Messiah of every kind of sickness and distress, wonderful physical beauty and vitality for the children of Israel, and[10] a fabulous productivity of soil and plants. Women will give birth to children daily.[11] Men will be twice as tall as Adam, who measured one hundred ells in height: even the dwarfs among them will reach to the pinnacles of the Temple.[12] No bunch of grapes will produce less than thirty casks of wine.[13] Barley will attain the height of the palm-tree and scatter meal about, already ground on demand, without any need of harvesting first.[14] If roasted pigeons are added, then the measure of the Messianic blessings will be full—a veritable fairy life in fairyland.

Shall it therefore be said that the rabbinical attitude towards the Messiahship had only earthly and political characteristics and none that were also deeply religious? God forbid! That

---

[1] *Pesachim* 54 a.   [2] *Shir rabba* on 1, 5.

[3] *Baba bathra* 75 a b; *Sifre* 65 a; *Pesikta* 143 a b.

[4] *Pesikta* 144 b.

[5] The world-power to be destroyed by the Messiah is, according to the entire rabbinical theology, the Roman Empire (see Weber, 365; Schürer, ii, 532; Bousset, 204).   [6] *Sifre* 86 a.

[7] *Tanchuma* 19; *Shemoth rabba* c. 35.   [8] Bousset, 216.

[9] Schürer, ii, 537. Unfortunately, Schürer in his magnificent work has not clearly enough distinguished between the rabbinical and the eschatological and apocalyptic conceptions.

[10] *Bereshith rabba* c. 12 and 26; *Shabbath* 30 b; *Pesachim* 68 a.

[11] *Shabbath* 30 b.   [12] *Baba bathra* 75 a.

[13] *Kethuboth* 111 b.   [14] *id.*, 111 b.

would be a complete misapprehension. Rabbinical Judaism has never failed to recognize the importance of its historical plan of salvation. It was, as we have said, convinced that the Messiah would lead the Jews to the exact observation of the religious Law of God in the Torah, and also would bring those who were not Israelites to recognize it. Precisely in that did the Synagogue see the spiritual worth and essential character of the Messianic age and the Messianic kingdom. The supremacy of the Torah, which, according to rabbinical interpretation, was one with the supremacy of God, was to make itself felt everywhere over the whole earth. So far as this the pharisaical idea of the Messiah was thoroughly religious, and even religious in a universal sense.

And not only in theory, but also in the practical conduct of life, did the Jews show a great, in fact, an unheard-of zeal for the hoped-for " kingdom of *God.*"[1] One must allow that under the leadership of the Pharisees they were more enthusiastic for the kingdom of God than ever, and sought to usher it in, not merely through a punctual observation of the Law, but through an acceptance of the rabbinical " yoke."[2] Precisely in order to increase the practical observance of the Law and yoke, and so to bring about the *Malkuth Jahwe* more speedily, they also developed that intense missionary activity of theirs, and compassed sea and land to make one proselyte (Matt. xxiii, 15).

The immense mistake lay in the fact that this Messianic conception, whether practical or theoretical, was applied to a kingdom of God which in a secular and political sense had acquired a changed value. The Judaists understood by this, in spite of all pious phrases and pharisaical hypocrisy, essentially a sudden change of things in the sense of the materialized, thoroughly worldly and particularly Jewish-Davidic supremacy. They endured the Law and " yoke " principally because these were the means to this political and national purpose. The Messiah was longed for by all classes because he was to hasten and assure the advent of their national dominion through the enforcement of the Law. And even Jehovah, who was to assume the government of Israel, must for this purpose place himself exclusively at the service of the Jewish national aspirations. He must become (excuse the expression, since it is absolutely correct) a thorough-going

[1] *Malkuth Jahwe.*

[2] Not only in the Gospels (Matt. xxiii, 4), but also in the *Talmud* the rabbinical fulfilling of the Law is always described as a " yoke " and " a heavy burden " (see Gal v, 1). Even one solitary commandment is exceedingly difficult to put into practice (*Mechilta* 110 a); but positive commandments are concerned with everything, yes, everything (*Sifra* on iii; Mos. 8, 25). Every object must be handled according to definite rules; every kind of work—for example, ploughing or planting—must be done in accordance with fixed, literal, theological instructions, otherwise a grave sin is committed (*Bammidbar rabba* c. 17).

Jew of the Law, must take upon himself in every way both Law and yoke, and put himself, with his heavenly royal court, entirely under the orders of the Jewish Sanhedrim.[1] Everything else that the Judaism of the Rabbis and Pharisees dreamed of, beyond their theocratical national power and its blessedness, was purely secondary, merely an accompanying phenomenon. The *Talmud* often expressly assures us: " There is no other difference between the present world and the era of the Messiah than the [present] servitude enforced upon us by the kingdoms [of the Gentiles]."[2]

Let it not be said that the Jewish conception of the Messiah first reached its sharply nationalistic and material climax in the period after Christ. It is, rather, proved from the most reliable sources that *already in the time of Christ the Jewish kingdom of God and expectations concerning the Messiah had sunk to a political and material level.* Even the Psalms of Solomon, which were composed half a century before Christ,[3] and express most ideally the Messianic conception of the Pharisees, do not rise above the level just described. According to their glowing pourtrayal, the Messiah will be a just king, taught by God, and filled with the Holy Spirit, who will rule a thoroughly holy and just people; that is, one that is law-abiding and well versed in the practice of the Torah.[4] He will govern Israel " in the fear of God and in the wisdom, rectitude and power of the Spirit "; he will lead it " in the path of righteousness, since he impresses upon all the fear of God." He will not extend his dominion only to the Gentiles. " He will direct nations and peoples with wisdom and equity. He will gather the nations together under his yoke, that they may serve him, and he will thus make Jehovah glorious over the whole earth."[5] The main thing, the essentially Messianic element in him is, however, his Davidic kingdom, the secular power with which he is to rule Israel, shatter its enemies and purify Jerusalem from the Gentiles.[6] Not a single non-Israelite is to dwell in the Messianic kingdom. Foreigners will be allowed only to bring gifts to Palestine for the children of Israel, and to stare enviously at their grandeur.[7] The Messiah is wholly a political ruler, and the Messianic kingdom a thoroughly secularized and nationalized " kingdom of heaven."[8]

We need only to open the *Gospel* to become convinced that this conception in the Psalms of Solomon of the kingdom and activity of the Messiah was by no means an isolated instance. Wherever the Scribes and Pharisees appear in the

---

[1] For the proof of this, see my *Die Krisis des religiösen Judentums zur Zeit Christi,* 10-12.   [2] *Shabbath* 63 a; *Pesachim* 68 a.
[3] Oskar von Gebhardt, *Die Psalmen Salomonis* (1895).
[4] *Ps. Salom.* xviii, 28-46.   [5] *id.,* xvii and xviii.
[6] *Ps. Salom.* xvii, 23-27.
[7] *Ps. Salom.* xvii, 30-34.   [8] *id.,* xi, xvii, xviii.

I.   II

Gospels, and wherever Jesus comes at all into contact with official Judaism in province or capital, we recognize the same materialized notion of the Messiah. We have had occasion to prove that sufficiently in the foregoing chapter.

Nor were these views limited only to the homeland, *Palestine. The Hellenistic Jews in foreign countries* thought the same. Flavius Josephus knows only a Messianic king, whom he, the renegade to Rome, hails in the Emperor Vespasian.[1] According to Philo of Alexandria (who died about A.D. 60), the Messiah has merely a military part to play, including a fight against the enemies of the Law and of the people of the Law, the victory and everlasting dominion of this people, and its attendant luxury, wealth, honour and corporate unity.[2]

The *rabbinical-Jewish Messiah* is also, on that very account, *merely a man,* both in origin and by nature.[3] Only the name of the Messiah—that is, the plan of his mission—is ancient. It is true, together with this ideal, the Palestine theology admits also a real pre-existence of the soul of the Messiah. This was, however, only in consequence of the rabbinical anthropology, which believes all human souls to have been created before the world, and kept in a sort of store-house in the seventh heaven until the moment of their union with the body.[4]

The Messiah is therefore a pre-existent and transcendental being in no other sense than all other men are. Also, the doctrine of the purely human origin and nature of the Messiah was not at all a more or less disseminated dogma, but was the common view of the rabbinical-jewish theology. The Jew Trypho assures St Justin very positively : " We all expect the Messiah as a man born from human parents, and as one who will receive from Elias, as soon as the latter shall appear, the kingly consecration."[5]

That this opinion did not first appear at a time subsequent to Christ is clearly evident from the Gospel, especially from the dispute of Jesus with the Jews, whom he wishes to convince out of Ps. cix that the Messiah is not merely an earthly descendant of David (Matt. xxii, 42 and parallels). Only through his zeal for the Law is he, like Abraham, Moses, Job and Ezechias,[6] superior to the average man, and he makes himself, precisely through this justification by the Law, worthy of accomplishing the work of the Messiah.[7]

If now we compare these rabbinical views, which were current among the contemporaries of Jesus, with *those of the*

1 *Bellum Judaicum* vi, 5, 4.

2 Philo, *De præmiis,* xiv-xx; *De execrationibus,* viii, ix, xix. Consult E. Brehier, *Les idées philosophiques et religieuses de Philon d'Alexandrie* (Paris, 1908); Lagrange, *Le Messianisme chez les Juifs,* 28-37.

3 *Targ. Jonathan* on Isa. xi, 1; *Shir rabba* 4, 8.

4 See Weber, § 46, 78.   5 *Dialog. cum Tryphone* c. 49.

6 *Bammidbar rabba* c. 14; *Bereshith rabba* c. 85.

7 *Bereshith rabba,* 85.

Old Testament, the result is a very wide difference. The narrow, national, materialistic power of the pharisaical Messianic kingdom, pertaining to this world only, stands in striking contrast to the world-embracing spiritual *kingdom of God.* It is true it based itself upon the religious fundamental Law of the Torah and had a theocratic character, but in principle it was conceived as thoroughly earthly and political.

The figure of the suffering and dying *Servant of God* was naturally no longer suited to this frame. It was the greatest conceivable annoyance to the Jews. Only rarely did a Rabbi dare to apply the descriptions of Isaias and the book of Wisdom (ii, 12-20) of the sufferings of the " just " to the Messiah. Rabbinical Judaism was deaf and blind to these Messianic prophecies. Dalman[1] and Lagrange[2] have clearly demonstrated this state of the case, which apologists even now often overlook. But the supernatural and supernational *Son of Man* of Daniel became also detached from the pharisaical notion of the Messiah, not to speak of *Emmanuel.* Only the *Son of David* remained, the purely earthly and Jewishly interpreted offspring of the great king, who was to lead the national power of the Torah to victory.

3. *The Apocalyptic and Eschatological Notion of the Messiah.*

Running parallel with the official Messianic notion of rabbinical theology, and of the great mass of the Jewish people was the eschatological and apocalyptic conception. This bore more the character of a conventicle religion, scarcely touched the masses, and represented a sect, in so far as it based its conclusions on apocryphal books, in contrast to the authoritative theology of the Synagogue, instead of evolving its doctrines, according to the rabbinical rule, only out of the canonical writings of the Old Testament.

The prevalence of *apocalyptic ideas* was in full swing from 160 B.C. to A.D. 120.[3] Its more important literary productions, in so far as they concern our purpose, are the following : The *Book of Henock,*[4] the original manuscript of

---

[1] *Der leidende und sterbende Messias der Synagoge im ersten nachchristlichen Jahrtausend* (Berlin, 1888).

[2] *Le Messianisme chez les Juifs,* 236-251, 259.

[3] For more exact information concerning the origin and age of the separate apocalyptic writings, see Schürer, *Geschichte des jüdischen Volkes,* iii, 190-293 (1898) ; E. Kautzsch, *Die Apokryphen des A. T.,* i (Tübingen, 1900) ; P. Holz, *Jüdische Eschatologie* (Tübingen, 1903).

[4] See Charles, *The Ethiopic Version of the Book of Enoch* (Oxford, 1906) ; a Greek-German edition by Radermacher and Flemming, *Das Buch Henoch* in *Die griechischen christlichen Schriftsteller der drei ersten Jahrhunderte* (1901) ; German translation by Beer, " Das Buch Henoch," in E. Kautzsch's *Die Apokryphen und Pseudepigraphen des A. T.* ii, 117-210 ; L. Gry, *Quand furent composées les paraboles d'Hénoch,* 103-141 (Muséon, 1909), and *Le Messianisme des paraboles d'Hénoch et la théologie juive contemporaine,* 143-154 (Muséon, 1909).

which dates from the time of the Machabees, and whose most important parts, the metaphorical discourses,[1] originated in the last decades before Christ; the *Book of Jubilees, or the Little Genesis,* from the time of John Hyrcanus;[2] the *Assumption of Moses,* written about six years after Christ;[3] the ante-christian Jewish portions of the *Sybilline Oracles;*[4] and, finally, two manuscripts concluded only after the destruction of Jerusalem—viz., the *Apocalypse of Esdras,*[5] also called the " Fourth Book of Esdras," and the *Apocalypse of Baruch.*[6]

The *Messianic ideas* in the *apocalyptic writings* are certainly often amalgamated with the rabbinical. Pharisaical and apocalyptic views at the outset whirl about in a confused mass. The older apocalyptic writers still held fast, however, wholly or in part, to the earthly, temporal Messianic king of the Synagogue; but when the prospects of the realization of the Messianic-Davidic kingdom, after the downfall of the Machabees and the beginning of the time of Herod, vanished more and more, many zealots doubted whether they should live to see it in this thoroughly corrupted world. They clung now narrowly and exclusively to the prophecy of Daniel about the Son of Man, who was to appear in transcendent might only at the end of the world, in order to place himself at the head of a supermundane kingdom of God.

In contrast to the hope of the future, previously held, which had kept wholly within the limits of the present world, all the Messianic ideas were now transported into the supermundane and the hereafter. With the coming of the Messianic age a new phase of the world will begin in the cosmological sense. This phase of the final period is, in all respects, in violent contrast to the present one. This temporal phase is under the dominion of the powers hostile to God—viz., Satan and his visible and invisible confederates. The future phase, in the world hereafter, will be under the dominion of God and his Messiah only. Both epochs are absolutely separated. The earthly condition of the world must first be destroyed before the supermundane Messianic phase can be ushered in.

Hence the Messianic salvation will come entirely from above, to the exclusion of all earthly relations whatsoever. The earth, on which it appears, will first be renewed from above, or else

---

[1] c. 37-71.

[2] Charles, *The Book of Jubilees, or the Little Genesis* (London, 1902).

[3] Charles, *The Assumption of Moses* (London, 1897).

[4] I use the edition of Joh. Geffken, *Die Oracula Sybillina,* in *den griechischen christlichen Schriftstellern der ersten drei Jahrhunderte* (Leipzig, 1902).

[5] *The fourth Book of Ezra* (Bensley, 1895); Leon Vaganay, *Le problème eschatologique dans le quatrième livre d'Esdras* (Paris, 1906).

[6] Fritzsche, *Libri apocryphi Veteris Testamenti* (Lipsiæ, 1871), German translation by Victor Ryssel; *Die Apokalypsen des Baruch,* ii, 402-457).

be let down directly from heaven. The blessings of the Messianic age, even those which are wholly sensuous, will be stored up in heaven until the coming of the Messiah. Above all, however, the Messiah himself is, in his origin, nature, life and work, entirely transcendental, pertaining exclusively to the other world. Pre-existing in heaven, he will descend thence at the conclusion of this earthly period, merely to decide the fate of men, as Judge, and to set himself up as the Messianic regent of the new world. In a word, while the popularly conceived Jewish Messiah and his kingdom are thoroughly earthly, and develop their activity in this world and period, the apocalyptic Messiah belongs entirely to the other world, produces his stage-effect (for one cannot call it by any other name) by ushering in a new phase of world history, and founds his dominion as a *post-mundum* kingdom of heaven.

Many apocalyptic writers think that this kingdom will last for ever, while others suppose that it will be relieved after a longer or shorter period by the resurrection of the dead, the Last Judgement and a condition of eternal duration in heaven or hell.[1] Hence the modern writers on the subject are wont to call the *apocalyptic Messianic ideas eschatological* because in them everything is concentrated on the last things, on the end of this period of the world and on the succeeding transcendental Messianic world.

The eschatological element is also the only difference between the *rabbinical and the apocalyptic Messianic standpoints*. The stage manager, the stage itself and the *mise en scène* are different in both; but fundamentally the same piece is played, whether in one place or another—namely, that of putting Israel, in a strongly materialistic sense, into a position of *national world supremacy*. One would not believe it possible, yet it is really so. The Messiah will first subdue all the enemies of God's people and drive the kings from their thrones and kingdoms[2] by the mere breath of his mouth and the sharpness of his purely forensic judgement.[3] Then he will award to the pious Jews dominion "over the whole earth, which is under heaven, and they shall reign over all nations ᴀ ᴛ ᴀ and shall possess the whole earth."[4] All the

---

[1] See the representations of the eschatological apocalyptists in W. Bousset's *Jesu Predigt im Gegensatz zum Judentum* (1892), and *Die Religion des Judentums im neutestl. Zeitalter*, 230-273 (1903); Paul Volz, *Jüdische Eschatologie von Daniel bis Akiba* (1903); W. Baldensperger, *Die messianisch-apocalyptischen Hoffnungen des Judentums* (1903); Hugo Gressmann, *Der Ursprung der israelitisch-jüdischen Eschatologie* (1905); Gustav Hönnike, *Das Judenchristentum im 1 u. 2 Jahrhundert*, 69-74 (1908); Lagrange, *Le Messianisme chez les Juifs*, 37-136 (1909).

[2] *Oracula Sybillina* iii, 652 ff.; *Henoch* 46, 4-6; 52, 4-9; *Apoc. Baruch* 39, 7-40, 2; 70, 2-10; 72, 2-6.

[3] *Henoch* 45, 3; 55, 4; 62, 2-11; 69, 27; IV *Esdras* 13, 25-28, 32-38.

[4] *Jub.* 32, 19; cf. *Henoch*, 92, 4.

Gentiles shall fall down before them, shall render them homage, cry to them for mercy and listen to their every word.[1] They will cut the throats of sinners and mercilessly kill them.[2] The Lord will deliver their enemies into their hands, and their yoke shall weigh heavily upon them.[3] " Then shalt thou be happy, O Israel, and shalt mount on the neck and wings of the eagle."[4] " And God will raise thee on high and make thee float in the starry heaven, and thou shalt look down upon thine enemies on earth, and thou shalt recognize them and rejoice."[5]

Simultaneously with the national world supremacy, Israel will be inundated with an abundance of all the sensible blessings conferred by the Messiah. The old Jerusalem, the object of longing to every Israelite, will be pulled down and superseded, and the Messiah will bring a new Jerusalem[6] which had existed before the Fall in Paradise, had since then been preserved in heaven, and from there will now descend.[7] This new Jerusalem will far surpass the ancient one in beauty and splendour.[8] The Messiah will gather together in it all pious Israelites.[9] " All who have been killed or dispersed " shall be brought home again in chariots on the wings of the wind.[10] In Jerusalem, around the Temple, the tower of which will stretch upward to heaven,[11] the happy Israelites will revel in the protection and blessing of the Messiah.[12] " Bliss will everywhere manifest itself, and peace will appear. . . . Health will descend in the dew, and sickness will depart. . . . And joy shall prevail over the whole earth."[13] The wild beasts will come to serve mankind.[14] Nature will be fabulously prolific.[15] On one vine-stock there shall be 1,000 vines, and on one vine 1,000 bunches of grapes, and on one bunch 1,000 grapes, and one single grape will give a cask of wine.[16] People will not become old and weary of life. At the age of 1,000 years they will still be as children and boys.[17] They will live till they have gotten 1,000 children.[18] Women will bear children without pain; reapers shall not become weary, nor shall builders be exhausted.[19] All the pious shall swim in

---

[1] *Henoch,* 90, 30.   [2] *id.,* 94, 7; 98, 12.   [3] *id.,* 95, 3-7.
[4] The Roman eagle is certainly here meant. See Schürer ii, 540.
[5] *Assumptio Mosis* 10, 8-10.
[6] *Henoch* 53, 6; 90, 28, 29; cf. *Jub.* 1, 17, 27, 29; *Orac. Sibyll.* iii, 657, 776.
[7] *Apoc. Baruch* 4, 2-6; IV *Esdras* 7, 26; 8, 52; 10, 44-59.
[8] *Henoch* 53, 6; 90, 28; IV *Esdras,* 7, 26.   [9] *Henoch* 90, 30.
[10] *id.,* 57; 90, 32.   [11] *Orac. Sibyll.* v, 426.
[12] IV *Esdras* 7, 27-28; 12, 34; 13, 48-50.   [13] *Apoc. Baruch* 73, 2.
[14] *Orac. Sibyll.* iii, 787-794; *Apoc. Baruch* 73-74.
[15] *Orac. Sibyll.* iii, 620-623; *Henoch* 10, 18-19.
[16] *Apoc. Baruch* 29, 5-8; see Papias in *Irenæus* v, 33, 3, where instead of 1,000, 10,000 is the figure given.
[17] *Jub.* 23, 27.   [18] *Henoch* 10, 17; *Apoc. Baruch* 73, 3.
[19] *Apoc. Baruch* 73, 2-3; 7, 74, 1.

riches.[1] The Messiah will bestow upon them all the joys and pleasures which they can possibly desire.[2]

We see that all this sounds as genuinely rabbinical as the rabbinical hopes of the Messiah to be found in *Mishna,* the *Talmud* and *Midrash* itself. Like the rabbinical ideas of the Messiah, those of the apocalyptists are also a product of narrow Jewish patriotism.[3] In both cases the kingdom of the Messiah and the kingdom of God are looked upon as essentially a national, sensuously glorious world-power, at the head of which Jehovah and his representative, the Messiah, are to reign.

The eschatological and apocalyptic conceptions of the Messiah are far inferior to the general Jewish conceptions characteristic of the Synagogue. Although the Messiah of the Rabbis is more or less identical with the national king, he had, nevertheless, a very real and (viewed from the standpoint of Jewish patriotism) also an ideal significance. He was, by his own personal holiness and justice, to make himself the Redeemer of the nation, though certainly only in a purely earthly sense. He was himself, then, finally to consummate the great national act, and so, with good reason, wield the sceptre over Israel. The whole Messianic national drama is, therefore, psychologically, from beginning to end, not badly constructed by the Rabbis, even if it does remain only a drama. But nothing of this applies to the eschatological and apocalyptic Messiah. *He* does nothing, teaches nothing, redeems nothing, and does not even exist on this earth. He merely springs upon the stage as a *Deus ex machina,* drives those who are not Jews out of the theatre, and amuses himself at their expense, together with the remaining pious Israelites. No wonder that this illogical Messianic rôle is not found at all in many of the apocalyptic writings, and that they do not even mention the Messiah, but only bring about the shifting of the scenes—from this world to that, and from pagan to Jewish power—by means of unnamed agencies, or even by Jehovah himself, the God of the Jewish covenant.

With the Old Testament notion of the Messiah the eschatological-apocalyptic notion has nothing more to do. The latter takes from the Old Testament only the model of Daniel's Son of Man, yet it detaches this from the Son of David, the Servant of God and Emmanuel, as well as, in general, from the whole teaching of the Old Testament concerning the kingdom of God, and retains only an imaginary, ethereal figure instead of the complete portrait of the Messiah.

---

[1] *Orac. Sibyll.* iii, 783.

[2] IV *Esdras* 7, 28; 9, 7-8; 12, 34; *Apoc. Baruch* 40, 2; 73, 1.

[3] It cannot, however, be denied that apocalyptic literature contains, nevertheless, also many golden grains obtained from the Prophets or from a tradition which had been nourished by the Prophets.

We have herewith completed our pourtrayal of the Jewish notions of the Messiah, one of which may be called the official rabbinical Messianic conception, the other the eschatological conception, officially forbidden by the rabbis. It remains to be said that, together with the views which have been just mentioned, and which culminate essentially in the expectation of a theocratical political kingdom under the supremacy of the Torah as interpreted by the scribes, there were present occasionally others also which struck a much more ideal and deeply religious note.

And yet, although it is certain that these neighbouring currents of thought existed, it is difficult to indicate them in detail. Jewish literature leaves us almost in ignorance in this respect. Yet some rays of light from the Gospels illumine these *circles of pious Jews, whose ideal of the Messiah was derived principally from the predictions of the Prophets, and therefore was far superior to the common Jewish notion in simplicity and spirituality.*

At the commencement of the Gospel of St Luke we at once meet with such a circle. Zachary, the father of John the Baptist, utters his views of the Messiah in the following words : " Blessed be the Lord God of Israel : because he hath visited and wrought the redemption of his people; and hath raised up an horn of salvation to us in the house of David his servant; as he spoke by the mouth of his holy Prophets, who are from the beginning : salvation from our enemies, and from the hand of all that hate us; to perform mercy to our fathers, and to remember his holy testament; the oath which he sware to Abraham our father, that he would grant to us, that, being delivered from the hand of our enemies, we may serve him without fear, in holiness and justice before him, all our days. And thou, child, shalt be called the prophet of the Highest : for thou shalt go before the face of the Lord to prepare his ways; to give knowledge of salvation to his people, unto the remission of their sins, through the bowels of the mercy of our God, in which the Orient from on high hath visited us; to enlighten them that sit in darkness, and in the shadow of death; to direct our feet into the way of peace " (Luke i, 67-79).

Here the Messianic-davidic kingdom already has spiritualized features; holiness, righteousness, knowledge of salvation and redemption of the people of Israel are essential characteristics of the Messiahship. Yes, the Messiah will bring salvation, light and peace to the Gentiles also, who sit in darkness and the shadow of death. This is a high level of Messianic conception, very remote from the average Jewish mind; and yet it was so purely Jewish in sentiment and expression that it could not possibly have been invented by the Christian Evangelist. The Christians who had witnessed the Saviour's suffering, death, resurrection, and ascension, thought and spoke quite differently of the glorified Messiah.

A similar conclusion is reached by a study of the Messianic ideas of the aged Simeon, who was a just and devout man waiting for the consolation of Israel, and the Holy Ghost was upon him. And it was revealed unto him by the Holy Ghost that he should not see death before he had seen the Lord's Christ (Luke ii, 25). He now takes the child Jesus in his arms and praises God, saying : " Now thou dost dismiss thy servant, O Lord, according to thy word in peace, because my eyes have seen thy salvation, which thou hast prepared before the face of all peoples ; a light to the revelation of the Gentiles, and the glory of thy people Israel " (Luke ii, 28-32).

Here also the Messiah is no longer merely the glory of the people of Israel which is to make the Gentiles feel the theo-cratical kingdom of the Torah ; he is also the light which is to bring the religious revelation to the Gentiles as well as to the Israelites. Instead of the glorious Messianic kingdom, Simeon foresees in spiritual vision even the persecution and suffering of the Messiah, when he says to Mary : " Behold this child is set for the fall and for the resurrection of many in Israel, and for a sign which shall be contradicted. And thy own soul a sword shall pierce " (Luke ii, 34, 35).

It is true it can with reason be objected (but not from the side of rationalistic liberalism) that Simeon and Zachary had attained to a higher conception of the Messiah by means of a special divine illumination. But it is none the less true that the divine illumination was bestowed upon them precisely because it found in them an instrument which had not been weakened by narrow political and worldly views of the Messiah. There were, therefore, certainly in Judaism at that time spiritual oases in which the Messianic ideas of the Prophets still lived.

We may go still further and assert that *the number of those who did not regard the national theocratic kingdom as the chief characteristic and the principal work of the Messiah was greater than might appear at the first glance and in the light of the rabbinical and apocalyptic literature.* Adolf Harnack remarks in reference to this point : " Among all those in whom the moral and truly religious elements began to gain the upper hand, the image of the political and warlike king must have withdrawn itself, and that of the *prophet,* which had always gently influenced their imaginations, must have taken its place. It was hoped that the Messiah would bring God near, would create, in some way, justice, and would free souls from their torturing spiritual burdens." That there were then among the Jewish people those who believed and expected such a Messiah, or did not at least reject him in advance, already explains to us the history of John the

Baptist as we read it in our Gospels.   How elastic the conceptions of the Messiah must have been—if this utterly un-
kingly preacher of repentance in a mantle of camel's hair, who
announced to the degenerate people merely the approaching
judgement, could be himself taken for the Messiah!   And
when we further read in the Gospels that not a few among
the people took Jesus for the Messiah, only because he
preached powerfully and healed by working miracles,[1] how
thoroughly changed the Messianic picture appears!   It is true
they saw in these works of the Saviour only the beginning,
and expected that the worker of miracles would soon discard
the last veil of concealment and " establish the kingdom; but
this was enough for them to be able to greet, as the Promised
One, a man with whose origin and previous life they were
acquainted, and who had done nothing but preach repentance,
announce the nearness of the kingdom of heaven and heal
the sick."[2]

Nevertheless, when it really came to the point of recognizing
him definitely as the Messiah, in spite of the fact that he had
positively repudiated the establishment of the earthly Messianic kingdom, the higher conception of the Messiah, even
in that class of the people, did not stand the test, but rejected
him who dared to say : " My kingdom is not of this world."

II.—Christ's Idea of the Messiah.

1. Rejection of the Messianic Notions of the Rabbis and Apocalyptic Writers.

In view of the explanations thus far given concerning the
Old Testament, rabbinical and apocalyptic conceptions of
the Messiah, it should now no longer be very difficult to
determine in what sense Jesus claimed to be the Messiah.

The most obvious thing to be done is, first of all, to compare the Messianic ideas of Jesus with those of the Rabbis,
because these were nearest to him in point of time, were
everywhere in circulation around him, met him wherever he
went, were on everybody's lips, and were firmly rooted in the
heads of almost all his associates and of his people.   It is
easily comprehensible that the evolutionary historical view,
according to which Jesus simply developed out of the Jewish
society of that time, makes the Saviour at once adopt the
generally understood, common idea of the Messiah held by
his rabbinical contemporaries.

But nowhere has the evolutionary theory suffered a more
decisive defeat than here.   *Between rabbinical pharisaism and*

---

[1] That the Messiah would prove himself to be such by miracles and
prophetic knowledge was the opinion of all Jews.   This is shown both
from rabbinical literature and from many passages in the Gospels.

[2] *Wesen des Christentums*, 86 f.

Jesus exist the greatest differences imaginable. The more important critics of modern times have not been able to shut their eyes to this consideration. To-day almost all of them give up the idea of seeing in the Messianic notions of the Pharisees the model which Jesus is said to have copied.

It is true some Jewish scholars[1] still maintain that Jesus united in his person simply pharisaical thought with a Galilean temperament. Also, according to Ed. von Hartmann, " it never occurred to him to make the slightest change in the popular expectation and conception of the Messiah and his task."[2] A. Neumann[3] and Otto Pfleiderer[4] assert, all facts to the contrary, that Jesus adopted the ideal of the Messiah with all the characteristics which it had for his time. Only they prudently add that he did reject the warlike side of the rabbinical notion of the Messiah, and that he did not wish to be a Messianic king in the sense of a liberator of the people and a conqueror of the Gentiles.[5] But the popular notion of the Messiah had essentially only this one side, as is clearly demonstrated by what we have previously adduced. Late critics, therefore, who still describe the Saviour as the rabbinical Messiah, are able to do so only from ignorance of what the rabbinical notions of the Messiah really were.

The question is, moreover, settled by the undeniable fact that Jesus was persecuted and condemned to death by his pharisaical contemporaries because he prohibited the popular rabbinical conceptions of the Messiah, and opposed to them his own personal, fundamentally different Messianic ideas.

But did this Messianic idea of Jesus agree, perhaps, with the eschatological and apocalyptic notions of the Messiah? The evolutionary school must evidently assert this, unless it is willing to give up the idea of seeing in Jesus only a splendid personification and further development of ideas already existing at the time. Hence the strong eschatological tendency in the latest research into christology. Albrecht Schweitzer, the historian of this research, entitles the chapter of his book dealing with this subject " Logical Eschatology," and proclaims himself the most extreme and decided leader of the eschatological school.[6]

The eschatological view of the life of Jesus had been already

---

[1] *Revue des Etudes Juives,* t. lii, 9 (1906).

[2] *Das Christentum des Neuen Testaments,* 58 (1905).

[3] *Jesus, wer er geschichtlich war,* 154 (1904).

[4] *Das Urchristentum,* 2nd ed., i, 665; *Die Entstehung des Christentums,* 58 (1905).

[5] Neumann, *l.c.;* Pfleiderer, *Entstehung,* 101.

[6] Albrecht Schweitzer, *Von Reimarus zu Wrede* (Tübingen, 1906), and also previously in his pamphlet, *Das Messianitäts- und Leidensgeheimniss; eine Skizze des Lebens Jesu* (Tübingen, 1901).

introduced by Reimarus,[1] Keim,[2] Colani,[3] Volkmar[4] and Wilhelm Weissenbach.[5]

Wilhelm Baldensperger[6] undertook to judge all the Messianic utterances of Jesus from the viewpoint of eschatology. For him Jesus is the fiery prophet who announces simply the apocalyptic final catastrophe, in the sense of the Book of Henoch, as immediately at hand, and represents himself as the man who will speedily appear in the clouds of heaven to carry out this catastrophe.

Johannes Weiss[7] connects the views of Jesus concerning the kingdom of God entirely with this catastrophe. The kingdom of God, instead of being a Messianic organization of quiet and gradual development, which grows here on earth as divine seed, and at the end of the world will be brought to heaven as a precious harvest, whirls thither, according to Weiss, in an apocalyptic hurricane, which destroys heaven and earth, in order to create for itself room for a new world era.

Now, last of all, comes Schweitzer, who reproaches his predecessors because they acquiesced in the idea of interpreting the Messiah and the kingdom of God eschatologically instead of " letting the whole public activity of Jesus, and the events connected or not connected with it, be elucidated by eschatology."[8]   Thus he drags the whole Gospel over to the volcanic ground of the apocalyptic writings, attributing to the Saviour a specially apocalyptic soul, and making him out to be an apocalyptic fanatic who sees, thinks, preaches and hopes for nothing else than a frightful cataclysm.[9]

In Germany the eschatologists were joined, among others, by G. Dalman,[10] Hollmann,[11] Zimmermann[12] and the Zürich professor Arnold Meyer.[13]   In transferring the ideas of the German to French soil, Alfred Loisy evaporated them in his usual way.[14]

---

[1] Schweitzer, *Von Reimarus zu Wrede*, 16-20.   [2] *id.*, 211.

[3] *Jésus-Christ et les croyances messianiques de son temps* (Strassburg, 1864).

[4] *Jesus Nazarenus und die erste christliche Zeit* (Zürich, 1882).

[5] *Der Wiederkunftsgedanke Jesu* (1873).

[6] *Das Selbstbewusstsein Jesu im Lichte der messianischen Hoffmungen seiner Zeit*, 2nd ed. (Strassburg, 1892). A third edition with another title appeared in 1903.

[7] *Die Predigt Jesu vom Reiche Gottes*, 2nd ed., 58-175 (Göttingen 1900).   [8] *Von Reimarus zu Wrede*, 347.

[9] *id.*, 347-395.   [10] *Die Worte Jesu*, 259 (Leipzig, 1898).

[11] *Welche Religion hatten die Juden als Jesus auftrat?* 73 (1905).

[12] *Der historische Wert der ältesten Ueberlieferung im Markus evangelium*, 97, 128 (Leipzig, 1905).

[13] *Das Leben nach dem Evangelium Jesu*, 5 (1905).

[14] Loisy, *L'Evangile et l'Eglise*, 53 ff. (Paris, 1902); *Les Evangiles synoptiques*, 192 f., 212 f., 242 f. (Macon, 1907). He was joined by Chapuis, *Revue de Théologie et de Philosophie*, 15 f. (1904); Monnier, *La mission historique de Jésus*, 39, 82 f. (1906); A. Causse, *L'Evolution de l'espérance messianique dans le Christianisme primitif* (Paris, 1908).

We must be grateful to the latest eschatologists that they, in contrast to the halfway attitude of their predecessors, knew how to adapt the Jewish apocalyptic ideas in their full extent to the entire life of Jesus. As Johannes Weiss and Albrecht Schweitzer both rightly claim, the watchword can be only "Either eschatological or not eschatological."[1] Either the apocalyptic eschatology can be carried out logically, genuinely, and without exception, or we cannot suppose Jesus to have been under the influence of the apocalyptic notions of his contemporaries at all.

But this clear, resolute and logical statement of the case at once amounts to a *refutation and decided rejection of the eschatological and apocalyptic thesis*. Merely a glance into the Gospel, on the one hand, and into Jewish apocalyptists, on the other, is sufficient to let us see the impossibility of logically interpreting the life of Jesus eschatologically. The life of Jesus is radiant with bright, sunny optimism; his whole being is, together with the greatest moral seriousness, full of joyous, cheerful sentiments which even scandalize the sanctimonious Pharisees. The Jewish apocalyptic ideas, on the contrary, emit poison through their gloomy pessimism, which considers the whole world as hopelessly lost, since it looks upon it as not only morally but physically evil. The Gospel of Jesus, in spite of its strong tendency to deal with the future and with the next world, is full of much that is real and valuable in relation to this one. It is a unique union of the Now and Then, so that the cleavages between this life and the next are all bridged over, and its whole view of the universe impels man towards something broad and great—a mighty line passing through time and eternity.

The apocalyptic views are those of a somnambulist, to whom the present is merely an appearance and an illusion, without any connection with the æon beyond this world of time. Life in the present, therefore, is without value or reality—merely a mode of reckoning with the future and trifling with an approaching ghost. The Gospel of Jesus insists strongly upon moral improvement, religious depth, sincere piety and inward holiness (" Be ye perfect even as your Father in heaven is perfect "), and promotes this perfection through untiring and undaunted teaching and admonition from person to person, from circle to circle, from infinitely patient labour on a small scale to intensive work upon the masses. The apocalyptic school, however, does not take a step to further the improvement and the ennobling of man, and conceives the future Messianic age from a purely cosmological standpoint, devoid of any higher religious life and any deeper union with God, and meanwhile thinks of nothing but awaiting with open mouth and folded arms the signs from heaven of the final catastrophe—" The Jews require signs "

[1] Schweitzer, 235.

(1 Cor. i, 22). The Gospel of Jesus, who works among the people and suffers and dies upon the Cross for sinners, instead of, like the apocalyptist, sitting down in a corner and writing one of those wonderful books which can never sufficiently gloat over the drastic punishment of the Gentiles and the beatification of Judaism—the Gospel of Jesus, although imbued with all possible love for its ancestral soil and for the chosen people of God, is nevertheless thoroughly universal and remote from all Jewish narrowness, and, above all, is opposed to the national, political and material Jewish dreams. The eschatological apocalyptist has eyes and ears only for petty, limited Jewish patriotism and the chauvinistic, sensuously intoxicating music of the future. Truly, to try to bring together and to blend in one the Gospel of Jesus and the later Jewish teachings of the apocalyptists, is to turn the facts completely upside down.

The best connoisseurs and historians of later Judaism, like Bousset, Schürer and Wellhausen, all of whom also belong to the liberal Protestant school, pronounce every such attempt hopeless.[1]

In fact, the eschatologists accomplish their artistic feat only by diminishing the differences of both sides. To Weiss, Schweitzer and Loisy the apocalyptic appears only in its eschatological, futuristic form, while its national and political soul is entirely, or almost entirely, overlooked. Baldensperger places such a different estimate on the eschatological and apocalyptic views that they can finally be defined as a Messianic expectation, freed from the earthly political ideal, and transported into the region of the supernatural.[2] That the eschatological catastrophe, with the appearance of the Messiah for the Last Judgement, is only the mould or melting-pot which contains the worldly patriotic hopes of Judaism, is forgotten by the rabid eschatologists.

They refashion the Gospel also in a similar way. Whatever in any way suits their ideas of eschatology is retained as genuine Gospel truth and the word of the Lord; but the utterances and motives of Jesus, which are not eschatological, are interpreted in an eschatological sense, and all that is unadaptable in this way is discarded as an unhistorical accretion. Thus they succeed in forcing the toned-down likeness of Jesus on to the toned-down model of the apocalyptic. But as soon as the complete Gospel is compared with the complete

---

[1] W. Bousset, *Jesu Predigt in ihrem Gegensatz zum Judentum* (1892); *Die jüdische Apokalyptik in ihrer religionsgeschichtlichen Herkunft und ihrer Bedeutung für das N. T.* (1903); E. Schürer, *Das messianische Selbstbewusstsein Jesu Christi* (1903); Jul. Wellhausen, *Israelitische und jüdische Geschichte,* 373, 386, 6th ed. (Berlin, 1907); *Skizzen* vi, 187 ff.

[2] Baldensperger, *Die messianisch-apokalyptischen Hoffnungen des Judentums,* 173 (Strassburg, 1903).

apocalyptic, the alleged kinship between them, to say nothing of their alleged identity, vanishes.

This applies especially to the Messianic passages in the Gospel. Eschatology would prove itself correct only if all the Messianic utterances, without exception, identified themselves with apocalyptic ideas—that is, if Jesus did not claim to be the Messiah in the present world, but hoped to become so only in the future at his second advent, and by means of this second advent to preside over the Last Judgement. But the utterances of Jesus in the Gospel say just the contrary.

Already, in his earthly life, his activity, his suffering and death, Jesus claims to be the Messiah, and wishes to be considered as such. His return for the Last Judgement is only the solemn conclusion, the highest and final triumph of his Messianic revelation.

John the Baptist sends messengers to inquire of Jesus whether he is the One who should come—that is, the Messiah —and Jesus answers by pointing out the miracles wrought by him, which, according to tradition, indicate the coming and the presence of the Messianic era, and prove the performer of these miracles to be the Messiah, who has already appeared and is active (Matt. xi, 5; Luke vii, 22; Isa. xxx, 5; lxi, 1). If John, as the eschatologists assert without cause,[1] in making his inquiry, had thought of the apocalyptic Son of Man coming for the Last Judgement, then it is only so much the more significant that Jesus energetically brings his answer down to the level of present-day realities, and proves himself to be the Saviour, who has *already come* and is already engaged in Messianic activity.

In Cesarea Philippi, Jesus inquires what the views of the multitude and the disciples are concerning the Son of Man as he was then living before them. Peter confesses at once : " Thou *art* the Messiah, the Son of God." And Jesus commends the Apostle, declares that his faith has been supernaturally revealed to him, and corroborates it without the slightest qualification. " Then he commanded his disciples that they should tell no one that he *was* Jesus, the Christ " (Matt. xvi, 20).

The woman of Samaria says to him : " I know that the Messias cometh (who is called Christ) : therefore when he cometh, he will tell us all things." The woman of Samaria, therefore, is not speaking of the apocalyptic Messiah, who will come only to judge the world, but the Messiah who " will tell us all things," who will appear as a prophet, and who is moved by love for his people, not by speculations about the approaching end of the world. And Jesus declares : " I *am* he who am speaking with thee." The Samaritans, however, fascinated by the charm of his speech, believed on him on

[1] Loisy, *L'Evangile et l'Eglise*, 54.

account of his teaching, and said : " We ourselves have heard him, and know that this is indeed the Saviour of the world " (John iv, 25 and 41, 42).

Jesus asks the man who was born blind : " Dost thou believe in the Son of God?" He answered and said : " Who is he, Lord, that I may believe in him?" And Jesus said to him : " Thou hast both seen him, and it is he that talketh with thee " (John ix, 35-37). Thereupon the Jews in the Temple surrounded him and said to him : " How long dost thou hold our souls in suspense? If thou *be* the Christ, tell us plainly." Jesus answered them : " *I speak to you* and you believe not. The works that I do in the name of my Father, they give testimony of me " (John x, 24). Therefore, Jesus not only claims to be the Messiah already here on earth, but he casts in their teeth the fact that he has given the most real and infallible proofs of his present Messiahship.

Soon after he has to justify himself before the highest tribunal of the nation for this very confession. The High Priest asks him : " *Art* thou the Christ, the Son of the blessed God?" " *I am,*" was the answer (Mark xiv, 61, 62). Caiphas presses the question under the most solemn oath : " I adjure thee by the living God, that thou tell us if thou be the Christ, the Son of God." " Thou hast said it," affirms Jesus (Matt. xxvi, 63). " *Art* thou, then, the Son of God?" " You say that *I am,*" replies Jesus (Luke xxii, 67-70), and adds : " You shall see the Son of Man sitting on the right hand of the power of God, and coming with the clouds of heaven " (Mark xiv, 62).

Both question and answer are astonishingly clear. In vain do the eschatologists assert that Jesus, by these last words, wished to explain the confession that he is the Messiah in the apocalyptic sense, that he will not become the Messiah until he returns for the Last Judgement.[1] Rather does Jesus say most emphatically that he *is already* the real Messiah, and that he *will* come again, as the Messiah, at the end of the world.

The Saviour expresses himself in precisely the same way before Pilate. The Prefect asks him : " Art thou the king of the Jews?"—that is, the Messianic king?[2] " Thou sayest it," answers Jesus affirmatively (Luke xxiii, 3 ; Mark xv, 2 ; Matt. xxvii, 11). Yet he at once repudiates the possible misconception that he claims to be an earthly, worldly Messianic king : " Thou sayest that I am a king. Yet my kingdom is not of this world. For this was I born, and for this came I into the world, that I should give testimony to the truth " (John xviii, 36, 37). Thus Jesus claims to be the king of

[1] Loisy, p. 54.

[2] That this is the correct interpretation of the question appears from Luke xxiii, 2.

truth, the spiritual Messiah, and this already now; in fact, from the first moment of his earthly existence; not that he will become the Messiah only at the future judgement. His Messianic kingdom is not *of* this world, but it does exist already *in* this world.

2. *Adoption and Extension of the Old Testament Notion of the Messiah.*

We come thus unexpectedly to the positive development of Jesus' notion of the Messiah. This is proved already to a considerable extent from the negative, repellent attitude of the Saviour towards the rabbinical and apocalyptic Messianic ideas of his contemporaries, just as every step which we have still to take in regard to the Gospels signifies, at the same time, a renewed rejection of these notions.

First of all, Jesus' conception of the *Kingdom of God.* According to the statements previously made, it may be considered certain that Jesus did not wish to found either a worldly theocracy of a political and material nature, in the rabbinical sense, nor a *post-mundane* theocracy of that nature in the apocalyptic sense. Rather does everything indicate that his ideal was directed to a spiritual, religious kingdom of God, in this world at its commencement, in the next world at its completion, and in its nature wholly supernatural. All the positive utterances of Jesus regarding the kingdom of God are confined within this compass.

The forerunner John had announced *the nearness of the kingdom.* " Do penance, for the kingdom of heaven is at hand " (Matt. iii, 2). Thereby he points to Jesus. Jesus himself takes up the same line of preaching. " He came preaching the Gospel of the kingdom of God, and saying : The time is accomplished, and the kingdom of God is at hand; repent and believe the Gospel " (Mark i, 14, 15). He also sent out the Twelve at first with the simplest announcement of the near approach of the kingdom into the world : " Preach, saying, The kingdom of heaven is at hand " (Matt. x, 7). The coming of Jesus and the commencement of his activity are equivalent, therefore, to the coming and beginning of the realization of the kingdom of heaven.

The preaching of the coming of the kingdom is immediately connected with the revelation of the miraculous powers of the Saviour. Not only does he himself make his own steps conspicuous by miracles, but he transmits the power of working them to his disciples and fellow-preachers of the kingdom : " Heal the sick, raise the dead, cleanse the lepers, cast out devils " (Matt. x, 8 and parallels). Through the performance of these Messianic deeds the proof will be established, not only that *the kingdom is approaching* (Luke ix, 10), but that

I.

it is already present : " If I by the Spirit of God cast out
devils, then is the kingdom of God come upon you " (Matt.
xii, 28). He considers his victories over the devils as so many
blows directed against the kingdom of Satan, and as a
triumph of the kingdom of God which has already arrived.
In exactly the same way he also calls his other miracles into
the lists as proofs for the kingdom of heaven which has
already begun (Matt. xi, 4-6).

At the same time he sets about *proclaiming the law of the
new kingdom*. Moving through cities and hamlets, he
preaches his doctrine everywhere, in the synagogues, in the
market-places, on lakes and on the slopes of mountains. This
doctrine is so truly the *Magna Charta* of the kingdom of
heaven that it is laconically called the " glad tidings [Gospel]
of the kingdom of God " (Matt. iv, 14; Luke viii, 1), " the
mystery of the kingdom of God " (Mark iv, 11), " the preaching of the kingdom of God " (Luke ix, 2); " the Law and the
Prophets were until John; from that time the kingdom of
God is preached " (Luke xvi, 16). Even the humblest of those
who accept the message of the kingdom is, therefore, greater
than John himself, who was only a forerunner of the kingdom
(Matt. xi, 11; Luke vii, 28). Referring to his own person and
his Gospel, Jesus can say to the Pharisees : " Lo, *the kingdom
of God is within you* " (Luke xvii, 21).

*A fundamental condition, therefore, for admission into the
kingdom* is faith in, and acceptance of, the Gospel (Mark
xvi, 16; John iii, 18, 36). To this is added the spiritual second
birth, " of water and of the Holy Spirit " (John iii, 3, 5), for
the forgiveness of sins (Mark iv, 12), as well as a new manner
of life on the ground of this spiritual second birth and in
accordance with the commandments of the Gospel (Matt.
vii, 21; xix, 8). Thus the kingdom of God presupposes a
complete spiritual transformation in every individual, and
requires, therefore, a decidedly chivalrous sentiment and
energy. Whoever does not prize and seek the " kingdom
of God and his justice " above everything (Matt. vi, 33),
whoever " putteth his hand to the plough and looketh back "
(Luke ix, 62), whoever does not put into the background,
and, if need be, abandon everything (Matt. v, 29; Luke
ix, 61; xviii, 29), and whoever is not ready to stake his own
life also (Luke xiv, 26) in order to gain the kingdom of God,
is not fit for it.

It is, therefore, easy to understand that the *kingdom of God
can extend only slowly and by constant efforts*. It will neither
announce itself by an earthly *coup d'état*, in the sense of the
Rabbis, with lightning speed and great external pomp, nor
will it fall from heaven as a complete *Malkuth*, in the apocalyptic sense (Luke xvii, 20). At its beginning it will be small
and inconspicuous, so that the great ones of the earth will not

notice it at all. Very gradually, however, it will grow, like the grain of mustard seed, until it becomes a tree, and will work from within outward, like the leaven, till it has transformed the whole world (Matt. xiii, 31; Luke xiii, 19). As the grain quietly germinates, sends up its blades, grows into ears, blossoms and finally is garnered in its maturity, so it is with the kingdom of God (Mark iv, 26-29) and with the children of the kingdom (Matt. xiii, 38). The Jews prove themselves to be unfruitful soil; therefore the kingdom of God will be taken from them and given to a nation yielding the fruits thereof (Matt. xxi, 43). *" And this Gospel of the kingdom shall be preached in the whole world for a testimony*[1] to all nations, and then shall the consummation come "—the judgement (Matt. xxiv, 14).

The judgement is the gate of entrance into the kingdom of God in the next world. It is closed against the kingdom of Satan, and condemns to the punishment of hell all those who on earth have belonged to the kingdom of evil. On the other hand, it is opened to the children of the kingdom of God, who finally inherit the kingdom prepared for them from the foundation of the world (Matt. xxv, 34). The kingdom of God on this earth is, both in its entirety and in its application to the individual man, only a commencement, a preliminary step, a preparation, for the everlasting kingdom of heaven in the world to come. In its final perfection, therefore, the kingdom is not yet complete. It is only in the act of approaching, and we must continually pray for its coming: " Thy kingdom come " (Luke xi, 2). As often as Jesus speaks of entry into the kingdom of God, he presupposes the kingdom, in this sense, to be a future event (Matt. v, 20; vii, 21). Whenever he pronounces the children of the kingdom of God on earth blessed he promises them the kingdom of God in the next world as a reward: " For theirs is the kingdom of heaven." " For they shall see God." " Then shall the righteous shine

---

[1] In opposition to the assertion made by some radical critics that Jesus wishes, in narrow chauvinism, to limit the kingdom of heaven to the Jews, Max Meinertz, *Jesus und die Heidenmission* (1908), and Fr. Spitta, *Jesus und die Heidenmission* (1909), prove that the Saviour wished to extend his Messianic salvation also to the Gentiles. See J. B. Major's " Did Christ contemplate the Admission of the Gentiles into the Kingdom of Heaven?" (*Expositor,* 385-399, Nov., 1909). Spitta, who is certainly beyond suspicion, expresses himself thus (p. 109) : " In direct opposition to Harnack's judgement, that the mission to the Gentiles did not lie within Jesus' field of vision, I am not content with the opinion that he imposed it on the hearts of his disciples after his resurrection, but I maintain that this task formed the desire of his soul from the very beginning, and that he not only did not abandon it when Gentiles came in his way, but actually sought them out by travelling where they were. One can, therefore, speak of Jesus as being really the first Christian missionary, who not only laid the foundation for Christian missions to the Gentiles by his ' intense universalism ' but whose own activity signifies its beginning."

forth as the sun in the kingdom of their Father." " And there shall come from the east and the west and the north and the south and shall sit down in the kingdom of God " (Luke xiii, 29). " That you may eat and drink at my table in my kingdom " (Luke xxii, 30). " I will not drink from henceforth of this fruit of the vine, until that day when I shall drink it with you new in the kingdom of my Father " (Matt. xxvi, 29).

If in this description of the blessedness of the kingdom there are some discordant tones which remind one of sensuous and earthly enjoyments, they are to be interpreted only metaphorically. *The whole teaching of Jesus in reference to the kingdom is so essentially spiritual, and he so effectually excludes from it the coarse ideas of his contemporaries, that we must see in the above expressions merely a strikingly figurative representation of the supersensuous bliss and blessedness of the kingdom of heaven.*

It could not have been explained otherwise, either to the disciples, who were thoroughly earthly in their ideas, or to the Oriental, who always wants to speak figuratively and can scarcely learn in any other way. Hence Jesus always pourtrays the kingdom of heaven under the metaphor of a Passover feast, a wedding feast, or a joyful feast, which he prepares for his disciples, and at which he himself goes about to serve his guests (Luke xxii, 16, 18). The unveiled picture of the blessedness of the kingdom of God, invisible to mortal eyes and incomprehensible to the carnal mind, is " *the eternal life* " near God and with God, together with the ineffable joys which are connected with it.

Accordingly, *the most important part and the completion of Christ's idea of the Messianic kingdom are located in the future,* not in the present. Jesus always directs our gaze upward and forward, from the kingdom itself and life in it, both of which go forward under many difficulties here below to the blessed perfection of the kingdom of heaven. Hope, expectation, longing for infinite perfection and blessedness in the world to come—these form the fundamental character of the religion of Christ and of Christianity.

Not exclusively, however. *The founding of the kingdom and its growth are accomplished in this present world.* The divine kingdom's grain of mustard seed is cast into the earth, germinates there, and grows and ripens its fruit before it is brought into heaven by the harvesting of the Last Judgement (Matt. xiii, 39). There will there be garnered only what was here sown (Gal. vi, 7). Time on earth for the sowing, eternity in heaven for the harvest, and between them the great day of judgement, when the sowing and the reaping will be estimated and valued according to their merits. In the Messianic kingdom of Jesus there is nothing sudden, nothing irregular, nothing partial. The idea of Christ and Christianity concerning the kingdom is that of a spiritual supremacy of God in man and over man on earth, and eternal supremacy over him in heaven, and, on the other hand, a spiritual approach to God on the part of man here, and an indissoluble union with God above; and all this through the mediation of Jesus.

In conformity with this is the interpretation which Jesus gives to the title *Son of Man*. We know that he bore by preference this Messianic title.[1] In Daniel vii, 23, etc., however, this appellation denotes the Messiah exclusively as a supernatural judge of the world and a glorious prince in the future kingdom of God. It is true Jesus claims to be the Son of Man in this complete sense, and, indeed, in this sense before any other;[2] but not exclusively. He prefers the title Son of Man precisely for the reason that it, on the one hand, in accordance with prophecy, expressed the *future dignity and glory of the Messiah,* while, on the other hand, according to the meaning of the word, it could be applied without difficulty to the *entire activity and life of the Saviour in this world.*

Thus Jesus enlarges this official name for the Messiah earthward and earthwide. As the Son of Man he becomes the herald of the glad tidings of the kingdom and the bringer of the work of salvation (Matt. xi, 19; xii, 32; xvi, 13; Luke vii, 34; xi, 30). As the Son of Man he has the power to forgive sins (Matt. ix, 6; Mark ii, 10; Luke v, 24), and, in contrast to the Mosaic Law, to declare his own authority as a teacher, and his own mode of action (Matt. xii, 8; Mark ii, 28; Luke vi, 5). As the Son of Man he sows the seed of the kingdom of God in human souls (Matt. xiii, 37), and calls sinners to form a part of this kingdom (Matt. ix, 13; Mark ii, 17; Luke v, 32). As the Son of Man he is come, not to destroy, but to rescue; not to be ministered unto, but to minister and to give his life a ransom for many (Matt. xviii, 11; xx, 28 and parallels). As the Son of Man he has not where to lay his head (Matt. viii, 20). As the Son of Man he must suffer much, must be rejected by the people, must be condemned by the scribes and High Priests, must die, and on the third day rise again.[3] Only then does he come as the Son of Man in the clouds of heaven, attended by angels, in view of the whole earth, in order to judge the world, to inflict the merited punishment of hell upon the wicked, and to bring home the good into the kingdom of his Father. Accordingly, Jesus certainly does not assume the name and title of the Son

---

[1] See F. Bard, *Der Sohn des Menschen. Eine Untersuchung über Begriff und Inhalt und Absicht solcher Jesus-Bezeichnung* (Wismar, 1908).

[2] Matt. ix, 27; x, 23; xiii, 41; xvi, 27; Mark viii, 38; xiii, 26; xiv, 62; Luke ix, 26; xii, 8, 40; xvii, 22; xviii, 8; xxi, 27, 36; xxii, 69.

[3] Matt. xii, 40; xvii, 9, 12, 21; xx, 18; Mark viii, 31; ix, 8, 30; x, 33; Luke ix, 22, 44; xviii, 31; xxiv, 7, 26; John iii, 14; viii, 28; xii, 34.

of Man merely in the eschatological meaning which it possesses in Daniel, but he puts into it the whole Messianic vocation and the entire Messianic activity, which begins with the incarnation and is fully consummated only in eternity.

Thereby the Son of Man takes the place of the *Son of David*. Everything of spiritual truth which, according to Old Testament prophecy, was found in the Messianic expression " Son of David," is carried over by Jesus into the appellation " Son of Man." The purely temporal, earthly and political conception of the Son of David, as it was held by most of his contemporaries, had to be rejected by the Saviour. In fact, in order to prevent an absolutely wrong idea of his Messiahship, and not to become a traitor to his own person and cause, *Jesus saw himself compelled to renounce, in part, even the formal title " Son of David," based though it was on the Old Testament.*

God had from the beginning announced the Messianic salvation as a dominion and a kingdom, and, correspondingly, the Messiah as a ruler and king. This was the happiest figure of speech that he could have chosen, and it also corresponded perfectly to reality, in so far as it was conceived as spiritual, not material and earthly. In order to make it still more accessible, comprehensible and popular to the chosen people, he announced the Redeemer as the King of Israel, and a king from the most brilliant dynastic family—that of David—who should rule for ever and bring an exuberance of blessings to both land and people. Although these promises appear, for the most part, in the garb of highly coloured temporal power and splendour, yet they were evidently intended to be merely, or at least chiefly, the figurative shell and external form of the spiritual blessings and benefits of the Messianic age. Even in those passages of the Old Testament, in which the Messianic ideals assume the most intense national and material colours, the Son of David still always appears as a worker of miracles, a priest and teacher of truth and righteousness, equipped with the choicest spiritual gifts of God, and sent for the salvation and prosperity of all nations.

Unmistakably, however, the increasing tendency of the Israelites to interpret the Messianic kingdom and its Prince, the Son of David, more and more in a national and political sense is revealed in the Old Testament; and when Jesus appeared men understood by the " Son of David," as we have seen, for the most part, only a national hero of the Jewish race. Judaism had taken the shell and the form for the essence and content of the Messianic prophecy.

Hence Jesus was obliged to shatter the shell, in order to preserve the real, intrinsic substance of his Messianic person and mission. *He only suffered men to call him the Son of David,* and caused the figure of the Son of David to retire behind that of the Son of Man; in fact, to disappear almost entirely.

It is true he is announced in advance by the angel as the " Son of the Most High, to whom the Lord God will give the throne of his father David, and he shall reign over the house of Jacob for ever, and of his kingdom there shall be no end " (Luke i, 32). Yet there follows immediately the thoroughly spiritual interpretation of this supremacy : " Thou shalt call his name Jesus, for he shall save his people from their sins " (Matt. i, 21). It is also true that the descent of Jesus from the house of David is continually emphasized (Matt. i, 1-6; Luke i, 27, 32, 69; ii, 4). For an abandonment of this lineage would have been, not only a denial of the historical fact, but would also have been equivalent to the abandonment of his Messiahship, since the Messiah must come from the house of David (John vii, 42). Also, when the multitudes greet him as the Son of David (Matt. xxi, 9, 15; Mark xi, 10), he may not refuse the ovation without denying his Messianic claims. And even when the blind and distressed implore him, as the Son of David, for help (Matt. ix, 27; xv, 22, 30), he heals and helps them, not only from the infinite tenderness of his heart, but because the Messiah, according to the prophet, was to prove himself a worker of miracles (Isa. xxix, 18; xxxv, 2; lxi, 1).

Yet he decidedly opposes the pharisaical supposition that the Messiah, by nature, is only David's natural descendant, and in his vocation only a successor to David in a worldly kingdom (Matt. xxii, 42 and parallels), and *he never once in his whole life calls himself the Son of David,* in order not to recognize the distorted rabbinical portrait of the Messiah as correct.

Moreover, the glorious title " Son of David " was less suitable to the Saviour also because he claimed to be here on earth, before all else, the *"Servant of God," the Redeemer and the Saviour of sinners,* in the literal meaning of those words.

Before he could enter upon his royal supremacy over the kingdom of God, he must first bring it into the world and again enrol individuals as well as humanity as a whole in that kingdom, which, through sin, had been destroyed. First, Mediator and Founder of the kingdom, then its King. In this way, then, Jesus claims to be merely the Mediator, Saviour and Redeemer. As the Hellenic world conferred these titles on its victorious hero-kings who brought to it political freedom, so does Jesus also claim for himself the names of " Saviour " and " Redeemer." He translates for himself the word Messiah by the other title, " Saviour of the world " (John iv, 25, 42). But for him it is a case of spiritual redemption from sin and guilt. Of him the angel had said : " Thou shalt call his name Jesus (Saviour, Redeemer, Deliverer), for he shall save his people from their sins " (Matt. i, 21). Now, Jesus himself confirms this interpretation of his name, and thereby outlines *the principal programme of his Messianic activity as that of redeeming people from their sins:* " The Son of Man is come to seek and to save that which was lost " (Luke xix, 10; Matt. xviii, 11).

No one who has read the Gospels will be able to doubt that fighting against the sin of guilty man, and bringing him back to God, formed the one great occupation of the life of Jesus. Not only was his religious activity concentrated in this, but even the physical benefits which he conferred and the miracles he wrought had always that *one* aim of redemption from sin and its forgiveness. He heals the paralytic at the Pool of Bethsaida, and admonishes him : " Behold, thou art made whole : sin no more, lest some worse thing happen to thee " (John v, 14). He frees the woman taken in adultery from the hands of her pharisaical accusers, and says : " Go and sin no more " (John viii, 11). He takes the sinful woman in the house of Simon under his protection, gives to her the comforting assurance, " Thy sins are forgiven thee," and remarks to the astonished Pharisees : " Many sins are forgiven her, because she hath loved much " (Luke vii, 47). And when the Pharisees regard this as an intrusion into the domain of God's power, and, accordingly, as an act of blasphemy, Jesus asserts and proves by the miracle that follows that " the Son of Man hath power on earth to forgive sins " (Mark ii, 1-13). In a word, *the Saviour's activity aims practically ever and always at effecting through his mediation the forgiveness of sins and at dispensing it himself.*

But also, and above all, it aims at *earning and meriting the remission of sins for men.* We know that the mediator, in the book of Isaias, is described as the Servant of God, who takes upon himself the sickness and sin of the people, and atones for them by his vicarious suffering. The Gospel applies this prophecy concerning the Servant of God to Jesus, and this is done in an especially remarkable way in one passage of the first Gospel (Matt. viii, 17). It is said there that the miracles of healing which Jesus worked on men were done for the purpose of fulfilling the words of Isaias : " Surely he hath borne our griefs and carried our sorrows." With profound truth *the whole life of Jesus is thereby applied to the central Messianic thought—that of vicarious atonement and redemption from sin and its consequences.*

Nevertheless, *the suffering and death of Jesus remain the real act of redemption.* We have already seen that Jesus looks upon his Messianic vocation, above all, in the light of his suffering, death, and subsequent resurrection. Even his teaching and all the rest of his Messianic announcements and activities pale before the stupendous fact of his suffering. At the same time he declared continually that only thus can the Old Testament prophecy be fulfilled, according to which the Messiah must suffer and die, and in this way enter into his glory (Luke xviii, 31 ; xxiv, 26 ; Matt. xvi, 21). He will thus atone for the sins of mankind and redeem humanity through his vicarious suffering as the Servant of God in the sense of the Psalms and of the writings of the prophet Isaias.

Still more emphatically does he state this purpose of his Messianic vocation in the words of John's Gospel : " As Moses lifted up the serpent in the desert, so must the Son of Man be lifted up ; that whosoever believeth in him may not perish, but may have life everlasting. For God so loved the world as to give his only begotten Son, that whosoever believeth in him may not perish, but may have life everlasting. For God sent not his Son into the world to judge the world, but that the world may be saved by him. . . . I am the good shepherd. The good shepherd giveth his life for his sheep " (John iii, 14-17 ; x, 11).

The answer which, according to the synoptic Gospels, he gave to the sons of Zebedee is exactly similar : " The Son of Man is not come to be ministered unto, but to minister, and to give his life a redemption for many " (Matt. xx, 28).

With this great utterance in regard to his plan, into which he compresses, at the commencement of the Passion Week, the whole doctrine of redemption, are connected those other words spoken on the night immediately before his death. At the Last Supper he took bread, gave thanks, broke it and gave it to his disciples, saying : " This is my body, which is given for you " (Luke xxii, 19). Likewise he took the cup, after the meal, and said : " This is my blood of the new testament, which shall be shed for many unto remission of sins " (Matt. xxvi, 28). There is no need of explanation, and still less of proof, that Jesus himself, by these words, represented his death as an atonement for the sins of mankind and a redemption from sin.

It is, however, also just as certain that modern liberal theology has no use for an atoning, sin-destroying Messiah. Not only because it regards the Saviour as a mere man, who is not in the least capable of such an atoning act, but, above all, because it cannot concede to the man Jesus a real Messianic vocation, on account of its preliminary denial of a supernatural revelation. It therefore sought, first of all, to ignore entirely the Johannine words of Jesus and to brand-mark the already quoted synoptical utterances about his aton-ing work and death as later interpolations into the Gospels, or as subsequent partial refashionings of the Gospel text.[1] But no grounds are to be found for the critical rejection of these

---

[1] Thus Johannes Weiss, *Die Predigt Jesu vom Reiche Gottes*, 197-201 (1900) ; H. G. Hollmann, *Die Bedeutung des Todes Jesu nach seinen eigenen Aussagen auf Grund der synoptischen Evangelien*, 142-148 (1901) ; Loisy, *Les Evangiles synoptiques*, i, 181 (1907). Previously Loisy still maintained the genuineness of the passages of the synoptics on this subject, but altered his views in union with Andersen, *Das Abendmahl in den zwei ersten Jahrhunderten nach Christus* (1902).

synoptic passages. The Leipzig professor Ludwig Ihmels justly remarks[1] that the whole reason for it lies in the fact that these passages do not harmonize with the portrait of Christ which the critics have fashioned. Their genuineness is also recognized almost universally by the leaders of liberal criticism,[2] and finally it is readily adopted by all critics, provided, on the other hand, that we consent to let the passages in question pass for interpolations from the Pauline theology.

This only is the point that is seriously contested. *Paul continually announces in new ways and with the greatest emphasis the forgiveness of sins and the removal of sins through the death of Christ.* That is the principal theme of his Gospel, "that Christ died for our sins" (1 Cor. xv, 3); that "Christ died and rose again, that he might be Lord both of the dead and of the living" (Rom. xiv, 9); that "Christ died for all, that they also who live may not now live to themselves, but unto him who died for them and rose again" (2 Cor. v, 15); that "Christ hath redeemed us from the curse of the law, being made a curse for us" (Gal. iii, 13); that "there is one mediator of God and men, the man Christ Jesus, who gave himself a redemption for all" (1 Tim. ii, 5, 6). Harnack says: "The death on the cross was of the greatest importance to all Christians, but for Paul it was simply *the* act and *the* work of Christ. . . . His preaching was the proclamation of the redemption effected by the cross and the resurrection. This furnished him with such an inexhaustible amount of consolation and exhortation that everything else in comparison sank into insignificance."[3]

In this all are agreed, and the fact is evident in all the writings of the Apostle to the Gentiles. Opinions begin to differ when the question arises as to the relation of the Pauline doctrine of redemption to the doctrine found in the Gospels and the writings of the Church. While all the New Testament texts and all the subsequent Christian centuries give us to understand that St Paul brought into a fully and universally developed system the doctrine of redemption, given in its germ and foundation by Jesus himself, and proclaimed far and wide by the first disciples, the modern critics (according to whom the Messianic work of Jesus is reduced to the eschatological announcement of the kingdom) tell us that *Paul is the inventor and creator of the doctrine of the atoning and redemptive death of Jesus.* It is claimed that it is owing to his preaching, his writings and his powerful influence that in so short a time the whole primitive Church conformed to the new dogma of Christ's redemptive work. Soon, it is said,

[1] *Wer war Jesus?* 57 (Leipzig, 1908). See also K. Müller, *Unser Herr,* 31-33 (Berlin, 1906).
[2] Harnack, *Wesen des Christentums,* 101; O. Holtzmann, *Leben Jesu,* 365 (1901); Wellhausen, *Das Evangelium Matthäi,* 122 (1904).
[3] Harnack, *Ueber die Glaubwürdigkeit der evangelischen Geschichte,* in *Christliche Welt,* 319 (1905).

he succeeded in bringing the whole Christian doctrinal system
into harmony with this theory of redemption, and even the
first three Evangelists had been no longer able to resist this
impressive thesis of Paul. They took, we are told, the idea
of the atoning death of Jesus from the Pauline Epistles, which
were already in their possession, and in particular they borrowed from the first Epistle to the Corinthians the decisive
words uttered at the Last Supper. In this sense Johannes
Weiss,[1] Hans Heinrich Wendt,[2] Georg Hollman,[3] Paul
Wernle,[4] Bolliger,[5] Hausrath,[6] and other Protestant investigators have lately expressed themselves, and Loisy[7] undertook to proclaim their hypothesis as dogma, in the name of
criticism.

And the reasons for this? We may well be astonished to
hear them : " From all appearances the text of Mark concerning the redemption of many through the death of Christ (Mark
x, 45) must have been inspired by Paul, and it seems as if this
Evangelist's report of the Last Supper had been enriched by
Paul with the idea of redemption ; Jesus seems to have
presented the chalice and the bread with reference to his
approaching death and the future reunion with his own in the
kingdom of God, without, however, setting forth the atoning
character and redemptive significance of his death. The words
of Jesus, as given by Luke (xxii, 19), which refer to his atoning death, appear to have been introduced subsequently from
the Epistle of Paul to the Corinthians (1 Cor. xi, 24). Mark's
representation of the Last Supper (xiv, 22, etc.) appears to be
based on a narration, similar to that of Luke, only what he
says of the ' blood of the new testament ' must have been
introduced in accordance with the doctrine of Paul. The
second Gospel, so influenced by the editing given it by Paul,
must then, in its turn, have influenced the first Gospel of
Matthew. Originally a shorter account of the scene of the
Last Supper had, therefore, preceded the synoptic representation of it, in which, it is true, the thought of Christ's
approaching death was present, but not the Pauline features
of the atoning character of that death."[8] We can hardly
believe our eyes in beholding this artificial construction
of history. "It appears. . . . it should be. . . . it would

---

[1] *Die Predigt Jesu vom Reiche Gottes,* p. 197 ff.

[2] *Die Lehre Jesu,* 505 (Göttingen, 1901).

[3] *Die Bedeutung des Todes Jesu nach seinen eigenen Aussagen auf
Grund der synoptischen Evangelien* (Tübingen, 1901).

[4] *Die Anfänge unserer Religion,* 79 (1904).

[5] *Das Messiasgeheimniss bei Markus,* 98-132 (Schweiz. theol. Zeitsch.,
1906).

[6] *Jesus und die neutestamentalichen Schriftsteller,* i, 300, 308 (Berlin,
1908).

[7] *L'Evangile et l'Eglise,* 69-73 (1902); *Autour d'un petit livre,* 122,
237 (Paris, 1903); *Les Evangiles synoptiques,* i, 96, 100, 116, 181 (1907);
ii, p. 540 (1908).

[8] *L'Evangile et l'Eglise,* 72; *Autour d'un petit livre,* 237

be . . . it must be . . . it could be . . . ." That is all!
And from this is drawn the conclusion that the passages of the
synoptists bearing on this point do not, therefore, belong to
the Gospel of the Saviour, but to the theology of Paul! A
more groundless criticism of the Gospels can scarcely be
imagined.

A closer comparison of the report of the Last Supper given
by Paul (1 Cor. xi, 24), on the one hand, with the accounts
given by the synoptists, on the other, in spite of the great and
essential similarity of all these reports, reveal differences of
such a nature that the hypothesis of the Evangelists having
borrowed from the Epistle to the Corinthians is excluded.
This is especially true in regard to the atoning character of
the death of Jesus. Luke, the " Paulist " among the synoptists, omits, in describing the presentation of the chalice, the
words, " This do ye, as often as you shall drink, for the com-
memoration of me "—words which are found in the report by
Paul; instead of them the Evangelist introduces the words :
My blood, " which is shed for you " (Luke xxii, 20), a conclusion which is not found in Paul. Mark and Matthew, on their
part, give expression to the idea of atonement at the presentation of the chalice, but not at the offering of the bread, while
in Paul we observe the exact opposite. According to these
two synoptists, Jesus adds to this the statement that his blood
will . . . be shed "*for many,*" while the Pauline report of
the Last Supper does not contain these words. The second
synoptic principal passage, according to which Jesus " gives
his life a redemption for many," has no parallel in Paul. To
be sure, 1 Tim. ii, 6 is very similar, " Who gave himself a
redemption," yet there follow the additional words "*for all,*"
instead of the synoptic formula, " for many." Certainly
both expressions are substantially the same, but the difference
in form excludes borrowing on the part of the Evangelists,
especially if we reflect that the synoptic passage stands in
the midst of the description of an episode which in Paul
is wanting. In view of this context, the synoptists could not
have been borrowers, and Paul only could have been so, if
there were any borrowers at all. *Hence the passages in the
Gospels which contain express statements about redemption
through Christ do not find their origin in the Pauline Epistles.*

Moreover, the *doctrine of redemption* in itself cannot have
originated first from Paul and through him have been transmitted to the synoptic Gospels. Our opponents could support
this assertion, at most, by the fact that the synoptic doctrine
of redemption does not differ essentially from the Pauline
doctrine. From this harmony they then unhesitatingly draw
the conclusion that the synoptists do not transmit to us the
views of the Saviour, but the theory of Paul. Remarkable!
If the Pauline idea of atonement were *not* to be found in the

writings of the Evangelists, then they would doubtless say :
"You see that Paul must have imputed this idea to the
Saviour, otherwise we should find it also in the Gospels."
But since it *does* form a part of the Gospels also, they say :
"You see that the Evangelists ascribe these views to the
Saviour in order to please Paul."

Evidently there is only one correct conclusion to be drawn
from the agreement of the Gospel and Pauline accounts—that
both report the same thing in accordance with two different
but concurrent sources of information, which can have had
their origin only in the reports of the first disciples, and therefore go back to the utterances of Jesus himself.   Willingly or
unwillingly, almost all the critics now acknowledge this to be
the case.[1]

Moreover, we should arrive at a similar result even if the
doctrine of redemption were found only in Paul, and were not
at all recorded by the Evangelists, or only in connection with
Paul.   For it is certain that "in the preaching of Jesus
Christ . . . no differences existed between Paul and the early
Apostles.   We may be certain, therefore, that what Paul
actually reports of Christ is nearly as reliable and valuable
as if the disciples of Jesus had themselves related it in
person. . . .   A controversy over these facts never occurred
among the Apostles."[2]

This fundamental view of Harnack about the Pauline
tradition of Christ is most clearly demonstrated in the question that here concerns us.   Paul does not bring out the
doctrine of the redemptive death of Jesus as his own view,
which is for the first time struggling for recognition in the
apostolic Church.   Rather does he everywhere take it for
granted that *it is familiarly known to all the churches to which
he writes, and forms a fundamental part of apostolic preaching*.   He expressly says : "I delivered unto you first of all
which I also received ; how that Christ died for our sins"
(1 Cor. xv, 3).   This central doctrinal point of the Pauline
Gospel existed, therefore, before he wrote.   The first
witnesses for Christ all preached it both before and contemporaneously with the Apostle to the Gentiles.   It belonged to
the treasure of saving truth, held by the oldest Christian
generation.

[1] See Jülicher, *Zur Geschichte der Abendmahlfeier in der ältesten
Kirche* (1892) ; A. Harnack, *Dogmengeschichte,* 64 (1894) ; E. Haupt,
Ueber die ursprüngliche Form und Bedeutung der Abendmahlsworte
(1896) ; F. Schultzen, *Das Abendmahl im N. T.* (1896) ; R. A. Hoffmann, *Die Abendmahlsgedanken Jesu Christi* (1896) ; P. Lobstein, *La
doctrine de la sainte cène* (1899) ; W. Schmiedel, *Die neuesten Ansich-
ten über den Ursprung des Abendmahls, Protestantische Monatshefte*
(1899) ; J. Wellhausen, *Das Evangelium Matthäi,* 122-126 (1904) ; *Das
Evangelium Lucä,* 121 (1904).

[2] Harnack, *Ueber die Glaubwürdigkeit der evangelischen Geschichte,
Christliche Welt,* 319 (1905).

These facts are asserted, not only by the more orthodox critics such as Karl Müller,[1] Paul Feine[2] and Julius Kaftan,[3] but also Wilhelm Wrede[4] and Johannes Weiss,[5] who try to create artificially an antagonism between Christ and Paul, but are unable to produce evidence that Paul's doctrine of redemption did not exist essentially in the first Christian community. In fact, Adolf Jülicher is obliged to recognize the fact that Paul " has the support of the original Christian community in his teaching about Christ and the doctrines of satisfaction and redemption." Accordingly " the cleft between Paul and ante-pauline Christianity has diminished remarkably," and " we see sometimes Jesus, sometimes the first Apostles, hold out the hand to him over the graves."[6]

A glance into the non-pauline writings of the New Testament confirms this statement. " The blood of Jesus Christ his Son cleanseth us from all sin " (1 John i, 7). " You are redeemed . . . with the precious blood of Christ, as of a lamb unspotted and undefiled " (1 Pet. i, 19). Thus and similarly do the writings of the first disciples speak to us, and what we know in general of the first preaching of the Gospel from the Acts of the Apostles amounts almost entirely to this—that in Christ alone is salvation, deliverance, redemption and forgiveness of sins. Again, Harnack cannot but acknowledge that " the confession of the Christian Church is that in none other is there salvation, and that no other name is given to mankind by which we can be saved, than the name of Jesus Christ. With this confession it began; for this confession its martyrs died; and from this confession it still derives its strength to-day, as it did 1,800 years ago. It connects with this Person the whole substance of religion, life in God, the forgiveness of sin and consolation in suffering."[7] And elsewhere : " That these two doctrines [death and resurrection for our sins] were for the primitive Church the principal dogmas, no one has yet doubted; even Strauss has not denied it, and the great critic, Ferdinand Christian Baur, has recognized that the oldest form of Christendom was built up from a confession of faith in them."[8] Christendom has never known any other Gospel.

Whoever departs from it, puts himself at once outside Christianity. But whoever asserts that this Gospel was the work of Paul presupposes something impossible to have really happened—namely, that at once, only a few years after

---

[1] *Unser Herr*, 42 f.
[2] *Paulus als Theologe*, 76-78 (Berlin, 1906).
[3] *Jesus und Paulus* (Tübingen, 1906).
[4] *Paulus*, 2nd ed., 96 (Tübingen, 1907).
[5] *Paulus und Jesus*, 5, 51 (Berlin, 1909).
[6] *Paulus und Jesus*, 34 (Tübingen, 1907).
[7] *Das Christentum und die Geschichte*, 5th ed., 3 (Leipzig, 1904).
[8] Harnack, *Wesen des Christentums*, 98.

the death of Jesus, the Gospel of the Saviour was placed upon an entirely different and essentially and knowingly incorrect foundation, with the common, unanimous consent of the first disciples, and, indeed, by means of a man who did not belong to the circle of the disciples, but who, on the contrary, humbly confessed himself to be a novice, and was universally known as such. A criticism which must condescend to such a monstrous alternative is thereby simply annihilated. It proves more clearly than all orthodox statements that the redemptive death and the redemptive doctrine belong to the innermost core of the Messianic preaching of Jesus.

Let us now sum up the results which we have gained. First of all, it has been shown to us that the Messianic views of Jesus were wholly foreign to the Judaistic conception of the Messiah, entertained by his contemporaries. He had, in common with the rabbinical and apocalyptical theology, only the thought of the Parousia—the view of his return at the end of the world. He rejected in the most decided manner the national-political conception of the Messiah in every form, and with it repudiated also in principle the only thing which apparently still united him with the Judaism of his time—the doctrine of the Parousia, conceived by it as something equally national and political.

It is easy to see, therefore, that the more obstinately his people adhered to the late Jewish Messianic expectations, which were so fundamentally different from those of the Old Testament, the more incomprehensible did Jesus as the Messiah remain to them. The Judaism of the Synagogue could acknowledge as the Messiah only a thorough-going Rabbi, whose words, works, conduct and interpretation of the truth adhered strictly to the narrow Talmudic system of ordinances, and whose kingdom was a world power with a purely Jewish provincial policy. The Saviour came, however, relying neither on official rabbinism nor on an equally narrow Jewish eschatology, but on the divinely laid foundation of the Old Testament, and repudiating the erroneous ideas of the Messiah which the Jewish narrow-mindedness of later years thought that it found in the Old Testament.

Nothing is more evident from the Messianic utterances of Jesus than his consciousness of the fact that he is upholding and fulfilling in every respect the *Old Testament* notion of the Messiah. Whenever he alludes to his " having come " or " having been sent," and however he may express himself concerning his Messianic beginning, and whether he speaks of his entry into the world, his teaching, his miracles, his suffering, his death, or his resurrection, he always remains conscious that he is fulfilling the prophecies and announcements of the Messiah, given in the Old Testament; that the whole Scripture must be fulfilled in him; and also that not a word had been spoken of the Messiah by Moses and the Prophets which was not to be realized in him.

If we compare the Messianic elements of the Old Testament which we have disclosed with the Gospel's actual Messianic confessions and recorded events, the essential unity of the Messianic conceptions, found in the Old Testament and the Gospel, becomes at once evident. In both we find the Son of David, the Son of Man, the suffering Servant of God, the Founder and King of the kingdom of God in this world and the next.[1] Hence Jesus is able continually to appeal to the Old Testament in proof of his Messiahship: "Search the Scriptures; and the same are they which give testimony of me" (John v, 39). With such and similar words he seeks to turn the Jews, who are offended at his Messianic activity (John v, 9-47), from their rabbinical pedantry in regard to the Law to the real Messianic truth of Old Testament revelation.

Yet the Messianic idea of Jesus is not identical with that of the Old Testament. He *interprets* prophecy concerning himself quite independently. It is undeniable that, together with the intellectual, religious, universal and supernatural upper current of Messianic prophecy, there flows also through the Old Testament an adjacent current, which is very natural, earthly and chauvinistically national. It is true subtle intellects and stout hearts account for this by saying that the latter is only the covering and symbol of the former. But it was Jesus who first freed the Messianic idea entirely from the bonds of all that was national, earthly and secular, and with masterly decisiveness declared that every other conception of the prophecy and expectation of the Messiah was absolutely erroneous. This we have sufficiently proved.

Jesus also *harmonizes* the Old Testament Messianic notion. It was certainly no unimportant and no easily comprehensible circumstance that all the Messianic prophecies refer to one and the same person, and can find their fulfilment only in that person. Hence the songs of Isaias about the "Servant of God" were never, until the time of Jesus, referred to the Messiah, so far, at least, as we can judge from the Jewish writings still existing. To identify the Son of Man in Daniel with the Son of David, and the kingdom of God, the construction of which was so difficult, with the glorious and perfected kingdom, appeared possible, indeed, only to a very few. But Jesus unites all this in genuine harmony in his own person and work. He is the thoroughly supernatural, pre-existing Son of Man in Daniel, but at the same time the truly incarnate Son of Man, human in every particular. Both as the Son of Man and Son of David he will enter upon his Messianic power and

---

[1] Of Emmanuel and Jesus the Son of God we shall have something to say subsequently.

supremacy, but only after he shall have preached, suffered and submitted to death for the sins of humanity as the humble Servant of God. By his teaching he enlists disciples for the kingdom of God, by his death he makes possible the entry into that kingdom, and in his resurrection and glory he takes possession of it. Thus in him one prophecy after another falls into line in the most perfect harmony, and the whole Messianic conception of the Old Testament becomes *one* continuous prophecy; and this does not form a mere theory with so many paragraphs, but is a living organism, incorporated in the one living person of Jesus Christ himself.

Jesus has thereby also *idealized* the Old Testament idea of the Messiah. Nowhere does he try merely to copy prophecy literally. On every occasion he fulfils the prediction in a sublime and masterful way, without letting himself be always limited by the same restrictions. He shows himself to be the Lord of the Old as well as of the New Testament, saying : " It was said by them of old time. . . . But *I* say unto you . . ." That is a declaration of majesty not to be mistaken. And he acted accordingly. What the men of old neither conjectured nor conceived, he elevated till it became the chief commandment of his kingdom of God—namely, Love. What the ancients did not regard as feasible, he made at once a fact—the proclamation of a Gospel of grace in contrast to the law of fear. What men, in any case, had formerly expected only as a secondary matter, he put in the foreground of his Messianic teaching and activity—the redemption from sin and guilt through the vicarious suffering and death of the Messiah. The Old Testament prophecies of the Messiah may have appeared before the coming of Christ as a powerful and brilliant light, but through their fulfilment in Christ this light shone forth with such supernal splendour that it appeared less as an illuminating touch than as a shadow of Jesus thrown back from Christ upon the Old Testament.

This is the *specifically Christian idea* of the vocation, work and person of Jesus the Messiah, with the exception that the divinity of Jesus has not yet been brought into consideration. It is the fulfilment and the blessed and glorious revelation of the Old Testament Messianic conception, and at the same time the correction and most positive rejection of the Judaistic conception, as it was held by most of the contemporaries of Jesus, whether of the rabbinical or apocalyptic stamp. The *modern* idea of the Messiah, advanced by the latest higher criticism, has nothing to do with it. To this school of criticism Jesus is merely a successful impersonation of the Judaistic ideas of the Messiah prevailing in his time. According to this school, Jesus must have evolved either from the rabbinism of the Pharisees or from apocalyptic eschatology, and must

L.

have incorporated now one and now the other of these, enhanced by his strongly individual and gifted personality. That is all. It is comprehensible, therefore, that the modern theory of evolution—for which no supernatural revelation whatsoever exists, but only natural development—cannot possibly furnish any other solution of the Messianic problem, even though such a solution contradicts, as we have seen, the facts of history and in particular the testimony of Jesus to himself as the Messiah.

CHAPTER III

ORIGIN OF THE MESSIANIC CONSCIOUS-NESS OF CHRIST

I.—Origin of the Messianic Consciousness of Christ according to Modern Criticism.

THUS far we have demonstrated the fact that Jesus bore witness to himself as the Messiah during his whole public life in an ever-increasing and ever more emphatic revelation, and interpreted the essential character of his Messiahship also with a unique and thoroughly sublime self-reliance.

But the more striking and remarkable these wonderful facts are, the louder and more forcibly do the critics ask : " How came Jesus to regard himself as the Messiah? Whence did he derive the conviction that he was the Messiah in the sublime sense indicated? Where and how did his Messianic consciousness originate?"

Not only in the opinion of orthodox believers, but also in that of sceptics and unbelievers, this question forms " *an essential part of the inquiry into the essence of Christianity in general.*"[1] With the answer to this stands or falls either the Christian conception, or the modern critical conception, of the Person of Jesus.

For believing Christians the answer to this question is a very simple one. They see in Jesus Christ the eternal Son of God, who was sent by the heavenly Father into the world, to redeem fallen humanity, as the Messiah. In this way the entire mystery of the origin of the Messianic consciousness of Jesus is solved. Jesus brought his Messianic vocation with him from heaven to earth. His Messianic consciousness, therefore, has its origin in his antecedent, pre-existent life. It forms the root and basis of the incarnation and the earthly life of Jesus, and is very far from having originated in this life and having been gradually developed here.

Very different, however, is *the opinion of the higher criticism, from the religious-historical and religious-psycho-logical point of view.* Since it considers Christianity merely as the result of the natural evolution of humanity, and as a period of transition in the moral, intellectual and religious development of the human race, it also considers the Saviour Jesus Christ as only a member and a factor of this natural evolution. It sees in him a mere man, without any previous

[1] Ernst Kühl, *Das Selbstbewusstsein Jesu,* p. 86 f. (Berlin, 1907).

195

life in heaven or any divine nature—a man like all the rest of men. Only this man (whether in consequence of some fanatical self-deception, or through divine interposition remains undecided) believed that he had an extraordinary Messianic life-task to perform, and actually did fulfil this life-task for the blessing of mankind.

Yet modern criticism, in claiming this, is placed before the problem of how the consciousness of such a task and of such an absolutely unique and unheard-of vocation could arise in the man Jesus. Both the sceptical and half-sceptical schools of criticism are bound to solve this problem, because otherwise their whole conception of the Messiah and of the person and work of Jesus Christ remains entirely without foundation. If they do not succeed in giving to this a thoroughly satisfactory and complete explanation, that is the best and most convincing proof that those schools of criticism have taken the wrong course in offering to the Christianity of all the centuries a thoroughly human conception of the nature and person of Jesus.

It is clear from the outset that *our opponents must explain the Messianic consciousness of the Saviour psychologically, as the result of a gradual evolution of the inner life of Jesus, and that they cannot possibly explain it in any other way, and ought not to attempt to do so.* On the one hand, they wish to confine even the Messiah-Jesus within the limits of natural development and of the purely human view of history. On the other hand, they proceed from the conviction that Jesus really did not at first and from his own nature possess any Messianic consciousness, although this undeniably appeared in him at a later date. It revealed itself, therefore, midway between the early and the later periods of his life. And because this could not possibly have happened through a supernatural revelation and the gift of divine grace (for our opponents deny the possibility of these, on principle), the Messianic consciousness of Jesus must have evolved itself from his own natural experiences; that is, out of the incidents of his external life and out of his inner ethical qualities and condition of soul. It is on this standpoint, then, that the rationalistic and rationalizing school of inquiry concerning Jesus really places itself.

Rationalism denies any objective Messianic vocation of Jesus, and accordingly supposes the Man of Nazareth to have worked himself more and more into the Messianic consciousness, grossly self-deceived, impelled by his deeply religious nature, urged on by his associates and his successes, and allured by his own imagination.

The classical example of this "psychological explanation" of Christ's Messianic consciousness is always Ernest Renan's *Vie de Jésus.* The French romanticist regards the extraordinarily perfect idea of God held by Jesus, and the spiritual union with God resulting from it, " as to a certain extent the potential germ of his whole power,"[1] and as the point of departure for his later religious and Messianic development. In contrast to Judaism,[2] Jesus recognizes in God his Father, and feels himself united with him in such a constant and profound intimacy as can only unite a child with his father.[3] " God does not speak with him as with a stranger; God is in him; he knows himself to be one with God, and he derives from his own heart what he says of his Father.   He lives in the bosom of God by means of an uninterrupted revelation; he sees him not, but he hears him. . . .   He believes that he stands in immediate intercourse with God; he considers himself to be the Son of God. . . .   Not as if Jesus had come at once to this high opinion of himself.   It is, however, probable that he thought from the very first that he stood in that relation to God in which a son stands to his father."[4]

This blessed conviction of his conscious filial relation to God forced him to convey to his fellow-men the same happiness. He taught them, accordingly, to recognize God as a Father, and to have intercourse with him as children and sons.   That seemed to him to be the true kingdom of heaven prophesied by the Prophets—the ardently expected kingdom of God.[5] The founder of this " true kingdom of God, the kingdom of the meek and humble, is the Jesus of the first days, those modest and unclouded days when the voice of his Father found a purer echo in his heart.   At that time God really dwelt upon this earth, for some months at least, perhaps for a year."[6]

Then came the unhappy change.   Influenced by the preaching of John the Baptist, by the extravagant Messianic hopes of the class of people around him, and much more even by the evolution of his own ideas, Jesus substituted for the inherent kingdom of God, consisting of a sweet, childlike consciousness of God, an external, realistically and at the same time transcendentally conceived kingdom.   An actual, theocratic kingdom was to be founded, and in order to make the founding of this possible the present sinful world was first to be transformed by a sudden catastrophe into one that would be supermundane and heavenly.   A second and equally sudden catastrophe was then at once to complete the supremacy of God upon the new earth.[7]   A radical revolution, which extended itself even to nature, was henceforth the fundamental thought of Jesus.[8]

That he himself was called to carry this revolution into effect he could not for a moment seriously doubt.   Yet, as has been said, " the conviction that he was the Son of God, the

---

[1] *Vie de Jésus*, 53.
[2] *id.*, 53, 54.
[3] *id.*, 54.
[4] *id.*, 55.
[5] *id.*, 56-63.
[6] *id.*, 57.
[7] *id.*, 81-93.
[8] *id.*, 85.

confidential agent of his Father and the executor of his Father's will, was so deeply implanted in him, that it probably had not developed gradually, but had had its origin in the very roots of his being."[1] If, however, he was called to complete the Messianic work of founding the kingdom of God, he was evidently also called to rule this future kingdom as the Messianic king. He was, therefore, in the full sense of the word, *the Messiah*.[2] " Possessed by this idea, which dominated him ever more and more, from this time on, with a truly fatal calmness, he pursued the course which his astonishing genius and the extraordinary circumstances of his life had indicated,"[3] everywhere proclaiming the glad tidings of the immediate coming of the kingdom of God and preparing men for it.[4] With his unexampled enthusiasm he awaited every day the glorious dawn of the new age of the world.[5]

Yet he was soon to see that he had deceived himself in supposing that he could conjure up the kingdom of God triumphantly and without great difficulties. Besides a small community of believing disciples, there was also the great mass of the people, and, above all, the party of the Pharisees, which felt itself aggrieved by the fact that he set aside the representatives of Mosaism, forced the Law itself into the background, and dreamed of a Messianic kingdom, which stood in violent contrast to their politico-national ideas of the Messiah. And the more clear and profound the ideas of Jesus concerning the kingdom and its coming became, the more intense grew the opposition to the pharisaical Jews. These already assumed a threatening attitude, and it could be foreseen that the issue would be an ominous and, indeed, a fatal one for the Nazarene. Thus Jesus familiarized himself first with the suggestion, and finally with the definite thought, that he could not, as the glorious Son of Man prophesied by Daniel, establish and rule the kingdom of God at once, but only after preliminary suffering and passing through death and the grave.[6] In reality, however, the idea of such a kingdom of God was buried with him with his death. " This realistic view of the coming of God had been merely a cloud, a passing error."[7]

This error, and consequently the Messianic consciousness of Jesus itself, is, it is claimed, really only explicable and excusable when the psychological constitution of Jesus is taken into consideration. Jesus was an enthusiast, an eccentric, an *exalté*, an ecstatic, a visionary.

" Carried away by an enthusiasm soaring to prodigious heights, and compelled to adopt every day a more ecstatic mode of preaching, Jesus was no longer free. . . . One was often tempted to believe that he was irrational. He suffered from feelings of anguish and spiritual distress. The impres-

---

[1] *Vie de Jésus*, 85. [2] *id.*, 94. [3] *id.*, 93. [4] *id.*, 93.
[5] *id.*, 219-228. [6] *id.*, 229-293. [7] *id.*, 57.

sive vision of the kingdom of God flickered constantly before his eyes and made him dizzy. . . . His unusually passionate temperament carried him at every moment beyond the bounds of human nature. His work was no longer a rational one. . . . Sometimes he was hard and strange. His disciples no longer understood him, and were seized with a certain feeling of fear in his presence. . . . At times they regarded him as a madman."[1] "The madman in him bordered on the inspired man; only the madman has never had any success. Never until then had insanity succeeded in exercising, as Jesus exercised it, a decisive influence on the progress of humanity."[2]

In this last confession lies Renan's own condemnation of his hypothesis of the origin of the Messianic consciousness of Jesus. Quite apart from its being in contradiction to the facts of the Gospel, a psychology of Jesus must be false which stamps as a madman, or at least as a visionary simpleton, one " to whom everyone of us owes what is best in him;"[3] " who has created a movement, at the beginning of which a man of colossal dimensions must have stood;"[4] " who has united in himself all that is good and sublime in our nature;"[5] "who stands at the summit of human greatness;"[6] " who is for ever unsurpassable, whatever the future may produce;"[7] and " whom all coming centuries will acclaim as the greatest of the children of men."[8]

From such a double-tongued, contradictory and senseless theory even the *liberal-protestant school* of critics turned with an emphatic gesture of disapproval. In France itself Edmund Stapfer, the dean of the Protestant theological faculty at Paris, wrote the following forcible sentences : " Jesus professed to be the Messiah. That is proven; that is certain. How did he come to do this? Through insanity, or not? It seems to us that this is the only alternative that henceforth presents itself to distinguish believers from unbelievers."[9] "Renan has said : ' Blinded by his success Jesus regarded himself as the Messiah.' He was rational at the beginning of his activity, but was no more so at its close, and his history, as Renan relates it, is, in spite of all the excuses which the latter brings forward for it, the history of the ever-increasing over-excitement of a man who began with the sober sense, clear vision and moral soundness of a beautiful and noble genius, but who ended with a morbid mental exaltation bordering on insanity. The word insanity has not been uttered by Renan, but the thought of it is stamped on every

[1] *Vie de Jésus,* 226, 227. [2] *id.,* 55. [3] *id.,* 202.
[4] *id.,* 319. [5] *id.,* 326. [6] *id.,* 320. [7] *id.,* 327.
[8] *id.,* 327. The thorough refutation of the psychiatrical and the psychopathological criticism of Jesus follows in the second volume of this work.
[9] E. Stapfer, *Jésus-Christ avant son ministère,* 2nd. ed., xi (Paris, 1896).

page. Yet the facts certainly contradict such an explanation."[1]

Thus does Stapfer ally himself with the "believers"; that is, by rejecting the harsh standpoint of the rationalists, he assumes that Jesus did not imagine that he was the Messiah, but that he was so in reality. Yet in this there is no mention of the supernatural Messiahship of faith, either by Stapfer or by any adherent of the liberal school. To them Jesus is merely a genius, richly endowed by nature, or, if one prefers, by natural providence, called to promote the evolution of humanity in a religious direction, precisely as Plato and Aristotle were called by God to promote scientific, and Michael Angelo and Goethe artistic, evolution. Accordingly, if Jesus, with all his greatness, was a mere man with a Messianic vocation, not exceeding the human standard, human powers and human nature, then his Messianic consciousness also must have been developed by degrees and psychologically.

We see, then, that in reality the Man of Nazareth undergoes, at the hands of the liberal school, exactly the rationalistic treatment of Renan, with the sole difference that it endeavours to represent his Messianic evolution as being based on something objective, not as the phantasy of an overstrained mentality. Essentially the holders of the liberal theory of evolution have learned nothing since the time of Renan. It resembles in almost every particular that of the French "decorative painter."

Stapfer, like Renan, denies that Jesus possessed at first a Messianic consciousness. It is true Jesus stood in an intimate moral connection with God, and this union was so profound and tender that God appeared to him as a Father and he knew himself to be ethically a Son of God.[2] On this account he felt himself impelled to accomplish something great for God, his Father, and to bring about for others also their adoption by God as children. Ever stronger and more emphatic became this question of his inmost heart : " For what purpose am I in this world? What is my mission? What is the vocation of my life?" And parallel to this question was the other : " Who will be the Messiah? When will he appear? What work will he accomplish?" Eighteen years of such reflections pass, and slowly but surely he comes to the steadfast conviction : " I myself am the Messiah."[3] The crisis takes place at his baptism. There he thinks he hears from above the voice of his Father, which gives the decisive, affirmative answer to his inward filial feeling and Messianic enthusiasm for God : " Thou art my beloved Son. In thee am I well pleased." Now his Messianic vocation had become a fact.[4]

[1] Jésus-Christ pendant son ministère, 2nd ed., 300 (Paris, 1897).
[2] Stapfer, Jésus-Christ avant son ministère, 89-91.
[3] id., 92.   [4] id., 152.

But how was he to interpret the Messianic vocation? He was still firmly rooted in the earthly and political ideas of the Messiah common to the Jews. The temptation, which " was not one separate and passing phenomenon, but extended itself over the whole period of the life of Jesus following the baptism," freed him " from the false ideas and all the incorrect political views regarding the Messiah, which he had shared with his entire people. He came out of the period of the temptation with the conviction that he must be a spiritual and moral Messiah . . . that he will establish his kingdom in the hearts of men and accomplish a purely religious work."[1] Finally, his persecution at the hands of the Pharisees familiarized him also more and more with the thought that he must suffer and die, and that only after this he would come in glory as the Messiah and find full recognition.[2]

Loisy,[3] Réville[4] and some German critics of liberal tendencies reject, for the most part, this last-named development, asserting that Jesus conceived his Messianic vocation, in a spiritual sense, at once after the baptism, and that the idea of suffering also was not absent from his mind. Yet in the main they all agree with Renan and Stapfer. They suppose that the Messianic consciousness of Jesus is not to be regarded as having formed from the first a part of his nature, but as the result of a gradual evolution. The foundation for it had been laid in the first period of his life, through the consciousness of sonship, which then appeared in him; through the occurrence at his baptism this became a positive certainty; and the succeeding period of his public life, with its temptations and experiences, strengthened, confirmed and clarified the consciousness of his Messianic vocation. In regard to these main points, we find, with some slight variations, a substantial agreement in the views of Otto Pfleiderer,[5] Willibald Beyschlag,[6] Adolf Harnack,[7] Johannes Weiss,[8] Hans Wendt,[9] Oskar Holtzmann,[10] Bernard Weiss,[11] Paul Wernle,[12] Konrad Furrer,[13] Adolf Julicher,[14] P. W.

---

[1] id., 162-176.   [2] Jésus-Christ pendant son ministère, 222.

[3] L'Evangile et l'Eglise, 55 (1902); Le IV Evangile, 233, 252 (1903); Les Evangiles synoptiques, i, 165, 183-186, 192, 206, 212, 242 (1907).

[4] Jésus de Nazareth, ii, 3, 13-20, 198, 208 (Paris, 1897).

[5] Religionsphilosophie, 2nd ed., ii, 186 ff.

[6] Das Leben Jesu, 215-255, 3rd ed (1893).

[7] Das Wesen des Christentums, 86-89 (1900).

[8] Die Predigt Jesu vom Reiche Gottes, 154-158 (1900).

[9] Die Lehre Jesu, 91-102, 2nd ed. (1901).

[10] Leben Jesu, 106-115 (1901).

[11] Das Leben Jesu, i, 271-328, 4th ed. (1902); Lehrbuch der biblischen Theologie des N. T., 61, 7th ed. (1903).

[12] Die Anfänge unserer Religion, 27-38 (1904).

[13] Das Leben Jesu Christi, 51-55, 70, 81-83, 2nd ed. (1905).

[14] Die Religion Jesu u. die Anfänge des Christentums, in Die Kultur der Gegenwart, No. 4, 55 (1906).

Schmiedel,[1] Otto Schmiedel,[2] Wilhelm Weiss,[3] Wilhelm
Bousset[4] and P. W. Schmidt.[5]

Wendt describes, perhaps most clearly, the evolution of
the Messianic consciousness of Jesus as follows : " We may
assert, on the ground of the religious self-consciousness, in
accordance with which Jesus later judged and acted, that he
always felt himself a son in relation to God, so far as his
consciousness went backward to his childhood.　Certainly this
filial feeling formed itself within him and grew broader and
deeper only gradually ; but he did not work his way out from
an original condition under the dispensation of the Law,
characterized by a slavish spirit towards God, to reach, only
at a later date, a condition under the dispensation of grace
and free adoption.　From the first he lived in the condition
and consciousness of a child of God. . . .　During the period
of his public activity his view of the fatherhood of God, and
his consciousness that he himself stood in a purely filial relation to the heavenly Father, was the firm foundation of his
certainty that now the kingdom of God was coming, and that
he himself was the Messiah in this kingdom.　In the period
which preceded his public appearance, however, this intimate
relation in which his knowledge of the fatherhood of God
and his own life in a state of sonship to God stood to the
establishment of the kingdom of God and to his Messiahship,
must have been still hidden from him. . . .　The knowledge
that he himself was called by God to be the Messiah of the
promised kingdom of salvation had not been completely possessed by him for a long time previous to the commencement
of his Messianic work.　He became aware of this revelation
which established his Messianic consciousness when he followed the call of John the Baptist to the Jewish people, to
prepare, through penance, for the immediate coming of the
Messiah, and, as an evidence of such preparation, to be
baptized in the Jordan. . . .　At the moment when he underwent the baptism of John he received the revelation, which
imparted to him his Messianic consciousness.　The perception
was then given him that the Spirit of God, whose bearer and
representative the Messiah was to be, had been bestowed
upon himself. . . .　As the Son of God, in whom was first
perfectly revealed the promised relation of salvation between
God and humanity, he must be the Messiah, whose task it was
to bring to the rest of mankind the knowledge and realization
of this saving relation, and thus to bring about the establishment of the promised kingdom of God.　The assurance of
his Messiahship, thus suddenly and miraculously received,

---

[1] *Protest. Monatshefte,* 267 (1906).
[2] *Die Hauptprobleme der Leben-Jesu-Forschung,* 96-99, 2nd ed. (1906).
[3] *Jesus von Nazareth,* 9 ff. (1906).　　[4] *Jesus,* 79 f., 87 f. (1907).
[5] *Die Geschichte Jesu erzählt,* 49-52, 57-59, 114, 120-122, 126 (1909).

was, however, followed by disturbing doubts. . . . And that which made such a conflict possible for him, and threatened to confuse him as to his Messianic vocation, was the number and variety in the Jewish conceptions of the Messiah, which until then had been kept hidden from him, and which he now recognized would not be realized if he himself should appear in that sense of the Messiahship and with the spiritual power revealed to him at the baptism. . . . The net benefit accruing to Jesus from his preliminary struggle with the temptations, which were directed, immediately after the baptism, against his consciousness of his Messianic vocation, consisted in his having acquired for his own sure possession the suddenly gained certainty of that Messianic vocation. Thereafter he was not subject to ever-new mental agitation, caused by inward scruples and doubts, whenever, in the practice of his Messianic calling, he encountered temptations originating in the prevalent Jewish conception of the Messiah or in the obstacles continually presented both by his disciples and by his enemies. Since he had at the start rejected this temptation, not briefly and superficially, but, on the contrary, had overcome it quietly and thoroughly during a period of spiritual conflict lasting for weeks, he could take up his public work and teaching with wonderful clearness and consistency, and with an immovable certainty of his Messianic consciousness and of his conception of the kingdom of God."[1]

From these statements it is evident that *the liberal school is indeed willing to oppose to the merely imaginary Messianic consciousness of Jesus one that is founded upon facts, yet represents this, exactly as Renan does, as the result of his subjective, psychological evolution.* It begins with a protest against rationalism, and ends with the final results of rationalism.

The liberal-conservative group of Protestant theologians recognizes in Jesus "the Son of Man and Son of God from heaven," but does not recognize the real Son of God and his divinity, and raises "a most emphatic protest against all attempts of the liberal school to apply to Christ the thought of development found in the modern theory of evolution. . . . The consciousness of Jesus that he was the Son of God and the Son of Man mocks at all attempts at a religious-historical explanation, and every theory of its evolution must be checked by it. If not, it should comprehend clearly that it must first destroy that consciousness of Jesus if it wishes to explain it in its way."[2] We should hardly believe it possible to meet with such words as these at the conclusion of an investigation in which the liberal-conservative theologian of Königsberg, Ernst Kühl, represents the self-consciousness of Jesus, quite

[1] Wendt, 94, 95, 97, 98, 99, 101-102.
[2] Ernst Kühl, *Das Selbstbewusstsein Jesu*, 86 (Berlin, 1907).

in the sense of the liberal school of criticism, as the result of a gradual development. The filial consciousness of Jesus has, it is true, according to Kühl " its ultimate rootlets in the depths of his own being, which it outgrew organically by what might be called a natural, spiritual necessity."[1] That is, however, all. Not even once is Jesus' consciousness of sonship made identical with his consciousness of his own nature. The latter is, rather, only the fostering soil in which the former grows. Hence " we are never able to decide whether the filial consciousness of Jesus took possession of him through some intervention of God at a definite period of his former life suddenly, irresistibly and overpoweringly, or whether (which is for us psychologically more comprehensible) it came into being gradually, like a mature fruit, after long evolution. And if it did ripen thus in long evolution, did this development proceed quietly, continuously and harmoniously? Or was it connected with severe spiritual struggles and inward conflicts? All these are questions for the answers to which no means of historical and psychological demonstration are available."[2]

According to Kühl, we know only that the filial consciousness, " this inner feeling and condition of kinship which raised him above all other men and united him with God, was already a characteristic of Jesus when he came to his baptism."[3] In Kühl's opinion, also, it cannot be doubted that Jesus' consciousness of being the Messiah originated in his consciousness of sonship, and, indeed, in consequence of his experience at his baptism. " Only this is certain—that the consciousness of his sonship took on the form of Messianic consciousness in consequence of the baptism."[4] His baptism must " surely be considered as the natal hour of his Messiahship, and at the same time also that of his Messianic consciousness."[5]

" From the moment of his baptism Jesus was convinced of his Messianic vocation and of his call to found the Messianic kingdom.[6] The day and hour of the coming of the kingdom and of his final Messianic triumphs he patiently left to God, because, by reason of his consciousness of sonship, he acquiesced entirely in God's will.[7] During his first Messianic work for his people, which was taken up and completed with enthusiasm, Jesus certainly never doubted that these triumphs would be, sooner or later, granted him by God. On this point even the hostility of the leading circles could not shake his confidence, so long as he had the sympathies of the people on his side. But when the great change in the people took place, when the flame of enthusiasm for him was extinguished . . . then he saw that the day and hour of the completion of the kingdom was to be postponed, and that all that the Prophets

---

[1] *id.*, 43.   [2] *id.*, 42.   [3] *id.*, 40.   [4] *id.*, 40.
[5] *id.*, 39.   [6] *id.*, 44-61.   [7] *id.*, 61.

had written of the Son of Man, even all that Isaias (chapter liii) had written of the suffering Servant of God, would find its fulfilment in the Messiah; then he made the thought of suffering a part of his self-consciousness, in voluntary submission to the divine will and in clear agreement with it. That was the really great, bold and heroic act of Jesus."[1]

When Kühl makes the thought of his coming suffering a development of Messianic consciousness, which came to Jesus only subsequently and, indeed, at a very late date, he goes beyond even most of the representatives of the liberal school which he attacks, *and reverts directly to the rationalism of Strauss and Renan.*

Thus the immense labour, in which the criticism of the last two decades has wellnigh exhausted itself in trying to explain intelligibly the consciousness of Jesus by the theory of psychological evolution, ends in a pitiful absurdity. It started out with indignation at Renan, who had dared to describe the Messianic consciousness of Jesus as the result of purely psychological development, and it closes, since it brings out the same assertions with various modifications, by saying that Jesus had by nature no Messianic consciousness; that the consciousness of sonship preceded the Messianic consciousness as a preparation; that Jesus first acquired his Messianic consciousness at the time of the baptism and by means of it; and that this Messianic consciousness was evolved to completion during the subsequent period of his public life.

But all this in substance the French rationalist had also said. Indeed, it will be shown that the modern critics themselves do not escape the absurd consequence resulting from declaring *Jesus, in the same breath, to have been the most perfect flower of human intelligence, yet at the same time a visionary suffering from insane phantasies.* This criticism of the modern evolutionary theory, pronounced upon itself, is the sharpest subjective criticism imaginable. Its advocates have certainly given themselves sincere and almost inconceivable effort to prove the psychologically false portrait of Jesus which Renan merely sketched, as an unsurpassable artist, to be a real, scientific and historic picture. They have not succeeded in the attempt. The "psychological" development-portrait of Jesus remains always an artificial construction. A serious and unprejudiced examination of the separate positions held by our opponents will fully convince us of this. Let us begin with the alleged evolution of the Messianic consciousness of Jesus during his public life.

[1] *id.*, 61-62.

II.—Evolution of the Messianic Consciousness of Christ during his Public Life.

We are acquainted with our opponents' views about the evolution of the Messianic consciousness. It is, however, necessary to examine still more closely their lines of thought and their " proofs " for the assertions made by them, in order to judge of them with certainty. The transformation in the Messianic ideas of Jesus begins, according to the modern critics, after the episode of the baptism. Jesus, they say, left the scene of the baptism with the firm consciousness that he had been chosen for the Messiah. Our opponents of all shades of opinion are, in fact, unanimous in thinking that " Jesus, when he made his public appearance, had already fully made up his mind both as to himself and his mission."[1] " No competent judge of the matter who has respect for tradition will, therefore, dare to cast a doubt upon the constant Messianic consciousness of Jesus after his baptism."[2]

We are assured, however, on the other hand, with equal positiveness, that *Jesus, immediately after his baptism, was not yet sure " of the nature of his Messiahship "*[3] or of the precise task which he, as the Messiah, had to perform, or of the manner of his Messianic activity. " Even if his experience at his baptism did settle the great and vital question of his being the Son of God, who had been growing to manhood in obscurity, another scarcely less important question forced itself upon him : In what sense was he to be the Messiah of Israel?"[4] The Messianic consciousness of Jesus has still always " two souls. . . . His vocation means for him a problem which only the future can solve. . . . An immense burden was thereby laid upon his soul, and a problem confronted him, the solution of which must have sometimes appeared very difficult."[5] " The perception of the task which the Father had entrusted to him could develop only by work and by victory over every sort of resistance."[6] " To such a degree did Jesus, his whole life long, elaborate and purify the Messianic title, assumed at first by inward compulsion."[7]

It was at first a question whether he should look upon his vocation in the sense of the Jewish nationalistic conception of the Messiah, involving the religious-political liberation of his people, and hence the establishment of a secular and earthly Messianic kingdom, or in the sense of a religious and spiritual

---

[1] Harnack, *Wesen des Christentums,* 88.
[2] Johannes Weiss, *Die Predigt Jesu vom Reiche Gottes,* 157 ; see also Julius Kaftan, *Jesus und Paulus,* 13.
[3] Hess, *Jesus von Nazareth,* 11.
[4] Willibald Beyschlag, *Das Leben Jesu,* i, 231.
[5] J. Weiss, *Die Predigt Jesu,* 156.   [6] Harnack, *Wesen,* 89.
[7] Wernle, *Die Anfänge unserer Religion,* 34.

liberation and the establishment of a Kingdom of God founded in the hearts of men. And if the latter course were chosen, then he must again ask himself whether he could found this kingdom now, in his earthly life, moving from victory to victory and from triumph to triumph, or whether he could do so only after having passed through suffering, death and the grave, and only at his second coming from heaven as the Messianic Son of Man? These were the two problems, to which the following period of his public life was gradually to furnish the solution.

First, the question *whether he was to be a political or a spiritual Messiah, and to found a political or a spiritual Messianic kingdom.* That this alternative weighed upon the mind of the Saviour very seriously is proved, our opponents say, by the Gospel history of his temptation, concerning which the critics assure us " that it was not one single passing fact, but that it extended over the whole life of Jesus following the baptism."[1] " The same spirit which had given him the certainty of his vocation drove him with great violence into the desert,"[2] where he was exposed to unheard-of conflicts with the devil. According to the enemies of supernatural revelation, this cannot, of course, be the historical report of a real external fact, but only the " symbolic veiling " of an inner psychical crisis[3] in Jesus, "a psychological experience of Jesus in a condensed symbolic form."[4] " Translated into our mode of speech or thought, the powerful exultation and blessed joy which he feels under the outpouring of divine love and strength from above, yield suddenly to a profound agitation. Doubts and cares press upon him. On all sides possibilities are revealed to him, which he feels are temptations and sinful paths. In short, violent inward struggles replace the first blessed certainty and enthusiasm."[5] The history of the temptation " is certainly the result of an inward conflict in Jesus, through which, at the beginning of his public life, he was forced to fight his way to a clear apprehension of the course which he must follow in his vocation."[6]

" What does this mean? Evidently the repudiation of a false, sensuous ideal of the Messiah. That is particularly evident in the third phase of his temptation, the purport of which was the offer of universal dominion at the price of doing homage to the prince of this world. The ideal of an immediate visible Messianic kingdom, a world kingdom which, proceeding from Sion, should unite all nations under his sceptre, presents itself before the mind's eye of the newly anointed. But he sees that such a kingdom can be established

[1] Stapfer, *Jésus-Christ avant son ministère,* 152; *cf.* Kühl, *op. cit.,* 13.
[2] J. Weiss, *op. cit,* 156.   [3] Stapfer, *l.c.*
[4] Loisy, *L'Evangile et l'Eglise,* 20.
[5] J. Weiss, *op. cit.,* 156.   [6] Kühl, *op. cit.,* 13.

only by the aid of the Evil One and by the instrumentality of worldly violence and intrigue, not by the agencies of spirit and truth, which are alone divine. Accordingly he rejects it. But the two preceding phases of his temptation also belong to the same false ideal—a Messiah who, by the arbitrary use of his miraculous powers, could remove any external want that he might feel, and who could avoid the burden laid upon him by his vocation, and who then, by a bold act of daring, crowned with success by God's assistance (perhaps the attainment of the nation's independence), could capture at a stroke the faith of the people. Such a Messiah was the necessary preliminary requisite for erecting that Messianic world kingdom of which the people dreamed. Starting from such apparently innocent and insinuating preliminary conditions, therefore, Jesus at that time examined point by point the Messianic ideal, which the spirit of his people and of the age had given him, until at last, fully realizing the point aimed at and the means necessary to attain it, he saw its incompatibility with a divine purpose, and consequently recognized in the spirit, which thus counselled and demanded, the tempter, Satan, the opponent of God. To recognize him as such meant for Jesus his instant rejection. . . . Jesus had, therefore, first to test those popular expectations, which may perhaps have exerted upon him a certain alluring charm, and hence he had no fixed, definite Messianic ideal, which would in advance have excluded those expectations."[1]

"It appears that Jesus himself subsequently related figuratively to his intimates (to whom such instruction could be only a blessing, in view of their ever-renewed hopes of a Jewish kingdom) how the first profound contact of his soul with the Messianic thought was a temptation to sin, a temptation to consider the flesh as his weapon, and to attempt the path to the Messiahship by means of insurrection and the sword. These had already, it is true, been tried before his day unsuccessfully, but would not God perhaps allow him, Jesus, by these means to succeed? . . . This temptation to be untrue to himself was not a mere passing one; he had first to experience it, and finally to subdue it thoroughly. But the result was a victory for his better, divinely begotten self. . . . Jesus remains true to himself and to the thoughts which had urged him onward at the beginning. God wishes to create the new, blessed era from within, out of the hearts of the pious."[2]

Stapfer, Beyschlag, J. Weiss, Kühl and P. W. Schmidt inform us, therefore, that *Jesus had to fight out an actual spiritual conflict with the Jewish political Messianic ideal, which up to that time had been also his own.* Only after this

---

[1] Beyschlag, *Das Leben Jesu,* i, 234-236.
[2] Schmidt, *Die Geschichte Jesu,* i, 59, 60, 114.

long-continued crisis had been overcome did he arrive at the firm conviction that his task was a purely religious and spiritual one.

This assertion, however, *contradicts in a twofold manner the most positively assured facts.* It is certain from the synoptic reports[1] that the temptation came to Jesus only outwardly, without the slightest spiritual conflict, and without in the least disturbing the equanimity and serenity of his soul. Equally evident is it, from the history of the temptation, that we are not justified in harbouring even the faintest suspicion that Jesus could have cherished any sort of inclination to the political Messianic idea of his people. Rather does everything indicate that he already then must have rejected every profanation and secularization of the Messiahship with the same decisiveness and the same inward aversion with which he rejected them in the whole of his subsequent life.

This fact is so clear and incontestable that *most of the critics see themselves compelled to refuse adherence to Stapfer, Beyschlag, J. Weiss and Schmidt.* "They were not fancies and ideals which had arisen from an evil, selfish nature hostile to God, and from an inclination in Jesus to be self-opinionated; an inference of those temptations from the soul of Jesus in this sense is certainly to be repudiated. But they were Messianic conceptions and ideals which had come to him from without—that is, from the prevailing views and traditions of his countrymen. . . . From the baptism on, one of his fixed ideas was the perception that the true kingdom of God was not a kingdom of earthly supremacy and the enjoyment of external prosperity, but rather that those who wished to participate, as true children of God, in the eternal life of the kingdom of God, must, instead of ruling, serve others out of love, and for the sake of heavenly blessings must give up striving after earthly treasures. Since he could conceive of his Messiahship only in connection with this idea of the nature of the kingdom of God, and with the object of establishing a kingdom of God of this sort, he was obliged from the very beginning to recognize the necessity of himself, as the Messiah, giving proofs of this loving service and of this renunciation for the sake of the kingdom of God in a specially high degree."[2]

Like Wendt, Oskar Holtzmann,[3] B. Weiss,[4] Wernle[5] and other liberal investigators also maintain that the illusion of the political rôle of the Messiah only reached his ear and played around his fancy from without. It found no echo in his soul. Rather did he recognize it " unhesitatingly as

---

[1] Matt. iv, 1-11; Mark i, 12 f.; Luke iv, 1-13.
[2] Wendt, *Die Lehre Jesu,* 90, 489 f.
[3] *Leben Jesu,* 112, 113 f.   [4] *Leben Jesu,* i, 314.
[5] *Die Anfänge unserer Religion,* 32 f.; see Harnack, *Wesen des Christentums,* 21 f., 88 f.

Satanic,"[1] and cried out : " No, those are voices of the devil which appeal thus to my Messianic feeling. Away with them !"[2]

But if that is the case, where then remains the alleged transformation and progressive evolution of the Messianic consciousness of Jesus from the political to the spiritual ideal? Both before, during and after the temptation Jesus immovably, and in spite of all delusions to the contrary, holds fast to the conviction that he is called to found a purely spiritual and religious kingdom of God. The temptation brought to him no new conception and no evolution of his Messiahship whatsoever. That is the epitomized meaning of all that has been said.

Moreover, for the sake of argument, we have always taken it for granted that *in the Gospel account of the temptation it was merely a symbolical representation of a spiritual experience* and of a discord which had gradually arisen in the soul of Jesus, either from within (as Stapfer, J. Weiss, Beyschlag and Schmidt maintain), or from without (as Wendt, B. Weiss, Harnack, O. Holtzmann, Wernle and others assert). But this presupposition stands *in direct opposition to the words of the Gospel*. The synoptists speak of a strictly *historical occurrence,* not of a dramatization of psychical conditions in the soul of Jesus. This occurrence takes place outside the soul of Jesus. In fact, it turns upon a dialogue between two real persons—between the Saviour on the one hand, and Satan the tempter on the other. It is sufficient to read the Gospels in order to perceive this, and hence to acknowledge that their text excludes any psychological change in Jesus regarding the Messiah.

If, on the contrary, that supposition can be in any way justified, then the literal historical text must be given up and travestied into a parable of the soul-struggles of Jesus. The origin of such a thought can only have been the wish to establish an evolutionary historical progress in the life of the Lord, and, above all, the liberal theologians' fear of the devil. Everyone will understand that this " critical " difficulty does not deter us from holding fast to the Gospel text.

All the more is this justified because the conflict of Jesus with Satan after the baptism corresponds perfectly to the whole situation, and denotes a real and true advance in the life of the Saviour. Even Loisy has recognized this correctly : " The consecration to the Messiahship, conferred at the baptism, had, as its consequence, the temptation of Christ. Avowedly the Messiah was to contend with Satan and conquer him. . . . The decisive conflict, from which he was to emerge as victor, was death. But if after his baptism he was already considered as the Messiah, the opportunity of an encounter

[1] Weiss, *op. cit.,* 314.   [2] Wernle, *op. cit.,* 33.

with the devil had even then to be given him. Hence the great scene of the temptation in the desert."[1] It also agrees with the attitude which evil spirits henceforth assumed towards Jesus by seeking to publish abroad his Messiahship prematurely, and thereby to frustrate it.[2] Our opponents have, therefore, no ground whatever for suspecting that the history of the temptation was only a parable in which the spiritual struggles of Jesus concerning his Messianic vocation are allegorized.

If, nevertheless, one is determined to hold to such an interpretation of the passages in the Gospels, then the problem must first be solved how it happened that the psychological experiences of Jesus were represented in the form of an actual temptation by the devil. The answer can only culminate in the alternative—either the orthodox tradition given by the Evangelists has pictured to itself the temptation of Jesus thus, or else Jesus himself has regarded the action of his spiritual thoughts and feelings as an outward temptation by the devil. The first of these hypotheses is plainly inadmissible for liberal criticism, which proceeds from the fundamental standpoint that the orthodox tradition of the earliest time has done everything to glorify the human historical portrait of Jesus by making it a heavenly and divine representation of Christ. Here, however, in the history of the temptation, Jesus, on the contrary, is lowered even to the sphere of diabolical machinations. Tradition, and therefore the Evangelists, cannot have invented that history. It originates with Jesus himself.

Holtzmann expresses himself on this point as follows: "Jesus informed his disciples of the inward conflicts which he had experienced after the revelation of his Messiahship at his baptism, making thereby the happiest use of some distinct individual reminiscences in the classical form of this kind of narration."[3] Then, however, he would have to be characterized as a rhapsodist and visionary, consequently as a man whose consciousness is clouded by irrational ideas.[4] On this point we agree again with Renan, and we say that *the Liberal idea of the evolution of the Messianic consciousness of Jesus during the period of temptation thereby surrenders its own position.*

There now ensued, according to our opponents' theory, an interval of hopeful activity, during which Jesus believed that he could establish the spiritual kingdom of God without delay and without provoking a crisis. Then began a period of

---

[1] Loisy, *Les Evangiles synoptiques*, i, 185-186.
[2] See p. 138 of this vol.   [3] *Leben Jesu*, 118; *cf.* 110 f.
[4] Beyschlag also remarks: "The visionary interpretation of the history of the temptation attributes the story to the soul of Jesus; but if these visions had come from his own natural heart, that would have been a centre of evil thoughts; and if God had suggested them to him, no one would know why and for what purpose," *op. cit.*, p. 233.

desertions and of difficulties occasioned by the people, the Pharisees and the leaders of the nation; and *now there first gradually dawned upon the consciousness of Jesus the thought that he must enter into his Messianic glory and supremacy through suffering and death.* This, according to some isolated critics, is the second stage in the psychological evolution of Jesus during his public life.

" It was very natural for those who held the old conception of the life of Jesus to attribute in advance the divine plan for establishing the kingdom of redemption, as it subsequently, in the course of events, came to be known—that is, God's determination to sacrifice his Son for the salvation of the world . . . to the soul of Jesus also, as a plan of which he was fully conscious. Such a conception is at once repugnant to us moderns. . . . To one who considers the matter without prejudice and historically, it is evident that Jesus could grasp the thought that he was fated to die only when, through experience, the knowledge of an irresistible antagonism between what he had to bring and the spirit prevailing in the people forced itself upon him, and thus the inevitable breach between himself and his people revealed itself. . . . The public life of Jesus began under other constellations than those which indicated the death of the cross. Jesus hoped to save a people as such, which, of course, was possible only if it did not reject its Messiah and nail him to the cross."[1]

According to Wernle, " the Messiah was associated, in the imagination of the Jews, with unalloyed heavenly and earthly glory. . . . In the soul of Jesus bitter experience with his people ripened the thought of the necessity of suffering and even death. . . . The Messianic glory became for him now an aim, which does not fall to the lot of a favoured man through any special fortune, but rather must be won by endless effort, renunciation, and even death, in obedience to the moral law."[2]

Bousset remarks : " The scene of Gethsemani points backwards. This clear apprehension of his fate, this submission to God's will, can have been given to Jesus only little by little, as a result of severe conflict. Intimations, constantly growing stronger, must have passed through his soul already long before Gethsemani. The more clearly Jesus surveyed the lack of results arising from his work among his people, and the stronger the certainty became in him that this people was travelling along the path to destruction and had been abandoned by God, the darker must have seemed to him also the fate of his own life, and the more certain the feeling that his activity must have a disastrous ending."[3] " Into the sunny picture, full of the highest hopes of victory, the gloomy,

[1] Beyschlag, *op. cit.,* 237-239.　　　　[2] Wernle, *op. cit.,* 34.
[3] Bousset, *Jesus,* 87 f.

menacing forms of his enemies force themselves upon the gaze of Jesus—the Elders, the High Priests, the scribes, the whole Sanhedrim and those of the people who blindly obey it. That they will pronounce excommunication upon him is doubly certain if he claims his kingdom—excommunication and death."[1] Stapfer,[2] J. Weiss[3] and Ernst Kühl[4] also subscribe to these opinions.

If we ask their reasons for this, we are given only one—namely, that Jesus began to speak openly and unreservedly of his death only after the end of his Galilean activity; that is, after the day of Cesarea Philippi. From this one fact that Jesus did not earlier disclose his consciousness of approaching suffering, the conclusion is drawn that he had had no such consciousness at all. Every beginner in historical criticism knows, however, how uncritical such an *argumentum ex silentio* is.

It is rejected also by the most important liberal investigators. Wendt, for example, says: "From the fact that Jesus first spoke to his disciples of his suffering and death after the confession of Peter, it of course does not follow that he himself, precisely at that time, first recognized the destiny of suffering that awaited him."[5] "From this it does not follow that the thought of death had now for the first time, or only a little while before, occurred to Jesus."[6] "Jesus believes himself to be the Messiah. But he knows that the Messiah is to come in the clouds of heaven when he brings the kingdom of God. So he himself, therefore, must be lifted up to God before his glorious appearing. Whether he thought from the very beginning that this would be effected by his death we do not know."[7] *It cannot, therefore, be proved from the Gospel that the consciousness of his (coming) suffering and death came to him only gradually.* This might well satisfy us, for this is the very point to be determined in our inquiry.

But we can go still further and conversely say that *from the facts stated in the Gospels it is evident that Jesus, already before the confession of Peter at Cesarea Philippi, was aware of the tragic end awaiting him.* The conviction of this breaks forth already at Cesarea so definitely, so forcibly and so naturally from the depth of his heart, that, far from being an idea which comes to him now for the first time, it had been in his mind secretly for a long time. Both Wendt and B. Weiss remark this. "The inward certainty with which he asserts the necessity of this fatality, and rejects the remonstrance of Peter (Mark viii, 32), proves that he had already fought out and conquered the temptation which this destiny of suffering

---

[1] Schmidt, *op. cit.,* 120; *cf.* 122-126.
[2] *Jésus-Christ avant son ministère,* 222 ff.
[3] *id.,* 158.   [4] *id.,* 61 f.   [5] Wendt. *op. cit.,* 489.
[6] B. Weiss, *id.,* ii, 261.   [7] O. Holtzmann, *op. cit.,* 139.

offered to his Messianic consciousness and his Messianic faithfulness."[1] Mark, moreover, " especially emphasizes the fact that Jesus began to speak then for the first time openly and unreservedly of his death, not that he had not spoken of it at all."[2]

He had already repeatedly informed his disciples in regard to it, although less forcibly and in the form of allegory. Before the confession of Peter he had told them that he would give them his flesh and blood as food and drink, and that he would go back to his Father in heaven (John vi, 48-63). Still earlier he had represented himself as the sign of Jonas : " For as Jonas was in the whale's belly three days and three nights, so shall the Son of Man be in the heart of the earth three days and three nights " (Matt. xii, 39, 40). And at a still earlier date he had, in reference to his body, spoken of the destruction of the temple (John ii, 19-21), and announced that the Son of Man must be lifted up like the serpent in the wilderness, that whosoever believed on him might have life everlasting (John iii, 14, 15).

In fact, according to the unanimous testimony of the synoptists, already at the beginning of his public work he intimated to his disciples that they would lose him by death : " But the days will come when the bridegroom shall be taken away from them, and then they shall fast in those days " (Mark ii, 20 ; Matt. ix, 15 ; Luke v, 34).

Accordingly, there was never wanting sufficient, even if less positive, information regarding the suffering and death of Jesus. Long before the Galilean crisis arose, and especially long before the partisan fury of the Pharisees and of the inflamed populace led anyone to imagine his ultimate fate, Jesus was well aware that he must suffer and die.

Thus the psychological solution of the problem of Christ's suffering, as given by liberal investigators, is unmasked as historically untrue. It is not *the increasing crisis that familiarizes the Saviour little by little with the thought of suffering*. His consciousness of coming suffering was present earlier and independent of his successes or failures, and it grew out of the depths of *his own being*. Moreover, he announced his destiny of suffering, first in parables and as it were through a veil, and then clearly and forcibly, not because the opposition to him was at first small and later increased in hatred and in numbers, but, on the contrary, *this revelation*, as we have shown elsewhere, *stood wisely related to his whole system of instructing* his disciples. This began by directing their attention to the Messiah, and then by awakening and strengthening their faith in him. Only then could teaching concerning the import of the Messiahship be begun and the transformation of their Jewish ideas of the

---

[1] Wendt, *op. cit.,* 489.　　　　[2] B. Weiss, *op. cit.,* 260 f.

Messiah be gradually accomplished. And the greatest, the most difficult, and final step, consisted in making them familiar with the idea of the Messiah's suffering and death, which was most antagonistic to their Jewish sentiments, and which they could only fully grasp after Jesus had died and risen again.

It is at once clear that holders of the nationalistic theory must claim at any price a continuous evolution of the Messianic consciousness of Jesus, and that this evolution must keep step precisely with the external circumstances of his life. Otherwise, how could they still defend their favourite thesis, according to which the Messiah Jesus was essentially a florescence of his age and civilization, and his Messiahship merely a result of that florescence? But *let them not assert such an evolution of the Messianic consciousness during the public life of Jesus in the name of Gospel history!* Even Loisy writes : " The Gospels contain actually no grounds for supposing an evolution which completed itself in the Saviour's consciousness and with relation to his manner of fulfilling the task given him by providence. For such an evolution there was lacking sufficient time, in view of the brief duration of his public activity. . . . The very simple stock of thoughts and impressions which constitute his Gospel appears to have been present from the beginning—a purely religious and moral conception of the kingdom and of the conditions which lead to it. Jesus appears perfectly equipped for his task as soon as he begins to preach. The obstacles which he encountered taught him nothing new, either regarding the import of his mission or the essential conditions of fulfilling it."[1]

The hypothesis of the evolution of the Messianic consciousness of Jesus during his public life must, therefore, be rejected. There remains, however, the question : What are we to think of the alleged origin of this consciousness before the public life of the Saviour?

III.—ORIGIN OF THE MESSIANIC CONSCIOUSNESS OF CHRIST AT HIS BAPTISM.

Modern liberal criticism holds almost throughout firmly to the supposition that *the baptism of Jesus marks the moment of the birth of his Messianic consciousness.*

Among the more important investigators, only Karl von Hase[2] and lately Bernhard Weiss[3] are of the opinion that the faith of Jesus in his Messianic vocation was formed in him at least subsequently to his twelfth year, and that it surely came to absolute certainty before his baptism. The other critics either explain with great positiveness the baptism in the

[1] *Les Evangiles synoptiques,* i, 212 f.
[2] *Geschichte Jesu,* 285 ff.   [3] *Leben Jesu,* i, 279-283, 294 ff.

Jordan as the original "natal hour of the Messiah,"[1] and the history of the baptism of Jesus as the "historical birth of his Messianic consciousness,"[2] or else they consider as "probable"[3] and "in the highest degree likely" the view that assigns the awakening of the Messianic consciousness to a time previous to the baptism.[4]

If we ask the reasons for such an interpretation, the majority of the critics forthwith refer us to the fact that *the simplest, and, indeed, the only possible way is to represent the Messianic consciousness as something historical and evolutionary.* Jesus is said by them to have felt, during his quiet life at Nazareth, more and more that he was the "Son of God," and accordingly to have "thought himself into" Messianic ideas and situations. The Baptist's preaching of the kingdom, and the popular movement called forth by him, raised this psychological conception to the highest degree, and when Jesus allowed himself to be baptized he thought that he perceived inwardly, through God's agency, the confirmation of his psychical emotions, and so "experienced" his Messianic vocation.

The representation continually recurring in these writers, with but few divergences, is somewhat as follows : " Jesus had concentrated all his thoughts and mental powers upon the smallest and most inconspicuous point—the secret relation of his life to God. . . . Then the news from the Jordan produced an overwhelming impression upon the heart of Jesus. He carried with him to the Jordan a secret question which was to be addressed to God, and into which his whole previous spiritual life condensed itself—namely, whether his hour also had not now come to speak of what had been revealed to him in secret communion with his heavenly Father. The solemn agitation in his soul increased at sight of this community of the baptized, these crowds of people without a leader and yet susceptible to prophetic exhortation. It waxed stronger on beholding the august form of the Baptist, who with impassioned words was exerting to the utmost all his powers, and to this was added a consciousness of the incomparably great moment. Modestly and unobserved, Jesus also advanced to request baptism—the Galilean before the preacher of repentance ! But an overwhelming emotion secretly flooded his heart, and when he emerged from the water, praying for and vowing purity of soul in every temptation to sin, the ecstasy seized him. He saw from the opened heavens the Spirit of God descending upon him, and perceived signs from heaven, which at last assured him that God was calling him to proclaim his new faith among his people. . . . Jesus knew that he

---

[1] Johannes Weiss, *Christus*, 23.
[2] Regensburg, *l.c.*, i, 219.
[3] Loisy, *Les Evangiles synoptiques*, i, 206.   [4] Bousset, *Jesus*, 80.

had been sent to bring to completion the final era of the world.''[1]

We receive no further explanation. But that is regarded as sufficient, since the Messianic consciousness of Jesus must be merely the result of natural development, and this development cannot be made credible otherwise than by the above psychological fabrication.

But the question is precisely *whether this psychological fabrication, and with it the audaciously asserted origin of the Messianic consciousness at the time of the baptism in the Jordan, can be justified historically.* Where the liberal investigators conclude their explanation a great interrogation point must be placed. How and on what grounds can it be proved that the subjective view of the defenders of the evolution theory corresponds to the objective facts in the life of Jesus?

Only a few critics, particularly Willibald Beyschlag[2] and Oskar Holtzmann,[3] find it worth their while to furnish this proof. Proceeding from the conviction that Jesus, subsequent to his baptism, had undoubtedly a positive Messianic consciousness, they try to prove, on the one hand, that this consciousness had been unknown to the Saviour before that occurrence, and, on the other hand, that the communication of that consciousness took place *in connection with* the baptism.

On the latter point Beyschlag writes : " The narrative of the baptism, uniformly placed by the synoptic Gospels at the beginning of the public life of Jesus, is evidently intended to inform us of the origin of his Messianic consciousness. It describes how the Spirit of God descended upon him, and, therefore, how he became the spiritually Anointed One, or the Messiah, for that indeed is the meaning of this name. . . . Heaven—that is, the upper, immaterial world—opened above him as he was baptized by John, that it might send down upon him in abundant measure its highest gift ; gently, as it were upon the wings of a dove, the Holy Spirit descends upon him, whom, as a prophet, it will not visit only temporarily, but upon whom, as the spiritually anointed, it will remain ; and what the symbols bring before his inward vision a divine voice within him explains to his spiritual ear, combining the words of Ps. ii, 7 and Isa. xlii, 1 thus : " This is my beloved Son, in whom I am well pleased "—that is, my chosen Messiah.[4] Oskar Holtzmann[5] interprets the events at the baptism in a precisely similar manner.

The *fact itself,* therefore, that Jesus was recognized, at his baptism, as the Son of God, and that the Holy Ghost was

[1] P. W. Schmidt, *Die Geschichte Jesu,* i, 53, 56-57 ; similarly, Hess, *Jesus von Nazareth,* 11 ; Bousset, *l.c.,* 80 ; Stapfer, *l.c.,* 152 ; Loisy, *Les Evangiles synoptiques, i,* 206, 408, etc.

[2] *Leben Jesu,* i, 224 ff.   [3] *Leben Jesu,* 99 ff.

[4] Beyschlag, *op. cit.,* pp. 216, 218.   [5] *op. cit.,* p. 104.

then communicated to him, is supposed to prove the simultaneous awakening of his Messianic consciousness. But this fact permits of another interpretation also, which has been given to the occurrence at the baptism both by the Evangelists and by all the Christian centuries—namely, that at his baptism Jesus received, in presence of the forerunner John, his divine attestation as being the Messiah, his visible, spiritual consecration to the Messianic vocation, and therewith also the supernatural announcement that the time appointed by God for the fulfilment of the Messianic vocational work had begun. "That Jesus became the Messiah, as Luther became the reformer—inwardly prepared for it, yet without having any premonition of it—that the realization of his vocation . . . came over him one day suddenly and with unexpected and overpowering divine power,"[1] and that " at the moment of baptism the consciousness of his Messianic calling was awakened and came into existence through a meeting and contact of his soul with his heavenly Father,"[2] does not at all appear from the events at the baptism. Rather does everything indicate the contrary. As Bartmann significantly indicates : " Christ himself receives it (the divine revelation at the baptism) in thankful prayer, yet without excitement or inquiry. For him it is no beginning, no turning-point in his sonship, no revelation of a secret, no matter of faith concerning which he might subsequently have doubts, no lofty height reached by a moral struggle from which he could be again thrown down, and no light from above which the earthly man in the darkness of this life, of which even a spiritually endowed Paul complains, longingly seeks for and joyfully retains. For him it is the confirmation of an existing fact."[3]

To this, it is true, Oskar Holtzmann objects that the way in which the events of the baptism took place indicates that it was a matter of a real change and transformation of the consciousness of Jesus. Holtzmann assumes at once that the heavenly voice and the communication of the Spirit on that occasion were not historical events perceptible by the senses, but merely a vision, an inward, ecstatical experience which " happened only in the soul of Jesus, and throughout had reference to Jesus only."[4] The effect of this inward and visionary seeing and hearing must, accordingly, also have been an inward, " complete transformation of his life " and consciousness.[5]

But this conclusion does not all result from Holtzmann's premises. However the events of the baptism may be interpreted, whether as an external or an internal experience, and whether this was known to Jesus only or to other persons

---

[1] Beyschlag, *op. cit.,* 225. [2] *id.,* 231.
[3] *Das Himmelreich und sein König,* 124 f.
[4] *op. cit.,* p. 105. [5] *op. cit.,* p. 106.

also, does not alter the facts at all. In any case, the question would remain whether Jesus actually received the Messianic consciousness at his baptism, or whether only the final consecration was conferred upon him by the heavenly voice and the indwelling of the Holy Ghost; and in any event this latter supposition would have to be answered affirmatively after due consideration of the reasons already given.

But how about the premises themselves which Holtzmann lays down? In the first place, was Jesus the only witness of the heavenly voice and the descent of the Holy Ghost, as Holtzmann and Wendt,[1] among others, assert? The Gospels deny this; Matthew (iii, 16) and Mark (i, 10) simply tell us that Jesus saw the heavens open and the Spirit descend upon him. Whether the Baptist was also an eye-witness of this is not said. It seems, however, to be taken for granted, since it is at once remarked quite objectively of the heavenly voice: " And behold a voice from heaven saying, This is my beloved Son in whom I am well pleased." The representation also makes the impression of having originated from the Baptist, who also saw and heard these things. Still more is this the case in Luke's narrative, where the whole scene is related from the standpoint of the observing Baptist: " Heaven was opened, and the Holy Ghost descended in a bodily shape, as a dove upon him (Jesus), and a voice came from heaven: Thou art my beloved Son; in thee I am well pleased " (Luke iii, 21-22). In the Fourth Gospel the report of the baptism is actually attributed to John the Baptist, who appears as an eye-witness. John relates that the Baptist had long ardently desired to meet among his neophytes him whom he, without knowing him personally, had proclaimed as the Greater One—that is, as the Messiah. God had revealed to him: "He upon whom thou shalt see the Spirit descending and remaining upon him, he it is that baptizeth with the Holy Ghost." As now Jesus comes before him and receives the baptism of water, John perceives the Holy Ghost descend like a dove and abide upon him, so that he can say of him positively: " I saw and I gave testimony that this is the Son of God " (John i, 26-34).

Thus the four Gospels report in entire unanimity that both John and Jesus were eye and ear witnesses of the event. Even Beyschlag recognizes the impossibility of limiting this to Jesus only.[2]

The proof also has been already furnished that O. Holtzmann, even though receiving for it the approval of the whole liberal school of criticism,[3] is wrong in interpreting this as

[1] *op. cit.,* p. 97.　　　　[2] *op. cit.,* p. 218.
[3] Thus Furrer, *Das Leben Jesu Christi,* 69, 2nd. ed.; W. Baldensperger, *Das Selbstbewusstsein Jesu,* 160 ff.; H. Wendt, *Die Lehre Jesu,* 97; *System der christlichen Lehre,* ii, 289 f.; Bousset, *Jesus,* 2 f.; H. J. Holtzmann, *Neutestamentl. Theologie,* i, 271; E. Schürer, *Das*

a mere vision. How could both John and Jesus have had at the same time precisely the same ecstatical experience, and (according to the liberal theory) have merely imagined that they saw the heavens opened and the descent of the Holy Ghost, and that they heard the voice of God from heaven? Rationalistic theologians will hardly accept this double psychological miracle at a moment when, through their fear of miracles and a divine revelation, they are contesting the reality of the events of the baptism.

In addition to this, we have also the arbitrary attempt to represent Jesus as a visionary, in contradiction not only to the whole personality of the Saviour, but to the whole Gospel account of the baptism, against the credibility of which a valid argument has never yet been brought. Even critics like Beyschlag and Kühl reject the hypothesis that Jesus beheld a vision at his baptism, because " the tendency to see visions, as we should have to suppose here in the case of Jesus, is found nowhere else in his life,"[1] and because " the whole impression of the personality of Jesus . . . makes the supposition of visionary conditions in his life quite impossible."[2]

Beyschlag and Kühl, therefore, change somewhat the unfortunate hypothesis of a " vision " by limiting the abnormal and fantastic convulsion (for there can be no question among the naturalistic critics of any divinely produced ecstasy) to the Baptist only, and add " that, corresponding to the vision of the Baptist, Jesus had an experience, by means of which he acquired at once, as a spiritual certainty, what the Baptist learned through a vision."[3] But that is truly to fall from the frying-pan into the fire. How could Jesus learn inwardly exactly what John beheld in an ecstasy, and *vice versa,* without a real supernatural coincidence? Of the contradiction between this pretence at getting out of the difficulty and the representation of the Gospel we will say nothing. The free-thinker, Friedrich Spitta, passes judgement on it with commendable frankness : " The traditional view, held by critical theologians, that in the events of the baptism it was a question of a vision referring to Jesus only, and beheld by the Baptist,

messianische Selbstbewusstsein Christi, 13; B. Weiss, *Leben Jesu,* i, 299, 303; P. W. Schmidt, *Die Geschichte Jesu,* 57; W. Beyschlag, *Leben Jesu,* i, 218 f.; H. Zimmermann, *Der historische Wert der ältesten Geschichte Jesu,* 86 ff.; Fritz Scholl, *Prot. Monatshefte,* 180 (1907); J. Bornemann, *Die Taufe Christi durch Johannes in der dogmatischen Beleuchtung der christlichen Theologie der vier ersten Jahrhunderte* (1906); Loisy, *Le quatrième Evangile,* 229; *L'Evangile et l'Eglise,* 20, 2nd ed.; *Les Evangiles synoptiques,* i, 185; Réville, *Jésus de Nazareth,* ii, 5 ff.; E. Kühl, *Selbstbewusstsein Jesu,* 39 ff. On the contrary side, Fritz Barth, *Die Hauptprobleme des Lebens Jesu,* 140 ff.
[1] Beyschlag, *op. cit.,* 219.   [2] Kühl, *op. cit.,* 41.
[3] Kühl, *op. cit.,* 42, and similarly Beyschlag, *op. cit.,* 219.

has been rightly rejected by A. Merx[1] as a modern illusion. A voice from heaven and the appearance of a dove are there, so that they may be heard and perceived by those present."[2]

Thus every attempt to explain the events of the baptism as if they really gave to the Saviour the consciousness of his Messiahship fails. On the contrary, everything indicates that the baptism denotes, not the beginning of the Messianic consciousness, but the commencement of the Messianic activity. This conviction could be invalidated only by the proof that *Jesus, before his baptism—that is, when he came to the Baptist—did not as yet possess the Messianic consciousness.*

Once more it is O. Holtzmann who undertakes to furnish this proof. In company with Strauss, he makes the Saviour enter upon his journey to the region around Jordan for baptism as a sinner in need of salvation, and as a man, who, like all others, needed a change of heart and forgiveness of sins, and who hoped to become, through baptism by water, a member of the coming Messianic kingdom, and was far from regarding himself as the appointed founder and future Lord of this kingdom—namely, the Messiah.[3] In fact, Holtzmann holds that the thought that he was the Messiah was so far from the mind of Jesus that he had not joined this movement towards baptism of his own accord, but had let himself be urged into taking part in it by the example of those around him : " As Luther was actually forced into the Reformation, so Jesus had to be forced into his work. It is, as it were, from a presentiment of persecution, flight and death on the cross that he dreads to meet the mighty preacher of penance, whose words are to unloose the forces still slumbering within him. . . . Like so many others, Jesus also lets himself be baptized. A determination thenceforth to live only in accordance with God's will, and the hope of thus participating in the kingdom of God, have urged him also to baptism."[4]

In proof of these assertions, Holtzmann appeals to merely one passage in the apocryphal " Gospel to the Hebrews," in which it is said : " Lo, the Mother of the Lord and his brethren said to him [Jesus] : John the Baptist is baptizing for the forgiveness of sins ; we want to go and be baptized by him. But he said to them : In what have I sinned, that I should go thither and be baptized by him? Anything wrong that I have said must have been said through ignorance. . . ."[5]

Now it would be very easy to point out that this text of the Gospel to the Hebrews presupposes in Jesus sinlessness and

[1] *Die Evangelien des Markus und Lukas,* 14.

[2] Spitta, *Das Johannes-Evangelium als Quelle der Geschichte Jesu,* 425 (Göttingen, 1910).

[3] Holtzmann, *Leben Jesu,* 99-103.   [4] *id.,* 102, 103.

[5] Nestle, *Novi Test. Græci Suppl.,* 76; Hennecke, *Neutest. Apokryphen,* 19.

Messianic consciousness, not sinfulness and need of redemption. It would, however, be a pity to waste a single word over it. One can only feel amazement that so serious a critic as O. Holtzmann does not blush to draw his conclusions from so dark a source when the historical tradition of the canonical Gospels flows so clear and limpidly.

This is not the place to demonstrate the absolute sinlessness of Jesus from his life in the Gospels. It is sufficient to point out that, according to the most indubitable representation of Jesus in the Gospels, he did not at all come to his baptism as a sinner and a seeker for salvation.

The two oldest reports of the baptism in the Gospels of John and Matthew[1] express this with all the simplicity and clearness that could be desired.

According to the Fourth Gospel, the Baptist publicly and officially (John i, 19-25) announced the approach of the Messiah, whose forerunner he was : " I baptize with water, but there hath stood one in the midst of you, whom you know not. The same is he that shall come after me, who is preferred before me, the latchet of whose shoe I am not worthy to loose " (John i, 26, 27). " The next day John saw Jesus coming to him, and he saith : Behold the Lamb of God, behold him who taketh away the sin of the world ! This is he of whom I said, After me there cometh a man who is preferred before me, because he was before me . . . that he may be made manifest in Israel, therefore am I come baptizing with water " (John i, 29-31).

While the Fourth Gospel adheres so steadfastly to the scene in which John, after the baptism, makes the people acquainted with the sinless and sin-forgiving Messiah who has thus made his appearance, Matthew relates his meeting with Jesus before the baptism. He had just pointed the latter out with the words : " I indeed baptize you in water unto penance, but he that shall come after me is mightier than I, whose shoes I am not worthy to bear ; he shall baptize you in the Holy Ghost and fire. Whose fan is in his hand, and he will thoroughly cleanse his floor, and gather his wheat into the barn ; but the chaff he will burn with unquenchable fire " (Matt. iii, 11, 12).

The Messiah is a judge and an avenger of what is evil, a bringer of salvation and one who baptizes with the Spirit. John recognizes as such the man who, immediately after this, comes from Galilee to the Jordan to be baptized. In his presence the Baptist becomes conscious of his own poverty of soul and sinfulness, and instead of offering baptism for the forgiveness of sins and for a preparation for the kingdom of God to him, he asks to be himself baptized by him : " I ought to be baptized by thee, and comest thou to me ?" (Matt. iii, 14).

---

[1] Beyschlag also, *Leben Jesu*, i, 219, and B. Weiss, *Leben Jesu*, i, 295, 300 f., declare that the representation given by John, in connection with Matthew, is the oldest, and originates with the Baptist himself.

This, at all events, presupposes sinlessness. Otherwise we should have to suppose that the severe preacher of penance, who cast the reproach of sin into the faces of the greatest of this world, had wished to flatter obsequiously a sinful man from Nazareth.

And Jesus does not reject the words of the Baptist as unsuitable. On the contrary, he confirms this view of John that he has no need of baptism and forgiveness, yet asks for baptism for other reasons : " Suffer it to be so now, for so it becometh us to fulfil all justice " (Matt. iii, 15). He is willing to submit to the baptism of John voluntarily, since it was the will of God that all Israel should meet the coming kingdom of heaven in the spirit of repentance (Matt. iii, 1-6).

Thus Jesus himself pointed out that baptism by water was neither the only thing necessary nor especially a sign and acknowledgement of sinfulness, but was, above all, the symbol of a decided turning of the will towards God and the approaching kingdom of heaven. Therefore it was fitting that precisely he should receive it who, sinless and at one with God's will, wished to call all men to the kingdom.

Wendt rightly says : " If the main purpose of John's baptism of repentance had been the confession and bewailing of sins hitherto committed, we should have to regard the coming of Jesus to this baptism as very strange, and would be able to see in it either an argument against the immaculate purity of his religious consciousness or the exhibition of a certain false modesty. But what John aimed at was evidently a change of heart from sin to the positive purpose of properly fulfilling the will of God. Hence it is quite comprehensible that Jesus, not only in spite of, but precisely because of, his consciousness of making a sincere effort to fulfil God's will in childlike obedience, felt himself compelled to let the baptism of John be applied to him also. Thereby he put the seal upon his determination to have in mind only the fulfilling of the will of God, and gave to this moral and religious volition of his a definite application to the approach of the Messianic kingdom of salvation announced by the Baptist."[1]

B. Weiss expresses himself in a similar way. " The symbolism of John's baptism," he writes, "denotes merely the complete termination of the life hitherto led, and the beginning of a new and entirely different one. For the sinful people it was the ending of their previous life of sin and the commencement of a new, sinless existence, together with the solemn confirmation of a thorough change of disposition. This for one who was devoid of sin it could not be ; but it confirmed in his case also the conclusion of his former life and the beginning of an entirely new one. It is true this previous life, which he now wished, as it were, to bury in the waters of the Jordan, had not been for him a sinful one, but it had been

[1] Wendt, *Die Lehre Jesu*, 96 f.

devoted to the natural relations of his life, to his former human professional calling and to his previous training. The new life to which he rose from the baptismal waters was distinguishable from his former life, not by his sinlessness, but only by the fact that it was thenceforth to be consecrated entirely to his supreme, divine vocation. In this sense Jesus saw, precisely in the command of God which summoned him also to baptism, the long-expected sign from his Father that it was now time to begin his Messianic career. It is true this solution of the question also presupposes that when he came for baptism he was already fully aware of his destined vocation to be the Messiah of Israel."[1]

In reality the going of Jesus to baptism is only fully comprehensible through this presupposition. If Jesus was conscious of his Messianic vocation, then he came for baptism as the vicarious penitent for the sins of others and as the Servant of God, who made satisfaction for mankind, and of whom it had been written in the fifty-third chapter of Isaiah that he would not separate himself from his sinful people, whose sins he would take upon himself, and whose unrighteousness he would destroy by his own righteousness. This conception alone corresponds to the line of thought found in the synoptic Gospels, and is expressly and unequivocally represented by John the Baptist in the Fourth Gospel as the only correct one. Jesus there appears for the baptism by water as the long-desired Messiah (John i, 27, 30) and as he who will confer, not the preparatory baptism by water, but the Messianic baptism of the Spirit (John i, 26), and as the " Lamb of God " upon whom the sins of humanity are laid, and who " taketh away the sin of the world " (John i, 29).

Only in this light also do we understand the progressive revelation of God in the events of the baptism. Jesus comes before the Father in personal holiness and perfection, and completely prepared to consummate for sinful humanity Messianic penance and Messianic righteousness. Then heaven opens, acknowledges him as the Messiah and God's beloved Son, and his vicarious atonement as being pleasing to God, while the Holy Ghost, according to prophecy (Isa. lxi, 1), seals this beginning of the Messianic work by descending upon the Saviour and abiding upon him. The evolutionary hypothesis, on the contrary, according to which Jesus came to his baptism not only without any Messianic consciousness, but even with a consciousness of personal sinfulness and need of redemption, not only has no basis of fact, but explains nothing and confuses everything, including its own line of reasoning concerning the evolutionary theory. The artificially woven thread of the natural development and preparation of Jesus, the equally natural end of which was to lead finally to the birth of the

[1] *id.*, p. 208. Similarly Furrer, *Das Leben Jesu Christi,* 68 f., 2nd ed.

Messianic consciousness at the baptism, is promptly and violently cut, and instead of the evolution so highly praised by our opponents there comes a complete revolution in the Saviour's consciousness. For "there is no psychological transition possible from the consciousness of being a sinner in need of salvation, like all men, to that of being the Saviour from sin for all men."[1]

In consideration of this, the theory of Holtzmann is now rejected by all eminent representatives of the liberal school of investigation. Adolf Harnack expresses himself in regard to it as follows : " Unless everything deceives us, there lie behind the period of Jesus' life which is known to us no violent crises and storms and no abrupt break with his past. Nowhere in his sayings and discourses, whether he threatens and punishes, or cordially invites and summons, or whether he speaks of his relation to the Father or to the world, do we perceive traces of spiritual revolutions which he has suppressed or scars of a fearful conflict. In him everything flows forth as a matter of course and as if it could not be otherwise, as a spring bursts forth from the depths of the earth, clear and unimpeded. Show us the man who at thirty years of age can speak thus if he has survived intense conflicts of the soul, in which he finally burns what he once adored, and adores what he once burned ! Show us the man who has broken with his past in order then to call others to repentance, but who, in doing so, never speaks of his own repentance ! This observation excludes the possibility of his life having been passed in spiritual contrasts."[2] Similarly do B. Weiss, Beyschlag, Konrad Furrer, Wendt and others repudiate every attempt to support the hopelessly lost position of those who make the Messianic consciousness of Jesus originate from the baptism by saying that Jesus had been, before his baptism, himself a sinful man in need of salvation.

IV.—Preparation of the Messianic Consciousness of Christ in the Consciousness of his Sonship.

The general endeavour of those who hold the evolutionary theory is rather to make the previous life of Jesus a continual preparation and increasing training for the subsequent reception of his Messianic consciousness. The central point and soul of this preparation is said to be his *consciousness of being the Son of God.* Jesus, it is said, brought with him out of his youthful years and out of Galilee such a highly developed consciousness of sonship that from it, under the influence of the popular movement towards baptism in the Jordan, the Messianic consciousness had necessarily to make its appearance, as the flower develops from the bud under the quicken-

---

[1] Beyschlag, *op. cit.*, i, 228.   [2] *Wesen des Christentums,* 21 f.

ing rays of the sun. Here we get at the root of all efforts to explain the Messianic consciousness of Jesus as a result of gradual evolution.

The unorthodox Christian view is simply forced to eradicate this root of its system unless it is willing to surrender and give up its naturalistic explanation of the belief of Jesus in his Messianic vocation. We have to do here, therefore, not with individual groups, but with the whole school of rationalistic and rationalizing investigators of the life of Jesus. They all inform us exhaustively how, from the inward disposition of the boy Jesus, and from the external circumstances of his environment, the conviction little by little arose in his mind that he was the Son of God—that is, that he stood in a loving or childlike relation to his Father in heaven, which was not, it is true, based upon a physical sonship, yet signified a very peculiar ethical sonship. Our opponents, indeed, assert that the title Son of God, as Jesus understood it, has exclusively this sense, and never means in Jesus essential divine sonship—that is, his real divinity. We shall investigate this problem later. For the present it is a question only of the origin of this consciousness of divine sonship and of its relation to his Messianic consciousness, however the former may be understood. This conviction already showed itself fully developed in the twelve-year-old Jesus in the temple. Little by little this consciousness of sonship increased so much under his own moral activity and under the influence of the ideas of his time and surroundings, that he asked himself more and more whether he was not called to make his fellow-men also children of their Father in heaven, and thus to render the Messianic work and kingdom a reality. His baptism gave, then, the conclusive answer to this question by finally merging his consciousness of divine sonship into his consciousness of being the Messiah.

Out of many dramatic descriptions[1] of this psychological development of Jesus let us select only one of the most significant, at least in its main features.

Konrad Furrer represents it thus : " It stands to reason that in his father's house he received early in life impressions of a very vital piety. . . Father and mother, teachers in the village, and instructors in the law, shared in the task of instructing the children in the Scriptures. We may, there-

---

[1] See, for example, Hess, *Jesus von Nazareth,* 4-9; Schmidt, *Geschichte Jesu,* 52-56; Wendt, *Die Lehre Jesu,* 91; J. Kögel, *Das Messiasbewusstsein Jesu,* in *Reich Christi,* viii, 403-420; Stapfer, *Jésus-Christ avant son ministère,* 89, 188; Loisy, *L'Evangile et l'Eglise,* 56; *Les Evangiles synoptiques,* i, 408; Beyschlag, *Leben Jesu,* i, 175; ii, 57; B. Weiss, *Leben Jesu,* i, 279. Strangely enough, B. Weiss, 280-283, expresses the view that the Messianic consciousness developed from that of sonship before the baptism, while Beyschlag, i, 224, supposes a sudden transition at the moment of baptism.

fore, without hesitation, suppose that Jesus had early absorbed all the treasures of this wonderful collection of writings. . . . We cannot say in what year for the first time a higher perception of God awoke in that young soul. . . . The Gospels give us only one, though certainly a very significant, report of the child Jesus, when twelve years old, in the temple. There the boy felt as if he were in heaven. He forgot the whole world in order to let himself be instructed about God and divine things by the wisest and most learned of his people. That was for him an unspeakably great joy. In order to understand it we need only to remember how great and distinguished artists often show in early youth a consuming desire for their art. . . . Who has not read something of the kind of the renowned sculptor Canova or of Thorwaldsen and others? As, therefore, these highly gifted artists exhibited in their tender years an ardent longing for art, so did the boy Jesus have a powerful yearning for the closest and most lasting communion with God possible. . . . Jesus felt the majesty of God most profoundly, and yet out of the depths of his soul was forced this cry : ' Wist ye not that I must be about my Father's business?' In the whole history of the world there is no more certain fact than this, that Jesus felt himself to be the Son of God, and that in obedience to the strongest impulse of his soul he could not do otherwise than call God ' Father ' and himself his Son. . . . How comes it that Jesus with such positiveness and steadfastness calls himself the Son of God? To this we have only one answer : His spirit, as no other since him has done with equal force, felt and experienced in himself pure goodness, holy love and limitless compassion as the supreme good. . . . With his consciousness of divine sonship Jesus stands absolutely alone in his time and in his world, for even the most pious men among his contemporaries in their attitude towards God were penetrated only by a consciousness of being his servants. Hence there must have developed in him, out of his own spiritual needs, a lofty sentiment, by reason of which he knew himself to be called to perform a great and unique task in the future. In other words, his Messianic consciousness has been formed out of his consciousness of sonship.''[1]

This prettily devised hypothesis, condensed into three short sentences, means that Jesus in earliest childhood acquired his unique consciousness of divine sonship through the influence of his disposition and education, but that his filial consciousness, which was already complete in the twelve-year-old boy, had nothing to do with his Messianic thoughts. On the contrary, that consciousness developed itself more and more, from his twelfth to his thirtieth year, in line with a combination of ideas regarding the divine sonship and the Messiah,

[1] Konrad Furrer, *Das Leben Jesu Christi*, 46-55, 2nd ed.

and so became the germ out of which, at the moment of the baptism, his final Messianic consciousness sprang into being. We must examine these three statements separately.

First, the alleged gradual *development of the consciousness of sonship to the Messianic consciousness, from the twelfth to the thirtieth year of Jesus.*

This is, in brief, a necessary invention, unless, indeed, we call it a necessary lie, inherent in a confused way of manufacturing history. We actually possess not a single particle of information about this period of Jesus's life. The years of his youth and early manhood are years of sacred stillness and profound seclusion. Out of them not a sound reaches us. The so-called " Gospel of Christ's youth " breaks off abruptly with the report of the twelve-year-old Jesus in the temple. Moreover, the liberal critics insist upon recognizing in that whole " Gospel of Christ's youth " only the scene in the temple as genuine and credible.[1] Indeed, when it appears to them advantageous to do so, they deny or ignore even the scene in the temple, or indulge in exaggeration concerning it in the name of " criticism." " With the baptism we tread for the first time in the life of Jesus on historical ground,"[2] or, " Tradition has not preserved for us anything certain about his development; scarcely does it lift even once the veil which is spread over his childhood, passed in the midst of numerous brothers and sisters; hardly once does it name him " carpenter,"[3] or, flatly, " We know nothing of the history of Jesus in the first thirty years of his life. . . . Never shall we discover through what inward development Jesus passed from the certainty of being the Son of God to the other certainty of being the promised Messiah."[4]

Very well; only this sort of criticism should then be honourable enough to confess that the representations which it gives describing the passing of Jesus from the consciousness of sonship to that of the Messiahship have their origin only in the pleasing realm of fancy, and that the whole hypothesis referring to them is every word pure invention.

Moreover, the presupposition also on which this hypothesis rests is itself merely an artificial fabrication—*namely, the contrast between the filial consciousness of the twelve-year-old lad and his Messianic consciousness.*

In order to understand this, we must again bear in mind

---

[1] We shall take up the question of the genuineness and credibility of the Gospel of Christ's youth in Part III. The account of the twelve-year-old Jesus is almost universally regarded as historical by our critical opponents. See, for example, B. Weiss, *Leben Jesu,* i, 253; O. Holtzmann, *Leben Jesu,* 76; Wendt, *Die Lehre Jesu,* 94; Stapfer, *Jésus-Christ avant son ministère,* 58; Furrer, *Leben Jesu Christi,* 46.

[2] Hess, *op. cit.,* p. 11

[3] Deissmann, *Evangelium und Urchristentum,* in *Beiträge zur Weiterentwickelung der christlichen Religion,* 83 (München, 1905).

[4] Harnack, *Wesen des Christentums,* 20, 87.

that, previous to his baptism, Jesus had spoken only once of this filial relationship to God before he began his public activity. It was precisely that voluntary confession of his: "Did you not know that I must be about my Father's business?" (Luke ii, 49). That this consciousness of being the Son of God excludes the consciousness of also being the Messiah cannot, however, be deduced from the words of the child Christ.

The very contrary appears to be the case. For what is the Messianic vocation of Jesus other than exactly his exclusive absorption in his "Father's business"? Even O. Holtzmann interprets the reply of the child Jesus thus: "The narrative portrays to us the growing lad Jesus in a way exactly corresponding to his future activity."[1]

We shall see later that the twelve-year-old boy really revealed even a divine consciousness, and that, therefore, any doubt of his having then been aware of his Messianic destiny is impossible.

If, however, for the time being we do not interpret Jesus' consciousness of sonship in the temple in that highest divine sense, its Messianic import can nevertheless be certainly discovered. We need only to ask how Jesus subsequently in his public life understood the title "Son of God" in its relation to the title of Messiah. From this consequence we can and must then draw our inferences in regard to the opinion held by him previously.

Now there is not the least doubt that for Jesus the name "Son of God," from the time of his baptism to the day of his death, was always equivalent to "the Messiah." Whether it does not mean still more—namely, his metaphysical, essential unity with his Father—must, as has been said already, be investigated elsewhere in this work. Our exposition regarding "the fact of the Messianic consciousness of Jesus" furnishes for this unqestionable evidence. Indeed, our opponents themselves are so convinced of it that they invoke and obstinately defend the absolute identity of the titles "Son of God" and "Messiah," as soon as the conservative critics show signs of seeing in Jesus the Son of God, more than the Messiah.

Already, in the account of the baptism and temptation— where the name Messiah is not yet found at all, but only that of the Father or of the Son—all liberal and rationalistic critics interpret the expression Son of God as a title of the Messiah. Why, then, should they hesitate to adopt such an exegesis only precisely in the story of Jesus' youth? For this reason, and for this reason only: that the defenders of the theory of evolution wish to have it so, and must have it so. If the Messianic consciousness of Jesus has not been developed step by step from his consciousness of sonship, then the entire

[1] *Leben Jesu*, 76.

foundation would be completely taken away from the evolutionary thesis in regard to Jesus. This calamity must, therefore, be prevented at all hazards, even at the cost of all psychology and all genuine history.

The third assertion of the development of the *consciousness of sonship in the child Jesus* is to be attributed finally to the same theoretical evolutionary hobby. Ostensibly, according to the modern school, the consciousness of sonship developed, in accordance with psychological necessity, from the temperament and *education* of the child of Nazareth. Now it is, of course, certainly true and evident that Jesus grew up and was educated amid God-fearing associates and in the atmosphere of the Holy Scriptures, like all pious Jews. But how was it that precisely Jesus, and he alone, in distinction from all his youthful contemporaries, educated in the same way, found in this education and environment the proper soil to nourish his consciousness of sonship? That is the mystery. Why did such an ordinary and universal cause have in him, and in him only, such an extraordinary and unique result?

Modern criticism replies : " Because that cause met in him an absolutely unique *temperament,* inclined to recognize profoundly the fatherhood of God and to experience the truth of it spiritually." The existence of such a temperament can be at once conceded. Yet thereby the question recurs with double force : How could Jesus in his earliest years, and almost in the cradle (for the psychological process is supposed to have ended with twelve years), how could he, at an age which antedates all serious contemplation and experience, have attained to such extraordinary, unheard-of and unique knowledge and experience concerning his filial relation to God? Every attempt to solve this psychological problem must be condemned in advance as nonsensical and as doing violence to normal human intelligence.

Yet, apart from this, our opponents' attempt to reconstruct psychologically the beginnings of Jesus' consciousness of being the Son of God could be taken seriously only under the presupposition that we possess no historical information about those beginnings. But this presupposition does not correspond to the facts. The evidence of Jesus' consciousness of being the Son of God, in Part III of this volume, will show that the Saviour gave very definite information on this subject, and that his estimate of himself contradicts the fantastic views of modern investigators.

Among these, some of decidedly liberal tendencies have also this impression. Gustav Dalman acknowledges that the utterances of Jesus concerning his filial relation to God " sound as if Jesus had never known any beginning of it. It appears to form naturally a part of his personality that he, in distinction from all others, expects to acquire the domination of the

world, and possesses an immediate knowledge of God, just as
a son by the right of birth becomes an heir, and by growing
up in close intimacy with his father from childhood comes
into a spiritual relation to his father peculiar to a child."[1]
Wendt says still more decidedly : " On the ground of the
religious self-consciousness in accordance with which Jesus
subsequently judged and acted, we are justified in assuming
that, so far back as his consciousness extended, he had always
felt like a son towards God. . . . From the very outset he
lived in the consciousness as well as in the condition of divine
sonship."[2]

V.—Origin of the Messianic Consciousness of Christ in the Consciousness of his Nature.

After these explanations, no further proof is really needed
of the fact that the consciousness of divine sonship and the
consciousness of Messiahship were naturally present in Jesus
from the beginning, or, in other words, that they coincided
with his consciousness of his own being and personality.

As we have thus far sufficiently seen, *all attempts to represent them as the result of a gradual evolution break down
completely.* The rationalistic and rationalizing school of
research has made every effort to prove the beginnings and
development of the Messianic consciousness in the youth,
baptism, temptation and separate stages of the public life of
Jesus. And yet the result is always the same. When one
thinks one has discovered a further development or even the
beginning of this consciousness, or finally even a preparation
for it, every time, by a more careful investigation, there gushes
forth the full, clear spring of the Saviour's perfect, complete
conviction of his Messianic work and vocation. The Messianic
consciousness of Jesus is and remains a mystery, before which
all evolutionary attempts to explain it prove worthless.

Willingly or unwillingly, the modern critics must themselves
confess this, since they have in vain strained every nerve to
support their theories. H. J. Holtzmann brings against these
critics the reproach of having " recently given to research into
the life of Jesus the reputation of a being psychologically disposed to a game of riddles and to an uncertain groping about
among odd fancies and suppositions."[3] Deissmann thinks that
" history has modestly and wisely let the natal hours of Jesus'
self-consciousness remain for us a mystery."[4] Harnack adds :
" How he came to the consciousness of the unique character
of his filial relation, and how he arrived at the consciousness
of his power and of the obligation and the task which were

---

[1] *Die Worte Jesu,* i, 233.   [2] *Die Lehre Jesu,* 93 f., 2nd ed.
[3] *Das Messianische Bewusstsein Jesu,* 42 f. (Tübingen, 1907).
[4] *Evangelium und Urchristentum,* in *Beiträge zur Weiterentwicklung der christlichen Religion,* 106.

involved in it, that is his secret; no psychology will discover
it. . . . How Jesus came to the consciousness that he was
the Messiah we are unable to ascertain."[1] "All that the
critics have said on this point," remarks Albrecht Schweitzer,
"rests plainly on experiments."[2] Still more clearly Paul
Wernle writes : "It is only honourable to confess that this
origin (of the Messianic consciousness of Jesus) is for us a
mystery, and that we know nothing about it. We can at
most say how the Messianic consciousness did not originate
in Jesus. Not through gradual reasoning and reflection ; these
never give certainty. From them may come, perhaps, the self-
consciousness of a clever theologian, but not that of the Son
of God. Not through the influence of his environment; the
voices of demons and of the world might have been able to
make his spirit falter, but never to impart to it divine certainty. Both explanations break down before the fact that from
the very beginning Jesus appears with perfect steadfastness
and unshakable certainty as the ambassador of God. Nowhere
is there a trace of hesitation, doubt, or a development from
presentiment to certainty. . . . He acts all his life under the
pressure of necessity. He knows that he is sent and impelled
by God; he has only the choice whether to obey or not."[3] In
regard to this, Wernle expresses a further thought, which,
considered in itself, confirms the idea that the Messianic consciousness of Jesus did not originate either earlier or later,
but was inherent in his nature. The Messianic consciousness
bears throughout the characteristics of his nature. *Self-consciousness and Messianic consciousness are in Jesus one and
the same thing,* equally deep, equally certain, equally steadfast, equally unchangeable, equally natural, as only an innate,
never an acquired, consciousness can be.

From this impression also rationalistic scholars cannot
escape. Renan has already called attention to the fact that
"the first thought of Jesus—the thought that he is the Son of
God, the trusted agent of his Father, and the executor of his
will—was so deeply implanted within him that this conviction
probably did not originate gradually, but went back to the
very roots of his being."[4] The Messianic consciousness of
Jesus is indicated, in the opinion of Loisy, by "a splendid
certainty of his faith,"[5] and is distinguishable as a "simple
and profound intuition." Deissmann says : "The Messianic
certainty of Jesus is his self-consciousness."[6] Harnack adds :
"In him everything streams forth as a matter of course and
as if it could not be otherwise. Thus does a fountain come
from the depths of the earth, clear and unimpeded."[7]

[1] *Wesen des Christentums,* 81, 88.   [2] *Von Reimarus zu Wrede,* 7.
[3] *Die Anfänge unserer Religion,* 31, 2nd ed.   [4] *Vie de Jésus,* 85.
[5] *Revue d'histoire et de littérature religieuse,* 91 (1904).
[6] *Evangelium und Urchristentum, op. cit.,* 106.
[7] *Wesen des Christentums,* 21.

Ernst Kühl expresses the same thought thus : " We nowhere come upon an act of Jesus which gives us any information about the origin or development of his self-consciousness. We find everywhere the same calm, steadfast opinion regarding himself, and we receive everywhere the same clear, uniform and complete impression of his personality. . . . In any case, this much is certain, that one can judge fairly of the peculiar nature of Christ's consciousness of his divine sonship,[1] with its serene clearness and its equable certainty in all the situations of his life, only if one recognizes without any mental reservation or restriction the fact that its ultimate roots lie in the depths of his own nature, out of which it has grown organically, and, if we may say so, by a spiritual natural necessity."[2] " If Jesus found the Messiah in his own person, he followed only a spiritual necessity of his being."[3]

We may go still further and say that *Jesus was positively aware that he was both the Son of God and the Messiah, not only after the commencement of his earthly human life, but that he was convinced that his divine sonship and Messiahship, like his nature, had their roots in the supernatural world and in eternity.* He claims not only to have been chosen from all eternity to be the Son of God and the Messiah by a call from heaven, but to have himself come from heaven into this world as the Messiah.

For the explanation of this statement we refer to the thorough demonstration of his supernatural pre-existence, which will soon follow. We can the more readily relieve ourselves of the trouble of proving it here in relation to his Messianic consciousness, as our opponents must agree with us on this point also. Jülicher says : " The Evangelist who makes Jesus declare that no man knoweth the Son but the Father, and, on the other hand, that no man knoweth the Father but the Son, presupposes in him also a consciousness which originated from another world and era."[4] Gustav Dalman, by a philological estimate of the utterances of Jesus, comes to the conviction that he derives his Messianic consciousness from his supernatural divine sonship : " For one who reads the words of Jesus without dogmatic prejudices, no other meaning can be found than that the Messiah is in reality the Son of one higher than David—namely, God."[5] B. Weiss holds a similar opinion : " However far Jesus looked back into his past life, he knew of no moment when the love of God had been bestowed upon him, and when God's selection of him had become an historical fact ; he was conscious of

---

[1] What is true of the consciousness of his divine Sonship is, according to our explanation, true also of his Messianic consciousness, since both blend in one.

[2] *Das Selbstbewusstsein Jesu,* 38, 43.

[3] H. J. Holtzmann, *Das messianische Selbstbewusstsein Jesu,* 78.

[4] *Jesus und Paulus,* 31.   [5] *op. cit.,* p. 234.

having possessed that love, ever since he had learned for the first time to look up to God, and in that love he knew that he had been chosen to be the Messiah. That, however, must have led Jesus of himself to the consciousness that he had possessed that love of God before his existence on earth began, and that his life, as well as his selection for his mission, had their origin in the depths of eternity."[1]

In wonderful harmony with this stands the *Gospel's account of the childhood of Jesus, in which the Messiahship and divine sonship are attributed to a supernatural origin, birth and nature.*

The angel Gabriel already brings from heaven the announcement of the coming forerunner (Luke i, 5). The latter is called John (Jochanan), which means " From the grace of Jehovah," because with him the Messianic day of salvation dawns, and because he will prepare his people for the coming of the Messiah. On that account the angel prophecies to Zachary : " Thou shalt have joy and gladness, and many shall rejoice in his nativity. For he shall be great before the Lord . . . and he shall be filled with the Holy Ghost even from his mother's womb. And he shall convert many of the children of Israel to the Lord their God. And he shall go before him (before the Messiah, the Lord) in the spirit and power of Elias, that he may turn the hearts of the fathers unto the children, and the incredulous to the wisdom of the just, to prepare unto the Lord a perfect people " (Luke i, 13-18).

Six months later the same angel Gabriel announces to the Virgin Mary the supernatural conception and birth of the Messiah and Son of God himself : " Behold thou shalt conceive in thy womb, and shalt bring forth a son ; and thou shalt call his name Jesus. He shall be great, and shall be called the Son of the Most High ; and the Lord God shall give unto him the throne of David his father ; and he shall reign in the house of Jacob for ever, and of his kingdom there shall be no end. . . . The Holy Ghost shall come upon thee, and the power of the Most High shall overshadow thee ; and therefore also the Holy which shall be born of thee shall be called the Son of God " (Luke i, 31-35). Joseph, the bridegroom of Mary, is also then informed, through the apparition of an angel, of the divinely supernatural conception of the Messiah in the Virgin's womb : " Joseph, son of David, fear not to take unto thee Mary, thy wife, for that which is conceived in her is of the Holy Ghost. And she shall bring forth a son, and thou shalt call his name Jesus, for he shall save his people from their sins " (Matt. i, 20, 21).

And again it is an angel who announces to the shepherds near Bethlehem the birth of the Messiah Jesus with the words :

[1] *Das Leben Jesu,* 4th ed., i, 281.

" Fear not, for, behold, I bring you good tidings of great joy, that shall be to all the people. For this day is born to you a Saviour, who is Christ the Lord, in the city of David. . . . And suddenly there was with the angel a multitude of the heavenly army, praising God and saying : Glory to God in the highest; and on earth peace to men of good will " (Luke ii, 8-14).

In the succeeding account of the child in the temple, Jesus is likewise hailed as the Messiah by the aged Simeon, " a just and devout man, waiting for the consolation of Israel," and who " had received an answer from the Holy Ghost that he should not see death before he had seen the Christ of the Lord " (Luke ii, 25, 26). Now, " when his parents brought in the child Jesus . . . he also took him into his arms, and blessed God and said : Now thou dost dismiss thy servant, O Lord, according to thy word in peace. Because my eyes have seen thy salvation, which thou hast prepared before the face of all peoples, a light to the revelation of the Gentiles and the glory of thy people Israel " (Luke ii, 27-32).

As is well known, all the liberal critics are exceedingly hostile to this wonderful garland of supernatural testimonials which, according to the Gospel account of Christ's childhood, enwreathes the announcement, the conception and the birth of the Messiah Jesus. They contest in particular the supposition that Jesus, as the Messiah and Son of God, was pre-existent and supernatural and supermundane in origin, nature and vocation. As has been already said, we shall discuss this criticism of the Gospel's representation of Christ's childhood at a later point, when we consider the divine consciousness of Jesus, because we can then first fully estimate the whole profound import of those passages in the Gospels of Matthew and Luke. The rejection of the Gospel's history of his childhood is, from the philosophical and doctrinal standpoint of rationalism and liberalism, a cardinal principle of self-defence and self-preservation, however unhistorical and unjustifiable such a procedure is. Any school of sceptical criticism which would accept the Gospel's account of Christ's childhood, and therewith the supernatural, supermundane origin of the consciousness of Jesus, would stultify itself.

Only—and this is the curse of the whole system—this same school of sceptical criticism is none the less compelled to surrender its position if it rejects the supernatural interpretation of the consciousness of Jesus. For, as we have proved after a serious examination of all the attempts of our opponents to solve the question, and as many of our opponents have themselves had to confess, there is no natural explanation of this consciousness. Jesus claims that he did not gain his conviction that he was the Messiah and the Son of God by a gradual evolution of his spiritual nature, and all the problems and hypotheses by which it is nevertheless asserted that this consciousness of his has been proved to be the result of a slow development and evolution have broken down lamentably. Thus the modern school of research into the life of Jesus is compelled either to believe in that evolution of Jesus against the evidence of all the historical and psychological facts, or else to doubt its own system.

There is only one way out of this dilemma—namely, that of *attributing the Messianic and divinely filial consciousness of Jesus to an ecstatic, visionary or absolutely deranged mental condition of the Saviour;* in other words, by claiming that Jesus, in a state of ecstatic excitement, gradually worked himself into those Messianic ideas, or in consequence of such mental crises believed in a supernatural Messianic vocation intended for himself from time immemorial.

Since the days of Renan and Strauss this assertion has appeared repeatedly, down to the time of O. Holtzmann,[1] who speaks of a not irrational ecstasy of Jesus, and to Loosten[2] and Emil Rasmussen,[3] who represent Jesus as insane and epileptic. Rasmussen, the barbarian from the Scandinavian north, declares that without exception all men who proclaim themselves prophets are deranged, and that the " Messiahs " are still worse; and finally, in speaking of Jesus's Messianic consciousness, he is guilty of writing the following disgusting sentence : " Just as the man who suffers from constant irritability is a chronic grumbler, and as the man who cannot escape being pursued by megalomaniacal ideas suffers from megalomania, so a man who proclaims himself a Messiah or a prophetic figure, or that he possesses a Messianic nature—is also a deranged person."[4]

However monstrous such coarseness is, and however repellent we find every attempt to represent the Saviour as an *exalté*, ecstatic or epileptic, and however energetically many liberal investigators protest against it, the rationalistic school of criticism cannot deny its responsibility for such aberrations. O. Holtzmann is right, from a liberal standpoint, when he[5] asserts with Johannes Weiss :[6] The Messianic consciousness of Jesus "would be wholly incomprehensible psychologically if it did not appear accompanied by religious ecstasy." If Jesus, from a mere man with purely human consciousness, had developed into the Messiah, and had attained to the consciousness that he was an ambassador from God and the Son of God, more exalted than all the Prophets, and that he came from heaven and united in himself all power in heaven and earth, then he would have been not

[1] *War Jesus Ekstatiker?* (Tübingen, 1903).
[2] *Jesus Christus vom Standpunkte des Psychiaters* (Bamberg, 1905).
[3] *Jesus, eine vergleichende psychopatische Studie* (Leipzig, 1905).
[4] *Jesus*, 135.   [5] *Id.*, p. 10.
[6] *Predigt Jesu vom Reiche Gottes*, 155.

only an ecstatic visionary, but, in the full sense of the word, a madman, as the most radical critics maintain.

This blasphemous assertion, which we shall refute in the second volume of our work, really condemns itself.   "The facts contradict such a declaration," we hear the Protestant liberal Stapfer reply to Renan.[1]   Since sceptical criticism is forced again and again to fall back upon this historically untrue psychology of Jesus, it has lately once more demonstrated its inability to interpret the consciousness of the Saviour historically by the evolutionary theory.   Moreover, it proves thereby that it is utterly impossible to judge of the Messiahship of Jesus scientifically and with fairness if he is regarded merely as a man.

We come thus to the consideration of Jesus' consciousness of his divinity.   First, this will throw complete light upon his Messianic consciousness, for first and only from the standpoint of Christ's divinity do we come to understand how the Saviour was able to apprehend from the very beginning his whole Messianic vocation and activity.   And first and only on the ground of Christ's divinity can the question be raised and answered whether and to what an extent his human knowledge concerning his Messiahship was capable of development and increase, in accordance with the words of the Evangelist : " And Jesus advanced in wisdom and age, and grace with God and men " (Luke ii, 52).

[1] See p. 200 of this volume.

PART III

THE DIVINE CONSCIOUSNESS OF CHRIST

CHAPTER I
THE DIVINITY OF CHRIST IN HIS LIFE

I.—THE DIVINE CONSCIOUSNESS OF CHRIST AS A WHOLE.

1. *Friends and Enemies of the Divinity of Christ.*

THE question of the Messiahship of Jesus is immediately connected with that of his divinity. His Messiahship and divinity form, in fact, the two pivotal points of christology. Both are alike infinitely important and essential in the conflict raging about the incomparably sublime personality of our Saviour. Only we will go, wherever it is possible, still more deeply into this question of the divinity of Jesus—to the central point of it, that is, to the very heart of Christ and Christianity. Here also, therefore, we collide more violently than elsewhere with the two fundamentally different and conflicting views concerning Christ—on the one hand, the positive Christianity of faith and the science of faith, and, on the other, the liberal pseudo-christianity of modern criticism.

The true, essential divinity of Christ has always been, is now and will ever remain the ultimate criterion of christology, and this again the decisive characteristic of positive Christianity. This is recognized, not only by Catholics and orthodox Protestant investigators, who still make a resolute stand[1] against a falling away in non-catholic Christendom from the belief in the only-begotten Son of God, but also by the most radical critics, who still have for Christ himself and Christianity at most a smile of pity.

Eduard von Hartmann, the philosopher of the Unconscious, declares that Harnack's attempt to understand the *Essence of Christianity* without Christ's divinity and without Christ at all is a senseless comedy. He says: " The essence of

---

[1] In recent times the divinity of Christ has been especially defended in orthodox circles by Johann Kunze, *Die ewige Gottheit Jesu Christi* (Leipzig, 1904); by Karl Müller, *Der Glaube an die Gottheit Christi, Biblische Zeitfragen,* II Serie, i (Berlin, 1906); Johann Steinbeck, *Das göttliche Selbstbewusstsein Jesu nach dem Zeugnis der Synoptiker* (Leipzig, 1908); F. Godet, *Commentaire sur l'Évangile de St Jean* 4th ed. (Neuchâtel, 1904); and the English theologians G. B. Stevens, *The Theology of the N. T.* (1901), and *The Teaching of Jesus* (1902); R. L. Ottley, *Doctrine of the Incarnation,* in J. Hastings's *Dictionary of the Bible* (Edinburgh, 1898-1904); W. Sanday, *id.,* see *Jesus Christ;* C. Fouard, *The Christ, the Son of God* (London, 1908); W. Hoyt, *The Lord's Teaching concerning his own Person* (London, 1908); H. P. Liddon, *The Divinity of our Lord and Saviour Jesus Christ* (London, 1908); W. M. Macgregor, *Jesus Christ, the Son of God,* 3rd ed. (Edinburgh, 1909).

Christianity is contained in christology, or nowhere. Whoever rejects christology rejects also the essence of Christianity."[1]

W. von Schnehen, although a pantheistic Monist, answers the question whether the liberal portrait of Jesus can be characterized at all as " Christian " with an emphatic " No," and adds : " Christianity is faith in Christ . . . the Saviour and the Son of God—that is, the Son of God and the Saviour in the true meaning of those words, and not in any modernized interpretation of them, which robs them of the religious characteristics of their old, unequivocal meaning, and substitutes for them a sort of general phraseology, which in reality says nothing. In a word, Christianity is the religion of Christ, and is faith in redemption only through the true Son of God, Jesus Christ. . . . Truly one must either be blind, or have most peculiar and no longer practical but purely personal reasons, not to recognize in all this the ' Essence of Christianity.' For a millennium and a half it was certainly always understood so. The faith of Christians is faith in the divine sonship and the redemptive work of Jesus Christ. To-day, also, it is still the rule that the consciousness of the Christian Church reckons with this fact. . . . Indeed, outside of Christendom one always understands by Christians those who believe in the divinity of Jesus Christ, and in this sense pray to him. The non-christian philosophy, in its most distinguished representatives, agrees absolutely with the orthodox Churches in this view; the adherents of other religions, so far as they know anything at all of Christianity, are of the same opinion; and it has been reserved only for the liberal rationalistic theology of the last 150 years to invent for its own special need an entirely new ' Essence of Christianity.' "[2]

In the case of genuine *rationalists,* who will soon almost without exception belong to history, we do not find this strange, and just as little so in the case of the most modern radicals, who are becoming more and more the heirs of liberal Protestantism. Both frankly confess that they wish to be non-christians and to work as such, and to try, both in principle and in practice, to dechristianize Christianity. Truly the rationalists, from Reimarus to Strauss and Renan, when they contested revelation only, were still genuine dogmatists in comparison with the radicals of to-day—Eduard von Hartmann, W. von Schnehen, Albrecht Kalthoff and others—who repudiate every objective idea of God and all real religion. But those, as well as these, acknowledge that their work is that of a destructive undermining of the foundations of Christianity.

With the *liberals* it is quite different. They all assume the

1 *Die Gegenwart,* 7, 210 (1901).
2 *Der moderne Jesuskultus,* 7 f. 2nd ed. (Frankfurt, 1906).

robe of Christian theologians, clothe their modern ideas and ideals in a Christian garb, and claim the honour of having unveiled to the world Christianity cleansed of all impurities, and of having portrayed it in its true " essence." In reality, however, they throw away precisely what the whole world regards as the deepest and most spiritual import of the Christian religion, and, in particular, its soul—the divinity of Jesus.

This reproach is applicable to all the liberal critics and accommodating theologians. *All of them, from the extremest left to the furthest right wing of the school of Ritschl, deny, in the name of true Christianity, the divinity of Jesus Christ.* This is, of course, comprehensible from the radical liberals, who at the present moment set the pace in the Protestant camp. Harnack has uttered for them the significant words : " Not the Son, but the Father only, has a place in the Gospel which Jesus proclaimed. The sentence, ' I am the Son of God ' did not find its way from Jesus into his Gospel, and whoever inserts it there, as a sentence in connection with others, adds something to the Gospel. But whoever takes up this Gospel and strives to know him who gave it to us will testify that here divinity has appeared in as pure a form as it ever can upon this earth."[1]

Only in appearance do the more *conservative members of the Ritschl school* reject this formula of Harnack. They talk much of the divinity of Christ and are able on occasion to grow quite eloquent in favour of it. But Albrecht Ritschl himself did not at all understand by this the eternal and essential divinity of the Saviour. His Son of God is a creature with limited powers, not essentially different from us Christians. " In the affirmation of his divinity the religious valuation of Christ finds only a very limited expression."[2] Christ is called God only in so far as he is historically the first in the community of the kingdom of God, and thereby unique of his kind.[3]

It is true Julius Kaftan remarks very positively, " So long as a Christology exists it will be the doctrine of the divinity of the Redeemer "; yet Kaftan makes the divinity of Jesus resolve itself into a natural endowment, by means of which the Saviour came into such a perfect spiritual unity and communion with God as no other human being ever experienced.[4] Beyschlag speaks in a precisely similar way of the " unique majesty of Jesus, for which, in the last analysis, the erroneous yet authorized name of divinity is not too high."[5] Lipsius

[1] *Wesen des Christentums,* 91, 92.
[2] Ritschl, *Lehre von der Rechtfertigung und Versöhnung,* iii, 389, 3rd ed.
[3] *id.,* 425 f., 438.   [4] Julius Kaftan, *Dogmatik,* 424 f., 437 (1897).
[5] *Neutestamentliche Theologie,* i, 77, 2nd ed.

and Nitzsch dispute this, remarking that one may indeed speak of a "unique existence of God in Christ," although the affirmation of the divinity of Christ "is inexact and not without error."[1]

Even Bernhard Weiss, who is looked upon as a kind of intermediary between the liberal and positive schools of thought, explains away the metaphysical consubstantiality of Jesus with the Father into a merely moral similarity of nature, by means of which he, above all other men, is qualified to bring the highest revelation of God to mankind.[2]

If the theology of the Ritschl school ever concedes the divinity of Jesus, it conceives it, at most, in the sense of the old monarchical theory, according to which the man Jesus became God only in time and by means of his Messianic vocation. "Christ is for us God. Jesus has become God by becoming Christ," writes Schulz;[3] and Reinhold Seeberg, in closest adhesion to Schleiermacher, declares: "The will of God, conducting the history of humanity to salvation . . . united itself with the man Jesus from the first moment of his existence . . . and permeated his feelings, thoughts and will. Thus did the man Jesus become the Son of God."[4]

If the essential and eternal divinity of Jesus is even seriously considered, Julius Kaftan[5] and other enemies of the left wing of liberal theology do not think thereby of the divinity of Jesus himself, but of the divinity of the Father standing behind him. With this Harnack also can, of course, agree. He wishes to substitute for the expression "Christ is God" the formula "God was in Christ."[6] In some such way every critic finally succeeds in acknowledging a divinity of Christ and at the same time in denying the divinity of Christ. Edmund Stapfer even calls Protestantism fortunate on account of this confusion : "I am convinced that this individualism is to-day the wisest and the only possible thing for us. Every Protestant believer manufactures his own christology for himself, because every believer conceives of the divinity of Jesus Christ in his own way, which is not the way of his neighbour."[7]

The *Modernists,* who have abandoned Catholicism, especially Alfred Loisy,[8] agree with this entirely.

---

[1] Lipsius, *The Theology of Ritschl,* 9; Nitzsch, *Lehrbuch der Dogmatik,* 497, 2nd ed.

[2] *Lehrbuch der biblischen Theologie des N. T.,* 58 ff., 6th ed. (Berlin, 1895); *Leben Jesu,* ii, 145 f. (Stuttgart and Berlin, 1902).

[3] *Die Gottheit Christi,* 725 f.

[4] *Grundwahrheiten der christlichen Religion,* 115 ff.; *Die Kirche Deutschlands im 19 Jahrhundert,* 47.

[5] *id.,* 438. [6] *Preussische Jahrbücher,* i, 588 (1903).

[7] *La mort et la résurrection de Jésus-Christ,* 340; *Jésus-Christ pendant son ministère,* 314.

[8] See the good delineation of him by Lepin, *Jésus, Messie et Fils de Dieu,* 238-267 (Paris, 1906) : *La Divinité du Christ d'après M. Loisy.*

All the modern enemies of the divinity of Jesus are united only in the main point of view that Jesus Christ himself did not claim to be God. Nowhere and never in his life, they say, did he utter a word indicating a really divine consciousness. Only after his death did the doctrine of his divinity gradually originate in the Christian Church, although in no way based upon the teaching of Christ himself. Let us examine these assertions.

2. *The Human and Divine Consciousness of Christ.*

The enemies of the divinity of Jesus will, in advance, have nothing to do with the orthodox Christian position. Instead of investigating the Christian point of view, according to which Jesus professed and proclaimed himself to be God, they oppose to it at once the negative antithesis " that Jesus himself did not claim to be God on earth . . . and that he bluntly declined the attribute of divinity and divine perfection."[1] In proof of this they appeal merely to the fact that he emphasized his *human consciousness* with great clearness as compared with his divine consciousness. Renan asserts that " Jesus does not for a single moment express the sacrilegious idea that he is God." " It is beyond all doubt that Jesus never thought of professing to be an incarnation of God himself. . . . There is not a trace of such a thing anywhere in the synoptic Gospels. The Evangelists make him act merely as a man. He is tempted; he is ignorant of many things; he corrects himself; he changes his views; he begs his Father to spare him trials; he is submissive to God as a son. He, who is to judge the world, does not even know the day of the judgement. He takes precautionary measures for his safety. Shortly after his birth he has to be saved by flight, to rescue him from men who wished to kill him. . . . All this proves the fact that he was only an ambassador from God, a man protected and privileged by God."[2]

The liberal criticism of to-day has remained true to Renan on this point. Some of Harnack's sentences sound very much like those of Renan : " He [Jesus] characterized the Lord of heaven and earth as his God and Father, as greater than he, and as the only one who is good. He is certain of having from this Father all that he has, and all that he is to accomplish. He prays to him, he submits to his will; and in an intense struggle he seeks to discover this and to fulfil it. His aim, strength, insight, success and his hard necessity, all come from this Father. So it stands recorded in the Gospels ; and there is nothing there which can be altered or falsely interpreted. This personality that feels, prays, acts, struggles

---

[1] Arnold Meyer, *Was uns Jesus heute ist,* 21 (Tübingen, 1907).
[2] Renan, *Vie de Jésus,* 54, 173, 179 f. (Berlin, 1863).

and leads is a man, who unites himself with other men also in relation to God.''[1]

Many others speak in essentially the same way, among whom (to mention only a few) are Wellhausen,[2] W. Bousset,[3] H. J. Holtzmann,[4] Chamberlain,[5] Paul Wernle,[6] Zimmermann,[7] K. Thieme,[8] and Alfred Loisy,[9] the latest mouthpiece of the Liberal school.

It cannot occur to us to deny that Jesus, before everything else, felt and showed himself as man, and that his human consciousness expressed itself in his life with plastic force and fulness. First his humanity in its entire reality, then his divinity in its spiritual fulness of truth; first the humanly comprehensible, then the divinely supernatural, which becomes known through and in the human nature of Jesus. It is for this reason that Jesus comes into this world as an infant in a manger, flees from his persecutors, and grows in age, wisdom and grace in the sight of God and men (Luke ii, 40, 50 f.). It is for this reason that at the beginning of his public life he submits like an ordinary sinner to the baptism of repentance, with the remark that he must fulfil all justice (Matt. iii, 15). For this reason he is led by the Spirit into the wilderness, where he fasts, is tempted and shows that he is hungry (Matt. iv, 2 and Luke iv, 2). On this account he endures all the days of his activity the human weaknesses of hunger, thirst, fatigue, sleep and other human afflictions. For this reason also he is moved by all the varieties of feelings known to the human soul—sympathy, tenderness, friendship, pain, grief and tears. He feels drawn to the young man who asks of him the way of life (Mark x, 21). He is moved by compassion for the widow whose only son is being carried forth upon a bier (Luke vii, 13). He has compassion on the multitude which has remained with him for three days, and suffers hunger in the desert (Matt. xiv, 14 and parallels). He groans in spirit, shudders and weeps at the death of his friend Lazarus (John xi, 33, 35), and sheds tears over obdurate Jerusalem at the thought of its ruin (Luke xix, 41). In the garden of Gethsemani an indescribable sadness overpowers him in view of his approaching end; his soul is sorrowful even unto death; he falls in agony, and drops of sweat exude

---

[1] *Wesen des Christentums*, 80.

[2] *Skizzen und Vorarbeiten*, vi, 188 (Berlin, 1899).

[3] *Das Wesen der Religion dargestellt an ihrer Geschichte*, 251 (Halle, 1903).   [4] *Neutest. Theologie*, i, 268 (Leipzig, 1897).

[5] *Grundlagen des* 19 *Jahrhunderts*, i, 209, 3rd ed. (München, 1901).

[6] *Die Anfänge unserer Religion*, 26-37, 2nd ed. (Leipzig, 1904).

[7] *Der historische Wert der ältesten Ueberlieferung von der Geschichte Jesu im Markusevangelium*, 144 (Leipzig, 1905).

[8] *Die christliche Demut*, i, 131, 170 ff. (Giessen, 1906).

[9] *Autour d'un petit livre*, 116; *Simples réflexions*, 72 (1908); *Quelques lettres sur des questions actuelles*, 148 (1908); *Les Evangiles synoptiques*, i, 193.

from all the pores of his body (Matt. xxvi, 37 and parallels).
He is, indeed, willing to die the most frightful of deaths and
to be buried in a rock-hewn tomb in order to complete the
tragedy of his human life.   Even after his resurrection his
paramount desire is to furnish irrefutable evidence of the fact
that he has risen from the grave as a living human being.
The disciples at Emmaus recognize him in the breaking of
bread (Luke xxiv, 30).   To the astonished Apostles he shows
his perforated hands and feet for them to handle, and he
eats with them honey and fish (Luke xxiv, 39-43).   Thus
Jesus, from the first to the last hour of his life, stands as
a true and perfectly human man among men.

Just as plainly does he show himself as man in his intercourse with God.   In his will (Matt. xxvi, 39), in his words
(John viii, 28, 38), and his work (John v, 19), and in his
moral (Matt. xix, 16) and intellectual (Matt. xxiv, 36) perfection, he subordinates himself to his Father in heaven
as every creature ought to subordinate itself to him.   The
glorification which comes to him in such abundance from his
miracles he wishes to transmit to the Father (Mark v, 19), as
he seeks, indeed, in everything to enhance the honour of the
Father (John viii, 49; xiv, 13).   Like an ordinary mortal, he
turns to God the Father partly in order to pay him the tribute
of adoration, partly to beg for his help and support.   The
Evangelists mention repeatedly his ardour in prayer (Matt.
xiv, 23; Luke ix, 18, 28).   He passes whole nights in prayer
(Luke vi, 12).   He can ask of his Father to send him more
than twelve legions of angels for his defence (Matt. xxvi, 53).
Also in working his miracles he often first raises his eyes to
heaven in prayer before he acts (Mark vii, 34; John xi, 38, 41).
In his prayer on the Mount of Olives he expresses the
sharpest distinction between his human will, which shrinks
from suffering, and the paternal will of God, to which he
submits in profound obedience (Matt. xxvi, 39 and parallels).
In his last agony on the Cross he finally feels himself forsaken by God his Father, and, dying, commends his spirit
into his hands (Matt. xxvii, 46 and parallels).

Thus does Jesus Christ reveal himself as man in every
respect and in all the situations of his life.   In his body and
soul, in his will, intellect and actions he is a man like us
other men, "in all things made like unto his brethren, yet
without sin " (Heb. ii, 17; iv, 15).   In fact, his human nature
appears in the self-consciousness of Jesus and in the representation of that consciousness in the writings of the Evangelists in such perfect naturalness, that we must see therein
a new, transparently clear proof of the fact that here everything is described in accordance with reality; not, as the
liberals believe, in the twilight of history, already refashioned
by faith.

But—and this is the question which we have to do with here—can liberal criticism legitimately draw the conclusion from the fact that Jesus shows himself so decidedly as man that he did not claim to be also God? Certainly not. Whether Christ was God or not, the human side of his nature and person would have had to come to expression in any case just as decidedly. Not only because Christ was also a real man, but also because, his divinity being presupposed, his divine nature could reveal itself only in his human nature and by means of his human nature, because he was *God-Man—incarnate God.*

An incarnate God thinks, wills, speaks and acts as man, even when his thinking, willing, speaking and acting cannot be explained merely from his humanity, but have their origin in the depths of divinity. A man who, casting aside at once the capacities, talents, forces and manners peculiar to his race, should appear before us with a claim to be God, would thereby also give us a proof that he understood the part he was playing very superficially and that he was nothing but a comedian, a *Deus ex machinâ.* The incarnate Son of God, whether he presented himself to his fellow-men or to God, remained the Son of Man, even when he gave proof of his pre-existence with the Father, of his supernatural nature, his likeness to God and his divinity in word and work. So it becomes at once comprehensible that he had not only to evince a decidedly human consciousness, but also to show that this human consciousness revealed itself with much greater clearness and publicity than the consciousness of his divine nature and being, and why. *Not only the theological, but also the purely psychological estimate of the person of Christ forbid the idea of his playing off his clearly marked human consciousness against his divine consciousness.* "Monsieur Renan, that clown in psychology," as Friedrich Nietzsche once called him, enticed subsequent liberal critics, in this respect, into a very dubious path.

Even the few texts which apparently favour our opponents' conception of the consciousness of Jesus, and to which they always again and again appeal with tenacious narrow-mindedness, do not alter these facts.

Above all, the meeting of Jesus with the rich young man is supposed to be decisive (Mark x, 17; Luke xviii, 18). "When the rich young man addressed him with the words, 'Good Master,' Jesus answered, 'Why callest thou me good? None is good but one, that is God.' He has with these words disavowed bluntly divinity and divine perfection." Thus does Arnold Meyer[1] decide, according to Harnack's statement.[2] Alfred Loisy[3] also, W. Bousset,[4] and even the orthodox-

---

[1] *Was uns Jesus heute ist,* 21 (Tübingen, 1907).
[2] *Wesen,* 80.   [3] *Autour d'un petit livre,* 148.
[4] *Das Wesen der Religion,* 251; *Jesus,* 92, 3rd ed. (Tübingen, 1907).

inclined Ernst Kühl[1] hold the same opinion—incorrectly. In the eyes of the rich young man Jesus was precisely not God, but merely a wise Rabbi, exactly as he is in the eyes of our rationalists and modernists. That being presupposed, it was typical both of the nature and of the deep humility of Jesus to give to God alone the honour by declining this expression of human praise.

Moreover, Jesus, who saw in the form of address given him by the young man merely a vain compliment, greatly coveted by the Pharisees (Matt. xxiii, 7), "rejects this ambitious and superficial habit of bestowing titles, without giving a thought to the question, whether he has a right to the appellation 'good' or not. The rejection of that distinction has, therefore, nothing to do with the self-consciousness of Jesus, but is a revelation of feeling, from which one perceives how far removed he is from the Scribes and Pharisees."[2] Provided the expression does not contain the praise of men, but a worthy recognition of God, Jesus lays a definite claim to the name of "Lord and Master" (John xiii, 13), and wishes to have it used in the sense of a good and absolutely perfect Master, in which sense God in heaven is called Father and Lord of all men (Matt. xxiii, 8, 9).

Furthermore, our opponents take refuge in the *remark of Christ concerning the coming of the day of judgement:* " But of that day or hour no man knoweth, neither the angels in heaven, nor the Son, but the Father " (Mark xiii, 32). Here is clearly and distinctly expressed the underlying thought which Jesus wishes to impress upon his hearers—God alone knows the day of the Last Judgement. No creature, even though it is one possessing pure intelligence, has knowledge of it. Even to the Son this secret is not made known, in so far as he speaks merely from his own knowledge as a creature. In so far as his humanity is connected hypostatically with his divinity, and, above all, in regard to his divinity itself, he also certainly knows this secret. But neither as man, nor as God, does he know this for men. He has no commission from the Father to communicate it to mortals. For, as he explains elsewhere, " It is not for you to know the times or moments which the Father hath put in his own power " (Acts i, 7).

Finally, the *complaint of the dying Saviour* on the cross : " My God, my God, why hast thou forsaken me?" (Matt. xxvii, 46). He who in his greatest agony breaks out in this cry of distress is the Son of God, hypostatically united with the human nature, which is struggling with death. It is,

---

[1] *Das Selbstbewusstsein Jesu,* 12-16 (Gr.-Lichterfelde, Berlin, 1907).
[2] Johann Steinbeck, *Das göttliche Selbstbewusstsein Jesu nach dem Zeugnis der Synoptiker,* 39 f. (Leipzig, 1908); R. A. Hoffmann, *Das Selbstbewusstsein Jesu nach den drei ersten Evangelien,* 6 f.(Königsberg i. Pr., 1904).

therefore, the man who feels himself forsaken, and who can
call God his God, and cry to him for help. The divinity of
Jesus is in no way excluded by the fact that his humanity
reaches here its highest, last and tragic expression.

Accordingly, when the liberal critics, together with Harnack, sum up the evidence against the divinity of Jesus in
the words, " This sensitive, active, struggling and suffering
personality is a man who unites himself with other men in his
attitude towards God," they have thereby really proved
nothing against the divinity of Jesus, but have only uttered
the truth well known to every reader of the Gospel, that Jesus
was truly and really man. Nevertheless, the question whether
Jesus was also God is not settled thereby, but, on the contrary, is now put forth for the first time. Now, first we must
ask whether all the utterances and actions of Jesus can be
explained by his human consciousness, or whether they, on
the contrary, find their explanation only in the fact that his
divine nature was united with his human nature in the one
person of the incarnate God and the divine Messiah.

3. *The Expressions of the Divine Consciousness of Christ.*

In approaching the answer to this question, we abstain for
the present from Christ's express designation of himself as
the Son of God, and take into consideration only the expressions of his divine consciousness in general. That this consciousness cannot be measured by the standard of ordinary
men is recognized also by our critical opponents. Renan,
the master of fine phrases, is forced to the acknowledgement :
" The faith, the enthusiasm and the constancy of the first
generation of Christians become comprehensible only by the
fact that at the beginning of the whole movement was placed
a man of colossal proportions. . . . This sublime personality, which even now, day after day, directs the destinies
of the world, can permissibly be called divine, not in the
sense that Jesus had absorbed into himself all that is divine,
or that he was identical with the divine, but in the sense that
Jesus is that individual who has brought his species nearest
to divinity. . . . The position which he ascribed to himself
was that of a supernatural being, and he wished to be considered as a being who stood in loftier relations with God
than other men."[1]

The most modern of the critics in the liberal camp share
the views of this rationalist. Paul Wernle certainly speaks to
them as if he had read their thoughts when he says : " Christianity originated from the circumstance that a layman, Jesus of
Nazareth, appeared with a more than prophetic self-consciousness, and drew men so closely to himself that they were able,

[1] Renan, *Vie de Jésus,* 54, 319, 325 f. (Berlin, 1863).

even after his ignominious death, to live and die for him. . . .
It is clear that from these words [of Jesus] there speaks a
superhuman self-consciousness. And this is the secret of the
origin of Christianity. . . . Always modest, humble, moderate, and yet with a superhuman self-consciousness. It is
absolutely impossible to invent such a spiritual life as this.
Revelation, redemption, forgiveness, help—all these he has
in himself and imparts them to those who yield to the impression of his person. And just as his statements about
himself far surpass the ordinary, so also does his manner
of life. . . . If he passes nights in solitary prayer, if in
preaching and healing he forgets food and rest, if he inter-
feres with nature, or if, himself moved by its mystery, he
seems to his associates as a being from another world and
to his puzzled relatives as one possessed of the devil—everywhere we have the same impression of the superhuman."[1]
P. W. Schmiedel confesses that "the synoptists also depict
it (the portrait of Jesus) likewise with a sublimity, which
exalts him appreciably above human standards."[2]

Yet the same critics declare that Jesus does not claim to be
a superhuman being, much less God. "He stands throughout
as a man among men, with a feeling of the distance which
separates all creatures from God."[3] "He does not surpass
the limits of the purely human. Before his soul Almighty
God remained in his entire sublimity, he did not force himself
to a place beside him. . . . He drew the dividing line
sharply."[4] Everything extraordinary and superhuman in his
words and works has its foundation in the Messianic consciousness of Jesus. In his nature he feels himself merely
human, but in his Messianic vocation exalted above men.
That is all. "The mediator is throughout a man, without
exception, but he has received from God a special vocation
and commission for men, and thereby he surpasses them."[5]
Only that? Really no more than that? Let us briefly collect
the most important expressions of self-consciousness of Jesus
in order to enable ourselves to form an independent opinion in
regard to them.

Jesus makes plain to us his superhuman and absolutely
divine consciousness by *comparisons,* in which he contrasts
himself, on the one hand, with the created world, and, on the
other, unites himself closely with God.

In all his humility and modesty he yet knows himself to be
exalted above all creatures. He is greater than Jonah and

[1] Paul Wernle, *Die Anfänge unserer Religion,* 26-29, 2nd ed. (Tübingen, 1904); E. Stapfer, *Jésus-Christ pendant son ministère,* 324, 337,
2nd ed. (Paris, 1897); Fritz Barth, *Die Hauptprobleme des Lebens
Jesu,* 256 ff., 3rd ed. (Gütersloh, 1907); W. Bousset, *Jesus,* 90 f., 3rd
ed. (Tübingen, 1907).
[2] *Das vierte Evangelium,* 19 (Tübingen, 1906).
[3] Wernle, *op. cit.,* 28.
[4] Bousset, *op. cit.,* 91.   [5] Wernle, *op. cit.,* 28.

Solomon (Matt. xii, 41); greater than Moses and Elias, the witnesses of his glorification (Matt. xvii, 3); greater than all the ambassadors of God in the Old Testament (Matt. xii, 41). In him his disciples behold what prophets and kings had in vain longed to see (Luke x, 24). The least in his kingdom is greater than John the Baptist, who, nevertheless, was more than all the prophets, yes, the greatest of all men born until that time (Matt. xi, 9-11). David himself, whose son the Messiah was to be, looks up like a servant to Jesus his Lord (Matt. xxii, 43-45). No man and no angel can stand comparison with him. He is served by angels (Matt. iv, 11); a word from him would be sufficient for the Father in heaven to send him twelve legions of angels (Matt. xxvi, 53). The angels are, in general, as much his as are the angels and servants of the Father (Matt. xiii, 41; xvi, 27). At the last day they will form his retinue of honour, like the household of a king (Matt. xvi, 27; xxv, 31). At a wave of his hand they will assemble the whole world before his face (Matt. xiii, 41; xxiv, 31). He is something different from men and angels. Exalted above both, he takes a rank and position close to the heavenly Father (Mark xiii, 32). He admonishes the disciples forcibly that they should call no one on earth Master or Father: "For one is your Father, who is in heaven; . . . one is your Master, Christ . . . and all you are brethren" (Matt. xxiii, 8, 9). Jesus conceives of the two designations, Father and Master, as parallel; applies one to himself, the other to the Father in heaven; and contrasts with both the men who, while different from Christ and the Father, are among themselves brethren.

If these comparisons between Jesus and the created world already point, not only to a superhuman vocation, but to a nature in the Saviour which is throughout superior to that of created beings, still more definite are *those utterances in which he compares himself directly with God*. With marvellous educative wisdom he starts out with the Old Testament idea of God and the Old Testament's divine revelation, because these were intelligible to the disciples and known by all. He places himself on a par with God, and applies the utterances concerning Jehovah to himself. As Jehovah alone is Israel's Lord to whom the nation is wedded, so Jesus is the bridegroom of his followers (Mark ii, 19; John iii, 29), and not merely the groomsman who is to lead the people to God. While the Old Testament never speaks of the people of a divine ambassador, such as Moses or Josue, but only of the people of Jehovah (Num. xvi, 3, etc.), Jesus calls the society of his believers exclusively *his* Church (Matt. xvi, 18). As was said of Jehovah in the Old Testament (Isa. xxxi, 5), so Jesus wishes to gather the children of Jerusalem to himself, as a hen gathers her chickens under her wings (Matt. xxiii,

37). With the same absolute authority, exclusively his own, with which God in the Old Testament sent out the bearers of his revelation, Jesus also says : " I send to you prophets and wise men and scribes " (Matt. xxiii, 34 ; Luke xi, 49). As Jehovah gave to Moses for himself and his brother Aaron the assurance, " I will be in thy mouth and in his mouth " (Exod. iv, 15), so Jesus also encourages the bearers of his Gospel : " I will give you a mouth and wisdom, which all your adversaries shall not be able to resist and gainsay " (Luke xxi, 15). Jesus never introduces his discourses after the manner of the prophets, " Thus saith the Lord," but, to the greatest amazement of his hearers, speaks like Jehovah himself, always in his own person, " as one having power " (Mark i, 22). As Jehovah is the Lord of the Old Testament Law, and as this forms his own peculiar and inalienable right, so Jesus declares himself to be the absolute Lord of this same Law. Over against all human authority he sets his word of command : " The Son of Man is Lord of the Sabbath " (Matt. xii, 1-8). In other words, the Son of Man not only puts aside the Old Testament by virtue of his Messianic power and vocation, but he stands above the Old Testament, as its Lord and Lawgiver who revealed himself indeed in the Old Testament by his word and his prophets, but in the New Testament has himself come to mankind in the person of the Son of Man.[1] Jesus applies, therefore, the Old Testament utterances of Jehovah to himself without any limitation and in solemn asseveration compares himself to the God of the Old Testament. Hence, it is only a furtherance and deepening of this thought when Jesus, as we shall soon see, removes every essential difference between himself and God the Father in heaven by his utterances in reference to the Son of God.

Secondly, Jesus expresses his consciousness of his divine nature in the *demands* he makes on mankind in regard to his person. Most remarkable is the *demand of faith*. This forms the basis of all his discourses and actions. What he seeks among the Israelites, but does not find in sufficient measure, is faith (Matt. viii, 10). That which qualifies the Gentiles to enter the kingdom of heaven before the Israelites is their greater readiness to believe (Matt. viii, 10-12). To make his disciples strong in faith is the principal aim of his admonitions,[2] the most desired result of his prayers (Luke xxii, 32).

[1] See the detailed proof of the correctness of this exposition in Schanz, *Markuskommentar*, 142 (Freiburg, 1881) ; Knabenbauer, *Commentarius in Ev. secundum Matt.*, i, 471 (Paris, 1892) ; *Comment. in Ev. sec. Marcum*, 89 ff. (Paris, 1894) ; Tillmann, *Der Menschensohn*, 126 ff. (Freiburg, 1907) ; Anton Seitz, *Das Evangelium vom Gottessohn*, 408-413 (Freiburg, 1908) ; Wünsche, *Jesu Konflikt mit den Pharisaern wegen des Aehrenausraufens,* in *Vierteljahresschrift für Bibelkunde,* i, 281-306 (1904).

[2] Matt. ix, 2, 22, 29 ; xv, 28 ; xvi, 8 ; xvii, 19 ; xxi, 21 ; Mark iv, 40 ; v, 34 ; x, 52 ; xi, 22 ; Luke vii, 50 ; viii, 25, 48 ; xvii, 5, 19 ; xviii, 8, 42 ; John xi, 15, 25, 40-48 ; xii, 36-46 ; xiv, 1, 10.

Only twice do the synoptists inform us that Jesus marvelled; once at faith and the other time at unbelief (Matt. viii, 10; Mark vi, 6). In considering his second coming, he is especially impressed by the thought whether he shall find faith on the earth (Luke xviii, 8). Now, one could, of course, easily understand his demand of faith in his words and his mission from God, even if he were no more than a human Messiah. But his claim to men's faith refers not only to his words and his vocation, but directly to his person. "Blessed is he, whosoever shall not be scandalized in me" (Luke vii, 23). Faith in the person of Jesus is the way to escape eternal ruin and to have life everlasting (John iii, 15-18). Faith in him is the work required by God (John vi, 29), and unbelief in him the sin of the world (John xvi, 9). Exactly in the same way as the disciples believe in God are they to believe in him (John xiv, 1); faith in the person of the Father and in the person of Jesus are practically the same. Still more, they blend into each other : "He that believeth in me doth not believe in me but in him that sent me" (John xii, 44). Whoever does not believe in Jesus proves thereby his complete unbelief in God (John v, 37). In a word, Jesus demands not only that men should believe in him and his message, but that they should believe in him and his person. The Last Judgement will deal first of all with unbelief in his person, and then only with unbelief in his teaching : "He that shall be ashamed of me and of my words, the Son of Man also will be ashamed of him, when he shall come in the glory of his Father with the holy angels" (Mark viii, 38). *He makes himself the object and the substance of faith.* That would be absolute idolatry if Jesus were merely a man with a supernatural vocation, and not real, incarnate God.[1]

Together with the demand for faith Jesus lays claim also to unlimited *love*. He reproaches the Jews not only with unbelief, but also with want of love for his person (John viii, 42). He continually admonishes his disciples to distinguish themselves through their love to Jesus (John viii, 42; xiv, 15, 21, 23). It is, however, not merely a natural love that he requires of his followers. On the contrary, every merely natural love must be subordinated to the love to Jesus. "He that loveth father or mother more than me is not worthy of me; and he that loveth son or daughter more than me is not worthy of me" (Matt. x, 37). Even the bonds of the closest natural love must be torn asunder when love to Jesus would thereby be lessened. "If any man

---

[1] How unprejudicedly the liberal critics oppose Jesus's demand for faith is shown by the laconic remark of Wrede : "That he (Jesus) made himself the object of faith or doctrine must be doubted, *notwithstanding some words in the Gospels which say so.*" Wrede, *Paulus,* 94, 2nd ed. (Tübingen, 1907).

come to me, and hate not his father and mother and wife and children and brethren and sisters, yea and his own life also, he cannot be my disciple " (Luke xiv, 25). No man, no man sent by God even, may speak thus. The commandment to love one's neighbour says only : " Thou shalt love thy neighbour as thyself." Jesus demands much more; whosoever does not love him more than himself, whosoever does not love him above all else, cannot be his disciple (Matt. x, 37-39). Jesus demands for himself the love of the whole heart, of the whole soul and of the whole mind, the love which we owe to God alone, and asks that we give it in the same way. He claims that men shall fulfil towards his person the first and greatest commandment which is incumbent on them in respect to God. Whoever fails in this love to Jesus fails too in his love to God (John v, 42). Whoever hates Jesus hates thereby God himself (John xv, 23). *Both blend in each other and both are alike—love to Jesus and love to God.* That is a claim to divine rights which penetrates life profoundly.

Moreover, Jesus allows himself to be *worshipped.*[1] We read frequently that the friends of Jesus "fell down before him and worshipped him," an homage which the Saviour not only accepted, but praised and rewarded with miracles. It is true, the expression " fall down and worship " may not, as a matter of course, be interpreted as an expression of religious, divine adoration. In itself it can mean merely the oriental salaam; the homage of deep reverence which the servant renders to his master and the subject to his king, and consists in the fact that the former falls on his knees before the latter and touches the ground with his forehead. This conventional homage is meant when the Gospel says that the servant " fell down and besought him ;"[2] when the wise men from the East and Herod himself wished to adore the new-born King of the Jews as a king (Matt. ii, 2, 8, 11); and when the Roman soldiers " bowing their knees, adored him," in order to mock Jesus as a pretender to the position of King of the Jews (Mark xv, 19).

But, provided the expression προσκύνησις, " obeisance," is transferred from the profane to the religious sphere, and hence becomes a form of religious homage, it means, according to the usage employed in the language of the Gospels, in the highest sense the *latreutic worship* which is due to God alone. No man and no angel allows such a religious obeisance to be offered him. When the centurion Cornelius " falls at his [Peter's] feet and adores him," the prince of the Apostles reproves him with the words : " Arise, I myself also am a man " (Acts x, 25, 26). When St John before the angel of

[1] See A. Seitz, *Die Anbetung Jesu als Gottessohn in den Evangelien,* in *Theologie und Glaube,* 286 ff. (1910).

[2] Matt. xviii, 26, according to the Greek original : *adored.*

the Apocalypse "falls at his feet, to adore him, the angel says: 'See thou do it not; I am thy fellow servant and of thy brethren. Adore God'" (Apoc. xix, 10; xxii, 8, 9). To fall down in homage is the highest act of worship which the believer performed to the honour of Jehovah in the temple at Jerusalem (John iv, 20-22; xii, 20; Acts viii, 27), and which the ancients continually render at the throne of God (Rev. iv, 10; v, 14; vii, 11), and that "adoration in spirit and in truth" which Jesus demands from the "true adorers of the Father" (John iv, 20-24), and of which he says: "Thou shalt adore the Lord thy God, and him only shalt thou serve" (Matt. iv, 10; Luke iv, 8).

Now, Jesus allows the *obeisance* or kneeling adoration to be offered to him many times and on very different occasions. The question is only whether it was, at those times, a matter of *religious* adoration or merely of worldly homage. If we leave out of consideration the concrete cases, as they are reported in the Gospel, it may be supposed that the Jews with their secular and political ideal of the Messiah might have adored the Saviour, now and then, as the expected Master Rabbi and national liberator, and therefore may have done homage to the Messiah-King who was to destroy the Romans, according to the secular manner of a court. Nevertheless, the Gospel, as far as we see, contains not a single case of obeisance of this kind. Jesus would have refused it just as decidedly as he did the title and name of an earthly Messiah-King, and protested against being called Lord and Master after the manner of the Rabbis and being honoured as such. As he considered his whole work and the significance of his person as exclusively religious, he could also consent to receive the honour offered to him only as religious homage.

Yet not only did he himself consider it so. In the subjective feelings of those who paid him homage, the worship offered him was always of a religious nature. It is true, in various degrees. It sometimes happened that people who honoured in the Saviour the possessor of supernatural miraculous powers fell down before him involuntarily in religious awe and hope without being in any way aware of his Messiahship or of his divinity. That may have occurred in the case of the Canaanitish woman, who adored him and said: "Lord, help me" (Matt. xv, 25); and perhaps also in the case of the leper, who "adored him, saying: 'Lord, if thou wilt, thou canst make me clean'" (Matt. viii, 2). In other cases, adorers cast themselves down before Jesus because, overwhelmed by the power of his teaching, his person and his miracles, they looked upon him as the Messiah in the true, religious sense, sent from God, and endowed with divine wisdom and might, without, on that account, regarding and acknowledging him decisively and for more than a moment as God. Such was the man who was born blind, who, after being healed and instructed by Jesus, hails Jesus as the Son of God, "falls down and adores him" (John ix, 35-39). Jairus also, the leader of the synagogue, was for a moment animated by a similar religious sentiment when he adored Jesus and begged for the resuscitation of his dead daughter (Matt. ix, 18); and likewise the man from Gerasa with the unclean spirit, who cried aloud to him for help, addressing him as the "Son of the most high God" (Mark v, 6, 7); and the disciples who, after the stilling of the storm on the lake, and the walking of Jesus on the water, "adored him, saying : ' Indeed, thou art the Son of God '" (Matt. xiv, 33). In such circumstances, if he knew himself not to be God, Jesus could not have allowed a purely religious adoration to be offered him. For, in so far as it stood opposed to something divine or even to a momentarily excited faith in his genuine deity, it rested—under the aforesaid supposition that he knew that he was not God—on superstition only. But in so far as it was applicable to the Messiah as merely a religious ambassador of God, it was a sin which Jesus, the jealous defender of the rights of his Father, was compelled to reject, as energetically as Peter and the angel of the Apocalypse rejected the religious adoration offered them. But if Jesus did not reject it, and allowed himself to be adored as the Messiah, he showed thereby a complete consciousness of his incarnate divinity. So much the more is this true of those cases in which, as we shall subsequently see, it is a matter of adoring Jesus as the Son of God in the strictly christo-logical sense of the word. So was it with the women and disciples after the Lord's resurrection (Matt. xxviii, 9, 17; Luke xxiv, 52). It is clear that Jesus by accepting this adoration confessed himself to be essentially God.

A third series of revelations of the essentially divine con-sciousness of Jesus relates to his *almighty works*. Omnipo-tence is the most convincing attribute of God and the most comprehensible proof of divinity. Jesus himself sees therein the manifestation of divinity, since he declares of God, in contrast to men, that with him all things are possible (Matt. xix, 26). But whoever reflects impartially upon the portrait of the Saviour given in the Gospels receives undoubtedly the impression that Jesus was omnipotent. Neither men, nor circumstances, nor the powers of nature are able to interfere with his life and actions. He never had to give up doing anything which he had resolved to do, nor did he ever suffer or experience anything which he himself had not wished. Never and nowhere, as happened occasionally to the disciples, did he lack the ability to complete, at will, even the most difficult task, surpassing the powers of any mere creature.

His *working of miracles* is a proof of this. With unique,

I.   17

divine omnipotence he heals every phase of suffering and every disease of humanity, brings the dead to life, commands evil spirits and compels the forces of nature to obey him. (See the chapters on the "Miracles of Jesus," in vol. II of this work.) Every attempt to explain the miracles of Jesus otherwise than by having recourse to divine omnipotence breaks down completely. Jesus also is well aware that his works are those of omnipotence and not the works of man. "Thou canst not make one hair white or black," he says (Matt. v, 36) of all men without exception, while he works as the Lord of life and death, and this *from his own inherent power*. If he sometimes indicates his miracles as works of his Father (Mark v, 19; John v, 19, 20, 36; xi, 41; xiv, 10), performed by the power of the spirit of God (Matt. xii, 28; Luke xi, 20), he nevertheless identifies this power with himself, and bears in himself the essential plenitude of divine miraculous power. This proceeds from him as his own personal power and characteristic. Whoever comes near to him has this feeling (Matt. xii, 28). The power to perform miracles, therefore, is his to use at any moment. He can employ it without first appealing to God, when, how and as often as he wishes. One single word is sufficient to accomplish the most miraculous result. Miracles appear as a perfectly natural expression of the inborn power within him. They stream forth as from a limitless, inexhaustible spring, without in the least exhausting or even diminishing its flow. This inexhaustible, ever fresh source of divine omnipotence he possesses so independently and so personally, that he imparts unlimited power also to his disciples to work miracles *in his name and by his orders* (Matt. x, 1; Mark iii, 15; Luke ix, 1). "Heal the sick, raise the dead, cleanse the lepers, cast out devils; freely have you received, freely give" (Matt. x, 8). With these words he sends his disciples out into the world. And their deeds correspond to the assurances given them. They do cast out devils and heal all infirmities and sicknesses (Mark vi, 13; ix, 37; Luke ix, 6). They are able to report joyfully to the Saviour: "Lord, the devils also are subject to us *in thy name*" (Luke x, 17). After the death of their Master, the Apostles continue *in the name of the Lord Jesus Christ of Nazareth* to heal the sick, to cast out devils from those possessed by them and to raise the dead (Acts iii, 6, 16; iv, 10, 30; ix, 34-42).

Still more astonishing than physical miracles is the spiritual power of *forgiving sins* used by Christ. No prophet had ever done that. At most, the prophets announced forgiveness in the name of Jehovah (2 Kings xii, 13). Everywhere in the Old Testament the forgiveness of sins is reserved for God alone, as he alone can judge sinners. Not once did Judaism ascribe the power to forgive sins to the expected Messiah.[1]

[1] G. Dalman, *Die Worte Jesu*, i, 215 (Leipzig, 1898).

The Pharisees, contemporaries of Jesus, thought the same. They denounced as downright blasphemy the arrogance of any man forgiving sins (Matt. ix, 3; Mark ii, 7; Luke v, 21). Jesus silently confirms the correctness of this view. But in order to show that the Messiah is more than a man and claims divine privileges, he not only forgives sins (Matt. ix, 2 and parallels), but expressly ascribes to himself the right to forgive them, and proves by a miracle that he possesses this absolute power in his own person (Matt. ix, 5-7 and parallels). Indeed, he goes so far as to transfer this divine right of forgiving sins in his name to his disciples : " Whose sins you shall forgive, they are forgiven them; and whose sins you shall retain, they are retained " (John xx, 23). " Amen I say to you, whatsoever you shall bind upon earth shall be bound also in heaven; and whatsoever you shall loose upon earth shall be loosed also in heaven " (Matt. xviii, 18).

The power to forgive sins comes, moreover, only from the essential Messianic vocation of Jesus of being the *Redeemer and Saviour of sinners.* Jesus is come to seek and to save that which was lost (Luke xix, 10). The saving consists in the rescuing men from the condition of being eternally lost, in which man finds himself in consequence of the guilt of sin weighing upon him. It is accomplished, however, not by any means merely by the fact that God announces forgiveness to the sinner and pardons his sins. Rather are this forgiveness and remission connected with the sacrifice of the life of Jesus. Jesus expressly says that " his life is a ransom for many " (Matt. xx, 28), and that his blood is the means for the remission of sins (Matt. xxvi, 28 and parallels). Jesus has, therefore, the full consciousness of such a value pertaining to his life, his blood and his personality, that their sacrifice in death forms a complete substitute for the offence given to God, which is inherent in sin. It would be madness and blasphemy if a mere man, and in any case a creature, should assume such importance. " The man who fulfils the prophecy that God will redeem his people from all their sins, the man who in his own person steps into the gulf which yawns between God and the world, the man who ascribes to his own life a value that can replace the infinitely great shortcomings of mankind, and whose importance to the world is like that of God, is the incorporation in a human person of God's willingness to save "[1]—*the divine Redeemer in the form of man.*

With the right to forgive sins and with the sin-destroying work of redemption there is immediately and logically connected the right, which Jesus reserves for himself, of at some time pronouncing the final sentence on the living and the dead,

---

[1] J. Steinbeck, *Das göttliche Selbstbewusstsein Jesu nach dem Zeugnis der Synoptiker,* 55 (Leipzig, 1908).

as the *Judge of the world*. He has appeared to redeem the world in humility and poverty; but he will come again at the last day to judge the world, in divine glory and in " his majesty and that of his Father and the holy angels " (Luke ix, 26 and parallels). He will not only take part in the judgement, like the angels, the Apostles and the just, but he, and he alone, in his own person will carry out the judgement in divine omnipotence (Matt. vii, 23 and parallels). The judgement and the final sentence are so exclusively his task that even the heavenly Father will not participate in it : " For neither doth the Father judge any man; but hath given all judgement to the Son, that all men may honour the Son, as they honour the Father " (John v, 22).

If Jesus, as Judge of the world, merits the same divine honour and adoration that belong to God the Father, it is evident that the Judge is not merely a human representative of God, but God himself, just like the Father. For divine honour and adoration cannot be transferred to any creature, not even to a merely human representative of God. As man, even as merely a humanly-considered Messianic Son of Man, he would, moreover, be at most capable of carrying out, in the name and by the order of God, the sentence pronounced by God as Judge. Christ, on the contrary, will try the heart and the reins and judge with omniscient keenness (Matt. x, 26 and parallels); he will judge men not alone from their outward works, but from their innermost thoughts and sentiments, known to God only (Matt. xii, 36), and he will, as an independent sovereign, render to each, according to the measure of his deserts or of his guilt, everlasting life or everlasting punishment (Matt. vii, 23; xvi, 27; xxv, 32-46). Only the all-wise, all-just and almighty God can judge the world thus.

In fact, the whole Old Testament also, down to the time of Christ, had already announced that Jehovah, the Lord, the true God, would execute the judgement of the world in his own person. The judgement day is " the great and dreadful day of the Lord " (Mal. iv, 5). " In the glory of his majesty " the Lord shall rise to execute judgement (Isa. ii, 19; lxvi, 15, 16). The Lord will gather together all nations and tongues, that they may see his glory (Isa. lxvi, 18). " The Lord my God shall come and all the saints with him " to the judgement (Zach. xiv, 5). " The Lord, the God of gods, our God shall come " openly to the judgement, " and the heavens shall declare his justice; for God is judge " (Ps. xlix, 1-6). " The Lord shall judge the ends of the earth " (1 Kings ii, 10). The Lord shall judge the world with justice and mercy, and the nations with truth and equity (Ps. xcv, 12; xcvii, 8). " The Lord standeth up to judge : and he standeth to judge the people " (Isa. iii, 13). In short, every doubt is excluded that it is Jehovah, the Lord God, who, according to the Old Testament, will personally conduct the judgement of the world. Since, therefore, Jesus Christ confirms the Old Testament teaching concerning the Last Judgement and applies it to himself, and represents himself as the only Judge of the world, he thereby unequivocally proclaims himself to be God.

We have thus far considered the superhuman consciousness of Jesus as to his nature in general, without speaking of his testimony to himself as the Son of God. It still remains necessary to show in what *spiritual connection this revelation of his divinity stands with his Messianic consciousness*. All the utterances of his supernatural consciousness which have been specified are made by Jesus Christ in his character of the Messiah. No one who studies them carefully can doubt this. Even our opponents agree with us on this point. On the other hand, they assert that Jesus, as the Messiah, reveals thereby no superhuman consciousness as to his nature, but merely a superhuman consciousness of his vocation. Christ, they say, has been fully aware that he was, by nature, a genuine man like all other men, only he imagined that he had received from God a Messianic vocation. From this Messianic rôle can be explained the extraordinary and superhuman character of all that Jesus asserted and thought about himself.

But, as we have seen, with such an explanation we arrive at no result, especially if, like the liberal school, we look upon the Messianic vocation of Jesus from a purely Jewish point of view—that is, if we make the Saviour proclaim himself to be the Messiah only in the sense of contemporary Judaism. But also every other conception of the Messianic idea, unless it holds firmly to the divine Messiah, will not do justice to the superhuman consciousness of Jesus. The utterances in which Jesus, by his comparisons, on the one hand, definitely distinguishes himself from the world of creatures, and, on the other hand, puts himself on a level with God; the practical demands which Jesus makes upon men's faith, love and honour; and the actual proofs of his divinity, which he furnishes by his deeds of omnipotence, as a worker of miracles, the forgiver and destroyer of sins, and judge of the world—point not only to the Saviour's consciousness of a divine vocation, but also to his consciousness of a divine nature in its fullest extent. Only by the fact that we recognize in Jesus Christ the Messiah-God is the whole problem of his supernatural self-consciousness solved. Accordingly, Christ not only elevated the Messianic idea, characteristic of his age and surroundings, from the low level of the national-Jewish and worldly political views, but at the same time brought to us the certainty that he, as the Messiah, must be also in every particular the Messiah-God, and actually God. His Messianic consciousness is, therefore, divine consciousness; His Messianic revelation is a divine revelation; and the Son of Man is the Son of God.

II.—CHRIST'S CONSCIOUSNESS OF HIS DIVINITY.

1. *Christ's General Consciousness of being the Son of God.*

Together with the Messianic testimony for his divinity thus far considered runs also a direct *revelation of his divine sonship.* Whoever has read the Gospel knows that Jesus calls himself therein the Son of God and allows himself to be so called. Even the most radical critics almost unanimously concede the fact that Christ's characterization of himself as the Son of God goes back not only to the disciples, but to Jesus himself. Only the meaning of this designation is questioned. Does Jesus wish to represent himself as the Son of God by nature, or has the expression on his lips another subordinate significance?

Judged by our manner of thought and speech, this question would be easy to answer. In the West we usually give the name " son " only to one who in the literal sense has been begotten by his father. With the Eastern, and especially with the Semite, it is otherwise. For him the name of son has not only the above-named meaning, but also a much more extensive one. It is used in order to express every close connection and kinship, every physical and moral communion or relation, which in any way resembles the relation between son and father. The Holy Scriptures throughout hold tenaciously to this linguistic usage. Whoever has been anointed with oil is called a " son of oil " (Zach. iv, 14); whoever has deserved death, or has been condemned to death, is called the " son of death " (1 Kings xx, 31; 2 Kings xii, 5). The word " son " is also transferred to the physical relations of lifeless things. Thus the arrow is the " son of the bow," or " son of the quiver " (Job xli, 19; Lam. iii, 13); the threshed out grain of wheat is the " son of the threshing-floor " (Isa. xxi, 10). Morally considered, the pupils of the prophets are " sons of the prophets " (3 Kings xx, 35); evil men are " sons of Belial " (Deut. xiii, 13; 1 Kings ii, 12), " sons of perdition " (John xvii, 12); the damned are " sons of hell " (Matt. xxiii, 15); the enemies of Jesus are " sons of the devil " (John viii, 44); while Jesus calls the Apostles " my sons " (Mark x, 24; John xiii, 33).[1]

Similarly and in an analogous sense we find also the expression " son of God " or " sons of God." Above all, it was natural to call the angels " sons of God " in consequence of their close connection with God (Job i, 6; ii, 1; xxxviii, 7;

---

[1] In the English version the words τέκνα and *filioli* are often translated by the word " children."—TR.

Ps. lxxxviii, 7). For the same reason just men and true
servants of the Most High receive the title " sons of God "
(Wisd. ii, 13; Eccl. iv, 11). In this sense it was allowable to
distinguish the Israelites by calling them " sons of God," [1]
and the people of Israel the " son of God " (Exod. iv, 22;
Osee xi, 1). With still greater appropriateness the name
" son of God " was transferred to the representative of God
among the chosen people, to the anointed king in the service
of Jehovah (2 Kings vii, 14). The kings and judges of this
world in general receive this title (Ps. lxxxi, 6).

It is, therefore, evident that the King of kings, the anointed
of God in the highest sense of the term, the longed-for
Messiah, deserved to be called the " Son of God." It is true
that he appears in the Old Testament only seldom under this
name, most distinctly in the second Psalm. Yet the title
" Son of God " was certainly known and used as a Messianic
title about the time of Christ. The Book of Henoch and the
Fourth Book of Esdras testify to this fact (Henoch cv, 2;
4 Esdras vii, 28). [2] It is no less evident from the Gospels that
the Jews who were contemporaries of Jesus regarded the title
" Son of God " as Messianic (John i, 49; vi, 70; Matt. xvi, 16;
Mark xiv, 61). By this they meant for the most part only that
the Messiah was the Son of God in the moral, metaphorical
sense of the word—namely, that, as God's ambassador who
brings salvation to Israel, he was superior to all mortals.
Sometimes, indeed, they thought of a metaphysical sonship
with God on the part of the Messiah, and, in connection with
the second Psalm, remembered the Emmanuel of Isaias, and
recalled the Logos-doctrine of the Books of Wisdom, and
the positive prophecy that God himself would come to rescue
Israel. Justin, the philosopher, still testifies of the Jews in
the second century : " If we bring up to them the [Old Testa-
ment] passages which speak of the suffering of the Messiah,
of his being worthy of adoration and of his divinity, they are
compelled to confess that all that was prophesied of the
Messiah; yet they deny that Jesus was the Messiah, although
they recognize that the Messiah was to come, to suffer, to
rule and to be worthy of adoration, as God." [3]

How, then, did Jesus himself understand the title Son of
God, and ascribe it to himself? The whole Christian world
has at all times maintained that this was done in the highest,
metaphysical sense, and that Jesus has testified to the fact

[1] Deut. xiv, 1; Isa. i, 2; xlv, 11; Jer. iii, 22; Os. ii, 1; similarly in
the N. T. the disciples and believers, Matt. v, 9, 45; Luke vi, 35;
John i, 12; xi, 52; 1 John iii, 1; v, 2.
[2] Also in the Sibylline books (iii, 776), Messiah is called " Son of the
great God." Yet this passage may have been a Christian interpolation.
See Geffken, *Die Oracula Sibyllina,* in *Die griechischen Schriftsteller
der ersten drei Jahrhunderte,* 87 (Leipzig, 1902).
[3] *Dialogus cum Tryphone Judæo,* c. 67.

that he was by nature the Son of God. The new school of destructive criticism thinks otherwise. It asserts that Christ's consciousness of being the Son of God in no way overstepped the limits of a purely human relation of Jesus to God the Father.

Individual modernists, and among them in particular Alfred Loisy,[1] think themselves justified in supposing that Jesus understood by his divine sonship nothing but his Messiahship, and this only in the sense of a purely human, Jewish-apocalyptical Messiahship; that in Jesus the Messiah and the Son of God are synonymous ideas, and because the Messiah belongs to the order of creatures only, so in regard to Jesus, as the Son of God, one must not think of a kinship of nature or of entire consubstantiality with God.

This certainly means turning things entirely topsy-turvy. Even if it should be proved that the title Son of God was for Jesus synonymous with the title Messiah, it would not by any means follow that Jesus, as the Son of God, was not a super-human being. For the enemies of orthodox Christianity, who at once decide in advance that the Messiahship is to be brought down to the level of the purely human, the above-mentioned conclusion is certainly and cogently evident. But we have already demonstrated that Jesus, as the Messiah, had not only, in the highest sense, a superhuman consciousness as to his vocation, but also a thoroughly superhuman conscious-ness as to his divine nature. If, therefore, his divine sonship were to prove equivalent to his Messiahship, we should, precisely for that reason, have to recognize him as *by nature* the Son of God.

But the view that Jesus understood by his divine sonship merely the Messiahship is plainly false. It is true, those who were possessed of devils, those whom he healed, the astonished masses of the people and sometimes also the disciples called him the Son of God, without thinking of anything but his Messiahship. But that does not come into consideration here at all. It is, rather, merely a question in what sense Jesus himself applied the expression Son of God to his own person. Did Jesus, when he called himself the Son of God, think simply of his Messianic vocation? Loisy and those who are of his way of thinking maintain this. But such an assertion cannot find support in one single utterance of the Saviour,[2] while, on the contrary, the most of the utterances about the

---

[1] *L'Evangile et l'Eglise*, 42, 53-57; *Simples réflexions*, 72; *Les Evan-giles synoptiques*, i, 243; a brilliant refutation by Lepin, *Jésus Messie et Fils de Dieu*, 280 ff. (Paris, 1906); *Les Théories de M. Loisy*, 304 ff. (Paris, 1908).

[2] Loisy appealed formerly to the confession of Peter and the utterances of Jesus about the judgement. Now he confesses in his *Evangiles synop-tiques*, ii, 363, 604-609, that these two texts also about the Son of God are to be understood in the metaphysical sense. Hence, he bluntly pro-claims them not genuine.

Son of God stand in no direct connection whatever with the Saviour's Messianic utterances.

Even those who positively deny the divinity of Jesus recognize this. Harnack writes : " Jesus himself has given to the idea of the ' Son of God ' a meaning, on account of which it almost falls out of the Messianic scheme or does not absolutely need this scheme for its comprehension."[1] They go, for the most part, so far that, exaggerating the facts of the case at the expense of the Messiahship of Jesus, they assume that the Messianic consciousness of Jesus has only grown out of the consciousness of his divine sonship.[2] However monstrous such an assumption is, the statement underlying it is nevertheless correct (as we shall soon convince ourselves)— namely, that Jesus did announce his divine sonship already before his Messiahship and independently of it.

The modernist equation—The Son of God = the Messiah, and the Messiah = a man—must accordingly be entirely rejected. It attributes Jewish notions of the time to Jesus Christ quite arbitrarily. According to the Jewish opinion of that age, it is true, the appellation Son of God was for the most part merely an honorary Messianic title, and the Messiah was also merely a man—in both cases because official Judaism at the time of Christ adhered to an earthly, national idea of the Messiah. Jesus Christ, however, as we have shown, conceived his Messianic vocation as something so supernatural and divine that a merely human person was insufficient for its realization, but rather a divine man, a divine Messiah, was required for that purpose. Hence, it is evident that he plainly gave to the expressions " Son of God " and " Messiah " an equally divine meaning; and, in fact, that precisely his essential divine sonship was the foundation and condition of his divinely Messianic mission and person. That this conception of the doctrine of the divine sonship is really the same as that of the Saviour, the following investigation will show. For the present we affirm only that *the divine sonship of Jesus ought not be judged of by his Messiahship, and still less by the Jewish idea of the Messiah.*

In this, as has already been remarked, most of the opponents of the divinity of Jesus are agreed. They are convinced that the utterances of Jesus which relate to his divine sonship must be investigated by themselves and independently of the Messianic question. We can obtain certainty as to what Jesus understood by his divine sonship only by examining the mean-

[1] *Wesen des Christentums,* 80; Wendt, *Die Lehre Jesu,* 421, 2nd ed. (1901).

[2] Renan, *Vie de Jésus,* 76 ff., 120 ff.; Edmund Stapfer, *Jésus-Christ avant son ministère,* 88 ff., 187 ff. (Paris, 1896); Harnack, *Wesen,* 80 f., 87 f.; B. Weiss, *Das Leben Jesu,* i, 280 (1902); *Lehrbuch der biblischen Theologie des N. T.,* 62, 288 (1903); J. Kögel, *Das Messianische Bewusstsein Jesu,* in *Reich Christi,* viii, 403-420.

ing of his utterances in regard to it. In doing this the aim in view must always be directed to the one alternative into which the whole problem of the Son of God resolves itself : *" Did Jesus claim to be the Son of God in a sense wholly transcending the limitations of time and the powers of a human creature, or did he reveal himself as the Son of God within the limits of a creature's purely human relations to the Father in heaven?"*

Hostile critics assume in advance the latter supposition. In their evolutionary view of the world, history and religion, they declare at the outset, as a basic principle, that Jesus applied to himself merely the common Jewish idea of the Son of God prevalent at the time, although certainly in a somewhat more intensive way than that in which the divine sonship could have been described by the average Jew. Heinrich Weinel, among others, expresses himself on this point as follows : " According to the use made of the word ' son ' in the Hebrew and Aramaic languages, one is not compelled to think of a peculiar kind of origin for the ' son,' but certainly must think of an especially intimate relation to the ' Father.' Jesus spoke freely of others also as ' sons of God '—that ye may be ' children ' of your Father in heaven. And he undoubtedly conceived this title in this sense, and fulfilled its significance with the whole intensity of his love to God."[1] In other words, Christ's divine sonship is to be interpreted according to the idea of divine sonship common to his contemporaries and his fellow-men. As in the Old Testament the angels, the kings of Israel, and the Israelites themselves, and in the New Testament the disciples and Christian believers are called sons and children of God in consequence of their intimate moral relations to God, so Jesus is said to have conceived the title Son of God, not as an expression of his natural relation to the Father, but as a token of his special spiritual and ethical nearness to God. According to O. Pfleiderer, " Christ, although he is called the only begotten Son of God, nevertheless appears as essentially the same kind of model, known from earliest times, of pious men in general, filled with the spirit of God."[2] According to Harnack, the deeper " knowledge of God is the whole import of the name of son " as used by Jesus. " Jesus is convinced that he knows God, as no one else has done before him, and he knows that he has the vocation to impart to all others this knowledge by word and deed, and therewith to inform them of their adoption as children by God. In this consciousness he knows himself to be the Son, called and appointed by God, hence the Son of God."[3] Reinhold Seeberg expresses the same idea in direct

---

[1] *Jesus im neunzehnten Jahrhundert,* iii (Tübingen, 1907).
[2] *Die Entwicklung des Christentums,* 31 (München, 1907).
[3] *Wesen des Christentums,* 81 ; so Bousset, *Jesus,* 99, 3rd ed.

support of the hazy christology of Schleiermacher and Ritschl :
" The will of God, leading the history of mankind to salvation . . . united itself with the man Jesus from the first
moment of his existence . . . and penetrated his feelings,
thoughts and will. Thus did the man Jesus become the ' Son
of God.' "[1] Bernhard Weiss also substitutes for the metaphysical consubstantiality of the Son with the Father a moral
similarity of nature, whereby the man Jesus is qualified above
all other men for the most intimate acquaintance with the
purposes of the Father and for their accomplishment in his
Messianic vocation.[2] Finally, Emil Schürer, in agreement
with these ideas, finds that the relation of the Son to the
Father is " not a natural, physical or metaphysical, but an
ethical relation . . . analogous to the relation of all God's
children to their heavenly Father, and yet having an intensity
which was unique by reason of a unique kind of knowledge
of God " and having also a corresponding call to reveal it.[3]

This selection of quotations is sufficient to give us an insight into the ideas of modern liberal theologians concerning
the Son of God. All of them, including the modernists, who
agree with Loisy admirably as to the equation, " the Son of
God = the Messiah," interpret *Christ's consciousness of divine
sonship as a spiritual and moral relation of the man, Jesus,
to the heavenly Father,* precisely as every man can come into
connection with God and become a child of God. Only Jesus,
as the Son of God, stands one step higher than other men.
As his knowledge of God and his fidelity to his Messianic
vocation have in them something extraordinary, so the divine
sonship, resulting from it, is extraordinary. Yet it has not
transcended the limits of the purely human, nor broken
Christ's purely natural relation, as a creature, to the Father.
Jesus is said also not to have professed to be the consubstantial Son of the Father in the sense of Christian dogma.

If we examine more closely in what way and by what means
the modern theology about Jesus arrives at this result, we find
again that it proceeds according to its usual rule of an
" exactly critical " treatment of the text. In advance one
must regard as already established what one wishes under all
circumstances to establish—namely, that the Son of God,
Jesus, has worked his way out of purely human conditions
and remains within the limits of those conditions. The utterances of Jesus in the Gospels which do not lend themselves
to this view are unhesitatingly rejected as not genuine, but
those which show an appearance of complaisance are pressed

[1] *Die Kirche Deutschlands im* 19 *Jahrhundert,* 294 (Leipzig, 1903).
[2] *Lehrbuch der biblischen Theologie des N. T.,* 58-60 (Berlin, 1895);
Leben Jesu, ii, 145 f. (Stuttgart and Berlin).
[3] *Das messianische Selbstbewusstsein Jesu,* 10 ff. (Göttingen, 1903);
similarly, Réville, *Jésus de Nazareth,* ii, 11 (Paris, 1897).

with violence into the procrustean bed of the "natural" theory of the Son of God.

In accordance with this "critical" method of procedure, the utterances of Jesus in regard to the Son of God in the Gospel of John are entirely, and those of the synoptics partly, eliminated or mutilated. Then these theologians announce, with a superior air of unprejudiced research : " It is neither paradox nor yet rationalism, but a simple statement of the facts, as they lie before us in the Gospels, that not the Son, but the Father only, belongs to the Gospel, as Jesus preached it."[1] That is true for one who is pledged to a Gospel trimmed, fashioned and interpreted to suit the desires of the liberals. But on every other kind of investigator such a procedure makes the impression of an attempt at strangulation. Only that solution deserves to be considered which deals seriously and honourably with all the utterances concerning the Son of God found in the critically sound texts of the Gospels.

If, then, we first take a hasty *general view of these utterances of Jesus concerning the Son of God,* it is palpably evident that our opponents' supposition is fundamentally false—that the Saviour called himself the Son of God after the manner of men, " in analogy with the relation of all God's children to their heavenly Father." Rather do we receive the very opposite impression. *Jesus claims to be the Son of God in an entirely different sense from that which says that all men are children of God, and that his filial relation to the Father is such that it finds no application to men.* As often as Jesus speaks of his relations with his Father he uses constantly and without exception the expression " My Father "; and as often as he calls the attention of the disciples to their childlike relation to God, there is the equally definite characterization, " Your Father." Never does he associate himself with the disciples and with men by the natural form of speech, " Our Father." It is true, in the Lord's Prayer he teaches the Apostles to pray, " Our Father, who art in heaven " (Matt. vi, 9). Yet Jesus only puts this prayer into the mouth of the disciples. He himself does not pray so. This is clear both from the distinct command, " Thus therefore shall ye pray," and also from the added conclusion in reference to forgiveness, in which again at once the term " Your Father " is used : " For if you will forgive men their offences, your heavenly Father will forgive you also your offences " (Matt. vi, 14). Even on those occasions in which Jesus unites himself with the disciples before God, and when therefore it would be certainly expected that he would use the collective expression, " Our Father," there stands, on the contrary, " My Father " : " I will not drink from henceforth of this

---

[1] Harnack, *Wesen des Christentums,* 91.

fruit of the vine until that day when I shall drink it with *you* new in the kingdom of *my Father*" (Matt. xxvi, 29). "And I send the promise of *my Father* upon *you*" (Luke xxiv, 49). "Come, ye blessed of *my Father,* possess you the kingdom prepared for *you* from the foundation of the world" (Matt. xxv, 34). Thus and similarly does Jesus distinguish unequivocally between his divine sonship and that of the disciples and men in general.

Gustav Dalman, the best-informed scholar in respect to the Aramaic language, spoken by Jesus, sees himself forced to this confession : "Nowhere do we find that Jesus proclaimed himself to be the Son of God in such a way that merely a religious and ethical relation to God is meant, which others also could and should also in reality possess. . . . Jesus has given men unmistakably to understand that he is not only ' a,' but ' the ' Son of God."[1] The examination separately of the most important utterances of Jesus concerning the Son of God will strengthen this opinion.

2. The First Revelation of the Son of God by Christ in the Temple.

The first words which have come down to us from Jesus refer to his filial relations with the Father. At the age of twelve Jesus had made the first Easter journey with his parents to Jerusalem. After the conclusion of the seven days' festival the boy remained behind in the temple, where his anxious parents, distressed by his absence, found him after three days, sitting among the Rabbis and astonishing the teachers, already grey in service, by his knowledge of the Law. In the agitation caused thus to her tender mother's heart, Mary addresses to him the mild reproach : "Son, why hast thou done so to us? Behold, thy father and I have sought thee sorrowing." Whereupon came this remarkable reply from the wonderful child : "How is it that you sought me? Did you not know that I must be about my Father's business?" (Luke ii, 48, 49).

It does not matter whether Jesus meant " in the house of my Father," or " in intercourse with my Father," or, finally, " in the sphere of work or nature of my Father "; evidently he means all that at the same time by the quite unlimited expression : " In what pertains to my Father." Yet, however we may exegetically circumscribe or extend these words, in any case Jesus expresses in them his full, certain and complete consciousness of being the Son of God, just as we find it in his whole later life and in all his words and deeds. No

---

[1] *Die Worte Jesu, mit Berücksichtigung des nachkanonischen jüdischen Schrijtums und der aramäischen Sprache erörtert,* i, 230, 235 (Leipzig, 1898).

one can seriously doubt this. Even the harshest enemies of the divinity of Jesus must confess : " Already, as a twelve-year-old boy, he felt himself to be the Son of God in the unique sense of the term."[1]

If that is the case, then it is, above all, certain that Christ's consciousness of divine sonship is not the result of a gradual psychological development. Jesus did not, little by little, through progressive knowledge of God and continued conduct pleasing to God, come to the conviction that he was in a unique sense the Son of God. And still less than inward reflection did external circumstances, such as the eager Messianic expectation of his contemporaries or his own successes, help to awaken and more and more to develop and strengthen his consciousness of divine sonship. No, before such an evolution could in any case have begun, Jesus' consciousness of divine sonship was complete in the tender years of childhood.

It is evident, however, that in these circumstances it also cannot be called merely a moral consciousness of divine sonship. As every human ethical relation is developed and strengthened and grows gradually through moral thinking and acting, so the unique ethical relation of Jesus to the Father, which our critics like to call the divine sonship of Jesus, could only have germinated in his youth, grown in his adolescence, and have come to maturity and full development in complete manhood. It contradicts all the laws of the psychology of children that a boy of twelve years, who had been brought up in the humblest, most ordinary and most obscure circumstances, should feel himself exalted above all men, and actually know that he was the Son of God in a unique ethical sense. Liberal critics remark very ingenuously in regard to the words of the twelve-year-old boy : " Here a premature consciousness of divine sonship and of vocation is taken for granted."[2] Certainly the natural, human explanation can make simply nothing out of such an early consciousness of divine sonship. It must either, in defiance of all criticism, declare the passages in the Gospels bearing on the subject ungenuine, or concede that the consciousness of divine sonship in the child Jesus was not inculcated and acquired but was innate, because it was present before and above any moral development ; in other words, that it consisted not of a merely ethical, but of a physical, or rather a metaphysical relation.

The mere fact of the existence of a consciousness of divine sonship in the child Jesus already reveals the glaring unnaturalness of the natural explanation of this consciousness.

[1] Bernhard Weiss, *Leben Jesu,* i, 279, 4th ed.
[2] Wilhelm Hess, *Jesus von Nazareth in seiner geschichtlichen Lebensentwicklung,* 5 (Tübingen, 1906).

If we, in addition to this, consider the depth and the import of the consciousness of divine sonship in the twelve-year-old boy the last doubt disappears. Jesus claims to be the Son of the heavenly Father precisely in that physical sense in which he passed in the world as the son of Joseph. To the definite words of Mary, "Thy father and I," he makes the equally definite explanation, "my Father" in heaven. The *tertium comparationis* is not an ethical, but a physical, fatherhood. Just for the reason and only for the reason that God in the proper, physical sense is the Father of the child Jesus is this child exalted above the mere sonship characteristic of creatures which connects him with Joseph and Mary. As a creature, Jesus should have spared his mother and foster-father the anxiety and trouble which he caused them by remaining in the temple. The words, "How is it that you sought me? Did you not know that I must be about my Father's business?" would appear very unchildlike in his mouth if Jesus were merely a human child. No gentle child would have allowed itself to speak and act in such a way towards its parents.

The ethical divine sonship of the human child Jesus, which is asserted by our opponents, required above all that he should not neglect his duty towards his parents. For such an offence is equivalent to an injury to God, and includes, therefore, the denial of his alleged ethical filial relation to God. Only by reason of the fact that Jesus is the Son of God physically, and hence is himself God, do his earthly parents become subject to him, and he can say with full right : "Why do you treat me like a mere human child? Do you not know that I, as the Son of God, am raised above all human relations?" Well considered, therefore, the conduct of the child Jesus in the temple and his announcement that he is God's Son are comprehensible only if Jesus is in the full and proper sense of the words the Son of God and also God. By the supposition of a merely ethical divine sonship, the scene in the temple would be inadmissible, in fact—may I be pardoned the expression—immoral. The explanation of the freethinkers invalidates itself.

Against this at most one objection could be raised—the possibility that Jesus, although merely human, had been instructed by God in his earliest years in regard to his future Messianic vocation, and that he, relying on such a supernatural revelation, had felt himself exalted above the usual childish, human relations and obligations, and had already then assumed the rôle of the Messiah. In fact, there are not wanting critics who take refuge in the supposition that Jesus received his vocation "conveyed to him by revelation in a condition of ecstasy. The beginning and the ending of his Messianic consciousness, and therefore those of his consciousness of divine sonship also, pertain to the transcendental."[1]

We do not need, however, to prove that the freethinker's view, which contests, on principle, all revelation, and wishes especially to explain the self-consciousness of Jesus as something purely natural, cannot be seriously entertained. But, apart from that, it is impossible that God should appoint a boy as his ambassador and let him make his appearance as the Messiah. Moreover, not one of the Evangelists looks upon the episode in the temple as a scene pertaining to the Messianic vocation. All the Gospels place the beginning of the Messianic *activity* in the mature years of Jesus's life. Even Luke, who has preserved for us the incident with the twelve-year-old Jesus, remarks later expressly : " Jesus was beginning about the age of thirty years " his Messianic public appearance and activity (Luke iii, 23 and parallels). Finally, even our opponents are unanimously of the opinion that the Messianic *consciousness* of Jesus had its beginning and the commencement of its development only with his baptism. The consciousness of his divine sonship at the age of twelve has in itself nothing at all to do with the Messianic consciousness. The former appears much earlier and independently of the latter. Son of God and Messiah cannot, therefore, properly be described as equivalent expressions, as is claimed by the school of Loisy. On the whole, every explanation which applies to the Saviour's consciousness of divine sonship only the standard of human relations fails completely. Already the child Jesus in the temple reveals a consciousness which must be considered, in view of its origin and import, as a strictly metaphysical divine sonship.

3. *Commencement of the Revelation of the Son of God to the Disciples.*

Almost twenty years elapsed before Jesus expressed himself further about his divinely human person. It is as though he wished to lift the veil no more from the mystery which is so difficult for mankind to comprehend. Yet, after the Baptist had publicly acknowledged him to be the Son of God (John i, 34), after the voice from heaven had sounded, " This is my beloved son, in whom I am well pleased " (Matt. iii, 17), after the tempter had divined in him the Son of God, and those possessed of devils had hailed him as the Son of God (Matt. iv, 1-11), and the first disciples had joyfully greeted him as such (John i, 41, 45, 49)—although certainly without apprehending the deep significance of the divine sonship—Jesus felt himself compelled to unveil more and more the idea of the Son of God. This took place first in the masterful inter-

---

[1] Wilhelm Schulz, *Protest. Monatshefte,* 443 f. (1906).

view with the Pharisee Nicodemus. An honoured teacher, Nicodemus belonged to that minority of the pharisaical party which drew near to the Saviour to a certain degree so long as he made no especially high demands upon their faith. By his benevolent sentiment and high education Nicodemus was capable of gaining a deeper insight into the person of Jesus than was the case at that time even among the disciples.

In the first place, the Pharisee frankly acknowledges the standpoint of himself and of the group that shares his views in regard to the Saviour : " Rabbi, we know that thou art come a teacher from God; for no man can do these signs which thou dost unless God be with him " (John iii, 2). He sees, accordingly, in the Saviour *some teacher sent by God— a prophet.* Jesus takes up this acknowledgement, as a starting-point, in order, in a wonderful dialogue, which in method adapts itself to the usages of the school of pharisaical Rabbis, to lead his questioner from that commencement up to the heights of his divine and Messianic revelation.

Recognized as an ambassador from God and a prophet, he directs the conversation immediately to the central idea, which is the import of the whole prophetic revelation and the aim of all the doctrinal teaching in Israel—namely, the kingdom of God and the Messianic revelation. He unfolds to the astonished " master in Israel " the fundamental requisites for the foundation of the Messianic kingdom and the fundamental conditions for entering into that kingdom, and thereby makes always more clear his claim to be not only *a* prophet, but *the* prophet—the God-appointed *Messiah of the world* (John iii, 3-10).

This being taken for granted, he now prepares the way for the proper knowledge of his Messianic person. In opposition to the hybrid idea of the Rabbis, who expected in the Messiah merely a man illumined and favoured by God—a " son of God " in the sense of our liberal theologians—Jesus declares that he is a *transcendental, supermundane and heavenly Being.* The Messianic perception of God which he brings to men, he draws from his own personal knowledge, not from a revelation and communication by the grace of God. The divine message which he brings from heaven, and the profoundest mysteries of the Godhead which he discloses, he has seen with his own eyes. " Amen, amen, I say to thee that we speak what we know, and we testify what we have seen " (John iii, 11).

He who is thus acquainted with heaven, and knows everything pertaining thereto, from direct observation, must evidently have been there. And, in reality, Jesus declares, by referring to Daniel's prophecy of the Son of Man, that he was in heaven before his life on earth, that he came down from heaven and that he will return again to heaven—in a word, that he is a heavenly being. "No man hath ascended into heaven, but he that descended from heaven, the Son of Man who is in heaven" (John iii, 13).[1] Thereby the modern liberal idea of the Messiah and Son of God, which sees in Jesus only a man especially favoured by God, is at once excluded.

Jesus, however, goes a step further, and lays before Nicodemus the keystone of the gradually developed revelation of his person. After having elevated his person, his will and his existence above everything merely human and mundane, he now lifts himself also above all created beings both in heaven and on earth, and affirms positively his *essential, metaphysical, divine sonship*. He plainly declares the Son of Man to be the *only begotten son of God* whom the Father has sent into the world. It is true, the expression "the only begotten Son of God" in itself allows always the double meaning—ethical sonship through the gracious selection and adoption of the man Jesus instead of a child, or essential sonship through the communication of the divine nature. But in the peculiar connection in which the designation "only begotten Son of God" here stands, the first meaning is not to be thought of. Jesus himself excluded it in advance by declaring precisely his superhuman nature, and by representing himself as a heavenly being, who had existed with the Father before all worlds. In fact, he already positively referred to his participation in the divine spiritual nature by ascribing to himself in his life on earth a direct knowledge and perception of God and of the divine : "We speak what we know and we testify what we have seen." Now he takes up this thought again and reveals fully its divine content. Not only must the world believe on the only begotten Son of God because his knowledge and his words proceed from a personal vision of God, but the world must also believe on the Son of God because he is the whole import and object of divine faith. And, accordingly, blessedness and eternal life are not only announced to believers through the only begotten Son of God, but the world becomes blessed through him, and in him possesses eternal life. "As Moses lifted up the serpent in the desert, so must the Son of Man be lifted up, that whosoever believeth in him may not perish, but may have life everlasting. For God so loved the world, as to give his only begotten Son, that whosoever believeth in him may not perish, but may have life everlasting. For God sent not his Son into the world to

[1] Jewish tradition held firmly to the real pre-existence of Daniel's Son of Man in accordance with the Book of Henoch xlviii, 6, "For this purpose the Son of Man was selected and hidden in him (God) before the world was created, and he will be with him to all eternity." See Paul Fiebig, *Der Menschensohn, Jesu Selbstbezeichnung mit besonderer Berücksichtigung des aramäischen Sprachgebrauches*, 122 (Tübingen and Leipzig, 1901).

judge the world, but that the world may be saved by him. He that believeth in him is not judged; but he that doth not believe is already judged, because he believeth not in the name of the only begotten Son of God " (John iii, 14-18). It would be absolute blasphemy if an ordinary human being, were he ever so gifted by divine grace, should use such language. Only an essentially divine man can speak thus of himself.

It is true, some exegetes, among them recently also Johannes Belser,[1] doubt whether the last quoted passages are to be regarded literally as the words of Jesus, or as the reflections of the Evangelist. Yet this doubt rests really only on the arbitrary supposition that Jesus at such an early stage and in the presence of a Pharisee could hardly have had such a deep insight into the mystery of his divinity—a view which does not require to be refuted. But even if it were well grounded and just, the interpretation which we have given would not thereby be at all weakened. For what John makes the Saviour say in this passage, Jesus Christ said repeatedly, later on, in other passages of the Gospel of John. In his report of the conversation with Nicodemus, John confirms, as Belser himself remarks: "the essential import of the utterances of Jesus. . . . The words of the Evangelist are really nothing but the words of Christ, which we meet with in the subsequent discourses reported by John."[2]

Not only that. We encounter them in substance also in the discourses of Jesus given by the synoptists (Matt. xi, 27; xvi, 16; xx, 28; xxi, 37; Luke x, 21). Whoever, therefore, like the liberal critics, appeals to the synoptists, excluding John, will be taught by them that Jesus on other occasions and before other hearers spoke substantially the same words that he uttered to Nicodemus in the wonderful conversation by night.

Thus, on a par with that conversation, in respect to time and content, is the revelation of himself which Jesus made to the *seventy-two disciples* on their return from their first missionary effort.[3] The messengers of the Gospel joyfully related to their master the miracles which they had performed in his name. Then Jesus rejoiced in spirit, and broke out into a loud and deeply touching prayer, in which he thanked the Father and glorified him because he had hidden the kingdom of God with its blessings from the wise and prudent of this world, and had nevertheless revealed it to the simple and to babes. Then he turned to the disciples with the words : " *All*

[1] *Das Evangelium des hl. Johannes*, 107 (Freiburg, 1905). On the other side are Schegg, Schanz, Fillion, Keil, Weiss, Knabenbauer, etc.

[2] Belser, pp. 107, 110.

[3] Matt. xi, 25; Luke x, 17. See H. Schuhmacher, *Die Selbstoffenbarung Jesu bei Matt.*, xi, 27 (Freiburg, 1912); Leop. Kopler, *Die johanneische Stelle bei den Synoptikern und die Gottessohnschaft Jesu*, in *Theol. Quartalschrift*, 1913-1914.

things are delivered to me by my Father, neither doth anyone know the Father, but the Son and he to whom it shall please the Son to reveal him " (Matt. xi, 27). These words are found not only in Matthew ; Luke transmits them exactly the same in substance, in spite of a small variation : " All things are delivered to me by my Father. *And no one knoweth the Son, but the Father ; and no one knoweth who the Son is, but the Father, and who the Father is, but the Son and to whom the Son will reveal him* " (Luke x, 22).

This joyful utterance of Jesus gives us a surprisingly deep insight into his consciousness of divine sonship and his most intimate relations to the Father. " All things are delivered to me by my Father." Jesus thinks here probably first of the power which he has received from the Father to work miracles and to overcome the kingdom of Satan. For he had himself, shortly before, given this power to the disciples, and now the seventy-two come to him with the joyful statement that they had been able in his name actually to have dominion over sickness, death and Satan. The Master takes occasion from this to lead his disciples a step further, and to declare to them that the Father has given him not only the sphere of divine power, thus far tested, but really divine omnipotence. " All things are delivered to me by my Father," or, as he will express himself subsequently : " All power is given to me in heaven and in earth " (Matt. xxviii, 18). Even our most pronounced opponents, like Heinrich J. Holtzmann,[1] Loisy,[2] Richard A. Hoffmann,[3] and Eduard von Hartmann,[4] see themselves compelled to acknowledge that Jesus in this passage thinks himself in full possession of divine omnipotence.

But the words of Jesus are not exhausted by these citations. Among the " all things " which are delivered by the Father to the Son is not only omnipotence but also *omniscience—* absolutely divine knowledge. Not only because Jesus says universally and without reservation, " all things," but because he still expressly adds : " No one knoweth the Son, but the Father, neither doth anyone know the Father, but the Son and he to whom it shall please the Son to reveal him." The knowledge and the fulness of truth and of the divine nature in the Son is so infinite that only the Father can fathom it—" No one knoweth the Son, but the Father." On the other hand, the knowledge of the Son is so perfect that he and he alone comprehends and fully grasps the divine knowledge and nature of the Father, and that all the divine knowledge and divine perception of his creatures flows from the divine know-

[1] *Neutestamentliche Theologie,* i, 274 f. (Freiburg u. Leipzig, 1897).
[2] *Evangelium und Kirche,* 63 (München, 1904).
[3] *Das Selbstbewusstsein Jesu nach den drei ersten Evangelien,* 25 (Königsberg i. Pr., 1904).
[4] *Das Christentum des N. T.,* 66, 111 (Sachsa i. Harz, 1905).

ledge of the Son, as from an inexhaustible source. " No one knoweth the Father, but the Son and he to whom it shall please the Son to reveal him.'' "The Son," remarks Loisy, " recognizes only God, the Father, as perfect, and precisely for the reason that he is the Son, exactly as God, the Father, only knows Christ, his Son, because he is the Father—God. The fundamental thought is the same as in the passage in John : ' No man hath seen God at any time ; the only begotten Son who is in the bosom of the Father, he hath declared him.' "[1]

In a word, the Son has a godlike, divine knowledge of the Father, precisely as the Father also has a divine knowledge of the Son. The knowledge of both, that of the Father and that of the Son, is identical ; both are equally divine and equally infinite—two immeasurable suns, which mutually illumine each other.

Jesus is, therefore, conscious of possessing the two attributes of nature and action, which belong to God alone, and in which the nature, the activity and the life of God are merged— omnipotence of will and power, and omniscience of intellect and perception. There can, therefore, be no more talk of his being a mere man whom God, out of grace and compassion, has endowed more richly than other human beings. *The unlimited divine knowledge and power of the Son can have their representative and find their explanation only in the divine nature of the Son of God.*

This becomes still clearer through the absolute *universal equality*, which, according to what has been said, exists *between Father and Son.* No more explanations and proofs are needed, but simply an unprejudiced examination of the words of Jesus, in order to gain the positive impression that Jesus was conscious that the Father is as the Son, and the Son as the Father, with the single exception of the personal relation conditioned by fatherhood and sonship. In other words, there exists between Jesus and the Father in the closest, natural sense that relation which exists between the Father and his only begotten Son—equality according to nature, difference in respect to the two persons. It detracts nothing from this that Jesus says, " All things are delivered to me by my Father.'' On the contrary, every son must speak so of his father. He has everything from the Father, his nature as well as the personal relation, which distinguishes him from the Father and at the same time unites him with the Father.

That Jesus claims to be the Son of God, as set forth in our text, in this and in no other sense, the best known critics in the camp of our opponents do not dare to deny. Gustav Dalman, who investigates the words of Jesus only from the standpoint of the philologist, writes : " Between Father and

---

[1] *L'Evangile et l'Eglise,* 47 ; H. Wendt, *Die Lehre Jesu,* 418 (1901).

Son there exists such a unique, complete and mutual relation
that, of necessity, others can gain a share of this full knowledge of the Father only through the mediation of the Son.
The two sentences about the knowledge of the Son by the
Father and about that of the Father by the Son are not to be
divided and interpreted separately. They are to be regarded
merely as a formal oriental expression for the reciprocity of
perfect knowledge. . . . That which is true of a father and
son in general is at once applied to Jesus and his heavenly
Father. Here also the relation to God which was peculiar to
Jesus is one that cannot be transferred or changed. . . . It
appears to be bound up with his nature."[1] Contemporaneously,
Edmund Stapfer, the liberal-protestant theologian of Paris,
writes : " Let us recall the great statement of Jesus, ' No one
knoweth the Son, but the Father.' I say that on the strength
of these words it is impossible to define Jesus. He remains
exalted above and outside of all subtleties, or better, above all
the impossibilities of metaphysics ; and he retains by reason of
these words, ' No one knoweth the Son, but the Father,' an
incomprehensibility, which is one of the surest signs of his
divinity, and is a necessary element for all true worship."[2]
Harnack, with no less frankness, acknowledges that " a formal
equality of Father and Son, who are separated only by their
names, and a relation between Father and Son, which never
had a beginning and remains always the same, are now
expressed [in the words of Matthew and Luke]. . . . If
Matthew has already written thus, then his own christology
resembles very closely that of John in one of the most important points [the divinity of Jesus], even if the passage
is interpreted more conservatively."[3] Alfred Loisy also is
ready to concede that " in the words, ' No one knoweth the
Son, but the Father, and no one knoweth the Father, but the
Son,' the actual divinity of the Son is taught."[4] " The
equality of Christ with eternal truth is declared therein. . . .
The mutual knowledge of Father and Son is not represented
as a relation which has come into existence in time and is
now realized; it has rather the immemorial character of the
analogous utterances which one finds in the Fourth Gospel;
it does not establish the pre-existence of Jesus, but rather
takes it for granted."[5]

Now, however, that the liberal critics have seen the im-

1 *Die Worte Jesu*, 232 f.
2 *La mort et la résurrection de Jésus-Christ*, 340, 2nd ed. (Paris, 1898).
3 *Sprüche und Reden Jesu*, 210, 211 (Leipzig, 1907). Thereby Harnack
also demolishes the interpretation which he gives to the same text in his
Wesen des Christentums, 81, which Loisy had refuted and declared to
be " a factitious and superficial explanation of the divine sonship of
Jesus "; Loisy, *L'Evangile et l' Eglise*, 41-44.
4 *Autour d'un petit livre*, 130.
5 *Les Evangiles synoptiques*, i, 194, 909 (1907).

possibility of interpreting the passage in the Gospels otherwise than in the sense of the true divinity of Jesus, this
passage must also at once be called by them unauthentic, and
for the simple reason that in it the divinity of Jesus is taught,
and because it destroys the jugglery of the liberal exegetes.
Loisy does not feel inclined to seek for the proof of the
unauthenticity of our text, but relies simply on his fundamental principle that all those texts must be unauthentic
which contain the divinity of the Son, or in any way put
the Son on an equality with the Father.[1] By virtue of this
principle, the words contained in Matthew and Luke cannot
be the words of the Saviour, but were subsequently ascribed
to him, as a wrongful justification of the oldest faith of
the Church in the divinity of Christ.[2] Because these words
in the Gospels remind one of the poetically conceived utterances in the Psalms and Prophets, they are supposed to represent an old Church poem.[3] Already before Loisy, Brandt[4]
and Pfleiderer[5] had resorted, in their extreme embarrassment,
to the same supposition. Their "critical" attempt was,
however, either ignored or directly repudiated by their own
partisans, since these words of the Gospels in their poetical
form are not unique in the utterances of Jesus; on the contrary, not a few utterances of his are so framed.[6]

Wellhausen,[7] Paul Wilhelm Schmiedel,[8] and after them in
particular Harnack,[9] seek, therefore, another way out of the
difficulty. Forced to the confession that the text quoted is
entirely authentic, and "belongs to the best sources of information about Jesus that we possess"[10]—namely, the so-
called *Discourses* of Jesus, from which it passed into the first
and third Gospels, they try to break off from it at least a
fragment. The portion, "No one knoweth the Son, but the
Father" (according to Matthew), or "No one knoweth who
the Son is, but the Father" (according to Luke), did not have,
according to them, its origin in that oldest source, but was
brought in from some other.[11] Therefore, this portion does
not contain the absolutely authentic words of our Lord!

Nevertheless, no critic can bring forward a single argument
to prove that the *Discourses* did not contain this portion; nor

---

[1] *Les Evangiles synoptiques,* i, 243.

[2] *L'Evangile et l'Eglise,* 41; *Autour d'un petit livre,* 130; *Les Evangiles synoptiques,* 909.   [3] *L'Evangile et l'Eglise,* 45-46.

[4] *Evangelische Geschichte,* 561 f., 576 f. (1893).

[5] *Urchristentum,* i, 435, 576, 667 (1902).

[6] Harnack, *Sprüche und Reden Jesu,* 191 (Leipzig, 1907); *cf.* Fritz
Barth, *Die Hauptprobleme des Lebens Jesu,* 264 f. (Gütersloh, 1907).
Against Loisy, especially Lepin, *Jésus, Messie et Fils de Dieu,* 323-332.

[7] *Das Evangelium Matthäi,* 57 f. (1904).

[8] *Protest. Monatshefte,* 2 ff. (1900); *Das vierte Evangelium,* 48
(Tübingen, 1906).

[9] *Sprüche und Reden Jesu,* 189-216.

[10] Harnack, *id.,* 215.   [11] Harnack, *id.,* 192.

is it possible to prove it, for we are entirely in the dark about the *Discourses* themselves. If it be conceded, however, that the passage in dispute was not taken from the *Discourses,* but was introduced from some other source, it does not at all follow from this that it is not just as truly an utterance of the Lord as the whole remainder of the text. The *Sayings and Discourses of Jesus* are also, according to Harnack, only the second source from which the Gospels of Matthew and Luke are derived. The question whether both these Evangelists took our text exclusively from the *Discourses,* or have made use of still other sources for it, is merely a problem pertaining to the history of manuscripts, and has nothing to do with the credibility of the Gospel report. That credibility would be endangered only if the whole, complete text in question had not from the first existed in the Gospels themselves. Now, however, Harnack writes, after investigating the manuscripts and the testimony of the Church Fathers : " All our witnesses for Matthew and for Luke have it. The most obvious, because the simplest, supposition, therefore, is that Matthew brought it into his text."[1] Because, on the other hand, one single manuscript[2] of Luke has by chance omitted the words, " No one knows who the Son is," these words are said not to have been written by Luke at all; and for that reason they are said not to have been written really by Matthew also; indeed, the whole passage in which they are found is to be regarded as questionable and as furnishing no more proof in favour of the divinity of Jesus. The theologian Fritz Barth, of Bern, thus disposes of this unheard-of failure in Gospel criticism : " Harnack's reconstruction of the passage is as little convincing as his restoration of the original ' Our Father,' and the conclusions which Schmiedel draws from the reconstructed text completely transform the sense of the passage almost into the very opposite meaning."[3]

It would be incomprehensible how able critics like these could adopt such abnormal views, if Harnack had not, at the conclusion of his treatment of our Gospel text, made the confession that he rejects it, not so much because of any critical reasons connected with the text, as because the divinity of Jesus is expressed in it : " That is indeed sufficient to see clearly the historical value of the utterances reported by Matthew. . . . The canonical interpretation of the utterance is Johannine and [therefore !] untenable."[4] In precisely the same way David Friedrich Strauss also had previously declared : " This utterance, which in the first and third Gospels stands quite isolated, suggests to us a fundamental view

[1] Harnack, *id.,* 204. [2] *Cod. Vercell.*
[3] *Die Hauptprobleme des Lebens Jesu,* 264. Equally sharply is Harnack's attempt repudiated by E. Kühl, *Das Selbstbewusstsein Jesu,* 22 ff.
[4] Harnack, *op. cit.,* 210, 211, note 2.

similar to that of the fourth Gospel, and appears *therefore* as an addition—the idea of Jesus . . . to exalt himself above the human," and must on that account be rejected.[1]   Such is "unprejudiced" criticism!

4. *Progress of the Revelation of the Divine Sonship to the Disciples and People in Galilee.*

The revelation of the divine sonship of Jesus moves in ever widening circles.   Towards the end of his Galilean activity it already addresses itself to the great *masses of the Galilean people.*

It is true, Jesus may not yet lead them into those depths of the mystery of the divine sonship into which he, according to our text, allowed the seventy-two disciples to gaze.   The people possessed then about that degree of knowledge concerning Christ which the Pharisee Nicodemus had when he addressed himself to the Saviour.   They regarded the Saviour as a prophet.   Some saw in him more than an ordinary prophetic figure, and extolled in him a specially endowed ambassador of God who was to precede the real Messiah.   Sometimes the multitude let itself be so carried away by the miracles of Jesus—though for a time only—that it hailed him as the expected national Messiah.   This view of the people was most forcibly expressed after the miraculous increase of the loaves of bread at Bethsaida, when the multitude wanted to proclaim him as the Messiah-King with the cry : " This is of a truth the prophet that is to come into the world " (John vi, 14).

Upon this Jesus takes occasion to give to the people in a wonderful discourse precisely the same instruction which he had once imparted to Nicodemus, who was of their opinion : Jesus is the true Messiah sent by God; as such, he is not a mere man, but a truly supernatural being, who had existed previously in heaven, who by his own power saves mankind, and is himself in his own person the salvation and eternal life of men.   " This is the work of God, that you believe in him whom he hath sent. . . .   My Father giveth you the true bread from heaven.   For the bread of God is that which cometh down from heaven and giveth life to the world. . . .   I am the bread of life. . . .   This is the will of my Father that everyone who seeth the Son and believeth in him may have life everlasting, and I will raise him up in the last day. . . .   Not that any man hath seen the Father, but he [the Son] who is of God, he hath seen the Father.   Amen, amen, I say unto you, he that believeth in me hath everlasting life. I am the bread of life . . . the bread which cometh down from heaven. . . .   I am the living bread which came down from heaven " (John vi, 29-51).

[1] *Leben Jesu für das deutsche Volk,* 203 f., *cf.* 198 ff. (1864).

This eucharistic prophecy and superhuman instruction in regard to the Son of God were too lofty for the people and even for most of the disciples. They wanted to recognize in Jesus only a son of God who had developed upward from mere humanity, and who, in spite of his divine sonship, still remained a mere man (John vi, 42); in a word, the son of God and the sonship of God in the sense of our liberal critics. On this rock their faith was wrecked. " After this, many of his disciples went back and walked no more with him " (John vi, 67).

Only the Twelve remained and stood this test of their faith. To the question of Jesus, " Will you also go away?" Simon Peter answers : " Lord, to whom shall we go? Thou hast the words of eternal life, and we have believed and have known that thou art the Christ, the Son[1] of God " (John vi, 68-70). To the renewed inquiry of the Lord, " Whom do you say that I am?" Peter answers with the equally definite acknowledgement : " Thou art Christ, the son of the living God "[2] (Matt. xvi, 16). And Jesus makes this testimony of Peter his own by praising it and pronouncing Peter blessed on account of it (Matt. xvi, 17-19).

What is, however, the import of this? In any case, it is certain that first of all and principally the *Messiahship* of Jesus is thereby pronounced. Not only does Peter's acknowledgement in regard to the Messiah stand in all four Gospels in the foreground, but Mark and Luke relate absolutely nothing but this acknowledgement. " Thou art the Christ " is the simple declaration in Mark's Gospel (viii, 29); while in Luke the statement is substantially the same, " Thou art the Christ [Anointed] of God " (Luke ix, 20). In John, the title " Son of God " is not positively certain, from the critical standpoint, but, on the other hand, the title " Messiah " is certain. And even Matthew, who gives the definite addition " Son of the living God," nevertheless finally lays again chief emphasis on the Messiahship. For, at the conclusion of his report, he informs us that the Saviour forbade the Twelve to speak publicly of what had happened, yet formulates this prohibition in such a way that it refers to the Messiahship only : " Then he commanded his disciples that they should tell no one that he was Jesus the Christ " (Matt. xvi, 20). *Peter's acknowledgement at Cesarea Philippi is, therefore, undoubtedly to be regarded primarily as an acknowledgement of Jesus as the Messiah.*

What, however, does the future prince of the Apostles think of the Messianic person and nature of Jesus? Is the

---

[1] According to one reading, " The Messiah, the holy one of God."
[2] The scene described by John vi, 27-70, and the synoptical description in Matt. xvi, 16, etc., Mark viii, 29 and Luke ix, 20, stand not only in close connection, but might be actually parallel passages. See proof of this in Seitz, *Das Evangelium vom Gottessohn,* 282.

Saviour for him a mere man, who conceives of the Messianic
vocation according to the rabbinical-Jewish or modern liberal
view, or is a heavenly, metaphysical nature united with the
man Jesus in one person, as the Christian faith supposes?
The answer really cannot be doubted. For fully two years
Peter had been a witness of the struggle of Jesus with that
humanized idea of the Messiah. In his parables, in the
demands which he makes on his hearers and in his whole
activity Jesus had more and more emphasized his supermundane and absolutely divine origin and nature. And now
he has just concluded the mighty discourse in which he
designates himself in direct terms, and also in the metaphor
of the bread from heaven, as the Messiah who, in accordance
with his origin and nature, emanates from heaven, who came
to earth only for the purpose of leading men to heaven, and
who is himself the eternal life of men. The Jews, who, a
moment before, had still given enthusiastic testimony to his
Messiahship (John vi, 14), turn away from him indignantly
because he requires them to believe in the superhuman,
metaphysical origin and nature of the Messiah Jesus. Yes,
even the disciples become disloyal to him at such a demand.
Only the Twelve stand firm. In contrast to Jewish unbelief,
which saw in the Saviour only an extraordinary prophet (Matt.
xvi, 14 and parallels), or was willing, at most for a moment,
to recognize him as a human Messiah (John vi, 14 and 65-67),
Peter from the midst of the Apostles raises his voice in the
decisive confession : " Thou art Christ; thou art the Messiah,
the anointed of God !" In such circumstances is it sup-
posable that he should have acknowledged the Master as the
Messiah merely in the Jewish-messianic sense of the term?

It is impossible, and Jesus himself assures us of the contrary. He had already on many occasions heard himself
hailed as the Messiah by the disciples, by those possessed by
devils, by those whom he had healed and by the astonished
multitudes, without ever showing any special joy on that
account. He was then hailed only as the supposed human
Messiah. Now, however, he congratulates Peter on his
confession of the Messiah, and derives this from a purely
supernatural revelation, in contrast to the Jewish, human
conception. He declares, therefore, unequivocally, *that Peter
believes in the superhuman, metaphysical personality of the
Messiah*—in the Messiah who has come from heaven, such as
Jesus had long and with ever increasing clearness in word,
work and life proclaimed himself to be. It is true, to conclude from Peter's subsequent conduct, he was still unable
to grasp the idea of the *full divinity of the Messiah—Jesus;*
but, even if he merely surmised it, it is, nevertheless, contained in his confession which comprised the entire divine
Messianic announcement of Jesus.

Therewith he throws also a clear light upon his additional designation of Jesus as the " Son of the living God." It is of little importance whether we have to do here merely with an added remark, which is equivalent to the Messianic indication, or whether " Son of God" stands as an independent title beside that of the Messiah. According to what has been said, the expression " Son of the living God" cannot be apprehended, in the sense of liberalism, as an ethical or theocratic son of God—that is, as a mere man who, in consequence of his better knowledge and the love of God, assumes the task of establishing the " kingdom of God." If the Messiah in this passage is regarded as thoroughly superhuman and metaphysical, the same thing must be true of the " Son of the living God." The height of Peter's faith in the Messiah indicates the height and depth of his faith in the Son of God.

If, therefore, we fix our attention upon this alone, without the other, we come to the same result. The Son of God, as Peter acknowledges him, stands in complete contrast to the Son of Man, as the Jews conceive of him. " Whom do men say that the Son of Man is?" asks Jesus. The disciples answer : " Some John the Baptist, and other some Elias, and others Jeremias or one of the prophets" (Matt xvi, 14 and parallels). Jesus said to them : " But whom do you say that I am?" Then Simon Peter answered and said : " Thou art Christ, the Son of the living God." The antithesis is as perfect as it possibly could be—the Son of Man in the question of Jesus; the Son of God in the answer of Peter. The antithesis lets us " perceive clearly that he who calls himself only the Son of Man is, in reality, the opposite of that— namely, the Son of God."[1]

If we take the title " Son of Man," as Jesus applied it to himself, as an expression of his true humanity and at the same time of his supernatural origin and nature, then the Son of God, standing above the Son of Man, must evidently be the Son of God in the proper sense of the word. Should one, however, wish, with the liberal school, to understand by the term " Son of Man" merely the *man* Jesus, the contrast between Son of Man and Son of God would be not less marked, since the Gospel " assures us that the Son of Man is at the same time the Son of God, and that the real humanity of the Saviour harmonizes with his divine origin."[2]

Only by this supernatural conception of Peter's acknowledgement of the Son of God does it become comprehensible that Jesus attributes this to a supernatural, divine source : " Blessed art thou, Simon Bar-Jona, because flesh and blood

---

[1] Dalman, *Die Worte Jesu,* 208 (1898); H. J. Holtzmann says the same in *Lehrbuch der N. T. Theologie,* i, 257 f. (1897); and Loisy, *Les Evangiles synoptiques,* ii, 3 (1908).   [2] Loisy, *id.*

hath not revealed it to thee, but my Father who is in heaven."
If Peter can have his confession, not from men, but only from
God, it necessarily exceeds the earthly, carnal views of men,
who represented the Saviour as a mere man.   However in-
complete the conception may have been which Peter formed
of the Son of the living God, his Son of God certainly surpassed any merely human standard.   But if his Son of God is
to any extent more than a man, then the liberal critics also
must concede that it is " a metaphysical idea, a name for a
divine being, who is other than men in general, and by nature
has originated from God "[1]—*i.e., is the essential Son of God*.
    " Thou art Christ, the Son of the living God."   In contrast
to the great number of the sceptical and half-believing mass
of the Galilean admirers of Jesus, Peter means by these words,
" Thou art the true, actual Son of God, and therefore the
Redeemer of the world."   It is only a literal repetition, a substantial confirmation and a deeper, clearer and profoundly
spiritual conception of his confession at Cesarea Philippi,
when Peter subsequently asserts his own faith and that of
his fellow Christians in " *Jesus Christ, our God and Saviour* "
(2 Peter i, 1).
    In fact, in the camp of our opponents the voices are in-
creasing in number which confess that in Peter's confession
at Cesarea the Messiahship and divine sonship are unhesitatingly expressed in the sense of Christian faith.   Among
others, Van Manen,[2] H. J. Holtzmann,[3] G. Dalman[4] and
very recently even Alfred Loisy[5] speak to the same effect.   So
soon, however, as sceptical science deigns to make the confession that faith and the Gospel harmonize in this point, at
once the usual assertion is made, that the Gospel comes here
into conflict with actual history, and that the Evangelists, in
particular Matthew, have let themselves be prejudiced in this
account by the christology of the oldest Church.
    This accusation is justified only by the fact that the tran-
scendental confession of Peter concerning the Messiah and
the Son of God, and respectively that of Jesus himself, who
approves of it, stands in contradiction to new rationalistic
theology about Jesus.   Formerly Loisy asserted that this
passage in the Gospels contains nothing more than the idea
of the theocratical human Messiah, on which account its
genuineness and credibility were not to be doubted.[6]   But
now Loisy is compelled to concede that this Gospel passage
teaches clearly the metaphysical divine sonship of Jesus, and
hence it is to be rejected as unhistorical and unworthy of

[1] P. W. Schmiedel, *Prot. Monatshefte*, 296 (1898).
[2] *Theol. Tijdschrift*, 184 (1894).
[3] *Lehrbuch der N. T. Theol.*, i, 257 (1897).
[4] *id.*, 208.
[5] *Les Evangiles synoptiques*, ii, 3.
[6] *L'Evangile et l'Eglise*, 42, 57.

belief.[1] Konrad Furrer, in an equally arbitrary manner, allows the words of Jesus to Peter to stand or fall according as they appear to testify for or against his own doctrinal opinion.[2] Against such a " critical " windmill it would be merely labour lost to tilt.

The liberal investigator, J. Weiss, who is certainly above suspicion, rightly characterizes it as " arbitrary radicalism " to try to invalidate the historical accuracy of Peter's testimony,[3] and Oskar Holtzmann says of the answer of Jesus to this confession : " What he [Jesus] replied to the confession is given us only by Matthew (xvi, 7-19) ; but the import of the words guarantees their genuineness."[4]

5. Intensification of the Revelation of the Son of God to the People and Disciples in Judea and Jerusalem.

The testimony to Jesus as the Son of God had caused much disturbance in Galilee. The mass of the people, and even most of the disciples, abandoned the Saviour ; but the Twelve came out of the crisis, on the contrary, strengthened in faith. Jesus now turned with them to the country of *Judea,* in order there, and, above all, in *Jerusalem* and in the *temple* itself, to proclaim before the people, priests and scribes his divine mission and divine sonship. He did this preferably at the great religious national festivals, to which the Jews from all parts of the country came in crowds. Already during the Galilean period of his activity he had once gone to the Holy City for a high festival, and on this occasion had begun his divine revelation. The time had not then come, however, to announce his divine sonship in metaphysical terms. He seized first upon the practical, palpable and therefore more comprehensible side of the subject; he testifies and proves by miracles that he does the *works* of his Father, is equal to his Father in heaven in respect to *power* and *efficiency,* and therefore is the divine Son of the divine Father. "Amen, amen, I say unto you . . . what things soever the Father doth, these the Son also doth in like manner. For the Father loveth the Son, and showeth him all things which himself doth. . . . For as the Father raiseth up the dead and giveth life, so the Son also giveth life to whom he will. . . . Amen, amen, I say unto you that the hour cometh, and now is, when the dead shall hear the voice of the Son of God, and they that hear shall live. For as the Father hath life in himself, so he

---

[1] *Les Evangiles synoptiques,* ii, 3.

[2] *Das Leben Jesu Christi,* 178, 2nd ed. (1905); similarly, Wilhelm Hess, *Jesus von Nazareth,* 60 f. (1906).

[3] *Das älteste Evangelium,* 50 (1903).

[4] *Leben Jesu,* 253 (Tübingen, 1901); also, W. Bousset, *Jesus,* p. 78, 3rd ed., says : " We have the right to regard this report as historically credible."

hath given to the Son also to have life in himself " (John v, 19-21, 25).

The Son does all that the Father does, even the Father's works of omnipotence. He does all this in accordance with his own will, like the Father, because he has seen it when with the Father, and he is able to do it all because he has in himself life, power and omnipotence like the Father. This announcement made by John, which Jesus subsequently repeats again and again in different forms, is only another variety of that revelation of his divinity to the seventy-two disciples, recorded in the synoptic Gospels : " All things are delivered unto me by my Father, and no one knoweth who the Son is, but the Father, and no one knoweth who the Father is, but the Son."

The same ability and power, proceeding from the same inward, divine source, which belongs to the Son as well as to the Father, prove *the divinity both of the Son and of the Father*. His Jewish hearers, in spite of their obstinacy, were well aware that Jesus declared himself to be in this sense the essential Son of God : " Hereupon therefore the Jews sought the more to kill him, because he did not only break the Sabbath, but also said that God was his Father, making himself equal to God " (John v, 18).

In reality, from this time on, the ferment which had begun among the people in Judea and the increasing hostility of their leaders press forwards ever more certainly to the catastrophe. Yet this was not to break out until Jesus had given a still more universal and incontrovertibly true proof of the divinity of his mission and of his nature. The Saviour makes use of the fact of his presence at the most brilliant annual festival at Jerusalem to take up again his teaching on this point.

In several violent discussions in the temple during the days of the Feast of Tabernacles, he gives further testimony in regard to his work and his person (John vii and viii). Amid continual confirmations of the more palpable proofs already given of his equality with God, he now at the same time promotes the *ideal, doctrinal knowledge of his metaphysical divine sonship*.

In the course of the dialogue the Pharisees put to him the question most plainly, " Who art thou?" Jesus gives the profound answer : " *The beginning,* who also speak unto you " (John viii, 25). Already just before he had given the unmistakable declaration : " You are from beneath, I am from above. You are of this world ; I am not of this world " (John viii, 23). He is supermundane and superhuman, not merely in his Messianic vocation, but also in respect to his origin and nature. Jesus answers the demand of the Pharisees to know something more precise regarding this nature and origin by characterizing himself as absolutely supernatural

and divine, as the principle of life and the first cause of all :
" I am, as I have always told you from the beginning, the
origin of all that exists." The Evangelist adds expressly
that *Jesus thereby spoke of his divinity,* but that he was not
understood by the Pharisees (John viii, 27).

As the origin of the universe, Jesus not only shared before
all time the glory of the Father before the world with all its
visible and invisible creatures existed (John xvii, 5), he had
shared it from all *eternity.* "Abraham, your father, rejoiced
that he might see my day," he said further to the Jews ; " he
saw it and was glad." Then they mocked him, saying :
" Thou art not yet fifty years old, and hast thou seen
Abraham?" Jesus said to them : " Amen, amen, I say to
you, before Abraham was made, *I am*" (John viii, 56-58).
Now, if he, who was not yet fifty years old, had already lived
before Abraham—that is, thousands of years previously—then
he must have had, besides and before his human mode of
existence, still another, older and supermundane existence and
nature. And if he says of this existence and nature, " I am,"
not " I was," or " I became," as Abraham, does not this
mean precisely that for him there is no time, that he is from
eternity? Does he not by this say of himself what God has
said of himself and alone can say of himself, " I am, that I
am "—the eternal being?

And thus also the Jews actually understood the Lord. They
were convinced that Jesus meant to make himself equal with
God. On that account they tried to inflict upon him the
punishment of stoning, assigned for the blasphemer (John
viii, 59). And Jesus does not retract his words. He therefore
confirms the fact that he really *professed to be God and, in so
far as that goes, was understood correctly by the people.*

In order to remove any doubt of the correctness of this
apprehension, he announces to the people that he is *the light
of the world.* " I am the light of the world. He that followeth
me walketh not in darkness, but shall have the light of life "
(John viii, 12). Thus speaks Jesus at the end of the Feast of
Tabernacles, which recalled the miraculous leading of Israel
through the desert and the revelation of God in the cloud of
light. For God is light. As the sun furnishes material light,
so God is the original abode and source of spiritual light—
truth. In many passages of the Old Testament, as well as of
the New, and in extraneous biblical literature, the being of
God is represented as light.[1]

Exactly so does Jesus conceive of his nature and his significance for the world. He is the essential, living and life-
giving saving truth, from which all salvation comes and in
which all salvation exists. Again and again he impresses

---

[1] Julius Grill, *Untersuchungen über die Entstehung des vierten Evangeliums,* i, 259-271, 308-312 (Tübingen, 1902).

this lesson on the Jews, and represents it readily by communicating, in close connection, to the man who was born blind, bodily light, as a symbol of the light that is spiritual and divine (John ix). Nor does he conclude the announcement of his person and his nature without again issuing to the blind masses of the people and their blind leaders the solemn warning : " Believe in the light, that you may be the children of light. . . . He that believeth in me, doth not believe in me, but in him that sent me. And he that seeth me, seeth him that sent me. I am come a light into the world, that whosoever believeth in me may not remain in darkness " (John xii, 36, 44-46).

No man, no divinely sent prophet—therefore also no son of God in the sense of the modern rationalists—can justly characterize himself as the Light of the World, or assert that he dispenses light out of his own abundance. Whoever does that must feel himself to be God. *For that reason, therefore, Christ also, as the Son of God and Light of the World, identifies himself immediately with the Father—with God.* " Whosoever seeth me, seeth the Father."

Light is *life* and imparts life. Light appears in the biblical revelation and, above all, in the words of the Saviour, as the effect and the cause of life, as a force at once bestowing life and conferring vitality.

God is, therefore, called the highest and only possessor and giver of this force, and also simply " the Life," " the Living One." In contrast to the lifeless idols of the heathen, and to creatures who are in need of life, the true God is defined in all the Holy Scriptures of both the Old and New Testaments as the essential Life and the Maker of the living.[1] The term " Living God " was the most unequivocal and most popular expression for the monotheistic idea of God. Jesus also loves to call his Father " the living Father," who " hath life in himself " (John vi, 58; v, 26).

But he immediately adds that the Son also is " living," like God, and that he has, like the Father, life in himself : " As the Father hath life in himself, so he hath given to the Son also to have life in himself " (John v, 26). Henceforth this doctrine occurs again and again in the most varied expressions, and is illustrated by many metaphors and examples, until it is finally moulded in the significant christological form : " I am *the* way, *the* truth and *the life* " (John xiv, 6). Quite unmistakably the Lord thus applies to himself the most popular and also in itself the most convincing attribute of divinity—absolute Being and Life.

Moreover, he is an absolute *Dispenser* of life. As his Father is the all-powerful Lord of natural life, and the in-

---

[1] See the exhaustive treatment of this subject by Grill, *Untersuchungen über die Entstehung des vierten Evangeliums*, i, 225-259.

finitely good Author and Accomplisher of the supernatural life of salvation, so the Son also is the personal principle of life and salvation for mankind. He proclaims himself to be the fountain of "living water," which "springs up into life everlasting" (John iv, 10); the Vine, from which everlasting vitality goes into the branches—that is, into the believers who are united with him (John xv); the "Bread of life" (John vi, 35, 48), the bread which came down from heaven (John vi, 51, 59), and "gives life to the world" (John vi, 33, 54). In divine omnipotence he can affirm, "Amen, amen, I say to you, if any man keep my word, he shall not see death for ever" (John viii, 51). "I give them [my sheep] life everlasting, and they shall not perish for ever, and no man shall pluck them out of my hand" (John x, 28).

As a proof that he is the supernatural, absolute principle of the life of mankind, he awakens Lazarus from physical death, and, turning to Martha, expressly says : "I am the resurrection and the life ; he that believeth in me, although he be dead, shall live ; and everyone that liveth and believeth in me shall not die for ever. Believest thou this? She saith to him : Yea, Lord, I have believed that thou art Christ, the Son of the living God, who art come into this world" (John xi, 25 ff.).

In fact, this is the only possible answer to the Lord's question. Whoever of himself creates physical life, and from himself imparts eternal spiritual life, and within himself bears essential life, cannot be a created being. "The vivifying action of the power streaming forth from the Son is not explicable merely by an intermediary action of the Son, but by the absolute character of the foundation and fulness of his life, willed and ordained by the Father himself. Whoever, like Jesus, restores the dead to life, must essentially be creative, life-giving power."[1]

Eternal First Cause, Light and Life, like the Father—therefore *consubstantial* and *one in nature* with the Father. "I and the Father are one" (John x, 30). In this the christological preaching of Jesus to the people reaches its climax. These words are not to be understood merely as indicative of the moral unity between Father and Son, but of the consubstantiality of both. Father and Son are one in the essential principle, which lies similarly at the basis of the divine activity of the Father as well as of the Son. They are one in the full metaphysical sense, so that Jesus can assert : "The Father is in me and I am in the Father" (John x, 38). The consubstantiality and oneness are thus so clearly declared that the Jews, shocked by the expression, cried out : "We stone thee for blasphemy ; and because that thou, being a man, makest thyself God" (John x, 33). Accordingly, the common people

[1] Grill, *op. cit.*, p. 288.

also understood the Saviour to claim by nature to be God— God in the same sense as the Father in heaven is God, in contrast to every creature. And Jesus affirms that this is the sense of his words, and that the people have understood him entirely correctly (John x, 33-39).

Modern opponents of the divinity of Jesus also cannot resist the same impression. They have only one thing to reply to it : that this revelation of Jesus to the Jewish people is related only by John. But, quite apart from the fact that the distrust of John, as we have demonstrated already, is not justified, the portrait of the Saviour drawn by John agrees in all its principal features with that of the synoptists. Thus, in particular, John's account of the teaching of Jesus to the people in regard to the Son of God is traced upon a synoptical foundation. Professor Fritz Barth, of Bern, has to confess : " We have not the right to reject this contribution of John ; for, although the ideas in the fourth Gospel may be more firmly grounded and clearer, . . . his portrait of Christ is, nevertheless, essentially the same."[1] *Precisely for the last period of his life, in which Jesus, according to the fourth Gospel, made to the Jewish people the conclusive revelations of his divinity, the synoptists also have preserved the corresponding episodes, which reveal the same truth not less clearly and with still greater lucidity to the people.*

In view of his coming condemnation, Jesus, at the beginning of Passion Week, relates to the Jews the *parable of the vintners:* " There was a man, an householder, who planted a vineyard and made a hedge round about it, and dug in it a press, and built a tower, and let it out to husbandmen, and went into a strange country. And when the time of the fruits drew nigh, he sent his servants to the husbandmen, that they might receive the fruits thereof. And the husbandmen, laying hands on his servants, beat one, and killed another, and stoned another. Again he sent other servants, more than the former ; and they did to them in like manner. And last of all he sent to them his son, saying : They will reverence my son. But the husbandmen, seeing the son, said among themselves : This is the heir ; come, let us kill him, and we shall have his inheritance. And, taking him, they cast him forth out of the vineyard and killed him " (Matt. xxi, 33-39 ; Mark xii, 1-12 ; Luke xx, 9-19).

No one could fail to understand the meaning of this parable. The householder typifies God, the vineyard signifies Israel, the husbandmen are the Jewish people, the servants are the line of prophets, and by the " son," the " one son, most dear to him," is meant Jesus himself (Mark xii, 6). Jesus, therefore, in contrast to the prophets, is not a servant, but the Son of God, and, moreover, the only, dearly beloved Son. If he were

---

[1] *Die Hauptprobleme des Lebens Jesu,* 266, 3rd ed. (Gütersloh, 1907).

merely a human Messiah—that is, a son of God in the figurative sense—he would then be only the greatest and latest in the ascending series of prophets. The contrast drawn between the servants and the only, dearly loved Son would then be quite absurd.

The rights pertaining to the Son reveal this still more clearly. " The position of the Son is . . . considered as one of right, which lays claim to the whole family property. In the case of the Son of God this can be a matter only of world supremacy, and, indeed, such a one as no Jewish emperor could exercise, but as God exercises it.''[1] Men, even the most esteemed, and prophets, have only duties as servants, but no rights. The Son, however, by reason of his nature, his birth and origin, comes into the absolute, divine joint-possession and co-regency of the world. There is evidently here no question of a mere adoptive relation, but only of the Son of God, Jesus, in the full metaphysical sense of the word.

Our opponents are not able to withstand this impression. Some of them, therefore, try again to dispute the *genuineness of the parable* of the vintners. First Jülicher affirmed that this parable was a pure allegory; that Jesus, however, never made use of the allegorical, but only of the parabolic form of discourse, and therefore he cannot have uttered the parable of the vintners.[2] It is true, the untenableness of this theory of the Marburg scholar has been strikingly proved even by liberal critics;[3] but that in no way prevents Alfred Loisy from printing it anew,[4] and he asserts with the greatest confidence that the parable of the vintners "belongs, it is true, to an ancient tradition, which originated even before the final editing of our Gospels; yet it is not warranted to be an utterance of Christ. . . . In its traditional form the allegory of the vintners appears to be a fragment of Christian apologetics.''[5] Because the allegory of the criminal vintners sounds " Johannine ''—that is, clearly declares the divinity of Jesus—it cannot be an utterance of the Lord, although it is attributed to the Lord unanimously by all three synoptists, and is also considered even by non-catholic critics, almost without exception, as a genuine utterance of Jesus.[6]

The High Priests and Pharisees felt themselves so hard hit by this parable of the vintners that they resolved to put the

1 Dalman, *Die Worte Jesu,* i, 230 f.

2 Jülicher, *Die Gleichnisreden Jesu,* Introduction (Freiburg i. Br.), (1886).

3 Among others by Chr. A Bugge, *Die Hauptparabeln Jesu* (1903); P. Fiebig, *Altjüdische Gleichnisse und die Gleichnisse Jesu* (1904).

4 *Etudes evangéliques,* 57 (1902); *Les Evangiles synoptiques,* ii, 318 (1908).

5 Loisy, *Evangiles synoptiques, l.c.*

6 Especially by H. J. Holtzmann, *Lehrbuch der neutest. Theologie,* i, 266; G. Dalman, *Die Worte Jesu,* i, 230; Wendt, *Die Lehre Jesu,* 419 (1901); O. Holtzmann, *Das Leben Jesu,* 333-335 (1901); B. Weiss, *Das Leben Jesu,* ii, 423, 4th ed. (1902).

Saviour to death at once (Matt. xxi, 45 and parallels). Then Jesus came with fearless candour into their midst, and once more put to them the decisive question : " *What think you of Christ? Whose son is he?* They say to him, ' David's.' He saith to them, ' How then doth David in spirit call him Lord, saying, ' The Lord said to my Lord, Sit on my right hand, until I make thy enemies thy footstool?' [Ps. cix, 1]. If David then call him Lord, how is he his Son?" (Matt. xxii, 42-45 and parallels).

Protestant criticism has, for the most part, tried to interpret these words of the Saviour as if Jesus wished to deny that the Messiah was to descend from David, and that he himself was a descendant of David.[1] Nothing is, however, more unjustifiable than such a supposition. Even Albrecht Schweitzer remarks : " Far from repudiating in these words the descent from David, Jesus, on the contrary, presupposes it in his case."[2] The conviction that the Messiah is David's son was, in fact, the common ground from which Jesus, as well as the Jews, proceeded, in order to prolong the discussion concerning the Messiah and concerning Jesus as the Messiah. It had never occurred to a Jew to question the fact that the Messiah would be a descendant of David, for the descent from David had been predicted too often and too clearly in the sacred books as a characteristic of the Messiah.

If Jesus had wished to disturb that belief, he would at once have stood before the people as a false Messiah and a heretic. On the contrary, he allows himself to be greeted and honoured as the " son of David." It is true, this Messianic official title, " son of David," did not designate merely a descendant of David, but, above all, the Messiah himself. Yet, "as a matter of course, it was thereby presupposed that the Messiah actually was a descendant of David, and Jesus would have hardly assumed that precise title if he had not found in his physical descent from David, according to prophecy, the verification of the appellation."[3]

---

[1] Wilh. Baldensperger, *Das Selbstbewusstsein Jesu,* 130 f.; H. J. Holtzmann, *Lehrbuch der N. T. Theologie,* i, 244 ff. (1897); P. W. Schmidt, *Geschichte Jesu,* 116, 156 f. (1899); Johannes Weiss, *Die Predigt Jesu vom Reiche Gottes,* 160 (1900); O. Holtzmann, *Leben Jesu,* 64, 319, 353 f. (1901); O. Pfleiderer, *Urchristentum,* i, 633, 2nd ed. (1902); Stärk, *Prot. Monatshefte,* 308 (1902); E. Schürer, *Das messianische Selbstbewusstsein Jesu Christi,* 17 (1903); Weinel, *Jesu im 19 Jahrhundert,* 285 (1903); Ed. von Hartmann, *Das Christentum des N. T.,* 55-60 (1905); W. Hess, *Jesus von Nazareth,* 97 (1906).

[2] *Von Reimarus zu Wrede,* 392 (1906); similarly, G. Dalman, *Die Worte Jesu,* i, 234, 260 (1898); H. Zimmermann, *Der historische Wert der ältesten Ueberlieferung von der Geschichte Jesu im Markusevangelium,* 89 ff. (1905); Hans H. Wendt, *Die Lehre Jesu,* 425, 2nd ed. (1901).

[3] Wendt, *op. cit.,* pp. 424-426. The real descent of Jesus from the race of David is historically beyond all doubt. Dalman, *op. cit.,* 262-266, and especially Peter Vogt's exhaustive monograph, *Der Stammbaum Christi bei den heiligen Evangelisten Matthäus und Lukas* (Freiburg, 1907).

But, however firmly the Saviour held to his Davidic origin and Messianic dignity, just as emphatically did he teach a supernatural origin and a divine dignity as the Son of God, far exceeding the former. And, in fact, the latter is to be conceived of as a true, essentially divine sonship, just as the former is to be regarded as a true and essential Davidic sonship. This alone is the meaning of the disputation of Jesus with the Pharisees. As the Son of God, he is the " Lord " of David, his ancestor; as the Son of God, he sits at the right hand of Jehovah and rules in divine power and glory. And only in his quality as Son of God is he able to be the Messiah—David's son. " He finds in the fact that David himself speaks of the Messiah, not as his son but as his Lord, a proof of the fact that what constitutes in the Messiah the basis and essence of his Messianic significance is not his descent from David, but something else much higher. The meaning of Jesus is that this something higher can be only the relation which the Messiah has to God—his divine sonship."[1] " For one who reads the words of Jesus without any dogmatic prejudice, no other meaning can result than that the Messiah is in reality the Son of one higher than David—namely, God."[2]   Even Alfred Loisy interprets this passage in the Gospels thus : " Jesus is not only the son of David, but the Son of God, and this latter sonship outshines the former."[3] This is, however, sufficient for Loisy again to find fault[4] with the text of the Evangelist, which is, nevertheless, recognized by all critics as authentic.[5]

6. *Conclusion of the Revelation of the Divine Sonship to the Disciples and Judges in View of his Death.*

After Jesus had announced his divine sonship to the people and their leaders without any enduring success, he addressed himself, in the last hours before his death, exclusively to the narrower circle of his disciples.   Ever since the days of Cesarea Philippi, the latter believed in his supernatural origin, and apprehended more and more also the divinity of the Master.   Now they were already so far advanced that Jesus could not only impress upon them the fact of his divine nature, but could partially disclose to them also his divine spiritual relation to the Father.   For the occasion of the quiet, sacred ceremony of farewell, the Lord had intentionally, as he himself says (John xvi, 5), reserved the profoundest and

---

[1] Wendt, *op. cit.,* p. 424.   [2] Dalman, *Worte Jesu,* 234.
[3] *Les Evangiles synoptiques,* ii, 363; also *Le quatrième Evangile,* 628 (1903).   [4] *Les Evangiles synoptiques, l.c.*
[5] See, among others, H. J. Holtzmann, *Lehrbuch der N. T. Theol.,* i, 258; Dalman, *op. cit.,* 234; Ed. Stapfer, *La mort et la résurrection de Jésus-Christ,* 29 (1898); O. Holtzmann, *Das Leben Jesu,* 353 f. (1901); B. Weiss, *Leben Jesu,* ii, 384, 4th ed.

most important revelations for his disciples. " As one, when
parting for ever from the friend nearest and dearest to him,
is impelled to pour into that heart, with which he is so
intimate, all that perhaps has been concealed within the shrine
of secrecy, even from him till then, so in like manner does
the Lord, in this solemn hour of his final instructions, impart
with unreserved confidence to his disciples all that they were
able to receive into their minds, not yet exalted, and their
hearts not yet expanded, by the Holy Ghost."[1]

*The basic thought of the wonderful farewell discourse and
of the accompanying high-priestly prayer is again, however,
the further initiation of the disciples into the knowledge of his
divinity.* So greatly does he advance this knowledge in that
last solemn hour that he can establish a complete contrast
between the faith of the disciples previously and now : " If
you had known me, you would without doubt have known my
Father also; and *from henceforth* you shall know him, and
you have seen him " (John xiv, 7). Scales fall, as it were,
from the eyes of the disciples. Working their way out of
the hybrid light of half-belief into the dazzling sunlight of
faith, they perceive that they know and behold the Father
himself in the Son, and the divinity of the Father in the
divinity of the Son. With ray on ray and flash on flash does
Jesus light up for them this truth. " He that seeth me, seeth
the Father also " (John xiv, 9)—that is, consubstantiality and
unity of Father and Son. " I am in the Father and the
Father in me " (John xiv, 11)—essential connection and
essential permeation. " All things whatsoever the Father hath
are mine . . . Father, all my things are thine and thine
are mine " (John xvi, 15 ; xvii, 10)—essential community and
essential reciprocity. The Son does the works of the Father,
who abideth in him. Whoever does not recognize and behold
the Son from and in his works, hateth both the Father and
the Son (John xiv, 10; xv, 24)—co-operation and reciprocity
in work. He that hateth the Father, hateth also the Son
(John xv, 23); and he that loveth the Father loveth the Son
also (John xvi, 27)—complete merging of the interests of the
Son in the interests of the Father, and *vice versa.* Jesus could
hardly have illustrated his divinity more clearly and more
forcibly.

And now, after he has opened his heart completely to his
disciples, and awakened in them the full consciousness of his
inward, divine life with the Father and in the Father, an
infinite longing fills him for a return to the glory of the
Father : " And now glorify thou me, O Father, with thyself,
with the glory which I had, before the world was, with
thee " (John xvii, 5). Only through voluntary humiliation

---

[1] Paul Keppler, *Unseres Herrn Trost. Erklärung der Abschiedsreden
und des hohepriesterlichen Gebetes Jesu,* 3 (Freiburg, 1887).

has the Son come forth from his majesty in the Incarnation (Phil. ii, 6 ff). His earthly life and suffering have merely cast a veil over his divine glory. This is by nature the inherent right and property of the Son from eternity, and will henceforth remain also for eternity. " When Jesus prays, ' Glorify thou me, O Father, with thyself, with the glory which I had before the world was, with thee,' δοξα (glory) indicates here the splendour of a divinely perfect, vital energy in conformity with absoluteness of being (John v, 26)—a splendour in which Jesus represented himself in his ante-mundane pre-existence as ' God in God,' and which is to come to him again after the transition from the physical to the purely spiritual and merely divine mode of existence. It is not a matter of the physical idea of the splendour of a transcendental substance of light, even if this also may have a share in it, but of the all-embracing (metaphysical and ethical) idea of the glory of an absolute personal life."[1]

Thus does Jesus utter, on the eve of his passion, in that intimate, family circle, *the last words concerning the mystery of his divinity;* although from all eternity the Son of God in the metaphysical sense and the possessor of the divine glory of the Father, he laid in the hands of his Father his glorious vesture, in order to complete his work on earth in a humble human form. Now he returns to the Father from his earthly pilgrimage in order, as God and Man, to enter again into the possession of divine glory, and through it to render his faithful disciples also blessed : " That they all may be one, as thou, Father, in me and I in thee ; that they also may be one in us. . . . The glory which thou hast given me, I have given to them, that they may be one, as we also are one. . . . Father, I will that where I am, they also whom thou hast given me may be with me ; that they may see my glory, which thou hast given me, because thou hast loved me before the creation of the world " (John xvii, 21-24).

An attempt has been made to diminish the force of the revelation of divinity contained in the farewell discourse of Jesus, by attributing this discourse to the Evangelist John. According to the theory of the liberal critics, John must have transformed the farewell thoughts of the Lord, in a free theological form, into the powerful address which we now possess. Such a subterfuge is, however, as unfounded as it is insufficient. Unfounded because, aside from all other reasons, the farewell discourse shows itself to be essentially an exact reproduction of the Lord's words.[2] Theodor Zahn writes significantly : " In reply to the charge that John some-

---

[1] Grill, *op. cit.,* p. 316.

[2] The passages quoted previously in regard to John's Gospel furnish proof of this. See also a short but very good exposition in Reppler's *Unseres Herrn Trost,* 6-14.

times lets the discourses of Jesus pass over a vanishing border-line into his own theological style of utterance, it is to be remarked that the very contrary can be proved."[1] But even if that charge were verified, it would still be insufficient to explain away from the farewell discourse the proof for the divinity of Jesus. Not only in its "Johannine" form which we possess, but in its wonderfully profound contents, even to its innermost core, this discourse is Jesus's own revelation of his divinity, and it is absolutely permeated and interwoven with it. It remains, therefore, the highest witness to the divine consciousness of Jesus, even if it be supposed that it has been freely remodelled by John. Only one who simply eradicates to the last letter the farewell discourse and the high-priestly prayer despotically from the Gospel can escape the impression of its complete christological and redemptive revelation.

The disciples were still under the impression of this full revelation when the Saviour came before the *judges of the Sanhedrim* for his last testimony to his divinity. Not as if he could have let those judges and the surrounding crowd of onlookers and agitators see into the depths of his divine nature and life which had just been beheld. No; he was obliged to begin again, where the incredulity of the Jews had remained. *He could let fall upon them merely the shadow of his divinely human personality.* And yet sufficient light lay in his shadow to let the judges perceive that *he claimed to be the true Messiah of the world and the true, supernatural Son of God.*

He testifies to this in the most public way and before the highest tribunal of the Jewish nation, the competence of which Jesus also had recognized (Matt. xxiii, 2). The members of the Sanhedrim had already been trying for a long time to destroy the obnoxious man from Nazareth (John vii, 44; viii, 59; x, 31, 39). Their plans, however, were without result, because the hour of Jesus had not yet come (John vii, 6). After the raising of Lazarus, their excitement rose to such a pitch that the assembled High Council passed a formal resolution in regard to the execution of Jesus (John xi, 45-57); and it was not to be long before they succeeded in getting him into their hands. Jesus was with all speed brought before the High Priest and the assembled Council, and the legal procedure against him was begun.

In the first place, however, it was not the duty of the Saviour to make a confession concerning himself, or even to let himself be interrogated. Jewish criminal proceedings did not aim at obtaining confessions from the accused.[2] The

---

[1] *Einleitung in das N. T.*, ii, 564 (Leipzig, 1899).
[2] The Mishna treatise on the Sanhedrim gives information concerning the legal proceedings of that body. This treatise was written, it is true,

latter must, on the contrary, be convicted of guilt by means of witnesses. Only after at least two witnesses, who had been found to be truthful, agreed in regard to the accusation, could he be pronounced guilty. If such evidence from concurring witnesses was not at hand, there was, it is true, a second means. Jewish law recognized as such the adjuration of the accused, in order to wrest from him an avowal.

So, then, a number of witnesses, hired by the councillors, appeared against Jesus, and brought forward many accusations, by reason of which he was said to have forfeited his life. But their testimony proved to be partly false and partly contradictory. A concurring testimony was not to be obtained (Matt. xxvi, 59-62; Mark xiv, 55-61). Consequently there remained only one other means of securing the condemnation of Jesus which had been determined on beforehand—the adjuration or confirmation by oath of the accused. Hence the High Priest rises from his seat, puts the Saviour on his oath, and addresses to him the greatest, most solemn and most decisive question which an earthly court of justice ever put, and by the affirmation of which Jesus would forfeit his life : " I adjure thee by the living God that thou tell us if thou be the Christ, the Son of God." Just as clear and definite as the question of the chief judge is the reply of Jesus : " Thou hast said it ; and[1] I say to you, hereafter you shall see the Son of Man sitting on the right hand of the power of God and coming in the clouds of heaven."[2] Then the High Priest rent his clothes, saying : " He hath blasphemed. What further need have we of witnesses? Behold, now you have heard the blasphemy. What think you? But they answering, said, He is guilty of death."[3]

---

only in the second century after Christ, yet its definitions were applied essentially already in the trial of Christ, as customary in lawsuits. See the admirable and illuminating monograph by A. Taylor Innes, *The Trial of Jesus Christ* (1899); and Stapfer, *Le Sanhédrin de Jérusalem au 1er siècle, Revue de Theologie,* Lausanne, 105-119 (1884); Jelski, *Die innere Einrichtung des grossen Synedrions zu Jerusalem* (1894); Schürer, *Geschichte des jüdischen Volkes,* ii, 188-214, 3rd ed. (1898); K. Kastner, *Jesus vor Pilatus* (Münster i. W., 1912).

[1] The Aramaic scholar, Dalman, in *Die Worte Jesu,* i, 255, thinks that merely the word " and " in the mouth of Jesus is due to the Greek πλην in Matthew and δέ in Luke, instead of the usual translation " yet," " however." In any case, the meaning of the passage remains the same.

[2] Matt. xxvi, 62-64; Mark xiv, 61 agrees with Matthew in his account with but one slight variation : " Art thou the Christ, the Son of the blessed God?" and Jesus said to him : " I am; and you shall see the Son of Man sitting on the right hand of the power of God and coming with the clouds of heaven."

[3] Matt. xxvi, 65 ff.; Mark xiv, 63 f. agrees : " Then the High Priest, rending his garments, saith, ' What need we any further witnesses? You have heard the blasphemy. What think you? Who all condemned him to be guilty of death.' "

This took place in an extraordinary night session of the Sanhedrim. Since, however, in criminal cases a death sentence could be pronounced only on the day on which the trial was begun,[1] a second session was appointed for the next day at daybreak (Matt. xxvii, 1; Mark xv, 1; Luke xxii, 66).[2] It is true, Jesus appeared there as a blasphemer, already condemned and therefore without legal rights.[3] Yet the Sanhedrists again repeated summarily the adjuration and interrogation, as well as the condemnation of the Saviour, in order to give to the trial a certain appearance of legality. They brought him before the Council, and said: "If thou be the Christ, tell us." And he saith to them: "If I shall tell you, you will not believe me. And if I shall also ask you [in order to lead you to a knowledge of the real facts], you will not answer me, nor let me go. But hereafter the Son of Man shall be sitting on the right hand of the power of God." Then said they all: "Art thou, then, the Son of God?" Who said: "You say that I am." And they said: "What need we any further testimony? For we ourselves have heard it from his own mouth" (Luke xxii, 66-71).

Then the whole Council rose, and they led him to Pilate (Luke xxiii, 1 and parallels), that the Roman procurator might confirm and carry out the sentence in the final tribunal.[4] It is true, the Jews endeavoured to bring up for his condemnation accusations of a political nature before the pagan Roman tribunal, which, for obvious reasons, did not care to bother itself about the alleged religious crime committed by the Nazarene (Matt. xxvii, 11 and parallels). But as these proved to be invalid, they demanded vociferously that Jesus should be put to death in consequence of the religious confession which he had just made, and on the ground of the Jewish religious law: "We have a law, and according to the law he ought to die, because he made himself the Son of God" (John xix, 7).

This inspection of the three stages of the trial of Jesus should be sufficient to give us the invincible conviction that

---

[1] Schürer, *op. cit.*, p. 211.

[2] Luke's account is only of this final session. See proof by Johannes Belser, *Die Geschichte des Leidens, der Auferstehung und Himmelfahrt des Herrn*, 282 f. (Freiburg, 1903). Moreover, in regard to form, both sessions were illegal: the first, because criminal trials, in which a death sentence was possible, could be appointed only in the daytime; the second, because the treatment of such cases was forbidden on the day preceding a Sabbath or a Feast Day (Sanhedrim iv, 1).

[3] In view of the ill-treatment which the members of the Sanhedrim and guards allowed to be committed against Jesus already before the session (Luke xxii, 63-65).

[4] Concerning the relation in regard to competence between the Jewish and Roman courts—that is, between the Sanhedrim at Jerusalem and the Roman governor—in the trial of Jesus, see Th. Mommsen, *Römische Geschichte* v, 512, 2nd ed.; *Röm. Strafrecht*, 240 note (1899); Innes, *l.c.*, 75 ff.

the Saviour confessed his true divinity before his judges.
Nevertheless, this is audaciously denied by the liberal school
of criticism.   The question of the High Priest, whether Jesus
is the Christ, the Son of God, must, it is said, be interpreted
from the usual Jewish point of view.   The Jews, and, above
all, the Sadducee, the High Priest Caiphas, had used the
words " Messiah " and " Son of God " as synonymous terms
for the same idea—namely, a Messianic king of the Jews, a
man especially beloved and favoured by God, who, precisely
because of this moral " divine sonship " is called to the
Messianic work, the re-establishment of the Davidical theocracy.   Accordingly, Jesus is said to have claimed to be such
a " Messiah " and " Son of God," and only such.[1]

Now, it is certainly to be conceded, and we have expressly
demonstrated it, that the Messianic idea of the Jewish contemporaries of Jesus did not for the most part exceed the
expectation of a political-theocratic king, and also that the
expression " Son of God " might mean only just this sort of a
Messiah-king.   Yet proof was also given at the same time
that the Saviour contended against that superficial and worldly
idea of the Messiah, held by the Jews, with the whole force of
his words and deeds ; that in accordance with his vocation, his
origin and his nature, he claimed to be the Messiah in the
supernatural sense of the word; yes, that the idea of the
Messiah, as personified in him, was precisely identical with
the divine Messiah.   Accordingly, he did not claim the title
" Son of God " after the standard of the ideas of the Messiah
common to the Jews at that time, but announced by ever
clearer and more definite revelations his supernatural divine
sonship.   A few days before, he had thereby brought the
masses of the people into a state of great excitement, and
the crisis which had now taken place was to be ascribed only
to his super-Jewish and supernatural revelation of the Messiah
and Son of God.   Should he now, all at once, descend from
the height of his confession hitherto made, and proclaim
himself as the Messiah of the world and son of God in
another less divine and indeed thoroughly human, worldly
and national sense?   Everyone can see that that is at once
unthinkable.

The confession of Jesus before the tribunal shows itself

[1] Thus argues not only the liberal-protestant school, but also Alfred
Loisy, *L'Evangile et l'Église,* 42, 57 ; B. Rose, *Etudes sur les Evangiles,* 105-197 (1902) ; Hermann Schell, *Apologie des Christentums* ii,
310-313, 2nd ed. (1908).   Rose and Schell concede, it is true, that only
the Sanhedrists have understood the answer of Jesus in the above sense,
while the consciousness of the divine sonship possessed by Jesus himself
referred to his essential divine sonship.   In contrast to his former
assertion, Loisy now acknowledges—*Les Évangiles synoptiques,* ii, p. 609
(1908)—that Jesus reveals at his trial a thoroughly divine consciousness,
on account of which the reports on the subject given in the Gospels are
not to be considered as historical.

rather to be a logical *revelation of his supernatural Messianic consciousness and of his metaphysical divine sonship.* Already at the first examination Caiphas puts the question : " Art thou the Christ, the Son of God, the Son of the Most Blessed?" Jesus does not content himself by answering the question in the affirmative. In order to exclude any possible misapprehension, he expressly declares in what sense he wishes to have both question and answer understood. " You shall see the Son of Man sitting on the right hand of the power of God, and coming in the clouds of heaven " (for the world-judgement). By these words Jesus unites his present confession directly with the one which he, shortly before, had made to his disciples and the Jews. He had, in connection with Psalm cix (Hebrew cx), and with Daniel vii, 13, declared that he was that Son of God, who, sitting at the right hand of Jehovah, takes part in the divine government of the world, and that Son of Man who will sometime come again to judge the world with divine power.[1] We have already seen that Jesus thereby really raises himself above the Jewish notion of the Messiah and son of God, and stamps himself as truly the divine Messiah and the essential Son of God. Now, under a sacred oath, he confirms this consciousness and profession of his personality.

Still more clearly is this the case in the second session of the tribunal, described by Luke. Here the Sanhedrim at first asks only about the Messiahship of Jesus. " If thou be the Christ, tell us." As Jesus confesses himself to be such, and adds that the Son of Man will sit on the right hand of the power of God, the judges understand at once that he thereby claims to be equal with God. For this reason they all immediately ask : " Art thou, then, the Son of God?" And upon the renewed answer in the affirmative they condemn the Saviour to death as a blasphemer. *The crescendo—Messiah, divine Son of Man and true Son of God is contained unmistakably in the words of Jesus.* This even very radical critics do not overlook.

According to Gustav Dalman,[2] " Jesus is in reality, according to his statement, precisely not the Son of ' Man,' but of ' God.' " Alfred Loisy[3] and N. Schmidt[4] similarly find that Jesus uttered, not only in Luke's Gospel but also in those of Matthew and Mark, his complete consciousness of divinity before the tribunal. If Loisy, Schmidt and other critics *on*

[1] That, together with Dan. vii, 13, the whole passage in Ps. cx is referred to by Jesus in his judicial confession, is explained also by Dalman, *Die Worte Jesu*, 254, and by O. Holtzmann, *Leben Jesu*, 374 (1901).

[2] *Die Worte Jesu*, 209.

[3] *Les Evangiles synoptiques*, ii, 609 f.

[4] Article *Son of God*, section 20, in Cheyne and Black, *Encyclopædia Biblica*, vol. IV, 4701 (London, 1903).

that account, and only on that account, doubt this report of
the Gospels, and assert that the synoptists, especially Luke,
have let themselves be influenced by the belief of their contemporaries in the divinity of Jesus, and have erroneously
represented the actual course of events at the trial, such an
" unprejudiced " criticism truly deserves not a word of refutation. Yet even Johannes Weiss[1] remarks : " One may think as
one will about the literary origin of the text of Luke [regard-
ing the judicial confession of Jesus], but one ought not to
reject with scorn the light which it gives." And W. Bousset
says : " The scene of the trial, in spite of all the objections
recently brought against it, is in its essence historical."[2]

It is, moreover, labour lost when the school of freethinkers
attempts to weaken the confession of the Saviour before the
tribunal, whether it be in reference to its historical credibility,
or to its dogmatic import. Even if that confession of Jesus
in regard to his divine sonship made in his own words did not
exist for us at all, the *members of the Sanhedrim themselves
and the populace, stirred up by them, give us clear information
concerning it.* They convince us, on the one hand, that they
wanted to extort from the accused Nazarene the confession
of his supernatural Messiahship and metaphysically divine
sonship, and, on the other hand, that they really succeeded
in obtaining this confession to the fullest extent.

If we wish to know what the views and intentions of the
Pharisees, Sadducees, priests and scribes were at the trial
of Jesus, we must consult again the Gospel and search for
the real cause of their hatred against the Nazarene. It lies,
as we again and again have had to prove, in the fact that
Jesus abruptly rejected the idea of a worldly and national
Messiah and Son of God, and offered to them in place of it
his thoroughly supermundane and divine consciousness. " He
was the Messiah (and Son of God), and claimed to be so,
but in a sense which seemed to the narrow horizon of contemporary Judaism as blasphemous."[3] Hence the movement
of hate against Jesus.

This movement degenerated into an attempt to murder
Jesus as often as he made the definite declaration that he was
the real, true Son of God. Ever since Jesus at the feast of
purification had distinctly uttered this consciousness of his
divine sonship (John v, 17) for the first time, " the Jews
sought the more to kill him, because he . . . said God was
his Father, making himself equal to God " (John v, 18).
Jesus' claim to divinity led at times, during the Feast of
Tabernacles and on the sabbatical Exhodion Feast, to renewed efforts to seize the hated Galilean and to stone him
(John vii, 44 ; viii, 59). And again, shortly before his trial,

---

[1] *Die Predigt Jesu vom Reiche Gottes,* 170 (1900).
[2] *Jesus,* 8, 3rd ed.   [3] Dalman, *op. cit.,* 259.

at the Feast of the Dedication of the Temple, an attempt was made to murder him, justified by the same testimony that he was the real, supernatural Son of God. "We stone thee, because that thou, being a man, makest thyself God" (John x, 33); thus spoke the same agitators who soon after were to sit in judgement upon Jesus.

If now, at the tribunal and for the purpose of obtaining a sentence of death against him, they despair of every other ground of accusation, and if they adjure the Saviour to tell them whether he is " the Christ, the Son of God " and the " Son of the Most Blessed," the meaning of their question is plainly furnished. They certainly aim at tempting him to make the same confession of his divine Messiahship and supernatural divine sonship, and not merely to the consciousness of being a national Messiah and a purely human son of God, which would have been useless in securing his condemnation and which had been repudiated by Jesus.

The Sanhedrists show, then, also by their sentence of condemnation that Jesus had actually made that confession. They find in the declaration of Jesus *blasphemy,* and condemn him to death for this reason and no other. In theatrical indignation " the High Priest rends his clothes and says : ' You have heard the blasphemy. What think you?' Who all condemned him to be guilty of death " (Mark xiv, 63 and parallels). In a moment the whole excited populace take up the cry, so that it echoes through the city, and rings in the ears of the Roman procurator : " We have a law ; and according to our law he ought to die, because he made himself the Son of God " (John xix, 7).

It is true, the Sanhedrists endeavour not to present to the pagan governor blasphemy alone as a reason for condemnation. They knew only too well that Pilate would neither mix up in their religious actions, nor pay any attention to the theocratical law of the Jews, which decrees the penalty of death for blasphemy.[1] Therefore they appeal, not only to the *crimen læsæ majestatis divinæ* (blasphemy), but to the *crimen læsæ majestatis humanæ,* alleged to have been committed by Jesus—an insult and an act of *lèse-majesté* against the Emperor. They say : "We have found this man perverting our nation, and forbidding to give tribute to Cæsar, saying that he is Christ the king " (Luke xxiii, 2). As, however, the latter accusation proves to be absolutely without foundation and false (Luke xxiii, 3 and parallels), the Jews in desperation go back to the real reason—blasphemy, on account of which they

[1] That Pilate will not meddle with the application of the religious, Mosaic, penal law, but lets merely the Roman State law constitute the rule of his court proceedings is perfectly clear, and is proved from the demand of the Procurator in John xviii, 31. When the Jews insist upon the death of Jesus by appealing to their law, Pilate answers ironically : " Take him you, and judge him according to your law."

have condemned the Saviour, and through the force of this they wish to obtain from Pilate the execution of the death sentence. "We have our law, and according to our law he ought to die, because he made himself the Son of God." *Blasphemy, and blasphemy alone, is, therefore, the only legal reason which the Jews finally and seriously invoke for their death sentence on Jesus.*[1]

Now, this confession of Jesus in the tribunal, before the Sanhedrists and the unbelieving Jews, could, in any case, *appear as blasphemy only if Jesus attributed to himself divine qualities, a divine nature and a metaphysical divine sonship.* The Mosaic Law orders in the case of a blasphemer : " The man that curseth his God shall bear his sin. And he that blasphemeth the name of the Lord, dying let him die. All the multitude shall stone him " (Lev. xxiv, 15, 16). However this law might or may be interpreted, it is clear, in any case, that it was not applicable to Jesus if he proclaimed himself merely as the Messiah in the sense of the popular Jewish expectation—namely, as a theocratical king and a son by the grace of God.

Such a Messiah and such a claim to divine sonship did not blaspheme or dishonour the name of Jehovah in any way. Otherwise the Messianic faith of the Jewish people and the Sanhedrists themselves would be liable to a charge of blasphemy. Of this our opponents are as firmly convinced as we. " A claim to be the Messiah is in itself, especially in respect to Jewish justice, no crime."[2] " The belief of Jesus that he was the Messiah might pass for madness or foolish conceit, but not for blasphemy, so long, at all events, as the opinion existed that a man of human origin would sometime appear as the Messiah."[3] " The mere affirmation of Messiahship could not certainly have led at once to a death sentence on

---

[1] Hermann Schell, *Apologie des Christentums,* ii, 311, 2nd ed. (Paderhorn, 1908), very naïvely asserts : " In what sense the High Priest and the Sanhedrim understood the divine sonship is proved by the effect of their accusation on Pilate and on his wording of the sentence. It was a question in the accusation of his claim to be ' King of the Jews,' not of his claim to a divine nature." Does not Schell really see, then, that the High Priests and the Sanhedrim accuse Jesus as King of the Jews only from a hypocritical motive, although the Saviour himself rejects this accusation so emphatically? And did not " the effect of their accusation on Pilate " consist in the fact that the Roman considered the attempt to blacken Jesus with the assertion that he was King of the Jews to be a thoroughly defamatory and inaccurate denunciation (Luke xxiii, 3 and following)? Finally, also the " wording of the sentence " does not prove that the Sanhedrists had the impression that Jesus claimed to be King of the Jews. Only with biting irony at the expense of the Sanhedrists (John xix, 20-22), who had charged the Nazarene falsely with this political *lèse-majesté,* did Pilate write above the Cross : " Jesus of Nazareth, the King of the Jews."

[2] P. W. Schmidt, *Die Geschichte Jesu,* 169 (Freiburg, 1899).

[3] Oskar Holtzmann, *Leben Jesu,* 375 (Tübingen, 1901).

Jesus. . . . No one would ever have made a crime of blasphemy out of a simple assumption of the title of Messiah."[1] "The law had no prohibition and no rule in the case of anyone declaring himself the Messiah; it was not forbidden."[2] "According to Jewish law, the fact of perjury or blasphemy, which is to be punished by stoning, and in presence of which the judges rend their garments, can only be conceded if an imprecation or abuse of the name of God is really uttered. Therefore, the mere assertion of Messiahship is, according to Jewish notions, not blasphemy at all."[3]

The assertion of Jesus that he was the Messiah and the Son of God, according to the Jewish, human conception, could at most have given occasion for an ecclesiastical trial, in which it would have had to be proved, on the ground of the acts of the Saviour, whether he was the true Messiah or a false one. Only the proof of his false Messiahship would have justified a condemnation.[4] But nothing at all in the trial of Jesus is said about anyone's having called for the signs of the Messiah and of having tested them in the case of the hated Nazarene. On the contrary, the Sanhedrists appealed, as a legal ground for condemnation, only to the confession of Jesus himself, that he was the Messiah and the Son of God, who would sit at the right hand of God and would come again sometime as Judge of the world. This testimony in regard to himself forces from them, without any further consideration, the cry of indignation : " He hath blasphemed. What further need have we of witnesses? Behold, now you have heard the blasphemy; he is guilty of death." The blasphemy worthy of death lay, therefore, according to the views of the stubborn Jews, in Jesus' confession that he was the Son of God, and in that only.

That presupposes, however, that Jesus, in his estimate of

---

[1] Dalman, *Die Worte Jesu*, 257.

[2] Adalbert Merx, *Die vier kanonischen Evangelien nach ihrem ältesten bekannten Texte. Übersetzung und Erläuterung der syrischen im Sinai Kloster gefundenen Palimpsesthandschrift*, II, i, 394 (Berlin, 1902).

[3] Wrede, *Das Messiasgeheimnis in den Evangelien*, 74 f. (Göttingen, 1901). Of the same opinion are Wilh. Brandt, *Die evangelische Geschichte und der Ursprung des Christentums*, 64 (1893); Alfred Loisy, *Les Evangiles synoptiques*, ii, 609 (1908); and all the prominent modern liberal critics. Only H. J. Holtzmann, *Lehrbuch der N. T. Theologie*, i, 265 f. (Leipzig, 1897), and *Das messianische Bewusstsein Jesu*, 31 ff (Tübingen, 1907), is of another opinion. " But he proves thereby only his own ignorance of the ideas of Jewish law," remarks Dalman pertinently.

[4] Perhaps by an appeal to Deut. xviii, 20-22, where the death penalty is prescribed for one who has been proved to be a false prophet. It is absolutely impossible that the Rabbis of the time of Jesus should have proposed anything lighter in regard to blasphemy and the death penalty. The later rabbinical law (Sanhedrim vii, 5) is, on the contrary, much more formal, so that finally a death sentence could be only seldom pronounced on a charge of blasphemy.

I.   20

himself, " ascribed to himself a grandeur which had never been attributed even to the Messiah "[1]—a grandeur which towered above every merely human conception of the Messianic nature, and apprehended the designation " Son of God " in a metaphysical sense. Only if he " meant that designation, Son of God, in a supernatural and metaphysical sense did there lie in the utterance of Jesus a detraction from the honour of God, and a blasphemous claim to equality with God."[2] " To say ' I am the Messiah ' was no blasphemy. To say ' I am the son of God ' did not mean to utter the name of God blasphemously. Only if he did not confine himself merely to the moral and religious idea of the sonship, but connected a metaphysical conception of it with the expression, Son of God . . . only then could the words of Jesus be considered as a blasphemy against God."[3] The Sanhedrists saw then in Jesus a false prophet, who blasphemed Jehovah, since he himself claimed divine rank, and enticed the people to follow a false God (Deut. xiii, 1-4). Such a false prophet should, according to the Law, be killed at once (Deut. xiii, 5, 10), " lest at any time the wrath of the Lord thy God be kindled against thee, and take thee [the people of Israel] away from the face of the earth (Deut. vi, 15). Hence, the counsel of the High Priest Caiphas : " It is expedient for you that one man should die for the people, and that the whole nation perish not " (John xi, 50). And on this account came the cry from the furious multitude : " Away with this man. Crucify him " (Luke xxiii, 18, 21). " We have a law, and according to this law he must die, because he made himself the Son of God."

But since they condemn the Saviour as a blasphemer by reason of his own confession, the judges prove officially and on oath that Jesus confessed not only that he was the theocratical Messiah-king and human son of God, but also that he was the divine Messiah and the essential Son of God, and that he on account of this confession was put to death.

1 Dalman, *op. cit.,* p. 257.
2 Wrede, *Das Messiasgeheimnis,* 75.
3 Loisy, *Les Evangiles synoptiques,* ii, 609. In order to escape the " historically impossible " conclusion (Wrede, 74), that Jesus understood the title " Son of God " dogmatically and metaphysically, Wrede and Loisy deny, at once and without any tenable reason, the credibility of these passages in the Gospels. The scene in question is said to have been invented by the Evangelist, or to have been retouched to harmonize with the faith.

CHAPTER II

THE DIVINITY OF CHRIST AFTER HIS DEATH

HITHERTO we have furnished proof that Jesus himself, during his mortal life, revealed himself as the true Son of God, as very God of very God. Not, indeed, in an immediate, lightning-like revelation, like a *Deus ex machinâ,* who springs down from heaven to earth. Rather does his revelation of himself stand in wonderfully wise harmony, on the one hand, with his *human-divine person,* in which he approached us, and, on the other hand, *with the human nature and limited mentality* of those to whom he announced his divinity.

Notwithstanding the fact that Jesus claimed to be God, he not only had to allow his real and entire humanity to develop, uncurtailed, but he was obliged to impose upon himself, in testifying to his own divinity, a certain modest and tender reticence. *In his human nature and through the medium of his human nature, he revealed himself as God.* Externally, however, in his whole appearance, he was only a man. Only his superhuman wisdom, perfection and omnipotence caused his divinity to shine through the human element in his person. Upon the human characteristics of Jesus the divine traits stamped themselves only in fine, transparent, spiritually transfigured lines of sublimity. Jesus could not, therefore, appear before mankind with the direct announcement : " I am indeed in my outward appearance a man, like all you men ; but in reality I am the eternal Son of God, begotten of the Father, the Creator and final aim of the universe, and I demand accordingly at once adoration and divine honour." Whoever thoroughly understands the situation in which Jesus, as man, found himself in relation to mankind will immediately feel that such language would have been unsuitable and not conformable to the eternal wisdom of God. Only as he actually did announce his divinity could he have done so—little by little, with an increasing unfolding of the truth, more practical than formal, rather through deeds than through words.

Still another equally important reason determined such a revelation of his divinity—*the spiritual disposition in which he found his Jewish contemporaries and, in particular, also his own disciples.* We have learned what this was sufficiently in connection with the Messianic problem. Apart from some elect souls, the people surrounding Jesus were so impervious to spiritual things, so full of earthly, sensuous, nationalistic, narrow-minded conceptions, that the Saviour could announce to them his Messiahship only little by little and in continual conflict with firmly rooted prejudices, and so indeed it was for the most part made known. What would have happened if it had been a question of the announcement of his equality with God and his own divinity? Then the difficulties to be overcome would have been twice as numerous before he could have reckoned on the slightest comprehension of it. It was necessary, first, to call the attention of his hearers slowly and gently to their prejudices, and to furnish them with proofs of his Messiahship through signs and wonders. At the same time, the Messianic notion of the disciples had to be reformed and brought up from the low level of nationalistic Jewish views. Together with this came the proof that the Messiah, precisely as the Messiah, must be God, and really a divine Messiah. And with this Messianic revelation of his divinity, Jesus then caused another to appear, according to which he proved himself to be the true Son of God in a metaphysical sense, independently of his Messianic vocation and destiny.

We have proved this testimony of Jesus to himself to be an historical fact, in spite of the modern criticism of Jesus, which audaciously asserts that the Saviour himself never and nowhere declared himself to be the true Son of God, and that only succeeding generations of his believing adorers had made him God. We were able to follow even the separate phases of the progressive revelation of the divine sonship of Jesus, beginning with his first appearance in the temple to his condemnation to death. Therewith our task is really accomplished. If, nevertheless, in what follows the line is still further advanced, and it is pointed out how the faith in the divinity of Jesus made its appearance in the early Church from the death of the Saviour to the end of the New Testament epoch, it is done in order to proceed to the very last positions of the enemy. He seeks precisely to assign the proofs of the divinity of Jesus in the earliest times to as late a date as possible, in order to draw thence the conclusion that the belief in the Son of God cannot belong to the treasure of revealed truth given by Jesus himself, but was a subsequent addition and an embellishment made by believers. In opposition to this it will be shown that this faith was at once the common property of the original Church, and therefore must be ascribed to the revelation made by Christ himself. *Faith in the divinity of Jesus, as it developed at once after the death of the Master, under their eyes and in consequence of the instructions of the risen Lord,* and as it immediately passed over to the first Christian generations as their most precious inheritance, *is only the reflection and echo of the divine self-consciousness which Jesus possessed during his earthly life.*

The faith of the earliest circle of disciples shows us, more clearly than anything else, what Christ thought on this point, and what he taught his disciples.

Fortunately the New Testament sources give sufficient, and in parts even abundant, information about the position taken in the first century towards the central truth of the Christian religion.   Of the forty days after the resurrection, during which Jesus appeared repeatedly to the disciples and associated with them, the last chapters of the Gospels provide us with information.   The Acts of the Apostles then tells us of the faith of the early Church in Christ, from Pentecost and the first instructions down into the fifties.   Meanwhile the great Epistles of Paul appear, which pourtray very fully the christology of the teacher of the Gentiles and of the Christian Church during the fifties and sixties.   Paul had not yet laid down his pen, when it was taken up by the synoptic Evangelists, who testify, as we have seen, just as clearly to their faith and that of their contemporaries, as they represent with historic fidelity Christ's own divine consciousness.   And soon after the synoptists, John appears upon the scene, and gives us, well on towards the end of the century, again as Apostle and Evangelist, an account of that "which was from the beginning and which he had seen with his own eyes of the Word of life," and what he and his brethren in the faith with heart and mouth confessed concerning the true Son of God, Jesus Christ.

I.—The Divinity of Christ after the Resurrection.

The impending death of the Master had been at all times the stumbling-block of the inner circle of his disciples.   Its occurrence depressed both the joy and the certainty of the faith of the Apostles.   With the resurrection, however, according to the representation of all the Gospels, their faith re-entered their hearts triumphantly and for ever.

One only hesitated—Thomas, the most incredulous and thoroughgoing critic of the Apostles.   He had not been present at the first appearance of Jesus after the resurrection, and to all the reports of his associates he remained sceptical. " Except I shall see in his hands the print of the nails, and put my finger into the place of the nails, and put my hand into his side, I will not believe " (John xx, 25).

Eight days after, the disciples were again assembled, and Thomas with them.   Then came Jesus, the doors being shut, stood in their midst and said, " Peace be to you."   Then said he to Thomas : " Put in thy finger hither and see my hands ; and bring hither thy hand and put it into my side.   And be not faithless, but believing."   Thomas answered and said to him : " *My Lord and my God.*"   Jesus said to him : " Because thou hast seen me, Thomas, thou hast believed ; blessed are they that have not seen and have believed" (John xx, 26-29).

Any doubt about the signification of this confession is impossible. For the first time in the Gospel Thomas gives to the Saviour the name "God" plainly; not merely "Son of God," but directly and emphatically "Lord and God." The appellation "Lord" which is added to the name of God is not at all accidental or of inferior value. We shall soon produce[1] from rich material the proof that the appellation "Lord" in the language of the disciples is identical with "Adonai-Jehovah," the proper name of God. *Both expressions together represent for the Israelite the full and complete name of God—"Lord God, Jehovah Elohim, Κύριος ὁ Θεός."* A more comprehensive and striking confession of the divinity of Jesus is not conceivable than this—"My Lord and my God." And Jesus makes this confession of Thomas his own, by expressly confirming it and by pronouncing those blessed who believe in his divinity without wishing to see with their eyes the evidence of what is believed.

However indubitable the meaning of Thomas's confession is, equally certain also is its *authenticity*. Apart from all other reasons, it finds its absolute confirmation in the Christian faith of the whole Christian community associated with the resurrection, of which we shall soon speak. On this account it is for the most part regarded as historical, even by those liberal investigators who are at variance with John's Gospel. Thus, for example, Johannes Weiss remarks : " The words of Thomas to the risen one in John xx, 28—' My Lord and my God '—are undoubtedly authentic."[2]

So much the more difficult, therefore, is it to observe in silence how these same liberal critics either pass lightly over the scene with Thomas, or, with a deep, sentimental groan, try to get around the essential point of the confession of the divinity therein contained. Thus, for example, Edmund Stapfer, the Dean of the Protestant faculty at Paris, makes, quite in the style of Renan, the following declaration : " In the presence of such a being, a being who has had such moral grandeur and such sympathy, who has possessed such absolute conviction, who has made such unheard-of demands, has shown such thorough devotion, and has enjoyed such a deep, intense and evidently certain life in and through God, the exclamation of Thomas is not too strong and escapes also from our hearts and lips. In the presence of Jesus we also break out into this cry of obedience and adoration, ' My Lord and my God !' "[3] Involuntarily one asks oneself how scholars

---

[1] In the chapters on " The Divinity of Christ in the Early Church " and " The Divinity of Christ and Paul."

[2] *Christus. Die Anfänge des Dogmas,* 29 (Tübingen, 1909).

[3] *Jésus-Christ pendant son ministère,* 351 (Paris, 1897).

with the reputation of Stapfer can seriously make acknow-
ledgements of this sort and yet, with apparently perfect sin-
cerity, deny the divinity of Jesus ! This riddle finds a solution
only in the words of Stapfer, in which he praises highly the
individualistic christology of modern liberal Protestantism,
and remarks : " In Protestantism every believer makes his
christology to suit himself, because every believer conceives
of the divinity of Jesus Christ in his own way, which is not the
way of his neighbour."[1]

*The Thomas episode mirrors instantaneously the faith of
the community of disciples from the morning of the resurrection to the day of the ascension,* on which Jesus departed from
this earth and returned to the Father. There is no doubt that
the faith of the disciples equalled that of Thomas. For we
cannot suppose that the " unbelieving " Apostle had more
faith than the disciples who believed. Moreover, and this is
the main thing, the disciples, as we shall soon see, already
after the day of Pentecost, appear with faith in Jesus as the
Messiah and " the Lord, Adonai, Jehovah," and exact the
same confession from all the new believers. They saw already,
in advance, therefore, in Jesus the Messiah and Lord, the
divine Messiah, and this faith must have developed powerfully
between Easter and Pentecost.

Whence came this change in the opinions of the disciples,
which up to that time had been partly unbelieving, partly
weak in faith ? Without doubt, the resurrection itself had
brought about this mighty strengthening of their faith. The
resurrection is always appealed to by the disciples as the
principal proof and justification of their faith in the Lord and
Messiah.[2] Jesus had, indeed, continually put forward his
resurrection as a guarantee for his personal revelation and his
claim to their faith. But even without this, the disciples
would never have been able to attain to the conviction that a
man who had remained dead in the grave was the Messiah
and Lord of the world. Therefore with the death of Jesus
every ground of support and every hope had vanished from the
disciples' hearts (Luke xxiv, 21), and only came back again
with the morning of the resurrection. He who claimed to be
Messiah and Lord must show in himself his power over death
and the world. The resurrection first became the sure pledge
that God's kingdom would triumph, and that the Lord would
bring the schemes of men to the fulfilment of his counsels
(Acts iv, 26). Proceeding from these considerations, the
disciples saw in the resurrection not merely a miracle, or even
the greatest of miracles, from which they concluded the truth

---

[1] *La mort et la résurrection de Jésus-Christ,* 340, 2nd. ed. (Paris,
1898).
[2] Acts ii, 24, 32 ; iii, 15 ; iv, 10 ; x, 40 ; xiii, 30 ; xvii, 31 ; 1 Cor. xv,
12 ; 1 Pet. i, 3, etc.

of Christ's Messianic and divine revelation of himself; they rather regarded the resurrection as his immediate installation into the position of the Messiah and Lord. They express this view even in the drastic words directed to the Jews—through the resurrection " God hath made both Lord and Christ this same Jesus, whom you have crucified " (Acts ii, 36). By this " it is not said that he during his earthly life had not yet been the Christ and Lord, but only that God had now raised him to a position and had glorified him in a living form in which he could prove to his Church that he is the Lord and Christ, which he had already been before."[1]

In this sense Harnack is right when he says : " Among the surest facts of history is this, that it was not the Apostle Paul who first brought into such prominence the importance of the death and resurrection of Christ, but that he, in making this recognition, stood in entire harmony with the early Church. . . . They were regarded already by the intimate circle of the disciples and by the original Church as fundamental. We can rightly affirm that the permanent recognition of Jesus Christ received its chief support here. On the ground of those two dogmas the whole system of christology has grown up."[2]

It is, however, incorrect to interpret this fact as if "the religion of Christ in the narrower sense " begins only with the resurrection and only in consequence of the belief in the resurrection.[3] It is not only the resurrection which first established the faith in Jesus as the Christ and Lord, but the resurrection in connection with the definite confession which Jesus made during his life—that he was the Christ and Lord. If Jesus had not given to the disciples this revelation before his death, and made upon them the impression that he was the Christ and Lord, even the resurrection could not possibly have brought that belief in his Messiahship and lordship into existence. That is so self-evident that even Johannes Weiss cannot but confess : " The appearances of the Lord, however important they may have been, would not *alone* have been sufficient to call forth a faith for which these men went to their death. . . . They must have been convinced that with their proclamation of this fact they were acting in harmony with Jesus. . . . The faith of the first disciples has its roots not only in their Easter experiences; it goes back behind Golgotha to the impression made by his personality. . . . The oldest faith in Christ extends back finally to the life of Jesus."[4]

Thus the faith in Christ and the christological confession

---

[1] Th. Zahn, *Skizzen aus dem Leben der alten Kirche,* 294 f., 3rd ed. (Leipzig, 1908).

[2] Harnack, *Wesen des Christentums,* 97.

[3] Thus Weinel in his *Paulus: Der Mensch und sein Werk,* 108 f. (Tübingen, 1904), and thus Harnack evidently wishes to be understood.

[4] Johannes Weiss, *Christus,* 10-12 (Tübingen, 1909) ; *Paulus und Jesus,* 9 (Berlin, 1909).

*of the Church of the resurrection are grounded in the life,
teachings and consciousness of Jesus himself.*   Not merely
the positive believers, to whom the resurrection was a fact,
but also "to crown all, even those who adopt the modern
view," and thereby deny the resurrection, must, as Johannes
Weiss acknowledges,[1] accept this explanation of the faith of
the disciples concerning Christ.   There is absolutely no other
explanation.   A consequence presupposes an antecedent.   The
faith of the Church after the resurrection points to a corresponding revelation of Jesus before his death.   Of so little use
is it for liberal criticism to strike out from the Gospel the
resurrection and the consciousness of Jesus that he was
Messiah and God.

With these words we have in substance pointed out and
explained the views concerning Christ, as they are found in
the Church of the disciples after the resurrection.   But reference must still be made in particular to the *form* in which,
then and subsequently, the faith in the divinity of Jesus was
for the most part expressed.   Thomas adored Jesus with the
words, "My Lord and my God," which was equivalent to
Lord God, *Jehovah Elohim*.   The other disciples also must
have often done so.   Most frequently, however, they use, as
appears from the closing chapters of the Gospels and the
opening chapters of the Acts of the Apostles, the address
and invocation, "Christ and Lord."   It has been said already,
and it will be thoroughly demonstrated in the next two
chapters, that both forms of confession mean the same thing
respectively, that the religious title "Lord," given to the
Saviour, signifies neither more nor less than Adonai-Jehovah
—the proper name of God.   This stands usually in the Old
Testament before the essential name of God (Lord God,
Jehovah Elohim),   but it indicated also, in itself alone, the
true and only Godhead with special reference to its divine
dominion, dignity and exaltation over the world.[2]

*Why did the disciples and the early Christians prefer this
expression for the divinity of Jesus, while they called the
Father simply God?*   The most obvious answer is to be sought
in the consciousness of the Apostles that this title best represents what is distinctive.   Since of the full double name of
God "Lord God" (Jehovah Elohim, Κύριος ὁ Θεός), the
first word is applied to the Son and the second to the Father,
the godhead is designated as the union of both, absolutely
and unequivocally, entirely in the sense of the monotheistic
formula of the Old Testament, "Hear, O Israel, the Lord our
God is one Lord."   But not only that.

In the name "Jehovah, Lord," the vocation and activity of

[1] *Paulus und Jesus,* 9.
[2] See subsequently in the chapter, "Divinity of Christ in the Early
Church."

Jesus, as the divine Messiah, found their most perfect expression. In accordance with our previous statements, we see that all the threads of the Messianic expectations in the Old Testament unite in the thought that the Messiah, as spiritual Founder and Prince of the kingdom of God, reigns over the whole world and is its Lord. Spiritual dominion over the world, divine power in the world, redemption of the world and judgement of the world—these are the great achievements and sovereign titles of the Messiah-King. That was already the infallible guarantee for the fact that the Messiah is identical with Jehovah, whose inalienable rights reached their culmination precisely in that absolute supremacy. Having attained that height, the Messianic prophecy then announces also: "The Lord Jehovah himself will come and save us" (Isa. xxxv, 4).

Now the disciples had certainly conceived this just as little as had the Jews contemporary with Jesus. It was almost impossible for their long secularized conception of the Messiah to rise to the Messianic ideal of the Old Testament. Even though they gave to the Master the name of Lord, they understood it, nevertheless, at first only as an expression of reverence and high regard, and as a substitute for the appellation "Master" (compare Matt. viii, 25 with Mark iv, 38; Matt. x, 24 and John xiii, 13 with Matt. ix, 11 and xvii, 23).

Jesus himself, however, taught them ever more plainly to call him Lord in an entirely different sense. He lets himself be addressed as "Lord, Lord," as Judge of the world (Matt. vii, 21; xxv, 37). And as there is only *one* Father, so he says that he also is the *one and only* Lord and Master (Matt. xxiii, 8). Then he performs, as an overwhelmingly convincing and withal a practical form of instruction, the masterful acts of God in a long and ever-increasing series—healing the sick, driving out devils, raising from the dead and forgiving sins. In close connection with this, he reveals in words his divine consciousness of being the Lord, which, immediately before his death, he clothes in the prophecy: "You shall see the Son of Man sitting on the right hand of the power of God and coming in the clouds of heaven . . . with great power and glory."

There can be no doubt that, with the wakening and growing faith of the disciples in the Messiahship of Jesus, their faith in his supremacy also awoke and grew. The resurrection gave to them palpable proof of the truth that Jesus was the "Christ and Lord." It was not they who had invented these sovereign titles and applied them to Jesus, but it was Jesus who had educated them to do so. Just as the faith of the Church of the resurrection in Jesus's essential divinity goes back to the impression of his personality and to his revelation before his death, so also this special form, in which the faith of the disciples makes its appearance, the faith in the Lord, goes back to the vitalizing instruction of the Saviour.

Also, after the resurrection, the christological teachings of Jesus are plainly designed to impress upon the disciples his essential divinity, and preferably in the form of his divine sovereignty.   The consciousness of being God and Lord pervades the message addressed to Mary Magdalen at the first appearance of Jesus after the resurrection : " I ascend to *my* Father and to your Father, to *my* God and to your God " (John xx, 17).   He who in a wholly personal way and in contrast to other men knows himself to be the Son of God, and is conscious that he can by his own power and in his own glory ascend to God the Father, must himself be God and Lord.

It is in a feeling of being God and Lord that he, on the day of the resurrection, shows to the two disciples on the way to Emmaus, step by step, how the whole announcement of the Old Testament concerning the divine Messiah refers to himself, and adds : " Ought not Christ to have suffered these things, and so to enter into his *glory?*" (Luke xxiv, 26).

His divinity and sovereignty also are revealed by him on Easter evening, when he ascribes to himself the unrestricted power to forgive sins—the highest divine and sovereign power —and transmits this, as a sovereign, to the Apostles with the words : " Receive ye the Holy Ghost.   Whose sins you shall forgive, they are forgiven them ; and whose sins you shall retain, they are retained " (John xx, 22, 23).

Eight days later he testifies that he has found among the eleven Apostles faith in his person as God and Lord, and he demands the same of the twelfth, Thomas : " Be not faithless, but believing. . . .   My Lord and my God. . . .   Because thou hast seen me, Thomas, thou hast believed ; blessed are they that have not seen and have believed " (John xx, 27-29).

Soon after, he elicits from Simon Peter by the Sea of Tiberias the acknowledgement of his divinity and sovereignty, and causes him to make good again his former threefold denial by a threefold confession of love for his Lord, and to crown this with the confession of the divine omniscience of Jesus : " Lord, thou knowest all things," even the hidden depths of my heart (John xxi, 15-17).

Jesus acts as Lord and God when he, by his own personal power, promises to send the Spirit of his Father : " I send the promise of my Father upon you " (Luke xxiv, 49) ; and he transmits to the disciples his own divine power of working miracles *in his name:* " In my name they shall cast out devils ; they shall speak with new tongues ; they shall take up serpents ; and if they shall drink any deadly thing, it shall not hurt them ; they shall lay their hands upon the sick, and they shall recover " (Mark xvi, 17, 18).

Finally, in the hour of his ascension there stream forth from his divine consciousness those sublime words : " All power is given to me in heaven and in earth. Going, therefore, teach ye all nations, baptizing them in the name of the Father, and of the Son and of the Holy Ghost. Teaching them to observe all things whatsoever I have commanded you. And behold, I am with you all days even to the consummation of the world " (Matt. xxviii, 18-20).

Jesus is the possessor and administrator of all power, supremacy and glory in heaven and on earth. That is, in fact, the most popular, and at the same time, scientifically, the most complete transcription of the idea of " Lord God," " Jehovah Elohim " ; the transcription that conveys the meaning which was familiar and perfectly comprehensible, especially to every Israelite, and to everyone acquainted with the Old Testament. Even Adolf Julicher remarks in regard to this : " When, in Matt. xxviii, 18, the risen Jesus takes leave of his disciples with the words, ' All power is given to me in heaven and in earth,' after he has already (Matt. iii, 17) been announced as God's well-beloved Son, and meanwhile, between his baptism and his last address to his disciples, has (Matt. xi, 27) imparted to them that his Father had given over everything to him—what else is that but the confession of Paul to the almighty Son of God?"[1]

And since Jesus closes his earthly existence and finishes his revelation " in the name of the Father and of the Son and of the Holy Ghost," he puts himself *on a level* with God the Father and the Holy Ghost. He unites himself with the Father and the Holy Ghost in the *one* mysterious Trinity, whose separate Persons possess the same divine sublimity, efficacy and nature, and for that very reason exist in the same divine unity : " *In the name* (not in *the names*) of the Father and of the Son and of the Holy Ghost." And if he, at the moment of his return to the Father and to the Holy Ghost, promises nevertheless to remain by and with his followers on this earth for ever, he proves thereby precisely that he is raised above time and space, eternal and omnipresent, and that he has, in his divinity, existed before all time in the bosom of the Holy Trinity, to which he now returns in his divinity and humanity.

Thus Jesus, as he takes leave of the world, and at the moment of his ascension and return to heaven, eliminates every merely human and creature-like conception of his person, his Messiahship, his sovereignty and his divine sonship.[2]

[1] Jülicher, *Paulus und Jesus*, 30.
[2] In regard to the genuineness of the trinitarian text, Matt. xxix, 19, *cf.* (apart from the " Introductions to the Gospel of Matthew ") Lepin, *Jésus, Messie et Fils de Dieu*, 334 ff. (Paris, 1906).

II.—THE DIVINITY OF CHRIST IN THE EARLY CHURCH.

1. *Its Representation in the Acts of the Apostles.*

Fortunately we know exactly how the original messengers of the Gospel executed their commission as teachers in regard to the person of Jesus, and how the early Church conceived its faith in Christ. The physician and Evangelist Luke relates it to us in his Acts of the Apostles. In that book the oldest historian of the young Church draws the portrait of Christ according to the discourses and deeds of the Apostles, beginning with the festival of Pentecost up to nearly the end of the first Christian generation. The Acts of the Apostles closes with the first Roman imprisonment of St Paul, which began very probably in A.D. 58-59, or, at the latest, 60.[1] Only the second part[2] of the book of Luke, however, falls in the fifties. The first and by far the greater part embraces only the first twenty years after the Saviour's death. We rely for what follows principally on this oldest portion of the Acts of the Apostles, since the period of the fifties is pourtrayed expressly through the Epistles of Paul. Indeed, we lay the greatest weight on the first nine chapters of the Acts of the Apostles, which begin immediately with Pentecost, describe events entirely within the year of Jesus' death and the year immediately succeeding it,[3] and contain especially the original teachings of Peter, Stephen and Philip.

It is, then, a matter of the greatest interest to see that *these old disciples proceed exactly as the Master himself had formerly done.* To their Jewish hearers, to whom their words were at first uttered, they declare with all possible intensity that Jesus is the Christ promised in the Old Testament: " Therefore let all the house of Israel know most certainly that God hath made both Lord and Christ this same Jesus, whom you have crucified " (Acts ii, 36). That is the fundamental tone of all the teachings of the earliest days (Acts iii, 18; v, 42; ix, 20, 22; xvii, 3; xviii, 5, 28).

To prove the true Messiahship of Jesus, these preachers of the Gospel make appeal to the miracles which the Man of Nazareth performed, and which were known to many of

---

[1] K. Kellner, *Wann waren Petrus und Paulus in Rom?* in *Katholik*, 11-38 (1887); P. Schanz, *Das Jahr der Gefangennahme des hl. Apostels Paulus*, in *Histor. Jahrbuch*, 199-222 (1887); Adolf Harnack, *Chronologie der altchristl. Literatur*, i, 233-239 (Leipzig, 1897); Belser, *Zur Chronologie des Paulus*, in *Theol. Quartschrift*, 353-379, (1898); Fr. X. Pölzl, *Der Weltapostel Paulus*, 431-452 (Regensburg, 1905).

[2] The first part ends in chap. xv, 35; then follows a transition to the second part, which begins chap. xvi, 6.

[3] Harnack, *Die Chronologie der altchristl. Literatur,* i, 237, puts the conversion and earliest activity of Paul, recorded in Acts ix, still in the year 30. Some other investigators suppose a somewhat greater interval between the death of Jesus and the conversion of Paul.

their hearers from having seen and heard of them. "Jesus of Nazareth, a man approved of God among you by miracles and wonders and signs, which God did by him, in the midst of you, as you also know" (Acts ii, 22, pentecostal speech of Peter). In particular they emphasize, as a most important feature, the fact that the Messiah Jesus had passed through suffering, death and resurrection into his Messianic glory (Acts ii, 36; iv, 27; x, 39; xiii, 23-37). It is constantly declared by them that Jesus has become Lord and Christ, or has been made so by God. Not as though during his life he had not been Lord and Christ, but that he has now been raised to a position, and has attained to a state of glory, in which he finally and in the clearest way proves to the world that he is Lord and Christ, and demonstrates it to his Church.

Starting from that point, however, these earliest preachers announced also the *divine sonship* of Jesus. Already in his Pentecostal teaching and the following speech of defence before the tribunal Peter says : "The God of Abraham and the God of Isaac and the God of Jacob, the God of our fathers, hath glorified his Son Jesus, whom you indeed delivered up and denied before the face of Pilate. . . . To you first, God, raising up his Son, hath sent him. . . . For a truth there assembled Herod and Pontius Pilate with the Gentiles and the people of Israel against the holy child Jesus, whom thou hast anointed. . . . Signs and wonders to be done by the name of thy holy Son, Jesus."[1] Philip demands faith in "the Son of God, Jesus," as the first condition for baptism (Acts viii, 37; it is true, the text of this passage is not wholly certain). Faith in Jesus, the Son of God, forms an essential

---

[1] Acts iii, 13, 26; iv, 27, 30. The Greek text of Luke does not, it is true, translate the Aramaic words of Peter in these four passages with *viós* (Son), but with παῖς, which, indeed, means first "child" or "son," but can also mean "servant," "menial." Yet it is certain that in Biblical or Septuagint Greek, παῖς is preferably used instead of *viós*, when the reference is to the Messiah; as, for example, in the Book of Wisdom ii, 13, compared with ii, 16 and 18. But also in the non-biblical literature of the first century after Christ, Jesus is sometimes called ὁ παῖς τοῦ Θεοῦ, when the "Son of God" is undoubtedly meant. So in the teaching of the Apostles, ix, 2, 3 and x, 2, and the Epistle of Clement of Rome to the Corinthians, lix, 2-4. But Luke, the author of the *Acts,* of all the New Testament writers, "stands nearest in his style to the Septuagint Bible; he lived in the Greek Bible" (Harnack, *Lukas der Arzt,* 120 note 2), and the teaching of the Apostles, as well as the Epistle of Clement, came into existence almost at the same time as the *Acts.* Where, therefore, in the *Acts* the Christ Jesus is called ὁ παῖς τοῦ Θεοῦ, this should certainly be translated "Son of God." So much the more as in two of these four passages divine things are spoken of the Saviour. In Acts iv, 30, Peter says that "Signs and wonders are done by the name of the holy Son (παιδός) of God, Jesus." Similarly, in Acts iii, 16, after Jesus had immediately before (Acts iii, 15) been called "the author of life." The Peshitto has on this account translated the παῖς, referring to Jesus, in all the four passages in the *Acts* by the word "Son."

element of the Gospel, as it was announced by the newly converted Apostle to the Gentiles. Immediately after his conversion, he " preached Jesus in the synagogues, that he is the Son of God " (Acts ix, 20, ὁ υἱὸς τοῦ Θεοῦ). He declares that it is written also of Jesus in Psalm ii : " Thou art my Son ; this day have I begotten thee " (Acts xiii, 33).

Jesus the Messiah and the Son of God—these are, there-fore, beyond a doubt cardinal points of the christology of the original Church. Just as certainly also can it be proved that the expressions " Messiah and Son of God " were not applied to Jesus in accordance with human standards, but *in the sense of a divine Messiah, a Son of God by nature, and a God-Man, Jesus.*

It is true, in the discourses of the Acts, the human element in Jesus is also strongly emphasized. The speeches of the early preachers of the Gospel represent him as a man to whom God has borne witness by signs and wonders, and whom he has anointed and consecrated with the Holy Ghost and divine power for his works (Acts ii, 22; x, 38). Of this same man it is, however, also asserted that he is " the author of life " (Acts iii, 15), and one who has in himself natural and super-natural life and imparts it to others; that in him " alone is salvation " and " that there is no other name under heaven given to men, whereby we must be saved (Acts iv, 12); that " all receive through his name remission of sins who believe in him " (Acts x, 43); and that " he is the Judge of the living and of the dead " (Acts x, 42). With such expres-sions one cannot speak of a mere man, however favoured and gifted. Such language is suited only to divinity.

Together with the Messiahship and divine sonship of Jesus, emphasis is also continually laid in the Acts of the Apostles, and already, in fact, in Peter's pentecostal speech, on his *sovereignty.* Jesus receives from all the original preachers of the Gospel and from the entire early Church throughout the name *Kyrios,* " Lord," " the Lord," " the Lord Jesus Christ," " our Lord," " our Lord Jesus Christ "—we meet these appellations on almost every page. *Kyrios* is the proper name of Jesus Christ. Anyone can convince himself of this who turns over the pages of the Acts, to say nothing of those writings of the New Testament in which the conditions of the second generation are more specially pourtrayed.

What means, then, in the Acts of the Apostles the title Kyrios, " the Lord," given to Christ? We have already elsewhere anticipated the meaning of this, and promised to produce at this place the proof of our interpretation of the name " Lord."

In itself the word " Lord " is a form of address which does not signify anything superhuman or even extraordinary. Precisely as in our language, so in that of the Semite (Matt.

xiii, 27; xxi, 30; John iv, 11; xx, 15), and of the Greek,[1] it can be used as a form of politeness towards an equal or as a sign of veneration and submission towards superiors. There is no doubt that Jesus in his earthly life was addressed in this sense, as Lord, by people who saw in him merely an ordinary man and teacher.

But the designation of Jesus as " Lord " by the first Christians had nothing to do with this simple form of address. It appears among them at once and continuously as a proper name of an exclusively *religious* import. What they wished to express by it must be shown by the linguistic usages of the time in the *Grecian, Jewish and Christian forms of speech.*

The Greek contemporaries of earliest Christianity bestowed the name *Kyrios* upon their gods, and, indeed, united with it the idea of special divine might and sovereign power. Accordingly, the God-fearing, pious man who had chosen some divinity as his particular defender and patron called him his *Kyrios,* Lord.[2] In so far as the Roman emperors allowed themselves to be made equal to the gods, they also claimed the title *Kyrios Dominus.* Augustus and Tiberius, it is true, declined the divine appellation. But their successors had themselves frequently enough entitled *Domini,* and, indeed, always in connection with the divine honours bestowed upon the living emperors.[3]

Since, therefore, the Christians designated and honoured Jesus as ὁ Κύριος, they placed him in opposition to the gods and lords of paganism, not only as the one and only God and Lord, but they placed Christ also especially "as the true, divine Lord in contrast to the 'God and Lord' on the imperial Roman throne."[4] Therefore, the investment of Christ with the title *Kyrios* denotes, in the light of the secular history of the time, a recognition of the divinity of Jesus.

We are not, however, restricted to this proof alone. The first Christians, indeed, justified their expression *Kyrios* by the usage of the Greek language; yet this expression had its origin in Old Testament and Jewish notions, and derived its very definite meaning from that source. The divine proper name Jehovah signified to the Jews living after the exile a word which one should not utter and cannot utter on account

---

[1] In Epictetus the physician is addressed as Lord (Diss. ii, 15, 5; iii, 10, 15) by his patient; the soothsayer by him who questions him (ii, 7, 9); and the rhetorician by his admirer (iii, 23, 19). In letters the father often receives from his son the title " Lord," as a relative does from his kinsmen, and a superior from his inferiors. See the vouchers for this in Adolf Deissmann's *Licht vom Osten, The N. T. and the newly discovered Texts of the Greco-Roman World,* 122, 125, 133, 152, 155 (Tübingen, 1909).

[2] Proofs in Deissmann's *Licht vom Osten,* 122 f., 128 f., 264 ff.

[3] See Gustav Dalman, *Die Worte Jesu,* 271; Deissmann, *op. cit.,* 114 ff 265, 274.

[4] Gustav Dalman, *op. cit.,* 271 f; Deissmann, *op. cit.,* 233 ff.

of its infinite majesty and sanctity. Accordingly, wherever the "unutterable name" Jehovah appears in the Bible text it is provided with the vowels of the word *Adonai* and spoken also as *Adonai,* "Lord." *Adonai,* Lord, has, therefore, the same signification as Jehovah, God.[1]

In the Septuagint, the Greco-Jewish translation of the Old Testament, both names, Jehovah and *Adonai* are rendered correctly and logically as *Kyrios,* "Lord." And, wherever in the original text *Jahwe ha Elohim* stands, the Septuagint translates it, according to genuine Jewish and Old Testament usage, by Κύριος ὁ θεὸς—that is, the Lord God. *Kyrios* is, therefore, the real proper name of the true God; and no Palestinian or Greek Jew ever understood by the religious designation "Lord, our Lord," anything other than the one true God.

The Acts of the Apostles leaves no room for doubt that the oldest Church adapted itself to this linguistic usage, by calling Christ *Kyrios,* or Lord. In the 110 passages in which we meet with *Kyrios* in the Acts, the designation in perhaps a third of them refers directly to God, in another third directly to Jesus Christ, and in the remaining third to God or to Jesus Christ. The expression is evidently used indiscriminately of God and of Jesus. For example, we find in Acts xi, 20 and 21 the surname *Kyrios* three times. The first time the reference is to Jesus, the second and third times to God and Jesus jointly. Very often it is impossible to decide whether the name "Lord" refers directly to God or to Jesus, or to both. The discourse glides imperceptibly from one to the other (Acts ii, 47; ix, 28, 31). This fact is a clear proof how the Lord Jesus is closely identified with the Lord God.

Moreover, in many places by means of further additions it is expressly indicated that the appellation *Kyrios,* "Lord" belongs to the Saviour as his own thoroughly divine name. The Lord Jesus, through the mediation of Peter, heals the paralytic (Acts ix, 34). The Lord Jesus strikes down and converts Saul (Acts ix, 5-27). In the name of the Lord Jesus and through the power of the Lord Jesus the disciples work all their miracles (Acts iii, 6; iv, 7-12; xvi, 18). In the name of the Lord Jesus they impart baptism for the forgiveness of sins (Acts ii, 38; x, 48; xix, 5). Faith in the Lord Jesus and the grace of the Lord Jesus bring salvation (Acts xv, 11; xvi, 31). For the name of the Lord Jesus Christ the disciples sacrifice their lives (Acts xv, 26; xxi, 13). To the Lord Jesus Stephen gave up the ghost (Acts vii, 59), just as the dying Saviour gave up the ghost to his Father (Luke xxiii, 46). The Lord Jesus is the "author of life" (Acts iii, 15), and "Lord of all" (Acts x, 36).

[1] See G. Hollmann, *Welche Religion hatten die Juden als Jesus auftrat?* 26 f. (Halle, 1905).

This sovereignty and dominion are, therefore, directly divine attributes. They include precisely what in the Old and New Testaments is looked upon as the mark of true divinity: God is Jehovah, *Adonai, Κύριος*—that is, the highest and unlimited Lord and Master of heaven and earth. Since the early preachers of the Gospel, from the first feast of Pentecost on, already proclaim, as a cardinal point of the Gospel: "Therefore let all the house of Israel know most certainly that God hath made both Lord and Christ this same Jesus, whom you have crucified" (Acts ii, 36), they put the Lord Jesus Christ on an equality with the Lord God.

This is proven also from another very important point of view—namely, from *the position which the "Lord" Jesus Christ holds in the inner religious life of the first Christians*. The Christians were recognized from the beginning as "invokers of the name of Jesus" and "worshippers of the Lord Jesus." Without infringing on the worship of the Father, which was, indeed, the same as the worship of the Son, the early Christians passed from the Old Testament worship of Jehovah to the worship of the "Lord" Jesus. It is true, the Apostles in Jerusalem still took part in the religious services practised by Israel, and paid visits to the temple at the usual hours for prayer, in order to pray to the God of their fathers with their people and for their people (Acts iii, 1; xxii, 17).[1] But together with this common bond, which still united the Christians with the Jews, the former brought their special knowledge of God also in their worship to an unequivocal expression. This was done by the adoration and invocation of the Lord Jesus. He formed, from the very first, the central point in the specifically Christian religion and piety.

To Saul first, at his conversion, comes the commandment of the disciple Ananias to call upon the name of the Lord Jesus as a fundamental condition of baptism and forgiveness of sins (Acts xxii, 16). Indeed, Saul had not yet been converted to the Lord, when the Christians in Damascus, as at Jerusalem, were already invoking the name of the Lord Jesus, and the whole number of believers, in reference to this worship of him, were simply termed the people who called upon the name of the Lord Jesus (Acts ix, 14, 21). And still earlier, the dying Stephen prays to the Lord Jesus for himself and his murderers—just as Jesus himself had, on the cross, prayed to his Father—"Lord Jesus, receive my spirit," "Lord Jesus, lay not this sin to their charge" (Acts vii, 59, 60). In fact, already at Pentecost Peter refers the words of the prophet Joel, "Whosoever shall call upon the name of the Lord shall be saved," to Jesus. For the discourse which the Prince of the Apostles connects with this prophetic text ends in the one

[1] See the account of Hegesippus concerning the indefatigable praying of James in the Temple, in Eusebius, *H. E.,* ii, xxiii, 6.

thought that Jesus Christ is the Lord, in whose name are forgiveness of sins, salvation and blessedness (Acts ii, 21-38). It is, however, doubtful whether Jesus or God is the Lord to whom the Apostles prayed *before* Pentecost, and said : " Thou, Lord, who knowest the hearts of all men, show whether of these two thou hast chosen " (Acts i, 24).

As we see, the early Christians do not content themselves with an enthusiastic veneration and glorification of their Master. No, they transfer to him *the genuine invocation of God and the adoration which is due to and is paid only to the Most High God*. They pray to the Lord Jesus, and expect from him an answer to their prayers, grace and forgiveness of sins, just as from God himself.

Of this central and thoroughly divine position of the Lord Jesus in the religious life and prayers of the oldest Christians, even the most pronounced enemies of the divinity of Jesus are convinced, and are surprised at it. Johannes Weiss, for example, expresses himself on this point as follows : " In order to explain what the use of the name ' Lord ' meant for the early Christians religiously, one would have to write out the whole New Testament. For the formula ' our Lord Jesus Christ ' contains the religion of the primitive Church in embryo. Obedient submission, reverence, a holy fear of wounding him, the feeling of absolute dependence upon him in all things, . . . gratitude, love, trust—in short, everything that man can feel in regard to divinity, all that is expressed in this name. . . . This looking upon God and Christ as being on an equality, which exactly corresponds to the joint sovereignty of both, is characteristic of the piety of the original Church. As the Christians cry ' Abba, Father,' and pray to him, so, undoubtedly, they have prayed to Christ in the most literal sense of the word, not only as an act of homage, but also in the form of a request. Of this invocation of the Lord we have several isolated instances ; but such prayers were surely vastly more numerous. The Christians, therefore, actually stand in regard to Christ as they do to God. . . . The moment when the first Christian addressed his prayer to the ascended Christ is the natal hour of that religion, which till the present day appears to many Christians as the true and only authorized Christianity. Other modern Christians may for themselves repudiate prayer to Christ and declare it to be an error, but the historian must say that Christianity from its earliest beginnings has practised the worship of Christ, together with the faith in God the Father, as the to it perfectly natural form of religion."[1] Like Johannes Weiss, a number of

[1] Johannes Weiss, *Christus*, 24 f. (Tübingen, 1909). See also the admirable treatment of the subject by Theo. Zahn, *Skizzen aus dem Leben der alten Kirche*, 271-308, 3rd ed. (Leipzig, 1908), under *Prayer to Jesus in the Apostolic Age*.

the most important Protestant investigators of various tendencies also recognize that "the Lord Jesus Christ" in the days of the original Apostles and the early Church is in every respect made equivalent to God. This is the opinion of Gustav Dalman,[1] G. B. Stevens,[2] B. Weiss,[3] K. Müller,[4] E. von Hartmann,[5] and Theodor Zahn.[6]

Jesus Christ, therefore, from the day of the Church's foundation, was venerated, invoked and prayed to in place of Jehovah; and the early Christians give significant and definite expression to this practical recognition of the divinity of Christ by transferring to Jesus the name Jehovah—Adonai, *Kyrios*, Lord. This is the christology of the Acts of the Apostles.[7]

2. *Historical Genuineness of this Representation.*

In order to weaken, or, when possible, to eliminate, the immense impression of this fact, one naturally takes refuge again in the stereotyped expedient, that the Acts of the Apostles was written comparatively late, and that it is questionable how far Luke gives us in it the portrait of Christ of the earliest generation, and how far this had been already refashioned by the faith of the later decades. This charge, which, in regard to the New Testament writings in general, has been already refuted, is in particular absolutely without foundation in reference to the conception of Jesus in the Acts of the Apostles.

No less a man than Adolf Harnack, the leader of the liberal Protestant school, has lately undertaken, in two masterfully designed and executed monographs, the defence of the Acts of the Apostles against the unheard-of accusation brought against it by representatives in other respects of his own views.[8] He describes the procedure of the latter with the words : "The book is alleged to be a comparatively late and motley compilation, in which the editor contributed a small but certainly a bad part; the autobiographical portions are not the work of the author, but excerpts from some source, or else purely literary inventions; historical mistakes are as numerous in it as are the rents and badly concealed reparations; the portrait of Paul is drawn with a bias, or from a lack of personal acquaintance, and the description in the first chapters

1 *Die Worte Jesu,* 271 f.
2 *The Theology of the New Testament,* 266 (London, 1901).
3 *Lehrbuch der biblischen Theologie des N. T.,* 133 (Berlin, 1903).
4 *Unser Herr,* in *Biblische Zeit- und Streitfragen,* 133 (1906).
5 *Das Christentum des N. T.,* 178 (1905).   6 *id.,* 275 ff.
7 See also Mangenot, *Jésus, Messie et Fils de Dieu dans les Actes des Apôtres* (Paris, 1908).
8 Adolf Harnack, *Lukas der Arzt, der Verfasser des dritten Evangeliums und der Apostelgeschichte* (Leipzig, 1906); *Die Apostelgeschichte, Untersuchungen* (Leipzig, 1908); *Neue Untersuchungen zur Apg. und zur Abfassung der synoptischen Evangelien* (Leipzig, 1910).

is hardly more than an imaginary painting; Peter is represented in the style of Paul, and Paul in the style of Peter—but
who can count all the accusations which have been raised
against this book? And if they were only tangible accusations! But since a large part of them have been conclusively
refuted, one has now almost more to do with a general mistrust of the book, and with fanciful ideas and patronizing
denials, than with definite objections; but mostly, however,
with the fruits of the mischievous method of hanging heavy
burdens on the slender thread of one single observation, and,
in the case of a New Testament writer, of making no allow-
ance for weakness or ignorance, but rather using these as
explosive material to blow up the entire book."[1]

It is, indeed, astonishing what violent attacks have been
made, even down to the most recent times, on the Acts of the
Apostles, solely because its contents, and more especially its
christology, have been to liberal critics a thorn in the eye.

In order to deal as they like with the contents of the Acts
of the Apostles, Luke, the pupil of the Apostles, must under
no condition be accepted as its author, although the unanimous Christian tradition, which can be traced back to the
middle of the second century, is in favour of Luke. In fact,
although investigators like Credner, B. Weiss, Klostermann,
Zahn, Renan, Hobart, Ramsay, Hawkins, Blass and many
others (to say nothing at all of Catholics) have proved the
correctness of this tradition, and although the liberals have
not been able to bring one valid argument against it, almost
all of them, from Königsmann, De Wette, Baur, and Zeller
to Wendt, Schürer, Pfleiderer, von Soden, Jülicher and John
Weiss, have agreed in denying the authorship of Luke. Only
since Harnack has spoken, and has brought forth an overwhelming mass of proof against the liberal critics in his
Luke the Physician, has the correctness of the tradition been
acknowledged.

Thereby also the *date* of the Acts of the Apostles has entered
a new phase. It is true, the fantastic wishes and assertions
of some critics, according to whom the " Acts " was not
written till the second century, had already given place to
the universal recognition that the book was written much
earlier. The liberals also are gradually, in considerable
numbers, approaching the views of orthodox investigators.[2]

Nevertheless, Harnack had, until 1906, firmly held the view

[1] *Die Apostelgeschichte,* 19-20.
[2] As for the date of the *Acts,* F. Blass assumes it to be between
64-70, *Acta Apostolorum, sive Lucae ad Theophilum liber alter* (1895);
B. Weiss gives it as about the year 80, *Lehrbuch der Einleitung in das
N. T.,* 3rd ed. (1897); A. C. Headlam assumes for it the year 70,
Dictionary of the Bible, vol. I, 30; Th. Zahn, about 75, *Einleitung in
das N. T.,* ii, 1899; Knabenbauer, as shortly after 62, *Commentarius
in Actus Apostolorum* (1899); R. B. Rackham, as the year 64, *The Acts
of the Apostles* (1901); Belser, as 63, *Einleitung in das N. T.* (1901).

that Luke wrote only between the years A.D. 78 and 93.[1]
Now, however, the Berlin critic himself contradicts the arguments brought forward for the above date,[2] and adduces
" very weighty observations " which favour the view " that
the Acts of the Apostles [and therefore also the Gospel] were
composed already at the beginning of the sixties."[3]   The only
reason which deters the rationalistic scholar from finally
agreeing to this date lies in the miracles and prophecies
narrated in the Acts ; for it would be almost impossible to
contest the historical authenticity of the records of those
miracles, and to declare them to be myths and legends, if the
Acts of the Apostles had appeared only from ten to thirty years
after the events described.[4]

If the Acts of the Apostles was already written at a time
when many witnesses of the events narrated in that book were
still alive, and could test the truth of the representation given,
the further charge that the author has drawn from thoroughly
unreliable or even imaginative sources falls at once to the
ground.   On the contrary, it can be proved with certainty
that Luke for the first part of the Acts relied on admirable
oral traditions and, indeed, on written sources also, while he
wrote the whole second half (chapters xvi to xxviii) partly as
an eye-witness, partly on the ground of the narratives of co-
operating witnesses.[5]

This material—a source of information both autobiographical and external, and written as well as oral—Luke
worked up with *historical fidelity*.   This is vouched for not
only by his own assertion and the demonstrable conscientious-
ness of the historian, but also by the whole content and form
of his book.   Luke makes throughout, not the impression of
" a wild enthusiast in the form of a physician," as the
extreme liberal critics describe him ; he is " neither uncritical
nor credulous. . . . Credulous and uncritical writers of that
period brought out very different productions !   Moreover,
this historian stands, in regard to the greater part of his work,
under a control than which one more severe can hardly be
conceived—namely, that of the Epistles of Paul.   That these
writings are the productions of the moment, and originate
from a man of the most marked subjectivity, increases even
more the severity of the test.   Yet only the over-scrupulous
and cavillers can fail to recognize that the Acts of the Apostles

1 Harnack, *Chronologie der altchristl. Literatur*, i, 246-250, 718 (1897) ;
Lukas der Arzt, 18, 115.   2 *Die Apostelgeschichte*, 217 ff.
    3 *id.*, p. 219.   4 *id.*, pp. 224, 225.
    5 Harnack, *Die Apostelgeschichte*, 131-198 ; *Lukas der Arzt*, 65-111 ;
Th. Zahn, *id.*, *Die von Lukas benützten Quellen*, 394-425 ; Belser, *id.*,
Die Quellen der Apostelgeschichte, 191-213 ; W. Hadorn, *Die Apostel-
geschichte und ihr geschichtlicher Wert*, 10 ff. (1906), *Das Evangelium
in der Apostelgeschichte* (1907) ; H. J. Andrews, *The Acts of the Apostles*
(London, 1908).

has, in many dozens of important and unimportant passages, stood the test which the Epistles of Paul mean for it. What still remains, apart from a few trifles, is the description of the apostolic council and that of the self-defence of Paul in the last speeches, and in general his attitude towards the Jews in his last sojourn at Jerusalem."[1]

But also these parts, which cannot be verified from the Pauline Epistles, are unassailable. In fact, precisely that which the critics have most contested in Luke "bears the stamp of historical reality," and the critics doubt it only because "they treat their fanciful notions about the book more respectfully than they do the great lines of the work which they in part acquiesce in, as a matter of course, and in part immediately criticize, because they know better."[2]

Harnack sums up his final judgement on the Acts of the Apostles, based on the most thorough analysis and painfully exact investigations, as follows : "Viewed from almost every possible standpoint of historical criticism, it is a solid, estimable and in many respects an extraordinary work,"[3] "a critically historical production which calls for the highest recognition,"[4] "a literary achievement of the first rank."[5]

In one point only does Harnack decide against the author of the Acts—namely, in reference to the belief in miracles and the reports of them.[6] And just in this point Harnack departs from the orthodox Christian opinion of the Acts of the Apostles. He cannot share the "prejudices" of orthodox investigators who take miracles seriously.[7] But whoever studies the *Apostelgeschichte* of the Berlin critic with an open mind will find that the tables are turned, and that Harnack approaches his judgement of the work of Luke with the prejudice that there are no miracles ; that this prejudice brings a painful discord into his otherwise admirable work ; that his explanations and arguments become both threadbare and astonishingly naïve when he endeavours to keep clear of the miraculous ; that he lets his judgement, as an historian, be obscured, and, in fact, finally be actually influenced by his philosophical view which is antagonistic to miracles ; and yet that he cannot, after all, either deny Luke's accounts of miracles, or prove them to be "legends growing with almost inconceivable rapidity,[8] or myths, or in any way explain them as natural events. Thus criticism will see itself compelled, not only, as Harnack says,[9] in all *other* points, but also in regard to the miracles in the Acts of the Apostles, to return

[1] Harnack, *Apostelgeschichte,* 17-18.   [2] *id.,* 10.
[3] *id.,* 222.   [4] *id.,* 10.
[5] *Lukas der Arzt,* 101.
[6] *id.,* 18. Nevertheless, he "absolves Luke from religious mysteries, tricks of magic, pious absurdities, etc."   [7] *id.,* 225.
[8] *id.,* 224.   [9] *id.,* 225.

to the traditional positions and to accept the work of Luke as in all respects a faithful reproduction of the history of the oldest Church.

This certainly means that the Acts of the Apostles, especially as regards christology, gives us historically positive information concerning those first days of the Church. After what has been said no more proof of this is needed. Jesus Christ—the Person and the Gospel of Jesus Christ—forms, after all, so emphatically the principal feature of the Acts of the Apostles that the work itself could not be historical if its christology were not historical. Moreover, the portrait of Jesus, as it is sketched by the different Apostles and disciples in the Acts, is, in spite of its general uniformity, so unique in its details that we cannot possibly suppose that Luke brought only his type of Christ—in case he may have had a type of his own—into his book and into the preaching of the first messengers of Christ. Even P. W. Schmiedel writes : " The portraiture of Jesus is more simple and agrees more perfectly with the most authentic passages in the first three Gospels than is elsewhere the case in the whole New Testament. It is hardly credible that this christology does not originate from the oldest source."[1] Moreover, the christology of the book of Luke is so intimately interwoven with the undisputed facts related in it, that one without the other is not to be thought of.

Even the formerly frequently asserted theory that the speeches in the first part of the Acts, which contain the most significant christological utterances of Peter, James, Philip, Stephen and the newly converted Paul, may not be historical but were composed by Luke himself, now proves worthless. Of course they bear the imprint of the style of Luke, since they were originally spoken in the Aramaic language. But, with all the fineness and freedom of his linguistic portraiture, Luke has altered his sources of information so little essentially that we distinctly feel the Hebraic mode of thought and expression of the original. Moreover, the added statements in regard to places, dates and incidents which are added to the story are so peculiar and exact that it would have been impossible subsequently to invent them. Furthermore, the separate speeches have throughout an individual stamp; so individual indeed that we find in them the character and personality of the different earliest preachers of the Gospel, Peter, James, Stephen, Paul and others.[2] Even Harnack, therefore, does not consider these speeches as inventions or plagiarisms from Paul's writings, but as an " original possession "[3] (of the Church), and he argues in favour of the existence of

---

[1] *Encyclopædia Biblica* (Cheyne and Black), article *Acts of the Apostles,* xiv, col. 48.

[2] See Harnack, *Apostelgeschichte,* 101-110.   [3] *id.,* 109 f.

written sources from which Luke derived them.[1]   In fact,
even if we were willing to concede that they were composed
freely only at a later date, their christological import would
still prove itself as belonging to the very first era.   They
contain, as Johannes Weiss correctly asserts, " such primitive
Christian characteristics, as refer back to the standpoint of
the oldest Church. . . .   Whether they originate at a later
epoch or not, they contain, precisely in their christology, very
ancient ideas."[2]

This must still be especially emphasized in regard to the
christology of the " *Lord,*" in which the divinity of Jesus is
expressed most clearly in the Acts of the Apostles.   Our
opponents hold firmly to the assertion that Luke borrowed the
titles *Lord, our Lord,* and *Lord Jesus Christ* from the
Epistles of Paul, and smuggled them into the original history
of the Church.   Against this two things can be said in reply.
First, the " Lord-christology " is such an essential part of the
Acts of the Apostles that the one must fall as an historic
monument if the other does.   Paul has not brought that
christology into the Church, but has himself found it
in the Church.   We meet with its first expressions already
before the ascension of the Lord—that is, at a time which
antedates the facts related in the Acts as well as the Epistles
of Paul.   Paul himself furnishes us the proof that Christ, in
the primitive epoch described in the Acts, and, indeed, already
in the first Jewish-Christian Church, was called " Lord " and
" our Lord."   This is made certain by the Aramaic formula
" Maranatha "—that is, " our Lord cometh," or " our Lord,
come !"[3] which " must originate from the original Church."[4]
Paul has, therefore, only reproduced " the name of *Kyrios,*[5]
which came down to him from the oldest Church."   Instead
of calling Paul the inventor of the " Lord-christology," and
Luke its Pauline heir and plagiarist, as most liberal critics
do, both Paul and Luke must, on the contrary, have learned
to designate Jesus Christ as the " Lord " from the early
Church.

Also the divine import which this name has in the Acts of
the Apostles was not at all, as the liberals wish to make us
believe,[6] taken from Pauline theology and by Luke construed
into the confession of the ancient Church.   Again, Paul's
Epistles themselves are a guarantee and a proof of the fact
that really the original Church in the very first years of its
existence saw and worshipped God in the " Lord " Jesus
Christ, as Luke reports.   It is an undeniable fact, which we

[1] *id.,* 136-139, 184-186.   [2] Johannes Weiss, *Christus* (Tübingen, 1909).
[3] 1 Cor. xvi, 22 ; Rev. xxii, 20.
[4] Johannes Weiss, *Christus,* 24.   [5] *id.,* 26.
[6] Even Harnack, *Lukas der Arzt,* 101, remarks of the author of the
Acts : " He who acknowledged Christ as the *Kyrios* . . . was a follower
of Paul."

shall soon demonstrate minutely, that about the fifties, when
Paul wrote his great Epistles, all Christians—old Apostles
and novices, Jewish and Hellenic Churches—everywhere
adored and invoked the Lord Jesus Christ—in short, offered
him a truly divine worship.[1]

Already, in the Epistle to the Romans, therefore, when
Paul is writing to Christians whom he has not taught, but
who had been previously converted and by other teachers
(Peter), he speaks of the divinity of Jesus as of a doctrine
which is universally known and conceded by all, and about
which there is still no dispute among Christians (Rom. ix, 5).

It is, however, clearly unthinkable that such a universal
phenomenon, which was regarded as the nucleus of the
Christian religion only twenty years after the death of Jesus,
should have merely a short time before found its way into
the Church.   On the contrary, Paul, already when he from
a persecutor became a confessor of Jesus, must have come
to know the disciples at Damascus and the Apostles at
Jerusalem as worshippers of the Lord Jesus.

Nothing, therefore, is more unwarranted than the supposition that faith in the divine nature of Jesus " was still
quite unknown to the oldest community of disciples."[2]   Even
Alfred Loisy recognizes, on the contrary, that the christological dogma " has been contained in the primitive tradition,
as the germ in the seed, as a real and living element."[3]   And
Smith, the radical American, professor of mathematics and
theological writer, declares frankly : " The Jesus Christ of the
original Christianity " (by which he means the Christianity of
the oldest period and the first days of the Apostolic preaching)
" was not human but divine, the King of all kings, the Lord
of all lords, the Saviour, the Redeemer, the protecting God."[4]

*The Christians, therefore, were from the beginning wor-
shippers of their Lord; and the Church, from the first hour
of its existence, regarded the adoration of its Founder as God,
as the distinguishing expression of its being.*   " There is no
Gospel of Christ which has not proclaimed him as a heavenly
Lord and King.   The same men who sailed with Jesus on the
Sea of Galilee, and ate and drank with him, have with death-
defying courage and irrepressible joy proclaimed this same
Jesus as the Lord exalted to the right hand of God, who has
given to his followers divine strength and life, and made them
certain of heavenly perfection.   The speeches of Peter in the
first part of the Acts bear eloquent witness to the fact that

[1] See, later on, our " Paul and the Divinity of Christ," as well as the
admirable treatment by Th. Zahn, *Skizzen aus dem Leben der alten
Kirche*, 271-308, 3rd ed. (1908), *Die Anbetung Jesu im Zeitalter der
Apostel.*
[2] Pfleiderer, *Entwicklung des Christentums*, 24, *cf.* 29.
[3] *L'Evangile et l'Eglise*, 162 (1902).
[4] *Der vorchristliche Christus*, 41, *cf.* 33 (1906).

the earliest apostolic portrait of Christ also was glorified with
divine splendour.''[1]   Even though the separate characteristics and the more minute elaboration of the divine portrait
of Christ may have been for many still very obscure, and
though the more exact execution and the theological and
speculative apprehension of it may have preoccupied the first
Christians but little, certain it is that the faith of the Church
in the divinity of Jesus Christ was already complete on the
first feast of Pentecost, and with that feast began its victorious march through the world.

*That points, however, with infallible certainty to the origin
of this faith—to Jesus Christ, to his own divine consciousness,
and to his own declaration of divinity.* "There is," writes
Sanday,[2] "nothing more wonderful in the history of human
thought than the quiet and unobtrusive way in which this
doctrine, which is for us so difficult, took its place without
struggle and controversy among Christian truths."   And the
wonder increases when we think that the first confessors of
the divinity of Jesus acknowledge this faith openly and without the least doubt immediately after the death of the Master,
although their Jewish ideas, which they had brought with
them out of the synagogue, must have encouraged anything
rather than a belief in the Messiahship and divinity of Jesus.
Their faith is and remains a riddle, in fact, a psychological
impossibility, if Jesus Christ himself had not educated them
up to this faith, and if he had not made upon the disciples immediately and directly the impression of a divine personality,
and had not proclaimed himself to them as God.   Hence it
must be true, when the first messengers of the faith assure
us that the supernatural and divine element, which they speak
of in Jesus, goes back to his own words and command : " He
commanded us to preach to the people, and to testify that
he . . . is the Judge of the living and of the dead '' (Acts
x, 42).

III.—St Paul and the Divinity of Christ.

1. *Pauline Christology.*

Already in the Acts of the Apostles we have found an out-
line of Pauline christology.   What especially interested us
in this were the beginnings of the christological views of the
Apostle to the Gentiles, which existed already before the
fifties.   Of how Paul subsequently preached about his Master,
and what he thought of him, his writings give us profound,
abundant and comprehensive information.   But, in addition,
they teach us what the whole Church at that time thought of
Jesus Christ.   For not only may the Pauline teaching be
regarded as an expression of the universal Christian doctrine,

---

[1] Feine, *Paulus als Theologe,* 44.   [2] *Epistle to the Romans,* 16.

but we gain from the writings of Paul the certainty that there was only one general Christian view of Jesus Christ, and that it did not occur to anyone to call it in question in any way. Thus the testimony of Paul becomes the testimony of all Christendom in the fifties and sixties.

We observe, in the first place, that in the following investigation we appeal to all the Pauline writings in the New Testament. The most of these are conceded by liberal critics to be, at all events, authentic. It is true, they still try to invalidate the genuineness of the pastoral Epistles and the Epistle to the Hebrews. But the reasons alleged for suspecting them are not at all tenable.

Moreover, the fact is, after all, admitted that the Epistles whose authenticity is thus doubted are in substance Pauline—that is, they elaborate Pauline ideas. And precisely the christological ideas of the pastoral Epistles and the Epistle to the Hebrews agree essentially with those of the other writings of the Apostle. Even if, therefore, we should wish to eliminate the former, the Pauline portrait of Christ would still remain essentially the same.

Then, however, the " non-pauline " writings, thus eliminated, would, nevertheless, have to be regarded as additional productions of the same period. Besides the one witness for Christ, Paul, a second and a third would thus announce themselves, and confirm and strengthen the utterances of the great Apostle; and so, instead of one problem, our opponents would have to solve two or three. They have, therefore, in any case no interest in placing the christological teachings of the pastoral Epistles and the Epistle to the Hebrews near to, yet apart from the christology of Paul.

Still less is it allowable to discern in Paul's writings a progressive christology. Our opponents, for the most part, make use of the well-known theory of evolution, adopted by the sceptical historians of religion in the case of Paul in order to make it more comprehensible how the Apostle has come, little by little, to the notion of his " Super-christ," in opposition to history and the real record of Jesus. He, who from the first had brought with him an almost superhuman idea of the Christ-Messiah, has, it is said, under the influence of the resurrected and exalted Jesus, in whom he erroneously believed, raised his ideal of Christ ever higher and higher; and every later Epistle shows such a christological progress and evolution in comparison with previous Epistles until finally the loftiest flight and climax of idealization and metaphysical speculation was attained.

Certainly a very prejudiced manipulation of history. There is also not a sign of justification for it, to say nothing of a single solid reason. Professor Karl Clemen, a biographer of Paul, who is certainly above suspicion, teaches his followers that "Paul preached already at the beginning precisely as he preached later; in the writings of Paul there is no evolution."[1]

Is, then, the doctrine of the divinity of Jesus Christ found in the Pauline christology?

The majority of liberal critics answer positively " No." According to K. Weizsäcker, the Christ of Paul is merely " a man in the sense of a higher, supermundane world, . . . with a spiritual body and an intelligence which thinks entirely in accordance with the spirit of God."[2] Bernhard Weiss explains him also as " a man, who before and after his earthly life enjoys a unique supernatural origin and existence, which, however, is in no way above the grade of a creature."[3] H. J. Holtzmann asserts that Paul teaches only a " man characterized by a divine life on earth, and consequently also, in a spiritual form of existence above the earth, in the sphere of God."[4] Otto Pfleiderer declares : " It is true, he [Paul], like the primitive Church, considered him to be a Son of David, a naturally born man and Jew; but that applied only to his outward manifestation, which formed merely a short episode in the heavenly existence of the Son of God before and after his life on earth." This Son of God is "a supermundane, spiritual being, a heavenly man, an exact likeness of God "— in fact, everything except the metaphysical Son of God.[5]

Julius Grill defines the Christ of Paul as a " celestial man, a pre-existing primitive man in the sphere of divine being." " The life of this celestial man is pure spirituality . . . in contrast not only to all earthly and material being . . . but also to every creature-like nature, in so far as it . . . frees itself from the primal source of spirit and life."[6]

Harnack calls the Christ of Paul temporarily certainly a " divine Being."   But that this expression must be interpreted in a human sense, appears immediately from this adjoining declaration of the Berlin critic : " Paul, led by Messianic dogmas and convinced by the impression thus made, has founded the speculative theory that not only was God in Christ, but that Christ himself possessed a peculiar, heavenly nature."[7]

[1] Karl Clemen, *Die Grundgedanken der paulinischen Theologie,* in *Theologische Arbeiten aus dem Rheinischen Predigerverein,* Neue Folge, 9 Heft (Tübingen, 1907); *Paulus, sein Leben und Wirken* (Giessen, 1904); *Die Entwicklung der christlichen Religion* (Leipzig, 1908).

[2] *Das apostolische Zeitalter,* 120 f., 3rd ed. (Tübingen, 1902).

[3] *Lehrbuch der biblischen Theologie,* 300 ff. (Berlin, 1895).

[4] *Neutest. Theologie,* i, 94 (Freiburg u. Leipzig, 1897).

[5] *Das Urchristentum,* 701 ff., 2nd ed. (Berlin, 1902); *Die Entstehung des Christentums,* 143 ff.; *Religionsphilosophie,* 264 f., 3rd ed. (Berlin, 1896).

[6] *Untersuchungen über die Entstehung des IV Evangeliums,* 68-70 (1902).   [7] *Wesen des Christentums,* 116.

Eduard von Hartmann finds that the Christ of Paul, before his earthly life, pre-existed not merely ideally but really, as a spirit, yet not as a celestial man, or (what is the same thing) as the Son of God, to which position he becomes exalted only by his resurrection, yet in such a way that he always remains a being subordinate to divinity."[1]

If we wish to lend credence to Adolf Jülicher, we find that Paul teaches, already working " with a mythological way of thinking," that " Christ is a celestial man . . . a man like ourselves, consisting of body and soul; both of which are, however, of a celestial substance—in fact, of precisely that substance which will also be ours in the period when all is made perfect. God has, in all his works, brought him forward as a Mediator."[2] H. Wendt says in different words the same thing, when he defines the Pauline Christ as an " Incarnation of a divine, pre-existent Spirit, in accordance with the Jewish conception of the Messiah;"[3] yet not to be spoken of as actually God.

O. Holtzmann similarly characterizes the christology of the Apostle Paul : " For Paul, in place of the real historic Jesus, appeared the image of the Son of God, who once had been active in the creation of the world, and who since then had dwelt with God in a divine form as the celestial man."[4]

For Arnold Meyer " the Christ of Paul is the celestial Son of God . . . a heavenly image of the Godhead; a mediator, through whom the sublime Godhead had relation with the lower world. . . . It has not been possible for Paul, however high his conception of Christ, to call him God."[5] " For Paul he is the new spiritual man, originating from heaven . . . who descended from heaven into this gloomy, earthly world, with its evil powers and dominions, to redeem us from them."[6]

This series of citations gives us sufficient information of how the liberal school of critics for the most part regards the Pauline christology. Among all their shades of views on other subjects, the majority of liberal critics maintain that Paul certainly teaches a Christ who pre-existed before his earthly life in some kind of form in heaven, and, after his death and resurrection, is continuing again his glorious life in heaven—a celestial man, the Messiah of the Jewish

[1] *Das Christentum des N. T.*, 218 f. note (Sachsa i. Harz, 1905).
[2] *Die Religion Jesu*, in *Kultur der Gegenwart*, i, 87, No. 4 (Berlin u. Leipzig, 1906).
[3] *System der göttlichen Lehre*, ii, 351 (Göttingen, 1906).
[4] *Christus*, 124 f. (Leipzig, 1907).
[5] *Was uns Jesus heute ist*, 7 f., cf. 5 ff. 18-23 (Tübingen, 1907); cf. *Wer hat das Christentum begründet, Jesus oder Paulus?* 25 (Tübingen, 1907).
[6] Bousset, *Jesus*, 97 (Tübingen, 1907); cf. *Der Apostel Paulus* (Tübingen, 1906).

Apocalypse; but that Paul does not concede to his Christ a divine mode of existence and a divine nature. Really not? *The Epistles of Paul,* examined without prejudice, say the contrary. *They teach the divinity of Christ clearly and expressly.*

First of all, they attribute to the Saviour a thoroughly *divine efficiency,* which he has exerted on this world of creatures before, during and after his earthly life. Before his life on earth, in union with God the Father, he created the entire world. Again and again Paul attributes to the pre-existent Christ the work of creation. The thing is so evident that it does not even occur to the liberal investigators to deny it. They do, however, assert that Paul regards his Christ— relying on Neoplatonism and the pagan-Jewish doctrine of spirits—only as a world-former, a demiurge, and an inter-mediary, through whom God organized the world. Christ is "the foremost of the mediating forces, through whom the universe has been brought forth from God to a separate exis-tence;"[1] there belongs to him only " a mediatorship in the creation of the world,"[2] "a cosmic mediatory rôle," since " God first forms the celestial man (Christ), and then, through the latter's mediation, the earthly man."[3]

But this means misunderstanding Paul thoroughly. Paul, on the contrary, teaches : " The Son of his love . . . who is the image of the invisible God, the first-born of every creature. For in him were all things created in heaven and on earth, visible and invisible, whether thrones or dominations, or principalities or powers. All things were created by him and in him, and by him all things consist " (Col. i, 13, 15-17). The Son of God " made the world " and " upholds all things by the word of his power " (Heb. i, 2, 3). Jesus Christ is the One, " for whom are all things and by whom are all things " (Heb. ii, 10). Therefore, he is not a mere world-framer, a spiritual being in human form, who is himself a creature, and plays merely the part of mediator. Rather is Jesus Christ the Creator of the world. He is the first-born Son of God, who was brought forth by God before all creation; all spiritual beings owe their existence to him; He is not the mere bearer of a mediatory rôle, the instrument which God made use of in creating the world, and which he then threw aside again, but he himself " made the world," " it is created by him," and " through the word of his power all things are upheld." " By him all things consist." And, as the world owes its origin to him, so he is also the divine final purpose of the world; " for him and by him are all things created." Exactly the same as Paul elsewhere says of God the Father : " To us there is but *one* God, the Father, of whom are all things, and

---

[1] Jülicher, *op. cit.,* 87.   [2] B. Weiss, *op. cit.,* 301.
[3] H. J. Holtzmann, *op. cit.,* i, 83 ff., 91 f.

we unto him, and *one* Lord Jesus Christ, by whom are all things, and we by him " (1 Cor. viii, 6).

And like the *Creator*, so is he also the *Redeemer* of the world, after it had through sin fallen from its origin and final aim : " God was in Christ, reconciling the world to himself " (2 Cor. v, 19). " When the fulness of time was come, God sent his Son, made of a woman, . . . that we might receive the adoption of sons " (Gal. iv, 4-6). " Even when we were dead in sins, [God] hath quickened us together in Christ (by whose grace you are saved), and hath raised us up together and hath made us sit together in the heavenly places, through Christ Jesus " (Eph. ii, 4-6). " In whom we have redemption through his blood, the remission of sins " (Col. i, 14). He is the source of grace and healing (2 Thess ii, 12, 13), of justification (Gal. ii, 17 ; Eph. ii, 14-18), of salvation (1 Tim. i, 15), of supernatural redemption and eternal glory (Col. i, 27 ; 2 Tim. ii, 10 ; iv, 18, etc.). Jesus Christ is, in a word, " the author of salvation " (Heb. ii, 10).

However, Paul is perfectly aware that " salvation," supernatural grace, redemption, blessedness and glorification are the work and act of God. " It is not of him that willeth, nor of him that runneth, but of God that showeth mercy " (Rom. ix, 16). "[God] hath mercy on whom he will, and whom he will he hardeneth " (Rom. ix, 18). From God comes the predestination, from God comes the calling, from God comes justification and from God comes glorification : " And whom he predestinated, them he also called ; and whom he called, them he also justified ; and whom he justified, them he also glorified " (Rom. viii, 30).

On the one hand, therefore, both the creation and the redemption of the world are the work and act of the Son of God and the Saviour, Jesus Christ. On the other hand, both creation and redemption are purely a divine act and a work of divine omnipotence. It is clear that Paul thereby proclaims the divinity of Jesus Christ.

But *omnipotence is only one of those divine characteristics* which Paul ascribes to the Son of God, Jesus Christ. He extols no less emphatically his *omniscience*. Christ is to him " the power of God and the wisdom of God " (1 Cor. i, 24). " In whom are hid all the treasures of wisdom and knowledge " (Col. ii, 3). Thereby is expressed in substance John's doctrine of the Logos, which reaches its climax in the statement that Jesus is the wisdom, knowledge and word of God. As such, the Christ of Paul has, of course, not only existed with God before his earthly life, but there belongs to him a pre-existence actually without a beginning—*Eternity*. Before all worlds were made, he was produced from God, as " the Son of his love, the image of God, the first-born of every creature " (Col. i, 15). And since by him the creation was effected, and

thereby time itself was created, the chronological order and
the transitoriness of created things become all the more the
standard by which to estimate the eternity and immutability
of the Son of God.   What is said of the eternity of Jehovah
in the Scriptures is now applied by Paul to Jesus Christ:
" Thou in the beginning, O Lord, didst found the earth; and
the works of thy hands are the heavens.   They shall perish,
but thou shalt continue; and they shall all grow old as a
garment; and as a vesture shalt thou change them.   But
thou art the selfsame, and thy years shall not fail " (Heb. i,
10-12).   As God is extolled in the sacred books as the in-
variable and unchangeable, and on that account eternal Being,
so similarly it is also said: " Jesus Christ, yesterday, and
to-day; and the same for ever " (Heb. xiii, 8).

The divine attributes of Jesus presuppose absolutely his
divine nature.   Paul affirms this by praising Christ as " the
image of God " (2 Cor. iv, 4), " the image of the invisible
God " (Col. i, 15), " the brightness of his glory and the figure
of his substance " (Heb. i, 3).

Christ is not merely made, like man, " *after* God's image "
(Gen. i, 26); no, he is, in accordance with his own nature, *the*
image of God, his own divine likeness.   Thereby he is exalted
above all human spheres; the essential image of God can be
only a divine being.

Paul brings up this thought, found in the Epistle to the
Corinthians, again in his Epistle to the Colossians.   He
asserts that the divine likeness in Christ finds its explanation
only in the fact that Jesus is the first-born of God.   In his
nature and substance Christ is born of God; in him " all the
attributes of the Father are concentrated."[1]

This thought is in harmony with what is said in the Epistle
to the Hebrews, when Paul speaks of Christ as " the first-
begotten " Son of God (Heb. i, 6), as the Creator and
Redeemer of the world (Heb. i, 2), and the " brightness of
God's glory and the figure of his substance " ; and therefore,
raised above all creatures, he " sitteth on the right hand of
the majesty on high " (Heb. i, 3).

As this image and essential likeness of the invisible God,
Christ is *one Godhead with the Father*.   In contrast to the
polytheism of the pagan world, the Apostle declares powerfully that " there is no God but one " (1 Cor. viii, 4).   But
he at once and very emphatically unites, as this one divine
being, the two Persons, God the Father and the Son Jesus
Christ: " Yet to us there is but *one* God, the Father . . . and
one Lord (Jehovah), Jesus Christ " (1 Cor. viii, 6).

Accordingly, Jesus Christ, who passed through this world
in human form, is not, after the fashion of men, a child and

---

[1] Johannes Weiss, *Christus,* 46 (Tübingen, 1909).   Therefore he is
" the firstborn before all creatures, the image of the invisible God."

son of God by divine grace, but a child of God by nature. And, in truth, he does not possess merely a portion, a ray, of the divine nature, as the Gnostic doctrine of emanations said of the world-framer. Rather does the whole and undivided nature of God belong to the Saviour Jesus Christ. " In him dwelleth all the fulness of the Godhead corporeally " (Col. ii, 9).

Only out of humble love to us has he assumed human nature and a human form, although he had already existed with the Father in a divine form of being, and even in that form of a human servant he remained fully conscious of his equality with God, and was entitled to divine honour and adoration : " Who, being in the form of God, thought it not robbery to be equal with God ; but emptied himself, taking the form of a servant, being made in the likeness of men, and in habit found as a man ; he humbled himself, becoming obedient unto death, even the death of the Cross. For which cause God also hath exalted him, and hath given him a name which is above every name ; that in the name of Jesus every knee should bow, of those that are in heaven, on earth and under the earth, and that every tongue should confess that the Lord Jesus Christ is in the glory of God the Father " (Phil. ii, 6-11).

Even scholars, who otherwise do not concede that the Christ of Paul is God, cannot help recognizing that, according to this passage in the Epistle to the Philippians, " Jesus Christ has existed from all eternity in the form of God in a godlike state of being,"[1] and that he is a " divine, pre-existing being,"[2] " a divine power,"[3] " a divine being."[4]

Having reached this high *ideal* point in his preaching of the Godhead of Jesus, Paul now goes on to the *explicit* confession that Christ is the *Son of God, Lord and God*.

Paul undoubtedly from the beginning conceived the naming of Christ as the *Son of God* in the metaphysical, not in the moral sense. For him the Son of God, Jesus Christ, is not at all a mere man, specially beloved of God, a child of adoption and grace. This is clear to every one who reflects that the apostle wrote and preached in the Greek language and for Greek readers. While the appellation Son of God, according to Semitic linguistic usage, could mean an adoptive son as well as a real, essential Son of God, the Greek connected with it only one—the latter—signification. Moreover, in the writings of Paul this conception of the title Son of God can be demonstrated particularly and in detail.

---

[1] H. v. Soden, *Der Brief des Apostels Paulus an die Philippäer,* 45, 2nd ed. (Tübingen, 1906) ; also Ad. Jülicher, *Die Religion Jesu, l.c.,* 86.
[2] Gustav Krüger, *Dreieinigkeit u. Gottmenschheit,* 86 (Tübingen, 1905).
[3] *id.*
[4] Weinel, *Paulus. Der Mensch und sein Werk,* 245 f. (1904) ; *cf.* Johannes Weiss, *Christus. Die Anfänge des Dogmas,* 27 ff. (Tübingen, 1909).

At the first glance, it strikes us as remarkable that the apostle uses the title Son of God in the most solemn passages of his Epistles and in the most sublime utterances about Jesus Christ. When he wishes to give prominence to the infinite love of the Father and the immeasurable humility and condescension of Jesus, which is involved in the incarnation (Rom. i, 1-3; viii, 3); when he wishes to prove triumphantly the sublimity and blessing of the Gospel of Jesus (Rom. i, 9; 2 Cor. i, 19); when he desires to extol in jubilant strains the certainty and divine blessedness of reconciliation and redemption through Jesus Christ (Rom. v, 10; viii, 1; Gal. iv, 6); when he wishes to reveal overwhelmingly the whole might and grandeur of the Saviour Jesus Christ (Rom. i, 4; Phil. ii, 9; Heb. i, 2); when he summons his readers to faith in Jesus Christ (Gal. ii, 16, 20); and to his invocation everywhere (1 Cor. i, 1-9); at the commencement and the conclusion of the Epistles, where he calls down upon the believers the grace and peace of God; in all these instances Paul calls Jesus Christ preferably the Son of God. And correspondingly he also calls God, in the most solemn moments and formulas of confession, " the God and Father of our Lord Jesus Christ " (Rom. xv, 6; 2 Cor. i, 3; xi, 31). All this points clearly to relations on the part of Jesus towards men and his Father in heaven entirely unlike those which could result from an adoption of the man Jesus, who is especially loved by God and is by him selected to be the Christ—that is, the Messiah.

If we inspect the subject still more closely, it can be easily seen how far removed Paul is from considering the title Son of God as equivalent to the liberal notion of a " Messianic child of God, through favour," or even to the orthodox notion of the Messiah—Christ. The expression Son of God in the writings of Paul nowhere passes for a synonym or expression for Christ. Rather does it describe the more intimate relations in which Christ, the Messiah, stands towards God the Father.

Now, it is true that in several passages the love of the Father to his Son is made especially prominent (Rom. v. 10; viii, 3, 32; Gal. iv, 4; Col. i, 15); but even H. Weinel frankly concedes that nevertheless " very often the words Son of God also stand, without any such sentiment, purely as a name for the divine nature of the Messiah."[1] And Johannes Weiss points it out as erroneous to explain the passages in which the love of God to the Son is strongly emphasized " in such a way that the sonship is only another expression for love, and that because God so loved this being he is the Son of God. On the contrary, because he is the Son, therefore God loves him. . . . Not a relation of affection, confidence or adoption, and not a figurative paraphrase of a moral or natural similarity

[1] Weinel, *Paulus,* 252.

of nature, but here [in the writings of Paul] 'Son' means what it is wont to mean—namely, descent from God. Not in the sense of a peculiar form of his human birth . . . his pre-existent Being has its origin already in God and certainly in a unique way."[1]

Still more frequently than with the appellation "Son of God," however, does Paul address the Saviour Jesus Christ as "Kyrios, Lord; our Kyrios, our Lord."

It is clear from the Pauline writings that the Christians of the time of the Apostle epitomized their faith in Jesus Christ most frequently in the name Kyrios, Lord. The confession of faith in Jesus, as the Lord, was considered as one of the holiest acts of a Christian. "No man can say 'the Lord Jesus' but by the Holy Ghost" (1 Cor. xii, 3). This confession is a necessary condition of salvation : "If thou confess with thy mouth the Lord Jesus, and believe in thy heart that God hath raised him up from the dead, thou shalt be saved" (Rom. x, 9). Hence this confession is to be on the lips of all : "That every tongue should confess that the Lord Jesus Christ is in the glory of God the Father" (Phil. ii, 11). From this it is evident that by the name "Lord" the Most High is meant.

In fact, we know that, for the contemporaries of St Paul and for his fellow-believers, Jewish and Greek as well, Kyrios was equivalent to Jehovah, Adonai, God.[2] Moreover, it can be positively proved that Paul regards the title "Kyrios" in the above sense and in no other.

Paul does not hesitate a moment by quotations from the Old Testament, unrestrictedly to apply to Christ the terms Kyrios, Jehovah and Adonai, which are there applied to God (1 Cor. i, 31). Jehovah, who led the Israelites out of Egypt and through the desert, is, according to the teaching of Paul, none other than Jesus Christ (1 Cor. x, 4). The word of the prophet Joel (ii, 32), "Every one that shall call upon the name of the Lord shall be saved," Paul refers directly to the Lord Jesus Christ (Rom. x, 13). In Ps. cii, 26, it is written of Christ the Lord : "Thou in the beginning, O Lord (Jehovah), didst found the earth, and the works of thy hands are the heavens" (Heb. i, 10). In short, Paul applies to Christ, the Kyrios, the Lord, what is said in the Old Testament of Jehovah.

If, therefore, the Kyrios-Christus is identical with the Old Testament Jehovah, then, according to the exposition of Paul, he is in the New Testament also on a par with God, is equal to him and identical with him.

We see this most clearly and, at the same time, most certainly from the *religious adoration and invocation* of the

---

[1] Johannes Weiss, *Christus,* 35.

[2] See the argument in the previous section, "The Divinity of Christ in the Early Church."

" Lord " by the Christians of the time of Paul. In contrast to the pagans, who honour many gods and lords, the Christians honour only one God, the Father, and one Lord Jesus Christ (1 Cor. viii, 5). Thereby is expressed " the divine position of Christ and the divine honour paid to him."[1]

This paying of divine honours to Christ as the " Lord " was, at the time when Paul wrote his great Epistles—that is, about twenty to twenty-five years after the death of Jesus— the distinguishing mark of all Christians and the bond which united them. Paul addressed the Christians at Corinth as " those called to be saints, with all that invoke the name of our Lord Jesus Christ in every place of theirs and ours " (1 Cor. i, 2).

Many things divided the Jewish Christians in Palestine, who still based their Christian piety more on the Mosaic Law, from the Gentile Christians in the Empire, to whom the Jewish forms of religious life were unknown. But all were united and harmonious in their worship of the Lord Jesus Christ. " There is no distinction of the Jew and the Greek; for the same is Lord over all, rich unto all that call upon him " (Rom. x, 12).

The invocation of the Lord Jesus was not made merely for the purpose of adoration and recognition of his glory, but also for the purpose of petition and prayer. It is the Lord Jesus from whom Paul and his fellow-Christians expect grace, help and mercy. The Apostle wishes and begs for the Churches grace and peace from God the Father and the Lord Jesus Christ (Rom. i, 7). By Jesus' personal mercy Christians are brought into the state of grace (1 Cor. vii, 25; 1 Tim. i, 12). All are saved through his mercy (2 Tim. i, 16, 18). The Lord Jesus Christ is the eternal High Priest, who, in consequence of his own experience in life, knows how to have, and really does have, sympathy with the believers in all their conditions and in all their need of help. For this reason everyone is to approach in prayer the throne of grace and compassion, and in prayer call upon God and the Lord and High Priest Jesus, enthroned with him, for pity and help (Heb. ii, 17 f.; iv, 15 f.; x, 19 ff.).

Paul commends himself also to the Lord Jesus in temporal and bodily afflictions and infirmities (2 Cor. xii, 7-9; Gal. iv, 13). He is conscious that all the vicissitudes and occurrences in nature and in human life depend upon the Lord Jesus and are his dispensations (1 Cor. iv, 19). This presupposes a faith that the " Lord " is the source of all grace, that he possesses divine knowledge and divine might, and that there is no sphere of human and worldly life, over which he has not supreme power. This faith in the universal participation of the Lord Jesus in the government of the

[1] Johannes Weiss, *Christus*, 26.

world Paul, in agreement with the early Church, sums up in
the formula, " sitting at the right hand of God " (Rom. viii,
34 ; Col. iii, 1 ; Heb. i, 3 ; viii, 4 ; x, 12 ; see Acts ii, 33 ; vii, 55).

So, then, Paul knows that he, even in regard to morals, is
thoroughly dependent on the Lord Jesus Christ, as the highest
and divine authority.   The word and command of the Lord
is the guiding line and binding rule for all moral thought and
action (1 Cor. vii, 10 ; xii, 25).   In every phase of his conduct
the Christian must seek the Lord : " Whether we live, we live
unto the Lord ; or whether we die, we die unto the Lord "
(Rom xiv, 8).

Professor Johannes Weiss, of Heidelberg—not an orthodox
theologian, but a very liberal thinker—epitomizes this whole
religious relation of Paul and of the Pauline Christian churches
in the following words : " For Paul Jesus himself is an object,
not only of faith, but of religious veneration.   For him who
begs for ' grace and peace ' not only ' from God our Father,'
but also ' from our Lord Jesus Christ,' Christ stands on an
equality with God ; . . . the practical piety of Paul and his
churches expects from him [Christ] the same as from God—
guidance, help, blessing.   It gives to him not only praise,
but also addresses prayers to him. . . .   Jesus is for the
Apostle not only a Mediator, Leader and Model, but also
absolutely the object of his religion."[1]

Now, this is self-evident, if Paul, in respect to the name
Kyrios, boasts of Christ that " God hath exalted him, and
hath given him a name which is above every name ; that in
the name of Jesus every knee should bow, of those that are in
heaven, on earth and under the earth, and that every tongue
should confess that the Lord Jesus Christ is in the glory of
God the Father " (Phil. ii, 9-11).   The name " Lord " is, therefore, the highest of all names, surpassing everything, towering above every name of created beings, and conferring the
right to the highest and unlimited veneration from all beings—
the name of Kyrios, Jehovah, Adonai, God.   Doubtless Paul
thinks here of passages such as Isaias xlii, 8 and xlv, 24,
and applies to Christ what God there says of himself : " I am
the Lord God [Κύριος ὁ θεός] : this is my name.   I will not
give my glory to another. . . .   Every knee shall be bowed
to me, and every tongue shall swear " (acknowledge God).
Even Johannes Weiss remarks, concerning this appreciation
of the name Lord in the Epistle to the Philippians : " Christ is
thereby exalted not only into a universal, divine sphere ; he
actually takes the place of Almighty God.   Here, therefore,
Kyrios can by no means have any less weighty meaning than
Theos."[2]

---

[1] Johannes Weiss, *Paulus und Jesus*, 3, 72 (Berlin, 1909).
[2] Johannes Weiss, *Christus*, 28 ; *cf.* J. Kögel, *Christus der Herr,*
Erläuterungen zu Philipp., ii, 5-11 (1908).

Other modern critics also recognize this fact. According to B. Weiss, the Christ of Paul is the Kyrios, who " at his second coming appears with divine omniscience, such as only the searcher of hearts can have " (1 Cor. iv, 5); who comes again with divine power to effect salvation at the last judgement, the administration of which itself already presupposes his divine rank (2 Cor. v, 10), in " contrast to all human mediation."[1] With the greatest clearness Eduard von Hartmann says : " The expression ' Lord ' is in the Pauline Gospel no mere polite form of address (as, for example, in Matt. vii, 21); but signifies the Lord of the universe (Rom. x, 12), to whom all things are subordinate, except him who has subordinated all things to him . . . (1 Cor. xv, 27). Paul uses the word Lord . . interchangeably for God and Christ."[2]

In order, however, to exclude the last doubt, Paul calls the Saviour and Son of God directly *God*. Thus we read in the Epistle to the Hebrews : " To the Son : thy throne, O God, is for ever and ever " (Heb. i, 8). In his letter to Titus he admonishes the believers, that they should show themselves wholly faithful, " that they may adorn the doctrine of God our Saviour in all things " (Titus ii, 10). Paul hopes for " the blessed hope and glory of the great God and our Saviour Jesus Christ, who gave himself for us, that he might redeem us from all iniquity " (Titus ii, 13). Jesus has been rejected by the Jews, " whose are the fathers, and of whom is Christ, according to the flesh, who is over all things, God blessed for ever " (Rom. ix, 5).

The opponents of the divinity of Christ feel, on the one hand, the full force of this confession of Paul, and, on the other, show their impotence against him. The God-Christ of the Epistle to the Hebrews, sharing the throne of the Father, is " no Pauline idea." Can that be proved? As if that idea were not repeatedly uttered by Paul in some other form ! In regard to the passage in the letter to Titus, Johannes Weiss remarks : " Yes, if we have the correct text, he [Paul] calls him absolutely our great God."[3] As if also there were a single trace of any other text in existence, which liberal critics like to call the " correct " one. Also one tries in vain to explain away from Christ the testimony of the Epistle to the Romans, that " God is over all things, blessed for ever " and to refer it to God the Father. Johannes Weiss is frank enough, in the face of such attempts, to affirm that the text " can refer only to Christ."[4] But he finds this confession of Paul " very remarkable . . . unthinkable." Therefore, it has been " rightly taken to be a violation of the text."[5] With the

[1] B. Weiss, *Lehrbuch der biblischen Theologie,* 285 f., 6th ed. (Berlin, (1895). [2] *Das Christentum des N. T.,* 178.
[3] *Christus,* 68. [4] *id.,* 29. [5] *id.*

right of the mailed fist of uncritical caprice, yes; for no one can appeal here to any other right.

That Paul calls the Saviour God is, however, in reality neither unthinkable nor remarkable, since he has used the equivalent expression *Kyrios* in countless instances, as referring to Christ, and, according to Johannes Weiss himself, " in the use of the name *Kyrios* lies the bridge to the last and highest utterances concerning Christ."[1]

On the other hand, it is also not remarkable that he does not call Jesus God more frequently. Later, too, and, indeed, down to the present time, Christ seldom receives from the Church the appellation " God," but almost universally that of the Son of God, or Lord. In the Apostolic period, however, the title " Lord " was just as exclusively, and even more so, the official and universally used title for Christ. It best expressed the divine position of Jesus towards the Father, as well as to the world and to mankind. Since of the full double title of God, "The Lord God" (Jehovah-Elohim, Κύριος ὁ θεὸς), the former was given to Christ and the second to the Father, the divinity and unity of both were clearly expressed. And, moreover, one thus avoided the danger of wounding the strictly monotheistic views of the Jewish Christians and also of giving to the Greek Christians any occasion for a polytheistic, or dualistic, interpretation of the Christian idea of God.

Thus can the christology of Paul be outlined in its main features. It really needs the courage of desperation, in face of this, still to maintain the almost stereotyped declaration of liberal criticism that the Christ of Paul is merely a preexistent, spiritual being, a celestial man, not essentially different from us men. The opponents of the divinity of Christ themselves cannot really believe it. Thus H. J. Holtzmann puts a great interrogation point before his Pauline celestial man by remarking that the Apostle knows " only of a man with a *divine element of life on earth*."[2] Pfleiderer examines the Pauline assertions about the " celestial man " Christ, and comes finally to the conclusion that " By them the essential foundation of his divine sonship in the super-theocratical metaphysical sense is positively laid."[3] It is all very well for Jülicher loudly to proclaim his conviction that the Christ of Paul " is a celestial man. . . . There remains the fact that Christ is the most exalted among the mediatory forces."[4] It must, however, also be conceded by him that " In the Epistle to the Philippians, chapter ii, the pre-existence of Christ Jesus in the form of God is unequivocally taught. Only when the time had come did he lay this aside and assume the form of a servant."[5] According to H. Weinel, the

[1] *id.*, 28.   [2] *Neutest. Theologie*, i, 94.
[3] *Das Urchristentum*, i, 227, 2nd ed.
[4] *Die Religion Jesu, l.c.*, 87.   [5] *l.c.*, 86.

celestial Son of God, Jesus, " stands, on the whole, still below
God "; he is "not himself God "; and yet Weinel must
acknowledge that the Christ of Paul is a "divine Being,[1]
and that we find the beginnings of this doctrine most clearly
in the writings of Paul."[2]

Paul Wernle concedes that Paul places his Christ on the
same footing with the God of Old Testament revelation.[3]
Then he continues: "What wonder, if now the fulness of
the Godhead dwells in him [Christ] corporeally? . . .   Son
of God, cross and resurrection are here [in the Pauline
Epistles] so interpreted that . . . the start is given for the
subsequent christological dogma."[4]   Arnold Meyer similarly
characterizes the Christ of Paul as " the celestial Son of God,
who did not belong to earthly humanity, but lived in glory
and divine resemblance to God.   The Son is the exact image
of the Father, and just as a Son—before all creatures—was
born in the likeness of his Father, and bears within himself
his entire fulness. . . .   At last, however, the Father allowed
him to descend to this earth in human form for the final
redemption of humanity and of the whole world. . . .   The
Christ of Paul becomes the God of this [Christian] people."[5]
And yet "this " (Pauline Son of God) "is not God " ![6]

The two radically liberal critics, Wilhelm Wrede and
Gustav Krüger, express themselves on this point more frankly
and with manly courage.   The former concedes at once that
Paul sees in Jesus, exactly as the orthodoxy of the Church
does, " a supermundane, divine being . . . an incarnate
divine being . . . a divine Christ."[7]   The latter acknowledges with equal frankness that "this Christ of Paul is a
divinely pre-existent being. . . .   It is true, the divine being,
of whom Paul speaks, is not yet called by him the ' Logos,'
but even though the word is lacking, the fact is nevertheless
there."[8]

This unavoidable conclusion forces itself even on the
rationalist Renan.   He says: " In the last writings of Paul
one finds a theory about Christ which presents him as a kind
of divine person; a theory which is thoroughly analogous to
that of the Logos, and which will subsequently take its final
form in the writings attributed to John. . . .   The earlier
and positively authentic writings of Paul contain the germ of
this new form of expression.   *Christ* and *God* are inter-
changed in them almost as synonymous beings; Christ exer-

---

[1] Weinel, *Paulus,* 250.   [2] *id.,* 243.
[3] *Die Anfänge unserer Religion,* 238, 2nd ed. (Tübingen, 1904).
[4] *id.,* 238, 243.
[5] *Wer hat das Christentum begründet, Jesus oder Paulus?* 25, 31, 95
(Tübingen, 1907).   [6] *id.,* 25.
[7] W. Wrede, *Paulus,* 84, 86, 87, 2nd ed. (Tübingen, 1907).
[8] Gustav Krüger, *Das Dogma von der Dreieinigkeit und Gottmenschheit in seiner geschichtlichen Entwicklung,* 86 (Tübingen, 1905).

cises divine functions; he is invoked as God; he is the connecting Mediator with God. . . . The veneration of Jesus . . . assumes in Paul the proportions of a real cult of adoration, which until then no Jew had shown to the son of a woman.''[1]

All this sufficiently proves that liberal critics do not accomplish the wonderful feat of eliminating the divinity of Christ from the theology of St Paul.[2]

2. Origin of the Pauline Christology.—Paul and Jesus.

It is precisely on this account that freethinking critics give themselves such unspeakable trouble to put the christological views of Paul in opposition to those of Christ and the first Christians, and to brand the former as the clumsy result of the most extravagant speculation and the morbid mentality of Paul. They construct an explanation of the origin and development of Paul's idea of Christ somewhat as follows :

Before his conversion on the way to Damascus, Paul was the most violent persecutor of Jesus, because he saw in him the exact opposite of what he venerated as the Messianic ideal. Saul was expecting the Messiah in the form of the apocalyptic heaven-sent man; and, basing his theory on the late-Jewish theory of angels, as well as on the Platonic-Alexandrian and old oriental mythology, he pictured to himself this heaven-sent man as a supermundane, spiritual being, as a pre-existing being intermediate between God and the world, as a world-framer, a second Adam, etc. With such a Christ the historical, earthly man Jesus had no similarity whatever. Hence he seemed to Saul the personification of the false Messiah.

Then suddenly occurred the great change near Damascus. In a fancied vision Saul thought that he beheld the hated Nazarene, Jesus, descending from on high in a celestial form of light, just like the Messianic celestial man, and that he spoke with him and declared that he was the Messiah so longed for by him. Saul regarded this inward experience as something actual, believed in it, and transferred his views of the Messianic celestial man and intermediate being to the historic Jesus.

Thus he became, after the event on the way to Damascus, the founder of an entirely new christology. This is not at all the continuation of the Christian line, which starts from Jesus and runs across the first Apostles and the original Church. On the contrary, it must be considered as a thorough transformation of that line. In contrast to the Gospel of Jesus

---

[1] Renan, L'Antéchrist, 76, 77, 79 (1873).
[2] See W. Beyschlag, Die Christologie des N. T., 176-256 (Berlin, 1866); Rich. Drescher, Das Leben Jesu bei Paulus (Giessen, 1900); F. Prat, La Théologie de St Paul (1908).

and the early Church, it is something new and secondary. Our principle must, therefore, be : " Away from Paul ! Back to the first disciples and to Jesus !"[1]

This, in bold outlines, is the development and explanation of the Pauline christology according to modern liberal criticism. In substance all these ideas are found already in the Tübingen rationalist, F. Christian Baur[2] and his pupil, Holsten,[3] and also in Hausrath.[4] Their successors rejected the hypothesis twice utterly, until it was completed in its present seemingly refined psychological form.

Its latest representatives are chiefly Brückner,[5] H. Weinel,[6] Paul Wernle,[7] Otto Pfleiderer,[8] Eduard von Hartmann,[9] and Wilhelm Wrede.[10] That the Damascus episode was only a vision, a religious experience, a revolution of the spiritual life, is supposed also by Clemen,[11] G. Krüger,[12] and Johannes Weiss.[13] The hypothesis of a vision passes now everywhere as a dogma of liberal investigation. From the standpoint of the " *modern conception* " the " experience " of Damascus *must* be a vision.

This psychological, or rather psychopathological conception, which is to make every supernatural influence of Christ on Paul unnecessary, and is to expose the Pauline christology as a figment of the imagination, is interesting as a drama, which could be entitled " The Tragedy (or, if preferred,

[1] This explanation of Pauline christology has been recently rejected on the Protestant side by Julius Kaftan in *Jesus und Paulus,* a friendly polemical pamphlet against the popular books on religious history by Bousset and Wrede (Tübingen, 1906); by Theodor Kaftan, *Der Mensch Jesus Christus, der einige Mittler zwischen Gott und den Menschen* (Berlin, 1908); Paul Feine, *Paulus als Theologe* (Berlin, 1906); *Theologie des N. T.,* 230-593 (Leipzig, 1910); Arnold Ruegg, *Der Apostel Paulus und sein Zeugnis von Jesus Christus* (Leipzig, 1906); McGiffert, *Was Jesus or Paul the Founder of Christianity? (Amer. Journal of Theology,* 1-20, 1909); W. Morgan, *The Jesus-Paul Controversy (Expositor,* xx, 9-12, 55-58). Of the above-named German investigators, however, only Feine expressly recognizes the divinity of Jesus in Paul's writings. Ruegg and Julius Kaftan know how to conceal their thoughts. Theodor Kaftan sees in Paul's Christ merely the human intermediary of salvation.

[2] *Paulus der Apostel Jesu Christi,* 2nd ed. (1866).

[3] *Evangelium des Paulus* (1880).

[4] *Der Apostel Paulus,* 126 ff. (1872); cf. *N. T. Zeitgeschichte,* ii. 442 f.

[5] *Die Entstehung der paulinischen Theologie* (1903).

[6] *Paulus. Der Mensch und sein Werk,* 243 ff. (Tübingen, 1904).

[7] *Die Anfänge unserer Religion,* 153-244, 2nd ed. (Tübingen, 1904): *Die paulinische Theologie.*

[8] *Die Entstehung des Christentums,* 111 f., 132 f., 143 ff. (München, 1905); *Das Urchristentum,* i, 226, 2nd ed.; *Religionsphilosophie,* 718 ff., 3rd ed.; *Entwicklung des Christentums,* 24 ff.

[9] *Das Christentum des N. T.,* 200 f., 2nd ed. (Sachsa im Harz, 1905).

[10] *Paulus,* 2nd ed. (Tübingen, 1907).

[11] *Die Grundgedanken der paulinischen Theologie,* 3 (1907).

[12] *Dreieinigkeit und Gottmenschheit,* 76-86 (Tübingen, 1905).

[13] *Christus; Die Anfänge des Dogmas,* 34-65 (Tübingen, 1909); *Paulus und Jesus,* 16 ff. (Berlin, 1909).

the Comedy) of Damascus, in three acts." Everything centres in the apparition of Damascus. *Previous to* that apparition, Paul is supposed to have already accumulated his christological ideas from Oriental, Greek and Jewish sources, and to have elaborated them inwardly. *On* the apparition at Damascus he transferred them, in consequence of a trick of the imagination, to Jesus of Nazareth; *after* the apparition, with even greater definiteness, in preaching and in speculative thought, he gave permanent form to the christology thus acquired, but with a total misapprehension of the doctrine of Jesus and the primitive, historical tradition concerning the real life of Jesus.

That is the Pauline show-piece of liberal criticism. Yet, after all, it is really only a *coup de théâtre,* and a very unreal one at that—only artificial work, not psychologically true art, and above all not history.

Paul is supposed to have derived part of his christological ideas from Oriental-Greek Gnosis and mythology, and to have found the rest of them in the Jewish theories about angels prevailing in his own land. But there cannot be any serious talk of a gnostic-mythological vein in the whole christology of Paul. Gnosis is nothing more nor less than the antipodes of the Pauline theology. The doctrine of Paul and oriental mythology likewise mutually exclude each other. Paul protests also in the most decided manner against every Gnostic and mythological addition, and, in fact, regards it as his life-work to contend most vigorously against the Gnostic and mythological view of the universe. It is to be hoped that this does not still need to be proved to anyone acquainted with the Epistles of Paul and the Acts of the Apostles.

The contrary opinions of modern critics seem to be nothing but interrogation points. For instance, Johannes Weiss accepts at once the " polytheistic, mythological character " of the Pauline christology, yet immediately adds the following astonishingly naïve confession : "*No one can prove* that it was precisely these Babylonian models, or whether it was Egyptian or Greek ones, which through innumerable agencies worked upon the Pauline idea."[1] Otto Pfleiderer writes similarly : "The conception of Christ, as a supermundane, spiritual being, as a celestial man exalted above the angels, and as a primeval Son of God . . . goes *perhaps* still farther back ; we cannot as yet assert anything *certain* about it, but *there is, nevertheless, ground for thinking* that already in Indian legend the celestial spiritual being, which appears in Buddha and other figures of redeemers, is designated as ' the great man,' and that in certain Jewish-Christian Gnostics the Redeemer-Spirit, which appeared in Jesus, is the same which was first incorporated in Adam. And with this there

---

[1] Johannes Weiss, *Christus,* 36.

was *perhaps* connected also the spiritual ideal man, whom Philo found taught in the first chapter of Genesis."[1]

More thoughtful investigators substitute for this repeated " perhaps " a categorical " no." A. Meyer acknowledges that Paul opposes his Christ, full of love and seriousness, to all other Gnostic powers.[2] Even the Logos doctrine of Philo, which would first of all have to be thought of, is, according to Paul Wernle, " too remote to come into consideration."[3] Bernhard Weiss[4] considers " the transference of any contemporary philosophical problem to Christ as undemonstrable," while H. J. Holtzmann smiles at the metamorphoses which Paul has already had to go through in modern criticism. " First, the origins of his ideas have been purely Jewish; then they became largely Greek; later on rather ' hellenistic'; soon again like those of the Old Testament. Now he forms an unswerving continuation of the life-work of Jesus, and now he makes a new start, which essentially ignores that life-work."[5] Paul Feine is finally no doubt right when he rejects the derivation of Paul's Christ from Greek, Hellenic and old Oriental sources with the remark : " It cannot be regarded as a sign of sound judgement if the attempt is made over and over again in critical theology to construct the Pauline christology out of that origin."[6]

The only real question is, whether the Apostle took his idea of Christ from the Jewish Apocalypse. If Paul would pourtray his Christ merely as an apocalyptic " celestial man," as our opponents allow, then we could at least talk seriously about it. But, as we have seen, the figure of Christ is, in the writings of Paul, thoroughly divine. The Jewish Apocalypse, however, does not know of any such figure. But also, quite apart from the divinity of the Messiah, Paul's teaching about Christ stands in most violent opposition to the apocalyptic theory of the Messianic celestial man. Not only orthodox theologians but the whole liberal school must concede that the chief characteristics of Paul's doctrine of the Messiah were the doctrine of grace and redemption, the love of Jesus for mankind, and his expiatory death for the sins of the world. There is not a single genuinely liberal critic who has not contested the Pauline christology for the very reason that it makes this doctrine of atonement, grace and redemption the central point of the Messiahship.

But this fundamental feature of Paul's doctrine of the Messiah is to the apocalyptic idea of the Messiah what fire is to water. It is, therefore, a flagrant contradiction of facts

[1] *Die Entstehung des Christentums,* 144 f. (München, 1905).
[2] *l.c.,* 19.   [3] *l.c.,* 239.
[4] *Die Religion des N. T.,* 140, 2nd ed. (Stuttgart und Berlin, 1908).
[5] H. J. Holtzmann, *Das messianische Bewusstsein Jesu,* iii (Tübingen, 1907).
[6] *Paulus als Theologe,* 32 (Gr.-Lichterfelde-Berlin, 1906).

when the liberal theologians designate the Christ of Paul as
an apocalyptic celestial man, and derive him from the Jewish
Apocalypse. Johannes Weiss now sets this forth with great
perspicacity, after surveying all the latest Pauline investigation. He writes : " Whence has Paul derived this portrait of
Christ? From Jewish tradition? Where in the Apocalypse
(of the Jews) is it written that the ' King-Messiah,' ' the Son
of Man,' the ' Judge ' is at the same time the incarnation of
the love and grace of God? The theory that Paul, having
come to faith in the Messiahship of Jesus, has transferred to
him only the marks of the apocalyptic Messiah, here breaks
down. He could not have taken this chief characteristic of
the portrait of Christ from Judaism ; here his own historical
experience has enlarged and transformed his Jewish portrait
of the Messiah in a most decided way."[1]

Moreover, Paul himself asserts expressly that he neither
took his portraiture of Christ from the Jewish Apocalypse,
nor had known it previously, from any other source whatever,
before the apparition on the road to Damascus. In the Acts
of the Apostles, as well as in his Epistles, his idea of Christ
appears to the persecutor as something entirely new, unexpected and direct. Even Wrede must confess that " Paul
cannot have been won over already through instruction beforehand, so that the vision would become merely a secondary
affair. He expressly denied human teaching to have been a
foundation of his faith, and, in any case, the apparition must
have had for him the character of something sudden and overpowering.[2]

But let us suppose that Saul, at the time when he was
travelling on the mountain road to Damascus, had taken with
him his portrait of Christ already completed. Can what
occurred near Damascus be explained thereby in a natural,
psychological manner? Can any explanation of the fact be
given that Saul now, suddenly, in consequence of self-suggestion and hallucination (for that is what our opponents assert),
transferred his ideal of Christ to Jesus, and believed it to be
incorporated in the hated Nazarene whom he was persecuting
(I Cor. xix, 9; Acts ix, 1; xxii, 3; xxvi, 9)? Evidently just
the opposite. Hallucination only strengthens the impressions
which a man has within him in a normal state. It would have
caused the hate of the Pharisee Saul to have been turned into
a veritable fury against Jesus and his claims to be the Messiah
and the Son of God. That would have been the only possible
result of the " vision " of Damascus. If Paul, on the contrary, in consequence of that vision, proclaims Jesus as the
Messiah, the Lord and God, it is not psychologically explicable; it is not natural, but either contrary to nature or super-

---

[1] Johannes Weiss, *Paulus und Jesus,* 51, 14.
[2] Wrede, *Paulus,* 10.

natural.[1] But if the conversion of Saul to faith in Christ cannot possibly be designated as a psychological result of the Damascus episode, it is thereby also proven that it cannot be merely a matter of a " vision " or of a subjective, imaginary apparition, or of " an inward view, an hallucination . . . a reflection of the soul, externalized, an objectifying of its own consciousness."[2]

For such a vision there is wanting all real presupposition. The liberal critics, it is true, are able to describe with great enthusiasm and almost statistical exactness how this vision occurred.   The christological problem, and the question whether Jesus of Nazareth was not, after all, the expected Messiah and Son of God, " might, we may suppose, have moved the spirit of Paul on the way to Damascus; doubt as to the right of his previous conduct and as to the truth of his former faith, pierced his heart like a fiery dart, and put his soul and body into a state of the most fearful excitement. If we add to this the nearness of Damascus, forcing him to make a speedy decision, and the lonely silence and scorching heat of the desert, we shall be justified in the conclusion, that in such circumstances the occurrence of a visionary experience was not at all out of the range of other analogous experiences."[3] " It was, indeed, no wonder that a notorious visionary and epileptic, in such conflicts of the soul, during a fever in the desert (which was connected with an inflammation of the eyes and perhaps an inflammation of the brain), was visited by an apparition of the Master of the Church which he was persecuting, as by an objective presentation of the doubts of his own conscience."[4] " All this is connected with the condition of nerves and brain, which caused him at times to have convulsions and to see visions. . . . In connection with this, he felt nervous twitchings, which he interpreted as blows from a messenger of Satan. When, therefore, he fell prostrate near Damascus, saw a light, heard Christ speak, and then was blind for some days, the analogy of experience demands that we here also think of a vision, in which a profound psychical process, which has reached the highest tension, is relaxed."[5]

These are nothing but phrases, which flatly contradict the truth, as well as the text of the New Testament authorities. Instead of being tormented by doubts and qualms of conscience about his own conduct, and about the possible truth of the utterances of Jesus, " Saul was breathing out threatenings and slaughter against the disciples of the Lord," when

---

[1] *Cf.* E. Moske, *Die Bekehrung des heil. Paulus, eine exegetisch-kritische Untersuchung* (Münster, 1907).
[2] Pfleiderer, *Die Entstehung des Christentums,* 111 f.
[3] Pfleiderer, *l.c.,* 138.
[4] Ed. von Hartmann, *Das Christentum des N. T.,* 201.
[5] A. Meyer, *Wer hat das Christentum begründet?* 36, 69 f.; *Die Auferstehung Christi,* 295-298 (Tübingen, 1905).

he set out for Damascus (Acts ix, 1). According to his own confession, he was actually foaming with a blind rage to persecute Jesus of Nazareth even at the moment when the apparition near Damascus occurred (Acts ix, 4; xxii, 4-8; xxvi, 14).

The "scorching heat of the desert" and the "desert-fever with inflammation of the eyes and brain" exist only in the heads of our critics, as also the desert itself.[1]

Moreover, whoever makes Paul a "notorious visionary and epileptic," as Hartmann, the philosopher of the unconscious, does; or a "sufferer from a disease of the nerves and brain," as A. Meyer supposes; or, finally, with the novelist, Gustav Frenssen, and the theologian and poet, Hausrath, makes him a "thoroughly ill man, tormented by serious nervous and mental disorders," and a "sentimental, even epileptic" subject of hysteria, will be branded as false by the work and writings of the great Apostle[2] as well as by expert medical opinion.[3]

It is true, Paul has had visions, but not in the sense of the vagaries of an unbalanced mind, as our opponents imagine them, but in the sense of supernatural "visions and revelations of the Lord," as Paul himself testifies (2 Cor. xii, 1), and such as often occurred in the first Christian Church with its wealth in gifts of grace.

Moreover, from such "visions," which he continually recognizes and designates precisely as such,[4] he wishes to keep the incident of Damascus perfectly distinct. This is for him a real, objective "appearance" of Jesus. It was a personal revelation of Christ, as real as the appearances of the risen Lord, of which Peter, James, the Twelve and five hundred disciples were witnesses (1 Cor. xv, 5-9). Jesus revealed himself to him to see and to hear (Acts ix, 17, 27; xxii, 14; xxvi, 16). During his entire life Paul never doubted that he had seen the living Christ. To everyone he put the challenging question : "Have I not seen the Lord?" (1 Cor. ix, 1). Supported by this conviction, he ranks himself unhesitatingly

---

[1] "For many hours south of Damascus there is no such desert at all. The region is, in fact, very well watered and fruitful, and was formerly much more so. Also that the simoon or sirocco has proved especially favourable to the creation of visions seems to me hardly probable in this locality."—Chr. E. Luthardt, *Allg. Ev.-Luth. Kirchenzeitung,* 396 (1906).

[2] "Are these writings the work of a fool, or a deceiver, or an epileptic affected by sunstroke, or a crazy enthusiast? Is such achievement, as his, psychologically comprehensible, as coming from such an origin?"—F. Ballard, König's translation, *Die Wunder des Unglaubens,* 194 (Gr.-Lichterfelde-Berlin, 1903).

[3] See the opinion of Dr. Blümke, in Rüegg, *Der Apostel Paulus und sein Zeugnis von Jesus Christus,* 108; Jülicher, *Einleitung in das N. T.,* 26 ff.; Simon Weber, *Die Gottheit Jesu u. die paulinschen Briefe,* in *Jesus Christus, Vorträge in Freiburg im B.,* 69 ff. (1908).

[4] Acts x, 9; xi, 5; xii, 7; xvi, 9; xviii, 9; xxii, 17; 2 Cor. xii, 1.

with the old Apostles, and is recognized by all as a disciple
and witness for Jesus of equal rights with them. Even hostile
criticism cannot invalidate this. " Paul certainly understands
by the revelation, which he had received, not merely a gradual
enlightenment of his way of thinking and feeling. For him
it is a matter of the wonderful procedure of a certain moment,
when he saw the Lord in radiant glory—in this the allusions
in his Epistles agree with the Acts of the Apostles."[1]

Not only that. We have, moreover, the incontrovertible
evidence that Paul did not deceive himself when he attributed
to the Damascus apparition objective reality. A proof of
this is the fact that the fellow-travellers of Saul were also
involved in the apparition; that "the light from heaven shone
also around his companions, a light which surpassed the
splendour of the sun "; and that under the powerful impression of the apparition all were thrown to the ground.[2] A
proof of the reality of the apparition is the blindness of Saul
in consequence of the brilliance, quite unbearable for his
physical powers of vision (Acts ix, 8); and a proof of the
reality of the appearance of Christ is finally the inward,
spiritual illumination and transformation, the moral and
religious new-creation of Paul, and his indestructible consciousness that he must thereafter serve Christ with body
and life, with all his senses and powers, and with the dedication to him of his entire being.

All this proves, as Bernhard Weiss acknowledges, that the
appearance of Jesus Christ to Paul " cannot be attributed to
a psychologically explicable vision."[3] Unless liberal criticism is willing to give up every sort of explanation, then
it must, willingly or unwillingly, deign to confess that an
actual, obvious apparition was vouchsafed to Saul near
Damascus, in which he saw with his own physical eyes the
risen and glorified Saviour, heard with his own physical ears
his voice, and received a corresponding inward revelation.

*Now, from this apparition and revelation—that is, from
instruction given by Jesus himself*—Paul, first of all, drew
the material for his Gospel. " The Gospel which was preached
by me is not according to man. For neither did I receive
it of man, nor did I learn it but by the revelation of Jesus

---

[1] A. Meyer, *Wer hat das Christentum begründet?* 35.

[2] Acts ix, 7; xxvi, 13. The unessential differences in the three reports
—Acts ix, 7; xxii, 9; and xxvi, 14—are explained without difficulty.
See the explanations of Joseph Knabenbauer, *Commentaria in Actus
Apost.,* 161 ff. (1899); F. X. Pölzl, *Der Weltapostel Paulus,* 38, note 1
(Regensburg, 1905); Ruegg, *Der Apostel Paulus,* 53; Anton Seitz, *Das
Evangelium vom Gottessohn,* 496, note 6 (Freiburg, 1908). Only one
who, with Baur, Wendt, Pfleiderer and other critics, wishes to make
it entirely plausible " that the details of this threefold narrative can
make no claim to exact historicity," can find a contradiction here.
Pfleiderer, *Die Entstehung des Christentums,* 132.

[3] *Lehrbuch der biblischen Theologie,* 203 f.

I.

Christ " (Gal. i, 11, 12). And the essential point of this revelation was again the christology, the mystery of the Person of Jesus Christ, as the Apostle all his life after the catastrophe of Damascus preached it. "When it pleased him, who separated me from my mother's womb and called me by his grace, to reveal his Son in me, that I might preach him among the Gentiles " (Gal. i, 15, 16). That is the first and most important source of the Pauline christology.

Of course, there can be no thought of Paul's having learned by that experience the whole Gospel and the whole historical life of Jesus. But Jesus drew him thereby into a vital association with his life, allowed him to have a wonderfully profound insight into his teachings, and convinced him of his Messiahship and real divine sonship. The evangelical and christological knowledge of Paul was supplemented and in all respects completed by the fact that he penetrated into the life and doctrines of the Master by the aid of *the original disciples, the original Church and the earliest traditions.* That was Paul's second way of approaching Christ.

The liberal critics bar this way. Although their "psychological" explanation of the Pauline christology before and at Damascus has proved itself an absurdity, they nevertheless wish to play out the third act of the drama. After the event at Damascus, Paul, it is claimed, further developed and elaborated his christology in a fantastic manner, without any regard to the real life of Jesus and to the historical tradition of it in the early Church, and did so in accordance with the imaginary vision on the road to Damascus, and on the ground of his preconceived ideas of the Messiah, which he had already brought with him to Damascus. His conversion " drew him away from all such connections, and also out of any connection with the first Apostles, as men (what they once were is, to him, a matter of indifference), and, indeed, from any connection with the earthly Jesus, who is also crucified, after the flesh, and is for him no more there. Paul lives only with the Christ whom he had come to know "[1]—that is, whom he imagined he had seen. "Thereby every human tradition is rejected, even that transmitted by the first Apostles. . . . Paul will learn nothing, but wishes rather to show and represent what he has done independently."[2] Paul has "woven into his Christian way of thinking, together with his own experience, current opinions of his own time, and also pagan, Greek, Oriental or Jewish-Gnostic traditions. . . . If Paul, as we suppose, grew up with such views from the time of his youth, he must, of course, have absorbed them, and cannot possibly have been subsequently aware whence he had derived them."[3] For the very reason that Paul uncon-

[1] A. Meyer, *Wer hat das Christentum begründet?* 72.
[2] id., 32. [3] id., 33.

sciously applied to Christ his own and others' non-christian ideas, and imagined that he had received everything, his whole, complete portrait of Christ "through the revelation of God," it can be finally again asserted that "it was not Paul who created his Christ, but that his Christ (the imagined one of his experience) laid hold of *him*, overpowered him, and became too strong for him. . . . Hence we stand before a mystery in religion, which mocks at every explanation."[1] That is the end of the "psychological explanation" of the Pauline christology. No liberal critic can give any other than Meyer has given. At most, they honour the "second founder of Christianity" with additional designations, such as "the involuntary product of rabbinical speculation and dialectics,"[2] a man with "the most extravagant speculations,"[3] a "theological premature birth,"[4] "a brother of the visionaries,"[5] "a man who had become a fool through boasting . . ." of "arrogant blindness . . . and proud self-sufficiency," which "scorned to learn doctrines from the lips of the personal disciples of the Master, before he preached them."[6]

That with such invectives the "mystery that mocks at every explanation" is not psychologically explained is patent to everyone. Moreover, the mere attempt to account psychologically for the final christology, as Paul presents it immediately after his conversion, proves itself immediately to be unpsychological. Only in so far as it could be established that Paul before the incident at Damascus carried about with him his conception of Christ already complete, and that he at Damascus simply transferred these ideas of Christ to Jesus of Nazareth of his own accord and independently, could the later Pauline christology be designated as a psychological product and psychological development of his former life. It has, however, been proved that this supposition is not correct. Whoever, in spite of that, builds up a theory upon it is building a castle in the air.

But also, quite apart from the incorrectness of our opponents' assumptions, the christology of Paul, after the Damas-

---

[1] Meyer, 33.

[2] Pfleiderer, *Die Entstehung des Christentums,* 141, 167.

[3] Wernle, *Die Anfänge unserer Religion,* 239, 2nd ed.

[4] Richard E. Funcke, *Die historischen Grundlagen des Christentums,* 244 (Leipzig, 1904).   [5] Wrede, *Paulus,* 15.

[6] Eduard von Hartmann, *Das Christentum des N. T.,* 171. Where it is possible, the hateful representation of Hartmann is surpassed by Fried. W. Nietzsche, *Morgenröthe,* 64-68, 182 (1881). The charge of Hartmann and A. Meyer, *Wer hat das Christentum begründet?* 32, that Paul, after his conversion, did not wish to go even once to Jerusalem to let himself be instructed, is contradicted by Ad. Jülicher with the remark : "He would have returned at once from Damascus to Jerusalem, but he knew that his former companions would quickly dispose of him if he surrendered himself to them."—*Paulus und Jesus,* 55.

cus episode, cannot be "psychologically" interpreted in the above sense unless we come into contradiction with the incontrovertible dates and facts of the Acts of the Apostles and the Pauline Epistles themselves. According to them, the great man by no means reasoned out and elaborated his christology merely from his experience at Damascus—whether this be regarded as a subjective vision of Paul or as an objective appearance of Christ—and with complete disregard of the real, historical life of Jesus and the tradition of the original Church, in which the historical Jesus continued to live.

Nothing is more untrue than the assumption that the historical life of the Saviour was a matter of indifference to Paul. True, it is hard to prove to what degree Paul in his missionary preaching referred to single events and single utterances in the life of Jesus. Certainly a mission to the Gentiles could not be carried on without the communication of abundant material from the life of Jesus for purposes of narration.[1] The Epistles of Paul do not contain much of it, for the precise reason that the historical life of Jesus was already known to the Churches to which those letters were addressed, and, again, because Paul did not wish to furnish in them historical details, but to express his views about the problems of Christian life. Nevertheless, there is sufficient evidence from the Pauline writings that Christ was the chief object of Paul's preaching—in fact, the person and teaching of Christ in just that historical conception which Jesus himself had given to it.[2] Paul declares that he has admonished the Church at Ephesus to remember "the words of the Lord" (Acts xx, 24, 35). "The word of Christ" is to be used in the Churches abundantly, and to be freshly brought to mind in the most varied forms of teaching and spiritual hymnology (Col. iii, 16). All instruction is to be joined to the "sound words of our Lord Jesus Christ" (1 Tim. vi, 3). In any case, Paul is conscious that his Gospel of Christ is identical with the Gospel which Jesus himself preached (Rom. xvi, 25). He expressly designates all preaching and all faith which do not agree with the historical, real truth of the life of Jesus as vain imaginings and as false witness against God (1 Cor. xv, 12-17). The highest guiding-star of his faith and his doctrine is "other foundation no man can lay, but that which is laid, which is Christ Jesus" (1 Cor. iii, 11)—that is, the historical Jesus.

As evidence for the charge that Paul placed no value on the historical Jesus appeal is made[3] to the confession : "Hence-

---

[1] Proofs in Johannes Weiss's *Das älteste Evangelium*, 33-39 (Göttingen, 1903).
[2] For the thorough proof of this, see Zahn, *Einleitung in das N. T.*, ii, 164-166 (Leipzig, 1899). 　　　[3] Weinel, *Paulus*, 244.

forth we know no man according to the flesh. And if we have known Christ (the Messiah) according to the flesh, but now we know him so no longer " (2 Cor. v, 16). But these words do not at all contain a depreciation between the so-called historic Jesus according to the flesh and the spiritual and celestial Christ. From the whole Pauline theology, as well as from the immediate context of this passage (see 2 Cor. v, 14, 15, 17), the antithesis of " flesh and spirit " is equivalent to Judaism and Christianity—that is, Paul's former Jewish, and now Christian, views of the Messiah. " As Paul also elsewhere reckons Judaism as a part of the category of the flesh, and declares it to be conquered and destroyed by Christianity, as the religion of the Spirit, so he passes judgement on the ideas of the Messiah, which he formerly had, whether they may have been really rather apocalyptic in general, or pharisaical in particular."[1] Thus, then, Paul does not express himself in the second Epistle to the Corinthians in favour of, but in the most decisive way against, the view of liberal criticism. He had not himself created his Christ by attributing to Jesus inveterate Jewish ideas of the Messiah, but his faith in Christ is genuine and early Christian, and rests on the real, historical life and work of Jesus himself. Jülicher also gives his opinion as follows : " An Apostle of Jesus Christ, who should not have wished to know anything of the earthly life of the Messiah, who, for the sake of his dogma, should have passed over contemptuously, as ' weakness of the flesh,' all that had become revealed through the submissive figure of the Son of God, is a creation of the modern habit of twisting conclusions, but not the Paul of history. The friendly co-operation of Paul with other Evangelists— for example, Barnabas and Mark—who certainly did not practise any such wonderful seclusion, excludes the possibility that the Gospel history remained essentially unknown to Paul."[2]

It can, then, also be actually proved from the Pauline writings[3] that *the Apostle to the Gentiles possessed a thorough and definite knowledge of the life of Jesus ;* that the historical person of the Saviour was always before his eyes; and that therefore his conviction and faith in regard to the divinity rested not only on the revelation of the glorified Jesus, which had come to him near Damascus, but also on the conduct of Jesus when on earth.

The assertion that " the Pauline theology was something almost wholly separate from the historical life and doctrines of

[1] Feine, *Paulus als Theologe,* 39.
[2] Jülicher, *Paulus und Jesus,* 55.
[3] See proofs in Feine, 45-50; Ruegg, 59; and especially in Titius, *Die neutest. Lehre von der Seligkeit,* ii, 12 ff.; Kölbing, *Die geistige Einwirkung der Person Jesu auf Paulus,* 111 f. (Göttingen, 1906); Johannes Weiss, *Das älteste Evangelium,* 33 ff. ; *Paulus und Jesus,* 10 ff.

Jesus,"[1] yes, that it was in error about the whole humanity of Christ,[2] stands in direct contradiction to this theology and to all the facts of Pauline preaching. Even Johannes Weiss pronounces untenable the statement " that Paul really had relations only with the celestial Christ, and, on the other hand, had known practically nothing of the earthly Jesus, who, in any case, played no part in his religious consciousness."[3]

Precisely, H. Weinel,[4] who has uttered literally this statement prohibited by Weiss, has finally again to avow that Paul has " preserved for us the portrait of Jesus sharp and clear. . . . We must not think that Paul knew nothing of Jesus. On the contrary, his Epistles contain so much of Jesus that he, even in the controversy which has just broken out again about the historical truth of the person of Jesus, is and remains the best and surest witness, and we must declare all his Epistles to be unauthentic if we would put aside his testimony. . . . And, however much he is occupied religiously with the exalted and living Christ, just as clearly do we find everywhere traces of his acquaintance with the narratives about Jesus as they were subsequently incorporated firmly in our Gospels."[5]

Moreover, the mere fact that shortly before and after the death of St Paul, and in the Churches founded by Paul in his missionary tours, the Gospels were written on the basis of the life of Jesus, up to that time related and preserved by oral teaching, proves exactly the whole absurdity of our opponents' hypothesis, which denies to Paul a knowledge of the history of his Master. How? The old Churches, in which Paul had preached, and which he had himself for the most part founded, possessed such an abundant knowledge of the words, deeds and suffering of the Lord that the synoptical Gospels could be composed out of it, and Paul, the head and educator of these Churches, was without this knowledge? To put the question is enough to answer it. This consideration alone would necessarily cause the final elimination from Pauline research of the liberal legend of Christ as merely an apocalyptic celestial man. " The thesis that the faith of Paul is connected by no living bond with the historical personality of Jesus will hardly disturb the theology of the future."[6]

In fact, Paul's acquaintance with the life of Jesus is so significant that sometimes the assertion has been made that

---

[1] Pfleiderer, *Entstehung des Christentums*, 185.

[2] Wrede, *Paulus,* 55. [3] Weiss, *Christus,* 32 f., 71.

[4] " In fact, Jesus hardly played any part for him (Paul) as a human being."—Weinel, *Paulus,* 244.

[5] Weinel, *l.c.,* 246, 249. Similarly, Weizsäcker, *Das apostolische Zeitalter*, 118, 3rd ed. : " Paul has doubtless known the Gospel tradition about Jesus. . . . That he knows the utterances of Jesus is proved by his citations. He uses them for the highest decisions in questions of life and faith." [6] Johannes Weiss, *Paulus und Jesus,* 72.

Paul derived it from a Gospel already put into written form. That is certainly not the case, and not a single tenable argument for such a supposition can be brought forward, although the Gospel of Matthew in Hebrew surely already existed. Also the view that the Logia—the *Discourses*—were already accessible at the time of the Apostle in the Greek Churches, and that Paul (as Resch tries to prove) is at every step dependent on them, is questionable. Paul himself may, however, be looked upon in a certain sense as the first Greek Evangelist. Only from twenty to twenty-five years after the death of the Master he has described his life in its most important outlines.

The source, however, from which he drew his knowledge was not, as our opponents assert, his own religious experience—Christ, psychologically learned by Paul—but *the tradition of the first disciples and the original Church.*

It is not merely an oversight, it is a gross and inexcusable error, when Professor Arnold Meyer writes: "Paul rejected all human tradition, even that of the first Apostles."[1] As if the history and the Epistles of Paul did not declare the very opposite of this! When Paul wishes to prove the reliability of his historical statements about Jesus, he appeals to the Twelve and to the hundreds of witnesses and hearers still living in the original Church (1 Cor. xv, 5-7). The historical knowledge of the separate facts concerning Jesus—events, circumstances, in short, all "the things that are of Jesus"[2] (Acts xviii, 25; xxiii, 11; xxviii, 31)—Paul received, like the Corinthians, through the narrations of others who, before him, had become acquainted with them (1 Cor. xv, 1-3).

Paul knew these bearers of the original tradition about Jesus from a most intimate association of many years. First, he gained exact information about Jesus during three years' residence in Damascus, from that ancient Church, closely connected with the mother Church in Jerusalem (Acts ix, 19-25). Then he remained a short time with Peter and James and the brethren at Jerusalem (Acts ix, 26-30; Gal. i, 18-20). Then he spent six or seven years more in the midst of the Church at Antioch, whose foundation the fugitives from the mother Church in Jerusalem had laid (Acts xi, 25-30; xiii, 1-3). On his missionary journeys also he was accompanied by the oldest members of the mother Church and was aided in his preaching by Barnabas, Mark and Silas. Finally, in order not to err in his Gospel concerning Jesus, he went specially a second time to Jerusalem to the first disciples (Gal. ii, 1 and following), in regard to whom he himself says:

[1] Meyer, *Wer hat das Christentum begründet, Jesus oder Paulus?* 32.
[2] This expression, τὰ περὶ τοῦ Ἰησοῦ, according to the linguistic usage of Paul and Luke, as well as grammatically, must be understood as the personal incidents in Jesus' life. See Eph. vi, 22; Col. iv, 8, etc.

" I communicated to them the Gospel which I preach among the Gentiles; but apart to them who seemed to be something, lest perhaps I should run, or had run in vain " (Gal. ii, 2).

By means of this chain of witnesses Paul stands so positively in connection with Jesus, his life and his teaching, that he can affirm that he had received his Gospel, as it were, from the Saviour himself : " I have received of the Lord, that which also I delivered unto you " (1 Cor. xi, 23).[1]

What is left, then, of the preposterous assumption that Paul has, on his own initiative, or, what is the same thing, according to his own subjective " experience," created a Christ, who stands in contradiction with the real person and history of Jesus and with the most ancient tradition? On the contrary, Paul proclaims with the whole force of his conviction that he preaches the divine man Jesus Christ precisely as the Saviour himself has revealed himself, and as the first disciples and the whole original Church preached him and believed in him. He knows himself to be in the full possession of the true portrait of Christ; he relies on the essential identity of his own revelation of Christ with that of the older Apostles and with that of Jesus, and even dares to excommunicate everyone, though he were an angel from heaven, who should preach another Gospel than that given by himself and by tradition (Gal. i, 8, 9). He verifies continually his preaching of Christ by that of the first Apostles, and lets this go so far as to have the correctness of his teaching confirmed by the assembly of the Apostles at Jerusalem, in order not to err himself or to lead others into error. It is abundantly proved from the old Christian sources that nowhere in the original Church—including the Jewish-Christian heterodox teachers, the enemies of Paul—was there heard a difference of opinion, or even a tiny discord, in regard to the way in which the person of Jesus was pourtrayed.

And in the face of all that, are we to suppose that Paul has, consciously or unconsciously, replaced the real, historical Jesus by a fantastic, subjectively-experienced—that is, an imagined—figure of Christ, separated it from all human relations, and clothed it with celestial dignity and a divine nature? And, furthermore, that he, the novice, completed this swindle already in the year of Jesus' death, and then continuously all his life repeated it in word and writing, without contradiction, but, on the contrary, with the universal approval of the first Apostles and the whole early Church, which itself must thus have committed this blasphemous deception with him, and allowed itself to be converted to the distorted Pauline portrait of Jesus? Everyone must see the incorrectness, let

---

[1] By this is meant—as Th. Zahn proves, *Einleitung,* ii, 171—not a personal revelation made to Paul—whether that of Damascus, or a later one—but the indirect revelation by means of tradition.

us say, the whole monstrous character of such a critical fabrication of history.

Paul, therefore, in his christology is at one with the immediate Church of the disciples of Jesus.[1] All the assertions that Paulinism grew outside of the latter, on Hellenic soil and out of a Greek-mythological sphere of thought, are excluded by Adolf Jülicher in the words : " No, the Christianity of Paul also has grown on the soil of the original Church at Jerusalem, and if Paul did once criticize the person of Peter, he never criticized Peter's Gospel. In every way he declares (1 Cor. xv, 11) that there exists no difference between the Gospel of Paul and that of the older Apostles ; at most there can be detected in his words (verse 8) a regret that they had come into possession of the complete revelation so much sooner than he."[2]

If anyone wishes to speak of a difference between Paul and the older Apostles, it can be only a formal one : " Paul elaborates more sharply what was already there in reality."[3] The Apostle to the Gentiles, it is true, pours the same thoughts that we find in the old disciples into other forms, and thinks them out to a conclusion, as was natural to his lofty mind and to the new world in the midst of which he proclaimed his Gospel. But he created no new Gospel and no new Christ. Even decided enemies of the divinity of Jesus are convinced of this. Julius Kaftan writes : " I sum up my judgement thus, that through Paul, and precisely through him and no one else, the Gospel of Jesus in primitive Christianity was preserved, and thus became a power that has changed the history of the world."[4] According to Weinel, Paul " has always preserved the connection with the first Apostles, and even in a difficult hour of his life resisted the temptation finally to tear away his Churches from the Jerusalem tradition and thereby from (the historic) Jesus."[5] Yes, the Jena critic rejects the hypothesis of a Pauline transformation of the earthly Jesus into a celestial-divine Christ so forcibly that he falls into the opposite extreme, and ascribes to Paul the credit for the fact " that the celestial Jesus has not entirely concealed the human Jesus."[6]

Accordingly, just as little as there exists any essential difference between the christology of Paul and the original Church, just so little is there any such difference between *Paul and Jesus*. Again Weinel is obliged to confess : " In the highest and last analysis Paul and Jesus are at one, however unlike their formulas may be, and however widely they differ in their entire nature."[7] This is a thought which

---

[1] See the monograph of A. Castellain, *St Paul, valeur de son témoignage sur le Christ, l'Eglise et la doctrine du Salut* (Bruxelles, 1909).
[2] *Paulus und Jesus*, 56.   [3] Feine, *Paulus als Theologe*, 52.
[4] *Jesus und Paulus*, 55.   [5] Weinel, *Paulus*, 244.
[6] Weinel, *l.c.*   [7] Weinel, *Paulus*, 117.

Adolf Jülicher puts into the following words : " Even if there are not a few differences between both [Jesus and Paul], nevertheless, Paul has understood the Master, whom he has never seen with his bodily eyes better than the Twelve, and he is nevertheless the heir to his true spirit. . . . In the main thing Paul is at one with Jesus. . . . For even the halfway unprejudiced it is hard not to see that Jesus is the Creator, and Paul the receiver."[1]

And yet Jülicher thinks that, in regard to christology, this unity between Paul and Jesus comes to naught : " If we gather together, as a whole, the scattered thoughts of Paul concerning his Christ, it is evidently impossible to derive them from the Gospel of Jesus, or even merely to put them at once into friendly relations with him. . . . The Christ-mythology of Paul appears like a ruthless violation of the portrait of Jesus, so great in its simplicity, which we have gained in the Gospels."[2] Assuredly the Christ-mythology of Paul, as Jülicher and the liberal critics like to represent it, is a ruthless violation of the portrait of Jesus in the Gospels, just as it is, as we have seen, a ruthless violation of the Pauline portrait of Jesus.

In opposition to it, the Apostle asserts in regard to his statements about Jesus : " I have received of the Lord that which I have delivered unto you " (1 Cor. xi, 23). And even Jülicher sees himself compelled to confess : " The declaration of Paul concerning his relation to Jesus referred of course to the simple dependence of the Apostle on the Lord. In his consciousness the all-dominating thing was that he might preach in the whole world precisely what Jesus Christ wished to have preached as his Gospel. . . . And he has not supplanted Jesus even unconsciously."[3]

Paul, therefore, has neither consciously nor unconsciously changed anything in the Gospel or the portrait of Jesus. Whoever honestly endeavours to compare the portrait of Jesus in the Gospels with Paul's portrait of him will perceive the essential unity of both. He will find that the Pauline preaching about the Son of God goes back to Jesus' own conception of his divine sonship and divinity, and that we possess in Paul a new confirmation of Jesus' own utterances concerning his exalted nature.

Hence the Berlin professor, Theodor Kaftan, is right when he says : " The watchword, which is given out to-day, ' Back from Christ to Jesus, and from Paul's preaching of Christ to the simple Son of Man of the Gospels,' is unacceptable. . . . This watchword is valueless, because it is based upon a false premise. The difference between the Christ of Paul and the Jesus of the Gospels, on which this watchword

---

[1] Jülicher, *Die Religion Jesu und die Anfänge des Christentums,* 89.
[2] Jülicher, *Paulus und Jesus,* 26, 27.   [3] *id.,* 11, 72.

relies, does not exist in the Scripture itself, but is dragged
into it.   The Jesus, whom this watchword opposes to the
Christ of Paul, is not the Jesus of the Gospels, but the Jesus
of a new theology."[1]   Similarly Julius Kaftan writes : " If
anyone to-day wishes violently to separate Jesus and Paul, to
appeal to Jesus and to repudiate Paul, it is, when seen from
the standpoint of history, a high-handed proceeding.   In
history they belong together, as the Lord, in whom we
believe, and the Apostle, to whom we owe the permanent
forms of this belief. . . .   The modern separation of Jesus
and Paul will prove to be, in the further development of
theology and the Church, a transient error."[2]   In fact, even
such a liberal investigator as Hermann von Soden already
designates this error as outlived : " The view formerly often
presented that Paul was in reality the founder of Christianity
is given up in scientific circles."[3]

IV.—THE SYNOPTISTS AND THE DIVINITY OF CHRIST.

1. The Divinity of Christ as Represented by the Synoptists.

We can summarize this briefly.   The synoptic representation agrees with the divine consciousness, which Jesus
himself reveals in the first three Gospels.   This consciousness
we have thoroughly and exhaustively estimated, beginning
with the revelation of divine sonship by the twelve-year-old
boy in-the temple to the hour of his ascension into heaven.
It is true, with these the corresponding texts in John's
Gospel were also continually taken into consideration, in
order to obtain a really organic picture of what Jesus Christ
said of himself.   Yet every reader can easily separate the
Johannine elements.   In this way, to use a somewhat unfortunate and unhappily too frequently employed expression,
he will have before him the characteristic " synoptic Christ,"
in distinction from the " Johannine Christ."

Only one thing is still wanting—the Gospel of the Childhood of Jesus.   Hitherto this has not been considered, because
it lies outside of, and previous to, the sphere of the direct
testimony of Jesus to himself.   Consequently it is more a matter
of merely arranging in logical sequence the divine features in
the Gospel of the childhood, in order to gain a comprehensive
idea of the divinely human person of Jesus held by the
synoptical Evangelists and by their Christian contemporaries.

While Mark opens his " Gospel of Jesus Christ, the Son
of God " (Mark i, 1), immediately with the appearance of the

---

[1] Theodor Kaftan, Der Mensch Jesus Christus, 3 (Gr.-Lichterfelde-
Berlin, 1908).
[2] Jesus und Paulus, 58.   Similarly, Scott, Jesus and Paul, in Essays
on some Biblical Questions by B. Swete, 375 f. (London, 1909).
[3] Die wichtigsten Fragen im Leben Jesu, 1, 2nd ed. (Berlin, 1909).

Forerunner, and while the Fourth Gospel, apart from the prologue, begins at once with the testimony of the already convinced John the Baptist to Christ, Matthew and Luke turn their gaze backwards, and pourtray historically the temporal beginnings of the life of Jesus by means of the oldest tradition. Matthew undertakes this task in order to weaken completely the caricature which Jewish and especially pharisaic fanaticism had already put into circulation concerning the life of the Saviour. Luke feels himself already, aside from this consideration, compelled to " diligently attain to all things from the beginning " in accordance with his very decided talent as an historian (Luke i, 3).

Liberal criticism, it is true, asserts the contrary. It affirms that both Luke and Matthew have allowed their judgements to be clouded by mythological or legendary stories of their contemporaries concerning the true and actual beginnings of the life of Jesus; and that their Gospel of the childhood, therefore, does not at all deserve to be taken seriously by historical criticism. That has been the unanimous opinion of rationalistic liberalism ever since the days of Gottlob Paulus, David Fr. Strauss and Ernest Renan down to H. Usener,[1] Hillmann,[2] P. Lobstein,[3] H. Holtzmann,[4] Harnack,[5] W. Soltau,[6] H. Gunkel,[7] Otto Pfleiderer,[8] Wellhausen,[9] Ed. von Hartmann,[10] and T. K. Cheyne.[11] These are really acrobatic feats, in which these and other more or less serious critics outbid themselves in their attempts, first to criticize the story of Christ's childhood out of the canonical Gospels, and then to make people believe that it was invented under the influence of Hellenic and Oriental mythology and freely imaginative Christian legend, and slipped surreptitiously into the Gospels by the synoptists, if not by some later irreverent hand.[12] This is not the place in which to deal with this

---

[1] *Religionsgeschichtliche Untersuchungen*, 69 ff. (1889); cf. *Geburt und Kindheit Christi*, in *N. T. Wissenschaft*, iv, 8 (1903).

[2] *Die Kindheitsgeschichte Jesu nach Lukas* (1891).

[3] *Die Lehre von der übernatürlichen Geburt Christi* (1896).

[4] *Lehrbuch der N. T. Theologie*, i, 414 (1897).

[5] *Zu Luk* i, 34, in *Zeitschrift für N. T. Wissenschaft*, 53 (1901); *Dogmengeschichte*, 95, note 2, 3rd ed.; *Wesen des Christentums*, 20.

[6] *Die Geburtsgeschichte Jesu Christi* (1902).

[7] *Zum religionsgeschichtlichen Verständnis des N. T.*, 63-70 (1903).

[8] *Das Christusbild des urchristlichen Glaubens*, 21 ff. (1903); *Entstehung des Christentums* 194 ff. (1905).

[9] *Das Evangelium Lucae übersetzt und erklärt* (1904).

[10] *Das Christentum des N. T.*, 23, 30, 59 (1905).

[11] *Bible Problems* (1905).

[12] The latter is the recent supposition of J. Wellhausen, since, in his commentaries on Matthew and Luke (Berlin, 1904), he frankly gives up the story of the childhood, although even Harnack, *Sitzungsber. der Königl. preuss. Akademie der Wissenschaft*, 547 ff. (Berlin, 1900), and Zimmermann, *Theol. Studien*, 250 ff. (1903), prove that the first two chapters of Luke's Gospel are from the same hand as all the rest of the Gospel.

hypercriticism. A renewed discussion of it is also not at all necessary. The full historicity of the Gospel of the childhood of Jesus has been sufficiently demonstrated[1] in recent years in numerous magazines and monographs by Protestants, as well as Catholics, while the liberal critics have not brought forth even *one* tenable argument against it, and maintain their own specious reasons only by continual mutual contradiction.[2]

The real and only reason why they attack the historical genuineness and credibility of the Gospel of the childhood is not at all an historical, but a philosophical one—the prejudiced, naturalistic and rationalistic view. According to this view, the texts of the Gospel are divided into two classes— one natural, the other supernatural. Whatever in the Gospels and in the Christ of the Gospels is merely and purely natural and human is pronounced genuine and credible. On the contrary, wherever in the Gospel and the life of Jesus supernatural, miraculous and divine elements come into consideration, a later insertion, or a myth, or at least a legend must absolutely exist. Only one who, starting from this "climax of arrogant assumptions," brings himself to restamp "the oldest monuments of Christian faith . . . as witnesses for modern views,"[3] can and must violently strangle in particular the Gospel of the childhood.

The Gospel of the childhood lies wholly in the sphere of supernatural revelation, and *Jesus Christ appears therein already as the divine Messiah and Son of God*. It is true, the human foundation of the portrait of Jesus shows itself

---

[1] This literature in German, French and English is completely set forth in P. A. Durand's *L'Enfance de Jésus-Christ d'après les Évangiles canoniques,* 65 ff. (Paris, 1908). Only the admirable book by Bardenhewer, *Maria Verkündigung, Biblische Studien,* vol. X (1905), has been overlooked by Durand. Since then have appeared : J. Pfättisch, *Der Stammbaum Christi beim hl. Lukas, Katholik,* 269-276 (1908); Simon Landersdorfer, *Bemerkungen zu Lukas,* i, 26-38, *Biblische Zeitschrift,* 30-48 (1909); V. Hartl, *Zum Stammbaum nach Lukas, id.,* 156-173, 290-302 (1909); Joseph Michael Heer, *Die Stammbäume Jesu nach Matthäus und Lukas, id.,* vol. XV (1910); F. X. Steinmeister, *Die Geschichte der Geburt und Kindheit Christi und ihr Verhältnis zu babylonischen Mythen,* in *N. T. Abhandlungen von Meinertz,* ii, 1, 2.

[2] Professor Richard H. Grützmacher, of Rostock, remarks, in regard to this contradictory criticism of the story of the childhood, in *Die Jungfrauengeburt,* 25 f. (Gr.-Lichterfelde-Berlin, 1906), the following : "Faith in the 'certain results of science' breaks down when one sees how its 'intellectual leaders' swear to the most pronounced contradictions on their scientific oath. Indeed, there is hardly one domain which, to such a degree as ours, can shatter even the simplest faith in the certainty of scientific results; provided, of course, that one works out the whole extremely voluminous literature (about the criticism of the Gospel of the childhood) in all its details, and enlarges one's knowledge also of one's own party limitations."

[3] Bardenhewer, *Maria Verkündigung,* 6.

there sharply and clearly. The child Jesus, according to the
record of Matthew and Luke, comes into this world as a
human being and is subject to all human conditions. He is
conceived and sheltered for nine months in the womb of the
Virgin Mary. He is born in a poor hut of refuge, laid in
a manger, circumcised after eight days, and later presented
in the temple of the Lord, and ransomed with the money of
humble people. Then he passes through all the phases of
the usual human child, grows and develops physically, morally
and spiritually. In regard to this entirely human side of the
life of the child Jesus, as it is depicted by the synoptists, the
Apostle Paul can say : Christ Jesus " debased himself, taking
the form of a servant, being made in the likeness of men and
in habit found as a man " (Phil. ii, 7).

Through his humanity, however, his divinity is already
discernible from the first hour. Not with obvious clearness,
as in his later life and activity, yet corresponding to the
beginnings and first steps of the personal revelation of
God.

The angel of God brings from heaven the first announce-
ment to the aged priest, Zachary, that he would receive a
Son, whom he is to call the Child of grace (Johannes, or
" Jehovah hath shown grace ")—a sign of the approaching
Messianic age of grace. Joy and gladness are to accompany the birth of John, "for he shall be great before the
Lord [Kyrios, Jehovah], . . . and he shall convert many of
the children of Israel to the Lord, their God [Jehovah-
Elohim], and he shall go before him in the spirit and power
of Elias . . . to prepare unto the Lord [Jehovah] a perfect
people " (Luke i, 5-18).

The Lord God, before whom John will be great, before
whom he will go in the spirit and power of Elias, to prepare
for him the way and the people, is undoubtedly the coming
Messiah, Jesus himself. Isaias (xl, 3) and Malachias (iii, 1)
had announced that the Messiah would send out a messenger
and guide before him. The prophet Malachias had especially added : "Behold, I will send you Elias the prophet,
before the coming of the great and dreadful day of the Lord.
And he [Elias] shall turn the heart of the fathers to the
children and the heart of the children to their fathers "
(Mal. iv, 5, 6). Relying on this utterance of the prophet,
everyone expected that Elias, or a prophet similar to him in
strength and spirit, would come to prepare the way for the
Messiah. This view is set forth already in the Book of Jesus
Sirach (xlviii, 10, 11). From the New Testament it is
evident that this belief was universal among its Jewish contemporaries (Matt. xi, 14; xvi, 14; xvii, 10; Mark vi, 15;
viii, 28; Luke ix, 8; John i, 21). The theology of the Rabbis
held fast to the appearance of the forerunner Elias as to a

dogma. This is evident from the Gospels as well as from the Mishna[1] (Matt. xvii, 10; Mark ix, 11).

Hence the aged priest Zachary could understand the angel's words only in the sense that his son, John, would be the ardently awaited forerunner of the Messiah, and that this Messiah was the Lord God in his own person. And in reality Zachary did so understand the message of Gabriel. In the prophetic song of praise which the happy father uttered after the birth of his son by God's grace, Zachary gives thanks from his deeply grateful heart for the dawn of the Messianic salvation, and adds, turning to John : " And thou, child, shalt be called the prophet of the Highest; for thou shalt go before the face of the Lord to prepare his ways; to give knowledge of salvation to his people, unto the remission of their sins, through the bowels of the mercy of our God, in which the Orient from on high hath visited us, to enlighten them that sit in darkness and in the shadow of death " (Luke i, 76-79). Here it is evident that John is not extolled in general as a forerunner and preparer of the ways of God, but very particularly as a forerunner and preparer of the ways of the Messiah. Not to God in general, but to the Messiah are therefore applicable divine names and attributes—The Most High, the Lord, the Bringer of Salvation, the Bowels of the Mercy of God, the Orient from on high, and the Light, which lighteth all things. In the mouth of the Jew every one of these names and titles was a powerful paraphrase of the divine name and nature of the Messiah.

Neither the Evangelists nor John the Baptist leaves the slightest doubt of this. All conceive the vocation of the forerunner, as well as the Person of the Messiah Jesus, in the sense of the prophet Isaias : " The voice of one crying in the desert : Prepare ye the way of the Lord, make straight in the wilderness the paths of our God. . . . Say to the cities of Juda—behold your God ! Behold the Lord God shall come !" (Isa. xl, 3, 9, 10; Matt. iii, 3 and parallels).

Six months after the announcement of the coming forerunner, the approach of the divine Messiah Jesus himself *is proclaimed by the word of an angel to the Virgin Mary:* " Hail, full of grace, the Lord is with thee ; blessed art thou among women . . . thou hast found grace with God. Behold, thou shalt conceive in thy womb and shalt bring forth a Son, and thou shalt call his name Jesus. He shall be great and shall be called the Son of the Most High. And the Lord God shall give unto him the throne of David his father ; and he shall reign in the house of Jacob for ever. And of his kingdom there shall be no end. . . . The Holy Ghost shall come upon thee, and the power of the Most High shall overshadow thee. And therefore also the Holy which shall

[1] *Edujoth* viii, 7 ; *Baba mezia* i, 8 ; ii, 8 ; iii, 4-5 ; *Shekalim,* ii, 5.

be born of thee shall be called the Son of God " (Luke i,
28-33).

The Son of the Virgin Mary will be Jesus, the Bringer of
Salvation, the redeeming, spiritual Messiah King. That is,
first of all, the fundamental meaning of the announcement to
Mary—the Messiahship of Jesus and his Messianic task and
work.

To this, however, is immediately joined the further explanation of the person and nature of the Messiah Jesus.
Already the utterance that he will be for ever the ruler of
the kingdom of God to be founded by him points to his
eternal and therefore divine nature. This knowledge is
strengthened by the fact that the angel emphasizes his
supernatural origin, towering far above all earthly and human
relations. Not from man will Jesus be conceived, but from
above, from God. The Holy Ghost will come upon the
Virgin, and influence her with divine power from on high,
and this influence shall be like an overhanging shadow,
much as in the Old Testament the cloud hung over the
tabernacle and the temple of God, while the glory of the
Lord filled it within (Exod. xl, 34).

If already the intimate connection of Jesus with divinity
has been obvious, the angel Gabriel now directly declares
this supernatural origin, establishes it, and takes for granted
the divinity of the Saviour. Jesus will be called the Son of
the Most High and the Son of God because he, without the
co-operation of a man, is to be conceived and born by means
of a perfectly unique miracle of divine omnipotence. The
basis of the divine sonship lies, therefore, not in the bestowal
of special favour upon Jesus, and in the acceptance of him
in place of a child, but in the origin and birth of Jesus in
his being and in his nature. Jesus is not an ethical, or
theocratic, but a metaphysical Son of God.

This the angel confirms, soon after, in substance also to
the future foster-father of Jesus, St Joseph, with the words :
" That which is conceived in her, is of the Holy Ghost. And
she shall bring forth a son; and thou shalt call his name
Jesus. For he shall save his people from their sins " (Matt.
i, 21). Hereto the Evangelist remarks : " Now all this was
done that it might be fulfilled which the Lord spoke by the
prophet, saying : Behold, a virgin shall be with child, and
bring forth a son, and they shall call his name Emmanuel,
which, being interpreted, is God with us " (Matt. i, 22, 23).
In reality, Isaias announces the future Redeemer and Son of
a Virgin as " God with us " : " Behold, a virgin shall conceive and bear a son; and his name shall be called Emmanuel " (God with us); and " Wonderful, Counsellor, God
the Mighty, the Father of the world to come, the Prince of
Peace " (Isa. vii, 14; ix, 6). To this announcement the angel

Gabriel alludes, and Matthew understands his words correctly, when he regards them as a fulfilment of that prophecy of Emmanuel. The import of the name given by the angel is, moreover, identical with that Emmanuel prophesied by the prophet and interpreted by the Evangelist. " Emmanuel " is equivalent to " God with us "; " Jesus " in the older Hebraic form is equivalent to " God is Salvation." " God is Salvation " means the Son of the Virgin, in that he " saves his people from their sins." " God with us " means the Son of the Virgin because he, who as a human being has entered into our race, is God.

Soon after the annunciation, Mary rose and went into the hill country to the parents of the future John the Baptist. " And she entered into the house of Zachary and saluted Elizabeth. And it came to pass that when Elizabeth heard the salutation of Mary, the infant leaped in her womb. And Elizabeth was filled with the Holy Ghost, and she cried out with a loud voice and said : Blessed art thou among women and blessed is the fruit of thy womb. And whence is this to me that the mother of my Lord should come to me? . . . And blessed art thou that hast believed, because those things shall be accomplished that were spoken to thee by the Lord. And Mary said : My soul doth magnify the Lord, and my spirit hath rejoiced in God, my Saviour " (Luke i, 39-47).

Elizabeth greets Mary as the mother of her Lord, her Kyrios. The still unborn child Jesus is the Kyrios of the highly favoured mother of the Baptist. That is so rare and extraordinary that evidently this title is not a mere polite address. Neither the Greek nor Aramaic linguistic usages permit one to address a child, and especially a still unborn child, even were it a prince, from motives of earthly reverence, as Lord, " Kyrios." Mary's child was, from a secular point of view, in any case, but especially for her relative Elizabeth, not a being to whom unusual reverence or any lordly rank at all was due. The form of address " Lord " can, therefore, have, on the lips of Elizabeth and in its application to Jesus, only a supermundane and religious signification. We know, however, that Lord, " Kyrios," as a religious form of address, was, according to Greek and Aramaic ideas, always equivalent to Jehovah, God. That it is to be so understood, particularly in this passage of the Gospel, is plain from the context. Within a few verses the expression " Lord " occurs again four times : " Behold the handmaid of the Lord " . . . " the mother of my Lord " . . . " blessed art thou that hast believed those things that were spoken to thee by the Lord " . . . " My soul doth magnify the Lord " (Luke i, 38, 43, 45, 46). In the first, third and fourth passage God is directly understood, and there is no doubt that also in the second passage Mary is called the Mother of the Lord, because her child is God—incarnate God.

Some months later, an angel proclaims to the shepherds the *birth of Jesus* with the words : " Fear not; for behold I bring you good tidings of great joy that shall be to all the people. For, this day is born a Saviour, who is Christ the Lord " (Luke ii, 10). A little while before, Mary had made the Saviour equal to God : " My spirit hath rejoiced in God my Saviour." Now the child Jesus is called the Saviour, therefore God. And still more definitely does the messenger from heaven designate him as " Christ the Lord "—Messiah, Jehovah, the divine Messiah.

Again a short space of time elapses. Then the saintly, aged Simeon in the temple takes the child Jesus in his arms and similarly praises God : " Now thou dost dismiss thy servant, O Lord, according to thy word in peace; because my eyes have seen thy salvation, which thou hast prepared before the face of all peoples, a light to the revelation of the Gentiles and the glory of thy people Israel " (Luke ii, 29-32). Jesus, the Salvation, the Saviour of the world, the Light of all nations, the glory of the people Israel ! We know all these attributes. They have not merely Messianic but absolutely *divinely* Messianic significance. They are simply titles, in which the pious Israelite transcribed the ineffable name of Jehovah, and which Jesus Christ applied to himself, in order to bring nearer to his disciples his divinely human personality. John the Evangelist uses them again, in order to clothe in them the highest mysteries of the christology and divinity of Jesus.

For the present, however, Providence closes the series of its revelations concerning the divinity of the child Jesus. It wished merely to call the attention of the world to the coming of the divine Messiah. And these manifestations were to remain limited to a small circle of chosen souls. Yes, even these chosen souls beheld the mystery of the divinity of Jesus only through a veil, and beheld it not by means of their own visual power, but, as is continually emphasized by the Evangelists, through the Holy Spirit, by a supernatural, miraculous illumination, or by means of instruction through heavenly messengers. Now the heavenly voices also are silent, and the illuminations of the mind cease. The hour of Jesus' own revelation had also not yet come. On the contrary. After all the miracles which surrounded his cradle, the divine child must even flee to Egypt from the persecutions of men. And after his return his juvenile life continued in deepest obscurity in Nazareth. Luke, after all his researches, can report of him only this : " The child grew and waxed strong, full of wisdom, and the grace of God was in him " (Luke ii, 40).

Then suddenly came a ray of divine light. The *twelve-year-*

old child of grace discloses in the temple for the first time his true, metaphysical divine sonship, as we have previously shown. Then another interval of silence up to the age when, in accordance with Jewish usage, the rabbinical teachers took charge of his public instruction. Then, all at once, is heard the *voice of the forerunner:* " I am the voice of one crying in the desert. Prepare ye the way of the *Lord,* make straight his paths, as was spoken by Isaias the prophet. Every valley shall be filled, and every mountain and hill shall be brought low . . . and all flesh shall see the *salvation of God* " (Matt. iii, 3 ; Luke iii, 4-6). " I baptize with water, but there hath stood one in the midst of you, whom you know not. The same is he that shall come after me, who is preferred before me, the latchet of whose shoe I am not worthy to loose. . . . He it is that baptizeth *with the Holy Ghost* " (John i, 26 ff. and parallels). As John, the next day saw Jesus coming to him, he said : " Behold the *Lamb of God, that taketh away the sins of the world.* . . . He must increase, but I must decrease. *He that cometh from above* [*Jesus*] *is above all.* He that is of the earth, of the earth he is, and of the earth he speaketh. *He that cometh from heaven is above all; and what he hath seen and heard, that he testifieth.* . . . *The Father loveth the Son, and he hath given all things into his hand. He that believeth in the Son hath life everlasting; but he that believeth not the Son shall not see life; but the wrath of God abideth on him* " (John i, 29, 36 ; iii, 30, 31, 35, 36).

From this testimony of John stream forth whole sheaves of divine and christological illuminating rays. Jesus is the Lord, prophesied by Isaias, " God with us," the mighty God : " Prepare the way of the Lord, as Isaias hath said." Jesus is the salvation of God, and " God is salvation " for all humanity. " All flesh shall see the salvation of God " cried John at the approach of Jesus. It is Jesus, who can, as he wills, dispense the Spirit of God, and hence disposes of divine power and force : " He will baptize you with the Holy Ghost." It is Jesus who can forgive sins and destroy the sins of the world : " Behold the Lamb of God, that taketh away the sins of the world." Jesus, externally a man like other men, nevertheless in his higher nature comes from above, from heaven, and is in consequence elevated above everything earthly : " He that cometh from above, from heaven, is above all." Jesus, as a man younger than John, is, in regard to this heavenly origin, older than his forerunner—a pre-existing being : " He that cometh after me, is preferred before me." Finally, Jesus is the well beloved Son of the heavenly Father, and, as such, is the object of faith, as is the Father himself : " The Father loveth the Son and hath given all things into his hands. He that believeth in the Son hath life everlasting."

Moreover, John proclaims Jesus' divine sonship, not from his own impulse and personal knowledge, but by the inward illumination of the Holy Ghost, and supported by the *divine manifestation* which occurred at the *baptism of Jesus,* of which the forerunner was the actual witness.[1] When Jesus came out of the water after the baptism, " Lo, the heavens were opened to him, and he saw the Spirit of God descending as a dove, and coming upon him. And, behold, a voice from heaven, saying : *This is my beloved Son, in whom I am well pleased* " (Matt. iii, 16 and parallels.)

These words form, from this time on, as it were, the sign-manual of *the whole synoptical consciousness of Jesus.* Jesus proclaims himself to be the Son of God in an increasing revelation of himself to the Apostles, the disciples, the Galilean people, the people of Judea and the Scribes and Pharisees in Jerusalem ; he corroborates this conviction of his entire life and teaching in the face of death with a sacred oath, and confirms it after the resurrection, until his ascension and return to the Father. And always and everywhere he declares that he applies to himself the title " Son of God " in the strictest sense of these words. He does not claim to be a mere child of God through grace, or a mere theocratic Son of God, but a true, metaphysical Son, of the same nature and substance with the Father. We have been able to ascertain this consciousness of divinity and of divine sonship everywhere, and to observe its development step by step. And, indeed, its essential characteristics are stamped not only on John's portraiture of Jesus, but on that of the synoptists as well. We do not need to prove this fact a second time. It is so clear and certain that not only conservative critics, but also the most important opponents of the divinity of Jesus in the liberal camp concede to-day that *the synoptic Christ is the true Son of God and really God.*

The hypercritical Professor W. Wrede proves that this is already the case in Mark, and Mark is regarded by Wrede, as well as by the liberal critics almost unanimously, as the oldest Gospel. If Jesus is attested from the time of his baptism, his temptation, and the confession of Peter down to the scene of the tribunal, as the " Son of God," this cannot be, in Wrede's opinion, " merely a theocratic name, and just as little an expression for the love of God for Jesus or for his human piety, but is the adequate designation of the supernatural being of Jesus, . . . supernaturally and metaphysically meant."[2]

[1] John i, 32-34. Because the utterance of the Baptist concerning the divine sonship of Jesus in John iii, 30, 35, goes back to this divine manifestation recorded by the synoptists, it is also based on the writings of the synoptists and may, therefore, be used here.

[2] Wrede, *Das Messiasgeheimnis in den Evangelien,* 73, 75, 76 (Göttingen, 1901).

It is true, Wrede tries to represent the texts of Mark, which speak in favour of the divinity of Jesus, as unhistorical opinions of the Evangelist. Johannes Weiss,[1] however, characterizes such an attempt as "morbid scepticism," and for his part expresses his conviction as follows : "Faith in the Son of God is the necessary preliminary for the understanding of the Gospel of the Cross " (Mark). Not first in John, but already in the critically incontestable Gospel of Mark, " the divine sonship is something supermundane, which can only be known, if one has, like the Christian Church, a faith which forces its way through the appearance of lowliness to its inner being."[2]

Wilhelm Bousset similarly says of Mark's Gospel : " This oldest of the Gospels is already written from the standpoint of faith (in the divinity of Jesus); for Mark, Jesus is already not only the Messiah of the Jewish people, but the miraculous, eternal Son of God, whose glory has illumined this world. And it has been rightly remarked that in this respect our three Gospels are different from the fourth only in degree."[3]

This view can also be read between and in the lines of Adolf Harnack's writings, however unwilling the Berlin scholar is to confess such an " essential retrogression " in our research into Christ. " Already," writes Harnack, " the Jerusalemite Mark has made of Jesus almost a divine apparition, or has found such a conception already existing," of course because " he and the authorities he cites have previously modified the tradition of Jesus according to the experiences of the Christian Church."[4] Even Adolf Jülicher rejects " the harshness of this view " of Harnack, and feels that " a divine apparition is an especially unfortunate expression for the play of colours about the head of Jesus, part heavenly, part human, which begins to manifest itself in Mark."[5] In an unguarded moment, also, Harnack comes boldly out from his game of hide and seek, and declares that Mark agrees with John " in the dominating intention of revealing the divine sonship of Jesus."[6] Of the third Gospel, however, he says : " Luke writes without any tendency, or, rather, he has only *one tendency*—to prove Jesus to be the divine Saviour. . . . In christology Luke approaches the kind of conception which we find in John."[7]

If, nevertheless, the liberal investigators even to-day still frequently preach an " evangelical " Christ, that is not God, the extremely radical pastor, Kalthoff, rightly ridicules this yes-and-no kind of theology. Catholicism and orthodoxy,

[1] *Das älteste Evangelium,* 51 (Göttingen, 1903).   [2] *Id.*
[3] Bousset, *Was wissen wir von Jesus?* 30 (Halle, 1904).
[4] Harnack, *Lukas der Arzt,* 86 note.
[5] Jülicher, *Neue Linien in der Kritik der evangelischen Überlieferung,* 70 (Giessen, 1906).
[6] *Lukas der Arzt,* 119 note.   [7] *Id.,* 117, 158.

then, would have understood Christ, from the first, more correctly than liberalism. They have, at all events, the Gospels on their side; and, indeed, not only John, but the synoptists as well, who represent Jesus as God and God incarnate. Only by an act of violence does liberal theology seek to render this state of affairs in the Gospels obscure.[1]

The radical, W. von Schnehen, pronounces a similar opinion : " The Jesus of whom these writings [of the Evangelists] tell us is throughout not a man, but at least a superman. Yes, more than that; he is the unique Son of God, the Christ, the coming incarnate God of the orthodox Church. In regard to the fourth Gospel, this is, indeed, universally recognized. . . . But the other Evangelists also have no idea of informing us merely of a ' man ' Jesus and of demanding faith and reverence for such a being. No, the miraculously born Son of the Virgin, pourtrayed in the Gospels of Luke and Matthew, the Jesus who has risen from the dead and ascended into heaven, as depicted in the first and third Gospels, is just as little a mere ' natural man ' as is the Christ of John."[2]

Honest criticism, however radically it may proceed, must therefore agree with this result, that *the synoptists believe in the divinity of Christ, and understand the historical person of Jesus as a divinely human Person—Jesus.* Mark, who, in the opinion of our opponents, sketched the oldest and historically the most correct portrait of Jesus, expresses only the principal import of his Gospel and, indeed, of the Gospels as a whole, when he introduces the history of the Master with the words : " The beginning of the Gospel of Jesus Christ, the Son of God " (Mark i, 1). And there can be no doubt that Mark, like Matthew and Luke, conceives the Son of God always and everywhere as "the one born of God,"[3] and that they derive this conception from the revelation of Jesus himself, and consider their representation as an absolute proof of the divine consciousness of Jesus.

This opinion of the synoptists concerning Jesus and concerning their own portraiture of the life of Jesus gives us at once the absolute *guarantee that we have correctly estimated the utterances reported by them of the consciousness of our Saviour, as the consciousness that he was God.*

Against all this one can object only that this fact does not appear with sufficient evidence from the synoptic revelation of Jesus Christ concerning himself; that the divinity of Jesus does not lie plainly enough on the surface of the synoptic Gospels; that not a single time in them does Christ call him-

---

[1] Albrecht Kalthoff, *Das Christusproblem,* chaps. ii-iv, 2nd ed. (1903); *Die Entstehung des Christentums,* chap. i (Jena, 1904).

[2] W. v. Schnehen, *Der moderne Jesuskultus,* 10 f., 2nd ed. (Frankfurt a. M., 1906).

[3] Gustav Dalman, *Die Worte Jesu,* 236 (Leipzig, 1898).

self God; and that, in fact, the synoptists themselves do not give him this title positively. They let the divinity of the Saviour be inferred rather from the words and works of Christ and from his whole physiognomy, than express it themselves unequivocally. And with all the divine sublimity of the synoptic figure of Christ, the human side of the Saviour's portrait, nevertheless, is much more prominent and clear than his divinity.

But this proves nothing against the fact that the synoptists were convinced of the divinity of Jesus, and that they read this out of the life of Jesus, but confirms, indeed, the fact anew that *the synoptic life of Jesus is truth, reality and history, and not an embellishment on the part of the Church.*

For the whole range of the synoptic Gospels this has been already demonstrated thoroughly and in detail, in reply to the modern evolutionary hypothesis of the liberal school. It has also been shown in another chapter of this book, with what infinite wisdom and prudence for the attainment of his purpose Jesus acted, by making prominent, first of all, in his revelation of himself, the human basis of his life and person, and then only little by little building up the mighty figure of his divinity. There is now still to be added here only the proof that *the personal conception and representation of the divine and human portrait of Jesus by the synoptists maintains itself on the same level of historical reality.*

2. *The Synoptic and the Real Portrait of Christ.*

The assertion of liberal critics that our Gospels and their views of Christ are to be considered merely as a reflection of the Church's Christ-legend, as it was forced upon them by the contemporaries of the Evangelists, runs counter to the incontrovertible observation that the synoptists nowhere refer back to the life of Jesus the views which they personally, and which all the Christian Churches of their time, then had of Jesus. When the synoptists wrote their Gospels, faith in the divinity of Jesus was an undoubted common possession of all true Christians, as it most certainly had been ever since the resurrection of Jesus. That is the one great fact which was established by our exposition of the divinity of Jesus after the resurrection, the divinity of Jesus in the original Church, and the divinity of Jesus as preached by Paul, which also results from a study of the synoptic Gospels.

Accordingly, the idea might actually suggest itself that the Evangelists had chosen this, their final point of view, as their starting-point. They could easily have been tempted to fashion their story of the life of Jesus in such a way as to make it appear that the Apostles and disciples had, from the very beginning of their calling and acquaintance with the

Master, believed in his Messiahship and divinity. Or, since this would be equivalent to an obviously incorrect and dishonest act, they could, nevertheless, have given to their representation an appearance, as if Heaven and the Saviour himself, from the beginning of his life to its close, had announced to all the world the Messianic and divinely human nature of Jesus with explicit, formal definiteness. Or, again, because such a portrait of Jesus was far removed from historical truth and the actual facts, they could and might have, nevertheless, finally followed the tendency—wherever the divinity of Jesus in reality reveals itself in the historical course of his life—to emphasize such traits strongly, and to seek out and pourtray these by preference.

If the synoptic figure of Christ, as the liberal investigators so confidently assert, was a pious attempt to embellish the historical portrait of Jesus, then not only the last alternative, but really all three of the above-mentioned alternatives, must be able to be proved in the synoptic Gospels.

The contrary is the case. Instead of pourtraying the later faith of the Apostles and disciples as existing previously, or, at the very beginning, we go with them through the whole unteachable apprenticeship of the original Apostles until they, under our very eyes, in a long, wearisome ascent and after many lapses, finally force their way out of the spell of rabbinical Judaism, to the recognition and confession of the Messiahship and divinity of Jesus. Instead of forcing the ways of Providence and consequently falling into the mistake of supposing that the sublime mystery of the person of Jesus had come suddenly, all at once, to a still unprepared humanity, and had blinded them by its splendour, the morning of the day of redemption, according to the synoptic representation, first dawned faintly, and that there then broke forth, modestly and prudently and with divine circumspection, one ray of everlasting light after another, until at Easter the brilliant sun of God's truth shed its radiance over all lands, and on Ascension Day stood high above the heavens. And instead also of bringing out and marking especially only the actual revelations and testimony of Jesus in regard to himself and his divinity, these find their support so naturally, so harmoniously and in such unaffected simplicity from the natural and supernatural course of Jesus' life, that we are almost as much astonished at the human fidelity and simple truthfulness of the representation, as at the divine events. This sincere character of the synoptic writings forms the sharpest imaginable refutation and repudiation of the modern liberal criticism of the Gospels, as well as the most positive and incontestable defence of the synoptic portrait of Christ.

This is shown most clearly from those very facts brought

forward by our opponents and exploited unjustly by them
against the divinity of Jesus—namely, that the man Jesus
stands so plainly in the foreground of the synoptic Gospels,
and that Jesus is never called directly God by the synoptists.

We know that among the Jews the real name of God " is
uttered more rarely in the time subsequent to the exile, and
finally is no more uttered at all,"[1] unless in the cult of the
temple and in quotations from the Scriptures, in which the
name Jehovah occurred. But also in these " Adonai " was
spoken, instead of " Jehovah," by an altered pronunciation.
As substitutes for the name of God, " general expressions,
such as the Holy One, the Almighty, the Exalted, the Great,
the Lord of Heaven, the Lord of lords, King of kings,
Glory, Great Majesty, were used, but also the mere word
' Heaven.'[2] Indeed, still more prudent and sometimes quite
colourless expressions were employed, such as the Voice, the
Height, the Place."[3]

Now, just as little as Jesus entirely forbade (Matt. xxiii, 2)
other Jewish religious usages, provided they had something
inherently good in them, just so little did he leave disregarded
the aforesaid custom of speaking prudently of God. It is
true, " superstitious ideas and such as were foreign to the
true revealed religion, in regard to the nature of the divine
name, may have been conducive to the introduction of this
custom. Because it was thought that the name of God, if
uttered, might draw down into this world the divine Person
magically connected with it, men had scruples about speaking
it. But the decisive reason was, after all, the commandment
of the Decalogue (Exod. xx, 7) : ' Thou shalt not take the
name of the Lord thy God in vain,' and behind this lay a
genuinely religious awe of the Judge of the world, enthroned
in heaven. This awe Jesus has not wished to abrogate,
according to Matt. x, 28 and Luke xii, 5, but has himself
intensified it."[4] In general, Jesus has broadly accommodated
himself to this habit of speaking of God more frequently in
indirect expressions, rather than always using the name of
God itself,[5] " yet has done so in such a way, that he thereby
reserved for himself a position peculiarly his own through his
preferred use of the designation of God as Father."[6]

After all this, one easily comprehends *that, and why, he
did not apply to himself the name of God*. He would, by so
doing, have given great offence to both the people and the
rabbis, quite apart from the fact that he would also have been
completely misunderstood. If he had called himself directly
God, his Jewish contemporaries would have understood it in

[1] Hollmann, *Welche Religion hatten die Juden, als Jesus auftrat?* 26.
[2] *id.*, 26 f. ; also Dalman, *Die Worte Jesu,* 159-167.
[3] Dalman, *op. cit.,* 167-191.   [4] *id.,* 190.   [5] *id.,* 150-167.
[6] *id.,* 190.

the sense that he claimed to be God and to identify himself with the Father in heaven. But it was quite unmistakable, when he, on the one hand, held exceedingly high the acknowledgement of the Father in heaven, but, on the other hand, also professed to be himself the Lord, the Almighty, the Truth, Salvation, the Judge of the world, and so forth. These were expressions in which precisely the Jew spoke of God, and from which he could undoubtedly conclude that Jesus wished to proclaim himself God.

When the synoptists wrote, no more consideration of the Jewish forms of expression respecting the name of God was any longer commanded. The Church had already almost exclusively devoted its attention to the Hellenistic Jews and to the Gentiles. Moreover, the Hellenistic synoptists felt themselves on this point just as little Jewish as on other points, and their Greek readers did not even know that linguistic usage of the Jewish rabbis. Already then was given also to the Saviour, in whose divinity the Christians from the first believed, the express title " God," although the appellations most in use were always " Redeemer," " Lord," and " Son of God." Remember only Paul and the Pauline christological terminology.

If the synoptists, nevertheless, *throughout and without exception avoid the name and designation of Jesus as " God,"* it is a manifest indication of the originality and historical truth of their portraiture of Christ.

This becomes still more evident in regard to the synoptic *representation of the humanity of Jesus.*

It is really very remarkable how strongly the human side of the life of Jesus is emphasized by the Evangelists. At the time when the synoptists wrote, Jesus Christ stood before the eye of faith as the first-born of the creation, as the ideal man, the divine man, the divine Messiah and the Lord of the world. He had proceeded from the bosom of the heavenly Father, had come to this earth only to redeem mankind, and had ascended again to the Father, in order to participate in his divine glory, to reign with him, and at some time to return with the whole heavenly host to judge the world. Liberal critics even maintain that the Christianity of that time, entirely abandoning the previous life of Jesus, now concerned itself only with the " Pauline christology of the exaltation."

If, therefore, the synoptic Gospels had been merely an echo of the theological speculation, or a result of the imagination of the Christians of that time, they would have had to pourtray the life and person of Jesus above all from that supernatural and superhuman point of view. The purely human and earthly element would have had to retire wholly, or for the most part, into the background.

But the synoptists bring the child Jesus into the world as a poor, wailing infant, in spite of his supernatural conception and heavenly origin.   And in spite of all the supermundane manifestations and proofs of his Messiahship and divinity, by which the history of the childhood and youth of Jesus is glorified, they everywhere indicate the genuinely human development of the boy Jesus.   The Evangelists, who allow us to behold, as through a veil, the divine countenance of the boy Jesus, find it important and necessary to relate to us how the Son of God at Bethlehem did not find even a shelter worthy of human beings, how he had to flee to Egypt from his persecutors, and how he grew up under the simplest conditions at Nazareth in the carpenter's family, and went through a purely human process of development in all respects.   Indeed, they several times express themselves in regard to this youthful period in such a way that we may suppose that Jesus carefully preserved the mystery of his divine inner life from his associates, and even from his foster-father and Virgin mother.   And in his later life also he revealed it only so far as it corresponded to the plan of Providence to disclose little by little the mystery of his divinity.   Yet the divine revelation of himself always runs along the thread of the naturally human destiny of Jesus, and, before it reaches its climax, it appears for a moment as if his divinity would be swallowed up in the nameless human misery, which overwhelmed the Saviour, until he had fully and completely paid to death the tribute of his human nature.

We have elsewhere furnished proof that the humanity and human traits in the life of Jesus form no argument against his divinity.   It is true, however, that this synoptic representation is a destructive criticism of our opponent's assertion that the synoptists do not present the history of Jesus according to its actual course, but that it is the Christ-legend of the second and third generation of the Church which they pourtray.

This assertion—only the old man's staff of senile liberalism —is so frail and rotten that truly candid liberal critics begin to throw it away.   " The traditions of Jesus, which are found in Mark and Luke, are older than is usually supposed," confesses Harnack.[1]   " The whole impression of the person of Jesus," Weinel asserts, " as we gain it from the first three Gospels, has already stood vividly before the soul of the Apostle Paul, and determined his course of action."[2]   And Pfleiderer confesses : " The three oldest Gospels, which, it is true, have been composed in an age subsequent to Paul, and partly under the influence of Pauline ideas, have for their

[1] *Lukas der Arzt,* 113.
[2] Weinel, *Paulus, Der Mensch und sein Werk,* 249 (Tübingen, 1904).

foundation the tradition of the original Church, concerning Jesus' life and teachings."[1]

Still more decidedly does Johannes Weiss reject the view that the post-Pauline Church, by reason of a disregard of the real life of Jesus, has dreamed of nothing but an exalted, glorified Christ, and that this way of considering him has dominated the synoptists also. He says : " The early Churches have, together with the formation of a theological doctrine concerning Christ, attached also the highest value to the keeping alive of the clear portrait of Jesus among them. . . . Even if the early Churches did direct their thoughts to the Exalted One, they had before their eyes a clear picture of him to whom they prayed. For either they belonged to those who had themselves seen Jesus, or they were under the impression of the tradition of his deeds and words. On the whole, the portrait, for which we are indebted to the love and fidelity of the oldest disciples, is a convincing and a truly human one. That the assemblies of these first Christians, their conversations and their quiet hours of solitude were filled with memories of the Master, and that they admonished one another with his words, encouraged one another by his example, and yearned for his love, we may take for granted, even though we have no direct testimony to that effect. For if they had not lived so loyally in the past, they would not have transmitted to us the precious collection of the words and narratives of the Lord so richly and admirably. . . . The post-pauline literature falls back more and more on reminiscences in the life of Jesus. . . . We have thereby come to the period when it proved necessary to give to the Church also a consistent portrait of the life of Jesus. The first Apostles and eye-witnesses had died, and it was essential to direct the flowing stream of oral tradition into a well-regulated bed. Thus originated the first Gospels."[2]

Adolf Jülicher summarizes the same conviction in the following words : " The whole tradition of the synoptists goes back, after all, to the ' Early Church,' and belongs in this sense to the time of Jesus. The Jesus whom the Church of Jerusalem had known is reproduced, even though with unequal degrees of clearness, in the first three Gospels."[3]

Hence the synoptic portrait of Jesus is only the replica of the real, historical, original life of Jesus, although, or rather precisely because, the synoptic Gospels are based upon the common Christian teaching, mirror the common Christian faith, and (especially Matthew's Gospel[4]) were themselves also books of the Church. Thereby falls to the

---

[1] Pfleiderer, *Die Entstehung des Christentums,* 185 f. (1905).
[2] Johannes Weiss, *Christus,* 69, 73 (Tübingen, 1909).
[3] Jülicher, *Paulus und Jesus,* 13 (Tübingen, 1907).
[4] Harnack, *Lukas der Arzt,* 120; *Die Apostelgeschichte,* 2 note.

ground not only the assertion that the faith of the synoptists in the divinity of Jesus does not go back to the early Church and to Jesus Christ himself, but it is also clear that the Christian tradition of later generations held firmly to the strictly historical life of Jesus; that, faith *in* the Saviour went hand in hand with the history *of* the Saviour; and that the contrast between the real Saviour and the alleged Saviour embellished by believers did not exist in the old Christian Church, but shows its ghostly form only in the imagination of modern critics.

V.—The Divinity of Christ as Represented by John.

1. *The Characteristic Form of the Johannine Christology.*

The Johannine christology differs from that of the synoptists by its *own special kind of representation* and by an *entirely new form of expression.*

The manner and representation of the synoptic christology is more practical than expository, more indirect than direct, more mediate than immediate, more insinuating than outspoken. The synoptists relate the life of Jesus simply, without specially bringing out in doing so those features in which the divinity of Jesus in particular revealed itself characteristically, and without expressly emphasizing the fact that, and how far, Jesus proclaims himself in his words and deeds as the real Son of God. The first Evangelists did not feel themselves at all called upon to speak of the divinity of Jesus in an explicit, demonstrative manner of pourtrayal. On the one hand, this doctrine appeared clearly enough from the simple Gospel of deeds and events; on the other hand (and this was the main thing), at that time within the Christian Church no one assailed the specific, fundamental dogmas of Christianity—the Messiahship and divinity of Jesus Christ. These truths were part of the undoubted possession of all the Jewish and Gentile Christian Churches and of all believers. We have been able to convince ourselves of this, particularly from the Epistles of St Paul.

Some decades later, things were otherwise. After the first enthusiasm was over, a reaction was visible among some adherents of the Christian religion, and sometimes even a partial return to the former Jewish and Gentile ideas, from which they had only just escaped. The Gentile-Christian elements in the Church, as is easily understood, were not entirely free from the formerly cherished religious views of the Greek popular philosophy. The Jewish Christians were drawn back to the national theology of the Synagogue, and above all to the rabbinical and apocalyptic views of the Messiah, which previously had held back the majority of their race from faith in Jesus, and which now drove even those who had become believers with irresistible power back again into the depths of racial, national-Jewish christology. After God's judgement on Jerusalem had come to pass and the visible nucleus of the indigenous nation had vanished, the Judaists held so much the more tenaciously to the ideal centre, to the nationally coloured portrait of the Messiah, while the Hellenic Christians frequently combined Jewish and Greco-Alexandrian elements with their Christianity. In this way the Jewish-Gnostic sects originated, which either questioned or bluntly denied the true divinity of Jesus, as well as his true humanity.

To meet these false doctrines of Cerinthus, of the Nicolaitans and other heretics, John saw himself compelled to lay express emphasis on the divinity and humanity of Jesus. Against them, according to the unanimous testimony of tradition, he wrote his Gospel.[1] It is true, he did this primarily neither for the purpose of proving the divinity of Jesus, nor in order to convert the heretics, but to strengthen the Christian sentiments of his Churches in Asia Minor, which possessed faith in Jesus Christ, by bringing as an authentic witness the divinely human life and the divinely human authentication of himself by Jesus vitally and forcibly before their eyes.

John expresses himself very plainly in regard to this *purpose of his Gospel,* and tells his readers that this is " *written, that you may believe that Jesus is the Christ, the Son of God, and that believing, you may have life in his name* " (John xx, 31).

In accordance with this purpose, the Evangelist unfolds immediately and in striking sentences in the *preface* to his Gospel, the *entire programme of the Christian doctrine of the God-Man*—his eternity, his divine qualities, his divine sonship, divinity and incarnation. Then he shows how this programme was developed throughout the entire life of Jesus. *John the Baptist* is a witness of it at the start, who proclaims the pre-existence of Jesus and his eternal being with God before all time (John i, 15, 27, 30), his celestial origin (John iii, 31, 32), his divine sonship (John i, 34) and his divine and Messianic work of redemption (John i, 29). And Jesus commends the Baptist for this christology and affirms that John " gave testimony to the truth " (John v, 33-36).

Beginning from this point, Jesus himself preaches continually the truth of his divine sonship in ever-loftier terms, and with ever-increasing emphasis. His mission from heaven and from God forms the ever-recurring subject of his conversation with his disciples and his public discourses to the people (John v, 38, 43; vi, 38; vii, 16, 29; viii, 42; xii, 49; xiv, 14). After he has granted to his hearers such

---

[1] Iren., *Adv. Hæres.*, III, xi, 1; Epiph., *Hær.*, LI, ii, 12; Hieron., *De viris illustr.*, 9.

a glimpse into his wholly supernatural nature, he explains to them his relation to God at length and under all aspects; he had a personal existence with God before he came into this world (viii, 58); he will return again to God as soon as he has finished his earthly work—the redemption of humanity (viii, 42; xvi, 28); he is the Son of God (iii, 16); and, indeed, the only-begotten, formed out of the substance of God and consequently a Son of like nature with the Father (i, 14, 18; iii, 16, 18); he is God, like the Father (v, 18; x, 30-36; xx, 28). In the unity of the being and nature of Father and Son are grounded the divine origin and character of the teaching of Jesus; what he himself, resting in the bosom of his Father, has heard and seen, that he speaks of and announces to the world (iii, 11; viii, 26; xv, 15). Out of the same unity of being and nature of Father and Son proceeds also the unity of their activity (x, 30, 38; xiv, 9; xvii, 21); the Son doth nothing which the Father does not do, as he, on the other hand, doth all the works of his Father (v, 19).

These works give to the utterances of Jesus about his divinity, first, decisive and infallible support. The Saviour himself appeals to his miracles as a reason for believing on him (John x, 25; xiv, 12. "These were signs of his high mission (ii, 23; iii, 2); they show in Jesus, who performs them, a higher, superhuman and divine power, point to his filial relation to the Father (v, 36; x, 38); and symbolize invisible precedents and truths. Thus the miraculous multiplication of the loaves was a symbol of the might and power of Jesus, in common with that of the Father, of imparting true life and nourishment of soul (vi, 26); the healing of the man born blind was a symbol that Jesus was the Light of the World (ix, 1, etc.), as God is, and brings to mankind spiritual illumination. The healing on the Sabbath day of the man who had been ill for thirty-eight years is not only a sign of his miraculous power, but symbolizes at the same time the truth that his activity is the expression of his perfectly harmonious work with that of the Father, and that this work consequently proves his right to sonship" (v, 17).[1]

In witness of the testimony which Jesus gives to his divinity in word and work *John brings forth his own experience and that of his fellow-apostles and believers.* Only through the oral and practical training of Jesus were the Apostles and disciples brought little by little to faith in the divinity of the Master, overpowered by the evidence of the grounds for faith which were furnished them. Still living near the Evangelist in Asia Minor were a number of the disciples of Jesus who had been witnesses of his preaching of his divinity, and of the proofs of divine power exercised to support the claim, and who confirmed the fact that the christology of John was a reproduction of the teaching

[1] Johannes Belser, *Einleitung in das N. T.,* 322 (Freiburg, 1901).

of Christ (xxi, 24). Above all, however, John can appeal to himself that, as an eye-witness, he gives his report concerning Jesus, his life, his humanity, his Messiahship and his divinity conformably to truth and reality. "And he that saw it hath given testimony," he says, "and his testimony is true. And he knoweth that he saith true, that you also may believe . . . that Jesus is the Christ, the Son of God, and that believing, you may have life in his name" (John xix, 35; xx, 31).

Thus the Gospel of John, in its commencement, in its centre and in its ending, is a forcible and well-grounded confession of the true divinity of Jesus. The first lines of this wonderful book express the divine christology in sentences worthy to be chiselled in stone. The same doctrine rings as a basic tone throughout the entire work, and in the final chord dies tremblingly away, to the effect that here on earth faith in Jesus, as the Messiah and Son of God, makes the Christian a Christian and is the pledge of his future eternal life. The confession of the metaphysical divinity of Jesus is so much the distinctive mark of the fourth Gospel that even sceptical critics acknowledge that the violent controversy which has raged for a hundred years about this Gospel is aimed only at the divinity of Christ proclaimed therein.[1]

Since John is presenting this Gospel of the divinity of Jesus to the Churches of Asia Minor, he presents to them again and very forcibly the same fundamental Christian fact in a personal letter. The genuineness of this *first Epistle of John* is, according to general critical opinion, conceded with that of the Fourth Gospel. Those critics who deny the Johannine origin of the Fourth Gospel see themselves forced, nevertheless, to the acknowledgement that the latter, as well as the three Johannine Epistles and the Apocalypse, belong "to the same school . . . the Johannine school."[2] Now, according to the first Epistle of John, the Son of God, who has given his life for us, is true God, and his mission and act of redemption are for that very reason the greatest proof of God's love for us: "By this hath the charity of God appeared towards us, because God hath sent his only begotten Son into the world, that we may live by him . . ." (1 John iv, 9). "And he is the propitiation for our sins; and not for ours only, but also for those of the whole world" (1 John ii, 2). "The blood of Jesus Christ his Son cleanseth us from all sin" (1 John i, 7). "In this we have known the charity of

1 Otto Schmiedel remarks very pertinently in *Die Hauptprobleme der Leben-Jesu-Forschung*, 17 (Tübingen, 1906): "For the last hundred, and especially the last sixty years, a bitter controversy has raged over this Gospel; and it is not strange, for the fight concerning the divinity of Christ is immediately connected with it."

2 Eduard von Hartmann, *Das Christentum des N. T.*, 246 (1905).

God, because he hath laid down his life for us " (1 John iii, 16).

Faith in the divinity of the Son and love of him is a divine commandment and the best proof of faith in, and love of, the Father : " This is his [God's] commandment, That we should believe in the name of his Son Jesus Christ . . ." (1 John iii, 23). " Everyone that loveth him who begot, loveth him also who is born of him " (1 John v, 1).

Faith in the divinity of the Son leads to the victory over the world, and confers eternal life : " Who is he that over-cometh the world, but he that believeth that Jesus is the Son of God?" (1 John v, 5). " And this is the testimony, that God hath given to us eternal life. And this life is in his Son. He that hath the Son hath life ; he that hath not the Son hath not life. These things I write to you, that you may know that you have eternal life ; you who believe in the name of the Son of God " (1 John v, 11-13).

But he that denies the divinity of the Son is a liar and antichrist, and accuses God the Father and the Son them-selves of false witness : " Who is a liar, but he who denieth that Jesus is the Christ? This is antichrist, who denieth the Father and the Son. Whosoever denieth the Son, the same hath not the Father. He that confesseth the Son, hath the Father also " (1 John ii, 22, 23). " He that believeth in the Son of God hath the testimony of God in himself. He that believeth not the Son, maketh him a liar, because he believeth not in the testimony which God hath testified of his Son " (1 John v, 10).

This divine christology of St John offers absolute certainty, because it corresponds to the original teaching of Christianity, and goes back to the testimony of the Apostle, as an eye-and ear-witness : " He that confesseth the Son, hath the Father also. As for you, let that which you have heard from the beginning abide in you. If that abide in you which you have heard from the beginning, you also shall abide in the Son and in the Father " (1 John ii, 23, 24). " That which we have seen and have heard, we declare unto you ; that you also may have fellowship with us, and our fellowship may be with the Father and with his Son Jesus Christ . . ." (1 John i, 3). " And we know that the Son of God is come. And he hath given us understanding that we may know the true God, and may be in his true Son. This is the true God and life eternal " (1 John v, 20).

Just as clearly does John announce the divinity of Jesus in the *Apocalypse*.[1] What the God of Israel had testified of

---

[1] For the thorough pourtrayal of the christology of the Apocalypse, see F. Büchsel, *Die Christologie der Offenbarung Johannis, Haller Dissertation* (1907); and especially Ermoni, *La Cristologia dell' Apocalisse, Rivista di scienze theolog.*, 369-383, 538-557 (1908).

himself by the Prophets, and what the same book of Revelation says of the heavenly Father (i, 8; xxi, 6), that can Christ also testify to himself: "I am Alpha and Omega, the first and the last, the beginning and the end. . . . I have the keys of death and of hell" (i, 18; ii, 8; xxii, 13). To him is due from all creatures in heaven and on earth the same honour and adoration as to God. The seer of Patmos, who once reclined trustingly upon the breast of Jesus, now falls, as if dead, before the throne of God and at the feet of the Son of God (i, 17), and describes with trembling hand the glory he had looked upon. "And I beheld, and I heard the voice of many angels round about the throne and the living creatures and the ancients, and the number of them was thousands of thousands; saying with a loud voice: The Lamb that was slain is worthy to receive power and divinity and wisdom and strength and honour and glory and benediction. And every creature which is in heaven and on the earth and under the earth and such as are in the sea and all that are in them, I heard all saying: To him that sitteth on the throne and to the Lamb, benediction and honour and glory and power for ever and ever. . . . Salvation to our God, who sitteth upon the throne and to the Lamb" (v, 11-13; vii, 10).

And this putting of Christ on an equality with God is found in a book in which even our critical opponents " have always believed they perceived the most authentic indications of the original Christian sentiment, which has become to us perhaps somewhat strange,"[1] and in a book which protests against any kind of apotheosis and adoration of created beings (xix, 10; xxii, 9).

John, therefore, brings forward the divinity of Jesus in his Gospel, in his first Epistle and in the Apocalypse in the most outspoken and demonstrative way conceivable. This mode of representation is in striking contrast to that of the synoptists, who, it is true, report the testimony of Jesus to his divinity, and let us see in their Gospels their absolute faith in his divinity, without, however, so frankly making the divine christology the sharply defined and clearly outspoken main thought and chief object of their writings.

The second difference which we notice between the Johannine and synoptical announcements of the divinity of Jesus lies in a form and conception, first met with in John, in the name and doctrine of the *Logos* (*Word*), into which John condenses all that he has to say to us of the incarnate Son of God.

Whoever has carefully read the three older Gospels is greatly

[1] Karl Müller, *Unser Herr*, 8 (1906). Ed. von Hartmann thinks that the Apocalypse " still stands entirely within the limits of Jewish Christianity, and shows scarcely any traces of Pauline influence."—*Das Christentum des N. T.*, 246.

astonished when, at the beginning of the Fourth Gospel, he reads the following remarkable and in the highest degree peculiar sentences : " In the beginning was the Word : and the Word was with God : and the Word was God. The same was in the beginning with God. All things were made by him : and without him was made nothing that was made. In him was life : and the life was the light of men. And the light [of the Logos] shineth in darkness : and the darkness did not comprehend it. There was a man sent from God, whose name was John. This man came for a witness, to give testimony of the light, that all men might believe through him. He was not the light, but was to give testimony of the light. That was the true light, which enlighteneth every man that cometh into this world. He was in the world : and the world was made by him : and the world knew him [the Logos] not. He came unto his own : and his own received him not. But as many as received him, he gave them power to be made the sons of God, to them that believe in his name. Who are born, not of blood, nor of the will of the flesh, nor of the will of man, but of God. And the Word was made flesh and dwelt among us, and we saw his glory, the glory as it were of the only begotten of the Father, full of grace and truth. . . . And of his fulness we have all received : and grace for grace. . . . No man hath seen God at any time : the only begotten Son who is in the bosom of the Father, he hath declared him " (John i, 1-14, 16, 18).

Before John proceeds to the narration of the human yet divine story of the earthly life and activity of Jesus, he wishes in this prologue, first of all, to characterize *the pre-existent personality of the Word,* and, indeed, at once, the *nature of the Word in itself* (John i, 1, 2). The Word is a pre-existent and transcendent being. To him belong *beginning and eternity* before all worlds. " In the beginning," when God had not yet created the world,[1] the Word was already with God.[2]   It is not a question here of a merely external proximity of God and the Word, but of an inner relation of being. The Word is a *being similar to God, a personal, divine being, God himself* (verse 1). Only as such, as a personal divine being, could the Word be with God from eternity (verse 2).

A divine *activity* also is characteristic of this divine nature of the Word (verses 3-5). The *creation* of the whole universe

[1] This Johannine expression, " In the beginning," refers plainly to Genesis i, 1.

[2] In the words, " In the beginning was the Word," the thought is, indeed, at first simply of the period before the world ; behind that, however, the idea of eternity merely, as it is included in that of divinity. Julius Grill, *Untersuchungen über die Entstehung des vierten Evangeliums,* i, 90 note, also 89-105 (Tübingen, 1902).

is an act of the Word, and in fact this creation of all things out of nothing is so exclusively his work, that nothing whatever came into existence save through him. Every theory of dualism as an explanation of the universe, and all thought of a created being acting as an intermediary, is thus excluded in advance (verse 3). To the creation is added the *revelation* of the Word. As he is the cause and origin of the material life and light, so is he also the bearer and dispenser of light and life—for the most part uncomprehended and rejected by men—wherever these shine and flow (verses 4, 5).

If, therefore, the Word has already directly, by his pre-existent work of creation and by his revelation before Christ's coming, outwardly manifested himself, so too he has appeared in the fulness of time *directly and in person in Jesus Christ, in order to complete the revelation of God to mankind and the spiritual re-creation of the world* (verses 6-18).

It was John the Baptist who first brought to men the news that the Word had come into the world in a personal form, and had presented himself as essential light and as a sun of revelation to mankind, so that all might believe in the Light, the Word (verses 6, 7). Some understood this erroneously, in that they mistook the mere man John for the Word, who is essentially God (verse 8). But in the divine Word, who is the true Light, that alone lighteth every man actually and truly, and to whom the whole world owes its existence, very few believed, when he himself appeared in his own world and among his chosen people (verses 9-11). The few, however, who did believe in him and received the Word through faith, were thereby united with him spiritually and therefore adopted as sons of God (12-13). This climax of revelation and redemption, however, could be reached only by *the Word, the only-begotten, metaphysical Son of God, assuming human nature and, as the true, God-incarnate Jesus Christ, pouring out in abundance his grace and truth upon mankind; and proclaiming and proving his divine glory visibly to men* (verses 14-18).

John now undertakes to relate how this revelation of the divine glory, truth and grace, and of the divine nature and personality of the Word, or Son of God, worked itself out in the life of Jesus, in his works, in his teaching and in his entire testimony to himself. *As his Gospel is nothing else than the testimony and proof of Jesus to himself as regards his human nature, Messiahship, and divine sonship, so it is also nothing else than a continuous commentary on the prologue about the Word* (Logos). Or, rather, this prologue about the Word is only John's synopsis of the Fourth Gospel, taken from the life, the words and the works of Jesus and concisely put together. It is not correct to say that John presents no doctrine of the Logos, although he uses the word

Logos;[1] nor is it right to assert that the Logos idea is found in John only in the prologue to his Gospel, while everywhere else the Anointed One, the Ambassador of the Father appears in its place.[2] The word Logos certainly does not recur again in the Gospel, at least, no more in the full significance of the prologue.[3] Yet the fundamental ideas of the Logos doctrine in the prologue—the pre-existence and eternity of the Logos, his activity in creation and revelation, his human nature, Messiahship, divine sonship, and divinity, and the Logos as true, divine Light and Life, the visible glory of God and the personified grace of God—these form the distinctive mark of the Fourth Gospel.[4] By the prologue, the reader of John's Gospel is conducted in a natural succession of steps from the eternity of the Word through vast antiquity and through that period of his activity which antedated the creation of the world and the birth of Christ to the present, in which the Evangelist, on the ground of his own experience, informs us of the manifestation of the divine Saviour. And, in fact, the result of this report agrees in all respects with the prologue—Jesus Christ proves himself by his life, words and work to be the divine Word, and the Light, Grace and Truth, as well as the Son of God, who became flesh for us, redeemed us through his suffering and will, through faith in him and love to him, confer on men continually eternal life and light.

The Evangelist himself declares authentically in his *first Epistle* that the whole life of Christ and the whole christology of the Fourth Gospel—in fact, everything that John on the strength of his own experience reports of Jesus on his own eye and ear testimony—is to be considered as Logos doctrine. At the very beginning of this Epistle he remarks with an evident retrospective glance at the Gospel and a clear outlook on the entire future import of his writings: " That which was from the beginning, which we have heard, which we have seen with our eyes, which we have looked upon and our hands have handled, of the *Word of Life* . . . that we declare unto you " (1 John i, 1, 3). Traces of the same Logos doctrine appear in the further course of the Johannine Epistle more than once.[5] In particular, the mystery of the three Persons of God is expressed in the formula " the Father, the Word and the Holy Ghost " (1 John v, 7).

Even the christology of the *Apocalypse,* which has been so frequently brought into conflict with that of the Fourth

[1] Theodor Zahn, *Einleitung in das N. T.,* ii, 535 ff. (Leipzig, 1899).
[2] Paul Schanz, *Apologie des Christentums,* ii, 633, 2nd ed. (Freiburg, 1897).
[3] Nevertheless, see John v, 38; viii, 55; x, 35; xvii, 6; xiv, 17.
[4] See the admirable and thorough presentation of the subject by J. Grimm, *l.c.,* 31-88, 285-384.
[5] See Grill, *op. cit.,* 301-303, 312.

Gospel, finds support in the Logos doctrine. Christ is for it the beginning of the Creation (iii, 14). He sits in glory on the throne of heaven (iv, 2; v, 1). He overcomes the world (vi). He is the sin-destroying Lamb of God, slain for humanity (v, 6, 8, 12; vii, 17). And "his name is called the Word of God" (xix, 13). Upon him the seer of Patmos confers the attributes of God and demands for him divine honour and adoration (see above).

St John uses, therefore, for the expression of his faith in the person of the Saviour and especially in his divinity a form peculiarly his own, which appears in no synoptic Gospel and in no older canonical book of the New Testament whatever. Not as if he depreciated the other usual designations for Jesus Christ, such as Son of David, Son of Man, Messiah, Son of God, God and so forth. We find all of these expressions in John's writings, and oftener than the term Logos. But what all these expressions say at the same time, John sums up in the one title used by him : the Word of God, the Word of Light, the Word of Life—the *Logos*. The title of Logos is for him the sum total of all christology, and in particular the precise expression for the metaphysical divine sonship and true divinity of Jesus. For this reason and in this sense the Johannine form of christology—the name Word, and the Logos doctrine itself—was handed down, as an inheritance, to the Church science of succeeding years.

2. *The Origin of the Johannine Christology.*

Liberal criticism clings to the fact, just stated, of the peculiar Johannine christology, in order to make people believe that John arrived at his doctrine of the divinity of Jesus in contrast to the teaching of Christ and of the older New Testament writings, and in connection with the Hellenic-Alexandrian philosophy. Pfleiderer, who represents this pet theory of the modern investigators of Jesus, most exhaustively and with the courage of desperation[1] sums up his view in the words : " The fourth Evangelist came to the apotheosis of Christ under the names of ' Logos ' and ' only begotten Son of God ' . . . not, of course, through historical tradition from the sayings of Jesus uttered for any such purpose, which are still not discoverable even in the oldest sources; and also not through mere reflection on the impression which the historical person had made upon him. . . . The explanation is much easier to find in the fact that the fourth Evangelist was under the influence of the Hellenic

[1] Especially in the following works : *Das Urchristentum,* ii, 25, 2nd ed. (Berlin, 1903); *Das Christusbild des urchristlichen Glaubens,* 12 (Berlin, 1903); *Die Entstehung des Christentums,* 215-240 (München, 1905).

and Gnostic fantasies, prevailing in his time and environment, which he sought to join on to the older Gospel tradition."[1]   The Zurich professor, P. W. Schmiedel, adds in
a spirit of mutual understanding the following : " It ought
never to be doubted that he [John] has borrowed the word
Logos and the ideas associated with it from Philo."[2] Accordingly, John carried over to the historical person Jesus the
pagan-Jewish Logos-ideas of Philo's religious philosophy,
and thereby made of the man Jesus a Son of God and a
divine person.   That this is not correct is evident from all
our arguments concerning the divinity of Jesus.   John is not
the first to teach the divinity of Jesus ; but this divinity was
testified to by Jesus Christ himself, was adored by the
original Church, and impressed upon it by Paul and the
synoptists, even if not in the Johannine form and style of
representation.   It is only a matter, therefore, of the secondary question, whether the fourth Evangelist derived this form
of his christology—the Logos doctrine—from a non-christian source—namely, from the Hellenic religious philosophy
of Philo.

The first philosopher who spoke of the " Logos " was
Heraclitus the " Obscure," of Ephesus, about 500 B.C.   The
Logos is, according to his hylozoistic and pantheistic view,
equivalent to " measure, law, reason and a rational order of
the world."   It is identical with the material, unconscious,
impersonal element (fire) which formed the world.

Anaxagoras, supported by the Heraclitian hylozoism and
pantheism, assumed, together with the material, world-forming element, an immaterial, transcendental and conscious
principle which fashions and organizes the material world, and
hence is called νοῦς—that is, reason or idea, not Logos.

Plato brings this reason, which he also calls νοῦς, not
Logos, into close relation with God.   The world-forming and
world-organizing reason is a quality of God.   God made use
of it for world-building, because he himself is too exalted and
abstract to be able to come into touch with the world.   The
Stoics restored the Logos to the place of the νοῦς, as a
world-forming principle, determining matter.   They approached again also the hylozoism of Heraclitus in so far as
the Logos, which they generally called God, was yet essentially identical with matter.   Everything that is, must, according to the Stoics, have in itself Logos (Reason); yet the
Logos must be thought of substantially.   The Logos is the
soul of the universe ; the universe is the body of the Logos.
The Stoics' theory of the Logos is higher than the panthe-
istic-materialistic Logos theory of Heraclitus only in so far
as the Stoics' Logos has intelligence and consciousness, and

[1] Pfleiderer, *Die Entstehung des Christentums,* 225.
[2] P. W. Schmiedel, *Das vierte Evangelium,* 118 (Tübingen, 1906).

is identified only with the finer elements, such as air and fire, not with the coarser elements, earth and water.[1]

Closely related to the Stoics' doctrine of the Logos is the Logos speculation of the *Alexandrian-Jewish religious philosophy.* While the Jews of Palestine kept themselves as much as possible aloof from Grecian thought, literature and teaching, the Jews of the dispersion saw themselves drawn into the Alexandrian religious and philosophical movement of the minds of the time. Partly from apologetic reasons, partly from a real inward enthusiasm for Greek philosophy, they endeavoured to unite Mosaic theology and Hellenic speculation, or, at all events, to shed light upon them through mutual contact, and to make them scientifically more profound. A rich and edifying theological-philosophical literature affords a proof of this. One needs only to remember the Alexandrian books of the Old Testament, as well as the Old Testament Apocrypha and pseudo-epigrapha.[2] The philosopher of religion, Philo, devoted himself in particular to this, more than to the dangerous reconciliation of Jewish faith with Grecian culture. In doing so, he took from pagan philosophy not only form and figure, but only too often also materials and ideas, whereby the revealed truth of faith was lost in Greek speculation. This was pre-eminently true in regard to the fundamental view of the universe.

The monotheistic view of the universe was for Philo not merely an inviolable truth, but precisely *the* truth, in opposition to Greek pantheism and materialism. Indeed, in order to remove himself as far as possible from the pantheistic and material idea of God, Philo, quite in the spirit of the contemporary theology of Judaism, conceived of God, not merely as an absolutely one, spiritual, personal, supernatural being, but as a being so exalted above everything earthly and material, that there exists between him and the material world a complete contrast. God is not merely different, but absolutely separated, from matter. The latter has always existed, as a second principle, together with God (Philo is not conscious of the fact that with this dualistic view he really gives up his monotheism), and when the world was to be formed and organized out of it, God could not himself directly come into combination with it in order to consum-

[1] Whoever wishes to inform himself more precisely concerning the Greek doctrine of the Logos will find ample information in the extensive literature referring to it. We mention especially Max Heinze, *Die Lehre vom Logos in der griechischen Philosophie* (1872); Aall, *Der Logos, Geschichte seiner Entwicklung in der griechischen Philosophie und der christl. Literatur* (1896-99); Ed. Zeller, *Die Philosophie der Griechen* (1869-1903).

[2] See the *Apokryphen und Pseudepigraphen des Alten Testamentes,* published by E. Kautzsch in union with numerous experts (Tübingen, 1900).

mate the world's formation. He employed for this an endless number of intermediary beings, called Logoi. The Logoi— that is, the sum total of the intermediary beings standing between God and the world—have their origin and find their unity in *the one true Logos*.

Now Philo defines this Logos as being connected, on the one hand, with the Platonic νοῦς, and, on the other, with the Logos of the Stoics. It differs from the latter only in the fact that, as in Philo, it is neither amalgamated with divinity, nor with matter, and therefore is not interpreted as pantheistic or materialistic. Philo tries to rescue his doctrine of the Logos from the swamp of Stoic materialism and pantheism by calling to his assistance the Platonic theory of ideas, world-reason and the world-pervading soul. According to him, the Logos is the sum total of the divine ideas, in accordance with which the world was to be formed—that is, the rational, divine plan of the universe. At the moment when God uttered in words this ideal world-plan or world-thought, the Logos issued from God into a union with matter. Through this union of the ideal world-plan with matter, the actual world came into existence. The Logos, therefore, became the world-creator, and remains continually the instrument wherewith God brings forth, preserves and governs the actual affairs of the world. In a word, " the Logos of Philo is the condensation and essential unity of all the forces which proceed from God, and thenceforth, independently and rationally—that is, wholly in harmony with the nature, thought and will of God—are working, world-creating, world-maintaining and ruling in both the infinitely great and infinitely little of the universe."[1]

It is evident that Philo has construed this doctrine of the Logos exclusively in accordance with the propositions of Greek philosophy. Only subsequently, and only so far as it is necessary and possible, does he try to gain support for it from the Old Testament, Jewish views and mode of expression. The double meaning of the Greek word Logos—reason (thought) and speech (word)—offered a point of connection with the Old Testament doctrine of the divine Word, or Word of God. In most cases where in the Old Testament reference is made to the word or speech of God, the corresponding Hebraic expression (*dabar*) of the original text is rendered in the Alexandrian Septuagint by Logos. The Logos, the Word of God, in consequence of the Old Testament, plays in the natural creation, preservation and government of the world, as well as in the supernatural revelation and mediation of divine salvation, a very prominent rôle ; in fact, in some passages, the Logos of God seems to appear

[1] Julius Grill, *Untersuchungen über die Entstehung des vierten Evangeliums,* i, 143.

almost as an individual being together with God. If we add that the extremely allegorical exegesis of the Alexandrian school was able to expand all the Logos passages at will, Philo could without great difficulty succeed in harmonizing the Old Testament Word-Logos with his Greek Reason-Logos.

Above all, however, Philo thought that he perceived in the Books of Wisdom in the Old Testament a direct analogue to the Logos of Reason. The " Sophia," or Wisdom of God, appears therein,[1] not only as a quality of Jehovah, but precisely as the highest hypostatical principle of the creation, guidance and government of the world and of all God's revelation to the world. For that reason, and, above all, because the " Sophia " is also occasionally called " Logos " in the Book of Wisdom itself,[2] Philo made the Old Testament Sophia equivalent to his philosophical Reason-Logos. " It is true, Philo once differentiates the Logos from the divine Wisdom, as if the latter were the former's mother; and he is pleased to represent this as the Mother of the universe, which has God for its Father; it has, from the seed, which it has received from God, given birth to the one, dearly beloved Son and to this world as well; but it is clear enough from a comparison of all his utterances that for him the Sophia and the Logos are not essentially different—only two designations of the same divine intermediary being, which he represents, according to the connection, either as the receiving, motherly principle, or as the active, creative principle."[3]

If now we compare the *Logos of Philo* with the *Logos of John,* it is at once evident that the fourth Evangelist has both the Logos name and also several Logos ideas in common with Philo and the Alexandrian-Jewish popular theology. This does not need to be demonstrated either in general or in detail. On the other hand, however, between the Hellenic Logos-doctrine of Philo (there is no need of considering the Greek doctrine), and the Logos-Christ of John, there yawns a mighty, impassable gulf.

[1] Especially Prov. viii; Eccl. xxiv; Wisdom vii, 9.

[2] ix, 1; xvi, 12; xviii, 15.

[3] Johannes J. Ign. Döllinger, *Heidentum und Judentum,* 845 (Regensburg, 1857). For the survey of the Logos doctrine of Philo, see Grossmann, *Quæstiones Philon. De Logo Philonis, q. altera* (1829); Gfrörer, *Philo und die alexandrinische Theosophie* (1831); Dähne, *Geschichtliche Darstellung der jüdisch-alexandrinischen Religionsphilosophie* (1834); Fr. Keferstein, *Philos Lehre von den göttlichen Mittelwesen* (1846); Siegfried, *Philo von Alexandria* (1875); Soulier, *La doctrine du Logos chez Philon d'Alexandrie* (1876); J. Réville, *Le Logos d'après Philon* (1877); *La doctrine du Logos dans le IV Evangile et dans les œuvres de Philon* (1881); Fr. Klasen, *Die alttestamentliche Weisheit und der Logos der jüdisch-alex. Philosophie* (1878); Drummond, *Philo Judæus, or the Jewish Alexandrian Philosophy* (1888); Ed. Zeller, *Die Philosophie der Griechen,* iii, 2 Part, 3rd ed. (1881); Julius Grill, *Untersuchungen über die Entstehung des IV Evangeliums,* i, 105-160.

In the first place, the Logos of John is, in the full sense of the word, a *person,* while the Logos of the Alexandrian philosopher, and of Greek philosophy in general, is only an abstract idea. It is true, occasionally it seems as if Philo were struggling with his own world of ideas, in the effort to conceive of the Logos as a personal—that is, a self-existent, conscious being. Some scholars even formerly believed that he brought this so far as to personify his Logos idea.[1] To-day, however, critics unanimously recognize that the Alexandrian-philosophical Logos is either a mere abstraction, or, in any case, that, half as an abstraction, half as a distinct, individual being, it " floats indistinctly midway between personal and impersonal entity."[2]

In contrast to this, the Logos of John has been with God before all worlds as a concrete, conscious person, has manifested himself as a personal, divine being in the creation of the world and in the history of salvation, and has finally " assumed in the Saviour a living, personal and distinctly visible form."[3] This is so evident that even the enemies of Christianity concede to us the proof of it. Only the Philosopher of the Unconscious undertakes to cast doubt upon the conscious personality of John's Logos, and to put him in this respect on a level with the Logos of Philo.[4]

With the personality, a second essential difference in the Logos of John is at the same time included—the *incarnation of the Logos.* " That the Logos could become flesh would have been for Philo an impossible idea."[5] " Philo had as yet known nothing of an incarnation of the Logos; it had no place in his sharply dualistic view of the universe."[6] " There can be no doubt that from these (philosophical) assumptions it was utterly impossible to arrive at the thought of an incarnation of the Logos."[7] This is so true, that the Christian Gnostics, precisely because of their falling back on Philo's ideas of the Logos, either directly denied the incarnation of the Logos in Jesus Christ, or allowed the divine Logos to enter into only an apparent and merely external connection with Jesus.

[1] Heinze, *Lehre vom Logos,* 291 ff.

[2] Zeller, *Die Philosophie der Griechen,* iii, 378, 3rd ed. Similarly, Soulier, *La doctrine du Logos chez Philon,* 162 f. ; Réville, *La doctrine du Logos dans le IV Evangile et dans les œuvres de Philon,* 26-29; Drummond, *Philo Judæus,* ii, 223-273; Aall, *Geschichte der Logosidee in der griech. Philosophie,* 217 (1896) ; Schürer, *Geschichte des jüdischen Volkes,* iii, 556 f., 3rd ed. ; Grill, *op. cit.,* 139-144, 170 f.

[3] Johannes Weiss, *Christus,* 64 (1909).

[4] " On the point whether the Logos is to be conceived as personal or not, John is no clearer than Philo."—Ed. von Hartmann, *Das Christentum des N. T.,* 284 (1905).

[5] P. W. Schmiedel, *Das IV Evangelium gegenüber den drei ersten,* 118 (Tübingen, 1906).

[6] Pfleiderer, *Die Entstehung des Christentums,* 227 (1905).

[7] Grill, *Untersuchungen,* 329.

In regard to this Gnosticism, as well as to its Philonian model, John speaks in his prologue these decisive words : "And the Word was made flesh and dwelt among us, and we saw his glory " (John i, 14)—that is, in the unity of the historical person, Jesus, it came to a real and abiding union of the divine Logos with the bodily and spiritual nature of a unique human being. This confession is for John fundamental towards every Gnostic denial or subtilization of the doctrine of the incarnation : " Every spirit which confesseth that Jesus Christ is come in the flesh, is of God; and every spirit that dissolveth Jesus is not of God " (1 John iv, 2). " For many seducers are gone out into the world, who confess not that Jesus Christ is come in the flesh. This is a seducer and an antichrist " (2 John 7). To prove the true incarnation of the Logos, John then sets to work to relate exactly what he had seen and heard of the Word of Life (1 John i, 1). The Fourth Gospel is nothing else than the concrete demonstration that the divine Logos has led a complete divine and human life in the human person of Jesus. The same Evangelist, who most fully represents the divinity of the Logos-Saviour, has also represented Jesus in all essential characteristics in his human nature, as scarcely one of the three synoptists has done.[1]

According to John, the Logos became flesh, and lived and worked as a man, because he was the Messiah, the personal instrument of God for the revelation to, and redemption of, mankind. The Logos of John is that almighty Word of God (" God's Logos "), by which the whole universe was called into existence; which has worked in the world ever since the beginning of creation in the most manifold ways; which came to the Patriarchs and Prophets; and which has gone, as a living being, through the whole history of the chosen people, and proclaimed himself everywhere as the future Messiah of the world (John i, v, vii, viii, ix, x). Finally, this divine Word has really become flesh in order to complete among us his Messianic revelation and work of salvation; to bring to us the grace of redemption by his whole earthly life, teachings and expiatory death; and to remain to all eternity the principle of all truth and grace.[2]

The Logos of Philo has nothing to do with the Messiah. The Alexandrian, it is true, shares fully the Messianic hopes and expectations of his race, especially the national-political

[1] See the detailed proof in Th. Zahn, *Einleitung in das N. T.*, ii, 539 Leipzig, 1899); Johannes Weiss, *Christus*, 83-86; R. H. Strachan, *Expositor*, 143 (Feb. 1910). One must truly be colour-blind to be able to assert, as P. W. Schmiedel does in *Das IV Evangelium*, 23, that the only noticeable human feature in John's portrait of Jesus is the utterance " Jesus wept " at the grave of Lazarus.

[2] See the prologue of John's Gospel, as well as the whole Gospel, as an elaboration of it.

hopes. He describes[1] with satisfaction and in glowing
colours precisely that kind of a Messiah and those Messianic
expectations, which we have learned to recognize as rabbinical and pharisaical Messianic ideas. In these, however,
the Logos is not mentioned in a single syllable. Indeed, "it
did not even occur to Philo to think of a connection between
this Logos idea and the thought of the Messiah."[2] His
whole conception of the Logos was opposed to the doctrine
of the Messiah. It is true, Philo tries, as we have already
said, to harmonize his Logos with the "Word of God" and
with the "Wisdom" of the Old Testament, so that we
expect that he must surely go on from that point to a
Messiah-Logos. But he brings the conceptions Word-Logos
("Word of God") and Reason-Logos ("Wisdom of God"),
which, in the great connection of the Old Testament, certainly belong to the order of Messianic prophecy,[3] into union
with the Logos theory only by way of an appendage, and
with a complete misunderstanding of its Messianic character.
His Logos is, in any case, only fastened on to the Old Testament. In its nature and origin it comes solely from Greek
philosophy; it is identical with the Logos of Heraclitus,
Plato and the Stoics, as world-soul, world-idea, world-reason.
    With this, however, the *divinity* of the Logos cannot be
compatible. The Logos has, in any case, a meaning and
place in Philo's system and is capable of playing its rôle as
world-framer and world-director, only if and because it is
not of a divine nature. The nature of God is, according to
Philo, abstract being, " an abstraction, leading the mind
beyond the idea of personality. . . . From this conception
of absolute being there resulted such a contrast between
divinity and the world of finite and material existence, that
the thought of an immediate relation of causation became
unrealizable. The practical foundation of the universe was
put outside the domain of God, and, so far as it was not
included in the dualistic assumption of eternal matter, was
recognized in the intermediary being of the Logos."[4] The
Logos is at once the dividing wall and the connecting link
between God and the world—no more. The making the
Logos equivalent to the "Word," the "Wisdom" of God
has also no more signification. On the contrary, Philo conceived precisely these two Old Testament notions absolutely
as intermediary beings, who stand in rank above the world,
but below divinity.

    [1] Cohn and Wendland's edition of *De præmiis et poenis*, 15 ff. (vol. v,
355 ff.) ; *De execrationibus*, 8, 9 (vol. v, 374 ff.).
    [2] Krüger, *Dreieinigkeit u. Gottmenschheit*, 100 (Tübingen, 1905).
    [3] See the article *Logos*, by Atzberger in *Kirchen-Lexikon*, viii,
97-125, 2nd ed.
    [4] Grill, *Untersuchungen über die Entstehung des IV Evangeliums*,
172.

The Logos of John, however, stands, as we have amply demonstrated, plainly higher, not only than all men, but also than all intermediary beings between God and men. He is, before all worlds and from eternity, the God of nature : " In the beginning was the Word, and the Word was with God, and the Word was God "[1] (John i, 1). With this, the sharpest conceivable antithesis to the Greek speculation of Philo about the Logos, the first verse of John's Gospel begins ; the following Logos-prologue carries this antithesis still further ; and the entire Gospel brings it to a comprehensive conclusion. This contrast is no less sharply defined in the first Epistle of John and in the Apocalypse. Gustav Krüger also is of the opinion that " for the Evangelist the Logos is the central idea, by which to reveal what Jesus Christ, in his divine characteristics, has been to him."[2]

If we summarize the main differences which in general separate the Logos of John from that of Philo and also from that of Hellenic philosophy, it is clear that the former cannot possibly be derived from the latter.

John denies and combats the Hellenic and Philonian ideas of the Logos, together with the Christian Gnostic ideas which were akin to them, by keeping remote from the Logos (Jesus Christ) precisely what is regarded in those speculations as an essential element of the Logos doctrine—namely, the Logos as an intermediary being, as a world-framer, a world-soul, and the shadowy, abstract Logos of reason. On the contrary, John predicates of his Logos, as essential, precisely that which is wanting in the Logos of Philo and the Gnostics. His Logos is that divine Person, who, un-

---

[1] J. Grill very rightly argues that this Johannine doctrine of the Logos resulted from the decided adherence of the Evangelist to the Personality of God, just as the hybrid Logos of Philo was a sequence of the abstract conception of the idea of God. " Since the Evangelist . . . holds firmly to the presupposition of a real, complete, personal life of God, even in feeling and willing, he arrives at a conclusion which gives to his Logos a signification thoroughly different from the nature of the Logos of Philo. If God is a personality, then he is not to be thought of without an object of his thinking and willing, knowledge and love. If he is absolute being, this object must be included in himself, and cannot come to him merely as an external being. If, however, the objective in God is to be an adequate object of his receptive and spontaneous activity, it must itself have just as truly the character of the Absolute as of the personal. . . . The one, absolute being appears thus as subject-object; not in a logically abstract sense, but, so to speak, polarized in the real relation of person to person. Thereby the idea of God has actually reached the highest possible degree of vitality, and the Logos is elevated above the level of the intermediary being."—*Untersuchungen über die Entstehung des IV Evangeliums,* 175. Thereby the liberal-Protestant scholar has at the same time suggested (the further argumentation is a matter of dogmatics) that, and why, John's doctrine of the Logos brings no dualism into the Godhead, although it indicates a number of divine Persons.

[2] *Dreieinigkeit und Gottmenschheit,* 97 (Tübingen, 1905).

created and eternal, is the primal cause of all creation and
of all divine revelation in the created world and in mankind;
and in the fulness of time this person became man, lived
and worked in Jesus Christ, and completed the redemption
of humanity.

It is not worth while, therefore, to designate, with
Pfleiderer, the Logos christology of John as an attempt to
connect the Gospel history with Hellenic and Gnostic speculation; or, with H. Holtzmann, to stamp it as "modified
Alexandrianism "[1]; or, even with Eduard von Hartmann, to
assert that the Logos of John was simply taken over "from the
allegorism of Philo, and above all from the confused whims
of the Gnostics,"[2] and that "all that John brings out about
the nature of the Logos is not only also said, but strongly
emphasized by Philo."[3] Such an estimate of the Logos-
doctrine of John contradicts the most fundamental facts of
the Fourth Gospel, and cannot be logically maintained by its
own advocates. Not to mention the caricature of the Johannine christology of Hartmann, which is not to be taken
seriously, Pfleiderer himself, who finds again the Logos-
Christ of John not only in Philo's writings but (to the great
astonishment of all critics) also in Jewish and Christian
Gnosticism—yes, in Greek, Eastern Asiatic, Babylonian and
Egyptian views[4]—sees himself finally compelled to concede
the decisive and essential difference between the Logos of
John and that of all other speculations.[5] Compressed into
one sentence, the whole wisdom of Pfleiderer would express
itself as follows : John has borrowed his doctrine of the
Logos from another source, but his doctrine of the Logos
is essentially the opposite of the doctrine thus borrowed.

The most important and circumspect opponents of the
divinity of Christ emphatically reject, then, even to-day this
"critical" explanation of John's doctrine of the Logos.
Julius Kaftan remarks : "In the prologue the point in
question is that of a loose connection with the Hellenic
Wisdom, without conceding to this a great influence in the
representation of the Christian thoughts in the Gospel
itself."[6] "In the sense of its author the Fourth Gospel is an
intellectual unity; . . . the framing of it by Hellenism a
chance event of contemporary history."[7]

Julius Grill, on the ground of a most thorough knowledge

[1] H. Holtzmann, *Das Evangelium des Johannes,* 45, 2nd ed.
[2] Von Hartmann, *Das Christentum des N. T.,* 284, 2nd ed.
[3] *id.,* 282.
[4] *Die Entstehung des Christentums,* 225. For similar obsolete and
discredited attempts at explanation from modern times, see Grill, *l.c.,*
206; von Hartmann, *l.c.,* 282.   [5] Pfleiderer, *l.c.,* 227.
[6] J. Kaftan, *Das Verhältnis des evangelischen Glaubens zur Logoslehre,* in *Zeitschrift für Theologie und Kirche,* viii, 3 (1897).
[7] J. Kaftan, *Jesus und Paulus,* 64 (Tübingen, 1906).

of the Philo-Hellenic doctrine of the Logos, as well as of that
of John, expresses his conviction as follows : " However striking the whole parallel connection is [between Philo and
John], it can hardly escape even a superficial observation that
a fundamental and essential difference in the Logos ideas of
the two writers makes itself felt throughout."[1]

The historian of dogma, Harnack, likewise declares : " The
reference to Philo and Hellenism is not at all sufficient here
[to explain John's christology], since it does not satisfac-
torily account for even *one* side of the problem.   Grecian
theologians have not been operative in the Johannine theology
—even the Logos has little more in common with the Logos
of Philo than the name. . . .   The prologue of the Gospel
starts out with a great being known to Hellenic readers—
the Logos ; recasts and refashions this—combating implicitly
false christologies—in order to substitute for it Christ—that
is, to disclose it as this Jesus Christ."[2]   The aged Weizsäcker has expressed himself in like manner concerning " the
relation between the Logos doctrines of John and Philo " :
" Nothing is easier than to point out the great difference
between the two doctrines, and to prove that they rest
on fundamentally different views.   And far be it from us,
indeed, to wish to avoid a recognition of the thoroughly
original Johannine formation. . . .   We may perhaps go
still further, and say not only that John has not borrowed
the Logos of Philo, but that his doctrine is exactly contrary
to it."[3]

If, in fact, we compare what the Johannine doctrine of the
Logos has in common with the Hellenic Logos-doctrine of
Philo, with what separates the two, we might well let the
following serve as the positive result : " The *name Logos* is
certainly common to both.   That John took this word from
the contemporary philosophy of the schools and people is,
however, not therewith proven.   Rather is it the case that he
had already found the name Logos used for Jesus Christ in
the Church.   This was so well known and commonly used
that the Evangelist simply assumed it, as it had been given.
But whether the Church took the name Logos over from the
Greco-Alexandrian philosophy, or from the Old Testament, or
from both together, must remain uncertain."

In a word, John has found at the time of his writing the
exterior frame, or *shell,* for his Logos doctrine all ready.
He adopted it, not merely because in itself it was very well
adapted to receive both the figure and the substance of the

[1] *Untersuchungen über die Entstehung des IV Evangeliums,* 139.
[2] *Dogmengeschichte,* i, 93, 3rd ed. ; *cf.* Harnack, *Uber das Verhältnis des Prologs des IV Evangeliums zum ganzen Werk,* in *Zeitschrift für Theologie und Kirche,* ii, 189-231 (1892).
[3] Weizsäcker, *Die johanneische Logoslehre,* in *Jahrbücher für Theologie,* vii, 708 (1862).

idea, but because, as a commonly understood point of departure for christological instruction, it was especially commendable,[1] and because the false Logos doctrine was assailable only by opposing to it the true doctrine, while retaining the Logos form. After he had purified it from all the slag which heathen philosophy, Jewish theosophy, and Christian Gnostic speculation had left in it, he poured into the " shell " the pure and wholly sublime contents of the Christian doctrine of the Logos, given by revelation, and placed in the frame, prepared for it by Providence, the thoroughly original Christian portrait of the God-Man, Jesus Christ.

We say the original Christian portrait of the God-Man, Jesus Christ. For however little the Johannine christology may, in its nature, be identified with any kind of Logos-speculation outside Christianity, *just as little may it be set up as opposed to the portrait of Jesus in the Christian Church, before John's Gospel,* and designated as a novelty on the part of the fourth Evangelist.

The modern talk—repeated *ad nauseam*—about the Christ of John being in contrast to the Christ of the older Christian writers—namely, the synoptists and Paul—is confused and confusing. It can be understood—and is for the most part also misunderstood—as if there had been in the Church during the first Christian century three essentially different conceptions of Christ—one Pauline, one synoptic, and finally one Johannine. This, however, does not at all correspond to the historical facts. True, Paul, the synoptists and John rely upon three special, though parallel, modes of teaching and traditions of the life and words of Jesus. The result of this is necessarily also three distinctly different representations. With John this form of difference is greater, because he not only can speak everywhere as an eye-witness, but sees himself confronted with the beginnings of the Christian-Gnostic heresy, which, in connection with the Jewish and Hellenic speculation about the Logos, denied the true humanity, Messiahship and divinity of Jesus. Thus he sees himself also compelled to elaborate the *portrait of Christ* as completely and decisively as possible, and especially to pourtray the divinity of Jesus more demonstratively and in the form of the true divine sonship and of the divine Logos; and this, as an eye-witness, he is qualified to do. We have already expressly demonstrated this Johannine peculiarity.

---

[1] The idea of the Logos must have been just as well known to the Church in its application to Jesus as the Logos name itself : " The self-evident introduction at the very beginning of a work plainly pursuing a new course shows unmistakably that the Evangelist thought that he might take for granted in his readers an acquaintance precisely with this idea."—Krüger, *Dreieinigkeit und Gottmenschheit,* 97.

But this peculiarity is purely external, and the differences resulting from it, as contrasted in the Pauline and synoptic christology, are thoroughly unessential, and do not affect the subject-matter itself. If we take away the Johannine frame of the portrait of Christ and the Johannine, that is, the contemporaneous, historical shell of the Logos doctrine, Jesus Christ stands before us in the Fourth Gospel as that divine Lord and Master who descends from the throne of his heavenly Father to this earth, becomes man, and lives, teaches and dies for us men, in order, as the Messiah, to redeem the whole world. In proof of this essential unity of the Johannine christology with that of the synoptists and Paul, we can appeal to the whole foregoing investigation, and conclude by pointing out that even hostile criticism does not succeed in establishing the truth of the liberal dogma of a christological antagonism between the Gospel of John and that of the synoptists and of Paul.

With regard to the *christological relation of the Fourth Gospel to the synoptists,* Adolf Harnack believes that he may call John a " glorified Matthew."[1] " Yet one can call him also just as well a glorified Mark and Luke; for he agrees with Mark in the dominant intention of bringing to light the divine sonship of Jesus."[2] Luke, however, " approaches in christology the type of conception found in John."[3] Harnack's Berlin colleague, Pfleiderer, expresses himself even more decidedly : " It must be acknowledged that all our Gospels stand, in principle, on the same standpoint, and that the difference between Mark and the other two synoptists and John is only a relative difference of degree between the various strata of theological reflection and ecclesiastical consciousness."[4] Bousset confirms this estimate, and writes : " The fact has rightly been brought out that in this respect (the doctrine of the divinity of Jesus) our three Evangelists are different from the fourth only in degree."[5] Edmund Stapfer goes still further : " The Christ of the Fourth Gospel in no respect exceeds the Christ which the synoptists let us surmise. He helps us to understand the latter."[6] Albrecht Kalthoff remarks : " The synoptic Christ . . . does not stand a hair's breadth nearer a really human conception of Christianity than does the Christ of the Fourth Gospel."[7]

These admissions, made by good liberals and even by ultra-radicals, agree, therefore, with those of the concilia-

---

[1] *Lukas der Arzt,* 119 note. [2] *id.* [3] *id.,* 158.
[4] *Das Urchristentum,* i, 666, 2nd ed. ; cf. *Entstehung des Christentums,* 186.
[5] *Was wissen wir von Jesus?* 30 f. (Halle, 1904).
[6] " Le Christ du IV Evangile ne dépasse en rien celui que les synoptiques nous font deviner. Il nous aide à l'apercevoir."—*Jésus-Christ pendant son ministère,* 326 (1897).
[7] *Das Christusproblem,* 21.

tory theologian of Berne, Fritz Barth, and of the orthodox
Protestant, Professor Johann Kunze, of Vienna: "We
have not the right to reject this Johannine contribution (to
christology); for even though the ideas in the Fourth Gospel
may be more strongly defined and more clarified . . . nevertheless, his portraiture of Christ is essentially the same."[1]
"It is true, differences exist between the three synoptic
Gospels and that of John, but if we do not exaggerate
them artificially, and if we do not lift the Christ of John
into the mists of heaven, and drag the synoptic Christ
down into the dust of earth, then still always for one of
religious sensibility there is only one Christ, and no essential
difference between the two portraits."[2] The same thing
is to be said about *the relation of the Johannine portrait of Christ to that of Paul.* "Jesus Christ, the Son of
God, the Redeemer of the world, is for Paul, as well as for
John, the nucleus and the star of Christianity."[3] Indeed,
the Pauline christology is still more closely related to that
of John than is that of the synoptists. It is not merely
identical with it, as far as the matter is concerned, but it
stands very near to it also in form. Fundamentally considered, we meet with the Logos doctrine of the fourth
Evangelist in all its principal points already in Paul,
although the Apostle to the Gentiles does not use the expression Logos. Anton Seitz has demonstrated this
thoroughly and profoundly.[4] It is, moreover, conceded by
our critical opponents. Ernest Renan has already called
attention to the fact that Paul "has set up a theory concerning Christ which is entirely analogous to the doctrine
of the Logos, and later found its final form in the writings
ascribed to John."[5] According to Harnack, the central
idea of the Logos-Christ was "prepared in advance, in fact,
necessitated by the Messianic speculations, as the Apostle
Paul and other old teachers had presented them."[6] Johannes
Weiss has "found the fundamental characteristics of the
Logos-christology already in Paul," and so effectually that
to him "the doctrine, after Paul, cannot say much more
that is new" on the subject.[7] The Johannine "idea of the
Logos, with which the prologue begins . . . connects itself
doubtless with the combination of Logos and Christ already
existing in the writings of Paul."[8] "This Pauline Christ,"
says Krüger, "is a divinely pre-existing being. . . . It is
true, Paul does not yet call the divine being, of whom he

[1] Barth, *Die Hauptprobleme des Lebens Jesu,* 266 (Gütersloh, 1907).
[2] Kunze, *Die ewige Gottheit Jesu Christi,* 22 (Leipzig, 1904).
[3] Paul Wernle, *Die Anfänge unserer Religion,* 447, 2nd ed. (Tübingen, 1904).
[4] *Das Evangelium vom Gottessohn,* 487-527 (Freiburg, 1908).
[5] *L'Antéchrist,* 76 (1873).   [6] *Das Wesen des Christentums,* 127.
[7] *Christus,* 65; *cf.* 43-65 (1909).   [8] *id.,* 87.

speaks, ' Logos,' but even if the word is wanting, the thing itself is, nevertheless, there.''[1] And P. W. Schmiedel adds : " What Paul has said with increasing definiteness, only without using the word Logos, is uttered here [in the prologue] by the fourth Evangelist.''[2]

If, then, the Johannine christology is different from that of Paul and the synoptists only in regard to the form—the " how " of its representation—since it says essentially and practically the same thing of Jesus which the earlier writers of the New Testament reported of him, one more consequence follows : *The christology of John is practically and essentially identical with the whole preaching and tradition of the early Church,* exactly as we have proved it to be in regard to the synoptic and Pauline christology. Agreement with the doctrine of the early Church is also for John the guiding principle in all his utterances concerning Jesus— a principle which bears the stamp of the Evangelist himself : " Whosoever denieth the Son, the same hath not the Father ; he that confesseth the Son hath the Father also. Let that which you have heard from the beginning abide in you. If that abide in you, which you have heard from the beginning, you also shall abide in the Son and in the Father " (1 John ii, 23, 24). And his old disciples assert positively that the Gospel of their master corresponds exactly to the original doctrine. " This is that disciple who giveth testimony of these things and hath written these things [his Gospel]. And we know that his testimony is true " (John xxi, 24).

The critics must subscribe to this decision concerning the origin of the Johannine doctrine of Christ, even if they are not willing to ascribe the Johannine writings to the Apostle. The conciliatory Berlin theologian, Julius Kaftan, expresses his conviction on this point in the following words : " Jesus and Paul are the first two members of that historic series in which the development of our religion shows itself. The Fourth Gospel, with the Epistles belonging to it, joins it as the third member—the theology of John. Between Jesus and Paul the preaching of the early Church, which Paul found already existing, forms the medium of transition. . . . Thus John joins Jesus and Paul as the third in the series. And this series forms a straight line. The change of direction lies not in the substance of the Fourth Gospel, but in its Hellenic frame, conditioned by contemporary history. . . . That which constitutes its principal import is the continuation of the line which leads from Jesus to Paul.''[3]

With this is included the fact that the *Johannine christology*—in its essence and content, not in the Logos-form of

[1] *Dreieinigkeit und Gottmenschheit,* 86.
[2] *Das vierte Evangelium,* 118; *cf.* 112 f. (1906).
[3] *Jesus und Paulus,* 63, 67 (Tübingen, 1906).

its representation—*is identical with the self-consciousness and self-revelation of Jesus,* precisely as we have proved it to be in regard to the Pauline, synoptic and, in general, to the original Church's portrait of Christ.   Indeed, the fourth Evangelist appeals not alone to this identity ; he can with more right than any other canonical writer appeal to *himself,* to his historical experiences, and to his own eye and ear testimony : " That which was from the beginning, which we have heard, which we have seen with our eyes, which we have looked upon and our hands have handled, of the Word of life.   For the life was manifested, and we have seen and do bear witness, and declare unto you the life eternal, which was with the Father, and hath appeared to us.   That which we have seen and have heard, we declare unto you, that you also may have fellowship with us, and our fellowship may be with the Father and with his Son Jesus Christ " (1 John i, 1-3 ; *cf.* John xix, 35 ; 1 John v, 20).

CONCLUSION

WE have reached the conclusion of our investigations of the consciousness of Christ. The results, to which we have come by the severest historical and critical examination of the proper sources of information, contradict throughout the views of the most modern sceptical students of Jesus Christ.

Proceeding from religious-philosophical and religious-historical considerations of the doctrine of evolution, the liberal school declares that Jesus himself never was, and never claimed to be, anything more than a man, highly gifted by nature, and destined for the further religious education of the human race. At most, conscious of his remarkable talents and high moral conduct, he applied to himself the contemporary Jewish ideas of a future theocratic founder of a kingdom, popularly called the Messiah, or Son of God. Of being the Messiah and Son of God, as Christianity has attributed these terms to Jesus, Jesus himself never had the faintest idea.

How he was subsequently able to be designated as the divine Messiah is, however, easily explicable, and can be read between the lines of the Gospels and other early Christian writings. The confession of the disciples of the Messiahship of their Master forms the beginning of the transformation of the man Jesus into the God-Man. " Since Paul and the first disciples had declared the man Jesus to be the Christ (Messiah), they now also ascribed to him everything that Judaism had, until then, believed and expected from the Christ. And a halo of utterances born of faith so quickly enveloped the young carpenter and peasant of Nazareth that soon his modest yet powerful figure almost completely vanished from this magic cloud."[1] " From the day on which ardent enthusiasm ventured to utter the words, ' Thou art the Messiah!' a mighty flood of faith rose to, and overflowed, this Jesus of Nazareth, and never came to rest until the confession, ' My Lord and my God ' had borne him upward to the throne of God himself."[2] " A deep gulf separates not only . . . the Johannine writings from the synoptic, but not less the synoptic history of Jesus from the real one. . . . The portrait of Jesus in our Gospels is entirely covered with a varnish, which in places allows absolutely nothing more of the original to be visible."[3]

[1] Weinel, *Paulus, Der Mensch und sein Werk,* 244 (Tübingen, 1904).
[2] *id., Jesus im XIX Jahrhundert,* 108 (Tübingen, 1907).
[3] Jülicher, *Neue Linien in der Kritik der Evangel. Überlieferung,* 70 f. (Giessen, 1906).

We have demonstrated, step by step, *the incorrectness of this pretended evolution of christology, and proved the historical truth of the Messianic and divine consciousness of Jesus.* Two main points have forced themselves upon us everywhere, and must be once more brought forward here in our conclusion.

First: There exist no " deep gulfs " between the christology of the early, and that of the later; generations and literary sources of early Christianity. It is true, the form and forcefulness of expression and representation, in which the portrait of Jesus is delineated, differs in the individual writers of the New Testament. Yet in them all, in Paul, as well as in the author of the Acts of the Apostles, and in the synoptists as well as in John, we found the unqualified confession that Jesus is the Messianic Redeemer and the true, essential Son of God. To this conviction the clearer-sighted investigators, holding otherwise the most varied opinions, can to-day no more close their eyes.

The Protestant conservative professor, Karl Müller, writes : " Nowhere in the New Testament is there to be found a trace of evidence that people, who really believed in Jesus, have in fact estimated him otherwise than as the Messiah of God, who is invoked as God himself, and before whom men prostrate themselves, as to the divine Lord."[1] The theologian of Rostock, Richard H. Grützmacher, expresses himself in precisely similar terms : " At the beginning of the twentieth century the unanimous result of the modern as well as of the ecclesiastical interpretation of the New Testament—and thereto later liberalism also gives its adherence in great measure—is this, that the Church's doctrine of the God-Man Christ is fully justified in appealing to the New Testament in its entirety, and has further developed its content only in form."[2] Adolf Harnack condescends to make at least this confession : " Already in the first two generations [therefore not first after the appearance of John's Gospel] everything was said of Jesus Christ that men are in general able to say."[3] Still more definitely does Harnack's colleague and kindred thinker, Johannes Weiss, remark : " A gradual evolution [of christology in early Christianity] is scarcely observable."[4] " Early Christianity is, at least in part, the religion of Christ—that is, the inward relation of faith to the exalted Christ stands in the central point. . . . I do not conceal the fact that I, together with the majority of modern theologians, profess the (contrary) view, and that I hope that this view will gradually prevail in our Church. But,

---

[1] *Unser Herr,* 10 f. (Gr.-Lichterfelde-Berlin, 1906).
[2] *Ist das liberale Jesusbild modern?* 30 (Gr.-Lichterfelde-Berlin, 1907).
[3] *Wesen des Christentums,* 97.
[4] Johannes Weiss, *Christus,* 4 (Tübingen, 1909).

as an historian, I must say that it is far removed from the view prevailing among the early Christians."[1]

The ultra-radical professor, Albrecht Kalthoff, of Bremen, summarizes the same conviction in the words : " The Christ, of whom the old Christian writings tell us, is throughout not a man, but at the least a superman, yes, more than this— a Son of God, a divine Man. From the Church's God-Man a straight line leads back through the Epistles and Gospels of the New Testament to the Apocalypse of Daniel, in which the Church's imprint of the portrait of Christ originated. But at every single point of this line the Christ has also superhuman traits, and never and nowhere is he what the theology of the critics has wanted to make of him."[2]

All the wonderful talk about the gradual evolution of the man Jesus up to the divine Man and divine Messiah-Christ in the course of the first century, and the digging of trenches between the original Christian, Pauline, synoptic and Johannine christologies, is, therefore, a matter of exceedingly hypothetical and fantastic dilettantism. We repeat once more, that there is a *formal* difference in the way in which the individual writers of the early Church expressed and represented their confession of belief in the Messiahship and divinity of Jesus. But there is no material, practical difference between the portrait of Christ in the first, second and third generations of Christian history. From the Church of the resurrection to the Church of John, the Christians unanimously beheld and confessed, in the Saviour, the Messianic Redeemer and true Son of God.

Secondly: This confession of the whole of primitive Christianity is not the result of a retouching of the portrait by believers; but goes back to the Messianic and divine consciousness and confession of Jesus himself.

The assertion that the portrait of Jesus has been little by little embellished through faith, and overlaid with a varnish of divinely human and divinely Messianic qualities, could be taken seriously only if separate strata of such legendary transformations could be proved. But this is by no means the case. From the pages of the whole New Testament only *one* portrait of Jesus confronts our gaze, as we have just seen—namely, the portrait of the divine man and the divine Messiah. This appears to us there at once complete, without the slightest approach to a gradual evolution from human-messianic to divinely Messianic and divinely human. Accordingly, it must be the essentially true reproduction of the original, historical portrait.

This is actually confirmed also by all the New Testament writers. What they report, after the death of Jesus, of the

[1] Johannes Weiss, *Paulus und Jesus,* 4 f. (Berlin, 1904).
[2] *Die Entstehung des Christentums,* 9 (Jena and Leipzig, 1904).

Messiahship and divinity of their Master, they do not at all
derive from the faith of their contemporary Church; no,
they are conscious that they are only testifying to the Messianic and divinely human consciousness which Jesus had
revealed during his earthly life. We have been able to prove
this fact clearly by the authors of the Acts and of the synoptic Gospels, as well as by Paul and John. Not only that—
the direct utterances of Jesus and his testimony to himself
regarding his Messiahship and divinity also spoke just as
loudly and unequivocally from the Pauline, synoptic and Johannine writings.

And even if we ourselves did not have these written records,
the unwritten testimony of the whole of primitive Christianity would undoubtedly say to us that Christ proclaimed
himself as Messiah and God. Even Harnack lays great
weight on the point that " outside of the four written Gospels
we possess still a fifth, unwritten one, which speaks in some
respects more clearly and impressively than the other four—
I mean the entire testimony of the first Christian Church.
We can gather from it what the general impression of this
person was, and in what way his disciples understood his
words and testimony to himself."[1]

If liberal criticism lightly asserts that precisely only the
supernatural side of the early Church's christology is not to
be regarded as the echo of the words and testimony of Jesus
to himself, then it is not the objective investigation of history,
but a secret wish that is father to such a thought. For the
subjective criticism which advocates the theory of historical
evolution—which is the basis of the denial of everything
supernatural—Jesus *cannot* be the Redeemer and incarnate
God. He *must,* as a mere man, have evolved himself from
the humanity surrounding him. Everything superhuman and
supernatural related of him *can* be only subsequent additions
and inventions of faith. Those books and passages of the
New Testament, which affirm the contrary, *must,* accordingly,
have come into it at a later date, or must in any case be
looked upon as legendary expressions of faith. If there still
remain any supernatural expressions concerning the person
and life of Jesus, this remnant also is either denied or newly
interpreted, until everything is made to harmonize with the
portrait of Jesus, which they themselves have drawn or
arbitrarily caricatured.

Thus, and thus only, according to the evolutionary theory
and the idea that Christ's life was merely a phase of
" religious history," does one succeed in explaining the
consciousness of Jesus and the earliest Christian reports
concerning the Messiah and the Son of God, Jesus. Sceptical

[1] *Das Christentum und die Geschichte,* reprinted in Harnack's *Reden
und Aufsätzen,* ii, 16 (Giessen, 1906).

criticism professes to have found and given to the world the historical Christ, but in reality it has constructed its own modern Christ *in opposition to real history.*

And also *in opposition to all psychology,* which is, if possible, still worse. The evolutionary, religious-historical theory insists especially on the fact that the man Jesus has been transformed into the heavenly Christ, the divine Man and the divine Messiah through the psychological experience of the disciples and the early Church. But if so, it is naturally bound to show the connecting lines which are supposed to lead from the purely human self-authentication of Jesus up to the divinely human and divinely Messianic portrait of him drawn by the disciples and early Christians. But this immeasurable gulf is bridged only with an unlimited amount of fantasy, not with legitimate psychology.

Indeed, how is it possible that the "young mechanic and peasant of Nazareth," whom the liberal investigators pourtray, could, shortly after his death, become exalted in the circle of the disciples to that heavenly Christ, the world-redeeming Messiah and the true Son of God? How is it to be explained that the same men, who, only a little while before, had eaten and drunk with him, and by reason of years of intercourse had become convinced of his mere humanity, could take him now for a superman and for the pre-existing and essential Son of God? How is it thinkable, that the Jews who were true to the Messiah, and to whom all idolatry of a creature was an abomination, ever folded their hands in prayer to the Jesus whom they had always heard pray to the Father, and that they could worship him whom they had seen live and die as a man? How comes it that all the Christians of the early times, the old disciples, like the synoptists, and Paul and John, all approved of this blasphemous deification of a human being and joined in it, and also that in the whole primitive Church not a sound of objection and indignation against it was raised? How is it, we ask with Kalthoff, how is it psychologically to be imagined that a "Protestant-liberal" type of Jesus was laid in the grave and that a "Catholic"[1] Christ rose from it?

Grützmacher rightly says : "Liberal theology has not yet comprehended that this religious-historical problem even exists, to say nothing of attempting then to solve it."[2] "In not quite one decade (for the rise of the Church's dogma is, on account of Paul, not to be put back beyond the death of Jesus) to enrol in the category of the gods a man about whom men were still perfectly well informed, and to hang about him every conceivable ornament of oriental mythology, is the exact opposite of gradual evolution."[3] How can it,

---

[1] Kalthoff, *Das Christus-Problem,* 26, 2nd ed.
[2] *Ist das liberale Jesusbild modern?* 39.   [3] *id.,* 40.

then, occur to the holders of the evolution-theory to cut so deeply into their own flesh by accepting such an unpsychological and abrupt hypothesis?

The liberal evolutionary theory can give to such questions at most the profound reply : That the exceedingly rapid embellishment of the man Jesus, which exalted him to the divine Man Christ, was brought about in consequence of the powerful impression which Jesus had made upon the disciples during his life, and in consequence of the visions of the resurrection, which they imagined they saw after his death. That, however, is not to solve the problem of abruptness, but only to push it into the background. On that very account, indeed, it is a question of how the disciples, after the ignominious death of their Master, could live with and worship him as the risen Lord and Messiah, unless he had previously made upon them the impression of being the *divine Messiah* as long as he dwelt among them. "For," as even the liberal, W. Bousset, remarks, "it is indeed comprehensible that the first disciples of Jesus, all of whose hopes had been shattered by the death and burial of Jesus, and all of whose views of the Messiahship of Jesus had been destroyed, *came back*, under the impression of their experiences with the risen Jesus, to the belief that Jesus was the Messiah, if they had gained this belief previously through the utterances and the conduct of Jesus. But it remains perfectly inexplicable how this belief could *originate for the first time* among the disciples after the great catastrophe; we should have then to suppose that those wonderful experiences of the Easter days had, in a purely magical way and without any psychological mediation, called to life something absolutely new in their souls. But, precisely from the standpoint of the strictly evolutionary-historical theory, this cannot be accepted."[1]

The mere attempt to explain the origin of the disciples' faith in the divine Messiah by this psychological enormity, and thereby to solve one riddle by another, is a direct blow to their own evolutionary theory, and a clear confession that the religious-historical and religious-psychological theory of the sceptics has here reached the limit of its art.

There is only one true religious-historical and religious-psychological solution of the existing problem—it is the derivation of the faith of the disciples in the divine Messiah from the divinely Messianic revelation of himself, made by their Master. If our opponents' form of science, known as the " strictly historical and strictly psychological school of criticism," wishes seriously to stand by its principles, then it must demand, still more decidedly than even we believing Christians do, that one should reason back from the faith of

[1] W. Bousset, *Jesus,* 77, 3rd ed. (Tübingen, 1907).

the early disciples and the original Church to the divinely
human consciousness of Jesus Christ. Then it will have to
acknowledge that " Jesus in his lifetime planted the only
seed from which Christianity grew into life after his death;"[1]
that the christological dogma, in the full meaning of the term,
" has its roots in the preaching and teaching of Christ;"[2]
and that " to that extent the Church's faith in Christ . . . is,
in the last analysis, the effect of the victorious, and even in
death unbroken, conviction and faith of Jesus himself."[3]

Thus do the desperate efforts of modern unbelief to deny
the Messianic and divine consciousness of Jesus lead irresistibly back to the conviction that *Jesus himself was conscious of being the Messianic Redeemer and true Son of God,
and proclaimed himself as such.*

[1] Jülicher, *Paulus und Jesus,* 69 (Tübingen, 1907).
[2] Loisy, *L'Evangile et l'Eglise,* 164 (Paris, 1902).
[3] Johannes Weiss, *Paulus und Jesus,* 9. (Berlin, 1909).

INDEX OF AUTHORITIES

INDEX OF SUBJECTS

*